HUAIYUN 40 ZHOU WANMEI FANG'AN

王艳琴　主编

怀孕40周完美方案

我们坚持以专业精神，科学态度，为您排忧解惑。

中国人口出版社

图书在版编目（CIP）数据

怀孕40周完美方案／王艳琴主编．－北京：中国人口出版社，2010.1

ISBN 978-7-5101-0309-4

Ⅰ.怀… Ⅱ.王… Ⅲ.①妊娠期－妇幼保健－基本知识 ②胎教－基本知识 Ⅳ.R715.3 G61

中国版本图书馆CIP数据核字（2009）第217086号

最轻松、最权威、最系统的
同步孕期读本

怀孕40周完美方案

王艳琴 主编

出版发行 中国人口出版社
印　　刷 北京振兴华印刷有限公司
开　　本 1020×710 1/16
印　　张 14
字　　数 150千字
版　　次 2010年2月第1版
印　　次 2011年1月第5次印刷
书　　号 ISBN 978-7-5101-0309-4
定　　价 26.80元

社　　长 陶庆军
网　　址 www.rkcbs.net
电子信箱 rkcbs@126.com
电　　话 (010)83519390
传　　真 (010)83519401
地　　址 北京市宣武区广安门南街80号中加大厦
邮　　编 100054

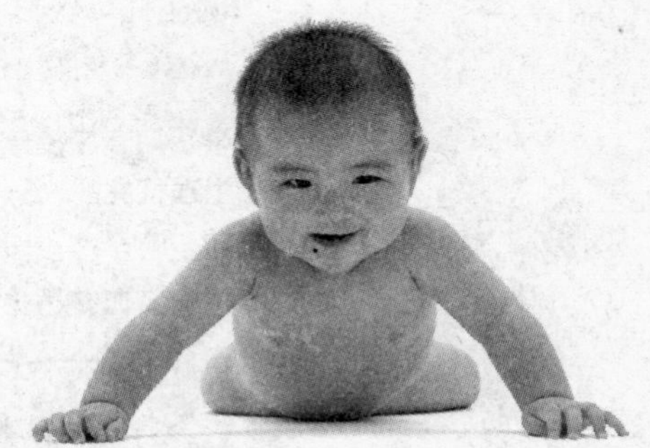

目 录

Contents

Contents

Contents

Contents

Contents

Contents

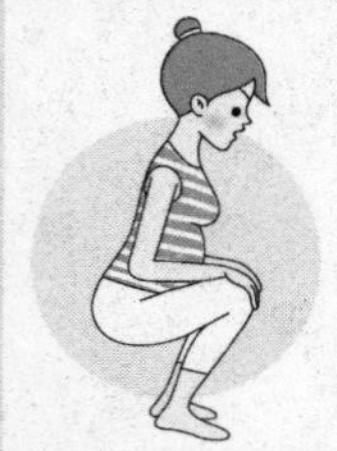

Contents

美国优生圣经49条

想做妈妈了吗？好好准备一下吧。
在科技发达的美国，给准妈妈都有哪些建议呢？

1. 孕前看医生，做检查。

2. 改变不良饮食习惯，多吃各种健康食品。

3. 孕前锻炼身体。

4. 接受怀孕教育。

5. 食用一些从未尝试过的新品种蔬菜。

6. 读一本怀孕方面系统知识的书籍。

7. 提前3个月放弃使用化学避孕方法。

8. 戒烟。

9. 服用产前维生素（含叶酸）。

10. 找一想做妈妈的同伴与你一起开始健康生活方式。

11. 留意月经周期，这会有助于你知道何时排卵及推算受孕时间，并能精确计算预产期。

12. 如果要更换自己的私人医生，请在孕前完成并去拜访。

13. 向朋友请教有关怀孕及做母亲的经验。

14. 避免接触可能对胎儿有伤害的化学物品，它们可能存在于你的工作和生活环境中。

15. 孕前请看牙科医生。

16. 如果你准备怀孕或可能已经怀孕，看病或体检时，请告诉医务人员，以避免不利于胎儿或孕期的检查及用药。

17. 不要再清洁猫窝。

18. 怀孕成功可能要花较长时间。如果你已超过35周岁，努力半年至一年仍未如愿，那么你应尽快去找医生。

19. 开始实施怀孕。

20. 孕后立即宣布怀孕。

21. 向父母请教有关经验，并将你的不同观点和想法告诉他们。

22. 注意休息，白天也小睡片刻。

23. 阅读一份杂志（孕期方面的）。

24. 若有呕吐、胃或心口灼热、便秘等症状，采用非药物疗法。

25. 注意饮水。

26. 再读一本有关的书。

27. 参加产前瑜珈或体育锻炼班。

28. 定期找助产护士或医生检查，以便发现问题及时处理。

29. 参加孕早期培训班。

30. 每日增加300～500卡热量。

31. 如果不打算在家分娩，应在参观几家要去分娩的医院或机构后再选定。

32. 记住并记录找医生的日程时间。

33. 做饮食记录，保证每日摄入所需热量。

34. 要装修房子或婴儿室，应避免油漆和壁纸的有毒气味。保持通风，不要干重活。

35. 多试着照看朋友的婴儿，学习一些护理新生儿的方法。

36. 及时报名参加分娩培训学习班。

37. 游泳对妊娠晚期妇女是项好运动，有助缓解疼痛，并使你觉得腹部重量减轻。

38. 参加母乳喂养学习班，以使你提前做好母乳喂养的准备。

39. 上床前请先做适当的伸展运动，这会防止你腿抽筋。

40. 坚持体育锻炼，感到累了可以放慢速度，但要坚持，这会使你产后快速恢复。

41. 写一份分娩计划，记下在你分娩过程中想要或需要的东西，并告知医生和那些当你分娩时应邀在你身边的人。

42. 准备一部照相机。

43. 避免心情紧张。

44. 让骨盆倾斜，这会有助于缓解疼痛，让胎儿处于良好的出生位置。

45. 如果你的预产期临近了，请准备好自己的东西，不要忘记带上保险证、预约住院的表格、照相机及分娩计划等。

46. 检查临产征兆。

47. 在分娩前照一张像。

48. 读书。

49. 吻你的小宝宝。

生命不易，怎不满怀期待

夜空里，繁星如一春花事，腾腾烈烈，开到盛时，让人担心它简直自己都不知该如何去了结。

繁星能数清吗？它们的历程能弄清楚吗？暂且不说夜空中的繁星，让我们反身自视，便会发现另一度宇宙——苍穹中数以亿计的小光点潮涌而前，奋力在深沉的黑暗中泅泳。尔后，众星寂灭，剩下的是那一颗唯一着陆的光体……

这其实是在描述精子和卵子的结合过程，那是生命最初的故事，是一切音乐的序曲部分，是美酒未饮前的潋滟和期待，是饱蘸水墨的画笔横飞纵舞前的蓄势。

卵子的一生（她是你的“孩子”）

看看孩子们在成为人之前的作为吧，原来他们早就很了不起啊！

女性体内共有两个卵巢，左右各一个，卵巢内住着卵细胞，卵细胞如同口袋包裹着卵子。早在女性出生以前，卵子就存在于温暖的卵细胞中了，她们沉着而安然地睡着，等待某年某月的某一天，成为某人的“新娘”。直到青春期以后，一个月一次的、不可思议的事情就发生了：那么多卵细胞中，只有一个也仅仅有一个卵细胞发展成熟。该月被选中的卵子，沐浴在卵细胞荷尔蒙中渐渐长大，等到她完全成熟的时候，大量黄体酮荷尔蒙就会生成，从而一直围护着新娘的卵细胞破裂了，于是她势如破竹般地从卵巢中飞跃而出，踏上了和精子哥哥相会的旅程——这就是“排卵”。

在人类的细胞中，卵子个头是很大的，直径大约有0.1毫米，凭肉眼就能看到一个白点。成熟的卵子从卵巢中飞跃而出后，输卵管开着像喇叭一样的大口向她发出引诱：“到这里来吧！”卵子很自然地流动着，进入了输卵管中。她在输卵管膨胀的部分等待着命运的相会。时间一刻一刻地过去，在宽大的输卵管中卵子等待着精子，她是焦急的，因为她的生命只有短暂的24小时。

一般来说，精子在射精后2～4天，卵子在排卵后24小时，是精卵结合的时限。在这段时间内，如果精子和卵子没有相会结合，卵子就只好在孤独和等待中枯萎、衰亡。

精子的历程（他也是你的“孩子”）

有一次，有一只小小的精子出发了，它的旅途并不孤单，和它结伴同行的探险家合起来有两三毫升（多的时候有五六毫升）。不要看不起这几毫升，每毫升的精子编制平均是两千万到六千万只，几毫升合起来便有上亿的数目了！这是一场机密的行军，所有的精子都如同赴命的战士，只顾奋力泅泳。它们虽属于同一部队，行军途中却没有指挥官。奇怪的是它们中的每一个都很清楚自己的任务——它们知道将要抢先攀登一块叫“卵子”的陆地，而且这是一场不能回头的旅途。除了第一个着陆的英雄，其他精子唯一的命运就是消亡。

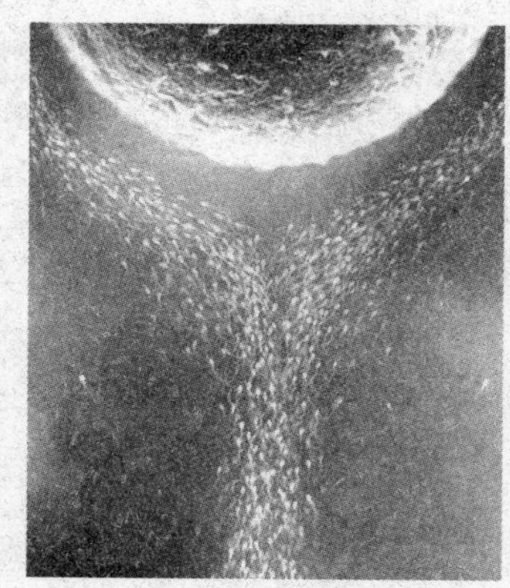

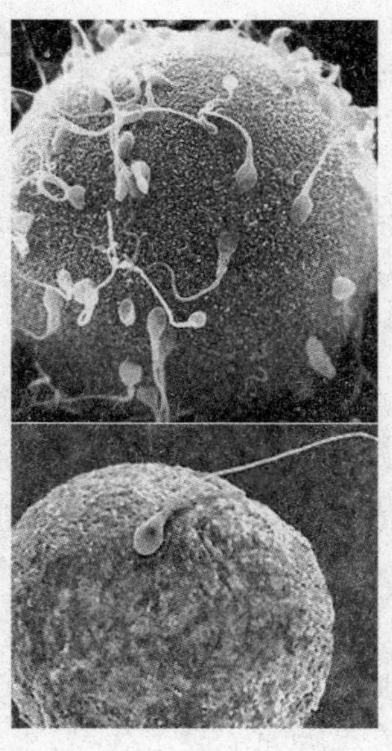

“抱着万一成功的希望”，这句话对它们来说是太奢侈了，因为它们是“抱着亿一成功的希望”全力以赴的。考场、球场都有正常的竞争和淘汰，但竞争淘汰的比率达到如此冷酷无情的程度，除了“精子之旅”以外，也很难在其他现象里找到了。

前行复前行，有些伙伴显然落后了，那超前的彼此互望一眼，才发现大家在相同中原来还是有小异的，其中有一批是X兵种，另一批是Y兵种。Y的体型比较灵活，性格也比较急躁，看来颇有奏凯的希望。但X稳重踏实，一种跑马拉松的战略，是个不可轻敌的角色。这一番“抢渡”，整个途程虽然不过25厘米左右，但相对于小小的精子而言，其行程也不逊于一次长征。精子如同一往无前的战士，一路行去。

这时，卵子的周围突然出现了骚动，她感觉到有很多东西包围在自己的四周。而且，一瞬间，就是这一瞬间，应该是大地倾身、上天动容的一瞬间。

这样说吧，如果你走在街头，有人请你买彩票，你随意买了一张，却中奖了，而且不是一般的奖，是头等大奖，你会怎样兴奋？更何况奖额不是几百万钞票，而是整整一部“生命”！

受精、着床

“是谁进入了卵子的体内？”

“是我。初次见面，卵子妹妹，我是你的精子哥哥。”

精子哥哥和卵子妹妹成为了受精卵，借助输卵管的运动，从相会的地方向定居地——子宫前进。在此期间，受精卵一边憧憬着到达子宫的幸福，一边像桑树的果实一样分裂。另一方面，子宫内为孕育新生命的准备也在紧锣密鼓地进行着。受精卵的床——子宫内膜，在女性雌激素的作用下变得像海面一样柔软、丰厚。

时间大约在受精以后一周，受精卵在子宫内膜中寻找到一个自己的家，并安然进入。当它完全嵌入子宫内膜而着床，这时妊娠才真正开始了。

事实上，在迁入新居前，受精卵也会遭遇困难。有时，恶魔的手会伸出来阻止精卵兄妹关系的稳定；有时，新家不够完善，使受精卵无法安心居住下来。人生遇到挫折，的确有点遗憾，这种妊娠不能成功的情况也常常会发生。

定居下来以后，精子和卵子的新生活开始了，也就是妊娠开始了。从此以后，结成一体的精卵兄妹将用40周的时间孕育成为一个新生命。

人类的受精、着床充满了生命的神秘感，人们并不知道在自己的身体里所发生的一切。一次次的偶然，一次次命运的安排，才促成精、卵的相会，从此才有了繁衍不息的新生命。

生命的产生如此不易，我们怎么能不满怀爱心地期待宝宝的成长呢？

从此以后，我的眼睛不眠地守望着，即使我没有看见你，而那凝望和期盼仍是甜蜜的。

我的心躲在雨季的绿荫中，期待着你的爱情，呵，宝贝，我总在惊奇地静听。你的光辉照亮了我的世界，我的心渴望和你合唱，这一辈子就注定要和你共风雨、同欢笑。风雨、欢笑是你我无休止的合唱！

婴儿是什么？

婴儿就是在你肚子里折磨你，让你吃不下、睡不好、玩不了，却要每天隔着肚皮给他听音乐、背唐诗的小东西。

婴儿就是曾经把你的纤纤细腰变成水桶，把你的妩媚小脸变成猪头，把你的炯炯双眼涂上黑眼圈，把漂亮房间变成狗窝的小魔法师。

婴儿就是彻底改变你好吃懒做、逍遥自在的生活，即使困得想骂、累得想哭，只要他一声哭叫，马上精神抖擞爬起来打点他的一切，而他整天作威作福，稍有不如意就耍赖的小磨人精儿。

婴儿就是坐在你怀里撒尿，骑在你头上拉屎，而你还得装出一脸幸福满足相的小“南霸天”。

婴儿就是可以让你端着饭碗研究他的大便，一边闻着臭气一边品味菜香的“小魔鬼”。

婴儿就是可以让你光天化日之下解开衣襟给他喂奶，而你从容自若，面不改色心不跳的小定心丸。

婴儿就是整天让你提心吊胆，吃多了怕撑着，吃少了怕饿着，穿多了怕捂着，穿少了怕冻着，有点风吹草动就吓得你睡不着觉的小捣蛋。

婴儿就是他笑你就开心，他哭你就难受，他疼你更疼，他生病你就恨不得那些该死的病菌全跑到你身上，充当他的“替病羊”的小晴雨表。

婴儿就是让你成为花钱如流水，一边咬牙切齿一边慷慨解囊的“购物狂”的小吸血鬼。

婴儿就是让你知父母恩知父母苦，理解“父母在，不远游”这个道理的小参照物。

婴儿就是他伤你若干却无所谓，你打他一下心里却疼好久的不公平产物。

婴儿就是他无意识的一声“妈妈”，随随便便的一个眼神，不经意的一个抚摸，睡梦中的一次皱眉，就让你热泪盈眶的小催泪弹。

婴儿就是他轻轻地挥动一下小手，小小的一声呼唤，就让你放下一切事情狂奔到他面前的小指挥官。

婴儿就是当你身心俱疲，他的一个笑容就能让你全身轻爽，马上灿烂起来的一束阳光。

婴儿就是风再大，雨再大，都能让你信心百倍等到彩虹的小天使。

婴儿就是他一天天长大，你一天天成熟，他一天天成熟，你一天天老去，却让你无怨无悔、不求回报的小可爱。

婴儿就是等到你白发苍苍，那个领着小孩让他叫你奶奶的人。

第1周

走近开始

第1周记：你坐在向南的露台上，我在昏暗的房间里不禁唱起歌谣。暮色苍茫，从窗口飘进湿润的绿叶的清香，似乎预示着某件事情将要发生。

生命的前奏　怀孕第一周，实际上只是你的月经周期进入第一周，此时你还谈不上怀孕与否。数周后当你知道自己怀孕时，根据妊娠期的算法，本周是第一周。妊娠期的算法是从末次月经第一天开始计算的，所以，在第一周里，夫妻实际上还是处在怀孕前的准备阶段。

准备好了吗?

精子和卵子的相遇、结合，这个创造神奇生命的重要过程，是在悄然无声中发生的。未出生的宝宝仿佛是一粒等待勃发的种子，准父母们正如在一旁日夜守候的园丁，满怀欣喜地期待着种子破土而出的那一刻。在父母内心里，每个宝宝的孕育、诞生和成长都是一个奇迹。为了孕育聪明、健康的宝宝，我们想在你即将实施的“造人”行动的第一周，回顾一下你应该提前做的准备工作，并根据情况给出一些建设性的意见。

1. 在过去1年或者说就在受孕前的3~6个月，你做了怀孕前的基本准备工作吗？比如说，是否做过孕前健康检查以及咨询，是否接触过烟酒、咖啡类饮料，是否接受过辐射（如照射X光），是否在对人体有害（如农药、麻醉剂、铅、汞、镉等）的环境中作业过，是否吃过禁忌药品，停服口服避孕药是否有半年的时间，是否使用过含雌激素的护肤品，是否养过宠物，如此等等。如果这些基本的准备工作，你不了解，甚至什么都没有做，那么，我们建议你再铺垫一段时间，因为小宝贝最好不是偶然受孕“结下的果实”。

2. 身体调养好了吗？ 怀孕前的几个月，夫妻双方饮食要健康，营养要均衡充足，这不仅是为将来的胎宝贝准备的，它还能使你更轻松地应对孕后及产后出现的各种变化。尤其是叶酸，在你打算受孕的前3个月，每天要补充400微克。如果这些工作没有到位，我们还是要建议你推迟时间受孕，补上这一课。

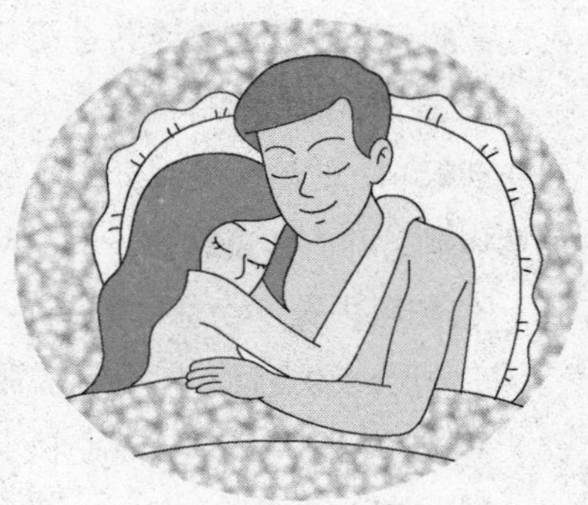

3. 作好思想准备了吗？ 首先和老公沟通好。夫妻双方是否能接受孩子的到来，经济条件是否许可，居所是否存在问题等等，都须要落实好。

如果所有的一切都准备就绪，那么我们就要恭喜你们了。新的生命的序幕即将拉开，祝你们好运！

孕前检查是一道命令

孕前检查非常重要，如果此前未作检查，本周就要“临时抱佛脚”了。另外人们往往有一个误区，只检查准妈妈而忽略了准爸爸。其实，宝宝是两人的结晶，因此准爸爸孕前检查也一样重要。

1.准妈妈孕前检查

检查时间早晨，空腹。

◎血常规（血型）：及早发现贫血等血液系统疾病，因为如果母亲贫血，不仅会出现产后出血、产褥感染等并发症，还会殃及宝宝，给宝宝带来一系列影响，例如易感染、抵抗力下降、生长发育落后等。

◎尿常规：有助于肾脏疾患早期的诊断。十个月的孕期对于母亲的肾脏系统是一个巨大的考验，身体的代谢增加，会使肾脏的负担加重。如果肾脏存在疾患，后果会非常严重。

◎便常规：消化系统疾病、寄生虫感染诊断，例如弓形虫感染，如果不及早发现，会造成流产、胎儿畸形等严重后果。

◎肝功能（两对半）：各型肝炎、肝脏损伤诊断。如果母亲是病毒性肝炎患者，没有及时发现，怀孕后会造成非常严重的后果，早产，甚至新生儿死亡。肝炎病毒还可垂直传播给孩子。

◎胸透：结核病等肺部疾病诊断。患有结核的女性怀孕后，会使治疗用药受到限制，使治疗受到影响。而且，活动性的结核常会因为产后的劳累而加重病情，并有传染给孩子的危险。

◎妇科内分泌全套：月经不调等卵巢疾病诊断，例如患卵巢肿瘤的女性，即使肿瘤为良性，怀孕后常常也会因为子宫的增大，影响了对肿瘤的观察，甚至导致流产、早产等危险。

◎白带常规：筛查滴虫、霉菌、细菌的感染，如果患有性传播疾病，最好是先彻底治疗，然后再怀孕。否则会引起流产、早产、胎膜早破等危险。

◎染色体检测：及早发现克氏征、特纳氏综合症等遗传疾病、不育症。

◎口腔检查：如果牙齿有问题，就要及时修补排除。孕期治疗牙病对宝宝会有不良影响。

◎全身体格检查：进行全身检查及生育能力评估，以便医生对准父母提出孕前科学指导。

2.准爸爸孕前检查

◎孕前精液检查：不少男性朋友嫌取精液麻烦而不愿检查，但是，与妻子的生育力检查的麻烦和费用相比，已经算是很方便的了。也正是因为平时体检不会检查精液，因此检查更有必要。

◎泌尿系统检查：泌尿生殖系统的毛病对下一代健康影响极大，如果没检查过，务必检查。

◎传染病检查：如果多年没有进行体检或者没做过婚检，那么肝炎、梅毒、艾滋病等传染病检查也是很必要的。

◎健康咨询：医生还会详细询问体检者及家人以往的健康状况，曾患过何种疾病，如何治疗等情况，特别要重点询问精神病、遗传病等，必要时还要求检查染色体、血型等。

如果发现问题，应该在医生指导下重新计划怀孕。准妈妈的疾病一定要在孕前诊断治疗，等到怀孕时才发现，对胎儿和母体危害较大。以上几项孕前检查都非常简单，只要花费半天时间，几乎所有医院妇产科都可以做，适合每个准妈妈。其他还有一些特殊的检查，是否需要进行，可向医生咨询。为了下一代，孕前检查对准爸爸准妈妈来说是一道必须执行的命令。

避开九大受孕“雷区”

1．情绪过度波动和精神受到创伤后；

2．烟酒过度、戒烟戒酒不足6个月；

3．生殖器官手术后不足6个月；

4．产后恢复时间不足6个月；

5．脱离有毒有害物质时间不足3个月；

6．照射x射线、放射线治疗、服用病毒性感冒药物或者慢性疾病用药后不足3个月；

7．口服或埋植避孕药停药时间不足3个月；

8．长途出差、疲劳而归不足2周；

9．天气酷热或暴风雨时。

小贴士……学量基础体温

基础体温（BBT）是指人在基础状态下的体温。一般是在睡眠6～8小时后，无任何干扰，如起立、活动、进食等的情况下，立即测量的口腔温度，夜班工作者可于睡眠6～8小时后测量。它能在某种程度上反应卵巢功能，是女性朋友自我检查内分泌功能和指导有计划妊娠和避孕的好方法。此法简单、易行，但需要坚持数月。

怎样测基础体温？

要测得准确的基础体温应正确执行以下几项：

1.准备一个水银温度计，掌握读表方法；

2.每晚临睡前将水银柱甩至35℃以下、酒精棉球消毒后放于床旁伸手可及处；

3.每晨醒后，即刻测量舌下体温5分钟。尽量固定在清晨5～7时测量，一般前后相差不超过半小时为佳。测温前严禁翻身、起床、大小便、吸烟、进食、谈话等，测量后将体温记录在表格中。

最初的叮咛（第1~4周）

怀孕计划一旦开始，生活上就有了讲究。对于最初几周，我们的建议是：

1．保持愉快的心情。

夫妻双方放松身心，多做有趣有益的活动，尽量减轻各种心理压力。丈夫多分担一些家务活，多做一些让妻子高兴的事情。

2．坚持良好的生活方式。

（1）不服用违禁药。

（2）戒除烟酒，戒除咖啡因饮料、碳酸饮料、浓茶。

（3）不要劳累，做轻松的活动，干轻松的家务，把家布置得温馨一些。

（4）不穿紧身牛仔裤、化纤质地的内衣裤。

（5）起床、睡觉、上下班、工作，合理安排，并适当运动。

（6）不要熬夜，保证睡眠8小时以上，最好晚上10时以前睡觉。

（7）做好个人卫生，尤其是生殖器卫生。丈夫不要频洗热水澡。

3.营养充足均衡。

(1) 摄入多种优质蛋白质、维生素和微量元素。不偏食。

(2) 少吃罐头、油炸、油腻食物、冷饮之类的食物，多吃蔬菜、瘦肉和豆制品。

(3) 每天补充400微克叶酸。

4．谨慎用药。

夫妻双方都不要随意使用药物，如果必须服药，要在医生指导下使用。

第2周

“幸孕时刻”

第2周记：迷朦中，我看见蝴蝶在阳光中飞舞，树叶在轻轻摇动，它们低唱着同一支歌。我独自蹒跚在果园中，倾听着，蝴蝶和树叶对我唱的什么，真是个难解的谜。

但是，我闻到果实飘香，它确已成熟了。

生命的前奏　怀孕第2周，实际上是你的月经周期进入第2周。此时准妈妈的身体正在很隐秘地发生变化，卵巢准备排卵以接受精子的到来。这段时间，要注意把握好“幸孕时刻”完成“幸福工作”，千万别错失良机！

顺利完成“幸福工作”

这几天，在排卵日之前，请保持良好的状态，准备“幸孕时刻”的“幸福工作”。注意留心最易受孕期，特别是排卵日这一天，是“黄金日”，是最理想的受孕日。从排卵期第一天开始，每隔一两天性交一次。研究证明，下午5时至7时做爱，是最佳“造人”的“幸孕时刻”，请把握住！

准备不足或临时出现情况不想怀孕，性生活就要错过排卵期。

月经期	排卵前安全期	排卵期			排卵后安全期
12345	6 7 8 9	10 11	12 13 14 15 16	17 18 19	20 21 22 23 24 25 26 27 28
不宜性交	性交不会怀孕	性交可能怀孕	最易受孕期。排卵日基础体温急剧下降，宫颈粘液拉丝最长，外阴部有明显的湿润感。把握住！	性交可能怀孕	性交不会怀孕

准确把握排卵日

1. 根据生理周期推算排卵日

正常育龄妇女每个月来1次月经，从本次月经来潮开始到下次月经来潮第1天，称为1个月经周期。28天是一般月经周期的平均日数。实际上，月经周期日数可能短至21天，或长至35天，只要其间隔是规则的即可视为正常。

排卵在一个月经周期中只发生于某一天。妇女的排卵日期一般在下次月经来潮前的14天左右（即从下一次月经的大概日期向前倒数14天）。离开卵巢的卵子在24小时之内受精能力最强，而男子的精子在女子生殖道内可维持2～3天的受精能力，故在排卵的前后几天里性交容易受孕。

根据排卵和月经之间关系，可以按月经周期推算出排卵期。

从下次月经来潮的第1天算起，倒数14天或减去14天就是排卵日，排卵日前5天和后4天，连同排卵日一共10天，称为排卵期。在排卵前的3天内和排卵发生后的1天内发生的性交，最容易怀孕，所以称为最易受孕期。

推算方法：例如，某女性的月经周期为28天，本次月经来潮的第1天在12月2日，那么下次月经来潮是在12月30日（12月2日加28天），再从12月30日减去14天，则12月16日就是排卵日。排卵日前5天和后4天，也就是12月11～20日为排卵期。

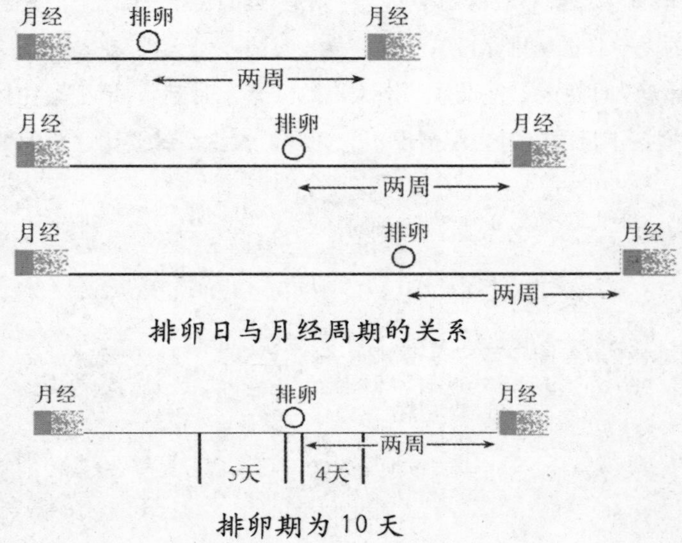

排卵日与月经周期的关系

排卵期为10天

2. 根据基础体温推算排卵日

基础体温是指人体在较长时间的睡眠后醒来，尚未进行任何活动(如说话、翻身或进食等)前所测得的口腔体温。清晨醒来时须立即测量。

正常育龄妇女的基础体温与月经周期一样，呈周期性变化，这种体温变化与排卵有关。正常情况下，妇女在排卵前的基础体温较低（36.6℃以下），排卵后因卵巢形成黄体，黄体分泌孕酮会使体温上升 0.3～0.5℃或更高一些，使体温呈现高低两相变化。高温期约持续 12～16 天（平均 14 天）。

正常妇女基础体温曲线上体温下降后急剧上升的一天就是排卵日。

如果没怀孕，黄体萎缩停止分泌孕酮，体温下降，回到基本线，月经来潮。如果已经怀孕，黄体受到胚胎分泌荷尔蒙支持，继续分泌孕酮，体温持续高温。如果卵巢功能不良，没有排卵也没有黄体形成，则体温将持续低温。

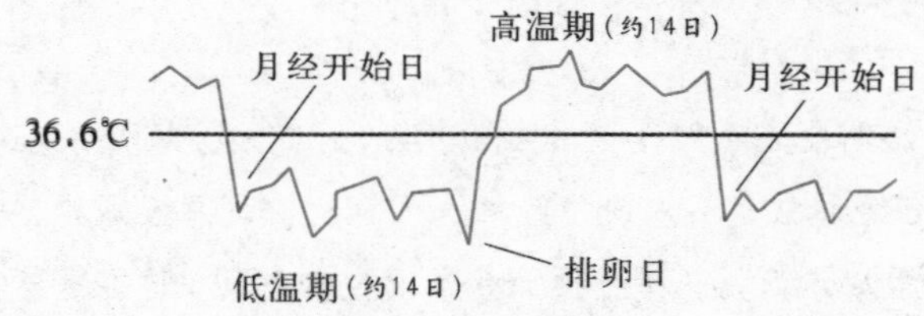

正常妇女基础体温曲线

3. 根据宫颈粘液推算排卵日

随着排卵和月经周期的变化，宫颈粘液的量和性质也跟着变化。在月经周期中，先后出现不易受孕型、易受孕型和极易受孕型 3 种宫颈粘液。

(1) 不易受孕型宫颈粘液：为月经周期中的早期粘液，在月经干净后出现，持续3天左右。这时的宫颈粘液少而粘稠，外阴部呈干燥状而无湿润感，内裤上不会沾到粘液。这种感觉的天数在每个周期里可发生变化，在长周期里可能天数很多，在短周期里可能很少，甚至没有。此为阴部“干燥期”，

(2) 易受孕型宫颈粘液：这种粘液出现在月经周期中的第9～10天以后，随着卵巢中卵泡发育，雌激素水平升高，宫颈粘液逐渐增多，稀薄，呈乳白色，这时外阴部有湿润感。干燥感的结束正是粘液的开始。如果月经后没有干燥日，表示粘液已经开始，分泌物发生变化，预示着可孕性。

可以妊娠的期间是，排卵前有粘液的日子到排卵日后的三天内。

(3) 极易受孕型宫颈粘液：排卵前几天，雌激素进一步增加，宫颈粘液

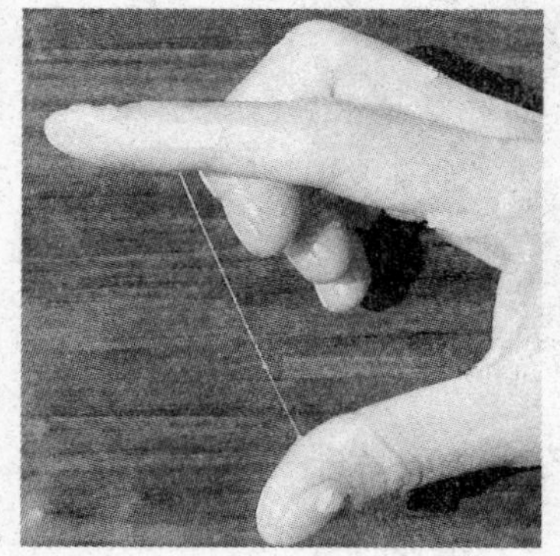

含水量更多，也更加清亮如蛋清状，粘稠度最小，滑润而富有弹性，用拇指和食指可把粘液拉成很长的丝状（可达10厘米以上），这时外阴部感觉有明显的湿润感。一般认为分泌物清彻透明呈蛋清状，拉丝度最长的一天很可能是排卵日，在这一天及其前后各3天为排卵期。

卵巢排卵后，黄体形成并产生孕激素，从而抑制子宫颈细胞分泌粘液，所以宫颈粘液又变少而粘稠，成为不易受孕型宫颈粘液，直到下次月经来潮。

小贴士……计算预产期

妊娠期自成熟卵受精后至胎儿娩出，一般为266天左右。为便于计算，妊娠通常是从末次月经第一天算起，足月妊娠约为280天（40周）。一旦确诊妊娠，便可预计孩子出生的时间，这在医学上称为"预产期"。大部分准妈妈在预产期前后2周内分娩。对于经期不准或是不太清楚经期的孕妇来说，用超声波来估计预产期特别有帮助。

计算预产期的步骤：

（1）找出最后一次月经的第一天日期。

（2）在月份上减去3或加上9，在日期上加7，就得到预产期的日期。如果日期得数超过30，月份顺延到下月，日期减30。

例如：末次月经是2004年2月5日，则月份=2+9=11；日期=5+7=12，即预产期为2004年11月12日。

又如：末次月经是2004年9月5日，则月份=9−3=6（或9+9=18，即相当于2005年6月）；日期=5+7=12，即预产期为2005年6月12日。

再如：末次月经是2004年2月25日，则月份=2+9=11；日期=32−30=2（即25+7=32，相当于下个月的2号），即预产期为2004年12月2日。

第3周

已经开始

第3周记：昨夜在露台上，你举起了青春洋溢的醇酒。我将杯儿放在唇边，合上双眼微笑了。你撩起我的长发，我宁静而又洋溢着柔情地将脸庞贴在你的肩头。

昨夜，月光梦一般漫溢在安睡的大地上。

生命起航 卵子和精子在最佳时刻结合了，这只是第一步，只是受精过程的完结，生命才刚刚步入旅程。受精卵需要旅行到子宫腔，并在那里安营扎寨，这一过程才算终结。在这个过程中，受精卵可能出现意外，也可能到了子宫腔而不能扎根。因此，你需要等待，直到好消息的到来。

只是第一步

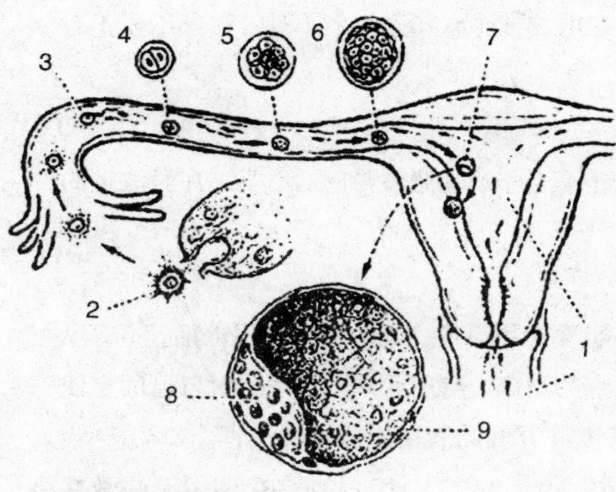

卵子受精与着床全程示意图

1精子 2排卵 3受精 4合子 5卵裂球
6桑堪球 7胚泡 8内细胞群 9原始滋养层

本周，当你工作、走路或睡觉时，你的体内却在发生神奇的改变。

受精卵在输卵管的蠕动和纤毛的推动下，向子宫腔移动，同时发生分裂（也称卵裂）。约经24小时完成第一次卵裂，变成2个细胞，继而分裂成8个细胞（称“胚球”）。第3天，分裂成16个细胞，形如桑椹，故称“桑椹胚”。第4天，受精卵进入子宫腔，发育成“早期胚泡”。进入子宫后2～3天，受精卵发育成“晚期胚泡”并开始“着床”，“着床”在11～12天内完成。所以，第3周是胚泡植入子宫“着床”的时候。但这时“着床”并未成，还不能说“怀孕”成功了。

为了有可能发生的“怀孕”，在这段认定的“受孕期”里，你可能要注意一些容易令人忽视的问题，营绝对安全的子宫环境。如果怀孕随后得到确认，你就要这样一直保持下去，直到宝宝安全降临人世。

营造安全的子宫环境

为了让宝宝顺利成长。必须努力创造出一个健康的子宫环境。具体事项如下：

1. 不服违禁药

(1) 怀孕期间，母亲不能服用禁药，如大麻、迷幻药、咖啡因等。

(2) 购买饮料之前，要阅读碳酸饮料罐上的标签，或问一问软饮料中咖啡因的含量。如果你喜欢喝热的饮料，试试喝热开水（可以加些柠檬）、热牛奶、热苹果汁或绿茶。

2. 远离射线

(1) 尽量不看电视、少用电脑。与电视机荧光屏的距离至少要保持2米；与电脑荧光屏要保持1米，每天在电脑前不宜超过1个小时。腹部不要正对荧光屏。

(2) 避免进行X线照射。

(3) 少用电磁炉和微波炉烹煮食物。启动微波炉时，不要站在微波炉的前方。

(4) 不要使用电热毯取暖。

(5) 尽量不使用无绳电话，也要少用手机。尽量少用公用电话，不得已时，讲话时尽量与话筒保持远一点的距离，使用后马上洗手。对自己固定使用的办公电话及家庭电话，要经常用75%的酒精棉球擦拭消毒。

(6) 睡觉时，不要将闹钟、随身听、MP3、MP4等放在枕头边，应放在距离自己1米以外的地方。

任何一种电器在不使用时，最好将其插头拔掉。经常开窗通风，可以让飘荡在室内空气中的电磁波及时排出。平时应多吃富含维生素A、维生素C和蛋白质的食物，比如乳类、蛋类、胡萝卜、瘦肉、动物肝、新鲜绿叶蔬菜等，能加强机体抵抗电磁辐射的能力。

3. 危险因素

(1) 要注意饮用的自来水是否含有有害的化学物质，如铅（如有条件，可饮用矿泉水）。

(2) 家庭清洁用品是否安全。洗衣要用肥皂，不宜用洗衣粉。

(3) 不要上美发店（不要电烫和染发，也不要涂指甲油、口红）。

(4) 将猫、狗委托别人带养（防止弓形体病传染给发育中的胎儿）。

(5) 如果邻近公寓正在喷洒除虫剂，请先离开一段时间，至少到你再也闻不到味道为止。

(6) 少入厨房。如果需要去，一定要尽量减少停留时间。可在厨房中安置排油烟机或排风扇，让厨房保持良好的通风，也可适当地多使用电炊具。如果你有煤炉或煤气器具，检查一下是否有漏气的可能性。

(7) 不要做大扫除或搬提重物。避免做剧烈运动。严禁从事骑单车、打网球、羽毛球、篮球、游泳等激烈运动。

4. 呼吸干净的空气

(1) 不要居住在繁忙的交通要道或向空气排放污染物的工厂附近，或者在总是充满烟雾的区域。如果烟尘指数过高，请留在室内，最好将窗户关上。

(2) 尽可能避免经过拥挤的街道，以及堵在排放大量废气的交通工具，如卡车与公共汽车之后。

(3) 如果有车，最好不要自己去加油。开车时紧闭车窗，尤其在交通拥挤时，关起窗户与天窗。

(4) 多在幽静的绿荫路上散步，有条件者最好经常置身于返璞归真的大森林中做“森林浴”。

5. 其他

(1) 用无污染、无毒制剂彻底洗净水果和蔬菜，并将外皮去除。

(2) 最好买施有机肥、没有喷洒除虫剂的蔬果。

(3) 远离含铅与水银的油漆、去漆剂，也不要使用香薰产品或芳香剂。

(4) 洗碗、淘米、洗菜时，不要将手直接浸入冷水中。洗碗要选用不含有害物质的洗洁精。

(5) 切勿憋尿不上厕所。

(6) 如果你有泡澡的习惯，最好改用淋浴，以避免泌尿生殖系统感染。

(7) 切生肉后一定要洗手。炒菜、吃涮羊肉时一定要把菜炒熟涮透。

(8) 避免穿牛仔裤、紧身裤及高跟鞋。

(9) 远离嘈杂的舞厅，若想听音乐、跳舞，可以在家里或环境安静、整洁、优雅的环境中进行。

(10) 不要到人群集聚的地方，避免与患流感、风疹、传染性肝炎等患者接触。

洗澡不再是随意的事了

洗澡对平常人来说，是一件小事。但对孕妇，尤其是对怀孕早期的孕妇，洗澡就不再是一件容易的事了。

1. 时间不适宜过长

妇女怀孕后，洗澡时间不要过长，因为洗澡时间过长会引起胎儿缺氧。

胎儿的氧气主要是通过脐带从母体获得。母体在缺氧的情况下，胎儿也会随之缺氧。洗澡时，浴室内由于通风不良，空气混浊，湿度大，再加上热水的刺激，使孕妇体内的血管扩张，血液流入躯干、四肢较多，进入大脑和胎盘的血液自然相对减少了，氧气供给也就减少了。因此，孕妇洗澡时间过长，就会造成胎儿缺氧。胎儿缺氧，若时间很短，一般不会有什么不良后果。但若时间过长，就会影响其神经系统的生长发育，轻者影响胎儿出生后的智力，重则出现唇裂、外耳畸形等先天性疾病。

孕妇每次洗澡时间不要超过15分钟，或以孕妇本身不出现头昏、胸闷为度。

2. 水温不宜过高

研究显示，怀孕前3个月，如果长时间让身体温度超过39℃以上，容易使发育中的胎儿发生脊髓缺损的危险性增加。在接近怀孕第一个月末，高温对胎儿伤害的可能性最高。

孕妇在怀孕期，不论是何种原因引起的体温升高，如感染发热、夏日中暑、高温作业、洗热水澡（尤其是热水泡浴）、剧烈运动等，都可能使早期胚胎受到伤害，特别是胎儿的中枢神经系统受害最为明显。所以，建议准妈妈采用其他方法替代泡热水澡，比如冲澡、泡脚等。冬季，最好利用空调或暖气来调节室内温度。

3. 不宜坐浴

孕妇如果洗澡采用坐浴方式，不仅会影响阴道的生理环境，还可能引起早产。

正常情况下，妇女阴道内保持一定的酸度，可以防止病菌的繁殖，起到防御外邪侵害的作用。这种生理现象与卵巢分泌的雌激素和孕激素有密切关系。坐浴时，浴液中的脏水有可能进入阴道内，容易引起宫颈炎、附件炎等，甚至发生宫内感染而引起早产。因此，孕妇不要坐浴，更不要到公共浴池去洗澡。妊娠后期的妇女，绝对禁止坐浴。

真实故事——怀上的经过

9月份，YJ（月经）后我们就计算着PL（排卵）日，我周期是32天，初步算出我的PL日在20号左右。

9月18号，早晨体温36.4℃，发现白带有拉丝现象。晚上我们就AA（同房）了，AA后老公帮我把臀部下垫高（放了个枕头），很难受地睡了一夜。

9月19号，早晨体温36.2℃，晚上我们也AA了。AA后，照样把我的臀部下垫高，很难受地睡到半夜，就上厕所了。

9月20号，早晨体温36.3℃，老公很累，没有AA。

9月21号，早晨体温36.2℃，我发现自己有一种无心想AA的感觉，不过AA后，还是照样把我的臀部下垫高，睡到半夜，就上厕所了。

9月22号，早晨体温36.2℃，没有AA。

9月23号，早晨体温36.4℃，RF(乳房)时常会感到涨痛。

9月24号，早晨体温36.5℃，发现我上厕所的次数比平时多得多，还有我的腰很酸，直都直不起。

9月25号，早晨体温36.8℃，腰酸，有点尿频，RF涨痛。

9月26号，早晨体温36.6℃，腰酸，有点尿频，RF涨痛。

9月27号，早晨体温36.8℃，腰酸，有点尿频，RF涨痛。

9月28号，早晨体温36.8℃，腰酸，有点尿频，RF涨痛，早晨起床快的话，有一种恶心感，不过可以忍一下，就可以过去了。

9月29号～10月2号，每天情况一样：

早晨体温36.8℃，腰酸，有点尿频，RF涨痛，有点恶心。

10月3号～10月5号，每天也情况一样：

早晨体温36.8℃，腰酸，有点尿频，RF涨痛，有点恶心，没胃口。

10月6号，早晨体温36.9℃，有点尿频，RF涨痛，有点恶心，感冒了。

10月7号，早晨体温37.0℃，感冒，腰酸，有点尿频，RF涨痛，有点恶心。

10月8号，早晨体温36.9℃，感冒，腰酸，有点尿频，RF涨痛，有点恶心。

10月9号，早晨体温36.9℃，感冒，腰酸，有点尿频，RF涨痛，有点恶心。去医院正式确定怀孕了。

天啊，我怀孕了，我真的怀孕了！

第4周

安营扎寨了

第4周记：如果卵子成功受精，受精卵边就会分裂边旅行，经过十来天，即在第4周，将在肥厚松软的子宫内膜着床，这时才意味着真正的开始。

我与丈夫的配合应该是成功的。

我的宝贝！我仿佛看见了你温柔地笑着，我仿佛听见了你咿呀地说着，我的心将听到了你话里的甜蜜。

夜色深沉，庭院宁静，他已入睡，我沉吟地微笑着，睡意全无……

生命起航　到第4周，胚泡已悄然在你的子宫里着床了。现在你的子宫内膜变得肥厚松软而且富有营养，血管轻轻扩张，水分充足。

胚泡在子宫内着床后，迅速向四周伸展，形成胚胎的原始内胚层、原始外胚层，两胚层呈现出圆盘状，即长约2毫米的“胚盘”。到第4周末时，在胚盘内、外两胚层之间，由外胚层分化出一层细胞，形成胚内中胚层，此时3个胚层就形成了，它们是胎体发育的原始基础，每一个胚层都分化为不同的组织。外胚层分化成神经系统、眼睛的晶体、内耳的膜迷路、皮肤表层、毛发和指甲等；中胚层分化成肌肉骨骼、结缔组织、循环系统、泌尿系统；内胚层则分化成消化系统、呼吸系统的上皮组织及有关的腺体，膀胱、阴道下段及前庭等。

如果“幸福工作”奏效，那么“胎儿”此时已经在你的子宫里安营扎寨了，除了在医生指导下继续补充叶酸外，要更加注意营养和休息。日常生活中的其他问题，参照前面讲的内容处理。

谨防药物致畸

怀孕以后，胎儿各器官发育时间不一，所以胎儿致畸的易感期也不同。例如，中枢神经系统的致畸易感期为受精后15～55天，心脏为20～40天，眼为24～39天，四肢为24～46天，外生殖器为36～56天。妊娠3个月以上的胎儿，各器官已经形成，此时外界环境的致畸影响大为减少。因此，为确保妊娠期母婴安全，应提倡在妊娠期（尤其是妊娠前3个月）少用药或不用药；凡属可用可不用的药物，应一律不用。

1. 用药准则

（1）一种药可以解决病痛的，不必用几种药；口服有效的尽量少打针。

（2）患病非用药物治疗不可时，一定要去医院经医生详细检查和明确诊断后，切实按照医嘱用药，千万不可自己随意滥用药物。

（3）即使是按照医嘱用药，但仍出现药物不良反应时，为了慎重起见，应立即停药并及时去医院再作检查与治疗，必要时应在医生指导下改用其他药物。

（4）对怀孕前曾引起过敏或其他严重不良反应的药物，特别是注明"孕妇慎用"或"孕妇禁用"的药物，包括中草药和中成药在内，均应慎用或禁用。

（5）多选用中草药，少用化学合成药。

（6）患有慢性病需要长期服药的孕妇，妊娠后应根据病情适当减少药物的用量，或者选用对胎儿影响较小的药物。

（7）药品疗效有争议的坚决不用。

（8）不要轻信药品广告，不要片面理解药物说明书，要听从医务人员的指导。

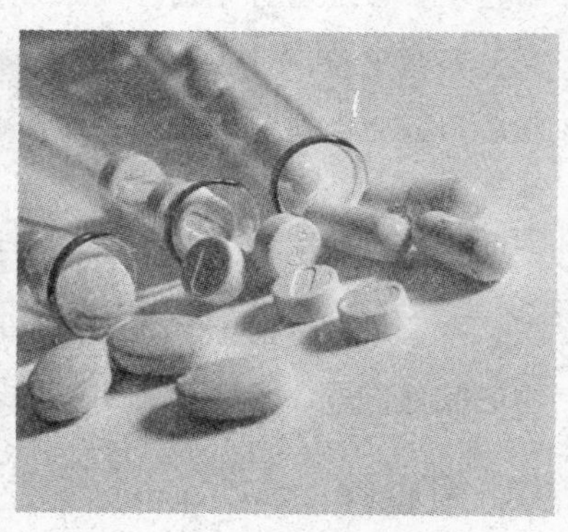

2. 注意的问题

（1）由于药物等因素有时还会影响器官的功能，如引起耳聋、肾功能减退等，所以，妊娠12周后用药还应十分慎重。

（2）用药要遵医嘱，既不要忌医禁药，又要谨慎用药。

（3）任何药物都要经医生指示才可服用。时间与剂量须遵照医生指示。

（4）除非经医生指示，否则不可以混合服用任何成药。

（5）考虑采用较安全的替代方式来代替服用药物。

坚果，为孕期加油

胎儿大脑发育需要的第一营养成分是不饱和脂肪酸，坚果含有丰富的不饱和脂肪酸。另外，坚果类食物中还含有15%～20%的优质蛋白质和十几种重要的氨基酸，这些氨基酸都是构成脑神经细胞的主要成分，同时还含有对大脑神经细胞有益的维生素B_1、维生素B_2、维生素B_5、维生素E及钙、磷、铁、锌等。因此，无论是对准妈妈还是胎儿，坚果都是补脑益智的佳品。

1. 核桃

补脑、健脑是核桃的第一大功效。它含有的磷脂具有增长细胞活力的作用，能增强机体抵抗力，促进造血和伤口愈合。核桃仁还有镇咳平喘的作用，尤其是经历冬季的准妈妈，可以把核桃作为首选的零食。

推荐食用方法：核桃可以生吃，也可以加入适量盐水，煮熟吃。

2. 花生

花生蛋白质含量高达30%左右，其营养价值可与鸡蛋、牛奶、瘦肉等媲美，而且易被人体吸收。花生皮还有补血的功效。

推荐食用方法：与黄豆一起炖汤，也可以和莲子一起放在粥里或米饭里。最好不要用油炒着吃。

3. 瓜籽

多吃南瓜籽可以防治肾结石；西瓜籽性味甘寒，有利肺、润肠、止血、健胃等功效；葵花籽所含的不饱和脂肪酸能起降低胆固醇的作用。

推荐食用方法：大多是炒熟了吃。

4. 夏威夷果

夏威夷果原产于澳洲，别名昆士兰果或澳洲胡桃。夏威夷果含油量高达60%～80%，还含有丰富的钙、磷、铁、维生素B_1、B_2和氨基酸。

推荐食用方法：夏威夷果可以鲜食，但更多的是加工成甜味点心。

5. 松籽

松籽含有丰富的维生素A和E，以及人体必需的脂肪酸、油酸、亚油酸和亚麻酸，不但具有益寿养颜、祛病强身之功效，还具有防癌、抗癌之作用。

推荐食用方法：单吃，或者做成美味的松仁玉米。

6. 榛子

榛子含有不饱和脂肪酸，并富含磷、铁、钾等矿物质，以及维生素A、B_1、B_2、烟酸，经常吃可以明目、健脑。

推荐食用方法：单吃，可以压碎拌在冰激凌里或是放在麦片里一起吃。

孕期饮食禁忌

1. 忌偏食挑食、追求高蛋白饮食

有的孕妇偏食鸡鸭鱼肉和高档营养保健品，有的只吃荤菜，不吃素菜，有的不喝牛奶，不吃鸡和蛋，造成营养单一，增加胃肠道的负担，并影响其他营养物质摄入，使饮食营养失去平衡。

2. 忌无节制地进食

有的孕妇不控制饮食。想吃什么吃什么，想吃多少吃多少，喜欢吃的东西拼命吃，造成有的孕妇胖、胎儿巨大。有的只是孕妇自己胖，胎儿却很小。

3. 忌食品过精、过细

孕妇是家庭的重点保护对象，一般都吃精白粉和精白米、面，不吃小米粥和粗粮、麦片，造成维生素B1严重缺乏和不足。

4. 忌摄入过多植物脂肪

如豆油、菜油等，造成单一性的植物脂肪过高，对胎儿脑发育不利，也影响母体健康。应提倡摄入适量的动物脂肪。

5. 忌高脂肪饮食

长期嗜食高脂肪食物，会增加大肠内的胆酸和胆固醇，可能诱发结肠癌。同时，高脂肪食物能增加催乳激素的合成，促发乳腺癌，不利母婴健康。

6. 忌吃刺激性食物

咖啡、浓茶、辛辣食品、饮酒、丈夫吸烟等均会对胎儿产生不良刺激，影响正常发育，甚至导致胎儿畸形。

7. 忌随意进补

孕妇经常服用温热性的补药、补品，比如人参、鹿茸、鹿胎胶、鹿角胶、桂圆、荔枝、胡桃肉等，势必导致阴虚阳亢、气机失调、气盛阴耗、血热妄行，加剧孕吐、水肿、高血压、便秘等症状，甚至引发流产或死胎等。

8. 忌食霉变食品

孕妇食用了被霉菌毒素污染的农副产品和食品后，不仅会发生急性或慢性食物中毒，甚至可殃及胎儿，导致产生遗传性疾病或胎儿畸形，如先天性心脏病、先天愚型等，有的甚至使胎儿停止发育而发生死胎、流产。

9. 忌长期素食

孕妇长期素食，不利于胎儿的生长发育。蛋白质供给不足，可使胎儿脑细胞数目减少，影响日后的智力，还可使胎儿发生畸形或营养不良；脂肪摄入不足，容易导致低体重胎儿的出生，婴儿抵抗力低下，存活率较低；对于孕妇来说，也可能发生贫血、水肿和高血压。

10. 忌高糖饮食

孕妇摄入过多的糖分会削弱人体的免疫力，使孕妇机体抗病力降低，易受细菌、病毒感染，不利优生。

11. 忌盲目补钙

孕妇盲目地摄入高钙饮食，如大量加服钙片、维生素D等，胎儿有可能得高血钙症。一般说来，孕妇在妊娠早期每日需钙量为800毫克，后期可增加到1000～1200毫克，补充钙剂前要明确剂量，需要在医生指导下增补。

12. 忌咸食

受激素水平变化的影响，孕期出现水钠潴留、妊娠后期一些人会出现水肿，咸食或腌制食品对减轻水肿不利，建议清淡饮食。

第5周

"好朋友"还没光顾

第5周记：例假晚了好几天没来，意味着什么？我找出很久以前买的试纸。老公和我一起盯着那试纸。它开始变化了，我们握着彼此的手，屏住呼吸。一条浅浅的蓝线慢慢显现出来，随后越来越深。我怀孕了！激动中我感到些许不真实和不安。

我们去了医院，大夫说，我已经怀孕5个星期了。天啦！精子和卵子在我的身体里相遇已经3周了，他们已分裂成无数的细胞——对了，大夫说，它们由胚泡现在已长成胚胎了。不知不觉中，我宝宝的神经系统、血管和心脏都已经形成了，他的小心脏，从今天起就开始在我身体里跳动了。

哦，天哪！

孕妈妈状况　已经进入第5周，"好朋友"还没光顾，你心情是欣喜还是紧张？生命的种子已种植在你的体内，如果你对孕育一个小宝贝是有备而来，从大约得知自己排卵那时起，你就会非常敏感地关注着自己的一切变化，期待着所希望的事情发生。由于荷尔蒙的作用，你可能未知怀孕就会觉得身体有了一种异样的充实感。果然，你的身体确实发生了变化，出现怀孕的征象。

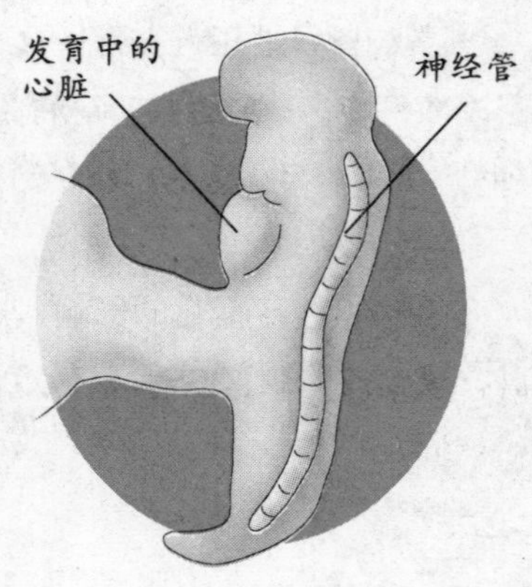

第5周（2月胎宝宝）

胎宝宝状况　本周，小胚芽才发育成胚胎，小胚胎大约长0.6厘米，有苹果籽那么大，外观很像个"小海马"。胚胎面部器官开始形成，眼睛的视网膜也开始形成，鼻孔可清楚地看到。

月经未至，即使还没有经过验孕确认，也要将自己作为孕妇，时时小心，尽量遵照专家提醒的注意事项行事。每天继续补充叶酸。丈夫也要处处关心妻子，进入准爸爸状态。

孕 2 月专家提示（第 5～8 周）

1．如果月经期过 7 天，就应到医院确证是否怀孕。

2．少量多餐，均衡饮食，多吃高蛋白、高纤维素、高铁、高维生素、高矿物质类食物，并摄取充足的水分。

3．避免感冒、受凉，避免出入拥挤的公共场所，也避免与宠物接触。

4．勿过度劳累、逛街或参加长途步行旅游等活动。也不要从事打高尔夫球、日光浴、泡温泉、三温暖、针灸、按摩、长程开车等活动。

5．每天增加 1 小时睡眠时间。

6．每天到绿地或林荫中散步 1 小时。

7．严禁烫头发或过度刺激乳头。

8.勿亲密接触患有癌症正在接受放射线治疗或化学治疗的亲朋好友。

9．不吸烟，拒绝饮用咖啡、浓茶、烈酒等饮料。

10．严禁服用镇静剂或安眠药。失眠时，可于睡前饮用温牛奶或听轻柔音乐以促进睡眠。

11．避免用力的动作（如搬家、搬晒厚重棉被等）。

12．最好理俏丽的短发。

13．丈夫要关心、体贴、照顾妻子，不要过性生活。

14．在医生指导下继续补充叶酸。

生理征兆

当你怀疑自己可能怀孕后不久，身体就会自动验证你是不是真的怀孕了。以下是怀孕早期常见的征兆，这些征兆出现的顺序常常因人而异。

可能会经历	说　明
疲倦	在怀孕的前三个月，你的身体会强迫你睡觉。常常在白天，你会感到极度的疲惫，让你渴望好好睡上一觉。在上午9点左右，你可能坐在桌前，不知不觉就睡着了。这种异常的疲倦通常过了前三个月就会消退。当你的身体渐渐习惯于怀孕时，就会恢复正常的精力。
晨吐	许多孕妇常经历的恶心、呕吐或腹部不适感，晨起常较明显。
月经过期	月经该来的时候没来。
厌恶某些气味	一些气味会让你觉得不舒服。你可能开始有饮食习惯的改变。你开始特别想要吃某些以前从来不碰的食物或以前认为没有味道的食物。
乳房改变	乳房变得更加柔软丰盈，乳晕变暗，乳房有胀痛感。
尿频	在怀孕早期，你会因为怀孕的激素改变而变得尿频（怀孕后期，尿频则是因为膀胱受到增大子宫的压迫）。

初步验孕

当女性发现月月要来的“好朋友”没来时，就要怀疑是否怀孕了。建议你先去药店购买早孕试条自行测试一下，或直接去妇产科请医生为你检查。

1. 初次问诊

“问诊”对第一次到妇产科检查的女性而言，极为重要。因为问诊没做好的话，原本35天一次月经的女性，可能会让医生误以为是28天来一次月经，这时医生为女性所做的验孕，就失去了准确度。

2. 如何验孕

想要验孕的女性，在第一次看诊时，都会被妇产科医生问到“最后一次月经何时来的？”并为你计算一下迟到天数，若超过14天，大部分会怀疑是

否有怀孕的可能。这时医生会请你拿纸杯到厕所自行收集尿液，再拿到检验科检验，5分钟内就会有结果出现。已证实怀孕的女性，医生会为你计算孕期周数，由于第5周的胚胎太小，准妈妈即使做了超声波也无法看到，所以，医生都会延后1周，再为孕妇做更详细的检查。

阴道出血并不少见

已经诊断怀孕后，发现阴道出血的现象并不少见。一旦发现就要及时到医院就诊，明确出血原因。如果是先兆流产，医生会给出你明确的具体建议。如果是其他原因导致的出血，医生会告知相关的注意事项。

真实故事……早孕测试

通过早孕测试纸测定怀孕后的几天里，我还没有出现妊娠反应，每天照样鲜活得很，鲜活得甚至让我自己疑惑起来：“我到底有没有怀孕啊？”老公被我一说也不由一愣：“可是有很多人知道你怀孕了啊，不要闹笑话哦！”

我是个超级敏感型动物，月经也比较规律，根据“经验”，而且又用测试纸测过了，基本上我是不怀疑的，但还是有点不安。老公晚饭后要去医院看病人，我立即就说：“再给我买两根早孕测试纸回来！”

他回来的时候，果然给带了两根测试纸。虽然知道要测晨尿才准，但是我还是急急忙忙抓了一根进了卫生间。一测，天，由于晚餐我喝了很多汤，排出的尿很清，明显不适合测试，结果迟迟不显现。几分钟之后，在灯光下仔细地看了又看，才看到另一道红杠杠，而且是淡淡的。这一晚我有些睡得不踏实了：“要是假阳性，我就要被人笑话了！”

第二天一早，我一到医院上班就去测了一个血，并且请求医院同事优先帮我化验。上午十一点多，结果出来了，相关的数值都明显升高，确定怀孕无疑！我笑了笑，也不知道是高兴还是尴尬。

第6周

终于有感觉了

第6周记：我总感觉想小便。大夫说，我的子宫有梨那么大，而我的宝宝还只不过是个小梨核儿。可就是这个小梨核儿压迫着我的膀胱。我整夜都睡不好，总是往厕所跑。

这些天，当我把手放在肚子上，想着我的宝宝，总是那样激动，但也免不了忧心忡忡。要做母亲了，真是人生的巨大变化！幸好，还有9个月时间让我来慢慢适应这巨大的变化。

我总有一天会把这个小东西抱在怀里，轻轻握着他的小手。我知道他们现在已经在我的肚子里形成了。

胎宝宝状况 在你的子宫里，小胚胎正在迅速成长。心脏已经开始有规律地跳动，初级的肾和心脏等主要器官都已形成，神经管开始连接大脑和脊髓。脑下垂体腺和肌肉纤维也开始发育。眼杯、听泡、鼻窝一一出现。四肢的变化也越来越明显。血液循环建立起来，形成胎盘雏形。“胎宝贝”已开始像蚯蚓那样蠕动了。不过这一切奇妙而微小的变化，你无法感受到。

孕妈妈状况 你的妊娠反应开始明显。由于雌激素与孕激素的刺激作用，你的胸部感到胀痛、乳房增大变软、乳晕有小结节突出且颜色渐渐变深。在月经逾期不至的10多天后，多数女性会时感困倦、排尿频繁，常在清晨起床后感到恶心或频繁呕吐，同时出现头晕、食欲不振、恶油腻食物等现象，但对酸性食物有了兴趣，或是突然非常想吃某种东西，且欲望难以遏止。这就是早孕反应，一般在怀孕12周后自行消失。

现在你的基础体温持续升高。如果还没有做早孕检查，该去医院了。日常生活中的问题，参照前面的叮咛。不要忘记在医生指导下继续补充叶酸。

为宝宝写日记

在将来的某一天，孩子们即将为人父母时，他们如果能看到你的孕期日记，读到有关他们在母体中的情况，以及孩提时代的记录，他们一定会非常激动。日记将成为最好的亲子通道。你的怀孕日记会成为你最珍贵的财产之一。你可以用精美的日记本，也可用你觉得合适的任意一个册子上。

日记写些什么或是怎样写，完全由你自己决定。写下你每一天的感受——欢乐、担心，或是做些什么会让自己感觉更舒服些。重点是你想写什么就写什么。你可能想要强调一些特别的事情，比如说发现怀孕了、第一次胎动、第一次买婴儿衣物、第一次子宫收缩等。告诉宝宝在这些重要时刻，你有什么样的感受。

我觉得怀孕是女人一生最伟大的一部分。在我怀孕期间，常觉得我的生活近乎完美，就好像我正在做我想要做的。在我一生中，从未像现在这样，感觉身为女人竟是如此美好，即使用全世界来交换这种感觉，我也不愿意。我更加感激我的母亲，我希望能够完全了解，她在怀我时的感觉是什么样的，当我年幼时，她是什么样的母亲。我真希望我的母亲能写下她当时的感觉。

同时，要鼓励你的伴侣记日记。毕竟，父亲也会有他的感受的。

珍贵的故事，只有你才能够把它流传下去。孩子在子宫内的时间，在他的一生中是很短暂的，但这段历程十分珍贵，值得记录并保留一辈子。

小贴士……好书推荐

科学技术文献出版社的《怀孕日记》值得推荐。

这是一本怀孕指导书，也是一本怀孕纪念册。你每天都可以从书中了解到胎宝宝当天的情况，并与他相互交流。你还可以贴上每个月的大肚子怀孕照片，也可以随时记下自己的感受。除了你自己贴上的孕照，全书没有一张别人的插图照片。所以可以说，这是一部完全属于你自己的怀孕纪念册。

上医院检查

怀孕是独一无二的，不管你具备多少怀孕知识，接受定期产检是绝对必须的。定期产检，不仅仅只是量量体重、血压、检测胎儿、验验尿而已。更重要的是发现问题，解决问题，让你准确地了解胎儿的现况，在精神层面上，给你一种安定感，让你怀着喜悦的心情，来面对怀孕期间的种种不适。

妊娠第6周或第一次正式检查，包括下列检查项目：

1．问诊：家族疾病史、过去疾病史、本胎不适症状。

2．身体检查：体重、身高、血压、甲状腺、乳房、骨盆腔检查、胸部及腹部检查。

3．实验室检验：血液常规、血型、Rh因子、VDRL、尿液常规、子宫颈抹片细胞检验。

4．例行产检：例行产检内容包括：

(1) 问诊内容：本胎不适症状如水肿、静脉曲张、出血、腹痛、头痛、痉挛等。

(2) 身体检查：体重、血压、腹长（宫底高度）、胎心音、胎位。

(3) 实验室项目：尿蛋白、尿糖。

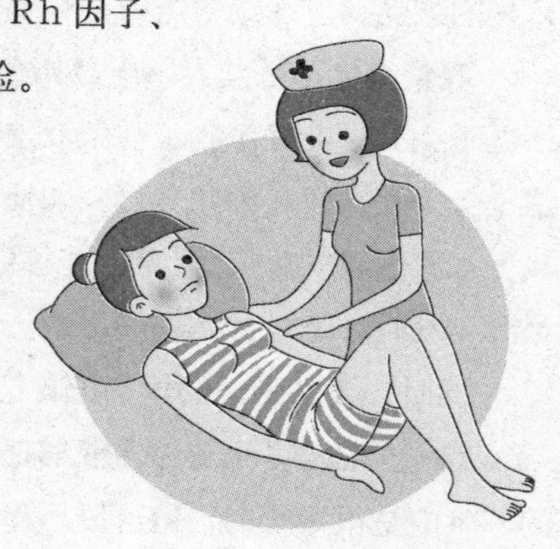

应对尿频

怀孕前三个月，由于子宫不断地长大，邻近的膀胱经常感觉到它的存在，在子宫扩大高出骨盆压迫在空膀胱上时，就会使你产生频繁的尿意，而且每次的排尿时间比平常略长。减轻这种情况的惟一办法就是每次入厕时，尽量将尿排干净。要达到这一点就要强化泌尿生殖系统相关的肌肉：

1．排尿练习：排尿时，试试看能否随意停止四五次。

2．重复做：一天练习4次，每次收缩与放松盆底肌肉10下。熟练一点后，每天依然做4次，不过每次可以增加到50下左右。

3．练习时间慢慢延长：可以先练习收缩盆底肌肉，然后从1数到5之后放

松。一次大概重复做10次就可以了。然后，再视情况慢慢增加收缩的时间。

4. 波浪式运动：由于部分盆底肌肉分别在尿道、阴道与肛门等部位形成回路，为了训练这些部位的肌肉，可以使用波浪的方式，从前向后收缩，然后再从后向前放松。

5. 改变姿势：越来越熟练之后，可以尝试使用躺姿、坐姿、蹲姿等不同姿势来练习上述运动。

早孕反应

约半数妇女于停经6周左右出现畏寒、头晕、乏力、嗜睡、流涎、食欲不振、喜食酸物或厌恶油腻、恶心、晨起呕吐等症状，称早孕反应。早孕反应多于妊娠12周左右自行消失。

许多孕妇常经历的恶心、呕吐或腹部不适感，很容易让怀孕的美好感觉变成痛苦。有些孕妇对某些味道重的食物，像大蒜、鱼或咖啡，闻之即呕；一瓶原来很喜欢的香水，很可能会让孕妇夺门而吐；原来喜欢的食物，现在也可能令人作呕。大约80%的孕妇有恶心、干呕、呕吐等现象。

许多孕妇发现下面的方法可以减轻早孕反应的不适：

1. 尽量避开刺激物

经过若干天的恶心，你就可以知道引发呕吐恶心的刺激物。安排日常生活时，尽可能地避开这些已知的刺激物。

2. 让每一天有个美好的开始

最好在每天晚上上床前，先吃点东西，这样第二天早晨起床时，肚子就不会空空如也。也可以在床边放一盘易消化又可口的饼干、小块水果，半夜醒来时，吃点东西。

告诉你一个小秘方：在脚落地之前，先在嘴里塞点东西。如果有必要，抱着你的食盒，吃它一上午。

尽量以一种轻松愉快的活动，像步行、冥想或阅读，开启一天的序幕，同时也让你的身体能度过你期望的美好一天。

3. 吃得让胃舒服

比较好的进食方式是少食多餐，一天六次。整天都吃易于消化的营养食

物，可以让你的胃舒服些。

(1)尽量避免吃难以消化的高脂肪或油炸类食物，如冰淇淋、薯条和炸鸡等。吃一些令人口渴的食物，如泡菜、薯条和苏打饼干，这样你就可以多喝点水，避免加重恶心的脱水。

(2)空胃对唾液非常敏感，一碰到就容易引发恶心。因此，不要将唾液吞到你空空的胃里，在吃容易引发唾液分泌的食物(咸的或干的食物)之前，应先喝牛奶或吃些稀粥等，将胃滋润保护起来。

(3)吃些瓜类、葡萄、莴苣、苹果、梨子、芹菜等水分多的食物。

(4)吃高热量的面包、麦片和饼干等。

(5)有时候你可能会不想吃也不想喝，但是如果不吃不喝，你可能会感觉更糟。吃些东西吧，什么都行。

(6)列出一份让你感觉舒服的食物清单。

4. 出门走走

新鲜空气、不同的景色、拜访朋友或看场电影，都可以让你分散注意力而感觉好些。如果你想要活动，那就活动吧；如果想休息，那就好好休息。

5. 把家务分出去

让丈夫做家务事，自己躺在床上吧。如果你想要吃什么，就叫丈夫去买。不要因为躺在床上觉得愧疚。记住，你正在为你们俩孕育一个新生命。对职业女性，怀孕是个从激烈的竞争中退下来的绝佳机会。

6. 穿舒服一点

穿宽松一点的棉质衣服。

7. 舒服的姿态

调整身体重心的位置，只要让胃的出口低于入口，逆流状况就会减轻。当你吃饱后，尽量直坐或是躺靠。平仰感觉不会太好。

8. 尽量多睡

嗜睡可以逃避恶心。为了避免起床后恶心，在休息之前，吃一些清淡的食物，首选水果或作用持久的谷类或面食等。

9. 保持乐观的心情

找些能与你分忧解愁的人聊聊。情绪不佳时，建议你用听舒缓的音乐或是与爱人一起散步的方法排遣。如果有一天，你无法将许多事安排妥当，仍要提醒自己：最珍贵的礼物就是肚子里的宝贝。

贴心·提醒

妊娠剧吐（严重的持续性呕吐）会导致脱水，甚至危及胎儿。如果出现下列的征兆，应立刻去医院：

呕吐持续；小便减少，小便颜色较深；嘴、眼睛、皮肤感觉干燥；觉得身体越来越疲倦，感觉越来越虚弱无力；意识逐渐不清；24小时无法进食或喝水。

缓解呕吐

下面的一些小措施可以缓解你的呕吐症状：

1. 多放些手绢、纸巾和塑料袋在你的手袋里，以备不时之需，避免一些尴尬。

2. 要吃早餐。即使你不想吃，也要少吃一点，哪怕是一片面包。这样，对你的胃有好处，可减少呕吐次数。

3. 如果你的血糖低或者总是感到饿，你可以随身携带、偶尔进食一些适合你的小零食，比如果汁会比茶或咖啡更适合孕妇。

4. 如果妊娠反应特别严重，要请几天短假在家休息。

5. 如果你是“一线”工作人员，如接待员、导购员等，要提前和你的同事或拍档打好招呼，以便他们在你去洗手间的时候随时接替你的工作。

第7周

外表没有变化

第7周记：我简直筋疲力尽。据说怀孕头三个月会非常疲惫，宝宝的主要器官都在这个时期形成。我算是体会到这种疲惫了。也许这是宝宝的脊柱正在形成，所以不停地要通过我的身体吸收大量叶酸，让骨骼可以长得坚固。近来情绪也不太好，不过这是早就料到的，因为我的荷尔蒙有很大变化。

只有一点好处——乳房丰满起来。真开心，因为我从来就不是个丰满的女人。但是它们也变得脆弱了，透过皮肤可以看到弯曲伸展的青色静脉，老公说像地图。

胎宝宝状况　胚胎细胞仍在快速地分裂。到本周末时，胚胎的大小有1.2厘米左右，形状就像一颗蚕豆。这段时期，胚胎的鼻孔开始形成，消化系统也在生长着，耳朵部位有些凹陷；四肢继续成长，手指也开始发育；心脏开始划分成左心房和右心室，每分钟的心跳可达150次；脑垂体也开始发育。

孕妈妈状况　虽然你的外表还看不出有什么大的变化，但在你体内的变化却是翻天覆地的。这段时间里，大多数孕妇在早晨醒来后会感到难以名状的恶心，嘴里还有种说不清的怪味道。你随时可能有饥饿的感觉，甚至会饥不择食地吃掉很多种食物——所以用不了多久，你就会发现自己的体态有所改观。此时切不可过多地考虑体形，因为目前这几周是“胎宝贝”发育的关键时期，维持胎儿生命的器官正在生长，一定要保证营养的供给。

最近一段时间，也许你的情绪波动很大，但要提醒你的是，早孕6～10周是胚胎腭部发育的关键时期，你焦虑的情绪会影响胚胎的发育，导致胎宝贝腭裂或唇裂。

日常生活中的其他问题，参照前面讲的内容处理。同时，不要忘记在医生指导下继续补充叶酸。

告别烦恼的方法

孕妈妈烦恼不安，情绪会传到胎儿的大脑中心，使胎儿的血管收缩，导致胎儿紧张。据调查，在孕7～10周内，孕妇精神极度不安，胎儿唇裂或腭裂的发生率较高。特别是前3个月，正是胎儿各器官形成的重要时期，如孕妇长期情绪波动，就可能造成胎儿畸形。

良好的心态，融洽的感情，是达到优孕、优生的重要因素。在夫妻感情融洽、家庭气氛和谐、心态良好的情况下，受精卵就会“安然舒适”地在子宫内发育成长，生下的孩子就更健康、聪慧。那么，怎样摆脱消极情绪呢？

1. 告诫自己

在孕期，要经常有意识地告诉自己不要生气，不要着急，宝宝正在看着呢！当你感到烦躁或焦虑时，有意识地花一些时间让自己平静下来，并把宁静的情绪传达给胎儿。尽管无法避免所有令人紧张的情况，却可以用更为积极的态度平衡这些情绪。这样做，其实就是在教育孩子如何表达不同的情感，这将为孩子今后的生活打下良好的基础。

如果你以前是爱较真的，对生活中的一些看不惯的小事儿，现在大可以睁一只眼，闭一只眼，让自己保持平和的心态。

2. 转移法注意力

有时候，消除烦恼的最好办法就是离开那种不愉快的情境，可以通过一项自己喜欢的活动，如听悦耳轻快的音乐、欣赏美术作品、多看美丽的景色、多读有利于心身健康的书刊，或者散步等，使你的情绪由焦虑转向欢乐。

3. 释放法

这是相当有效的情绪调剂方法，可通过写日记或向可靠的朋友叙说自己的处境和感情，使烦恼烟消云散，得到令人满意的“释放”。

4. 协调法

每天抽出30分钟的时间到住家附近草木茂盛的宁静小路上、公园散散步、做做体操，心情会变得非常舒畅，尤其是美妙的鸟鸣声更能帮助你消除紧张情绪，使你深受感染而自得其乐。

5. 冥想法

闭上眼睛，思想宝宝的可爱摸样、活动状况等，把你的精气和爱传达给胎儿。如果你内心一直维持平静与安定的状态，胎儿也会受到良好影响。

(1) 沉思前半个小时左右，不吃喝任何东西。

(2) 找一个温暖、安静稍微暗些的房间。

(3) 穿着宽松的衣服，背部挺直，找个舒适的姿势坐着。地上可放把椅子或是垫子。

(4) 把注意力集中在呼吸上，或是房间里的某个物体上，或者重复一句话或某个音节。

(5) 如果出现某些让你心烦或激动的事，随它们去，再把注意力集中在你所选的焦点上。

6. 社交法

将自己置身于乐观向上的人群中，充分享受友情的欢乐，使你的情绪得到积极的感染，从中得到满足和快慰。同别的孕妇及其配偶交谈，可以有效地舒缓紧张情绪。

7. 改善生活环境

布置一个温馨、宁静而又浪漫的环境并不困难，只要在房间的布置上做一些小小的调整就会很有效果。适当添一些婴儿用的物品，让那些从商店购买的可爱婴儿小物件（婴儿的衣服、浴巾等），随时提醒自己：一个小生命即将来到身边！

同时，可在床头的上方贴一张漂亮的婴儿画，有时候一边看这张画，一边想象自己的宝宝是什么样子？是不是像这个宝宝一样如此可爱、动人？

孕早期饮食指导（第1～3月）

孕早期，膳食要以重质量、高蛋白、富营养、少油腻、易消化吸收为其原则。一日少食多餐，以瘦肉、鱼类、蛋类、面条、牛奶、豆浆、新鲜蔬菜和水果为佳。可选择孕妇平常喜好的食物，但不宜食用油腻、油炸、辛辣等不易消化和刺激性强的食物，以防消化不良或便秘而造成先兆流产。进食时，最好将饮食中的固体与液体食物分开，即在正餐完毕后隔些时间再喝水或汤。

妊娠反应重的，可适当加服维生素B_1、B_6，每日服3次，每次10毫克，连服7～10天，以帮助增进食欲，减少不适感。

1. 孕早期要合理调配膳食

(1) 粮谷类食物：包括米、面、杂粮、赤豆、绿豆及含脂肪多的坚果类。这些食物可提供能量，供给蛋白质、无机盐、B族维生素、膳食纤维。每日最低摄入量应在200克以上。

(2) 蔬菜、水果类食物：它们主要供给孕妇维生素和无机盐，如胡萝卜素、维生素C、维生素B_2、钙和铁。每日摄入量至少应该在500克以上。

(3) 动物性食品：如猪、牛、羊、鸡、鸭、鹅肉及肝、肾、心、肚，水产类、蛋类。这些食物蛋白质含量高，容易消化吸收，是最重要的优质蛋白质的来源，还可提供一定的脂肪、脂溶性维生素和无机盐。每日摄入量至少在100克以上。

(4) 乳类和乳制品：它们是营养最完全的一类食品，富含蛋白质和容易吸收的钙。孕妇每日应尽量保证摄入乳类和乳制食品200克。

2. 准妈妈孕早期开胃食谱

(1) 西红柿炒豆腐：用开水把西红柿烫一下，去皮，切成厚片。把豆腐切成3厘米左右长方块。锅内放少许油，油热后放入西红柿小炒片刻，再把豆腐放入锅内，加少许酱油、白糖、盐滚几滚，待豆腐炒透即可装盘。

(2) 酸菜鲫鱼汤：鲫鱼去内脏，洗净后用油煎一下，放入2碗水煮开后，放入酸菜、葱、生姜。先用大火煮3～5分钟，然后用小火煮15～20分钟，汤变成乳白色即可。

(3) 自制酸黄瓜：黄瓜洗净后，切成细条，用盐腌15分钟，渍水，加入少许食醋、糖搅拌。用保鲜膜封住碗口放入冰箱内，30分钟后即可吃。如果觉得凉，可以放一会儿再吃。

3. 注意的问题

怀孕最初3个月，由于妊娠反应，吃不下很多东西，所以营养的补给是不充分的。一餐吃不了太多，可以少食多餐，什么时候想吃就什么时候吃。如果食欲较好，应尽量摄取足够的维生素B1、维生素C和钙及水等物质，比如喝牛奶、多吃干酪、新鲜蔬菜、水果等。

营养菜单——孕早期

1. 鱼片豆腐

材料：豆腐100克，鱼片150克，上汤900克，姜1克，油、料酒、精盐、胡椒粉各适量。

做法：热锅油熟后放姜、鱼片在锅中煎透，溅入料酒，加入豆腐条，入上汤。汤滚至奶白色，撒上精盐、胡椒粉即可。

2. 冬菇菠菜汤

材料：冬菇50克，菠菜250克，姜片、上汤、盐、糖各适量。

做法：冬菇用清水浸软，切片、菠菜切段。热锅下油爆香姜片，放入冬菇及上汤煲滚，文火煲约15分钟。下菠菜滚熟，放入盐糖调味即成。

3. 泥鳅鱼汤

材料：泥鳅120克，盐适。

做法：将泥鳅用热水洗去粘液，剖腹去内脏，用油煎至金黄。加水1碗半，煮汤至半碗，用盐调味即成。

4. 鲜菇肉丸

材料：鲜菇50克，青菜50克，瘦猪肉馅100克，上汤600克，盐、酱油、葱片、胡椒粉、水淀粉适量，蛋清1个。

做法：鲜菇、青菜洗净切细。瘦肉馅入酱油、葱片、水淀粉、蛋白、盐调匀。将锅洗净，注入二汤，放入鲜菇、青菜烧滚，把调即的瘦肉馅做成肉丸逐个迅速落汤烧滚至熟，用精盐、胡椒调味即成。

5. 蛋糕蒸鲫鱼

材料：活鲫鱼1尾，鸡蛋200克，料酒10克，盐1.5克，鸡油5克，葱段20克，鲜姜块（拍松），高汤150克，姜汁适量。

做法：

（1）把鲫鱼去掉鳞、鳃、鳍，从鱼的反面鳃下部用刀切一个三角口，取去内脏，要特别注意不要弄破苦胆，洗净鱼身；将鱼在开水锅中煮至5～6成熟时捞出，控净水

分。刀口朝下放在大碗中，并将葱段、姜摆放在鱼身上。

(2) 鸡蛋取蛋清用筷子搅散，加料酒、盐、姜汁、高汤，用筷子搅拌均匀，倒在鱼身上，盖上盖，放入笼屉蒸熟（不超过20分钟），取出后拣去葱姜，淋上鸡油即成。

6. 姜汁鱼片

材料:桂鱼500克，蛋清250克，姜50克，盐3克，香油适量。

做法：

(1) 将桂鱼从脊背处下刀剔去鱼骨，去皮、去头、剔成净鱼肉，把鱼片切成5厘米宽的段，再切成0.6厘米厚的片，加入盐、姜末、香油、打好底味，腌制数分钟，再加少许蛋清，淀粉抓均匀，姜切成末放在碗中，将香油烧热冲在姜末碗中。

(2) 锅内放入水，开锅后把锅端下分批下入鱼片，注意不要大开锅，鱼质很嫩，下入锅里有片刻即熟，然后再入第二锅，直到鱼片全部汆完为止，将鱼片放入托盘里，把香油冲的姜汁倒在鱼上即可。

7. 鱼豆腐

材料:鲫鱼3条，豆腐1000克，鸡蛋2个，青蒜少许，酱油15克，料酒20克，盐12克，花生油100克，水淀粉适量。

做法：

(1) 鲫鱼开膛洗净，取其中两尾鱼，剔下鱼肉，切片去皮，用刀背砸成细泥状，豆腐砸成泥状。葱切少许葱段，姜切少许，青蒜择洗干净切成末。

(2) 葱段、姜片放入碗中加放料酒、清水略泡片刻，把汁倒入鱼泥中，将鱼泥解散成稀糊状，用箩过一遍。再把豆腐泥和鱼泥和在一起调匀，加入蛋清搅匀。然后取一长方盘，先抹上油，把拌好的豆腐鱼泥倒入盘内，约摊11毫米厚（如果无盘可用屉布，四周用木条架起亦可)，上笼用中火蒸透，取出切成3厘米宽、4厘米长的条，放入盆内，用凉汤加入盐泡上。

(3) 锅烧热注入花生油，把剩下的鱼放入两面略煎一下（用油略炸一下亦可)，倒入漏勺。锅内放油，下花椒炸出香味，放入豆瓣酱（剁细）炒透，加汤、酱油、、料酒、葱花、姜末，放入鱼浇之，待鱼烧入味，用手勺在锅内把鱼搅烂，用小眼漏勺把鱼骨捞出，再用箩把汤过一遍。

(4) 把过好的鱼汤倒入锅内上火，把豆腐条滤掉汤轻轻推入锅内，用小火慢慢烧，待汤快要收干时，用少许水淀粉勾芡，撒上青蒜末，用手勺轻轻推匀，倒在盘内即可。

8. 糖醋白菜

材料：大白菜200克，胡萝卜50克，油、糖、酱油各6克左右，花椒2粒，团粉3克。

做法：将白菜洗好，切成斜片；将胡萝卜也切成斜片。将糖、醋、酱油、团粉混合在一起。油锅熬热后，先煸白菜，后放胡萝卜，待近熟烂，将糖醋汁倒入调匀即成。

9. 奶油白菜

材料：鲜牛奶50克，大白菜250克，盐与猪油各6克，团粉各1.5克。

做法：将白菜洗好，切成4厘米长的小段。把油熬热，稍凉，将白菜倒入，再加些肉汤或水，烧至7～8成烂，放入盐。将团粉用少量水调匀，再将牛奶加在团粉内混匀，倒在白菜上成为乳白色汁液，再烧开即成。

10.油豆腐油菜

材料：油菜200克，油豆腐50克，酱油6克，食油6克，团粉1.5克，糖、料酒各1.5克。

做法：油菜洗净切段，梗叶分置，油豆腐切成块。油熬热后先煸菜梗，加盐，再下菜叶煸几下，然后将油豆腐放入一同炒几下，加酱油和少量水烧开，再加入糖，最后再将团粉加水和匀，倒入锅中，调成稀汁状即成。

11. 清蒸大虾

材料：带皮大虾500克，香油10克，料酒、酱油各15克，醋25克，汤50克，葱、姜、花椒各适量。

做法：大虾洗净，剁去脚、须，摘除沙袋、沙线各虾脑，切成4段，葱切条，姜一半切片，一半切末。大虾段摆入盘内，加入料酒、葱条、姜片、花椒和汤，上笼蒸10分钟左右取出，拣去葱、姜、花椒装盘。用醋、酱油、姜末和香油兑成汁，供蘸食。

小贴士……不要乱服用维生素

近年来研究发现，孕妇过多食用动物肝脏，会导致体内维生素A摄入过多，可能会危及胎儿的健康，导致胎儿耳朵缺陷、头面形态异常、唇裂、腭裂、眼睛及神经系统缺陷。孕妇食用动物肝脏，每周1次。至于维生素A、维生素B和微量元素锌等，可以从其他食品中获得，如新鲜蔬菜、水果、鱼类、瘦肉等。

许多孕妇早期妊娠反应较强烈，恶心呕吐不能进食，医生往往允许服用少量维生素B_6以止吐。而有些孕妇以为维生素B_6是维生素，是人体所需物质，没有坏处，就较长时间地服用。其实，长期过多服用维生素B_6，可使胎儿对它产生依赖性，医学上称之为维生素B_6依赖性。

孕妇长期大量服用维生素C会导致流产。服用过多的叶酸也会对身体产生不良的影响，如可能影响体内锌的代谢而造成锌缺乏，致使胎儿发育迟缓。大量服用维生素A可能导致婴儿骨骼畸形、泌尿生殖系统缺损以及硬腭豁裂。服用维生素E过多会使胎儿大脑发育异常，过多的维生素D则会导致胎儿的大动脉和牙齿发育出现问题。

孕期补充维生素，提倡食补。补充维生素制剂，一定要在医生指导下服用。

第8周

腹部无明显改变

第8周记：天啦，我讨厌这样！我觉得恶心。书上说早晨会恶心，不知为什么我却总在下午有这种感觉。幸好我还没吐过，只是很不舒服。强迫自己吃几片面包能缓解一点恶心的感觉。当然，闭着眼睛想象我可爱的宝宝也能让我暂时忘掉难受。直觉告诉我"他"一定是个男孩！他的脸正在形成。他会像谁呢？

大夫告诉我他至少应有2.5厘米长了，和身体相比，他的头显得异常地大。所以，在我的想象中，他就是一只小海马，在我的身体里快乐地遨游。

胎宝宝状况　进入第8周后，胚胎已初具人形，但是小尾巴还没有完全消失。心脏和大脑已经发育得非常复杂，眼睑开始出现褶痕，鼻子部位也渐渐挺起，牙和腭开始发育，耳朵也在继续成形，小胳膊在肘部变得弯曲。手指和脚趾之间隐约有少量蹼状物。到第8周末，"胎宝贝"长到3厘米左右、体重约有4克。眼、耳、鼻、口已可辨认，胎盘和脐带形成。并会做踢腿、伸腿、抬手、移动双臂的小动作了——尽管你丝毫察觉不到。

孕妈妈状况　此时孕妈妈子宫增大，但腹部外观仍无明显改变，小腹微凸。体重比孕前增加约1.5～2.5千克。乳房发胀，乳头、乳晕变黑而敏感。

不要忘记在医生指导下继续补充叶酸。第8周，别忘记了到医院接受例行产检。

睡好踏实觉

你越感到怀孕，睡眠困难就越大。以下有几种方法，也许可以帮助你更好地享受夜间睡眠。

1. 别把工作带回家

不要把工作，至少不要把工作上的忧虑带回家。对工作的担忧可能会使你一夜睡不好。

2. 睡前吃些点心

(1) 睡前吃些清淡的点心，如全麦面包、乳制品、瘦肉（特别是火鸡肉）以及一些水果，会有助于安睡。

(2) 为减少夜里肌肉抽筋发生的几率，试着夜间服用钙补充剂。

(3) 晚上可以试着喝上一杯菊花茶，菊花茶具有镇静、安眠的功效。

(4) 避免食用含咖啡因食物、饮料。

(5) 睡前别喝酒，切忌服用安眠药。

3. 少吃含有利尿成分的食物

下午3点之后，避免食（饮）用一些具有利尿成分的食物或饮料，如含咖啡因的咖啡、茶、可乐等，或小红莓汁以及芦笋等。睡到半夜、感到有尿意时，马上爬起来把尿排掉，不要憋尿。

4. 选择舒适的床铺

(1) 尽可能挑软一点、大一点的床铺，让身躯得以做最舒适的伸展。

(2) 新鲜空气可以帮助入睡，睡觉时可以打开窗户。如果太冷不便开窗，不妨使用加湿器，尽量让房间空气保持湿润，这样就会觉得舒畅一些。

5. 保持良好的睡姿

怀孕前三个月，最好侧卧位。怀孕后三个月，朝左侧睡可能是最好的姿势。不必过于担心什么样的睡姿会影响胎儿的健康。事实上，大多数孕妇晚上睡觉的姿势都会变来变去，根本不可能整晚固定在同一种睡姿上。

6. 放松心情入睡

睡觉是一件很自然的事，不要强迫自己。如果你真的睡不着，以下几种方法也许可以帮得上一点忙：

(1) 随意阅读内容轻松的散文、杂志。千万别在这个时候读那些内容血腥、刺激、有悬念和使人高兴的小说！

（2）与丈夫轻松交谈一会儿。

（3）看部令人神经放松的电影。喜剧可使人发笑，而欢笑可松弛神经，看部至少是那种结局完美一点的片子。

（4）舒舒服服泡个热水澡(温度不要太高)，请丈夫帮你从头到脚按摩一番。

（5）听些能使你进入梦乡的歌曲。芭蕾和古典音乐都有缓慢升降的高潮和低潮，催眠作用很好；主题略显单调并有多次重复的乐曲也一样。你还可以试试听些声音单调重复播放大自然中声音的音乐，如潺潺的小溪流水声，或是海浪拍打岸边的声音。

7. 注意

（1）适度地增加运动可以帮助睡眠，但不要在睡前1个小时做剧烈运动。

（2）睡不着时，千万不要生气、心急，否则，更急更气更难入睡。

（3）也不要担心睡眠不足影响胎儿，其实，睡眠不足不会伤着宝宝。

家务劳动

1. 家务料理

（1）随着妊娠周数的增加，准妈妈的肚子越来越大，本身的负荷就很重，身体不那么灵活了，所以做家务时，要以“缓慢”为原则，以不直接压迫到肚子的姿势作为最基本的原则。

（2）做家务时不要长时间站立，建议做15～20分钟家务休息10分钟。

（3）有些准妈妈平时对家务要求严格的话，怀孕时就可以稍微降低标准了。当然，最重要的是，家中其他成员能分担家务，让准妈妈无后顾之忧。

（4）做家务应以不影响孕妇身体的舒适为原则，切忌过度。如果突然出现腹部阵痛，或是子宫收缩，要赶紧停止手里的活计，躺下休息。如果还不能缓解不适，就要赶紧就医了。

(5) 许多孕妇在孕初期的反应十分严重，根本无法做家务事。此时丈夫和家人应适时分担家务。

(6) 双手往上或往下的姿势太多，会牵扯到肚子，要尽量避免这些动作。

(7) 孕妇不适宜提太重的东西。

2. 打扫清洁

(1) 打扫卫生，最好能够使用不需要弯腰打扫的器具，要避免蹲下或跪在地上。

(2) 浴室内不仅很容易滑倒，而且清洗浴室需要许多弯腰的动作，就交给准爸爸吧！

(3)贴身的小衣物只需站在浴室的洗脸柜旁搓洗就可以了，至于大件衣物，就交给洗衣机吧！

(4) 晒衣服时，孕妇就要踮起脚尖来够衣架，很危险，最好使用可以升降的晾衣架，使用方便、安全。

(5) 收拾东西或擦桌子时，不要将腹部紧靠桌面，使劲地够向远方。宁可多移动身体，小块地擦，也不要想要偷懒而拉扯到腹部的肌肉。

贴心·提醒

1. 孕妇做家事，要分段进行，且不能以未怀孕前的标准来要求自己，最好动员丈夫和家人齐动手。

2. 出现下列情况的孕妇，不适合做家务：

(1) 体态臃肿、灵活度不够者。

(2) 医生告知有早产、需要卧床休息者。

(3) 正在有活动性出血或出现破水者。

(4) 即使只做简单家务，也会诱发子宫收缩者。

(5) 做家务时出现呼吸急促（每分钟超过30次）、心跳加快（每分钟超过100次）者。

上班路上

怀孕初期，许多孕妇还要到单位上班，在选择使用交通工具时需要学会保护自己和腹中的宝宝。

1. 骑自行车

怀孕初期和中期，很多孕妇骑自行车上下班，只要骑车时间不太长，还是比较安全的。但要注意以下几点：

(1)不要骑带横梁的男式自行车，以免上下车不方便。

(2)套个厚实柔软的棉布座套，调整车座倾斜度，让后边稍高一些。

(3) 骑车时活动不要剧烈，否则容易下腹腔充血，容易导致早产、流产。

(4)骑车时车筐和后车座携带的物品不要太沉。

(5)不要上太陡的坡或是在颠簸不平的路上骑车，因为这样容易造成会阴部损伤。

(6)在妊娠后期，最好不要骑车，以防羊水早破。

2. 乘公共汽车

乘坐公交车是最经济而且安全的选择，但乘车时间应该避开上下班乘车高峰，以免因为空气质量差而加重恶心的感觉。公交车后部比前部颠簸得厉害，所以应该选择前面的座位。

3. 自驾汽车

许多孕妇驾车时习惯前倾的姿势，容易使子宫受到压迫，产生腹部压力，特别是在怀孕初期和怀孕七八个月时，容易导致流产或早产。怀孕期间若短距离驾驶，不要采取前倾的姿势驾驶。如果路况不好，最好放弃长距离的驾驶。

舒服地工作

怀孕期，你在办公室做一些简单的布置，就可以舒适地工作了。每一点微小的变化都会给你带来一天的好心情，试试看吧。

1. 穿舒适的鞋，在办公桌底下放个鞋盒作搁脚凳。在办公室放双拖鞋是不错的选择。

2．穿宽松舒适的连衣裙。

3．找其他做过母亲的同事帮助。

4．多喝水，在你的办公桌上准备一个大水杯，随时填满你的喝水杯。

5．如果你不得不去洗手间，尽快去。

6．把你的桌椅调整得尽可能地舒适。

7．避免危险的工作场所。

8．自我减压，如果在工作场所不能自己调节压力，尝试一些办法去对付它，如深呼吸、舒展肢体、做简短的散步等。

9． 接受帮助，如果你的同事小心地照料你，你不要介意，应为有一个支持你的空间满意。在你的生命里，这是一个非常特殊的时期，所以不必感到害羞而拒绝别人的帮助。

10. 工作一段时间后要适当地做做伸展运动，抬腿并适当按摩小腿部以放松压力。

11．无论站着或是坐着，尽量保持一个端正的姿势会使你感觉更自信，也使你看上去没有那么笨重、气喘吁吁。

贴心·提醒

1．不要像孕前那样超负荷工作。

2．偶尔的小憩对你也是非常有用的。午休时间，可以打个盹儿。

3．一天工作过后，要充分休息，保持良好睡眠。

4．经常操作电脑的女性，最好穿上防护服。

第9周

现在是胎儿了

第9周记：从现在开始，不许再把我的宝宝叫胚胎了，大夫说，他已经是一个小胎儿了，他的肝脏已经开始制造血细胞。

近来，我有时会觉得头晕，大夫告诉我，因为这个时期由于激素的关系，血压会有一些下降，不要担心。

胎宝宝状况　从本周开始，曾经的“胚芽”已经开始是一个五脏俱全、初具人形的小人儿了，也就是“胎儿”。妊娠9周以后的时期，称为“胎儿期”。

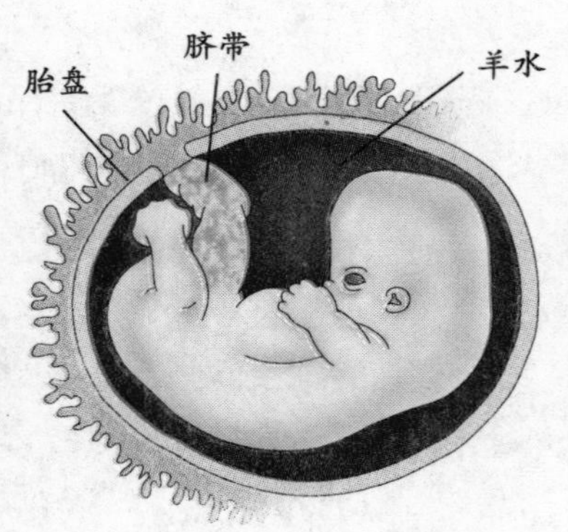

第9周（3月胎宝宝）

孕妈妈状况　这段时期是整个孕期的一个关键时期，胎宝贝的变化很大，首先是小尾巴消失了，且开始发育形成器官系统。胳膊已经长出来了，在腕部两手呈弯屈状，并在心脏区域呈交叉样。腿在变长，脚已经长到能在身体前部交叉的程度。小家伙会不断地动来动去，不停地变换着的姿势，但你仍然感觉不到。小家伙不仅有了人样，也开始有自己的精神，并孕妈咪的情绪息息相关。所以你要尽量让自己保持平稳、乐观、温和的心境，这就是良好的启蒙胎教。

现在胎儿还不能确定是男孩还是女孩，而你的下腹部也未明显隆起，但乳房更加膨胀，乳头和乳晕色素沉着更为明显。现在需要使用比孕前稍宽松的的文胸，才能让你的胸部感到更舒适——要选纯棉质地的文胸，它除了舒适以外，也不会产生细小的纤维阻塞乳头、防碍以后乳汁的分泌。

孕3月专家提示（第9～12周）

1. 要避免过度劳累或激烈运动。避免攀高取重物或提担重大物件。

2. 孕妇情绪暴躁、易怒、容易激动，宜进行适度的户外活动或参加自己有兴趣的文艺活动，以调适良好心情。

3. 温度适宜时每天到公园、绿地散步一小时。

4. 每天至少有8小时的睡眠，每天中午最好睡1～2小时。

5. 勿穿紧身衣裤，选择穿低跟及止滑的鞋子。

6. 选择做轻松的家务活，一次不要做太多。

7. 勿暴饮暴食。食物要清淡、爽口，多吃蛋白质含量丰富的食物及新鲜水果、蔬菜等。如果呕吐得厉害，要去医院检查，输液治疗很有效。

8. 饮食以低盐为主，每日的摄盐量以7～10克为宜。

9. 坚持早、晚认真刷牙、漱口。

10. 蚊虫叮咬后，切忌涂用清凉油。

11. 在医生指导下继续补充叶酸。

冬季保健

如何安度严冬，保障自身的健康与胎儿顺利成长，是人们所关心的。那么，孕妇将如何顺利度过严冬呢？

1. 注意保暖，严防病毒感染

冬季气温低，温差变化大，呼吸道抵抗力降低，易患风疹、流感等由病毒引起的传染病。早孕时，感染风疹、巨细胞病毒、水痘、流行性腮腺炎和流感等病毒，会对胎儿造成不同程度的损害。因此，孕妇应该注意衣着和起居，室温力求稳定，寒潮袭来时应多穿些衣服，外出时尤应严防着凉受寒。孕妇所在地区如发生上述疾病流行，不可随意外出．更不能到公共场所去。家中如有患者，要认真隔离，防止家庭内相互传染。

2. 注意饮食营养

冬季人体散热多而快，孕妇应该吃得更好些，以满足母子的生理需要。冬季孕妇应多吃些瘦肉、鸡、鱼、蛋类、乳类、豆制品和动物肝肾等营养丰富的食品。特别值得注意的是，冬季绿叶蔬菜极少，容易缺少维生素，孕妇应多吃些绿叶蔬菜和水果，以及含维生素A十分丰富的胡萝卜等。

3. 常晒太阳

孕妇需要比一般人更多的钙质。以保障胎儿的骨骼发育。钙在体内吸收与利用离不开维生素D，而维生素D需要在阳光的紫外线参与下由体内进行合成。因此，孕妇需要充足的阳光。但晒太阳不可隔着玻璃，因为紫外线不能通过玻璃。起不到上述作用。这就要求孕妇在冬季天气较好时，到户外去晒太阳。每天不应少于半小时。居住在西北房、平时与阳光接触较少的孕妇，尤应做到这一点。

4. 严防跌伤

北方的冬天，天寒地冻路滑，孕妇身重体笨，容易跌伤。所以，冬天里孕妇不可穿高跟鞋或塑料底的鞋，应穿布底、软底、底不滑的鞋。走路、乘车，特别是夜里去厕所，以及上下楼梯时，应格外小心，严防跌倒，以免发生意外。下雪天孕妇尽量不外出。若要上班工作则需要有伴同行。

5. 注意通风换气

冬天人们常将门窗紧闭，不注意换气，易造成空气污浊，氧气不足，孕妇会感到全身不适，还会对胎儿的发育产生不良的影响。另外，冬季用煤火取暖时，应注意通风，勤检查炉灶，预防煤气中毒。

夏季保健

三伏盛夏，赤日炎炎，一般人都在为食欲减退所扰，为暑气逼人所困，有着妊娠呕吐反应、身体笨重的孕妇更是为酷暑而苦恼。那么，孕妇将如何顺利度夏呢？

1. 合理饮食

酷暑，孕产妇不宜吃产热高的高脂肪食物。饮食宜清淡、凉爽可口，如大米绿豆粥（温）、大米百合粥、清蒸鱼、豆皮或腐竹拌黄瓜等。注意，孕产妇不宜多饮冷饮，不宜用啤酒和汽水等饮料解暑，更不可吃变质的东西。

2. 选择适宜的服装

要穿颜色素淡吸热差的衣服，以白、淡黄和浅绿色为宜。衣料要选用放热量大的麻纱和导热性能好的丝织品。另外，孕产妇衣服款式宜宽大、松软，切不可穿紧身衣裤。

3. 勤用水

为了安全、顺利度夏，更好地解暑降温，孕产妇应该比一般人更要勤用水。孕妇有条件的每天中午和晚上临睡前各淋浴一次，或用温水擦身各一次，不要嫌麻烦。

4. 创造室内舒适的“小气候”

影响健康和舒适的因素有室温、湿度、风力、辐射等，所以应着重从这几个方面改善居室环境让孕妇过得更舒适。孕妇的居室温度最好能保持在25～30℃，湿度宜保持在50%左右，避免中午太阳直射，经常通风，但不宜总开电扇直吹。室内空气干燥时，勤洒净水或放置一盆清水。睡觉时不要一直开着冷气，同时要注意选用手感舒服的床单和睡衣。

穿鞋之道

准妈妈穿鞋首先要考虑安全性，选择鞋子时应注意以下几点：

1. 最好穿大约 2～3 厘米的中跟鞋。
2. 鞋的前部应软而宽。
3. 鞋帮要松软，面料有弹性，如羊皮鞋、布鞋等。
4. 脚背部分能与鞋子紧密结合。
5. 有能牢牢支撑身体的宽大后跟。
6. 鞋底带有防滑纹。
7. 能正确保持脚底的弓形部位，宽窄、长度均合适，鞋的重量较轻。
8. 孕后期，脚部浮肿，要穿有松紧性、稍大一些的鞋子。
9. 孕妇弯腰扎鞋带不方便，应穿便于穿脱的轻便鞋。

内裤和胸罩

1. 内裤

孕妇阴道分泌物增多，宜选择透气性好、吸水性强及触感柔和的纯棉质内裤，对皮肤无刺激，不会引发皮疹和痒疹。切忌贴身穿化纤衣裤。

推荐两种适合孕妇的内裤：

（1）覆盖式内裤：覆盖式内裤能够保护孕妇的腹部，裤腰覆盖肚脐以上部分，有保暖效果；松紧可自行调整，随怀孕不同阶段的体型自由伸缩变化；弹性良好的伸缩蕾丝腰围，穿着更舒适；有适宜与多种服装搭配及穿着需要的款式和花色，如平口、灰色等。

（2）产妇专用生理裤：产妇专用生理裤采用舒适的柔性棉制作，弹性高，不紧绷。分固定式和下方可开口的活动式两种，便于产前检查和产褥期、生理期等特殊时期穿着。

2. 胸罩

（1）舒适：为适应乳房的胀大，最好选用可调整型的罩杯。所谓舒适合身的胸罩，在穿起来的时候，应该能够与你整个乳房紧密贴合在一起，乳罩的中央紧贴胸部，没有空隙。

（2）材质：以较透气的棉质胸罩为优先考虑，避免选购样式花哨、且可能会引起皮肤过敏的材质。也不要购买用化纤布做的不透气或不吸水的乳罩，以免发生湿疹。

（3）肩带：用心感受一下肩带在你胸廓上的位置。在背部的位置，应该是舒适地贴近你的肩胛骨下方；在胸部的位置，你也不应该会有任何的不适感；最后，再试着举起手臂或耸耸肩，感受一下是否会有什么不适感产生。

（4）吊环：最好是选用较宽、且有衬垫的吊环。

（5）夜间型胸罩：许多孕妇会在夜晚使用材质较轻的夜间型胸罩，让胸部有机会稍微喘息一下，缓解不适。

第10周

喜怒无常

第10周记： 宝宝已经开始经常活动了——虽然我还没有什么感觉。在水的世界里，小家伙大概会像鱼一样地游动吧，还有，他的脚是蹼状的，像鸭子的蹼。

这一段，我非常地想吃冰激凌——据说这种强烈愿望也是由荷尔蒙变化引起的。而且，因为时时恶心，凉的东西吃下去好像能让我舒服一些。昨天下午我打开冰箱，拿出了一块奶油冰激凌，结果被下班回来的老公撞上了，硬没让吃。

控制一下也好，我长胖了许多，衣服穿起来全都觉得紧了。

胎宝宝状况 孕10周，胎宝贝长到4厘米左右，外形就像一只小豆荚，体重约10克。身体所有部分已经“初具规模”，包括胳膊、腿、眼睛、生殖器以及其他器官。但还不能辨别胎儿性别。胎盘已经很成熟，可以支持产生激素的大部分重要功能。

孕妈妈状况 与上一周比，你的身材没有太大变化。通常这段时期的孕妈咪情绪波动会十分剧烈，甚至可以说是喜怒无常，这是孕期雌激素作用的结果。

日常生活中，要注意多喝水，不要空腹。如果很想吃冷饮，如冰淇淋等，要尽量控制。如果你发现白带增多，一定要妥善应对。可为自己准备专用的盆、浴巾，每天用温开水清洗外阴2～3次，清洗时不要用普通肥皂。阴道清洗问题，建议你咨询医生。没有医生的指示，不可擅自清洗阴道。

日常生活中的其他问题，参照前面讲的内容处理。不要忘记在医生指导下继续补充叶酸。

应对各种不良情绪

情绪是一种复杂的心理现象，而孕妇的情绪是否稳定，对胎儿的身心健康影响很大。

1. 不良情绪一：担忧和焦虑

你在孕育新生命的同时，可能会为宝宝和自己的未来担心忧虑，比如为宝宝的生育费用担心，为怀孕可能丢失工作而担心，为自己的体形日益臃肿而烦恼，等等。这些不良情绪很容易使你陷入无休无止的焦虑中。殊不知，这样久而久之就会让腹中的孩子的心理也产生变化。

危害：容易使孩子形成胆小怕事的性格，同时心理承受能力也降低，做事容易情绪化，可能会经常莫名其妙地大哭特哭。

怎么办：最好的方法自然是你随时调整自己的情绪，一旦发现自己正在陷入忧郁焦虑的泥潭，应立刻想办法疏导或转移注意力，可以通过看书和电视来缓解紧张的情绪，让自己开朗起来。

2. 不良情绪二：发怒

如果你总会有发怒的理由，如老公晚回家；邻居家的狗又跑过来撒尿；新买的裙子结果发现是次品等等。这些生活中遇到的琐事都可能让你大光其火，大发雷霆。殊不知，你发火之后心里是痛快了，可对宝宝的个性也造成了坏影响。事实上，一个容易动怒的妈妈，很可能会生出一个容易动怒的孩子。

危害：如果你常常发火的话，容易使孩子的性格更固执、更偏激，也更容易情绪化，说不定以后还会变成经常顶嘴或离家出走的麻烦孩子。

怎么办：最好的办法是，你一旦遇到可能会发火的时候，就告诉自己先等一等，然后可以喝点水，在屋子里走几圈，等这个过程完成后，你的火应该已经熄灭了。

为了减少发火的次数，你也可以在觉得自己要发火前，出门去散步，这样也有助于稳定情绪。

3. 不良情绪三：多愁善感

在怀孕期间遇到不顺心的事也是常有的，但不少多愁善感的准妈妈经常会将一些小挫折扩大为自己人生的失败，因此整天自怨自艾，愁眉不展。殊不知，这也可能会影响到孩子的情绪。

危害:准妈妈经常哭泣，伤感，容易使孩子形成胆小、懦弱、缺乏自信心的性格。

怎么办:最好的办法是你在伤心时找一些事来做,以分散自己的注意力，也可以看一些轻松愉快的电影、电视来缓解情绪。当然，如果伤感情绪严重的话，找人倾诉则是最佳的发泄方法。

4. 不良情绪四:自己吓自己

有些想象力特别丰富的准妈妈，在看完恐怖片或侦探小说后，就会变得疑神疑鬼，经常会有担惊受怕的情绪，比如一个人在家时总是担心有人来袭击，也有的人因为担心半夜有贼侵入而整夜整夜睡不着。其实，这也会对孩子的身心发展造成不良影响。

危害:准妈妈经常处于恐惧中，容易使孩子产生行为偏激、固执，自卑的性格，长大后这样的孩子在语言能力上可能会遇到困难。即使没有语言障碍，也不容易跟别人友好相处，沟通能力差。

怎么办:尽量不要看恐怖片或侦探小说，即便偶尔观看，也要在白天进行，因为晚上观看恐怖片往往容易造成失眠，对孩子的身心危害更大。

小贴士……孕期好心情4招

1. 逛街、散步——女人好心情的不变法则，孕期也同样适用。

2. 家人、老公、朋友的温馨陪伴、谈心。

3. 去做一件有意义的事，避免孕期闲散生活带来无聊的感觉。

4. 多看有关孕产养育的书籍、杂志，排除因为恐惧生育而产生的忧郁情绪。

舒缓压力

胎儿保健不仅应保证孕期母亲不生病、胎儿发育正常，还应当注重心理保健。孕妇的情绪，就像晴时多云偶阵雨的天气一般，很难捉摸。但是急躁、不安、紧张等负面情绪，不仅对胎儿不好，还会造成身心压力。下面介绍的几招有助于缓解情绪:

1. 早睡早起

放弃没有规律的作息，养成早睡早起的好习惯。早晨起床后，到室外散散步。

2. 倒倒你的苦水

怀孕后，由于生理上的原因，很多准妈妈变得比较脆弱，心里常会产生一些莫名其妙的失落感、压抑感、恐惧感，遇事容易发怒、焦虑、惊慌、悲伤等。当你碰到不愉快的事情时，一定要主动及时地说出来，让丈夫做做你的出气筒。

也可以约上几位好朋友，一起吃饭聊天，向她们宣泄心中的不快；或约上其他的准妈妈，一起交流“准妈妈经”。

3. 写日记

写孕期日记，你可以每天写，也可以二三天或四五天写一次。写的内容可随心所欲地发挥，什么都可以写，可长可短，比如早孕反应怎么开始和结束的、什么时候听到胎心音了、感觉到胎动了等。还可以不定期地让准爸爸给你拍一些照片，然后贴在日记里面，图文并茂，乐趣无穷。

4. 看书

日常生活中，经常阅读一些书籍，调节自己的身心。从胎教的角度考虑，准妈妈宜选择一些格调高雅、趣味盎然的读物，如时尚杂志、育儿杂志以及一些适合幼儿阅读的故事书等。准妈妈可以边看书边将内容讲解给肚中的宝宝听，千万不要以为宝宝和你隔着一层肚皮，跟她讲话是一件不可思议的事，只要你用“爱”来和宝宝交流，就能有效地刺激胎儿的脑部发育。

准妈妈最好不要看一些故事情节跌宕起伏的书，以免情绪随着情节波动。也不要用一个姿势长时间地看书。

5. 下午茶时间

每天享受一段悠闲的下午茶时间，一杯淡淡的花茶或一杯热牛奶，依自己的心情做变化。

6. 欣赏美好的事物

画展、摄影展、陶艺展等，都具有陶

冶心性的功能，不仅可以缓和心情、进行胎教，也可以从中释放压力。

7．不看恐怖片

恐怖片的悬疑情节，会造成孕妇精神紧张，过度刺激对孕妇和胎儿都有不良影响。

8．请老公按摩

某些孕妇由于腹部增大的缘故，大腿根部常会有疼痛感。请亲爱的先生帮忙按摩，是个促进感情、抒解疼痛的好方法。

9．唱歌、听音乐

孕妇的心情起伏较大，而随着歌曲的旋律与歌词，可以抒发心理的不愉快与烦闷。

听音乐是孕妇在怀孕期间保持心情愉快的最简单可行且有效的方法。比较适合准妈妈听的音乐有莫扎特的《小夜曲》；维尔第的小提琴协奏曲《恋人》第一乐章、《四季》第四乐章等。音乐以优雅、悦耳动听的轻音乐曲为佳。

10．冲个快乐澡

淋浴时，放个轻松的音乐，洗个轻轻松松、舒舒服服的快乐澡。

11．插一盆美丽的花

在家里插一盆鲜花，每隔一段时间，就变换不同的鲜花，让室内充满着清新的花香，令人赏心悦目、心情愉快。

贴心·提醒

孕妇高兴时不可以大笑，大笑会使腹部猛然抽搐，妊娠初期导致流产，妊娠后期会诱发早产。

第11周

草莓那么大了

第11周记： 我的小宝贝现在应该已经长到如同一颗大草莓那么大了。宝宝的脖子开始渐渐形成，这样他的头就不像以前那样看起来和胸连为一体。

我恶心的感觉好象也减轻了许多，食欲慢慢好起来。

胎宝宝状况　到本周末，胎宝贝身长增长到4～6厘米，体重增加到14克左右。头显得格外大，几乎占据了身长大部分。面颊、下颌、眼睑及耳廓已发育成形，颜面更像人脸。尾巴完全消失，眼睛及手指、脚趾都清晰可辨。由于皮肤是透明的，所以可清楚地看到正在形成的肝、肋骨和皮下血管。心脏、肝脏、胃肠更加发达，肾脏也发达起来，输尿管已经形成，这些器官包括大脑以及呼吸器官等维持生命的器官都已经开始工作。

胎宝贝幼小的四肢已经可以在羊水中自由的活动了：双手能伸向脸部，时常会做吸吮、吞咽等小动作，可以把拇指放进嘴里，或是尝尝小脚趾的味道如何。本周末，胎宝贝的性别就可以分辨了。

孕妈妈状况　你的孕早期就要结束了，这段时期想必你已经注意到自己"腰变粗了"，但还没必要穿孕妇装。胎宝贝已经大得充满了你整个子宫，如果你轻轻触摸你的耻骨上缘，你的手会感觉到子宫的存在。小腹部可能会出现一条浅色的竖线，颜色变深，这就是妊娠纹，不必太担心。阴道分泌物也较前略有增多，呈无色或淡黄色、浅褐色，属于妊娠生理反应，是正常的。但是，当分泌物的量如果增加得太多并有异味时，应马上告诉医生。

早孕反应开始减轻，你已经基本摆脱了怀孕初期情绪波动大、身体不适等症状的困扰。再过几天，恶心呕吐、食欲不振的现象就要结束。

本周是胎宝贝全面快速发育的时期，在以后3周里，他们的身长将再增长两倍。所以，均衡饮食是首要的，以保证充足的蛋白质、多种维生素、钙、铁等营养素的供给。由于胎儿骨骼的迅速生长，你的身体对钙的需求量大大增加。尤其是早孕反应严重的女性，更要加强钙和维生素D的补充，平时你可以多喝富含钙质的牛奶。

日常生活中的其他问题，参照前面讲的内容处理。不要忘记在医生指导下继续补充叶酸。

头发养护

头发属于皮肤组织的一部分，就像皮肤一样，它也会受到怀孕激素的影响而产生变化。如原来干涩的头发这时可能会更干涩，原来油腻的头发现在更油腻，甚至卷发会变成直发。怀孕中期是保养头发的好时期。只要懂得细心呵护，秀发便似清晨花叶上滚动的露珠，永远折射着鲜花的柔美和香甜。

1. 选择合适的发型搭配你的脸型

(1) 如果头发比较厚，脸型比较饱满，就适合留长头发，让脸看起来修长一点。

(2) 如果原本就留着长发，但是发质比较干燥，而且容易分岔或断裂，那么最好把头发剪短或是打薄一点。

(3) 如果是直发，自然分泌的发油可以让头发看起来更有光泽。

2. 试着换几种洗发精来洗头

(1) 如果头发比较干燥，可以减少洗头次数，并使用少量、成分温和的洗发精洗头。洗完头之后，也可以抹上一层保湿润发摩丝，以避免干裂现象的发生。

(2) 如果头发是油性的，可以洗得勤快一点。

3. 美发小技巧

(1) 头发油和头皮屑——柠檬焕发法：将护发素加柠檬混合，并将其涂在洗过的半干的头发上，固定好，戴上浴帽，5分钟后洗净。每周做3次，头屑及油腻现象就会大有改观。需要注意的是，混合后的护发剂，在头发上涂薄薄一层就行，不要贪心涂的太多。

(2) 头皮痒、敏感——芝麻油焕发法：取芝麻油适量，以清水轻轻弄湿头发，从发根至发尾涂上芝麻油并按摩头皮，包上热毛巾捂30分钟，再以温水洗头，进行一般洗发程序即可。

（3）头发易折断，脆弱，起静电——黄豆护发焕发秘法：将50克黄豆和2杯矿泉水一起煮开，水滚后改小火煮成一杯待用。除去黄豆，洗头后用黄豆水冲洗最后一次，洗后无需再用清水冲头发。每周采用这样的方法洗发之后，再使用少量免洗护发素，秀发就会渐渐恢复过来。

（4）掉发——酸奶焕发法：用洗发精洗头发，冲洗干净之后，用酸奶充当润发乳使用，秀发不但不会有洗发精残留的问题，摸起来还非常的柔顺，但务必要用温水冲干净。

4．其他

（1）用毛巾将头发擦干，会比用吹风机吹干更对发质有益。

（2）淋浴时，别忘了用指尖，轻轻地按摩头皮，以刺激头皮血液循环。

（3）不要用过热的水洗头。

（4）用木梳梳头：从前额开始向后梳，梳时要紧贴头皮部位，用力大小适中，动作缓慢柔和。梳头5～7天后，洗头一次。

指甲保养

怀孕激素会刺激指甲生长的速度，新生的指甲由于比较软，断裂的几率比平常要高。怀孕时，可以做一些指甲的保健工作。

1．平常多摄取一些含有胶质成分的食物。

2．勤剪指甲，尽量让指甲保持短短的。

3．就寝之前，使用一些保湿防护乳液，来保护手部肌肤与指甲的组织。

4．使用清洁剂做家事时，别忘了戴上手套，以免手或手指沾到刺激性强的清洁剂，造成过敏与伤害。

5．避免擦指甲油。目前市场上销售的指甲油，大多以硝化纤维为基料，配以丙酮、乙酯、丁酯、苯二甲酸等化学溶剂和增塑剂以及各色染料而成，这些化学物质对人体有一定的毒性作用。涂指甲油的孕妇用手抓食物时，指甲油中的有毒化学物很容易随食物通过胎盘进入胎儿体内，日积月累，可影响胎儿健康。

口腔护理

老话说："生一个孩子丢一颗牙"。的确，怀孕期是女性一个特殊的生理时期，由于女性内分泌和饮食习惯发生变化，体耗增加等原因，往往容易引起牙龈肿胀、牙龈出血、蛀牙等口腔疾病。因此，需要做好口腔护理工作：

1. 坚持每日2次有效刷牙。对容易感染蛀牙的孕妇，适当用一些局部使用的氟化物，如氟化物漱口液等。使用短软毛的牙刷轻轻刷牙，这样不会引起牙龈出血。

2. 每天用具有杀菌功能的漱口水多漱几次口，漱完口后将漱口水吐掉，千万别把漱口水当饮料一饮而尽。

3. 使用不含蔗糖的口香糖清洁牙齿，如木糖醇口香糖。如果能在餐后和睡觉前咀嚼1片，每次咀嚼至少5分钟，对于牙齿和牙龈健康是很有帮助的。

4. 少吃粘牙的糖果或甜点。

5. 每隔3个月检查口腔。如果自觉有口腔疾病，应随时就诊，及时处理，按医嘱做好保健工作。

贴心·提醒

1. 多吃富含维生素C的水果与蔬菜。含钙丰富的食物也有益于牙齿的健康。

2. 孕早期，不得进行拔牙、洗牙之类的治疗。孕中期，可以到医院处理治疗。

第12周

孕早期要结束了

第12周记：本周是怀孕第一个阶段的末尾了，流产的可能性也减小了。直到这个周，我才把自己怀孕的消息公开，告诉了朋友们，大家都非常惊讶，表示关心。

我今天去医院做了透视，当从透视仪器的屏幕上看到宝宝模糊的形状，我禁不住热泪盈眶——一个多么完美的宝宝，虽然可能不到7厘米。

胎宝宝状况 这一周，胎宝贝身长大约6.5厘米，大脑的体积越来越大，几乎占了整个身体的一半。小手小脚上的蹼状物消失，手指和脚趾已经能完全分开。一部分骨骼开始慢慢变得坚硬起来，出现了关节的雏形。膝盖、脚后跟清晰可见。为了适应出生后的生活，胎宝贝已经在忙着锻炼身体了，小小的脑袋会动了，抬起小脚的动作甚至可以和出生后的动作媲美。这时，肾脏、输尿管已经形成，胎宝贝可以排泄了；其他关键器官的发育也将在本周与下周内完成。现在胎盘基本形成，胎宝贝与孕妈咪的联系进入稳步发展阶段，发生流产的机会相应减小了。胎宝贝已经开始进入脑细胞迅速增殖的第一阶段——“脑迅速增长期”，即孕4～6月。

孕妈妈状况 孕3月末，大多数孕妈咪孕吐已缓轻，疲劳嗜睡阶段也已经过去。与前段时间比，你会感到精力已经恢复了。你可以时常真切地感觉到胎宝贝的存在，还可能会经常习惯性地轻抚你的小腹，与腹中正忙着或闲着的小家伙“交流”。也许你的皮肤会有些变化，比如脸和脖子上不同程度地出现了黄褐斑，你还可能注意到小腹部的妊娠纹渐渐变成黑褐色，不用担心，这是孕期的正常特征，待小宝贝出生后，它们就会逐渐消退。

日常生活中的其他问题，参照前面讲的内容处理。

本周别忘记进行例行产检，不要忘记在医生指导下继续补充叶酸。

第一次B超检查

从满11周开始至孕14周之间，通常进行第一次B超检查。可以测量胎儿鼻骨和颅后透明带，结合其他指标，初步筛查先天畸形。

补充铁剂

铁是人体生成红细胞的主要原料之一，孕期缺铁性贫血，不但导致孕妇心慌气短、头晕、乏力，还可导致胎儿宫内缺氧，生长发育迟缓，生后智力发育障碍，生后6个月之内易患营养性缺铁性贫血等。

孕妇要为自己和胎儿在宫内及产后造血做好充分的铁储备，因此，刚开始怀孕的时候，就需要补充铁质（如果能在怀孕前补充，效果一定更好），以便储存额外的铁质。补铁分药补和食补。

1. 补充铁剂 补充铁质药片（硫酸亚铁片）或铁剂，最好在医生指导下进行。如果铁剂刺激肠胃，加重便秘，可以将一天一剂分为数次服用。吃富含铁质、容易让人体吸收的食物也是一个好选择。

2. 食物补充 孕妇可多食一些含铁丰富的食物，如蔬菜中的黑木耳、紫菜、海带、芹菜、韭菜、苋菜、油菜、黑芝麻、莲藕粉；水果中的干杏、樱桃；谷类食物中的芝麻、大麦米、糯米、小米；豆类食物中的黄豆、赤小豆、蚕豆、绿豆，等等。瘦肉、猪血、动物肝脏、蛋黄中铁的含量更为丰富。

补充钙剂

孕妇对钙的需求量很高，因为胎儿所需的钙是从母亲这个“储备库”中获取的。孕妇缺钙症状包括腰酸背痛、手足麻木、肌肉抽搐、妊娠高血压、产后牙齿松动、骨盆疼痛、关节疼痛等。

1. 补充钙剂

计划怀孕的夫妇或已经怀孕的孕妇，可在医生指导下额外补充一定量的钙剂，如碳酸钙、葡萄糖酸钙等。

2. 食物补充

孕妇适当选择一些富含钙的食物如奶类、豆制品，基本可以补充钙质。

孕妇补钙的最好方法是每天喝200~400克牛奶。每100克牛奶中含钙约120毫克，牛奶中的钙最容易被孕妇所吸收，而且磷、钾、镁等多种矿物质搭配也十分合理。

富含钙的食物有海带、黄豆、冻豆腐、腐竹、奶制品类（包括酸乳酪、牛乳）、黑木耳、鱼（如带骨鲑鱼、鲔鱼、沙丁鱼）虾类、无花果、杏仁、花椰菜、甘蓝菜等。

贴心·提醒

1. 吃肉骨头炖汤，并不能很好地使钙吸收，如同时补充一定量的维生素D，就可使钙很好地吸收。

2. 孕妇服用钙片，应按医嘱进行。

3. 增加日光照射时间，防止维生素D的缺乏，促进食物中钙的吸收。

小贴士……关于维生素D

维生素D能促进食物中钙的吸收，并通过胎盘参与胎儿钙的代谢。我国建议孕妇每日应摄取10微克的维生素D，为了达到这个供给量标准，孕妇应注意多从食物中摄取维生素D，增加日光照射时间，以防止维生素D缺乏症的出现。

一般食物维生素D含量不丰富。含量较多的食物有海产鱼类、蛋类和黄油。天然浓缩食物主要是鱼肝油。孕妇在选择鱼肝油和维生素D强化食物时，一定要遵照医生的嘱咐，不可过量，以免引起中毒。

“吃”出健康宝宝

日常饮食中有很多食物看似平常，其实对孕妇具有非常好的保健作用。如果注意摄取这些食物，可以帮助孕妇健康地孕育胎儿。

1．富含维生素C果蔬——预防先兆子痫

先兆子痫是孕后期容易发生的一种严重并发症，影响孕妇和胎儿的安危。有关专家调查时发现，摄取维生素C少的孕妇，血液中维生素C水平也较低，她们发生先兆子痫的几率是健康孕妇的2～4倍。因此，专家建议孕期应注意摄取富含VC的新鲜蔬菜和水果，每天的摄取量最好不低于85毫克。

2．蜂蜜——促进睡眠并预防便秘

在天然食品中，大脑神经元所需要的能量在蜂蜜中含量最高。如果孕妇在睡前饮上一杯蜂蜜水，所具有的安神之功效可缓解多梦易醒、睡眠不香等不适，改善睡眠质量。另外，孕妇每天上下午饮水时，如果在水中放入数滴蜂蜜，可缓下通便，有效地预防便秘及痔疮。

3．鱼类——避免胎儿脑发育不良

鱼体中含有DHA，这种物质在胎儿的脑细胞膜形成中起着重要作用。调查发现，怀孕后经常吃鱼有助于胎儿的脑细胞生长发育，吃得越多，胎儿脑发育不良的可能性就越小。专家建议，孕妇在一周之内至少吃1～2次鱼，以吸收足够的DHA，满足胎儿的脑发育需求。另外，孕期每周吃1次鱼还有助于降低早产的可能性。

4．黄豆芽——促进胎儿组织器官建造

胎儿的生长发育需要蛋白质。黄豆芽中富含胎儿所必需的蛋白质，还可在孕妇体内进行储备，以供应分娩时消耗及产后泌乳，同时可预防产后出血、便秘，提高母乳质量。所以，黄豆芽是孕产妇理想的蔬菜。

5．鸡蛋——促进胎儿的大脑发育

鸡蛋营养成分全面均衡，七大营养素几乎完全能被身体所利用。尤其是蛋黄中的胆碱被称为“记忆素”，对于胎宝贝的大脑发育非常有益。鸡蛋虽是孕妇的理想食品，但非多多益善，每天吃3～4个为宜，以免增加肝肾负担。

6. 冬瓜和西瓜——帮助消除下肢水肿

怀孕后期由于静脉受压，足踝部常出现水肿，经过休息就会消失。如果休息后仍不消失或程度较重又无其他异常，称为妊娠水肿。冬瓜性寒味甘，水分丰富，可以止渴利尿。如果和鲤鱼一起熬汤，可使减轻孕妇的下肢水肿。西瓜具有清热解毒、利尿消肿的作用，经常食用可能帮助消除下肢水肿。

7. 南瓜——防治妊娠水肿和高血压

南瓜花果的营养极为丰富。孕妇食用南瓜花果，不仅能促进胎儿的脑细胞发育，增强其活力，还可防治妊娠水肿、高血压等孕期并发症，促进凝血及预防产后出血。取南瓜500克、粳米60克，煮成南瓜粥，可促进肝肾细胞再生，同时对早孕反应后恢复食欲及体力有促进作用。

8. 新鲜酸味水果——防止胎儿神经管畸形

杨梅、草莓、樱桃、猕猴桃、石榴、葡萄等都是带有酸味的水果。这些水果中富含叶酸，而叶酸是胚胎神经管发育的非常重要物质。如果孕期缺乏叶酸，就会影响胚胎神经管的发育和形成，导致脊柱裂或无脑儿。因此，在孕早期要注意多吃些新鲜酸味水果，降低胎儿发生神经管畸形的风险畸形。

9. 芹菜——防治妊娠高血压

芹菜中富含芫荽甙、胡萝卜素、维生素C、烟酸及甘露醇等营养素，特别是叶子中的某些营养素要比芹菜茎更为丰富，具有清热凉血、醒脑利尿、镇静降压的作用。孕后期经常食用，可以帮助孕妇降低血压，对缺铁性贫血以及由妊娠高血压综合征引起先兆子痫等并发症，也有防治作用。

10. 马铃薯——减轻孕吐反应

马铃薯富含维生素B6，具有止吐作用。如果多吃一些马铃薯，就可帮助孕妇缓解厌油腻、呕吐的症状，马铃薯也是防治妊娠高血压的保健食物。

11. 动物肝——避免发生缺铁性贫血

孕期血容量比未孕前增加，血液被稀释，孕妇出现生理性贫血。铁补充不足容易引起孕期贫血或早产。孕期一定要注意摄取富含铁的食物。各种动物肝铁含量较高，但一周吃一次即可。吃这些食物的同时，最好同吃富含维生素C或果酸的食物，如柠檬、橘子等，增加铁在肠道的吸收率。

预防便秘

1. 多摄取富含纤维素的食物 纤维素经过肠道时不被消化，起着像海绵样的作用，吸满液体。水分增加有助于粪便更快地移动，让粪便得以较轻松地排出体外。吃些水果，尤其是梅子、梨、无花果、杏。同时多吃蔬菜，特别是比较脆的蔬菜，如胡萝卜、小胡瓜、黄瓜、芹菜等，以及其他如全谷物，包括全麦和杂粮面包、豆类和玉米等。为了从水果和蔬菜中得到最多的纤维，尽量生食或略煮并保留皮。请购买或种植不含农药的有机蔬果。

2. 增加水分的摄取 如果你增加纤维素的摄取，就一定得随之增加水分的摄取，太多的纤维和太少的液体实际上能使粪便变得硬而使便秘的情况更加严重。因此，如果你喜欢喝果汁，就饮用新鲜果汁（如梅子汁、梨汁和桔汁），这样不仅增加水分的摄取量，另一方面也同时增加纤维素的摄取量。不过，要确保你每天再补充6～8大杯水才行，避免饮用含咖啡因的饮料。

3. 多运动 让全身动一动，你的肠道也动一动。经常运动可以让你的生理系统的“运动”更规律，使你的肠道功能不致失衡。

4. 定时排便 养成每天定时排便的良好习惯，每次排便时间不宜过长。不要在排便时看书，以免注意力分散延长排便时间，致使肛周静脉长时间处于紧张状态，影响血液回流。

贴心·提醒

1. 便秘时，尽量避免服用泻药，以免子宫收缩造成流产或早产。

2. 便秘严重时，在医生指导下用药。

第13周

孕中期开始了

第13周记：我相信小草莓现在已经有橘子那么大了，而我的肚子也能看出轻微的突起——虽然隔着衣服外人还看不出来。

我几乎不再觉得恶心，而且居然变得相当精力充沛。我头发上有一层奇异的光泽，皮肤变得平滑而且柔软。胎盘已经在我内形成，它会控制激素的生成，并且负责为宝宝提供营养。

由于脂肪层还没有生成，宝宝的腿会显得骨瘦如柴，做妈妈的却恰恰相反，我觉得自己像发酵的馒头。大夫特地告戒我不要穿紧身牛仔裤，因为会影血液循环，造成静脉曲张和肿胀。

胎宝宝状况　胎儿身长约7厘米甚至更长。眼睛在额上显得更为突出，眼间距逐渐缩小，但眼睑仍然紧紧地闭合。耳朵已经到位，内耳等听觉器官已基本发育完善，对子宫外的声音刺激开始有所反应。胎宝贝的条件反射能力加强，手指开始能向手掌握紧，脚趾与脚底也可以弯曲了。脐带可以进行营养与代谢废物的交换了。肝脏开始制造胆汁，肾脏开始向膀胱分泌尿液。如果你用手在腹部轻轻抚触，胎宝贝会随只之蠕动，但因力薄气小你无法感知。

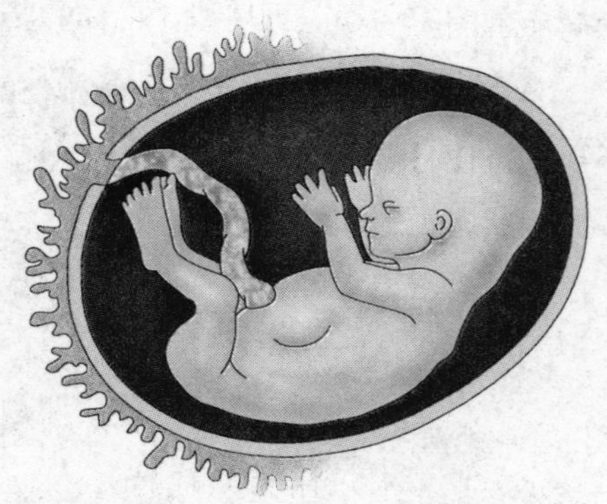

第13周（4月胎宝宝）

孕妈妈状况　经历了前3个月的磨难，孕中期的妊娠反应已经没那么激烈了，胃口一下子变得很好得好，很多美食都表现出出奇的好吃，那种美味的感觉恐怕此生只有在这段时间才能感觉得到。

不过对于崇尚美食的准妈咪来说，一定记住要吃得适可而止，否则把自己和胎宝宝养的太胖，会给自己顺利生产和产后的减肥带来无穷的麻烦。在享用美食的同时，你该准备宽松的衣裤了。

孕4月专家提示（第13～16周）

1．“害喜症状”已改善许多，情绪转好，食欲增加。应注意均衡饮食，特别是要多摄取蛋白质、植物性脂肪、钙、维生素等营养物质。不要过多地摄入糖类甜食等，以免影响主食的摄入量。适当限制盐的摄入，每天摄入盐15克左右。

2．由于阴道分泌物增多、新陈代谢旺盛，应勤换内衣裤，每天洗澡，保持身体清洁、舒适。

3．腰腹部位渐感沉重负担，甚至会引起酸痛不适，一次不要走太多路。晚上睡觉时腰部垫一小睡枕，可获改善。

4．外出购物时，不要提过重物品。

5．清洗浴厕或下雨天外出时，走路要格外小心，踏稳每一步，以避免滑倒。

6．母亲已能借着超音波听到胎儿的心跳声及感受到胎动，可和先生分享彼此的喜悦，并增进亲密关系。

7．保持自己轻松愉快的心情，看书、听音乐、公园散步都是很好的选择。

8．可以恢复性交生活，但应避免选择压迫腹部的姿位。

9．可上点淡妆。

10．洗发精选择植物性pH5.5～6.5之间。

11．服装色系以提高亮度为主，例如浅水蓝、淡紫色等。

12．可以依据自己的体力、精神状况，参加准妈妈辅导班或孕妇教室，学习有关妊娠、分娩及新生儿方面之医疗保健知识。

孕中期饮食指导（第4～7月）

孕中期，胎儿的生长速度逐渐加快，体重每天约增加10克左右，胎儿的骨骼开始钙化，脑发育也处于高峰期。此时孕妇的胃口开始好转，孕妇本身的生理变化使皮下脂肪的储存量增加、子宫和乳房明显增大，孕妇本身的基础代谢也增加了10%～20%。因此，饮食上要注意如下几点：

1. 膳食结构

食物品种应强调多样化，主食（大米、面）350～400克，杂粮（小米、玉米、豆类等）50克左右，蛋类50克，牛乳220～250毫升，动物类食品100～150克，动物肝脏每周2～3次每次50克，蔬菜400～500克（绿叶菜占2/3），经常食用菌藻类食品，水果100～200克，植物油25～40克。

从第20周开始，在饮食中要有意安排富含钙质的食物摄入，特别对于孕吐反应剧烈的孕妈咪更是如此。

2. 饮食成分

（1）鲜奶：牛奶、羊奶含有丰富的必需氨基酸、钙、磷、多种微量元素及维生素A、D和B族维生素。有条件者每日可饮用250～500克。应鼓励喝不惯奶的孕妇从少量开始喝奶，逐渐增加。食后如有胀气不适，可煮沸稍冷后，加入食用乳酸、醪糟汁或浓酸果汁制成酸奶食用。如喝奶后引起腹泻，也不要强求饮用。

（2）蛋：蛋是提供优质蛋白质的最佳天然食品，也是脂溶性维生素及叶酸、维生素B_2、B_6、B_{12}的丰富来源，铁含量亦较高，不仅烹调方法简单多样，甜、咸均可，并宜于保存。凡条件许可，尽可能每天吃鸡蛋1～3个。

（3）鱼、禽、瘦肉及动物肝脏：这些都是蛋白质、无机盐和各种维生素的良好来源。孕妇每天饮食中应供给50～150克。如有困难，可用蛋类，大豆及其制品代替。鱼和蛋是最好的互换食品，可根据季节选用。动物肝脏是孕妇必须的维生素A、D、叶酸、维生素B_1、B_2、B_{12}、尼克酸及铁的优良来源，也是供应优质蛋白质的良好来源，每周至少吃1～2次，每次100克左右。

（4）大豆及其制品：大豆及其制品是植物性食品蛋白质、B族维生素及无机盐的丰富来源。豆芽含有丰富的维生素C。农村或缺少肉、奶供给的地区，每天进食豆类及其制品50～100克，以保证孕妇、胎儿的营养需要。

（5）蔬菜水果：绿叶蔬菜如小白菜、豌豆苗、白菜、菠菜；黄红色蔬菜如甜椒、胡萝卜、红心红薯等都含有丰富的维生素、无机盐和纤维素。每天应摄取新鲜蔬菜250～750克，其中有色蔬菜应占一半以上。水果中带酸味者，既合孕妇口味又含有较多的维生素C，还含有果胶。每天供给新鲜水果150～200克。瓜果类蔬菜中黄瓜、番茄等生吃更为有益。蔬菜、水果中含纤维素和果胶对防治妊娠期便秘十分有利。

（6）海产品：应经常吃些海带、紫菜、海鱼、虾皮、鱼松等海产品，以补充碘。内陆缺碘地区应食用加碘食盐。

（7）硬果类食品：芝麻、花生、核桃、葵花子等，其蛋白质和矿物质含量与豆类相似，亦可经常食用。

3．避免吃的食物

（1）油腻而难以消化的食物，如油炸食物、熟猪肉制品，动物的头肉等。

（2）辛辣食物。

（3）易发生食物中毒的食物，如甲壳动物、淡菜、蚌类、野生蘑菇等，另外还有不新鲜的食物，剩饭剩菜。

（4）使人发胖的食物。

（5）生鱼、生肉、未熟的肉制品，如不太熟的涮羊肉、烤羊肉串、生鱼片、生肉片。

（6）酒精饮料。

（7）食品添加剂过多的食物和饮料。

（8）罐头食品。

（9）浓茶、咖啡及含咖啡因的饮料。

（10）山楂及山楂制品。

小贴士……食物过敏危害大

孕妇食用过敏食物不仅能导致流产、早产、胎儿畸形，还可致婴儿多种疾病。

有过敏体质的孕妇可能对某些食物过敏，这些过敏食物经消化吸收后，可从胎盘进入胎儿血液循环中，妨碍胎儿的生长发育，或直接损害某些器官，如肺、支气管等，从而导致胎儿畸形或罹患疾病。

食物过敏可从下面5个方面进行预防：

1. 以往吃某些食物发生过过敏现象，怀孕期间应禁止食用。

2. 不要吃过去从未吃过的食物或霉变食物。

3. 食用某些食物后如发生全身发痒，出荨麻疹或心慌、气喘，或腹痛、腹泻等现象，应禁止食用。

4. 不吃易过敏的食物，如海产鱼、虾、蟹、贝壳类食物及辛辣刺激性食物。

5. 食用异性蛋白类食物，如动物肝、肾、蛋类、奶类、鱼类应烧熟煮透。

营养菜单——孕中期

1. 阳春面

材料：鸡蛋面条100克，鸡蛋1个，青蒜苗3棵，香油5克，花生油、精盐适量，高汤适量。

做法：

(1) 鸡蛋磕入碗内搅匀；炒锅上火烧热，用洁布抹一层花生油，倒入蛋液摊成蛋皮，取出切成细丝；蒜苗洗净，切成2.5厘米长的段。

(2) 置火上，锅内加水烧开，下鸡蛋面条煮熟；捞出盛碗内，撒上蛋皮丝、青蒜段。

(3) 将高汤倒入炒勺中烧开，撇去浮沫，加精盐调味，再淋点香油，浇在面条上即成。

2. 鸡蛋家常饼

材料：面粉500克，鸡蛋250克，植物油100克，精盐10克，葱花100克。

做法：

（1）鸡蛋磕入小盆内，加入葱花、精盐搅匀。

（2）面粉放入盆内，加温水300克和成较软的面团，稍饧，上案搓成条，揪成5个剂子，用擀面杖擀开，刷上植物油，撒少许精盐，卷成长条卷，盘成圆形，擀成直径12厘米的圆饼。

（3）平底锅置火上烧热，把饼放入锅内，定皮后抹油（只抹一面），再烙黄至熟取出。

（4）将鸡蛋液分成5份，把1/5鸡蛋液倒在平底锅上摊开（大小与饼一致），将饼无油的一面贴放在蛋上，烙熟即成，食时切成小块。

3. 牛奶大米饭

材料：大米500克，牛奶500克。

做法：大米淘洗干净，放入锅内，加牛奶和适量清水，盖上锅盖，用小火慢慢焖熟即成。

4. 海米醋熘白菜

材料：白菜心500克，水发海米25克，花生油50克，花椒油5克，酱油10克，白糖30克，醋15克，精盐2克，水淀粉15克，料酒少许。

做法：将白菜心切成小片段，放入沸水锅内焯一下，捞出沥干水分。炒锅上火，放油烧热，下海米和酱油、精盐、醋、料酒、白糖，加入白菜片翻炒，加水少许，待汤沸时，用水淀粉勾芡，淋花椒油，盛入盘内即成。

5. 冬菇菜心

材料：油菜心250克，冬菇50克，鸡油25克，汤300克，盐、糖、料酒、胡椒面、姜、葱、淀粉适量。

做法：

（1）油菜心洗净，在沸水中氽透，过凉开水待用。

（2）冬菇泡透，去蒂洗净，先用沸水氽透，放在碗内，加葱、姜、料酒、汤、盐上屉蒸30分钟。

（3）锅内放鸡油、葱、姜煸香下汤，汤开后捞出葱、姜，放盐、糖、胡椒面，再放菜心烧入味，捞出码在盘中，冬菇拣净姜葱放在菜心周围，锅内的汤勾好芡，加入鸡油，浇在菜上即可。

6. 杞子煲红枣

材料：麦芽糖60克，枸杞30克，红枣20个。

做法：枸杞、麦芽糖、红枣加清水煮熟服用。

7. 四物炖豆腐皮

材料：豆腐皮250克，香菇10克，当归25克，枸杞25克，人参20克，红枣10颗，料酒、盐适量。

做法：

（1）将豆腐皮切成条，每条折成四叠挽成一个结。香菇泡软。

（2）将豆腐皮结、香菇和四种药材入炖锅内，加入料酒、盐煮沸。

（3）移至文火炖1小时即可。

8. 茄汁虾片

材料：净虾肉250克，黄瓜60克，番茄汁75克，盐5克，香油50克，葱姜各50克，糖适量。

做法：

（1）将净虾肉用刀从背脊外一剖两瓣，不要剖断，从虾尾部往前3毫米处，斜刀切片，每隔3毫米切一片，依次完全切好，放在碗里，加盐抓匀、腌制使其入味。

（2）锅内入上净油，至6成热油温，将虾片轻轻滑一下，捞出控油。

（3）葱姜切成末，锅内放香油为底油，油温后将葱姜末下锅，煸炒出香味，再放番茄汁煸炒，炒熟后，加入盐、糖，把过油的虾片倒入锅里，颠翻几下，打入明油即可。

（4）装盘时，把黄瓜洗净消毒，斜刀切成片，围边装入盘里，中间放入番茄虾片。

9. 炒芙蓉干贝

材料：干贝100克，鸡蛋清6个，料酒15克，盐7克，水淀粉50克，熟猪油75克，高汤250克，葱姜末适量。

做法：先将干贝洗几遍，将硬边去掉，再用温水洗净，上屉蒸烂、去汤搓碎，与蛋清、高汤、葱姜末、料酒、盐、水淀粉搅匀。炒勺上火加熟猪油，烧热放入干贝炒熟即可。

10. 炒芙蓉大虾

材料：净大虾肉175克，鸡蛋清15克，净南荠10克，料酒15克，盐5克，大油500克（净耗75克），水淀粉10克，高汤75克，葱末2克，姜末适量。

做法：

(1) 将南荠用刀拍碎抹成泥。大虾肉抹刀切厚片，用水淀粉、蛋清少许抓匀上浆。

(2) 把蛋清放入大碗中，加南荠泥、葱末、姜末、盐、料酒、湿淀粉、高汤，用筷子搅打均匀。

(3) 炒勺上火放入大油，烧至五、六成熟时，将虾片散开下勺，用筷子拨散，滑透倒入漏勺控净油，倒入鸡蛋清搅拌均匀备用。

(4) 炒勺再上火，放大油，油热后，将虾肉蛋清倒入勺中，晃勺推炒，不使粘底，蛋清凝固时颠勺翻个，顺着勺沿烹入高汤，再晃勺翻个，汤收尽即成。

11. 翡翠虾仁

材料：鲜河虾仁750克，马蹄100克，熟金华火腿40克，鸡蛋清2只，菠菜200克，料酒10克，精盐7克，干淀粉8克，鸡汤少许，葱白4克，花生油适量。

做法：

(1) 虾仁漂洗干净，骨结面吸干水分。菠菜洗净，切碎捣烂，用洁布挤出绿汁。马蹄、火腿均切成虾仁大小的丁。葱白切成马蹄形。

(2) 菠菜汁用火烧开，将浮在上面的一层绿色沫用小漏勺捞出，放入小盘内，其他水不要，将菠菜沫适量地放入虾仁内搅匀，待虾仁够绿后，再加入精盐、料酒、蛋清、干淀粉拌匀浆好。

(3) 炒锅上火，注入油，待烧至四成热时，下入虾仁拨散滑熟，起锅，倒入漏勺，滤净后炒锅至火上，加少许汤，下入马蹄、火腿、葱白、咯炒，倒入虾仁，烹入料酒，加入少许油，翻炒均匀即成。

12. 虾仁豆腐汤

材料：豆腐100克，鲜虾仁750克，蛋清1个，上汤900克，油250克，料酒10克，精盐、胡椒粉各适量，水淀粉10克。

做法：热锅下油，将虾仁放入拉油至熟放入汤盆待用，将余油出锅。锅内加入上汤、豆腐条。用精盐、料酒调味，撒上胡椒粉。用水淀粉打芡，加入虾仁，将打散的蛋清倒入搅匀即成。

13. 红萝卜牛骨汤

材料：牛骨500克，红萝卜1个，番茄2个，椰菜100克，洋葱半个，胡椒3粒。

做法：牛骨洗净斩块备用，红萝卜去皮洗净切大块，番茄洗净切块，椰菜洗净切块，洋葱洗净切片。瓦煲中放入胡椒3粒，加放牛骨、红萝卜块、番茄块、椰菜块、洋葱片，放入适量清水煲2个小时，调味即成。

14. 生菜滚鱼汤

材料：生菜300克，豆腐100克，鱼1条，姜1片。

做法：鱼剖开腹去内脏和鳞，洗净沥干水，生菜摘为寸长，豆腐切条。鱼下油煎黄铲起。放入姜爆香。加适量水烧滚，放入豆腐滚约15分钟，下生菜滚熟，放盐调味即成。

15. 泥鳅鱼汤

材料、做法参见50页。

第14周

胃口大开

第14周记：今天我听到他的心跳了！大夫把一只像麦克风似的仪器放在我的腹部，把另一头给我听。那声音听起来像一匹马在喘息——而且是以每分钟150次的频率。真不敢相信，比我自己的心跳要快一倍。大夫说宝宝已经有我的拳头那么大了。

我的乳头和乳晕都已经显出很深的褐色。真没想到，乳房也会发生那么大的变化。

胎宝宝状况 这一周，胎宝贝的身长有7.5～10厘米左右，体重不到30克。现在，胎宝贝的皮肤上覆盖有一层细细的绒毛，这绒毛通常会在出生后消失。头发也开始迅速生长。下颚骨、面颊骨、鼻梁骨等开始形成，耳廓伸出。小家伙已经可以做很多表情了：皱眉、做鬼脸、斜一斜小眼睛。

孕妈妈状况 你的体态还不太像个孕妇。不再晨吐了、也不恶心了，胃口也会变得好起来，但胃酸也将随之而来。有些孕妈咪可能会发现，自己的乳头能挤出少许乳汁，它看上去像分娩后分泌的初乳。

孕妈咪的胃口大开，但要注意科学地摄取各种营养素，不可胡吃一气。特别是有过严重早孕反应的孕妈咪。饮食一定要多样化，不可偏食、也不要挑嘴。每餐吃得不宜太饱，应少食多餐，细嚼慢咽，以利于消化吸收。

性生活

妊娠3个月以后，胎盘逐渐形成，妊娠进入稳定期；早孕反应过去了，孕妇的心情开始变得舒畅。由于激素的作用，孕妇的性欲有所提高。加上胎盘和羊水的屏障作用，可缓冲外界的刺激，使胎儿得到有效的保护。因此，妊娠中期可适度地进行性生活。

怀孕的第4～6个月，也称为怀孕的“蜜月期”，往往是她们人生中最值得回味的一段美好时光。舒心的性生活充分地将爱心和性欲融为一体。白天，丈夫给妻子或者妻子给丈夫亲吻与抚摸，爱的暖流就会传到对方的心田。这样对于夜间的闺房之爱大有益处。反过来，夜间体贴的性生活又促进夫妻白天的恩爱，使孕妇的心情愉快，情绪饱满。

妊娠中期的性生活以每周1～2次为宜。性生活时，丈夫务必注意卫生，以免妻诱发宫内感染。有自然流产和习惯性流产的孕妇，应避免性交。

性交时应避免压迫女方的腹部，要减少阴茎的冲撞力及深度。下列是一些适宜的姿势，是否适合你，可逐一试试：

1．女上男下式。

2．侧卧式：男方侧卧，女方仰卧，同时将双腿搭在男方双腿上。

3．男上女下式（避免压迫女方腹部）：男方在上面，但应注意双手支撑，以免对女方腹部造成压迫，这种姿势可一直运用到腹部隆起过大为止。

4．坐入式：做爱时女方面对面坐在男方双腿之上（适合腹部不太大的时期）。当腹部变大时，女方可转过身体用坐姿后入式。

5．后入式：女方四肢俯卧，男方采取跪姿后入式。

贴心·提醒

怀孕3个月内，少运动，以免影响坐胎。怀孕中期，散步要注意速度，最好控制在4千米／小时，每天1次，每次30～40分钟。怀孕后期，以稍慢的散步为主，速度以3公里／小时为宜，时间不宜超过15分钟。

小贴士……让自己更性感

1．让你自己看起来更加性感

虽然你的身体日渐丰腴，但这并不表示你就不应该看起来最好。好好地替自己设计个新发型、改变上妆与穿着上的造型，让你的丈夫耳目一新。

2．行为上更加妩媚一些

人类行为的变化，可以影响到感觉。比方说一个简单的微笑，可以刺激脑部，产生与你真正感到愉快时相同的化学物质，结果一时之间，你好像觉得心情真的不错。同样，如果你在行为上没有性感，就会让你的丈夫感觉不出性感，使他退缩。结果，就一直恶性循环下去。相反地，如果你能够在行为上更加妩媚一些，那么效果一定会出乎你的意料之外，你很快会吃惊地发现自己确实很性感！

3．有自信更能吸引丈夫

如果你总是觉得逐渐隆起的腹部会让丈夫丧失兴趣，那可就大错特错了。一般说来，男人多半会对妻子怀孕的肚子感兴趣，对妻子因怀孕身材上所产生的种种变化，也会大感好奇。

不要先入为主地认为，你的丈夫一定会对你性趣索然，相反地，他可能正想与你共度良宵呢！

4．共享身体变化的感觉

让丈夫以你身体上的变化为骄傲，比方说颜色变深的乳头、隆起的肚皮等。另外，你们也可以一起脱个精光躺在床上，专心去感受腹中的胎动，这是新手父亲从未有过的经验，相信他一定会觉得很有意思。

最好的方式，就是要丈夫帮忙，每个月都帮你照些各个角度的照片，将这重大的怀孕过程中你身体的所有变化用相片记录下来。

5．浪漫一下又何妨

婴儿出生前，经常定个周末约会。偶尔约会一下，相信一定能够增进你们小两口的生活情趣。因为孩子出生后，你们彼此就没有太多的精力了。

头痛怎么办

像恶心一样，头痛也是孕妇最常抱怨的现象。怀孕中期快结束时，头痛通常会减弱或消失。你可以试着在不吃药的情况下，用其他的方法来疏缓头痛：

1. 了解头痛的原因

当你发生头痛现象的时候，要仔细想一下，是不是因为你做了什么、吃了什么或在烦恼什么，结果导致头痛。你是不是常常将"这份工作真是烦死了"、"我一看到他就觉得头好痛!"之类的话挂在嘴上？结果，你可能因此头痛起来。

如果你整天都心烦气躁、忧心忡忡的话，试着放松自己，静坐、睡睡觉，也许可以帮助你疏解压力，进而减少头痛的发生。

2. 慢慢改变体位

任何能改变脑部血流量的动作，都会造成头痛。这种情况，在一大早起床时，或者从晚上舒适的躺椅爬起来的时候最容易发生。所以，为了让胎儿与你的脑袋可以同时取得足够的血流量，请尽量缓慢改变体位。

3. 保持血糖的稳定

血糖降低，也会导致头痛的发生，因此，你可以尽量以少量多餐的方式，或是随时给自己补充一些小点心，别让自己有饥饿感。

4. 保持空气的流通

(1) 避免呆在充满烟味的房间里。

(2)在人多的公共密闭场所里，应该尽量让自己接近门，以便能经常出去呼吸新鲜的空气。

(3) 冬天有暖气的时候，应该将最接近自己的一扇窗打开一点。

(4) 如果在密闭的办公大楼上班，尽量抽空往有窗户的楼道或茶水间跑，以多吸取一些新鲜空气。

5．在家休养

试着放松自己，在家里好好休养一下，也许症状很快就可以解除。下面是几种可以在家自我放松的一些小技巧：

（1）头部按摩：放松平躺在舒服的垫子上，请丈夫在你觉得疼痛的部位以划圈的动作按摩，力量要足够使皮肤在颅骨上移动为宜。

（2）保持鼻窦畅通。

（3）平心静气，闭目养神：只要一觉得头痛，马上选择到安静、光线较暗的房里平躺着休息。

贴心·提醒

1．孕期不要头一痛就马上服用止痛药，这很危险。

2．怀孕后期，如果还有严重、持续的头痛现象（尤其伴有视力模糊），这有可能是高血压前兆，应去医院检查。

预防痔疮

妇女妊娠后，容易患痔疮。如病情严重，会大量出血，导致贫血。如痔疮脱出肛门，还容易发生感染、嵌顿，出现疼痛、坏死，令人苦不堪言。

1．合理饮食

饮食要富有营养，注意多饮水，多吃新鲜的蔬菜、水果。忌食辣椒、大蒜、生姜、大葱等辛辣刺激性食物。

2．适当运动

适当活动，或做些轻体力的家务劳动。不宜久坐不动。

3．提肛运动

全身放松，端坐，将大腿夹紧，吸气时腹部隆起，呼气时腹部凹陷。呼吸5次后舌舔上腭，同时肛门上提，屏气，然后全身放松。如此反复，每天做2次，每次重复20遍。

4．定时排便

养成每天定时排便的良好习惯，每次排便时间不宜过长。不要在排便时看书，以免注意力分散延长排便时间，致使肛周静脉长时间处于紧张状态，影响血液回流。

5．痔疮的处理

(1)用医生建议的冰枕或冰棉球，防止痔疮，并可帮助收缩及减轻不适感。

(2) 痔疮刺激或疼痛很厉害时，采用膝胸姿势，当你正准备通过冰枕或其他治疗方法来解除疼痛时，这样的姿势可以暂时减轻肿胀血管的压力。

(3) 买一个救生圈，放在你的座位上，也可以坐在枕头上。

(4) 痔疮严重时，在医生指导下用药。

预防尿失禁

怀孕到中期，孕妇每次打喷嚏时，必须夹紧双腿，否则会有点尿失禁。这是因为打喷嚏、咳嗽或者捧腹大笑时，横膈膜会收缩并推挤腹部内容物和子宫向下压到膀胱。如果当时膀胱是胀满的，或是骨盆底部的肌肉处于疲倦状态，将会滴出尿来。不要担心，这个问题将会随着宝宝的诞生而消失的。下面一些方法帮助你尿失禁：

1．经常排尿，尽可能保持膀胱是空的。

2．排尿时，尽可能额外再压迫3次，使膀胱完全排出尿液。

3．咳嗽或打喷嚏时，张开嘴巴，这样可减少压迫到横膜的机会。

4．练习缩肛运动：排尿时，将尿液完全排干净，收缩肌肉几次，就像是要停止尿尿一样。

贴心·提醒

这段时期，如果实在有些问题，可以利用纸巾及棉垫解决由此引发的尴尬。

第15周

开始留心体重

第15周记：宝宝的皮肤依旧是透明的，并且有一种淡淡的红色。如果我能透过身体看到他，我就能看到他的血管。

我自己的皮肤颜色好像比以前深了，尤其是脸上的小斑点，更加明显了。有朋友告诉我，她怀孕的时候脸上长了蝴蝶样的斑点，我好像倒是没有。

我还知道，宝宝的骨骼也开始变得更坚固了。

胎宝宝状况 胎宝贝的身长已经长到10～12厘米，与上周相比，体重重了不少，达到50克左右。而接下来的几周中，小家伙的身长和体重可能会发生更大的变化，增长一倍甚至更多。胎宝贝的头顶上开始长出细细的头发，眉毛、睫毛也长出来了。腿的长度已经超过了胳膊。手指甲完全形成，手指的关节也开始运动。胎宝贝这时会练习打哈欠、打嗝了，不要小看这个小动作的练习，它能保证小宝贝在出生之后顺畅的呼吸。

孕妈妈状况 这个时期孕妈咪体内的雌激素水平较高，盆腔及阴道充血，白带开始增多，这是非常自然的现象。

应注意保持外阴部的清洁，每天清洗，避免使用刺激性强的皂液；内裤应选用纯棉织品且每天都要换洗。

这一周，要注意饮食，不要喝含咖啡因的饮料，别吃辛辣食物，少吃高糖食物和含有添加剂和防腐剂的食物。同时，注意口腔卫生。孕早期不能接受的拔牙、治疗牙病的情况，现在可以到医院解决了。

第15～18周之间是做产前诊断的最佳时期，这样做可以确定胎宝贝是否存在先天缺陷，进一步了解胎宝贝的健康状况。

体重增加多少

怀孕期间，体重增加太多，可能会出现妊娠问题和难产；体重增加太少，对胎儿不健康，还会增加发生早产的可能性。

孕妇体重的增加是进行性的：妊娠初期，体重增加不明显，3个月体重应增加1～2千克。妊娠中期，每周体重增加约350克，一般不超过500克，合计增加4～5千克。妊娠后期，每星期体重应增加500克左右，合计增加5～6千克。孕妇到足月妊娠分娩时，理想的体重是在原体重上增加9～11千克。一般身材较高瘦的孕妇，体重增加的幅度会比较少；相反，身材矮胖的孕妇，体重增加的幅度会最多。至于身材中等的孕妇们，体重增加的幅度居中。

怀孕后，叫丈夫到商店，买一个精确的电子磅秤。就是这件法宝，可以令你一直良好地监控体重增长。早晚跳上磅秤，将体重记在随身日历上。体重超重时，要控制体重的增加。

贴心·提醒

妊娠中期、后期，孕妇要经常测量自己的体重，密切观察体重的变化。如果每月体重增加不足1千克，或增加超过3千克，均应视为异常情况。

小贴士……不可强行减肥

蛋白质是人体的主要建筑材料，脂类同样是细胞膜、脑、神经组织不可缺少的构筑物质，各种维生素、无机盐、微量元素在胎儿旺盛的细胞分裂、组织增生、器官形成过程中不可缺少，这些物质需要源源不断地来源于摄入吸收。然而，减肥的孕妇恰恰断绝了这些物质的来源，势必影响胎儿发育。

专家指出：孕期肥胖是正常生理现象，不可以刻意减肥，更不可用药物减肥。

不发胖的秘密

饮食并非少吃就能减肥，进食的技巧、食物的烹调、外食的选择等，皆是控制体重的关键。

1. 进食行为改变

(1) 改变进餐顺序:先喝水→再喝汤→再吃青菜→最后吃饭和肉类。

(2) 养成三正餐一定要吃的习惯。

(3) 生菜、水果沙拉应刮掉沙拉酱后再吃，或要求不加沙拉酱。

(4) 只吃瘦肉。

(5) 不吃油炸食品。

(6) 浓汤类只吃固体内容物，但不喝汤。

(7) 带汤汁的菜肴，将汤汁稍加沥干后再吃。

(8) 以水果取代餐后甜点。

(9) 用开水或不加糖的饮料及果汁，取代含糖饮料及果汁。

(10) 吃完东西立刻刷牙，刷过牙就不再进食。

(11) 睡前3个小时不再进食（但白开水除外）。

2. 烹调方式改变

(1) 尽量用水煮、蒸、炖、凉拌、红烧、烤、烫、烩、卤的烹调方式。

(2) 以上烹调方式尽量不要再加油，可加酱油。

(3) 烹调时少加糖。

(4) 烹调时少用勾芡。

(5) 烹调时少加酒。

(6) 煮饭、买菜前，先算好吃饭人数及份量，避免吃下过多剩菜。

(7) 青菜可多吃，但最好以烫的为主，或将汤汁滴干以减少油脂的摄取（或用清汤、开水洗）。

(8) 吃饭勿淋肉燥、肉汤。

(9) 少用糖醋、醋溜、油炸、油煎的烹调方式。

3. 营养又不胖的食物构成

构　成	说　明	附　注
5份水果和蔬菜	日常饮食应该至少5份水果和蔬菜，才可以提供足够的维生素、矿物质和纤维，帮助消化，有效预防便秘。蔬菜不要煮太久，最好能生吃，这样可以最大程度保留蔬菜的营养价值。但一定要将蔬菜冲洗干净。	“份”的量因人而异，例如，如果每日摄取食物总量为1300克，蔬菜、淀粉和蛋白质的摄取比例为5∶5∶3，则每份食物为100克。也就是说每天应吃500克的水果和蔬菜、500克的淀粉类食物、300克的蛋白质类食物。
4～6份淀粉类食物	每天应该吃4～6份热量不高的淀粉类食物，如面包、马铃薯或者意大利面条等。这些食物是碳水化合物和纤维的重要来源。但过分加工会破坏这些食物中的营养成分，如有可能应尽量吃全麦面包或者是麦片。	
2～4份蛋白质类食物	怀孕期间，对蛋白质的需求会上升50%左右，因此日常饮食中应添加2～4份分富含蛋白质的食物，如肉类、鱼类、豆类和乳品。	

4. 营养又不胖的食谱

早餐（早上7∶00）	主食（包括面食、米饭、稀饭、粥类或面包）100克。 鸡蛋（可按自己喜欢的口味做成荷包蛋或炒鸡蛋等）50克。 蔬菜（西红柿、海带、黄瓜、卷心菜等）100克。
早午餐（上午10∶00）	牛奶或豆浆200克（也可以果汁或新鲜水果代替）。 饼干或小点心25克。
午餐（12∶00）	主食（米饭或面食）150克。 蛋类50克。 肉类100克。 蔬菜100～150克。
下午茶（下午3∶00）	果汁或新鲜水果200克（可以牛奶或豆浆代替，最好与早、午餐不同）。 点心50克。
晚餐（下午7∶00）	主食（米饭或面食）150克。 鱼类100克。 蔬菜150克。 夜宵（睡前1小时） 水果100克。

站、坐、行的姿势

现在，由于体重的增加和身体比例的改变，使得你身体重心位移，韧带也比从前柔软了，因此起坐、拿东西等动作都得“小心行事”。

1. 站立

孕妇平常站立时，应保持两腿平行，两脚稍微分开，把重心放在脚心处，这样不容易疲劳。如果长时间站立，可采取“稍息”的姿势，一腿置前，一腿在后，重心放在后腿上，前腿休息；过一段时间，前后腿交换一下，或者重心移向前腿。当由坐位、蹲位起立时，要注意动作缓慢。

2. 坐姿

孕妇如果做家务活或上班，尽可能坐着进行。要深深地坐在椅子上，后背笔直地靠在椅背上。坐在椅子边上容易滑落，如果是不稳当的椅子还有跌倒的危险。坐在有靠背的椅子上时，股关节和膝关节要成直角，大腿成水平状态。端坐时，不妨用小椅子来垫脚，两腿适当地分开，以免压迫腹部。切忌双腿交叠，因为这会阻碍血液的运行，影响胎儿的发育。坐椅子时，不要“扑咚”一下坐下去，应先坐在边上再一点点向后移动。

3. 行走

孕妇腹部前凸，重心不稳又影响视线，很容易摔倒，行走时要特别注意。

行走时正确的姿势是抬头，伸直脖子，下颌抵住胸部，挺直后背，绷紧臀部，好像把肚子抬起来似地保持全身平衡地行走。跨步时要足后跟先落地，足内侧后着地，待足大趾着地后方可再举足。不要猫腰或强挺胸姿势行走。

4. 立位改为坐位

当由立位改为坐位时，孕妇要先用手在大腿或扶手上支撑一下，再慢慢地坐下。如果是坐椅子时，要深深地坐在椅子上，后背笔直地靠在椅背上。可以先慢慢坐在靠边部位，然后再向后移动，直至坐稳为止。但不要坐在椅子的边上，容易滑落，如果是不稳当的椅子还有跌倒的危险。另外，坐有靠背的椅子时，髋关节和膝关节要呈直角，大腿要与地平线保持平行。

5. 坐位改为立位

由坐位站起时，要用手先扶在大腿上，再慢慢站起。

6. 拾起东西

将放在地上的东西拿起或放下，注意不要压迫肚子。不要采取不弯膝盖只倾斜上身的姿势，那样容易造成腰疼。

正确的姿势应该是先屈膝，然后落腰下蹲，将东西捡起放在膝上，再起立将东西拾起。放东西也是一样，先屈膝，然后落腰下蹲，放下东西后，双手扶腿慢慢起立。

7. 上下楼梯

由于居住条件不同，有的人必须上下楼梯。上下楼梯时不要猫着腰或过于挺胸腆肚，只要伸直脊背就行。要看清楼梯，一步一步慢慢上下。只用脚尖是危险的，特别是怀孕后期，隆起的肚子遮住视线，看不见脚下。注意千万不要踩偏，脚踩稳了再动身体。如有扶手，一定要扶着走。

8. 从床上起来

从仰卧的姿势起来时，先采取横卧位，再半坐位，然后起来，禁止使用腹肌以仰卧的姿势直接起身。

9. 提重物

用一手提重物跨步时，一定要使重物正好处于前后腿的中间，腰挺直，膝关节微屈，这样腰部和两足所承受的重量可以平衡。向上搬物必须两手持物，但应尽量避免向上搬物。

10. 洗澡

洗澡容易滑倒，是很危险的。出入澡盆时要抓住澡盆的边缘。还要察看一下铺在地板上的垫子或凳子是否会打滑。

10. 工作台的高度

熨衣服用的台子及厨房水池的高度，应以站立时，肘关节和台面保持垂直为最理想。每个家庭应根据具体情况加以考虑。

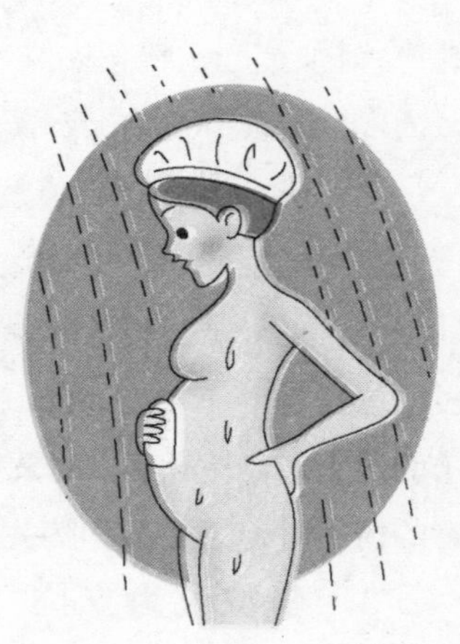

第16周

准备孕妇装

第16周记： 大夫说，宝宝身体的各种毛发都在生长，包括睫毛。我希望他有长长的眼睫毛和漂亮的眉毛。他身体上还覆盖着一层纤细柔软的胎毛，不过胎毛会随着他的成长渐渐消失。我想起姐姐的孩子，出生时耳朵上满是毛，一两周后才消失。

我几乎没有腰了，该到医院做全面体检了。在病床上，我就像是个小婴儿。当大夫把针刺进我的血管采血的时候，我忽然想到：生孩子的时候，我耐得住疼痛吗？

胎宝宝状况 胎宝贝的皮肤逐渐变厚而不再透明，现在的身长大约有12厘米，体重达到了150克。现在的小家伙"忙时"伸手、踢腿、舒展身姿，"闲时"揉脸、吃手、打哈欠。对于多数孕妈咪来说都可以感觉到胎动了，当小宝贝忙着做体操的时候，你会注意到小腹中那瞬间奇妙的感受。

孕妈妈状况 这一周，孕妈妈腹部略显凸，体重上升加快。以前的裤装或裙装穿有些紧张，要准备改穿宽松的服装。乳房比以前大而柔软，深色的乳晕很清晰。

16~20周，胎动通常会在此期间出现。当你感觉到第一次胎动时，一定要记录下时间，下次去医院体检时请告诉医生。

第16周，别忘记到医院例行产检。高龄孕妈咪在孕16周要注意到医院预约羊水穿刺检查。

穿出漂亮

初为人母的喜悦和心底涌动的温柔会让准妈妈们浑身充满母性的光辉。孕育一个生命，隆起的腹部和洋溢的幸福、满足，这就是身为女人最特别的美丽。怀孕的时候，虽然体形发生了变化，虽然总会有不能抵挡的臃肿时刻，但还是让我们一起来说："穿出漂亮，穿出好心情！"

怀孕4个月时开始考虑选购孕妇裙或孕妇裤。怀孕期购买的衣服毕竟利用率低，因此最好能精打细算，用最少的钱购置最合适的衣物。

1. 尺码大小

应以宽大为原则。怀孕使血液循环增加并加速，孕妇非常容易出汗，腿脚也常常浮肿。过紧的衣服不仅影响乳腺的增长发育，导致产后少奶或无奶，而且会因压迫下腹部减少胎盘血流量，对胎儿生长发育造成损害。因此，最好选择比身材大一号的衣服。

2. 衣料质地

选择衣料应以轻柔、耐洗、吸水、透气为原则，同时考虑到季节性。

孕妇的新陈代谢加强，易出汗，最好选择透气性强的天然材质，如纯棉、丝绸。尤其在夏天，纯棉更是首选，不仅透气，而且柔软、吸汗、耐洗。

冬季，孕妇的着装就要注意不让腹部和腰腿受寒，衣着要轻而暖，最好选用保暖性能好的毛料，也可以选择轻便柔软的羽绒服。

不管是在哪个季节，最好避免选用有化纤成分的布料。因为化纤布料在加工时使用化学药剂处理，如直接与孕妇皮肤接触，会因孕妇皮肤敏感性的增高而引起皮肤发炎，对胎儿也不利。

3. 衣装款式

衣服的款式以身体的活动不受拘束及方便为原则。家中的服装以舒适为第一前提，而工作时的孕妇装则多少要透些职业装的气息。

上衣的胸、腹部、袖口要宽松，宜前开襟或肩部开扣、V字领。传统的上小下大的连衣裙装，也因为适合不同月龄的孕妇而经久不衰。上下身分开的衣装非常易于穿脱，可以减少孕妇笨重身体的不便。

最流行的款式还有背带裤。背带裤的带子比较宽，不会勒到胸脯，比较适合孕期腹部膨隆的变化；又不会勒到腰部，穿在身上可以掩盖腹部、胸部、臀部的粗笨体形，给人以宽松自然的美感。

至于衣服的颜色和图案，则可根据个人的不同爱好和需要而选择。一般来说，选择穿浅色图案的衣服，粉红、浅蓝、浅绿……这些颜色能让孕妇看起来健康、可爱又不失母性的风采。如果衣服上有些小碎花之类的图案，可以掩饰一些突出的腹部。

小贴士……着衣保健小提醒

1. 出门别忘了戴上帽子，夏天可以防晒，冬天戴帽子可以防寒。

2. 夏天出门时准妈妈别忘了带一把遮阳伞，防止紫外线对准妈妈和胎儿的危害。

3. 多雨的季节一件风雨衣是十分必要的，可以对抗多变的天气。

4. 在有空调的地方办公，夏天别忘了为自己准备一件薄外套。

5. 淡绿、浅黄、湖蓝、粉红等柔和的颜色特别合适准妈妈穿着，这些颜色可以使人的心境平和，对胎儿的发育有利。

6. 容易感冒的准妈妈在天气转凉时为自己准备几条围巾，既可以御寒，还可起装饰作用。

留住美丽肌肤

四季交错，孕妈咪怎样才能让肌肤焕发出动人光彩呢？孕期生理变化引起的色素斑、妊娠纹、干燥……使曾经美丽不在。怀孕时，孕妇的皮肤可能会产生种种变化，如肌肤变得没有光泽，皮脂较多，皮肤变得粗糙。因此，孕妇不能忽视对肌肤的护理。

1. 避免长时间日晒

怀孕期间，尽量避免长时间曝露在紫外线下，以免将你的皮肤晒伤。

(1) 在户外活动的时候，尽可能待在阴凉的地方。

(2) 戴上能够将你整个脸都遮住的宽沿帽。

(3) 尽量避免在紫外线最强的上午11点至下午3点之间在户外活动。

(4) 避免使用任何含有香精或酒精成分的保养用品。

(5) 避免使用一些美容专用的人工紫外线照射工具。

2. 滋养皮肤

(1) 保持均衡的饮食习惯。

(2) 维生素C与B_6是皮肤再生重建最重要的两项营养素，每天可以补充25～50毫克的维生素B_6片（最好请医生推荐）。

(3) 使用保湿乳液，也可以使你的皮肤看起来更光滑柔顺。如果皮肤非常干涩，你可以摄取较多含有不饱和必需脂肪酸或亚麻油酸（一般常见于蔬菜类及鱼类）的流食，来改善干涩的肤质。

3. 皮肤保湿

(1) 大量饮水。

(2) 在暖气房里增加空气湿度，在办公室放一个加湿器。

(3) 尽量抽些时间到通风的地方，让皮肤能够透透新鲜空气。

4. 按摩肌肤

妊娠中，每天进行按摩既可加快皮肤的血液流通，增进皮肤的新陈代谢，又能预防皮肤病，保持肌肤的细嫩，使皮肤的机能在产后早日恢复。

(1) 先用净面膏擦掉脸上的污垢。

(2) 用香皂把脸洗净，用毛巾把水擦干。

(3) 在脸上涂上冷霜膏，用中指和无名指从脸的中部向外部螺旋按摩。

(4) 结束时，要用挤干热水的毛巾擦拭，用香皂洗脸，喷上化妆水或乳液。

5. 舒适穿着

(1) 避免合成纤维的衣料，尽量穿着宽松、透气的棉质衣料，让皮肤能够无障碍地进行呼吸。

(2) 避免穿着裤袜，以免造成大腿内侧、臀部等部位的皮肤，因为透气不佳而长出痱子。

(3) 穿戴胸罩前洒上一点不含香味的爽身粉，以减缓胸罩对肌肤的刺激。

6. 洗脸

洗脸是妊娠期最基本的美容手段。早晚各一次，使用平时常用的香皂，擦出泡沫来，要仔细洗，洗净后涂上化妆品。夏季易出汗，要增加洗脸次数。

7. 选用正确的沐浴乳

(1) 一般说来，清水通常不会引起肌肤的任何不良反应，但是过多的沐浴可能会刺激柔嫩的肌肤。洗澡时，应该控制冲澡的时间，别让手脚的皮肤都皱起来之后，才离开浴池。

如果你在怀孕之前就有湿疹的现象，待在浴缸的时间过长，就会加重湿疹的症状。

(2) 肥皂会将有益于保护肌肤的天然油脂去掉，应使用具有保湿成分的肥皂，且肥皂的用量越少越好。可选用市面上一些温和不伤肌肤、且不会彻底除掉肌肤油质的沐浴乳。

尽量避免直接使用肥皂清洗乳头及乳晕部位的肌肤。

(3) 沐浴之后，趁肌肤还保持湿润时，使用一些保湿乳液，让肌肤保湿的时间更持久。

8. 呵护敏感的肌肤

(1) 经常洗脸，保持面部清洁。

(2) 油性皮肤，可用些收敛性洗面乳清洁脸部；干性皮肤，最好不要用香皂，可选用滋润霜或婴儿用的面霜。

(3) 使用保湿乳敷脸时，可以以小面积画圆的方式，比平常多按摩脸部的肌肤几次。

(4) 避免使用油性的乳液、磨砂膏或者含有香精或酒精成分的清洁液等来洁净脸部的肌肤。

9. 正确化妆

准妈妈化妆要谨慎，因为化妆品使用不当，对胎儿的健康成长是一种潜在的隐患，如诱发流产、早产，导致畸胎及先天性疾病的发生。

(1) 可以化表情活泼的淡妆，避免化浓妆。要使用惯用的化妆品，不要使用新的化妆品。妊娠中，即使用惯用的化妆品，如果出现皮肤粗糙了，也要中止使用。

化妆可使用一些化妆水、雪花膏、粉扑等。粉底的油脂，由于油性较强，易妨碍皮肤呼吸，最好不要选用。

(2) 不宜滥涂口红：口红是由多种油脂、蜡质、染料和香料等成分组成的。其中油脂通常采用羊毛脂，是一种从羊毛液中回收和提炼而成的透明膏体。羊毛脂既能吸附空气

中各种对人体有害的重金属微量元素，又能吸附能进入胎儿体内的大肠杆菌等微生物，随着唾液进入人体内，使孕妇腹中的胎儿受害。因此，孕妇最好不涂口红。

小贴士……皮肤问题应对方法

1．皮肤油腻

孕妇新陈代谢缓慢，皮下脂肪增厚，汗腺、皮脂腺分泌增加，全身血液循环量增加，面部油脂分泌旺盛的情况会加重，皮肤变得格外油腻，"T"型区域更为显著。

（1）保持皮肤的清洁，不能用太强的洗剂，每天多洗几遍脸。

（2）多摄取含优质的动物蛋白和维生素A、B_1、B_2、B_6、C、E等食物；蔬菜、水果可使你的皮肤颜色更加漂亮。

（3）均衡摄入营养，使孕妇的头发和皮肤得到很好的保护。

2．干燥粗糙、易生暗疮

由于孕激素的关系，皮肤失去了以前的柔软感，而略呈粗糙，甚至会很干燥，有的会出现脱皮现象，脸部的色素沉淀也增加。

（1）干性皮肤的孕妇不要频繁地洗脸，最好改用婴儿皂、甘油皂洗脸。

（2）使用能给皮肤增加水分的护肤品，涂抹在干燥区内并轻轻地加以按摩。选用婴儿润肤膏或润肤露，防止皮肤干燥，保持酸碱度平衡。

（3）洗浴时不要浸泡太久，尽可能少用普通肥皂，可使用不含皂质、ph值属中性的沐浴露或婴儿香皂。

（4）沐浴后，在全身涂抹润肤油。

（5）注意饮食营养平衡，增加镁、钙等矿物质的摄取，如肉类、鱼、蛋；还要增加必要的脂肪酸和维他命，如绿色蔬菜、水果、坚果、谷物、牛奶、鱼油、豆类等。减少含兴奋剂如咖啡、酒、茶的摄取，多喝水。

3．妊娠纹

怀孕中期，在皮肤膨胀较为明显的几个部位，如腹部、乳房、大腿以及臀部等，开始有粉色妊娠纹的产生。

以下是几种帮助你在产后消除妊娠纹的小技巧：

(1) 经常锻炼，防止赘肉产生，控制体重增加。

(2) 保持均衡的饮食习惯，多摄取富含维生素C与蛋白质的食品。

(3) 在产后的3个月里，持续对产生妊娠纹的皮肤施以按摩。

让“蝴蝶”飞离

蝴蝶斑，又称为黄褐斑、肝斑、妊娠斑。之所以叫蝴蝶斑，是因为它呈现的外观常常像蝴蝶般对称；叫妊娠斑是因为妊娠妇女中有很多人会出现这样的皮肤症状；称之为肝斑，是因为它的出现，有时会伴随着肝部病变。当然，肝斑的出现并不一定是由于肝部疾病引起的。

女性怀孕后，内分泌系统功能重新调整，会使皮肤上出现色素沉着，尤其是鼻梁两侧的面部皮肤更为明显，这些黄色或褐色的斑点，就是名字听起来异常美丽的“蝴蝶斑”。大约有20%的女性怀孕后会在面颊部长出妊娠斑，这是怀孕过程中的正常现象，是因为怀孕后胎盘分泌雌性激素增多的缘故。一般来说，不需要任何治疗措施，生产之后体内雌激素分泌恢复正常状态后，大部分人的妊娠斑会逐渐变浅或消失。

几种帮助你防止蝴蝶斑的小技巧

(1) 防止在阳光下直接照射面部过久。可以使用有防紫外线作用的遮阳伞、戴遮阳帽、着长袖上装等。不使用防晒化妆品，尤其化学防晒剂配方的产品，以免化学成分对皮肤产生刺激。

(2) 不吃辛辣等刺激性强的食物，少吃动物脂肪。

(3) 每天早、中、晚至少洗3次脸，用优质天然洁肤品。

(4) 保持轻松、愉快、平静的心情。

(5) 睡眠充足、生活有规律，适当参加文体活动。

注意：怀孕期间，慎用祛斑霜治疗妊娠斑。

第17周

要小心行事了

第17周记: 大夫说到这个时候，宝宝小手可以自己握住了，而且有了属于他自己的独一无二的指纹。我想着我那只有鸭梨大小的宝贝，想着他的指纹，心里觉得真是奇妙啊。

我开始感觉背痛，这是因为我的韧带比从前柔软了。现在无论是拿东西还是起坐，我都得很小心才行。

胎宝宝状况　已经长成一个鸭梨的样子，长约有13厘米，重170克左右。大脑发育已经很充分，心跳变得更有力。循环系统和尿道完全进入正常的工作状态，肺也开始工作，能平稳地吸入、呼出羊水。可以做指尖并拢的动作了，平时除了玩玩小手和小脚，脐带也成了小家伙的新玩具——对它不是拉就是抓。

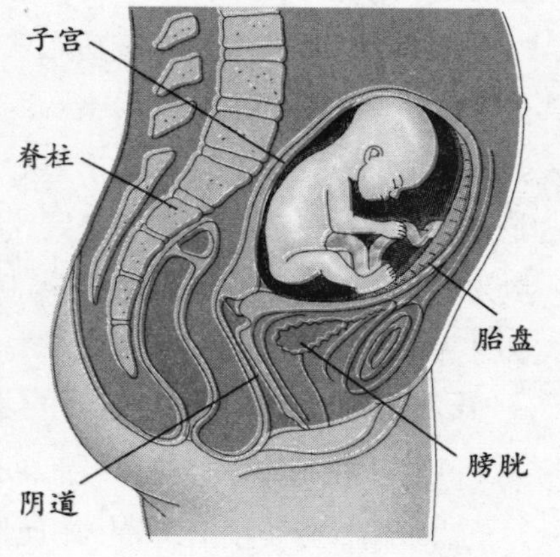

第17周（5月胎宝宝）

孕妈妈状况　现在你最少增加了2千克体重，有些孕妇也许会达到5千克。你的子宫长得很大，有时你会感到有一阵阵的剧痛，这种疼痛是因为腹部纫带伸拉的原因。因为韧带比从前柔软了，起坐、拿东西等动作都得“小心行事”。从这一周以后，你身体的重心就会随着子宫的不断增大而发生着变化，你觉得行动开始有些不大方便了。

你可以借助听诊器听到宝宝强健有力的心跳声了。这周，如果你再抚摸腹部，可能会较明显地感觉到小家伙轻微的反应，甚至可能会感觉首次胎动。现在你可以和丈夫一起着手对胎儿进行胎教了。

孕5月专家提示（第17～20周）

1．注意勿食用过多饮食，体重从第17周到第20周以增加1千克为宜，以免过胖。

2．开始穿着宽松衣服，选择数件自己喜欢的孕妇装换穿，保持心情愉快。

3．乳腺开始发达且乳房增大，有时甚至会出现乳汁分泌，宜清洁乳头使之舒适。

4．胎儿骨胳系统发育成熟，大量吸收母亲营养。母亲若患有蛀牙，宜安排牙科门诊时间接受治疗。

5．检查是否有贫血现象？若有，宜选用高铁饮食。

6．可安排短程或行程不紧凑的旅游，以调节身心，减缓压力。

7．可恢复平日喜欢的运动，但不可参与激烈的比赛。

8．整理棉被、开车、按摩、服用肠胃药或便秘药、朋友婚庆，只要不过度，皆可去。

9．烫衣服时最好选择烫衣台与孕妇同高者，站着烫，以免增加腰部的负担。

10．晾晒衣服时，宜将竹竿降到孕妇腰部之高度，切勿踮脚或弯腰。若发生小腿抽筋，宜尽快按摩腿肚或一手压住膝盖一手将脚指头往上用力压。

11．发型宜清爽样式，避免烫发及染发。

12．避免铅污染:不用印刷品包裹食物，尤其是报纸;不用带漆的筷子和容器;尽量少到马路上去，减少吸入汽车尾气。

关于胎动

胎动，是指胎儿在母体子宫内的主动性运动，比如呼吸、张嘴运动、翻滚运动等。如果是受到妈妈咳嗽、呼吸等动作影响所产生的被动性运动，就不算胎动。到孕8周的时候，宝宝初具人形，四肢已经长出来了，这个时候胎儿就会在腹中蠕动，按说，这才是最初的胎动，但非常微弱，所以孕妈咪是感觉不到的，只有在B超上才能见到。通常说的胎动，是指孕妈妈可以感觉到的胎动。

1. 何时开始

一般说来，胎动会发生在怀孕的第五个月，也就是第18周与第20周之间。有些孕妇会早在第18周之前，便已感受到宝宝的动作。当宝宝开始踢你时，只有你才会感受到他的存在。这是只属于你自己的最甜美的秘密。

2. 你的感觉

宝宝的第一踢并不十分明显。你所感受到的第一踢，很有可能只是心理作用而已。但不久之后，你会开始频繁感受到宝宝的动作，这是一种前所未有的感觉。到了后期，宝宝的动作逐渐强到会让你在半夜中惊醒过来。

3. 发生的频率

随着怀孕月份的增加，宝宝的动作会变得更加频繁，这种动作频率会在第七个月达到高峰。自此之后，频率开始降低，但在最后两个月动作的力量却会增强。

第20周时，宝宝胎动的频率十分不稳定，平均胎动次数大约在200次左右。晚上8点到翌日上午8点之间，是小宝宝在子宫中最为活跃的时刻。

4. 胎动位置

在第五及第六个月，宝宝的胎动是非常随意的，在小腹的任何一处，你都有可能会感受到这样的轻踢。大多数宝宝的姿势都是用背对着母亲的左边，所以如果孕妇以左侧睡姿躺在床上，这样就会在右边的肋缘处感到宝宝的脚在踢。除此之外，有时你还可感到宝宝在打嗝，这种力量有时比胎动还要大呢。

贴心·提醒

在你的怀孕日记中，记录下宝宝胎动的情况。这个感受的过程，将会是你怀孕中最值得回忆的一部分。

真实故事——最初的胎动感觉

俞女士：

第一次胎动不太明显，就像蝴蝶轻飞，小鱼游水，我总是不确定这是不是胎动，期待着宝宝更大的运动。

赵女士：

“咕噜，咕噜”就像小鱼在吐泡泡，心里泛起一阵阵幸福的涟漪，这是宝宝和我的第一次“有声”的交流。在此之前，我一直觉得宝宝和我分别在两个世界里，我是通过生理反应（呕吐，身体不适）来感知宝宝的存在，这一美妙时刻，我觉得宝宝是在用她独有的方式跟我打招呼。

周女士：

怀孕19周又6天了，我感受了宝宝的第一次胎动。以后，宝宝的活动力也越来越强。一般都是躺下来时，宝宝就会一直动一直动。最近连坐着宝宝也会踢哦！

有时候老公回来，我希望老公也可以感受到胎动，就会叫宝宝踢我！

老公笑着说我是被虐待狂。不过宝宝不太配合。可能要等到大一点，宝宝就听得懂了！

不过，宝宝啊，你踢归踢，不要太用力哦，不然，妈妈会痛痛的。

余女士：

第一次真切地感到胎动是在怀孕四个月，那天晚上刚吃过晚饭，空气中还残存着饭菜的气息。先生在厨房里收拾餐具，哗哗的流水声不时传出。我躺在床上休息，忽然感到腹内叽哩咕噜一阵乱响，猛然间又很特别地跳了几下。我惊得一下坐起来。

“喂！”我对着厨房喊。

“什么事？”水声仍没有停止。

“我感到孩子动呢！”我喊。

“什么？”水声止住了，他从厨房探头看我。

“胎动！”我说。

“是吗？我听听！”先生跑过到俯头倾听。

宝宝还挺赏脸，接连又跳动了几下。

“真的！”先生惊喜地叫道，“大概对涮羊肉挺满意。”

“去你的，你以为都像你呀！”我嗔道。

“那当然！儿子，你好！”先生虽然对我表白说男孩女孩都一样，但从他的称谓里我也看出了他的立场。先生对着我的肚子胡乱甜言蜜语了一阵，真有点似傻若狂的样子。

“他能听见吗？你这是白费力气！”我说。

“书上说能！”

也不知宝宝真听懂了，还是我们太神往了，腹部又特别地跳了几下。

俞女士：

由于近来找了些育儿方面的书“补课”，我了解了一些孕育方面的知识。很多书上说，初产妇16周时会感受到胎动。我已经屏气静心地注意好几天了。不过什么感觉都没有。

今天在学校监考。教室里安静得连落下一根针也会听见。我站在教室后走来走去，心里却开起了小差——甜蜜地想着肚肚里小宝宝。

突然，肚皮上有什么东西轻轻划过——从左到右！我停住脚步，屏住了呼吸。

从右到左，又来了一下——像一只小虫在飞，翅膀触到了我的肚肚！

胎动！

我笑了！一定是胎动！

看到对面另一位监考老师正奇怪地望着我。我赶紧低下头。但我相信，脸上飞起的红晕一定让他产生了联想——监考还做春梦！

张女士：

一个慵懒的傍晚，携着夕阳的余晖，我漫步在湖畔的柳林中，湖光、山色、落日、塔影、鸟鸣，生动祥和的画卷在面前展延。骄热的季节里因为怀孕，竟使我这平日活泼、粗心的人少了以往的躁动，多了些许宽容。深吸一口气，过滤掉城市喧嚣的羁绊，只留下一抹大自然的灵动，悠然感动之时，忽觉肚子里一阵怪怪作响，像是清风荡漾水面拂起的层层涟漪，“咦！”禁不住一声惊呼，我知道，一个小生命正在用行动告诉我他(她)真实的存在，这就是我怀孕4个半月感受的第一次胎动，那份激动至今难以言表。

与胎儿的沟通渠道

科学实验证明，胎儿在生长发育时并非“两耳不闻宫外事”，而是和母亲共享营养，共同欢乐，共同呼吸，既互通信息又互相干扰，母亲与胎儿的相互交流主要有以下几种方式：

1. 生理交流

胎儿是由母亲孕育的，因此母亲与胎儿血肉相连，息息相关。他们之间最早发生的沟通莫过于生理信息的传递。

胎儿的存在促进了母体分泌维持妊娠所需要的激素，并使母体产生必需的生理上的变化，如子宫增大、变软，乳腺增生。乳房增大，基础代谢加快，激素活动增加，以及全身各器官的生理机能增强等等，胎盘分泌的一系列激素可以维持妊娠的进行。总而言之，胎儿在积极地促使分泌一些物质，协助母亲维持自己的生命。当母亲有嗜烟、酗酒、滥用药物、暴饮暴食以及遭受外伤等情况时，会使胎儿的生长环境发生有害的变化，进而使胎儿产生恐惧的心理，表现为胎动异常，心动过速等。就这样，从胎儿到母亲，又从母亲到胎儿，彼此间完全对等地传递着生理信息，相互影响，相互作用。例如，当一个母亲生活在极为恶劣的环境中时，身体分泌的有害激素通过生理途径传递给胎儿，而胎儿接收到这种有害的信息后，则又反过来停止促进母体分泌维持妊娠所必需的激素，进而使胎儿发生身心障碍，甚至停止生命。

2. 营养交流

胎儿生长发育所需的全部养料（包括氧气）都是经过胎盘由母亲的血液中获得的，胎儿体内的代谢废物也得由母亲的血液循环帮助排泄。自受孕之日起，孕妇既要维持自身的营养需求，又要保证胎儿的生长发育，其体内代谢较孕前明显旺盛。

孕妇如果缺乏营养，胎儿的代谢物质来源不足，生长发育受到阻碍，这不仅表现在体形上发育迟缓，还会引起胎儿大脑发育不良，脑细胞数较少，日后孩子的智力受到影响。另一方面，孕妇若营养不良，缺乏蛋白质、铁、维生素等，容易发生缺铁性贫血或巨幼红细胞贫血，进而影响胎儿发育，出现流产、早产、死胎等。同时，孕妇因营养不良而抵抗力降低，极易感染病毒，细菌，也会影响胎儿发育。所以．孕妇应注意营养物质的摄取，既要进食肉、鱼、蛋、豆等富含蛋白质的食物，又要吃新鲜蔬菜、水果等。

然而，如果孕妇过多食用肉、鱼、甜食等，易使体液酸性化。血中儿茶酚胺水平增高，孕妇出现烦躁不安、突发脾气、易伤感等消极情绪，会促使母体内激素和其他有害物质分泌增多，易导致胎儿唇裂和其他器官发育畸形。

而孕妇过量服用维生素A、鱼肝油等，会影响胎儿大脑、心脏发育，诱发先天性心脏病和脑积水；孕妇补钙过多，易导致新生儿高血钙症，表现为囟门过早关闭，腭骨变宽而突出，鼻梁前倾，主动脉缩窄等畸形，严重的还伴有智力减退。

此外，孕期要忌食某些致畸食物，如发芽的马铃薯，可口可乐和咖啡等。

3. 情感交流

早在胎儿时期，母子之间不但有血脉相连的关系，而且还具有心灵情感相通的关系。母亲与胎儿分别通过不同的途径彼此传递情感信息。

胎儿能够通过母亲的梦，向母亲传递信息。看上去这种说法似乎荒诞可笑，但是在大量的医学文献中都曾记载过孕妇的梦成为事实的例子。其实这并不奇怪，因为孕妇的梦恰恰是她在清醒状态下的情绪和思维的反应。

同样，母亲的情感诸如怜爱胎儿，欢迎胎儿，以及恐惧、不安等信息也将通过有关途径传递给胎儿，进而发生潜移默化的影响。比如说，当母亲在绿树成荫的小路上散步，心情愉快舒畅时，这种信息便很快地传递给胎儿，使他体察到母亲恬静的心情，随之安静下来。而正当母亲盛怒之时，胎儿则迅速捕捉到来自母亲的情感信息，变得躁动不安。据报道，一些毫无医学原因的自然流产正是由于母亲的极度恐惧和不安造成的。

总之，母亲与胎儿之间是存在情感沟通渠道的。至于这条渠道是怎样建立，这些又是如何发生的，目前还是一个令人费解的谜。但是充分的事实已经证明，凡是生活幸福美满的母亲所生的孩子大都聪明伶俐，性格外向；而生活不幸福的母亲所生的孩子却往往反应迟钝，存在自卑、怯弱等心理缺陷。

4. 运动交流

胎儿与母体血肉相连息息相关，母体运动除了增加对胎儿氧的供给，增强血流循环，促进胎儿大脑及全身发育外，母亲选择运动和环境优美的大自然，对自然美的感受及运动后愉悦的情绪都对腹中胎儿产生美的潜移默化的感染，对胎儿乐观开朗性格的形成有很大关系。现代胎教研究证明，运动亦应从胎教开始训练，从有胎动开始，孕妇仰卧，全身放松，用手在腹部来回抚摸，然后用手指轻戳腹部的不同部位．观察胎儿的反应，几周后胎儿就逐渐适应了这种训练方法并做出一些相应的反应。

除了借助于抚摸引发出胎儿的交互作用之外。母亲自己本身要进行孕妇体操，或者是充分地括动身体，因为这些都会影响胎儿的运动能力。

5．语言交流

从怀孕5个月左右开始，就要尽量和胎儿说话。母亲可以用语言将现在的行动告诉胎儿，或者是唱歌、读书给胎儿听。最好一个月的时间都唱同一首歌、念同一本书。

可以用光照着腹部，告诉他："天亮啦！这就是光亮。"借以教导他明暗的区别。或者一边抚摸腹部，一边告诉他："头朝下，脚朝上。"

还可以告诉他："踢两次肚子。"教他数数。

6．行为信息交流

通过观察发现，每当胎儿感到不适、不安或意识到危险临近时，就会拳打脚踢向母亲报警。据报道，一位妊娠7个月的孕妇突然感到腹中的胎儿猛烈地冲撞自己，并且持续时间较长，经医生诊断。结果是前置胎盘。这是一种很可能导致胎盘与子宫分离引起大出血的妊娠。可见，胎儿已感到即将降临的危险，于是不得不竭尽全力通知他的母亲。

另一方面当孕妇因重体力劳动，大运动量活动，长途跋涉，以及繁重的家务等引起极度疲劳，或者因种种原因造成巨大的烦恼、气愤和不安时，也会自然而然地传递给胎儿，从而波及胎儿的健康和发育，严重时甚至使胎儿感到无法忍受而发生流产、死产等意外。因此，未来的母亲应重视孕期保健，注意分析来自胎儿的行为信息，以保证胎儿健康成长。

关于胎教

1.正确认识胎教

科学胎教是十分重要的，但目前有些人对胎教的认识还存在一些误区，有人甚至根本不相信胎教，认为胎儿根本就不可能接受教育。这是因为他们没有正确地理解胎教。

胎教不同于出生后的教育，胎教不是教胎儿识字、唱歌、算算术等，而是通过各种适当的、合理的信息刺激，促进胎儿各种感觉功能的充分发育，为出生后早期的感觉学习打好基础。这样来理解，您是不是认为胎儿有价值呢？另外，胎儿在母体中智能发育状况，人们并没有完全弄清楚，所以进行合理的胎教也许会产生意想不到的意义。

2.胎教的科学依据

胎儿具有惊人的能力，为开发这一能力而施行胎儿教育，近年愈来愈引起人们的关注。美国著名的医学专家托马斯的研究结果表明，胎儿在6个月时，大脑细胞的数目已接近成人，各种感觉器官起趋于完善，对母体内外的刺激能做出一定的反应。这就给胎教的实施提供了有力的科学依据。

胎教以是临床优生学与环境优生学相结合的实际运用与具体措施。

3. 胎教的准确含义

◎广义胎教：为了促进胎儿生理上和心理上的健康成长，同时确保孕产妇能够顺利地渡过孕产期所采取的精神、饮食、环境、劳逸等各方面的保健措施。因为没有健康的母亲，亦将不会出生强壮的胎儿。有人也把广义胎教称为“间接胎教”。

◎狭义胎教：根据胎儿各感觉器官发育成长的实际情况，有针对性地，积极主动地给予适当合理的信息刺激，使胎儿建立起条件反射，进而促进其大脑机能、躯体运动机能、感觉机能及神经系统机能的成熟。换言之，狭义胎教就是在胎儿发育成长的各时间，科学地提供视觉、听觉、触觉等方面的教育，如光照、音乐、对话、轻拍、扶摸等，使胎儿大脑神经细胞不断增殖，神经系统和各个器官的功能得到合理的开发和训练，以最大限度地发掘胎儿的智力潜能，达到提高人类素质的目的。所以，狭义胎教亦可称之为“直接胎教”。

怀孕时胎教是一项非常重要的工作，它会影响到胎儿以后的身心发展、人格智力。所以，准爸爸准妈妈从现在起就应该开始重视胎教。

第18周

感觉到了胎宝宝

第18周记：我感觉到他了，肯定是他。像一个泡泡在我肚子里拱了一下。当时我正在地铁里，那种感觉让我激动得差点要拥抱我身旁那个陌生男人。还好他正在看报纸，没有注意到我当时的失态。

就像第一次透视，第一次听到胎心，那一刻的感觉也成为了我怀孕过程中的一个纪念碑。我真正感觉到肚子里有一个小人了，这个小人儿现在至少有一支钢笔长了吧！

胎宝宝状况 胎宝贝已经长到14厘米左右了，体重大约200克。原来偏向两侧的眼睛开始向前集中。骨骼差不多已成为类似橡胶的软骨，并开始逐步硬化。大多数孕妈咪在这周都可感受到第一次胎动了，那感觉如同小蚯蚓在蠕动，或是像手放在鱼篮外但仍能感到里面的小鱼在跳动一样。

孕妈妈状况 从现在开始，大多数孕妈妈会真切地感受到胎儿的胎动，胃部感到飘来飘去，许多孕妇都记录下了第一次感到胎动的时间。你的兴奋一定会让丈心痒难耐，因为他体会不到胎儿在身体内的运动，当然，你可以让他把手放在你的腹部，让他感觉一下胎儿的存在。

从现在开始，小家伙需要你供给更大量的钙。所以，生活中要注意进食富钙食物、或是到户外晒太阳，特别是冬季。也可以向你的医生咨询，是否有必要补充维生素D和钙剂。要时刻记住，肚子里的小宝贝是个能听、能看、有各种感觉的小生命，对于外界各种刺激十分敏感，并能做出多种反应，从而具备了接受教育的基础。因此，一定要抓住这“天赐良机”，加强对小宝宝进行音乐、语言、抚摸、情绪、运动等胎教。

胎动的规律

正常情况下，一天之中，胎动在上午8～12点比较均匀，下午2～3点时最少，6点以后就开始逐渐增多，到了晚上8～11时最活跃。

胎动的强弱和次数，个体差异很大。有的12小时多达100次以上，有的只有30～40次。但只要胎动有规律，有节奏，变化不大，都说明胎儿发育是正常的。

胎动计数已成为孕妇进行自我监护的基本方法之一。孕妇可在固定时间，早、中、晚各计数胎动1小时，3次相加乘4即为12小时胎动数。正常胎动每小时大于等于3次或12小时大于等于30次。若当天的胎动次数较以往减少30%或以上者，为胎动减少。

孕16～20周	孕20～35周	临近分娩
运动量:小,动作不激烈。 妈妈的感觉:微弱,不明显。 位置:下腹中央。	运动量:大，动作最激烈。 妈妈的感觉:非常明显。 位置:靠近胃部,向两侧扩大。	运动量:大,动作不激烈。 妈妈的感觉:明显。 位置:遍布整个腹部。
孕16～20周是刚刚开始能够感知到胎动的时期。这个时候的宝宝运动量不是很大，动作也不激烈，孕妈咪通常觉得这个时候的胎动像鱼在游泳，或是“咕噜咕噜”吐泡泡，跟胀气、肠胃蠕动或饿肚子的感觉有点像，没有经验的孕妈咪常常会分不清。此时胎动的位置比较靠近肚脐眼。	这个时候的宝宝正处于活泼时期，而且因为长得还不是很大，子宫内可供活动的空间比较大，所以这是宝宝胎动最激烈的一段时间。孕妈咪可以感觉到宝宝拳打脚踢、翻滚等各种大动作，甚至还可以看到肚皮上突出小手小脚。此时胎儿位置升高，在靠近胃的地方了。	因为临近分娩，宝宝慢慢长大，几乎撑满整个子宫，所以宫内可供活动的空间越来越少，施展不开，而且胎头下降，胎动就会减少一些，没有以前那么频繁。胎动的位置也会随着胎儿的升降而改变。

小贴士……感受胎动的时刻

1．夜晚睡觉前

一般，宝宝在晚上是动得最多的，一方面比较有精神，另一方面，孕妈咪通常在这个时间能静下心来感受宝宝的胎动，所以会觉得动得特别多。

2．吃饭以后

吃饭以后，孕妈咪体内血糖含量增加，宝宝也"吃饱喝足"有力气了，所以胎动会变得比饭前要较频繁一些。

3．洗澡的时候

可能是因为洗澡时孕妈咪会觉得比较放松，这种情绪会传达给宝宝，他就比较有精神。

4．对着肚子说话的时候

准爸、准妈和宝宝交流的时候，宝宝会有回应，用胎动的方式表达自己的感觉。

5．听音乐的时候

受到音乐的刺激，胎宝宝会变得喜欢动，这也是传达情绪的一种方法。

了解胎教原则

胎教原则是人们进行胎教时必须遵循的准则，它反映了胎教的客观规律，同时也是千百年来胎教实践的经验的概括和总结，贯于胎教的整个过程之中，对具体的胎教活动起着极为重要的指导作用。自觉遵循胎教的基本原则，是胎教成功的前提和保证。

◎自觉性原则　自觉性原则要求孕妇在正确认识胎教的重要意义的基础上，主动学习和运用胎教方法，有目的、有计划地进行胎教。

◎及时性原则　胎教过程具有不可逆转性，因此胎教必须尽早地及时地进行。否则错过了胎教最佳的时机，再采取措施就难以弥补。一般来说，胎教的最关键时期是怀孕5～7个月。

◎科学性原则　以科学的教育学、心理学和生理学、优生学等理论为指导，根据胎教过程的基本规律，恰当地选择胎教方法，引导胎儿在母体内更顺利，更健康地成长。

◎个别性原则　根据孕妇本人及其家庭的具体情况，选择适宜的方式方法，由于孕妇本人的智力能力，气质性格等许多方面都存在着个体差异性，所以，胎教的途径的手段也应该随之而异。

此外家庭经济状况，文化背景和生活情趣等也会给胎教活动带来一系列影响。遵循个别性原则，能够扬长避短，收到较好的效果。

胎教方法盘点

如今的人们越来越注重使用胎教来促进孩子智力的发展，合理胎教的方法是值得推荐的，但专家提醒准妈妈，对于胎教过程不必过于苛求，最重要的还是保持心情愉快，这是胎教的基础和前提。给胎儿施加刺激信息时，要轻柔，要在胎儿活动期间。不可干扰胎儿睡眠。

归纳起来，孕期生活中实施胎教的方法主要有以下 8 种。

1.营养胎教

从广义的角度说，营养也是胎教。孕期必须注重均衡的饮食搭配，做好体重控制，针对不同阶段，做重点式的营养补充。孕早期（1～3个月）：补充叶酸和维生素，摄取容易消化、清淡的食物，可减缓怀孕初期的不适症状。怀孕中期（4～7个月）：因孕妇的食欲增加，应注意补充富含蛋白质、钙、植物性脂肪的营养食品。怀孕晚期（8～10个月）：应控制水和盐分的摄入量，并监控体重的增加。

适合周数：得知怀孕开始。

2.音乐胎教

建议妈妈选择舒缓、轻柔、明朗旋律、温和自然、有规律性、节奏和妈妈心跳相近的音乐或乐曲；莫扎特的EQ音乐、大自然的河川、溪流声、虫鸣鸟叫声等都是不错的选择，具有安抚胎儿、调节昼夜规律的作用。妈妈应尽量避免听吵杂或不当的音乐(胎儿不喜欢听到高振动频率的音波)。

适合周数：怀孕第 16 周开始。

3.美育胎教

经常欣赏艺术作品可以提高人的感受力；准妈咪可以带着肚子里的小宝宝，一同欣赏美丽的事物，当准妈妈感受到美的同时，也在无形中传达给宝宝了喔！

适合周数：怀孕第20周开始。

4.抚摸胎教

父母用手轻轻抚摸胎儿或轻轻拍打胎儿，通过孕妇肚皮给胎儿触觉上的刺激，促进胎儿感觉神经和大脑的发育。父母用手在腹部抚摸胎儿，用手指对胎体轻按一下，胎儿会作出反应。可边触摸，边说话，加深全家人的感情。

适合周数：怀孕第20周开始。

5.意念胎教

准妈咪在怀孕期间透过想象来勾勒宝宝的形象，这个形象在某种程度上，将与即将出生的胎儿相似。有些准妈咪很担心胎儿出生后，是不是有身体上的残缺，经常忐忑不安，不如在房间里贴一些可爱宝宝的画像或照片，可以帮助孕妇保持愉快的心情。

适合周数：怀孕第28周开始。

6.语言胎教

爸爸和妈妈每天都要跟肚子里的宝宝说说话，早上起床打招呼、不时地把看到的东西分享给宝宝等。这不仅是语言胎教的重点，也是建立亲子关系的关键。

适合周数：怀孕第24周开始

7.运动胎教

在进行时，准妈咪必须掌握好动作的幅度与运动量。

孕妇可以做一些胎儿小体操，在感觉到胎动时仰卧、全身放松，用双手从上到下、从左到右，反复轻柔地抚摸腹部，有时，也可以用手指轻压胎儿，并感觉胎儿随着指压轻轻地蠕动。除此之外，准妈咪每天做适量的运动，有助于顺产，并减少生产时会阴肌肉受损。

适合周数：怀孕第20周～36周。

8.光照胎教

胎儿的视觉发育大约要到36周大时，才能对光照的刺激产生反应。每天用手电筒紧贴肚皮一闪一闪地照射胎儿的头部，每次持续2分钟，胎儿出生后的动作行为、视觉功能及对昼夜的区分也表现得比较强。

适合周数：怀孕第32周开始。

小贴士……值得欣赏的10首胎教音乐

1.普罗科菲耶夫的《彼得与狼》——做个勇敢的宝宝

2.德沃夏克的e小调第九交响曲《自新大陆》第二乐章——抚平焦躁的心情

3.约纳森的《杜鹃圆舞曲》——特别适合在早晨睡醒后倾听

4.格里格的《培尔·金特》组曲中《在山魔王的宫殿里》——感受力度与节奏

5.罗伯特·舒曼的《梦幻曲》——感受清新与自然

6.约翰·施特劳斯的《维也纳森林的故事》—感受春天早晨的气息

7.贝多芬的F大调第六号交响曲《田园》——在细腻的乐曲中享受宁静

8.老约翰·施特劳斯的《拉德斯基进行曲》——激情澎湃中感受无限活力

9.勃拉姆斯的《摇篮曲》——妈妈无尽的爱，在乐曲声中与小宝宝说说话

10.维瓦尔第的小提琴协奏曲《四季·春》——体验春季盎然的感受

第19周

换上了孕妇装

第19周记：我的宝宝已经有小甜瓜那么大了。大夫说他的手指上甚至已经长出了指甲。哦，那他出生时，指甲一定该剪了吧。我暗暗地想，他会不会抓伤了自己的小脸呢！

我腹部的皮肤开始觉得有些痒。我在腹部擦了些润肤霜，好像还挺管用。如果痒得更厉害，我想就得去找大夫了。肚子越来越大了，我已将宽大的孕妇装换上了。

胎宝宝状况　小宝贝已经长到15厘米左右，差不多有200～250克了。开始能够吞咽羊水，肾脏已经能够制造尿液，头发也在迅速生长。最大的变化就是感觉器官开始按照区域迅速发展，从这周末开始，味觉、嗅觉、触觉、视觉、听觉会在大脑中专门的区域里发育。

孕妈妈状况　每天你都会明显感到胎宝贝不停地运作，甚至晚上会“折腾”得你无法入睡。你的肚子越来越大，腰身明显加粗，动作开始笨拙。有些孕妈咪腹部的皮肤会有些痒，试着擦些润肤霜也有用。如果痒得厉害，要及时问医生。你会注意到，随着的乳房的增大，乳腺也发达起来。

现在你就要注意乳头和乳房的保养了，以防止乳房组织松弛、乳腺管发育异常，否则有可能产后缺少乳汁。

每晚八九点钟的时候。每天坚持数胎动，想象小宝贝的各种神态和体态时，会得到小家伙的回应。

准爸爸辅助胎教4步曲

很多人都知道胎教并不是一个人的事，准爸爸在胎教中的作用很大。如果孕妇在妊娠期情绪低落、高度不安，孩子出生后会出现智力低下、个性怪癖、容易激动等状况。专家指出，从某种意义上说，诞生聪明健康的小宝宝在很大程度上取决于父亲。特别是在情绪胎教中，准爸爸所起的作用非常大。

丈夫应积极支持妻子为胎教而做的种种努力，主动参与胎教过程，陪同妻子一起和胎儿“玩耍”，给胎儿讲故事，描述每天的工作和收获，让胎儿熟悉父亲低沉而有力的声音，从而产生信赖感。

1、当好“后勤部长”

怀孕的妻子一个人要负担两个人的营养及生活非常劳累。如果营养不足或食欲不佳，不仅使妻子体力不支，而且严重地影响胎儿的智力发育。因为，宝宝的智力形成的物质基础，有2/3是在胚胎期形成的。所以丈夫要关心妻子孕期的营养问题，尽心尽力当好妻子和胎儿的“后勤部长”。

2、丰富生活情趣

早晨陪妻子一起到环境清新的公园、树林或田野中去散步，做做早操，嘱咐妻子白天晒晒太阳。妻子感到丈夫温馨的体贴，心情舒畅惬意，对胎儿的发育也有好处。

3、风趣幽默处事

妻子由于妊娠后体内激素分泌变化大，产生种种令人不适的妊娠反应，因而情绪不太稳定，因此，特别需要向丈夫倾诉。这时，丈夫要用风趣的语言以及幽默的笑话宽慰和开导妻子，这是稳定妻子情绪的良方。

4、协助妻子胎教

丈夫对妻子的体贴与关心，爸爸对胎儿的抚摸与“交谈”，都是生动有效的情绪胎教。

在胎教过程中，丈夫应倍加关爱妻子，让妻子多体会家庭的温暖，避免妻子产生愤怒、惊吓、恐惧、忧伤、焦虑等不良情绪，保持心情愉快，精力充沛。

真实故事——我的胎教

盼盼一岁七个月了。上个月的一天，奶奶带她下楼，出门时说:“盼盼，奶奶抱你下楼玩。”他回答说:“奶奶累了，盼盼自己走，下楼玩。”一连三个短句，吐词清楚，条理清晰，你能相信是一岁半孩子讲的话吗？前几天偶然的一次，爷爷抱着问他，爸爸、奶奶在干什么？他回答说:“爸爸炒菜，奶奶切辣椒，爷爷抱盼盼，阿姨上班了。”爷爷再问:“舅舅呢？”“舅舅也上班了。”

一连串的短句，不仅内容完整，一个“也”字的运用，充分显示其语言的成熟和表达的精确程度。如果不是我从怀孕4个月开始经历过“语言胎教”的实践，也许我自己也不会相信一岁七个月的孩子会有样的口才。

据胎教资料，胎儿5～6个月语言中枢已基本形成。因此，我从4个月起就有意识地对胎儿进行语言刺激。第一周训练发音：用手轻轻地有节奏地拍着腹部，发a、o、e等韵母和声母，每日早、中、晚三次，每次20分钟；第二周，发m—a—、ma—，b—a—、ba—……；三周起训练 ma—ma—，ba—ba— 等双音节词；第四周开始用很慢的速度讲短句，如“奶奶吃饭”、“宝宝睡觉”等等。尽管第一个月我感觉不出胎儿有任何反应，可我充满信心，天天坚持施教。

5个半月后感觉到胎动了，除每天坚持语言训练外，着重于观察力、记忆力的培养。主要通过户外散步、上下班路上和睡前对胎儿讲述所见事物的名称、外形等等，往往同一个地点、同一件事物我会专程去上三四次，每次至少要讲述3遍。第一二次去，着重给孩子介绍事物的名称、外形、颜色……我讲，胎儿听，让胎儿通过我的眼睛观察事物；第三四次重游，我就边讲边提问，好像与老朋友亲切地交谈。如“昨天我们在这里看到什么了？好多好多苹果是不是？红红的苹果，对不对……”到屋外散步，我们夫妻常边走边自言自语地告诉孩子看见些什么:“爸爸妈妈带宝宝出来散步，你看，到桃花苑了，这儿都是桃树；唷，好多桃花呀！”闻一闻(其实是我在闻)，“啊，真香！”

上下班路上，我也默默地自言自语和孩子说话，告诉他路上见到的一些新鲜事物。晚上，总是念儿歌、讲故事给他听。

怀孕到第7个月，胎儿的脑、四肢等器官均已形成，我开始用游戏的方法对胎儿进行语言和动作的协调训练。先给胎儿讲解一至二遍，再自己做示范动作，最后和他一起做游戏。例如早晨起床前，我每天都轻轻地拍着腹部说："宝贝，要起床了，你听见妈妈的话就动一动。"起初几天都没有任何反应，没想到了第4天，孩子果真用脚向我放手的部位踢过来了。你说我有多高兴啊！而后，只要我拍着肚子和他说话，他都会踢我。三周后我训练他左右两边踢，果真胎儿会随着我手的移动一左一右地踢我。乐得他爸爸直打哈哈。

怀孕到8个月，我侧重于训练胎儿的思维想象能力，常念一些琅琅上口散文诗般的儿歌，如《小雪花》："是谁，敲着窗户沙沙沙？是我，我是……"，由于这样的儿歌难度大，所以一有时间就念，每次念一首，一首念三天。

"胎教"作为"0岁教育方案"的一个重要组成部分，它对于培养人的潜在素质，对后天婴幼儿基本素质的提高，无疑有较大的影响。

乳房护理

乳房是未来婴儿营养的源泉，因此，保护好乳房十分重要。实际上，不管你是否决定哺喂母奶，在第19～20周时，都要进行乳房护理，以预防乳头破裂而导致发炎，同时矫正乳头凹陷。

1. 乳房的保健

妊娠期乳房逐渐变大、变重，如任其发展不管，会使乳房组织松弛，乳腺发育不正常。可选用合适的乳罩将乳房兜托起来。乳罩类型应以不过于压迫乳头、也不影响乳房的血液循环为原则，如选用背带较宽的大号乳罩，可使人感觉不到乳房的重量，也不至压迫乳头。

睡觉或休息时应取下乳罩，这样有利于呼吸及乳腺的血液循环。同时，应注意防止乳房受外伤、挤压并防止感染。如发现乳房红肿有硬块时，应及时热敷、按摩。

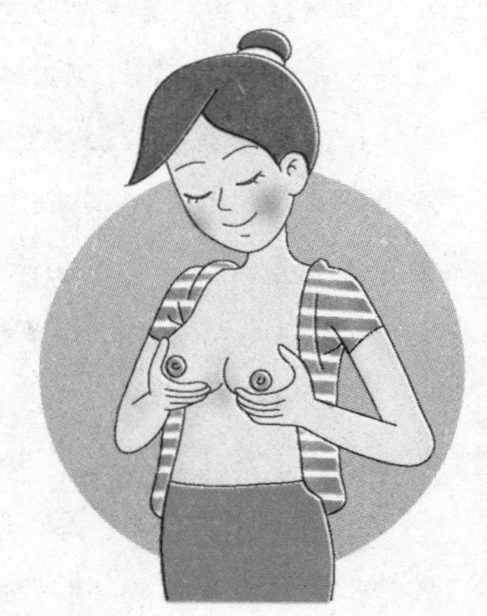

2. 乳头的保健

初次怀孕的人，乳头的皮肤很娇嫩、敏感，往往经受不住日后婴儿反复吸吮的刺激，哺乳时会感到奇痒或疼痛。为了克服这种现象，要从妊娠5～6个月起每日用肥皂水和温水擦洗乳头一次，擦除乳头上积聚的分泌物干痂，然后涂一些油脂，可增加皮肤的坚韧度和对刺激的耐受力，以防哺乳时发生乳头皲裂。妊娠后期也应经常用温水或酒精清洗乳头，保持乳头清洁，促进乳头皮肤老化，角质层增厚，对防止发生妊娠期乳腺炎大有好处。

乳头过短，甚至凹陷，或乳头有裂纹的孕妇，应及早采用乳头矫正法，矫正可从妊娠17周开始，方法如下：

(1) 揪出乳头，停留片刻，每日进行数次。如乳头揪出有困难时，可压乳晕周围，揪出后可按乳头保护法进行摩擦。

(2) 先把自己的手洗净，乳头两侧各放一个手指，先是上下，然后左右，轻轻地往相反方向牵拉乳晕皮肤及其下面的组织，重复进行，每日2次，每次5分钟。哺乳时可用中指食指按压乳晕部，以便使乳头凸起，给婴儿吸吮母乳创造良好的条件。

(3) 用上述方法不能矫正时，可使用乳头吸引器将乳头吸出。无吸引器时可用一副注射针筒连接一段小皮管，皮管接在眼药水瓶的小口上，大口对准乳头，针筒抽气后负压可将乳头吸出，维持一定时间，每天做2次。或用半个光滑的核桃壳扣压在乳头周围，以挤出乳头。

使用以上方法揪吸乳头时可能会引起宫缩，对子宫敏感、宫缩频繁的孕妇，或有反复流产、早产史的孕妇要特别注意。

(4) 使乳腺管通畅。为使乳腺管开通，乳汁流畅，从妊娠32周起要挤出初乳（即在正式泌乳前，乳房分泌的少量清稀的乳汁），提前这样做了就能预防郁乳、乳头裂伤，乳汁分泌不足等问题发生。但须注意是否有子宫收缩出现，必要时要中止或暂缓进行。

妊娠妇女定期产前检查时，应该注意乳腺的检查。

第20周

绰约孕生活

第20周记：孕育宝宝的路程，我应该已经走了一半了，我的肚子已经非常明显地隆起。

我做了第二次B超，是为了看看宝宝是否有什么不正常。谢天谢地，一切都很好。我很想知道宝宝的性别，但是大夫只是呵呵地笑。开电梯的阿姨盯着我瞧了半天，十分肯定地告诉我怀的是女孩。哈，我的直觉居然错了？我还是决定从今天起，改口叫"她"了。

我想象她在我的肚子里吮吸着大拇指的样子……

胎宝宝状况　胎宝贝已经长到16厘米左右，体重不到300克，生长趋于稳定。胎宝贝开始有了脑部的记忆功能，你和爱人的"温言软语"小宝贝都能记下来。皮下脂肪开始生成，味觉、嗅觉、听觉、视觉和触觉等感觉器官迅速发育。心跳已经十分活跃，小手小脚都能在羊水中自由活动了。

孕妈妈状况　从现在开始，你的腰部和腹部也开始膨胀了。宫底每周大约升高1厘米，到了让老公帮你测量每周宫高的时候了。如果宫高持续2周没有变化，就要及时请医生为你做检查。因为胎宝贝整天忙着在里面做伸展运动，要么伸伸胳膊、要么踢踢腿，你的肚子从表面上看去可能偶尔会有些凹凸鼓动。

食物花样要不断变换，注意营养的均衡。这时要适当地增加运动量了，运动可以增强心肺功能，使身体适应血液循环和呼吸系统不断增加的负荷。在医生指导下或是在孕妇学校学到的助产体操会有非常好的效果，它可以增强参与分娩的肌肉群的力量、放松骨盆关节，为今后能顺利分娩做准备。充分的全身性放松的运动可以使你保持身心愉快。

第20周，别忘了到医院做例行产检、B超检查。

B 超检查

超声波，是频率在 20 千赫以上超过人耳听阈的声波。在目前的超声波方法中，B 型超声波（B 超）检查法是最主要的方法。因为 B 超可以直接显示图像，涉及的内容广泛，在预防、诊断、治疗、康复、监护和普查人体疾病中有很高的实用价值。借助 B 超诊断胎儿是否畸形的准确率较高。

1．借助 B 超诊断胎儿是否畸形有五大优点

（1）对人体无创伤、无射线、无痛苦；

（2）能够清晰地显示人体软组织的解剖结构；

（3）可直接观察脏器的活动状态；

（4）施羊膜腔穿刺术时，可以帮助胎盘定位，避免损伤胎儿；

（5）简便、准确、容易被孕妇接受。

2．对于高度怀疑下列 5 种胎儿畸形者，可用 B 超进行诊断

（1）无脑儿：可在妊娠 3 个月后检出；

（2）脑积水：脑积水常合并羊水过多，易于检出；

（3）神经管畸形中的脑脊膜膨出；

（4）脐带异常，如脐膨出；

（5）消化道异常，如消化道闭锁、十指肠闭锁等。

B 超检查还可以依次对胎儿的身体各部位进行扫查，可诊断联体畸形、小头畸形等。高分辨率的 B 超甚至可对唇裂等微小畸形准确诊断。

3．为什么要进行 B 超检查？

（1）发现胎儿某些严重畸形，如体表畸形，少数内脏畸形等。但并非全部都可查出。

（2）确定预产期。孕妇月经周期不规律，可使用超声检查确定预产期。

（3）确定胎儿位置。使用超声检查确定胎儿在子宫内是否是臀位（即胎儿臀部靠近骨盆出口，对分娩不利），是一种最安全、快速的方法。

(4) 确定胎盘的位置。通常胎盘是植入子宫体的侧壁。如果胎盘植入子宫颈口附近，或覆盖子宫颈口，这种情况容易导致孕妇阴道出血。

(5) 发现并确认胎儿的数目。如是否为双胞胎。

(6) 了解胎儿生长发育情况。有时你的医生需要知道你的胎儿当前的生长发育情况，如果你的宫高测定经常偏小或过大，而超声检查能帮助医生较为准确地评估胎儿生长发育的情况。

(7) 了解羊水量。通过普通测定子宫的高度可以提示羊水量是否正常，但超声检查能准确判断羊水的多少。

(8) 评估胎儿宫内状态。超声波可获得生物物理切面图，可了解胎儿在宫内的状态，以消除疑虑。还能观察到健康胎儿的正常活动，并进行评分。

(9) 排除异位妊娠。有的孕妇胚胎种植在子宫外，如输卵管妊娠，这是很危险的妊娠。因为当胚胎不断长大时，随时有可以引起输卵管破裂。使用超声检查在大多数这样的病例中能清楚地观察到胚胎种植的部位。

(10) 协助孕期其他特殊检查。进行羊膜腔穿刺时，穿刺针的定位应在超声仪的指导下进行。

4. 注意的问题

(1) B超检查是常规产前检查的必做项目，也是使用得较多的产前诊断技术。但不适当的B超检查会损害胎儿的中枢神经。正常妊娠者应该根据医生建议，在适当的时间接受适当的B超检查，次数不宜过多（整个孕期不超过3次），每次检查时间不宜超过3分钟。

(2) 目前，国内一些医院竞相开展给肚子里的宝宝做B超“照相留影”，甚至做VCD，留下娘胎中的一颦一笑。这股时风，不但吸引了广大孕妇，也煽起了不少媒体的宣传热情。但是，专家告诫：超声的危险性从未“解除警报”，为了让宝宝免受伤害，这种冒险的“留影”还是不照为好。

孕期旅行

准妈妈要出门旅游，最好安排在怀孕中期（怀孕4～6个月）。旅游前最好先咨询产科医生，以确定是否适合旅游。此外，要注意交通安全，在汽车或飞机里一定要系好安全带，要有人陪同。若有任何不适，马上请当地医生检查。准妈妈若有不适合旅游的因素，最好不要勉强成行，以免在旅途中发生状况。非出远门不可时，应请产科医生将你的特殊情况写下，随身携带，一旦遇到不适，可马上拿给当地医生看，有助于医生立即采取正确的应变措施。

一般来说，怀孕的时候最好是不要出门，但现在的许多准妈妈都是忙碌的职业妇女，长长的十个月里说不定就要出公差，为了自己和胎儿的安全，一定要认真阅读下面的文字：

1. 制定合理的旅行计划

即使身体状况很好，准妈妈也不能太过疲劳，在行程安排上一定要留出足够的休息时间。此外，出发前必须查明到达地区的天气、交通、医院等，若行程是难以计划和安排的，有许多不确定的因素的话，还是不去的好。

2. 途中要有人全程陪同

准妈妈不宜一人独自出门，如果与一大群陌生人做伴也是不合适的。最好是由丈夫、家人或好友等熟悉你的人陪伴前往，不但会使旅程较为愉快，当你觉得累或不舒服的时候，也有人可以照顾你。

3. 衣食住行要多注意

（1）食：避免吃生冷、不干净或没吃过的食物，以免造成消化不良、腹泻等突发状况；奶制品、海鲜等食物容易变质，若不能确定是否新鲜，最好不要吃；多喝开水，多吃水果，可防脱水和便秘。

（2）衣：以穿脱方便的保暖衣物为主，还可以带上帽子、外套、围巾等，以预防感冒。若所去地区天气炎热，帽子、防晒油不可少。平底鞋、托腹带、弹性强的袜子可帮助你减轻疲劳带来的不适。多带一些纸内裤可以应急。

（3）住：避免前往海岛或交通不便的地方。蚊蝇多、卫生差的地区不可前往，传染病区更不合适准妈妈前往了。

（4）行：坐车、搭飞机一定要系好安全带，落座前最好找好洗手间的位置。准妈妈尿频，憋尿对准妈妈是没有好处的，最好能每小时起身活动十分钟。如果颠簸的厉害的话，就不要起身了，在座位上伸展一下身体。不要搭坐摩托车或快艇，登山、走路也都注意不要太费体力，一切宜量力而为。

4. 随身携带药品

胃肠药、治疗外伤的药水药膏、创可贴、花露水等，使用时要先看说明，有无准妈妈慎用的字样。

5. 运动量不要太大或太刺激。

运动量太大容易造成准妈妈的体力不支，因而导致流产、早产及破水。太刺激或危险性高的活动也不可参与，例如过山车、自由落体、高空弹跳等。

6. 旅途中随时注意身体状况

旅途中，若感觉疲劳请稍事休息；若有任何身体不适，如下体出血、腹痛、腹胀、破水等，应立即就医。此外，如果准妈妈有感冒发烧等症状，也应该及早去看医生。总之，不要轻视身体上的任何症状而继续旅行，以避免造成不可挽回的损失。

孕期写真照

孕妈妈拍专业写真照，在大城市已成了一种流行。孕期十月，你都可以留下孕影，但适合拍专业写真的时间要到7个月后，此时肚形与孕味才充分显现。在最后两个多月里，孕妈妈都应该找个机会去专业的孕妇馆拍摄。

孕妇写真的风格日益多样，孕妈妈可以与摄影师交流，也可以带着自己喜欢的样片与风格给摄影师看，以便摄影师创作。孕妇写真还是以记录为主，孕妈妈可以带些自己有纪念意义的衣服与装饰来拍摄，也可以带上为小孩准备的衣服与物件，这样出来的照片不但有自己的独特性，更有纪念意义，也使摄影师有更多的表现空间。

一位孕妈妈对写真的感言：

马上宝宝就要出世了，对于孩子的到来我有很多的憧憬。我想准妈妈们可能会给孩子准备很多东西，早早为孩子做好各种打算。不要忽略，拍孕妇写真也是重要的一项。我个人认为这个留念还是很有意义的，大多数人一生也就这么一次。它不像结婚照可以补拍，孕妇照只能在孕期拍摄，记录自己怀孕的体态。将来等到孩子大了，可以给孩子看看，当年你就是从妈妈的肚子里出来的。当你指着照片说：看，这就是妈妈怀你的样子。那是多么值得骄傲的事情啊！现在我的肚子都裂了，有很多的纹。也许很多人觉得有纹不好看，甚至拍后用电脑给修了。我不这认为，其实这纹正显示了孕妈妈的辛苦，将来给孩子看时可以理直气壮地说：看，妈妈多辛苦才将你个生下来的。那可就有凭有证了。

专业摄影师的拍摄小记：

孕妈妈对自己的写真都非常重视，下面是我遇见的其中两位。

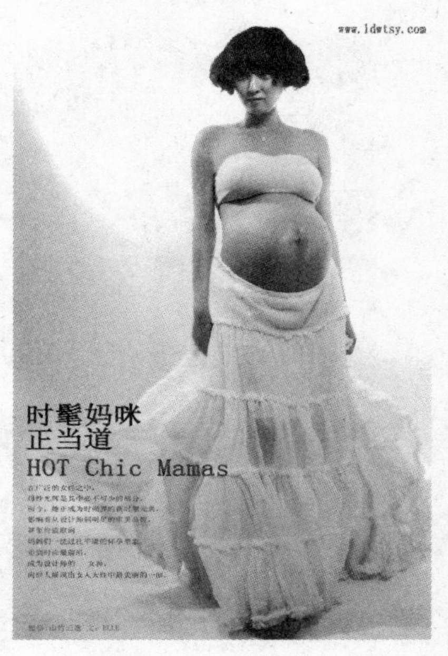

www.ldwtsy.com
时髦妈咪
正当道
HOT Chic Mamas

她是从怀孕开始就规划自己的拍照时间，离生小孩还只有一个星期的时候，来我们摄影馆拍摄，真是出乎我的意料，肚子已经是非常的饱满与壮观，但她摆设的动作很随意与自然。据她说，每年都拍摄写真，所以对拍照的感觉掌握的比较好。在出来的像册里，我们署上了“时髦妈咪正当道”的标题。取片时她与母亲一起来的，她母亲一定要把照片挂一张在自己的家里，对女儿这时的形象感到非常的自豪。

还有一位孕妈妈更使我记忆深刻。她已经住院了，时刻准备生产，可还是放不下这桩心事，瞒着家人与医生从医院里跑出来拍照。她说，我怎么着也要为自己此时的形象留个纪念，不然以后再也不可能了。

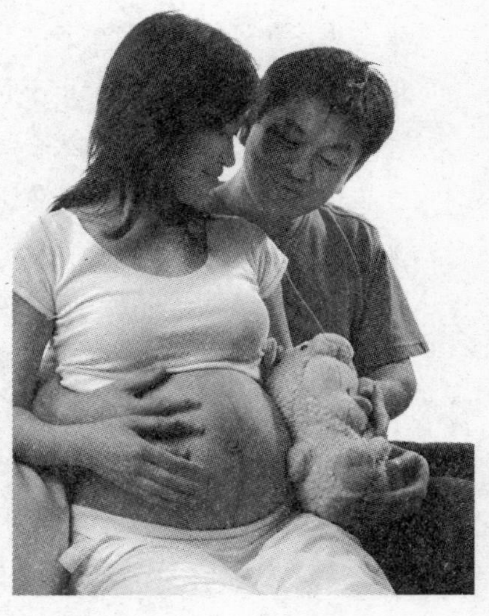

我为何执著孕妈妈写真？这得从一张黄历说起。

父亲留给我一张纸片：我出生那天的黄历，记载着我出生日期，有阴历也有公历，还有芒种和适合出门等信息。见到这一张发黄的纸片时，我已经 30 多岁了，当时眼里一阵模糊，非常感激父亲。它已不是一张轻薄的纸片，它承载着几十年的厚爱。我仿佛看见，我妈怀我时的形象与当时家里的各种桌桌椅椅。如果当时要留下照片多好啊！现在可能已经发黄了，母亲也是满头白发，可照片上的形象真真实实存在过，也鲜艳过。

因为这个遗憾，我拿起了相机，决心为令人敬爱的妈妈们留下最美、最动情的瞬间。

第21周

宝宝只有半斤重

第21周记：宝宝长得更大了，据说她的小乳牙已经开始在颌骨内形成。不过我的牙不大好，牙龈出血，我打算去看牙医。

宝宝的活动能更加明显地感觉到，她好象已经有了固定的活动和睡眠的周期。不幸的是，她的活跃期是在晚上，但愿她出生后可不要这样。

胎宝宝状况 胎宝贝身长约18厘米，体重300克左右。头发在迅速地生长，眉毛和眼睑清晰可见，渐渐变得"眉清目秀"。开始长出手指甲和脚趾甲。皮肤结构形成，变得滑溜溜的身上覆盖着一层白色、滑腻的物质，这就是胎脂。胎宝贝已经有了固定的活动和睡眠的周期，不过活跃期不一定都是在白天，也有可能在晚上或其他时间段。

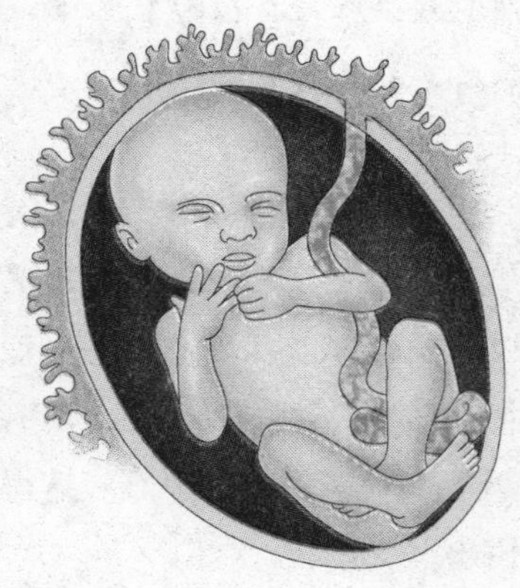

第21周（6月胎宝宝）

孕妈妈状况 这时，你的呼吸变得急促起来，特别是上楼梯的时候，走不了几级台阶就会气喘吁吁的。这是因为日益增大的子宫压迫了你的肺部，而且随着子宫的增大，这种状况也更加明显。此时胎儿和母体的生长发育都需要更多的营养，要注意增加铁质的摄入量。如有必要，也可在医生指导下补充铁剂。

选择一些好听的故事讲给宝宝听，也许将来这些故事会是宝宝出生后最喜欢的呢。

孕6月专家提示（第21～24周）

1．勿食用过多饮食，体重第21周～第24周以增加1千克为宜，以免过胖。

2．穿着宽松衣服，保持心情愉快。

3．穿戴合适胸罩，清洁乳头使之舒适。

4．避免长期站立，睡觉时可抬开双腿。

5.晾晒衣服时,宜将竹竿降到孕妇腰部之高度,切勿踮脚或弯腰动作。若发生小腿抽痉,宜尽快按摩腿肚或一手压住膝盖一手将脚指头往上用力压。

6．发型宜清爽样式，避免烫发及染发。

7．穿著平底鞋，以减轻腰部的负担，也降低母体重心，避免跌倒。

8．上、下楼梯宜踏稳脚步，将身体重心放在前脚，较不易跌落。

9．尽可能避免从事会使小腹用力的工作。

爱抚胎宝宝

抚膜胎儿是生命的亲昵。胎儿需要的是母亲的爱，不但需要优美的语言和乐曲，而且还需要有肢体的接触和亲昵。摸一摸胎儿，腹内的小宝宝可以感觉到。经常抚摸胎儿可以激发胎儿运动的积极性，你也许不会明显感到胎儿发回的信号，这种信号缓慢而有节奏，只有实践，才可能有清晰的感觉。

孕后6个月时，孕妇要经常抚摸腹部，与胎儿进行“交流”。

1．姿势

孕妇仰卧在床上，头不要垫得太高，全身放松，呼吸匀称，心平气和，面部呈微笑状，双手轻放在胎儿位上，也可将上半身垫高，采取半仰姿势。不论采取什么姿势，但一定要感到舒适。

2．方法

双手从上至下，从左至右，轻柔缓慢地抚摸胎儿，心里可想象你双手真的抚摸在可爱的小宝宝身上，有一种喜悦和幸福感，深情地默想或轻轻说出：

"小宝宝，妈妈真爱你"，"小宝宝真舒畅"，"小宝宝快快长，长成一个聪明可爱的小宝贝"等言语。

每次2～5分钟，一天2次。如果配以轻松、愉快的音乐进行，效果更佳。

如果胎儿以轻轻蠕动作出反应，可继续抚摸；若胎儿用力挣脱或蹬腿，应停止拍打抚摸。理想的抚摸时间，以傍晚胎动较多时，或晚上10时左右为好。

贴心·提醒

1．抚摸胎宝宝之前，准妈妈应排空小便。

2．孕早期以及临近预产期不宜进行抚摸胎教。

3．抚摸胎宝宝时，准妈妈避免情绪不佳，应保持稳定、轻松、愉快、平和的心态。

4．进行抚摸胎教时，室内环境舒适，空气新鲜，温度适宜。

5．有不规则子宫收缩、腹痛、先兆流产或先兆早产的准妈妈，不宜进行抚摸胎教，以免发生意外。

6．曾有过流产、早产、产前出血等不良产史的准妈妈，不宜进行抚摸胎教，可用其他胎教方法替代。

小贴士……听胎心

胎心的速率可以提示胎儿的健康情况，正常怀孕6个月后，可听到胎儿心脏跳动所发出的声音。

丈夫可使用胎心听诊器或简易的喇叭形听筒，贴在孕妇腹部听。每天1次，每次1分钟，可在孕妇脐部上、下、左、右四个部位听。

正常的胎心跳动为120～160次/分。如果每分钟胎心率大于160次或小于120次，或胎心不规律均为异常情况。可过一段时间再听一次，如果仍属异常，应及时到医院检查。

和胎宝宝做游戏

怀孕5个月的孕妇，可以与胎儿玩踢肚游戏。美国育儿专家提出了一种胎儿“踢肚游戏”胎教法，通过母亲与胎儿进行游戏，达到胎教的目的。

1. 姿势

孕妇仰卧在床上，头不要垫得太高，全身放松，呼吸均匀，心平气和，面部呈微笑状，双手轻放在胎儿位上。也可将上半身垫高，采取半仰姿势。不论采取什么姿势，都要感到舒适。

2. 方法

(1)胎儿踢肚子时，孕妇轻轻拍打被踢部位几下，然后等待第二次踢肚。

(2) 一两分钟后，胎儿会在拍打部位再踢。这时再轻拍几下，接着停下来。如果你拍的地方改变了，胎儿会向你改变的地方踢，注意改拍的位置离原胎动的位置不要太远。一两分钟后，胎儿会在改变后的部位再次踢。

(3) 每天进行2次，每次3～5分钟。

经过这种刺激胎教训练的胎儿，出生后学站、学走都会快些，身体健壮、手脚灵敏。婴儿出生时大多灵敏，拳头松驰，啼哭不多。与未经训练的同龄婴儿比，显得天真活泼可爱。

3. 注意

(1) 游戏前准妈妈应排空小便；避免情绪不佳，应保持稳定、轻松、愉快、平和的心态；进行游戏时，室内环境舒适，空气新鲜，温度适宜。

(2) 如遇到胎儿“拳打脚踢”强烈反应，表示胎儿不高兴，这时孕妇应停止动作。此时，可用爱抚法抚摸胎儿头部，安抚胎儿，一会儿胎儿就会安静下来，用轻轻蠕动来回答。

(3) 有不规则子宫收缩、腹痛、先兆流产或先兆早产的准妈妈，不宜进行踢肚游戏，以免发生意外。

(4) 曾有流产、早产、产前出血等不良产史的，不宜进行踢肚游戏。

第22周

胎动更频繁了

第22周记：今天我很担心，因为赶着去上班的时候，我走得快了些，忽然感到腹部剧痛。大夫说这是子宫肌肉伸缩引起的，是这个阶段常见的征状，以后慢慢会好起来。他建议我行动时要放慢动作。我想，这到是个很好的偷懒的借口。

胎宝宝状况　胎宝贝身长已经长到19厘米左右，体重大约有350克。小家伙的皮肤是红红的，为了方便皮下脂肪的生长，上面皱皱的。胎宝贝手部和手指的小动作多了起来，不是抓抓小鼻子、就是揉擦小脸、拍拍小脸蛋，有时还会撅撅小嘴巴。

孕妈妈状况　你的身体会越来越重，上楼的时候会感到呼吸有点儿困难。如果你走得快了些，腹部有可能会忽然感到一阵剧痛，这是子宫肌肉伸缩引起的，是这个阶段常见的症状，以后慢慢会有所好转，建议你暂且把行动节拍稍稍放慢。胎动更加频繁了，好像无论你做什么事，胎宝贝都在积极地出回应，让你感受到这个小家伙的存在。

为了防止会出现腰、腿部神经痛或膀胱刺激症，应格外注意下身的保暖了，特别是寒冷时节。贴身内裤应挑选保暖效果好的履盖式内裤（裤腰能履盖肚脐及以下部分），或者选用腹带，既能保温，又能从下腹轻轻托起增大的腹部，使身体稳定性增加。

每天听一段抒情幽雅的古典音乐，或是找些短小、有趣的童话，请老公一起配合，富有感情的朗读给小家伙听；也可以买一盘幼儿故事磁带，每天听一段。最好是反复地讲或听同样的音乐或是因定的几个小故事，这样才会加深小宝贝对“这段声音”的记忆，也许在小家伙出生后，那段声音会使得吃奶时胃口大开，或是能很快从哭闹中平静下来。

可以选择这个时间为自己和未来的宝宝采购一些必需的用品，比如婴儿床、婴儿车。

安全运动

孕妇明智地选择运动是很重要的，因为此时孕妇身怀六甲，无法再像过去那样，想做什么运动就做什么。

1. 爬楼梯

有的准妈妈会选择爬楼梯的方式来锻炼自己，这种办法有利于自然分娩。只要身体不觉得疲倦，这样的运动是很不错的。

2. 游泳

喜欢游泳的准妈妈也可以保持这个习惯，不过要注意选择卫生的泳池；在拥挤的时候不要下池游泳；游泳完毕后一定要注意保暖不要感冒了；游泳时间比平时要少一些。

3. 跑、跳、瑜伽

需要跑、跳和四肢充分伸展的运动对于不是职业运动员的准妈妈来说有一定的危险，最好不要参与，尤其是在孕期的前三个月和最后三个月。如果你有练习瑜伽或有氧操的习惯，最好向你的教练咨询一下，在练习中如果发现不适要立即停止并联络妇产科医生。

4. 每天散步 30 分钟

这是一项值得推荐的运动。最好选择清晨或黄昏去花园、绿地或其他空气清新、环境幽静的地方走一走，条件许可的话最好能有人陪伴。如果到了围产期，一定要有人陪伴或随身带好通讯工具，遇上突发情况可以在第一时间得到帮助。

5. 快步行走

快步行走与慢跑相比，不易损伤关节，也不易影响子宫内的胎儿。对于平常没有运动习惯的孕妇来说，每天只要能够快步走上30分钟，这样的运动量就已经很理想了。

贴心·提醒

1.孕期选择的运动完全可以按照自己平时的爱好来进行，不过，运动量要相对小一些。

2. 怀孕早期3个月内，少运动，以免影响坐胎。怀孕中期4～7个月，胎盘已经形成，可加大运动量。8个月以后，以稍慢的散步为主，速度上以3公里／小时为宜，时间上以孕妇是否感觉疲劳为度，最好别超过15分钟。

3.运动时，注意如下几点：

（1）穿宽松的衣裤、宽松的平底鞋。

（2）避免在水泥或柏油等硬质的地上从事运动，以减少运动伤害。

（3）运动前后各喝上两杯250毫升的果汁或矿泉水，补充一些点心，避免自己或胎儿血糖过低。

（4）怀孕前三个月，体温不要超过39℃。

（5）运动前，先做个5分钟暖身运动与缓和运动。

小贴士……运动量监控法

孕妇运动量是要合适，孕妇自己身体承受不了运动的负荷，胎儿一定也会觉得不舒服。一般来说，可以根据心率来判断运动量是否过量。母亲在运动时的心率，最好不要超过每分钟140次。可以利用以下方法，来判断运动量是否已经有过量：

1. 脉搏测量

可以用手腕上或下颚接近颈部位置的脉搏，来检测脉搏速度是否已经太快（只要轻按在脉搏上10秒，然后将所计算的脉搏跳动次数乘以6，就得到每分钟的心跳数）。运动时，脉搏不要超过140次／分，体温不要超过38℃。

2．说话试验

运动时，如果说起话来，已经有上气不接下气的感觉，就应该将目前的运动减缓下来，直到可以保持正常的说话速度为止。

3．运动试验

运动时，如果有头晕目眩、虚弱、头痛、呼吸短促、心悸、子宫收缩、阴道出血或漏液，或者身体任何部位感到疼痛，就应该立即停止。

分娩运动

运动可以保持体能、稳定情绪，更重要的是通过运动，可以增强与分娩相关肌肉与关节的力量，让孕妇在分娩的时候，对胎儿产生较大的推力，使宝宝出生得更顺利一些。

1. 盆底肌肉弹性运动

怀孕过程中，如果找不出一项适合你的运动，我们强烈建议你试试锻炼盆底肌肉弹性的凯格尔运动（Kegel）。

凯格尔运动是一位名为凯格尔的医生所发明的运动。通过凯格尔运动，可以强化骨盆底部肌肉的弹性，让它达到收放自如的境界。这样做的结果，不但可以预防或治疗小便失禁，而且可以避免分娩时阴道组织撕裂，使分娩更轻松顺利。另外，凯格尔运动可以增加阴道肌肉的弹性与敏感度，让性生活更美满。

盆底肌肉弹性是否良好，可以这样判断：尿到一半的时候，试着看看能否忍住，停止排尿，如果能够很轻易、快速地做到，表示这部分的肌肉弹性很好。如果做不到，可以试做几周凯格尔运动，就会看到成效显著：

(1) 排尿练习：排尿时，试试看能否随意停止四五次。这项运动无法训练大腿、下腹部以及阴道肌肉，是凯格尔运动的暖身操。

(2) 重复做：一开始，一天练习4次，每次重复10下收缩与放松盆底肌肉。熟练后，每天做4次，每次50下左右。

(3) 练习时间慢慢增长：先练习收缩盆底肌肉，然后从1数到5之后放松。重复做10次。然后视情况慢慢增加收缩时间。

（4）熟练后，可以尝试使用躺姿、坐姿、蹲姿等不同姿势来练习。

2．分娩肌肉伸展运动

锻炼所有与分娩有关的肌肉，使你分娩时，能够更顺利、更舒服一点。肌肉伸展运动就是针对腿部、下腹部肌肉、骨盆肌肉以及相关肌肉韧带的加强运动。

（1）蹲姿练习：每天先蹲10次，每次以1分钟开始练习，然后慢慢增加练习的时间与次数。清理冰箱、叠衣服甚至看电视时，可以顺便做蹲姿练习。

（2）随意叉腿盘坐：阅读、织毛衣时，可以练习叉着腿盘坐，每天二三次，每次10分钟。练习这种姿势时，背部要保持挺直。习惯后，可以慢慢延长练习时间。

（3）腿部伸展盘坐：背部倚靠墙壁或沙发，叉着腿盘坐，然后将盘坐的双腿抬起，让双腿的脚掌平贴在一起。然后，再将双臂自然放在膝盖上面。如果膝盖曾经有过毛病，最好别做此项运动。

（4）大臂绕圈运动：练习腿部盘坐姿势后，可以起身做大臂绕圈运动。绕臂时，手臂尽量放轻松一点。

（5）骨盆翘起运动：骨盆翘起运动是一种可以舒缓下背部压力的运动。有几种方式：

a.四肢着地：四肢着地，用双臂支撑重心，尽量不要摇晃背部。吸气时，要深入丹田，维持3秒钟左右。开始吐气时，可以变换成较舒服的平躺姿势，然后慢慢吐气出来。一天可以至少练习4次，一次重复练习50次。

b.站姿：站立，背部尽可能垂直贴靠在墙壁上，后脚跟与墙面保持约10厘米的距离。身体前倾，将下背部尽量向墙壁“顶”，保持5秒钟，然后重复三五次。

（6）膝胸伸展运动：膝胸伸展运动是一种消除下背部疼痛最有效的运动之一。每次5分钟即可。先将双手撑着地板，然后以膝盖跪着面向地板，接着在手肘与前臂处垫着枕头，以方便将手肘与前臂屈放下来。然后，慢慢将头部放低，放在屈贴在地板上的手肘与前臂之间。此时，臀部微微抬起，使下半身的重量用腹部的肌肉来做支撑。

第23周

真正的“大肚婆”

第23周记：望着日渐隆起的肚子，我祈祷自己不要留下妊娠纹。我妈妈就没有。据说这种东西是由遗传基因决定的，跟用什么护理品没太大关系。

今天我的腹部有一种好像跳动一样的奇怪感觉——他们说那是宝宝在打嗝。尽管她需要的所有氧气都是由我通过脐带输送给她的，但她好像自己也在练习呼吸和吞咽。

胎宝宝状况　胎宝贝长到了21厘米左右，体重大约450克。五官越发清晰，具备了微弱的视觉。胰腺及激素的分泌也正在稳定的发育过程中。肺中的血管形成，呼吸系统正在快速的建立。

孕妈妈状况　你会发现自己变成了一个真正的“大肚婆”，肚子不仅是大了，也变得非常能装吃的，可能连一些你以前本不喜欢的食品都能让你感到很有食欲。这时你常会有“烧心感”，在弯腰、咳嗽、用力时更容易发生，所以日常饮食要注意不要过饱，不要一次喝入大量的水或饮料，少吃辛辣性食物、过冷或过热的食物，用餐后不要立即躺下。睡眠时可将头部床脚下垫高15～20厘米，抬高上身的角度，这样做可有效减少胃液返流。排便时不要过于屏气用力，衣带裤带要宽松。

要注意生活细节：站立时两腿要平行、两脚稍稍分开，把重心放在脚心上。走步时要抬头挺胸，下颌微低，后背直起，臀部绷紧，脚步要踩实。上下楼时切忌哈腰、腆肚，下楼时一定要扶着扶手，看清台阶踩稳了再迈步，尤其到孕后期更要注意。坐下时要深而稳地坐在椅子上，后背伸直靠在椅背上，髋关节和膝关节呈直角状，切忌只坐在椅子边上。拾取东西要先曲膝、后弯腰，蹲好再拾，注意不要压迫肚子。避免站在小凳子上够取高处的东西、长时间蹲着做家务、双手拾重东西，或是做使腰部受压迫的家务等。

胎动次数有所增加，并更加明显。你可以试试和你腹中的宝宝做做游戏，当他（她）把你的肚皮顶起一个小鼓包时，你可以一边跟他（她）说话，一边也用手摸摸他（她），轻轻推一下，看他（她）有什么反应。经常这样做，胎儿会发现这是个有趣的游戏，会和你玩得很起劲。

孕妇胀气

由于怀孕时子宫的增大会压迫到大部分消化系统，因此消化道内会本能地产生气体与之抗衡。

减缓胀气现象发生的方法有以下几种：

1．时常让肠道保持蠕动

避免便秘可以减少胀气的产生。

2．细嚼慢咽

吃喝得很快时，很容易咽下许多气体。吞下的气体越多，已经迟缓的肠道必须应付的气体越多。因此，一定要细嚼慢咽。消化道上端加工处理得好，下端就容易发挥功能。

3．避免食（饮）用含气食物

常见的产气食品包括甘蓝菜、包心菜、花椰菜、芽甘蓝、豆类、青椒以及一些碳酸饮料，如汽水等。

4．避免食用油炸以及过于油腻的食物

含高油脂的食物由于较难消化，因此，停留在消化道的时间相对较久，从而导致胀气。

5．少食多餐

像小宝宝一样少食多餐要比一日三餐更有利于肠道的消化。大多数孕妇对每天吃五六餐感到更舒服。

头晕目眩

怀孕中期或接近中期时，你可能会觉得头晕目眩、头昏眼花，这是正常的怀孕反应。除非发生的频率越来越高，而且越来越严重。否则，不会造成什么不良的影响。

头晕目眩主要是由于脑部供血不足引起的，如孕妇的身体动作变化很大或是长时间坐着或站着保持一种姿势，都会造成脑部供血不足而引起头晕目眩感。如果你晕眩的次数十分频繁，就应该到医院进行检查，找出病因对症下药。

下面是预防和减少怀孕时发生晕眩现象的小技巧：

1．以少量多餐的方式，补充营养价值高的点心。

2．定期做产前检查。每次做产检时，别忘了测量血压、血液铁质含量是否正常。

3．避免长期保持同一站姿或坐姿。如果真的必须一直坐着，就别一直坐着不动，抬高腿部。在坐着的同时，做一些简单的腿部运动。如频繁前后或左右变换姿势；脚部尽量上下摆动；腿和脚做划圈运动；还可以分别将你的双腿交互举起、放下等。

4．进入怀孕后半期，尽量朝左侧躺着或睡觉。

5．不论从躺姿爬起来，还是从坐姿站起来，动作应该放轻放慢。

6．如果感觉到轻微头晕，最好能坐就坐，能躺就躺。躺下时，头部平躺，将腿部微微举高。

7．如果坐下之后，晕眩的现象仍然没有明显的改善，如果可能的话，最好设法找一处舒适的地方躺下。此时，头部应保持平躺，并且将腿部微微举高。

第24周

宝宝1斤重了

第24周记：我想到有本书上说，如果宝宝现在出生，她应该有机会能活下来，尽管她的肺还没有发育完全，而且身体上也没有足够保护自己的脂肪组织。她只有550克，需要靠各种现代医学手段才能生存。

我不该想这些的，这让我觉得心里不舒服。我现在几乎无法忍受在电视里或者书里看到生病的婴儿甚至医院。怀孕让我自己变得非常敏感了。

胎宝宝状况　胎宝贝长到25厘米左右，体重差不多有550克，开始充满孕妈咪的整个子宫。这时，小宝贝会用脚踢子宫，使羊水发生震荡，以引起大脑冲动从而促进皮肤发育。如果子宫收缩或受到外力压迫，胎宝贝会用力踢子宫壁，把这种信息传递给妈咪。

孕妈妈状况　你的乳房越发变大、乳腺功能发达，如果用手挤压会流出少量黏性很强的黄色乳汁。子宫进一步增大，宫高接近20厘米，子宫底已高达脐部，你自己用手就能明确的判断出子宫的位置。

要多多注意休息，休息时可将枕头、坐垫等柔软东西垫在膝窝下，避免做经常弯腰的活动或长久站立，穿柔软轻便的低跟鞋或平跟鞋，腰痛得厉害时可用热水袋热敷。睡眠时，正确的姿势是左侧卧位。注意补充铁质，多吃一些含铁、维生素C丰富的食物，以增进铁质的吸收。也可在医生指导下补充铁剂。

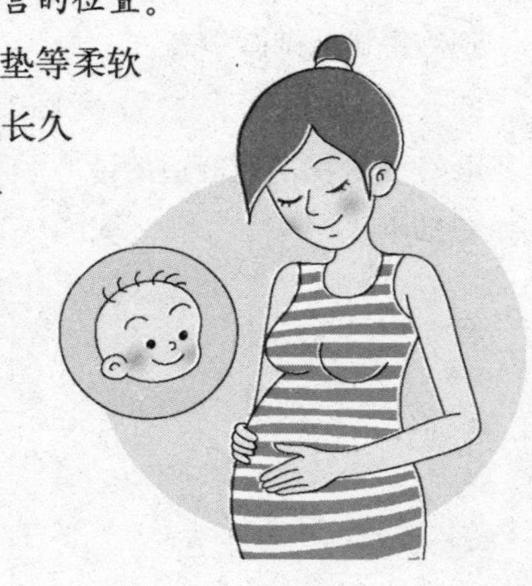

第24周，别忘了到医院做例行产检。准爸爸要协助妻子做好胎儿监测。

注意测试胎动

除了B超检查，孕妈咪是没办法通过眼睛了解生活在子宫里的宝宝的状况的，作为宝宝传达讯息的方式，胎动是孕妈咪了解胎儿健康状况的重要渠道。孕妈咪需要通过测试胎动，来了解胎宝宝的安危状态。所以，即使每天忙于工作和家庭，也要抽空温柔地触摸肚子，确认胎动情况，以防不测。

1．测试时间

怀孕第24周时可以开始。到28周后胎动更有规律，就应每天坚持。

2．测试方法

（1）方法一：计算达到某个胎动次数所需要的时间，以10次为标准。

测试开始：准妈妈早上起床后就开始测量胎动，达到10次后，就不再算了。你可以照常地上班、做家务。有些准妈妈1小时就有可能达到10次；也有可能到晚上才有10次。如果你到了晚上都没有10次胎动的话，建议去医院检查。

（2）方法二：记录每天的胎动次数。

测试开始：可以用画表格的方法进行记录。每天早上8点开始记录，每感觉到一次胎动，就在表格里做个记号，累计10次后，就不再做记录。如果到晚上8点，胎动次数都没有达到10次的话，建议你尽快去医院检查。

（3）方法三：计算固定时间内的胎动次数。

测试开始：准妈妈每天测试3小时的胎动。分别在早上、中午、晚上各进行一次。将所测得的胎动总数乘以4，作为每天12小时的胎动记录。如果每小时少于3次，则要把测量的时间延长至6或12小时。

（4）方法四：晚饭后的测量。

测试开始：准妈妈在晚饭后7～11点间，测量宝宝的胎动次数，看看出现10次胎动所需要的时间。如果超过3小时，胎动的次数达不到10次的话，就需要尽快去医院检查。

（5）方法五：累计白天的记录。

测试开始：准妈妈在整个白天，大约早上8点～晚6点间，能够有10次胎动的话，就可放心了，这是最简单的方法。

小贴士……如何把胎动数清楚？

数胎动时可以坐在椅子上，也可以躺在床上，双手轻轻放在腹部，专心体会胎儿的活动，从胎儿开始活动到停止只算一次。这样就容易数清楚胎动次数了。

异常胎动信号

准妈妈应该以24小时作为一个周期，来观察宝宝的胎动是否正常。因此，如果一天内，发现宝宝的胎动规律明显异于平时，就应该查找原因，及时到医院就诊。

1. 胎动突然减少

诊断原因：准妈妈发烧。

分析：一般来说，如果准妈妈有轻微的发烧情况，胎儿也因有羊水的缓冲作用，并不会受到太大的影响。值得注意的是引起准妈妈发烧的原因。如果是一般性的感冒而引起的发烧，对胎儿不会有太大的影响。如果是感染性的疾病或是流感，尤其对于接近预产期的准妈妈来说，对胎儿的影响就较大。准妈妈的体温如果持续过高，超过38℃的话，都会使胎盘、子宫的血流量减少，小家伙也就变得安静许多。所以，为宝宝健康着想，准妈妈需要尽快去医院，请医生帮助。

建议：

（1）怀孕期间，要注意休息，特别要避免感冒。

（2）有流行性疾病发生时，要避免去人多的地方。

（3）每天保持室内的空气流通和新鲜。

（4）多喝水、多吃新鲜的蔬菜和水果。

2. 胎动突然增加

诊断原因：准妈妈受剧烈的外伤。

分析：一般来说，胎儿在妈妈的子宫里，有羊水的保护，可减轻外力的撞击，在准妈妈不慎受到轻微的撞击时，不至于受到伤害。但一旦准妈妈受到严重的外力撞击时，就会引起胎儿剧烈的胎动，甚至造成流产、早产等情况。此外，如果准妈妈有头部外伤、骨折、大量出血等状况出现，也会造成胎动异常的情况发生。

建议：

（1）少去人多的地方，以免被撞到。

（2）减少大运动量的活动。

3. 胎动突然加剧，随后很快停止运动

诊断原因：胎盘早期剥离。

分析：这种情况多发生在怀孕的中期以后，有高血压、严重外伤或短时间子宫内压力减少准妈妈多容易出现此状况。症状有阴道出血、腹痛、子宫收缩、严重的休克。一旦出现这样的情况，胎儿也会随之作出反应：他们会因此突然的缺氧，胎动会出现短暂的剧烈运动，随后又很快停止。

建议：

（1）有高血压的孕妇，要定时去医院做检查，并依据医生的建议安排日常的生活起居。

（2）避免不必要的外力冲撞和刺激。

（3）保持良好的心态，放松心情，减轻精神紧张度。

4. 急促胎动后突然停止

诊断原因：脐带绕颈或打结。

分析：正常的脐带长度为50厘米，如果脐带过长则容易缠绕胎儿的颈部或身体。因为好动的小家伙已经可以在羊水中自由地运动，翻身打滚是常有的事情，所以一不小心就会被卡住。一旦出现脐带缠绕或是打结的情况，就会使血液无法流通，导致胎儿因缺氧而窒息的现象。有上述情况出现时，准妈妈会感觉到：胎动会出现急促的运动，经过一段时间后又突然停止，这就是宝宝发出的异常信号。

建议：

（1）一旦出现异常胎动的情况，要立即就诊，以免耽误时间造成遗憾。

（2）准妈妈要坚持每天细心观察胎动，如有不良感觉时，应马上咨询医生或去医院检查。

第25周

身体越来越沉重

第25周记：因为血液供应增加，我的心脏和肺都要承担比以前更重的负担。今天赶车的时候我稍稍加快了脚步，就不得不大口喘气。

我的孕妇特征已经非常明显了，在哪里都能得到人们的特殊待遇——比如在拥挤的车厢里给我让出一个座位。长的越来越庞大的不仅是我，还有我的宝宝，她的肌肉和脂肪组织也都在快速生长。

胎宝宝状况　胎宝贝身长大约有30厘米，体重不到600克。大脑发育进入一个高峰期，脑细胞迅速增殖分化，脑体积增大。视网膜发育完全，眼皮也会动了，小眼睛时睁时闭，这样的小动作能帮助完善睡眠的功能。舌头上的味蕾正在形成，这时小家伙能通过你尝到食品的味道了。

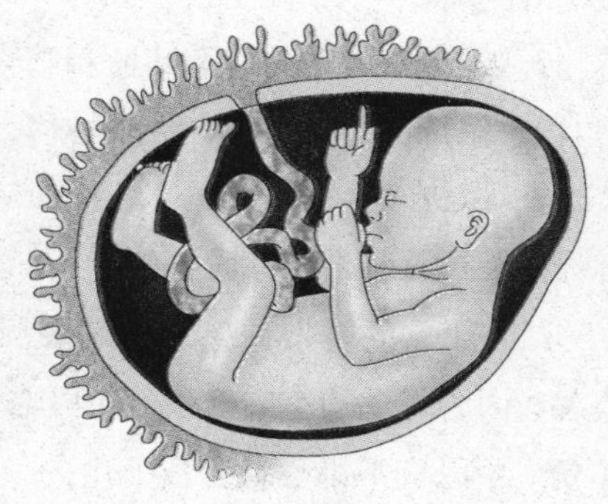

第25周（7月胎宝宝）

孕妈妈状况　身体越来越沉重，手脚也会出现酸痛。要多晒太阳，防止缺钙。因为胎儿大脑在飞速发育，你应多吃些健脑的食品，如核桃、芝麻、花生等等，但要注意适量，避免"上火"引起便秘。适当的运动能帮助你的大脑释放有益物质，通过血液进入胎宝贝体内，对大脑发育极为有利。

经常做适量下蹲运动，这种动作能加强骨盆肌肉运动，增加骨盆肌肉弹性，减少难产几率，虽然简单，却是最好的助产运动。运动一定要适度，不可过劳，严禁做剧烈活动，避免挤压和震动腰部。

孕7月专家提示（第2~28周）

1. 随着胎儿渐渐长大，母亲腹部也愈来愈大，腰背脊椎的负担也愈来愈大，走路时宜保持抬头挺胸正确姿势，坐时腰部要有支撑，时间皆不可过久。

2. 由于大腹顶住胃部，发生心口灼热感，此时进食后不要马上躺下，可采用半坐卧姿势较为舒适。

3. 若足踝或双脚浮肿厉害，可抬高双腿或穿著弹性袜改善，平时切勿久站或久坐，也不要长时间走路。

4. 穿平底鞋，以减轻腰部的负担，也降低母体重心，避免跌倒。

5. 因腹部渐大，上、下楼梯宜踏稳脚步，将身体重心放在前脚，较不易跌落。

6. 若宝宝出生用品尚未准备齐全，这个月还可安排时间选购，但要尽快完成。

7. 绝对禁止站在椅子上位于高处取物，或拿取位于高处的物品，此种姿势最容易因重心不稳而跌倒。

8. 避免腹部用力的工作，以免刺激子宫收缩，引起早产。

9. 变换姿势体位时，动作不要太迅速，以免引起晕眩而跌倒。

10. 此时期胎儿活动频繁，若产检被诊断为“胎位不正”时，可做“膝胸卧姿”改善（膝胸卧姿做法:选择一处硬又平的地面，将胸部完全紧贴地面;臀部提高，固定此姿势10~15分钟，早晚各1次，做到胎位正常为止）。

11. 口红色彩基本上不要鲜红色系，免得看起来脸型臃肿。

12. 穿宽松孕妇洋装、布料花色尽量简单。

糖筛查

满24周至孕28周之间进行糖筛查，即筛查妊娠期糖尿病，目前妊娠期糖尿病的发生率高达5~6%，此项筛查最好不要遗漏。

下肢静脉曲张

静脉曲张是怀孕期间许多不良反应之一。小腿更是特别容易产生静脉曲张，主要表现为下肢表浅静脉扩张、伸长和迂曲，像蚯蚓样伏于小腿或大腿部。最早可出现在妊娠3～4个月时，但大多数在妊娠后期发病，生完宝宝后的几个月内，都会消失。

1. 不要揉或用力按摩静脉曲张的血管，否则会引起静脉更进一步损坏，甚至会引起血栓。

2. 避免长时间站着或坐着，坐着时不要跷腿，并尽可能地把脚提高。

3. 多走动可促进血液循环。

4. 靠左侧躺着睡觉。

5. 穿着较宽松的衣物。避免穿紧身裤、束腰带、吊袜带、半统袜及任何会妨碍你血液循环的衣物。

6. 早上起床前，穿上护腿长袜。但不要穿高过膝盖的长袜，因为袜子上端的松紧带，会阻碍血液回流。

7. 摄取足量的维生素C。维生素C可以保持静脉的健康与弹性。

贴心·提醒

如果小腿下半部出现可以看见血管的地方，已经逐渐疼痛、红肿、发热或触痛，静脉可能已经感染了，这是一种可能导致血栓的"血栓性静脉炎"，最好到医院治疗。

第26周

宝宝1斤半了

第26周记：我的肚子现在看起来像是被塞进了一个足球。肚脐都有些凸出了——那是因为子宫在里面顶着它。

宝宝的眼睛已经可以睁开了，我希望她的眼睛能像老公那样迷人。她的耳朵应该也形成了，我希望耳朵像我——老公的耳朵我不喜欢，一对大大的招风耳了。

胎宝宝状况　小宝贝身长不到35厘米，坐高约为22厘米，体重800克左右。眼睛、嘴唇、鼻孔慢慢形成。这个时候胎儿的大脑对触摸反应很敏感，视觉神经的功能已经在起作用了，关节也渐渐灵活。

孕妈妈状况　日常饮食要注意保证优质足量的蛋白质，每天的摄入量要比孕早期多，且动物蛋白质应占全部蛋白质的一半以上。适当增加植物油的摄入量，也可以适当食些花生仁、核桃仁、芝麻等含必需脂肪酸含量较高的食物。

有的孕妇此时开始出现下肢水肿，预防的办法是：不要长时间站立或行走，休息或睡觉时要把脚垫高。

妊娠水肿

90%以上的女性在怀孕期间脚踝和腿部会出现肿胀现象，如果经过检查无子痫前症的症状，便可视为正常现象，不算什么疾病。这种现象一般在怀孕后期会好转。

1. 正常的水肿

(1) 在一天的不同时间，身体水肿的部位也不同（这就叫做“重力性水肿”)。如果你抬高足部1小时，腿部和脚踝的水肿就会减轻。

(2) 体重增加情况正常。如果体重没有原因的突然增加，表示可能有问题发生。

(3) 血压在正常范围内。

(4) 产检时的尿液检查没有尿蛋白。

2. 不正常的水肿

(1) 腿部过度肿胀：用手指按压肿胀部分，会遗留下明显的凹陷（称为“凹陷性水肿”)，这类的肿胀就算你把脚抬高1个小时，也不会消失。

(2) 体重增加太多、太快。

(3) 血压过高。

(4) 饮食不正常。

(5) 尿液检验显示有过多的尿蛋白。

(6) 常觉得不舒服或宝宝的成长不正常。

3. 减轻水肿的办法

(1) 避免长时间坐着或站立。

(2) 忙完一天回家休息时，将水肿的双腿大约抬高1小时。

(3) 坐在摇椅上放松身体，同时把双脚靠在小板凳上。

(4) 走路、游泳是促进手臂和腿部血液循环的绝佳运动。

(5) 避免仰躺睡姿。

(6) 穿着宽松衣物，避免有松紧带的长裤、袜子或其他衣物。

(7) 白天用小板凳把双脚垫高，夜间则用枕头。

(8) 坐着的时候可以抬高双手。

(9) 每天至少喝8大杯水（每杯250毫升)。留意尿液颜色，来决定每天是否摄取了足够的水分。如果你的尿液是无色或淡黄色，表示摄取的水分足够，如果尿液颜色比较深，像是苹果汁的颜色，表示你可能有脱水的现象。

日常饮食中，少食，忌食生冷、油腻食物；适当多吃些温阳的食物，如米、面、豆类、瘦肉、动物肝脏、鸡、鸭等。每次产检时，医生都会检查水肿的程度。因此，如果担心自己体内的水分含量不正常，可以咨询医生。若肿胀越来越重，伴头晕等不适，应及时到医院诊治。

营养菜单——水肿食疗

1. 番茄肉片煸扁豆

原料:番茄150克，扁豆100克，瘦猪肉50克，精盐10克。花生油10克，酱油15克。

制作:将番茄洗净，去皮去籽，切成块;猪肉洗净，切成片;扁豆收拾好，洗净，切成小段。锅置火上，放入油，油烧热，放入肉丝煸炒，然后放人扁豆，一同快炒，焖软，在快软时放人番茄、盐、酱油一同炒匀即成。此菜富含维生素 B_1、铁等多种营养物质。

扁豆有健脾化湿、利尿消肿作用。西红柿还有降压作用。此菜适于孕妇食用，以利消肿降压。

2. 白萝卜豆腐脑

原料:白萝卜、嫩豆腐各250克，香油、精盐、淀粉各适量。

制作:把豆腐放入沸水锅内烫片刻，捞出，切成薄片，待用。将白萝卜去外皮，洗净，切成细丝，沾上干淀粉后。放入温油锅里煸炒，加水煮至酥软，轻放入豆腐片，点入精盐调味，煮沸，着薄芡，淋上香油即成。

此菜能顺气化痰，消食利尿，主治妊娠水肿、消化不良、大便干结、咳嗽气喘等病症。

3. 花生红糖羹

原料:花生米250克，红糖、糯米粉各150克。

制作:将花生仁连衣冲洗净，待用。净锅置于火上，加清水适量，旺火煮沸，放入花生米，改用小火煮至酥烂，再用糯米粉加少许清水勾芡，以红糖调味，即成。

此羹营养丰富，常食对孕妇大有裨益。有理血利水的作用，主治孕妇妊娠水肿。

4. 赤小豆粥

原料:赤小豆、粳米、白糖各100克。

制作：将赤小豆拣去杂质，淘洗干净，用清水浸泡过夜后捞出，待用。把粳米淘洗干净，直接放入煮锅内。加入赤小豆、适量清水，先用旺火煮沸，再用文火煮至豆、米熟透。以白糖调味，稍煮片刻，即成。此粥有利于消肿、健脾养肝、益气固肾，适用于孕妇妊娠水肿、脚气浮肿、胃炎水肿等。健康人常食能减肥，并治疗肥胖病。

腿部抽筋

怀孕中期后，许多孕妇半夜会被小腿或脚抽筋给弄醒。

1. 预防抽筋

（1）整天穿长袜。避免长时间站立或坐着。

（2）上床前，运动小腿肌肉：把脚趾朝小腿的方向往上拉，将足跟往前推，这样能伸展最有可能抽筋的小腿肌肉。下述的抽筋舒缓活动亦是很好的预防方法，左右各做10次左右。

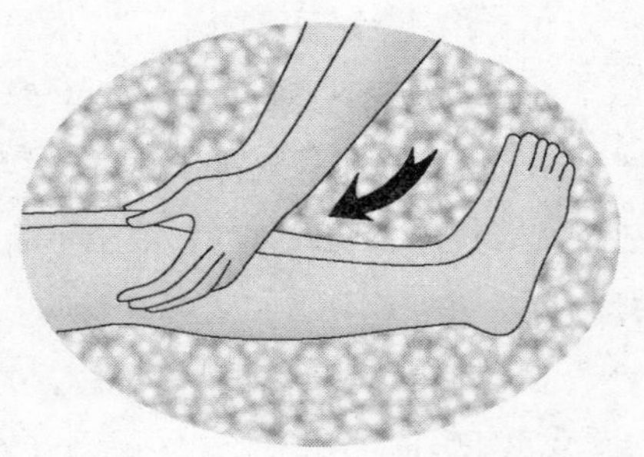

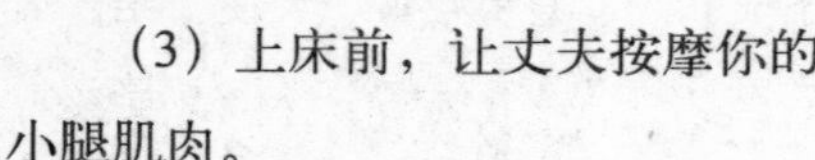

（3）上床前，让丈夫按摩你的小腿肌肉。

（4）睡眠时将腿放在枕头上。

（5）采用左侧睡姿。

2. 缓解抽筋

（1）抽筋时，按摩抽筋的肌肉或要你的丈夫磨擦它，以促进循环。

（2）抽筋时，起床活动，走一走或者站着或以靠着墙壁的姿势，做下列的伸展运动。

（3）如果抽筋很严重，则可以躺在床上，抓住疼痛的那一只腿的脚趾，保持膝盖伸直并尽可能地贴近床，按住它们朝你的头部方向慢慢拉。

如果你水桶般的肚子使你无法弯向前去抓到脚趾，那么可以伸直你的腿，压住你膝盖使其贴近床并且将你的脚趾弯向你的头。

3. 预防、舒缓抽筋的措施

腿抽筋时，以下的运动可以帮你舒缓该现象；如果坚持做这些运动，还可预防抽筋。

(1) 保持小腿伸展。把抽筋的那条腿放在另一条腿后。保持背部挺直，将未抽筋的那一侧，慢慢地屈膝，如此可以在保持抽筋那条腿伸直及足踏到地板时身体往前倾斜（前脚脚跟也要放在地板上），并缓一缓地伸展。

(2) 坐着让腿伸直。坐在地板上，把一只腿伸向一边，足部弯曲。把另一只腿折进来，足部伸向胯部。保持外伸的腿挺直，并弯身向前去拉脚趾头。保持这样伸展的姿态几秒钟，然后换另一侧并重复以上的动作。不要把脚趾头朝前、脚跟朝向你，因为这样会使已痉挛的肌肉产生收缩。

贴心·提醒

出现腿部抽筋时，该试着补充钙质。如果严重最好到医院检查后进行必要的治疗。

第27周

胎动像波浪一样

第27周记： 洗澡的时候，看着大大的肚子，有时表面会像波浪一样地动起来。老公也看见了，惊讶不小。睡觉的时候，我蜷着将身体贴在老公身后，他的宝贝女儿冷不防狠狠地一踢，正踢着他的腰了。这下子让他们父女俩切切实实地交流了一回，也使老公真实地感觉到这个女儿的存在——以前，对这个没有切身体验的父亲来说，宝宝好像只是看不见的微风。

胎宝宝状况 胎宝贝身长约38厘米，坐高约25厘米，体重900克左右。很多胎宝贝都已经长出了头发，眼睛也能睁开了。大脑活动在这一周非常活跃，很多专家认为从这周开始，小宝贝开始会做梦了，但是我们还不知道小家伙到底梦见了些什么。

孕妈妈状况 你的子宫接近了肋缘，这会让你们觉得气短，这是正常现象。饮食中，米、面、杂粮要互相搭配，保证孕妈咪摄入足够的营养。多吃海水鱼、奶类、奶制品、豆制品、动物肝脏及蛋黄等富含维生素D的食物。同时，注意吃些海带、紫菜，达到补碘的目的。

小宝贝的胎动有时会让你吃惊，你的腹部可能会像波浪一样地动起来。从现在开始，你最好有计划地学习一些关于分娩的知识、看些关于分娩的录像，或是参加孕妇学习班学习分娩课程。这样做有助于你更加了解自己、了解分娩，减轻产前的精神负担。

呼吸短促

怀孕期间，因为“一人呼两人吸”，因此，许多孕妇时常会觉得上气不接下气。这并不表示你或宝宝体内缺氧，只不过是表示你的肺没有足够的空

间扩张。到了怀孕后期，喘不过气来的频率和强度会增加，这是因为子宫膨大限制了肺部每次呼吸时的扩张能力。为了弥补下方被挤掉的呼吸空间，怀孕激素会刺激你多呼吸，这样才能确保你和宝宝都获得足够的氧气。

下面这些方式可以增加呼吸的效率和容量，同时能解决怀孕后期上气不接下气的问题：

1．觉得喘不过气来，马上改变姿势。

2．发现自己上气不接下气，就把动作放慢。

3．试试呼吸运动：站起来，深深地吸一口气，同时把手臂向外侧举和向上举。慢慢呼气，同时把手臂放回到身体两侧。配合呼吸，头部向上抬再向下看。

4．经常运动。怀孕早期即开始进行有氧运动，可以增加呼吸和循环系统运作的效率。

5．尝试各种坐姿或躺姿，找出有助于你呼吸顺畅的姿势。用正确的姿势坐在直椅子上（挺胸、肩膀向后）比起瘫软在躺椅上，肺部会轻松一些。采用半躺姿势入睡，可以靠躺在枕头上。或者采用侧睡姿势，并且在头下面多垫一个枕头来抬高头部。

如果突发严重的呼吸不顺畅情形，同时伴随胸部疼痛、呼吸快速、脉搏加快或深呼吸时胸部剧烈疼痛等，应迅速就医。

皮肤瘙痒

少数孕妇在妊娠期间，尤其在妊娠早期和晚期，会出现部分或全身性皮肤瘙痒。瘙痒感有轻有重，轻者不影响生活和休息，只是皮肤有痒痒，一般不被重视；严重者痒得人坐卧不安，难以忍受。

瘙痒有阵发性和持续性的，无论哪一种，都与精神因素有关。白天工作、学习紧张时，瘙痒可以减轻或不痒；夜深人静时，瘙痒往往加重，甚至越抓越痒，严重影响睡眠。妊娠期皮肤瘙痒，有的短期内会自行消失，有的一直持续到妊娠终止，分娩后很快会消失。这是妊娠期间特有的症状，所以称为妊娠瘙痒症。

孕妇有了皮肤瘙痒后怎么办呢？

1．用炉甘石洗剂，或用5%～20%黑豆馏油，或用10%～20%中药蛇床子溶液，或用75%酒精涂擦局部止痒。

2．尽量避免用手去搔抓痒处，以防抓破皮肤后引起细菌感染。

3．忌用肥皂水擦洗，防止不良因素刺激。平时孕妇的饮食宜清淡，多食新鲜蔬菜、水果，少吃刺激性食品。居室内保持一定的湿度，防止皮肤干燥，对预防皮肤瘙痒是有好处的。

4．在医生指导下适当用些镇静药和抗过敏药，局部瘙痒可外涂樟脑霜、樟酚酊、樟脑扑粉或肤轻松、地塞米松等药物。全身瘙痒可适当选用镇静剂或脱敏剂，如口服舒乐安定片，每日2～3次，每次1毫克；扑尔敏片，每日3次，每次4毫克等。如果加服B族维生素和维生素C以及静脉注射葡萄糖酸钙，疗效更佳。用药必须在医生指导下进行，自己千万不要滥用外用药和内服药。

第28周

孕程已过三分之二

第28周记：宝宝的身上现在覆盖着一层皮脂。书上指出，这层厚厚的蜡一样的东西能在她游动的水世界里保护她，而且还能防止她被脐带缠住。

医院的大夫说，宝宝现在已经能听到我的声音了，而且出生后还能记得我的声音。我想当我唱歌时，没准宝宝会盘算着弄两个耳塞戴上。我对自己的歌声实在没什么自信。

胎宝宝状况 胎宝贝身长约40厘米，坐高约26厘米，体重1100克左右。大脑已相当发达，可以逐渐控制自己的身体了。已形成自己的睡眠周期。小男孩的阴囊明显，睾丸已开始由腹部往阴囊下降；女孩的小阴唇、阴核渐渐突起。大脑皮层已变得发达，大脑发育进入第二个高峰期，已经建立起来的脑神经细胞可传导脑神经细胞的兴奋冲动。包裹胎宝贝的胎膜内羊水量与他们的身体相比，已达到妊娠最高峰。胎位不能完全固定，可能出现胎位不正。内耳与大脑发生联系的神经通路已接通，对声音的分辨能力大为提高。胎宝贝的动作可能比较频繁，常常活动筋骨或是干脆翻个身。

孕妈妈状况 孕妇由于身体新陈代谢消耗氧气量加大，活动后容易气喘吁吁。腹部向前挺得更为厉害，所以身体重心移到腹部下方，只要身体稍微失去平衡，就会感到腰酸背痛或腿痛。心脏负担也在逐渐加重，血压开始增高，静脉曲张、痔疮、便秘这些麻烦，接踵而至地烦扰着孕妈咪。

到本周，你进入了孕后期。你的血压这时期开始升高，要开始注意妊娠高血压综合征了。不要做过重的工作和家务，避免激烈运动，每天一定要保证8小时以上的充足睡眠和安静的休息，最好还有午休。情绪要稳定。少吃咸食，不要过多摄入动物性脂肪及碳水化合物，以免体重增长过快。

第28周，别忘了做例行产检。同时，建议你做葡萄糖耐受试验。

孕后期睡眠问题

怀孕后期，孕妇大多都存在睡不安稳的问题，其主要原因有三个：一是子宫变大，向上压迫到胃而引起胃灼热，向下压迫到膀胱，使孕妇夜间频繁地上厕所；二是睡眠周期改变，这一时期做梦较多，较易出现苏醒状态；三是小宝宝在肚子里敲敲撞撞，让孕妇不得不醒来。

休息不好会让孕妇很疲倦，影响以后的分娩和育儿，下面是一些争取更多睡眠的小技巧：

1．白天多找机会小憩片刻。

2．早点上床睡觉。

3．如果腿部抽筋使人半夜惊醒，你可以试试睡前按摩。

4．如果消化不良或呼吸短使你无法入睡，试试用枕头微微抬高上半身的姿势入睡。

5．如果因为不舒服而半夜醒来，就立刻变换睡姿，尤其是因子宫肌肉拉扯而造成的骨盆疼痛，或子宫压迫骨盆神经所引起的不适时更应如此。

6．倾听放松身心的音乐听些能使你进入梦乡的歌曲。芭蕾和古典音乐都有缓慢升降的高潮和低潮，催眠作用很好；主题略显单调并有多次重复的乐曲也一样。你还可以试试听些声音单调重复播放大自然中声音的音乐，如潺潺的小溪流水声，或是海浪拍打岸边的声音。

贴心·提醒

白天适度地增加运动可以帮助睡眠，但不要在睡前一个小时内做剧烈运动。

妊娠高血压综合征

简称妊高征，是妊娠期妇女所特有而又常见的疾病，以高血压、水肿、蛋白尿、抽搐、昏迷、心肾功能衰竭，甚至发生母子死亡为临床特点。妊娠高血压综合征按严重程度分为轻度、中度和重度，重度妊娠高血压综合征又称先兆子痫和子痫，子痫即在高血压基础上有抽搐。

发病时间一般是在妊娠20周以后，尤其在妊娠32周以后最为多见。冬春寒冷季节和气压升高的条件下，易于诱发。

1.易患妊高征人群

(1)年轻初产妇及高龄初产妇。

(2)体型矮胖者。

(3)营养不良，特别是伴有严重贫血者。

(4)患有原发性高血压、慢性肾炎、糖尿病合并妊娠者，其发病率较高，病情可能更为复杂。

(5)双胎、羊水过多及葡萄胎的孕妇，发病率亦较高。

(6)有家族史，如孕妇的母亲有妊高征病史者，孕妇发病的可能性较高。

2.对母体和胎儿的影响

(1)对母体的影响：妊娠高血压综合征易引起胎盘早期剥离、心力衰竭、凝血功能障碍、脑出血、肾功能衰竭及产后血液循环障碍等。而脑出血、心力衰竭及弥散性血管内凝血为妊娠高血压综合征患者死亡的主要原因。

(2)对胎儿的影响：重度妊娠高血压综合征是早产、宫内胎儿死亡、死产、新生儿窒息和死亡的主要原因。孕妇病情愈重，对胎儿的不良影响亦愈大。

3.如何预防妊高征

(1)实行产前检查，做好孕期保健工作。妊娠早期应测量1次血压，作为孕期的基础血压，以后定期检查，尤其是在妊娠36周以后，应每周观察血压及体重的变化、有无蛋白尿及头晕等自觉症状。

(2)加强孕期营养及休息。加强妊娠中、晚期营养，尤其是蛋白质、多种维生素、叶酸、铁剂的补充，对预防妊娠高血压综合征有一定作用。因为母体营养缺乏、低蛋白血症或严重贫血者，其妊高征发生率增高。

(3)重视诱发因素，治疗原发病。仔细想一想家族史，孕妇的外祖母、母亲或姊妹间是否曾经患妊高征，如果有这种情况，就要考虑遗传因素了。孕妇如果孕前患过原发性高血压、慢性肾炎及糖尿病等均易发生妊高征。妊娠如果发生在寒冷的冬天，更应加强产前检查，及早处理。

第29周

进入孕后期

第29周记：昨天晚上老公带我去看焰火。烟花在空中炸响的声音让可怜的宝宝几乎蹦起来。她对声音真的已经很敏感了。

近来，我又开始感觉到疲劳了。我想这是因为我已经进入孕期的最后阶段了吧。

胎宝宝状况 胎宝贝坐高27厘米左右，身长大约43厘米，体重已经有1300多克。这一周小家伙有个十分可爱的小动作不会被你查觉，那就是“微笑”。

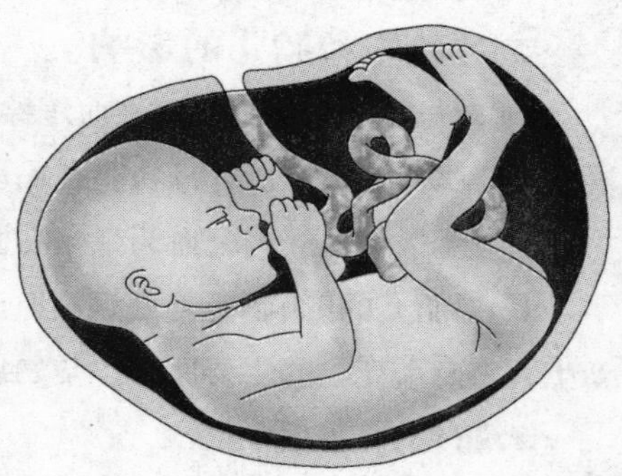

第29周（8月胎宝宝）

孕妈妈状况 孕妈妈肚子里的胎儿营养需求达到最高峰，这时的孕妈妈需要摄入大量蛋白质、维生素C、叶酸、B族维生素、铁质和钙质。可多喝牛奶，每天最好喝两杯(500毫升)。不爱喝牛奶的孕妇也可以喝豆浆，多吃豆腐、海带和紫菜，这些食物中钙的含量也很高，特别是海带和紫菜中还含有丰富的碘，有利于胎儿发育。缺钙比较严重的孕妇要根据医生的建议补充钙剂。

还在给你的胎儿讲故事、说童谣或听音乐吗？你觉得他(她)是不是有反应呢？你可以继续坚持下去。或许这会使你的宝宝出生后，比那些没有受到这种训练的宝宝更好带呢。你也可以让你的丈夫抚摸着你的肚子，和胎儿说说话，让未来的宝宝也熟悉一下爸爸的声音。

你现在可以为即将出生的宝宝缝制一些小衣服、小被子，或者想一想该给宝宝起个什么名字了。

孕8月专家提示（第29～32周）

1. 远游或长时间外出，一定要交代家人行踪，以策安全。

2. 提取重物宜将身体重心放在双腿上，切勿直接弯腰取物。

3. 平衡膳食，注意营养素的补充。

4. 只可做轻松的家务事，大扫除、清洗浴厕，请家人代劳。

5. 认识生产前征兆，避免过度劳累，万一发生早产情形，态度宜冷静沉着赶快就医诊治。

6. 睡眠姿势避免仰卧位，提倡左侧卧位。

7. 减少出入公共场合，人多或过度拥挤的地方要少去，不但可减少感染机率，也可避免母亲因情绪过度激动或受惊吓紧张而早产。

8. 注意皮肤泛油光，随时使用吸油纸擦拭。

9. 剪个线条利落的短发，并更注意清洁。

10. 可穿孕妇装，但长度不可太短，最好及膝或超过膝盖。

孕后期饮食指导（第8～10月）

孕后期，胎儿的生长速度进一步加快，尤其是细胞体积增加迅速；大脑发育加快；肺部进一步发育以适应出生后能进行呼吸和血氧的交换功能；皮下脂肪大量储存。另外，胎儿还需为自己出生后储备一定量的钙和铁等营养素。

1. 膳食结构

此期孕妈咪不仅需要增加热量的供给，更应注意优质蛋白质、铁、钙和维生素等营养素的补充。由于子宫快速增大压迫胃部，使孕妈咪的食量减少，所以宜采取少食多餐制，每日可增至5餐以上。

在孕中期膳食组成的基础上再增加50克禽、鱼和蛋，220克毫升牛奶或豆浆等。每天钙的需要量为1200毫克，有水肿的孕妈咪应限制食盐每日在5克以下。

饮食原则是食物品种多样，营养更为丰富。

2. 孕妇饮食要求

(1) 饮食中应以蛋白质和碳水化合物为主，除食入主食米、面和含蛋白质丰富的奶类、蛋、肉、鱼类等食物外，还要注意多食入动物肝脏、猪血、海产品、骨头汤、豆制品、新鲜蔬菜、胡萝卜、水果等含钙、铁、磷等微量元素及维生素的食物。

(2) 在妊娠的最后两个月，胎儿对铁质的需求量相对较多。可适当多吃富含铁的食物如肝、肾、红枣、桃干、杏干、菠菜等。

(3) 海带是矿物质营养素的大宝库，海带和紫菜中钙的含量很高，是一般蔬菜的10倍，此外还含有大量的碘，对孕妇和胎儿十分有益。所以，孕妇在最后两个月里，应尽量多食用海带和紫菜等海产品，既补充了营养，又不易增加体重。

(4) 注意适当晒太阳，以促进维生素D的合成，利于钙、磷的吸收及胎儿骨骼的生长发育。

(5) 妊娠后期，往往出现便秘，孕妇除了多吃些油菜、芹菜等含纤维多的蔬菜外，还要多吃些生津清热的水果、蔬菜，如苹果、香蕉、葡萄、西红柿、茄子等。

3. 勿乱补，控制体重

孕后期勿需大量进补，孕妇的过度肥胖和巨大儿的发生对母子双方健康都不利。孕妇在怀孕期的体重增加平均12.5千克为正常，不要超过15千克。

孕期能量和某些营养素的过剩，会对孕妇及胎儿产生不利的影响。孕期营养过剩，尤其是能量及脂肪摄入过多，则可能导致胎儿巨大和孕妇肥胖，增加难产机会。

如果出现超重或体重增加过多，应在医生指导下根据情况调节饮食方案，适当减少动物脂肪与碳水化合物的摄入量。

营养菜单——孕后期

1. 红烧海参

材料：发好海参500克，瘦肉200克，白菜300克，姜2片，葱2棵，红萝卜花数片。

煨海参料:盐、糖各半茶匙，生抽、酒各1茶匙，上汤1杯。

调味料:生抽、生粉各半茶匙，油半汤匙。

芡汁料:蚝油、生粉各1茶匙，麻油、胡椒粉各少许，清水3汤匙。

做法:

(1) 海参放入姜、葱、开水内煮5分钟，除去内脏洗净，滴干切件。

(2) 瘦肉切丝，加入调味料拌匀待用。

(3) 白菜洗净，以油、盐、水炒熟围于碟边。

(4) 烧热锅，下油两汤匙爆香姜、葱，加入煨料及海参煮至海参软烂，放入瘦肉，芡汁料兜匀上碟即成。

功效:海参的营养价值极高，含丰富的蛋白质、钙和碘，是滋补食品。具有补血调经的菌用，更有安胎及利于生产的功能，最适宜怀孕后期食用。

2. 核桃明珠

材料:去衣核桃肉150克，中虾400克，芦笋粒3汤匙，红萝卜粒2汤匙，蒜茸半茶匙，酒1茶匙。

调味料:盐、糖、生粉1/4茶匙，蛋白、油各1汤匙，麻油、胡椒粉少许。

芡汁料:蚝油1茶匙，生粉半茶匙，盐、糖1/4茶匙，麻油数滴，清水2汤匙。

做法:

(1) 核桃肉放入开水中煮3分钟，取出滴干，入暖油中炸至微黄色盛起。

(2) 虾去壳，切双飞去肠，用盐擦洗干净，冲水吸干水分，加入调味料拌匀，泡嫩油盛起。

(3) 烧热锅，下油一汤匙爆香蒜茸，加入芦笋、红萝卜略炒，放入虾，加酒，下芡汁料及核桃肉，兜匀上碟即成。

功效:核桃是滋养食品，有补血的功效，常吃能使皮肤光滑。虾含有大量蛋白质，可算是养生佳品，配合含丰富纤维的芦笋，最适宜怀孕后期食用。

3. 西芹鸡柳

材料:西芹、鸡肉各300克，红萝卜、姜花各数片，蒜肉（切片）2粒，酒1茶匙。

腌料:盐1/4茶匙，蛋白半只，生粉1茶匙，麻油、胡椒粉各少许，油1汤匙。

芡汁料：盐、糖各1/4茶匙，生抽1茶匙，生粉半茶匙，麻油、胡椒粉各少许，清水2汤匙。

做法：

（1）鸡肉切条，加入腌料拌匀，腌15分钟，泡嫩油待用。

（2）西芹去筋切条，以油、盐略炒盛起。

（3）烧热锅，下油1汤匙爆香姜片、蒜片、红萝卜，加入鸡柳，加酒，放入西芹及欠汁料兜匀上碟即成。

功效：怀孕后期常有便秘现象发生，应大量摄取纤维质含量丰富的蔬菜，如西芹、芦笋，更含有大量维生素，并有辅疗黄疸病和高血压的功效。

4. 营养牛骨汤

材料：牛骨1000克，红萝卜500克，番茄、椰菜各200克，洋葱1个，黑胡椒5粒。

调味料：盐适量。

做法：

（1）牛骨斩大件(买时斩好)，洗净，放入开水中煮5分钟。取出冲净。

（2）红萝卜去皮切大件，番茄切成4件，椰菜切大块，洋葱去衣切块。

（3）烧热锅，下油1汤匙，慢火炒香洋葱，注入适量水煮开，加入各材料煮3小时，下盐调味即成。

功效：牛骨含丰富钙质，对孕妇及胎儿都有益，孕后期是胎儿骨骼形成的时候，特别需要钙质，因此应常饮用牛骨汤。

5. 鲜番茄炒蛋

材料：鲜番茄200克，鸡蛋2只，食油25克，盐3克，料酒10克，高汤50克。

做法：

(1)番茄用开水泡一下，去皮，用刀切开，净籽，再切成丁，放在碗内待用。

（2）将鸡蛋打入碗中，用筷子搅匀，再下盐1.5克和料酒搅匀。

（3）锅烧热，放入油，即把番茄投入锅内，炒2分钟，加盐2克炒和，随即把蛋倒

卓越亚马逊发货单

订购日期：2011-04-21
发货库房：武汉库房
发货单号：Dt7MzW0QR
订单号：C01-9415970-4948851
是否已开发票：否
收货人姓名：王爱珍
国家：中国，省：河南，市：郑州市
区：金水区，邮编：450002
地址:郑州市金水区东风路4号院

序号	商品名称	货位号	单价(元)	数量	金额(元)
1	孕产禁忌专家忠告 B0036FU6FK	A-3	¥13.40	1	¥13.40
2	怀孕40周完美方案(升级畅销版) B0036FU6FU	A-3	¥13.40	1	¥13.40
3	胎教每天一页(畅销全彩版) B004F9PR50	A-3	¥15.30	1	¥15.30
小计				3	¥42.10

配送费(元)：¥5.00　　促销折扣(元)：-¥5.00　　订单总额(元)：¥42.10
礼品卡支付(元)：¥0.00　　已付款(元)：¥0.00　　应付款(元)：¥42.10

非常感谢您在卓越亚马逊 (http://www.amazon.cn) 购物，我们期待您的再次光临!
如果您想了解我们的商品验收、退换货等政策及流程，请访问卓越亚马逊帮助中心 (http://www.amazon.cn/gp/help/customer/display.html).
卓越亚马逊客服中心联系方式：点击网站首页右上边“帮助”--“帮助”页面右侧点击“联系我们”。

7/Dt7MzW0QR/-3 of 3-//MM/std-cn-d2d-mpos-avail/3693354/0422-19:00/0422-08:18/juanta 包装类型：BAG

入翻炒再加汤烧1分钟即成。

6. 蘑菇蛋卷

材料：鸡蛋3只，蘑菇20克，植物油25克，牛奶25克，精盐少许。

做法：将鸡蛋打入碗中搅散，放入牛奶和盐调匀，蘑菇洗净后切成薄片。炒锅置旺火上，下油烧热，放入蘑菇煸炒几下，再放入鸡蛋液，制成饼，折成卷，煎至呈深黄色时，出锅装盘。

7. 奶油扒白菜

材料：净白菜200克，细盐4克，牛奶75克，葱末25克，水团粉25克，料酒15克，高汤75克，大油60克。

做法：

(1) 将白菜头顺切1厘米宽、12厘米长的条。

(2) 先用开水将白菜煮烂，用漏勺控出，过入凉水中，将白菜条用手理顺，放在平盘中，挤去水分。

(3) 坐锅，打大油40克，葱末炝勺（葱不要炸老），加料酒，打高汤，加细盐，将白菜下勺，见旺火，焙至汤汁少许，用牛奶将水团粉和好，勾芡，打大油（20克），翻炒出锅。

8. 虾米烧菜心

材料：青菜1000克，笋30克，虾米10克，植物油35克，料酒0．5克，精盐5克，汤250克。

做法：

(1) 青菜去老叶，去菜根后，切7厘米长的段，切取菜心600克，洗干净。笋切成5厘米长、2厘米宽、0．4厘米的厚片。虾米用水25克浸透。

(2) 旺火烧锅，放进植物油，烧到六成热时，把菜心倒入锅。

(3) 菜心翻炒15秒钟，然后加入笋片、虾米和精盐，再炒15秒钟，放入料酒和汤。

(4) 把锅移到中火上烧约10分钟左右，等菜熟烂，翻个身出锅即成。

9. 黄瓜炒子虾

材料：子虾150克，黄瓜125克，白糖10克，精盐2克，酱油30克，熟猪油45克，料酒5克。

做法：将虾用水洗一下，剪去须和脚，黄瓜洗净切成3厘米长、0．2厘米厚的片。炒锅内放入猪油，用旺火烧锅，等油冒烟时放入虾翻炒两下，加入黄瓜片，料酒、糖、酱油、盐，再翻炒两下，加水45克，烧开，再翻炒几下即成。

预防早产

大多数早产的原因是无法控制的，如子宫颈闭锁不全、胎盘异常等。就算是没有危险因素的妈妈，也可能发生不明原因的早产，不过这类早产通常可以预防。

要预防早产，下面是一些值得你注意的事：

1．进行良好的产前检查。

2．不要抽烟，最好在怀孕前就戒掉。

3．尽可能不要饮用含酒精的饮料。

4．注重营养均衡的饮食，维持适当的体重增加。

5．避免服用禁药，非经医生许可，不要自行服用成药。

6．避免怀孕期间仍处在长期的精神压力之下。

贴心·提醒

一旦出现下列早产征兆，立即去医院就医：

1．羊膜破裂：指的是羊水从阴道滴出或冲出。

2．腹部紧缩感。

3．腰骶部酸痛。

第30周

宝宝3斤重了

第30周记：噢，这个小丫头太活泼了，小手小膝盖到处乱伸。躺在椅子上的时候，我把一杯橙汁放在肚子上，居然被她撞倒了，洒了我一身。

她已经约40厘米长了，体重也在不断增加——这点倒是和我一模一样。我不再坐地铁或者公交车了。老公负责开车接送我，不过每次系安全带都成了件麻烦的事。

胎宝宝状况　胎宝贝身长约44厘米，体重在1500克左右。头部还在增大，大脑发育非常迅速，大脑和神经系统已发达到了一定程度，一旦遇到强烈的声音刺激和震动，胎宝贝就会大惊失色，做出非常惊谔的样子，张开双臂好像要抓住什么。大多数胎宝贝此时对声音都有了反应，眼睛也可以自由开闭、能辨认和跟踪光源。小宝贝的头部逐步下降，进入骨盆。

孕妈妈状况　子宫已上升到横膈，孕妇会感到呼吸困难，喘不上气来，吃饭后胃部不适等。随着小家伙的脑袋逐步降入骨盆，不舒适的感觉会逐渐减轻。

孕后期胎宝贝在子宫内的正常姿势应该是头部朝下臀部朝上，以使分娩时头部先娩出。本周要注意的首要问题就是“胎位”，如胎位不正常，就要在医生指导下进行自我矫正。到了孕后期，白带会越来越多，护理不恰当就可能引起外阴炎和阴道炎。日常生活中要注意保持外阴清洁卫生。

第30周，别忘了到医院做例行产检。

胎位矫正

胎位，是指胎儿在子宫内的位置与骨盆的关系。正常的胎位应该是胎头俯曲，枕骨在前，分娩时头部最先伸骨盆，医学上称之为“头先露”，这种胎位分娩一般比较顺利。除此之外的其他胎位，就是属于胎位不正了，包括臀位、横位及复合先露等。

通常，在孕7个月前发现的胎位不正，只要加强观察即可。因为在妊娠30周前，胎儿相对子宫来说还小，而且母亲宫内羊水较多，胎儿有活动的余地，会自行纠正胎位。

若在妊娠30～34周还是胎位不正时，就需要纠正了。

可以自行在家进行的矫正方法：

膝胸卧位操：孕妈妈排空尿，松解腰带，在硬板上俯撑，膝部要尽量接近床面。每天早晚各1次，每次做15分钟，连续做1周。然后去医院复查。

做这种姿势可使胎臀退出盆腔，借助胎儿重心改变，使胎头与胎背所形成的弧形顺着宫底弧面滑动而完成胎位矫正。

注意活动姿势

到了怀孕后期，孕妇的行走、睡眠等等日常活动都会受到宝宝的影响，为了保证孩子的健康成长和维护孕妇自身的健康，怀孕以后应当注意保持正确活动姿势。

1．下楼时要握住扶手，防止身体的前倾、跌倒。上楼时拉住楼梯的扶手，可以借助手臂的力量来减轻腿部的负担。

2．平时行走时，应该抬头、挺直后背、伸直脖子、收紧臀部，保持全身平衡，稳步行走。

3．坐下时，最好选择用直背坐椅（不要坐低矮的沙发），先保持背部的挺直，用腿部肌肉的力量支持身体坐下，使背部和臀部能舒适地靠在椅背上，双脚平放在地上。

4．起立时，要先将上身向前移到椅子的前沿，然后双手撑在桌面上，并用腿部肌肉支撑、抬起身体，使背部始终保持挺直，以免身体向前倾斜，牵

拉背部肌肉。

站立的时候，要保持两脚的脚跟和脚掌都着地，使全身的重量均匀的分布在两只脚上，双膝要直，向内向上收紧腹壁，同时收缩臀部，双臂自然下垂放在身体的两侧，头部自然抬起，两眼平视前方。

5. 不要直接弯腰从地上拾起物品，以免用力过度导致背部的肌肉和关节损伤。应当先慢慢蹲下，拾起物品后再慢慢站起来。

6. 当需要拿高处物品时，千万不要踮起脚尖，也不要伸长手臂，以免不慎摔倒，最好请在家中的亲人帮助。

7. 睡觉的姿势往往会影响睡眠的质量，到了怀孕28周以后，要避免长时间的仰卧，以免增大的子宫压迫下腔静脉，影响宝宝的发育，一般以左侧卧为主。起床时，如果你原来的睡姿是仰卧的，应该应当先将身体转向一侧，弯曲双腿的同时，转动肩部和臀部，再慢慢移向床边，用双手撑在床上、双腿滑下床下，坐在床沿上，少坐片刻以后再慢慢起身。

贴心·提醒

1. 每天晚上至少要有8～9小时的睡眠时间，有条件的话，中午还可以小睡1小时。

2. 运动时要有限度，不要运动到令自己感到疲劳或上气不接下气的地步。不要尝试那些剧烈的运动，要避免任何有损伤腹部危险的运动。

第31周

更是“大肚婆”

第31周记：我在书上读到过，在这个时期，宝宝已经有了味蕾，对妈妈吃的所有东西都会有感觉。不会吧？难道羊水中会我吃的食品味道？

不过，这段时间我的胃口不是太好，吃一点点就吃不下了，就像吃饱了似的。我没有办法，大夫也没有招，只能少吃多餐，我还经常吃些小点心。我在想原因一定是子宫变大了，把我的胃挤小了吧。

胎宝宝状况　胎宝贝身长约45厘米，体重约1500～1800克。小宝贝身体和四肢继续长大，直到和头部的比例相当。皮下脂肪更加丰富，皱纹减少，看起来更像一个初生的婴儿了。各个器官继续发育完善，这时胎儿的肺部和消化系统已基本发育完成，可以分泌消化液。味蕾更加发达。这时小家伙喝进去的羊水已经可以经过膀胱排泄在羊水中，这是在为出生后的小便功能进行锻炼。

孕妈妈状况　孕妈咪无论夜晚睡眠还是白天躺卧，都应采取左侧卧位，避免长时间仰卧。这时你会感到呼吸越发的困难，喘不上气来。子宫底已上升到了横膈膜处，吃下食物后也总是觉得胃里不舒服，因此也影响了食欲。这时最好少吃多餐，以减轻胃部的不适。

腹痛

1.腹痛的原因

腹痛是因为子宫的不规则收缩引起的。从孕早期开始，一直到孕晚期，大部分孕妈咪都会有肚皮硬起来的感觉。其实这是子宫的一种不规则收缩，间隔时间、子宫收缩时间都有长有短，相对来说孕早期的子宫收缩时间会短一些，到孕晚期可能时间会越来越长。一般来说是不会感觉到疼痛的，但也有一部分孕妈咪能明显地感觉到。到孕中期以后，子宫迅速增大，子宫四周的韧带由原来松弛状态变为紧张状态，尤其是位于子宫前侧的一对圆韧带被牵拉，由此也可引起牵引胀痛。

2.腹痛的对策

腹痛时，如果没有出现阴道出血或破水，胎动也正常，那么请以休息为主，孕妈咪不必紧张，这只是正常的子宫收缩。如果腹痛时孕妈咪正在上班，先放下手头的工作，坐下来休息休息就可以了。如果腹痛剧烈，而且伴有阴道出血、破水，有可能是流产、子宫外孕或者早产的征兆，必须迅速就医。

3.腹痛的具体问题

(1) 腹痛跟睡姿有关系吗？

孕中期以后，随着腹部的不断隆起，有些孕妈妈睡觉的时候，常有腹部胀痛的感觉，这个时候如果我选择左侧卧，情况就会好一些。请问，腹痛跟睡姿有关吗？

睡姿是个人的习惯，腹痛其实与睡觉的姿势没有太大的关系。但是到孕晚期的时候，我们还是鼓励孕妈咪能左侧卧，这倒不是因为子宫收缩不收缩的关系，而是因为右侧卧容易压迫到神经，影响到胎儿，导致缺氧的症状。

(2) 怎么区分腹痛和胎动？

有些孕妇老是觉得胎动很多很频繁，动静也大，有时候还有隐痛感，如何区分腹痛和胎动？

如果在某一个时间段里(如5分钟)感觉胎动很厉害，就认为胎动太频繁，就会担心。其实只要真正学会数胎动的正确方法，就可以作出正确判断。可参见本书第17、18周的有关内容。一般的孕妇培训班也都会指导孕妈咪如何来数胎动。如果你感觉胎动超过了规定的数量，就要到医院去看看了。至于隐痛，如果持续时间短，不重复出现，应无大碍，否则就应找医生查明情况。

(3) 持续30分钟的腹痛正常吗？

一位怀孕23周的孕妈妈，凌晨1点左右突然感觉腹胀，感觉是子宫被横向纵向拉伸。侧卧在床上，不敢动弹，只好做深呼吸，直到半小时后才停止胀痛。这到底是怎么回事？

正常的腹痛或者说是子宫不规则的收缩，频率上可能有所不同，但持续时间一般都小于30秒。即使临产时分，阵痛的持续时间也不会超过1分钟。所以持续30分钟的子宫收缩是没有的。如果没有阴道出血、破水的情况，而持续腹痛30分钟的话，可能是有其它问题存在了，如胎盘早剥等，这种情况下应及早就医。

背痛

“我的背好痛！”是半数孕妇在怀孕后半程几乎会天天抱怨的症状。

怀孕期间，韧带组织因为要让宝宝比较容易通过骨盆，逐渐在放松，而松弛的韧带会造成肌肉负担过重，尤其是支撑脊柱的那些肌肉。另外，过度拉扯的腹部肌肉迫使孕妇依靠背部来支撑体重，从而增加了背部肌肉的工作负担。尤其在怀孕后期，一些工作过度的肌肉和背部韧带会因此产生疼痛。

1. 背痛预防

(1) 穿柔软合适的低跟或坡跟鞋，不要穿高跟鞋，防止下肢浮肿。

(2) 避免在坚硬的路面慢跑。

(3) 不要扭转脊椎。

(4) 避免长时间的站立或坐着，不要过多走路，下腹部使用腹带。

(5) 晚上睡的床垫应硬度适中。采用侧睡，每次醒过来就更换姿势。

(6) 以正确的方式搬重物，即在搬重物时，要像一个刚学步的孩子，用大腿使劲。不要把腰背部当成了起重机。

(7) 注意休息和睡眠，饮食方面多吃些猪腰、芝麻、核桃等补肾利腰之品。

2. 背痛治疗

(1) 在疼痛的地方冷敷或热敷。

(2) 淋浴时，用热水淋冲疼痛的地方。

（3）请丈夫按摩背部：沿着她的脊柱两侧，利用拇指按压的方式，由上往下按摩。接下来，继续往她的下背部两侧，沿着她的骨盆上缘按摩。最后按摩肩膀，揉捏她的颈部和肩膀肌肉，然后往下按摩她的脊柱，以及横向按摩她的下背部。

假如疼痛向下延伸到腿部，甚至到脚上，就应该去看骨科医生，进一步地检查和治疗。

腰痛

怀孕末期，孕妇的腰痛通常局限在下腰部，每天只痛一会儿，或每周只痛一次。有人则稍重一些，当站、坐、弯腰、提重物时，便感到腰痛。走路、打喷嚏、用力解大小便时，疼痛更加厉害，或引起臀部和大腿酸痛，以致不能走远路、做家务，极少数还需要住院治疗。

孕妇腰痛基本上是一种生理性反应，不必过于忧虑。怀孕前应注意经常锻炼，增强体质。要注意劳逸结合，特别是不要增加腰部负担。平卧睡觉的时候，可在膝关节后方垫以枕头或软垫，使髋关节、膝关节屈曲起来，帮助减少腰腿后伸，使腰背肌肉、韧带、筋膜得到更充分的休息。孕妇不要穿高跟鞋，防止因此加重挺腰的姿势，又影响足部的血液供应。

孕妇腰痛绝大部分不需要治疗，如症状严重，除了休息外，可以对症治疗。但要注意，不少治疗腰痛的中药常含有活血化淤的成分，孕妇不宜服用，也不宜贴膏药，以免影响胎儿发育，甚至流产。分娩以后，这些症状就会消失。

个别孕妇腰痛是患了腰椎间盘突出症，宜采用卧硬板床休息、牵引等方法治疗。

第32周

宝宝已经4斤了

第32周记： 大夫摸了摸我的肚子，告诉我，宝宝现在是头朝下了。但愿她会一直这样呆着，那么出生的时候就不会有太多麻烦了。我又开始频繁地去厕所，我的膀胱被挤地更小了。这倒是不奇怪，因为宝宝现在已经有40.5厘米了。

胎宝宝状况 胎宝贝身长约46厘米，体重1800～2000克左右。皮肤淡红并日益光滑起来，但皮肤皱折仍然很多，看起来像个小老头。胎动次数减少、动作也减弱，再也不会像原来那样在你的肚子里翻筋斗了，但只要你还能感觉得到小家伙在蠕动，就说明一切正常。

孕妈妈状况 这段时期，孕妈咪一定要注意饮食安排，体重每周不应超过500克。少吃过咸的食物，每天饮食中的盐应严格控制，不宜大量饮水；适当限制食糖、甜食、油炸食品及肥肉的摄入，油脂要适量；选体积小、营养价值高的食物，如动物类食品，避免吃体积大、营养价值低的食物，如土豆、红薯，这样还可减轻胃部的涨满感。

一些生活中的小细节也要注意，比如每天早晨起床后，先喝一杯凉开水再吃早餐，有助于预防便秘；每天晚上入睡前先做5分钟的乳房按摩，疏通乳腺管为哺乳做准备；枕头不宜太高，否则易使颈胸处弯曲过大，不仅不利于呼吸，还会压迫胎宝贝。

孕妈咪现在时常会感到疲劳，因此不要再独自一个人出远门，要服从自己身体的感觉，多休息，适当活动，比如饭后和丈夫一起在花园里散散步，或者做一做孕妇体操，缓解一下腰背的疼痛。

第32周，别忘了到医院做例行产检。

孕后期衣着

最后这近十周里，为了保持正常的日常起居，为自己选择适合妊娠后期特殊需要的着装，会显得很重要。

鞋：孕后期足、踝、小腿等处的韧带松弛，应当选购鞋跟较低、穿着舒服的便鞋。身体越来越笨重起来后，要穿平跟鞋以保持身体平衡。从现在起，足、踝等部位会出现水肿，可以穿大一点的鞋子。鞋底要能防滑。

内衣：应当选择大小合适的纯棉质的支撑式的乳罩。妊娠期乳房变化很大，婴儿出生或断奶后，乳房还容易下垂。需要能起支托作用的乳罩，背带要宽一点儿，乳罩窝要深一些。先买两副即可，然后可以根据乳房的变化情况再买合适的，同时可以备有几个夜用乳罩。

内裤：不宜再选用三角形、有松紧带的紧身内裤。宜选择上口较低的迷你型内裤或者上口较高的大内裤。内裤前面一般要有弹性纤维制成的饰料，有一定的伸缩性，以满足不断变大的腹部需要。

弹力袜：弹力袜能协助消除疲劳、腿痒等症状，防止脚踝肿胀和静脉曲张，尤其对于孕期需要坚持上班工作者，效果更明显。

上衣：上衣要保证宽大和长度，宽松下垂的T 恤、圆领长袖运动衫或者无袖套领恤衫，这类上衣看上去好，穿着舒适，分娩后仍然能穿。

背带装：选用质地、造型、款式适合的背带装，或裙或裤，从视觉效果上修饰日渐臃肿的体形。

裤子：运动装裤子既舒服又无拘束，只需要把裤腰处松紧带拆掉改为背带，做成宽大的背带裤，就能适应妊娠晚期变大的腰围。

节制性生活

进入孕8月，是妊娠后期的开始。此阶段胎儿生长迅速，子宫增大很明显，对任何外来刺激都非常敏感。孕后期，夫妻间应尽可能停止性生活，以免发生意外。

若一定要有性生活，必须节制，并注意体位，还要控制性生活的频率及时间，动作不宜粗暴。这个时期最好采用丈夫从背后抱住孕妇的后侧位。这样不会压迫腹部，也可使孕妇的运动量减少。

有自然流产和习惯性流产的孕妇，整个妊娠期间都避免性交，千万不要为一时的冲动造成永久的悔恨。

第33周

守候宝宝

第33周记：出门的时候，我得停下来休息好几次。

这些日子的确很疲惫！睡觉也变得困难，因为我总也找不到一个舒服的姿势。我不能趴着，当然不能了。但如果我仰面躺着，总觉得呼吸困难。我的肺受到压迫，而且由于子宫的关系，静脉受压，血液循环也不好。我只有侧躺着，在肚子下面垫个枕头，两腿间再垫一个。可是这样我翻身就又成了问题。老公说他觉得是和一条大鲸鱼睡在一起，好几次差点被挤下床去。

胎宝宝状况　胎宝贝身长约47厘米，体重2000～2250克左右。呼吸系统、消化系统发育已近成熟。对于初产妇，这时候胎宝贝的头部已经降入你骨盆，紧紧的压在子宫颈上；而对于经产妇，胎宝贝入盆的时间会较晚些。随着胎儿皮下脂肪的快速积累，他(她)的皮肤已经开始变得富有光泽，不再像个皱巴巴的小老头了。

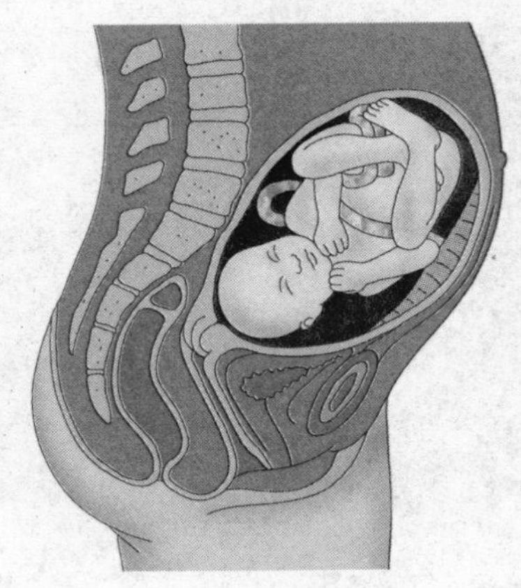

第33周（9月胎宝宝）

孕妈妈状况　子宫继续在往上、往大长，子宫底高达至28～30厘米，宫底位于脐部与剑突之间，在孕32～34周期间循环血量增加明显。腹部继续向前膨胀，越来越笨重的身体会给孕妈咪带来很多不适，比如稍多走点路就会感到腰疼、足跟疼；你的行动更加笨拙，这时一不留意便会引起腰外伤，造成腰椎间盘突出。已升到上腹的子宫顶压膈肌和胃使你不要吃得过饱。不少孕妈咪身体的一些部位会出现浮肿，须要注意。

清晨起床后，如果头一天肿起来的脸、手、脚、腿等部位还是没消肿或减轻，要及时向医生反应，同时要特别注意水的摄入量。

沉重的腹部会让孕妈咪不愿意走动，并且感到疲惫，这是正常现象，但是为了在分娩的时候更加轻松些，你至少要坚持每天的散步活动。

孕9月专家提示（第33～36周）

1．不要单独外出。若必须外出，则务必交代行踪及联络事宜。

2．备妥住院生产所需用物，最好是装放在一方便取用的背包内，以便随时紧急使用（背包内用物建议携带洗脸毛巾一条、洗澡毛巾一条、牙刷、牙膏、洗脸清洁剂、肥皂、保养品、换洗内衣裤3～5套、轻便休闲服2～3套、饮水杯、卫生纸、产垫、筷子、汤匙等进食用具）。

3.备妥住院生产所需重要证件，如健保卡、夫妻二人的身份证、孕妇健康手册、医院挂号证等。

4．若发生不正常出血或早期破水，宜马上前往医院待产，切莫拖延。

5．饮食宜多吃蔬菜、水果、低盐及高蛋白食物。

6．每天至少散步20～30分钟。有助产程之顺利进行。

7．可利用小耳环来搭配修饰脸型。

8．每周使用深层洗发精清洁并保持发型。

9．服装布料选择不容易产生皱折的质料。

产前运动操——腰、腿部运动

常用的产前运动操，包括腰部运动、腿部运动、腹式呼吸运动和闭气等等，其主要目的在于锻炼孕妈妈身体各部分肌肉能力，减少临产阵痛期的疼痛；减少生产时情绪及全身肌肉的紧张；增加产道肌肉的强韧性，以便生产更加顺利；并帮助缩短产程。运动施行时间太早没意义，一般在怀孕第8个月时可以开始。

1.腰部运动

目的：生产时加强腹压及会阴部的弹性，使胎儿顺利娩出。

动作：手扶椅背慢慢吸气，同时手臂用力，脚尖立起，使身体同时向上，腰部挺直，使下腹部紧靠椅背，然后再慢慢呼气，手臂放松，脚还原，早晚各做5～6次。

2.腿部运动

目的：加强骨盆附近肌肉及会阴部弹性。

动作：以手扶椅背，右腿固定，左腿做360度转动划圈，做毕还原，换一条腿继续做，早晚各做5～6次。

贴心·提醒

做运动前，先排尿，排空膀胱；最好选择硬板床或坐在地面上做，坐姿亦可；要穿着宽松的衣服，并且解开带扣；产前运动的具体时间，最好在就寝前和早餐前做；方法要正确，注意安全，不可蛮干；次数由少渐多，不宜过度劳累。

产前运动操——呼吸运动

做好呼吸运动训练，是为了提前了解、掌握和配合产程要素，进行顺利分娩的训练的必须内容，也能起到孕晚期自我锻炼和保健康的作用，做得越早、练得越熟，于分娩时的效果越好。

1.腹式呼吸运动

目的：在临产阵痛期，可以松弛腹部肌肉，减轻痛苦。

动作：平卧，腿稍屈，闭口，用鼻子深呼吸，使腹部突起，肺部不动，吸气时越慢越好，然后慢慢呼出，使腹部渐渐平低，每天早晚各做10～15次。

2.闭气运动

目的：配合临产时子宫口开全后用力，这项运动可以加强腹压，有助于胎力较快娩出。

动作：平躺后，深吸两大口气，立即闭嘴，努力把横膈膜向下压如憋排大便状，但要注意，练习时只可感受用并掌握力方法，不要真用力，每日早晚各做5～6次。

3.胸式浅呼吸运动

目的：临产时胎头娩出，做这项运动能避免胎儿快速冲出，而损伤婴儿或导致自身会阴部严重裂伤。

动作：平躺下把双腿伸直，张口做浅速呼吸，每秒钟呼气1次，每呼气10次必须休息一下，再继续做，早晚各做3～4次。

小贴士……孕后期运动注意

妊娠后期做运动时，要注意下面事项：

运动前做热身，运动后做放松练习；运动前后都要适当喝水，防止脱水。

做所有的运动都要舒缓而有节奏；运动时要连续呼吸，不要屏气；要避免猛力转身和用力过猛；避免坐姿抬双腿运动，因为会增加腹背肌的张力。

如果出现疼痛、恶心、眩晕症状，则是身体发出了停止或减轻运动强度的信号。

另外，尽可能和朋友或家人一起做运动，以保障安全。

第34周

给他安排点具体事

第34周记： 老公今天替我刮了腿上的毛。我一直有这个习惯，可现在自己没法弄了。我还习惯每天洗澡，但现在似乎不太可能了。算了，不想了。宝宝已经44厘米了。她那么大，压得我无法呼吸。我已经不上班了。

胎宝宝状况 胎宝贝身长约48厘米，体重在2300克左右。小家伙的头部进入骨盆，但这时胎儿姿势尚未完全固定，还有可能发生变化，需要密切关注。原本长满全身的胎毛逐渐消退。

孕妈妈状况 孕妈咪的小腿、脚背及外阴等部位会出现静脉曲张，使孕妈咪感到发胀、酸痛、麻木和乏力，严重时血液积聚成球状，血管壁菲薄，极易破裂。一旦破裂将会血流如注，对孕妈咪和胎宝贝都非常危险。因此，应在生活中你要多加防护。比如刚发生静脉曲张时，就不要长时间站立或久坐不动，要经常变换体位休息，注意常活动脚部。把双腿抬起以利静脉血回流，外阴静脉曲张时应适当卧床，取卧位休息。每天起床后趁静脉曲张和下肢水肿较轻时，穿上高弹力尼龙袜或在小腿缠上弹力绷带；外阴部可用弹力月经带，待到晚上取下；内衣不要过紧地勒在腹部。这样，即可减轻静脉曲张的症状，也可避免磕碰等外伤造成的出血及感染。

睡眠时用枕头垫高双腿，促使静脉血回流；避免用过冷或过热的水洗澡，与体温相同的水最为适宜；防止便秘，如有慢性咳嗽或气喘应彻底治愈，以减轻静脉压。外阴发生静脉曲张要及时就医，因为外阴静脉曲张常伴有阴道和子宫颈静脉曲张，若不及时采取措施，临产时胎宝贝的头经过时易发生静脉破裂出血。另外，要禁止骑自行车和房事。

这时你可不要一个人再走太远的路，如果你需要什么可以让你的丈夫陪你一起去，或是帮你去买。你可以把自己入院分娩和宝宝出生一周内需要的东西列出一个清单，交给丈夫去采购。

第34周，别忘了到医院做例行产检、超音波检查。

丈夫要做的事

越接近生产，准妈妈越容易因为不知何时会发生阵痛而感到焦虑。准爸爸应该了解这种不安，不要以为只要去医院，就会有医生照顾。因为你的一句话和体贴的心，往往能给予妈妈生小宝宝的力量。

准爸爸要为妈妈和宝宝做好下列几点：

1．早一点回家

让待产的妈妈最不安的就是夜晚独自在家，所以请准爸爸尽可能早点回家。

2．随时保持联络

晚回家时，一定要告知自己身在何处。不管是在加班，或是和朋友一起去喝酒，让太太知道你在哪里会比较安心。要回家时最好先打个电话告知："我要回家了。"在自己随身携带的笔记本上记下预定生产的医院、娘家和邻居的电话号码。

3．减少假日的应酬

预产期接近，假日最好尽可能陪在太太身旁。可以向周围的人说明原因，请对方理解。而且太太为了准备生产，应该有许多事需外出办理，不妨陪太太去买东西、帮太太开车或是提东西。

4．不要在意太太的任性

当产期越来越接近，不安、担心、害怕等往往会使太太焦虑不安。或许会变得有点任性，这时不妨睁只眼睛闭只眼睛。相信不久后，太太就会抱着宝宝展露美好笑容。

5．调整工作行程

知道预产期近了，爸爸也该有生产的准备动作。先将工作安排好，以利于有突发事件时，可借助同事之力使工作顺利进行。

6. 尽早交接家事

尽早询问家事的处理方法。如果已经有第一个孩子，不妨和孩子一起等待妈妈出院。不要忘了洗碗盘、清扫、洗衣等工作，不要以充满垃圾的房子迎接新生的宝宝。

准爸爸产前培训

准爸爸要关心孕妇的思想情绪，鼓励孕妇树立分娩信心，还要对自己的工作做好安排，做到亲自陪妻子去医院，并陪伴分娩。另外，还要参加医院产科门诊举办的爸爸会，掌握孕期保健知识、胎教和分娩知识，这样就可以更称职地尽到丈夫的责任。

准妈妈就要生孩子了，在这个关键时刻，作为孩子的父亲、妻子的老公，准爸爸可以做些什么呢？这个无法自己生孩子的大男人，他在女人的生育过程中，可以起到怎样的作用？

第一课：帮准妈咪调节环境

在分娩前后，大多数准妈妈都希望自己处在一个舒适的环境下：光线柔和，室温适宜，环境清静，有亲人陪伴，有舒缓的音乐……去医院时，准爸爸可以带上一些让她心理安慰的东西，比如她喜欢的娃娃、衣服、小摆设等，让她即使在医院里，也能感觉到家的温馨。

准备功课：临产前，和妻子一起去了解一下病房、产房的环境，熟悉自己的医生。熟悉的环境能让人感觉舒服、放松。

第二课：学会放松自己

第一次迎接新生命，任何人都会感到紧张，准爸爸虽然只能旁观，但他的紧张、忧虑也是很自然的。然而，在妻子面临分娩时，作为她的精神支柱，如果丈夫自己先紧张起来，就一定会影响到妻子的情绪，使她更加不安、惶恐。因

此，准爸爸一定要学会放松自己，自己先放松，才可能去放松临产阵痛的妻子，给予她最大的安慰与支持。

准备功课：了解足够多的有关生育方面的知识，平时多与妻子所在医院的医生交流、沟通，做到胸有成竹，心中不慌。

第三课：给予妻子积极的心理暗示

生孩子前，切忌自己吓自己。如果自己把分娩过程想象成可怕的经历，那么你在迎接挑战之前就已经打败了自己。因此，作为妻子精神上的支持者，丈夫一定要经常给予妻子积极的心理暗示，让她积极地面对这个自然的生理过程，而不要总是给她带来坏的消息，让她未战先怯。

人们常有这样的生活体验：当想到山楂时，口中就会感觉到酸，甚至会流口水。这就是一种心理暗示。你知道它是酸的，即使你没有真的吃到它，而只是想了一下，你也会感觉到那种酸的滋味。生孩子也是一样。如果妻子认为生孩子是痛苦的，那么在临产前，她就会不自觉地想到疼、想到各种危险与不顺利，那么，各种痛苦就会被她扩大，无形中给分娩加大了难度。所以，丈夫要经常给妻子带来好消息，不要去听信别人说的某某人生孩子的时候痛得死去活来。事实上，哪怕是经历同一件事，不同人的感受也是不一样的，而且每个孕妇的忍痛能力也影响着她当时的真实感受。只要你的妻子能认真了解分娩过程，做好各种准备，这些发生在个别人身上的痛苦经历就不会重现。

准备功课：多把正确、实用的生育知识告诉你的妻子。平时可以向那些有着顺利分娩经验的人请教，并把这些好的消息带给你的妻子。你还可以常和她一起想象孩子有多可爱，有了孩子以后，家庭是多幸福。

第四课：妻子宫缩疼痛时，丈夫帮助她的技巧

1. 疼痛时的思想转移

每个待产妇都要经历宫缩。宫缩给人的感觉是不适的，所有的人都会感觉到疼。刚开始宫缩时，每次宫缩时间较短，且宫缩间隔较长。然后，宫缩时间会变得越来越长，间隔时间变得越来越短，疼痛也越来越剧烈。这种疼痛要持续很久。这时候，丈夫给妻子讲笑话什么的就起不到任何作用了，因为她完全笑不起来。

准备功课：如果丈夫想了解孕妇在疼痛时最想身边的人做什么，不妨问

一下自己的妈妈以及妻子的妈妈，她们的切身感受一定会让你有所启发。

2．放松妻子的身体

妻子在宫缩时，腹部肌肉紧张是很正常的，此时，身体其他地方要尽量放松，这就需要丈夫来帮忙了。

时断时续的宫缩要持续8～10个小时。宫缩刚开始时，妻子还不需要入院，家里的环境可以让她感觉更好些。当她或坐或躺时，她的身体需要一些支撑，比如枕头、靠背。丈夫要确保妻子的肘、腿、下腰、脖子都有地方支撑，并检查她身体各部分是否完全放松。妻子可能无法顾及到这些，甚至懒得说话，所以丈夫要主动帮忙。等到了医院，丈夫也要随时关心妻子是否躺（坐）得舒服。

如果妻子因疼痛而感觉很紧张，丈夫可在一旁带她深呼吸，提示她一些保持轻松的要点。丈夫还可以为妻子按摩，以缓解她临产时的紧张与不适反应。

3．准备功课

（1）练习按摩：可先由妻子给丈夫做按摩。丈夫接受过按摩后，才会知道怎样的按摩最舒服有效。接下来，丈夫就可以试着给妻子按摩，双方可互相交换关于按摩的意见，使丈夫的按摩技巧逐渐改善。

（2）慢舞：搂着妻子在音乐下慢舞，想象着孩子在肚子里很快乐的样子。这种方式不仅能帮妻子克服紧张、害怕的情绪，还能帮助胎儿旋转，让它调整好胎位，从而更有利于他的顺利降生。

（3）爱：抚摩、拥抱、亲吻、赞美，这些都是丈夫对妻子的最好鼓励。不要吝啬你的情感表达，经历这样一个人生关口，你和她才真正融合为一家人。

（4）细心关怀：记得提醒你的妻子，在临产时，她需要大量喝水，注意排尿，适当走动，不要让她一直平躺着。如果她觉得不舒服，洗个澡也许有所帮助，适当的冷敷、热敷也可起到一定作用。

第35周

准备分娩用品

第35周记：据大夫说，宝宝的头现在已经在我骨盆的地方。那里空间很小，她应该会一直这么老实地呆着。现在她大概每天要长13克的分量。

很高兴我不用去上班，如果阳光很好，我就在露台坐一会儿，脚还得垫高。我的脚踝有些肿了。我闭上眼睛，把脸转向太阳，能感到眼前有温暖的红色光晕。

我想着宝贝，她是不是也能感觉到那阳光。

胎宝宝状况 胎宝贝身长不到50厘米，体重约2500克。小宝贝的两个肾脏已经发育完全，肝脏也具备了代谢功能。头部下降到骨盆里，因为那里空间较小，小宝贝显得老实多了。肺部发育已基本完成，如果这时小家伙“提前报到”，存活的可能性为99%。

孕妈妈状况 这周以后，子宫壁和腹壁变得很薄，当胎宝贝在你肚子里有活动时，你可能会看到小家伙的手、脚或是肘部关节在腹部突显的样子。

日常生活中要注意预防和积极治疗便秘，少吃辛辣食物、多吃含纤维素的蔬菜、水果和粗粮，少量多次喝水，保持排便通畅，减轻直肠静脉丛的淤血；最好养成早上定时排便的生物钟活动；不要忍便，便干结难以排出可喝些蜂蜜等；不能乱用泻药，以防引发流产。形成痔疮时要多卧床休息，不要久坐、久站，适当出去散散步，做些做力所能及的运动。经常做“提肛运动”，可改善盆腔血液循环，增加痔静脉丛血液的回流，从而减轻淤血使痔疮自愈。

如果你对日益临近的分娩感到忐忑不安甚至有些紧张的话，你应该努力使自己平静下来，注意休息，养精蓄锐，轻松的日子已经不多了，再享受一下二人世界的安静温馨吧，听听音乐，和丈夫聊聊天，讨论你们即将面临的育儿的重任，分析和安排可能遇到的问题。

准备宝宝用品

新生儿降临之前，父母要将孩子的衣、食、住、行用具准备就绪；以便迎接宝宝的到来。

1. 卫生用具

(1) 尿布：要求吸水性强，质料柔软。

(2) 棉垫：棉垫可用布和棉花制作。用浴巾折叠也可以。

(3) 小方毛巾：喂奶喂水时做围嘴使用，准备5～6块。

(4) 清洗用具：洗脸、洗屁股、洗澡盆各1个。所用毛巾各1块。浴布1条。此外，还要准备婴儿香皂、面霜、小儿爽身粉一盒。

(5) 酒精、眼药水：75%的酒精100毫升，0.25%的氯霉素眼药水4～5支。棉花棒若干，体温计1支。

2. 喂养用品

(1) 奶瓶：如果是母乳喂养，准备1～2个奶瓶，用以喝水、喝果汁。如果是人工喂养，需要准备5～6个奶瓶。喂水和喂奶的奶瓶最好分开使用。奶瓶以200毫升的耐热玻璃奶瓶为宜。

(2) 奶嘴：准备和奶瓶配套的奶嘴3～4个。根据婴儿月龄不同，决定奶嘴开孔的大小。奶嘴扎孔时要先用酒精擦洗缝衣被针，然后在奶嘴上扎1～2个孔。孔洞不可过大，以防呛奶。可将奶瓶倾斜45度以检查孔口的大小是否合适。倾斜时，内容物一滴接一滴地流出为合适。大一点的婴儿的奶嘴口可稍大一点，小一点婴儿的奶嘴口可稍小一点。

奶瓶、奶嘴使用前均要消毒，即把洗净的奶瓶、奶嘴放入锅内煮，奶瓶煮沸10分钟，奶嘴煮沸3分钟。然后把煮锅水倒去，奶瓶、奶嘴留在锅内盖好待用。

(3) 其他：小食匙、奶瓶刷、保温桶、大口玻璃瓶、电热杯和奶锅。奶瓶刷弹性要好，一定要专用。保温桶用于盛热奶供晚上孩子喝。大口玻璃瓶用于存放消毒后的奶嘴，可用罐头瓶，但要有瓶盖。电热杯为夜间热奶用。奶锅要带把的。

3．衣服

衣服以冬天保暖、夏天散热、穿着舒适、不影响生理机能（皮肤出汗、手脚的运动等）为原则。最好用纯棉布、薄棉布、薄绒布自制，也可以选用其他新生儿穿过的衣服。衣服要质地柔软、装饰物少、色彩浅淡、洗涤方便。衣服要洁净，存放时不要放樟脑丸。

衣服的胸围和袖口要宽松，以便穿脱。不要用扣子，而可以系带子。

新生儿不宜穿毛衣，天冷时可穿无领棉袄。夏装可为睡裙式单衣，高温天气可用布胸肚兜。还要有婴儿帽，以备外出时用。

4．寝具

（1）被褥：新生儿应有专用棉被，不可与成人共用。

（2）枕头：新生儿不一定要用枕头，吐奶和打嗝会不断弄湿枕头，可用折叠的毛巾代替枕头。

（3）床：婴儿不宜与父母同床，须用婴儿床。婴儿床的床板木条间距不得大于0.5或1厘米。栏杆高度至少要超过66厘米，栏杆之间的距离不可过大，也不可过小。

婴儿床可以紧挨着墙或放在离墙50厘米左右的地方。床下地上可铺上毯子等软垫，以防孩子跌落时碰伤头部和身体。

不要把布绒玩具、充气玩具放在婴床里。

5．居室

成人一直居住的房屋可以供婴儿居住，婴儿不需单独住室。住室要整洁、向阳、空气清新，经常通风和换气，但要防止过堂风。

不要让婴儿睡在客厅里，以防传染病的侵袭。

居室的门窗宜加上纱门、纱窗和窗帘，以避免蚊蝇侵扰和阳光的直射。

检查产前准备工作

在产前的最后几周，要把自己在分娩期间需要完成的事情交代给丈夫或其他亲人，同时要做好准备分娩的工作。

1. 可以唤起你记忆的检查表

(1) 把未完成的工作做个交接。

(2) 到医院预先登记。

(3) 参观分娩地点（产房）。

(4) 准备好宝宝的全套衣物。

(5) 购买舒适衣物的最后机会:睡衣和哺乳胸罩。

(6) 拟定生产计划。

(7) 询问医生什么时候该到医院。

(8) 购买汽车婴儿安全座椅（对有车的夫妻）。

2. 去医院之前应检查的事项

(1) 不知什么时候会有阵痛时，最好做一个紧急时候能联系的人的一览表。

(2) 事先确认去医院的略图和所需时间。

(3) 先跟认识的人打招呼什么时候用车（对无车的夫妻）。

(4) 经常洗头等身体保持干净。

(5) 对出血、破水等所有情况都要做好准备。

(6) 吃些容易消化的简单食物来储存体力。

3. 住院前确认的事项

(1) 整理住院时要带去的物品。

(2) 整理冰箱内部。

(3) 确保需要时能随时帮忙的人。

(4) 买些能保存的食物放着。

(5) 寻找出院后能帮忙的人。

(6) 准备放孩子的地方。

(7) 确认去医院的方法。

(8) 准备婴儿用品（生产用品）。

(9) 整理家里人的衣服和日常用品放在容易寻找的地方。

4. 住院需要的物品

(1) 医疗卡、现金。

(2) 最心爱的枕头。

(3) 录音机和最喜欢的音乐。

（4）按摩乳液或按摩油（无香精）。

（5）最喜欢的易消化的零食（例如蜂蜜、干果、新鲜水果、燕麦片）。

（6）热水瓶。

（7）衣服，拖鞋。

（8）卫生纸、水果刀等一般住院用品。

（9）梳子或其他梳理头发用品。

（10）肥皂、体香精、洗发精；牙刷、牙膏、唇膏。

（11）卫生棉（医院也会提供）。

5. 留给丈夫的信息

（1）把应该告诉丈夫的东西简单的记下来。

（2）告诉丈夫放衣服、内衣、日常用品的地方。

（3）告诉贵重品（存折、现金、印鉴）的保管场所。

6. 宝宝出院服装

（1）帽子、袜子、小靴子。

（2）一件内衣（纱布内衣）。

（3）连裤睡衣（也就是兔装）。

（4）婴儿浴巾。

（5）冬天须另备连腿睡袋、厚毛毯。

（6）尿片。

7. 其他

保险单、照相机或摄像机、入院登记单、最喜欢的书籍或杂志、电话卡、通讯录等。

第36周

了解一些生产知识

第36周记： 我买了一个专门哺乳用的乳罩。我的乳房已经非常大了。昨天好朋友来看我，我戴上那个乳罩给她们看，她们目瞪口呆。想想就要成为现实了，马上就能见到她了，我真是很激动。我的宝宝，我们就要相见了……

胎宝宝状况 胎宝贝身长约50厘米，体重约2800克。心、肝、肺、胃、肾等器官已经发育成熟。全身呈现淡红色的皮肤也没有了皱褶，体型圆圆胖胖的。手和脚的肌肉也很发达，头部进入妈妈的骨盆中，身体位置又稍稍下移。

孕妈妈状况 因为胎宝贝头部进入骨盆、子宫底部下垂，本周孕妈咪胃和胸部的压抑感慢慢会消失，前段时期的呼吸困难和胃部不适等症状开始缓解。受到压迫的膀胱使尿频的现象继续，白带会增多。你的子宫颈和阴道变得柔软，肚子有鼓胀感。有的孕妈咪会感到下腹部坠胀，甚至会有宝宝要出来的感觉，别担心，这些感觉是由小宝贝位置逐渐下降引起的。

随着体重的增加，你的行动越来越不方便，应保证足够的睡眠和休息，为分娩贮存体力和精力。因为随时可能分娩，不要独自出门太远；住院分娩要事先预约好，去医院的各种必须品要及时准备。坚持测胎心、胎动。不要因为胃口好转就酣吃酣睡，体重超重对分娩很不利，要控制在每周500克以下。注意观察早产征象，如腹部发硬，并伴随着腹部阵痛、阴道出血，要及时告诉医生。做家务时也一定要注意动作轻缓，不要过猛，尽量不要做弯腰和下蹲动作，更不能做有危险的攀高动作。

这时你应该了解有关临产征兆的知识，了解什么是宫缩、见红、破水，该如何处理等，因为现在你随时有可能临产。

从这周开始，孕妈咪要每周做一次产前检查。别忘了要到医院做例行产检啊。

分娩知识

掌握一定的分娩知识，有助于你今后的分娩。

1. 分娩时，学着放松肌肉

学会放松，可以使你有个毕生难忘的愉快分娩经历，否则这次分娩，可能就是你想尽快忘记的一个可怕的噩梦。

除了子宫肌肉收缩外，放松全身其他肌肉有助于缓解不舒服的感觉，并且加速产程的进行。在子宫收缩过程中，身体任何部位的紧张，尤其是面部和颈部的紧张，都会扩散到原本应该放松的骨盆肌肉。紧张的肌肉比松弛的肌肉更会造成疼痛，而且也更容易疲劳。因此，人们说："愉快的精神让身体健康，给灵魂力量。"

两次子宫收缩之间要放松，子宫收缩期间要放开。整个分娩期间，要牢记这个要诀。训练自己想一些可以放松肌肉，又可以让自己放掉身体戒备，让它自然运行的任何事情。一感觉到收缩开始，千万不要紧绷肌肉且全神贯注地准备迎战接下来的阵痛。相反地，要深呼吸、放松，然后放开自己。不断练习这两种"放"的运动，慢慢你就知道要告诉自己："要收缩了，放开身体。"而不是："喔，讨厌，又要开始痛了。"

（1）和你的丈夫一起练习放松身体

首先布置个舒服的场地，找一堆枕头来，然后告诉你先生，你希望枕头怎么摆。你可以用不同的姿势来练习下面的运动：站着、靠着你丈夫、靠着墙或是靠着家具等，或是坐着、侧躺、甚至四肢着地也可以。

练习一：检查身体的肌肉紧张程度——额头皱起、拳头紧握、嘴巴紧闭等都是显而易见的。接着有序地从头到脚练习放开每一组肌肉。先紧绷，然后放松，这样你可以了解这两种不同的肌肉状态。等你的丈夫示意宫缩开始，心里就想：放松、放开，然后去感受每一组紧绷肌肉渐渐松弛下来的情形。

练习二：怀孕的最后几个月要经常练习"触摸—放松"的运动。先找出哪些触摸、什么样的按摩最能让你放松，以练习一的方式，从头到脚循序渐进地做。先绷紧一组肌肉，然后让你的丈夫在该处施以温暖轻松的触摸，好让你试着把这组肌肉放松下来。这样你就不用一直听着你丈夫提醒你"放松！"的指令了。

只要你丈夫能在正确的地方予以适当的抚触，你就会放松该处的肌肉。你还可以这样练习：“我这里痛，你压（摸、碰）一下这里。”

（2）心智的想象

如果你能让心境澄明，又能想象各种安抚情绪的画面，就可以顺利地放松分娩中的身体——至少在两次收缩之间。

a.现在就想好哪些事情、哪些画面最能让你放松，然后经常练习想象这些画面，特别是在怀孕的最后一个月更要如此。这样在分娩的时候，你就会储存了相当丰富的短片，如果在两次宫缩之间，你需要几分钟的放松，就可以随时拿出来播放。很多产妇表示下面这些与分娩有关的想象很有帮助：滚动的波浪、瀑布、蜿蜒的溪流、和丈夫在海滩上漫步的情景等。你也可以把一些最愉快的记忆在心里储存起来，比如你和你丈夫是怎么认识的、过去约会对象中你最喜欢的人、做爱、一次难忘的假期等。

b.想象分娩中的各种情境。收缩开始的时候，想象你的子宫轻轻地拥抱小宝宝，宝宝可爱的小头也同时显露出来。在宝宝经过子宫开口的阶段，想象你的子宫颈每一次收缩就越来越薄，开口也越来越大。有些妈妈也成功地在娩出阶段运用这样的心理想象，她们假想阴道像一朵花一样地开放。

c.把痛苦的画面转为愉快的想象，试试所谓“包裹疼痛”的策略。把疼痛当成一团黏土一样抓起来，然后揉成一个小球，包装起来，放进氢气球里，然后想象它离开你的身体，飞上天空。对付使你沮丧的思绪也可以用这个方法：把它们包起来，想象它们飘走。

d.在剧烈的子宫收缩期间和两次收缩之间，想象你将获得的喜悦，而不是要必须经历的痛苦。想象宝宝出来的时候，你伸出手，协助医护人员把宝宝放到你肚子上，让宝宝依偎在你胸前。

（3）分娩时想喊就放开嗓子喊出

不必对自己发出的声音不好意思，只要能有利于放松就好。很多产妇在难熬的时候，放开嗓子喊叫、呻吟，或是怒吼，这些都可以给她们力量，让她们觉得放松和舒服。

2. 分娩时的正确呼吸方法

缓慢的深呼吸有松弛的效果，而且能为血液提供大量的氧气；快而短促的呼吸则效果相反。如果你发现自己在子宫收缩的时候呼吸得很快，这可能表示你正处于惊慌的状态。把呼吸速度放慢，你自然而然就会冷静下来了。

正确的呼吸就是对你有帮助的呼吸方式，也就是能以最省力的方式输送最多氧气给你和你的宝宝的方法。

(1) 必须做的事

①在两次宫缩之间自然地呼吸，就像你睡着时的呼吸一样。

②宫缩开始时，慢慢地深吸一口气，让气从鼻子进去，然后慢慢地以长而稳的方式通过嘴巴呼出来。呼气的时候要放松脸部肌肉，并尽量放松四肢，同时想象紧张焦虑离你而去，像大大松了一口气一样来做这个呼气的动作。

③到了收缩的顶峰，提醒自己继续放松、舒服地呼吸。

④要求丈夫在发现你因为剧烈收缩而呼吸急促时，千万提醒你要慢慢来。让他也跟你一起缓慢、放松地呼吸。

⑤如果觉得自己还是呼吸得太快，停一会，然后深呼吸，再跟着吐一口长而久的气，就好像你要吹凉热食冒出来的蒸汽一样。每隔一阵子就做一次这个动作，以提醒自己要慢下来。

(2) 不该做的事

①不要喘气。

②不要过度换气。

③不要憋气。

(3) 不要太担心分娩的时候要怎么呼吸。只要能临危不乱，到时候就会很自然地采用对自己以及对婴儿最好的方式呼吸。

“生”还是“剖”？

目前生产的方式主要有剖宫产和顺产。选择分娩方式前，医生会对产妇做详细的全身检查和产科检查，检查胎位是否正常，估计分娩时胎儿有多大，测量骨盆大小是否正常等。如果一切正常，孕妇分娩就可以采取自然分娩的

方式；如果有问题，则会建议采取剖宫产。

1. 自然的方式就是最好的方式

产妇若无不良指征，应尽可能顺产。

2. 剖宫产

剖宫产对母体的损伤大，术后腹壁伤口裂开，术后伤口感染；孩子没有经过产道的挤压，容易患有吸入性肺炎。

剖宫产的指征：

(1) 患有重度妊娠高血压情况危急；

(2) 35岁以上高龄；

(3) 母亲的骨盆出口窄小；

(4) 前置胎盘；

(5) 胎盘早剥、胎儿宫内缺氧而危及母婴安全的。

小贴士……剖宫产术的利与弊

剖宫产是产科的重要手术之一，也是解决难产及挽救产妇和胎儿生命的有效措施之一。剖宫产不是自然分娩的正常途径，对母婴有许多不利的影响，主要有如下几方面：

1. 麻醉意外

施行剖宫产术，须用麻药进行麻醉。目前。大多采用硬膜外腔连续麻醉，虽然这种麻醉方法比较安全，但也不是绝对安全，偶然也会发生麻醉意外而造成难以挽回的损失。

2. 出血量多

阴道分娩平均出血量为50～200毫升，而剖宫产平均出血量则在200～300毫升以上。如果术后发生子宫切口感染，可发生难以控制的子宫大出血。一旦发生这种情况，绝大多数要切除子宫才能解决问题，这给产妇在精神上和肉体上带来极大的痛苦。

3. 感染的机会增加

剖宫产的手术操作比较复杂。被切开和缝合的腹壁、子宫肌肉的层次要比阴道分娩多得多，手术后各种感染的机会也比阴道分娩多。

4. 住院时间长

由于手术和麻醉的影响，在剖宫产后头两天发生肠胀气，甚至不能进食，身体恢复和子宫复原比阴道分娩的要慢；加上腹壁切口的缝线，一般要到术后第7天才能拆除。平均住院时间为8~9天，而阴道分娩只要4天左右。

5. 给再次怀孕带来麻烦

做过剖宫产手术的妇女，不宜在短期内再次怀孕，因为子宫上有一手术疤痕，一旦怀孕，如做人工流产，容易引起子宫疤痕破裂。万一再次妊娠，在妊娠后期，由于子宫撑大，很可能使子宫上的旧疤痕裂开，如得不到及时抢救，可严重威胁母体和胎儿的生命安全。因此，剖宫产术后应采取可靠的避孕措施，如果需要再次生育，至少在两年内不能怀孕。

6. 偶然发生严重并发症

手术时如果发生羊水从子宫切口进入血液循环，则可引起羊水栓塞，甚至威胁产妇生命；手术后若长期卧床不活动，下肢血液容易淤滞，静脉内易形成血栓，一旦起床活动，由于血栓脱落，可引起肺栓塞；如果小肠粘在子宫上，可发生肠梗阻等各种近期或远期的严重并发症。

7. 对婴儿的一些不利影响

对大多数婴儿来说，剖宫产对其健康没有影响。但也有少部分剖宫产的婴儿，因为没有经过阴道分娩的挤压，出生后不能适应外界环境，有时可发生肺扩张不全或误吸羊水等情况而使婴儿出生后不能自主呼吸，甚至危及生命。

了解分娩过程

自然分娩包括三个阶段：

1. 第一产程（宫口开大）

从子宫出现规律性的收缩开始，直到子宫口完全开大（子宫口扩展到10厘米宽）为止。此期初产妇一般经历12~14小时；经产妇因子宫颈较松，扩张较易，需6~8小时。

（1）分娩初期：分娩初期（或潜伏期），孕妇看起来没什么明显的动静。有的孕妇甚至不知道自己已经开始分娩。对于大多数孕妇来说，分娩初期，宫缩每隔5～30分钟1次，每次持续30～45秒。

（2）活动期：如果宫缩强度让你没办法把一句话顺利讲完，那就表示进入活动期了。活动期的宫缩约3～5分钟1次，每次持续45～60秒。产妇们常形容活动期的宫缩像是波浪一样，从子宫的上方开始向子宫下方推进，或是从后面往前面扩散。这些波浪的强度波峰会在宫缩的中间出现，然后逐渐缓和下来。

活动期会持续3～4小时。子宫颈会张开4～8厘米。宝宝的头降到骨盆下方，因此会压破羊膜，造成羊水冲出。活动期牢记下面这些要点，有助于缓解不适感和促进产程：

①在宫缩之间休息以恢复体力。

②在宫缩期间放松与放开。宫缩一开始就深呼吸一口气，缓慢有节奏地从鼻子吸气，由嘴巴吐出。宫缩结束，再次深呼吸，把全身累积的紧张都释放出来。

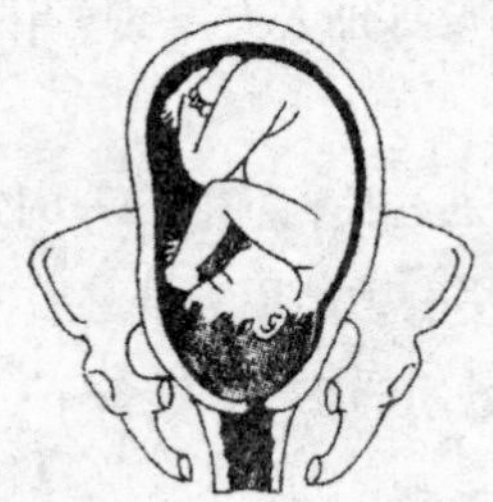

宫口开大2厘米时。阵痛间隔8～10分钟。阵痛间隔还比较长，所以这段时间要充分休息。

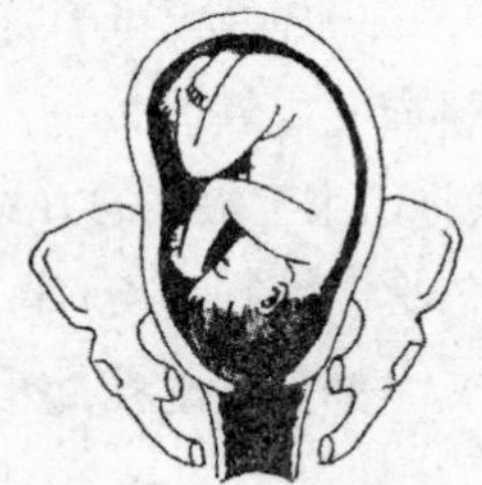

宫口开大6厘米时。阵痛间隔3～5分钟，阵痛加剧。子宫口开全还需2～3小时，到娩出还需7～8小时。

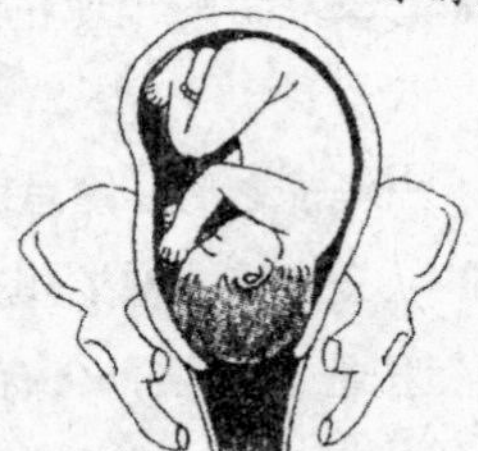

宫口开全时。阵痛间隔约1～2分钟，约持续40～90秒钟。此时的宽度可使胎儿通过。再过2～3小时胎儿将诞生。

第一产程：从有规律的宫缩到子宫口开全

③不断变换姿势。随机应变，只要有用就可以。

④每1小时就去排空膀胱。

(3)过渡期:过渡期表示你即将从分娩的第一阶段——展开骨盆通道，进入第二个产程，也就是推出宝宝的过程。过渡期是整个分娩过程中阵痛最强的时候，不过也是最短的时期，通常只维持15～90分钟。很多产妇过渡期的宫缩都不超过10次或是20次，大约每1～3分钟1次，每次宫缩持续约1～1分半钟。过渡期非常难熬，必须利用各种放松和缓解疼痛的方法：

①宫缩间隔充分休息。

②专心让身体松弛:想象你的子宫颈正在打开，同时往上拉，越过宝宝的头。

③利用不断吐气来克服想要用力的冲动。

2. 第二产程（胎儿娩出）

从宫颈口开全至胎儿娩出。此期初产妇约需1～2小时，经产妇多在1小时内完成。这个阶段一结束，你的宝宝就出世了。

(1) 孕妇能做些什么

①当你的直觉告诉你推的时候，你就用力，不要等别人大声喊“用力”的时候才推。

②推出宝宝最好的方式是尽你所能地推，但是别过头。短暂（5～6秒）、多次（每次宫缩3～4次）的用力。在连续5～6秒使尽全力地用力推之后，把空气全部从肺部吐出来，然后赶紧吸气，让肺部充满新的空气，准备下一次用力。

③宫缩一结束，抓紧时间好好休息。宫缩时或宫缩之间，想象张开、释放或是展开等画面。也可以借着想象高贵的玫瑰花瓣开放，来鼓励你的身心张开并释放出小宝宝。

(2) 宝宝出现了:用力推了一阵子之后，阴唇就会开始突出，再过一会儿，医生就可以看到小小皱褶的头皮出现，宫缩停止时就会缩回去，下次宫缩时又会出现。当阴唇和会阴在拉扯的时候，会有一种刺痛、灼烧的感觉，这种刺痛是身体要你暂停用力的信号，再过几分钟，宝宝头的压力会自然让你的皮肤神经麻痹，这时灼烧感就会消失。

再经过几次收缩，宝宝的头会随着肩膀通过耻骨下方而转向。再经过几次收缩，宝宝就会滑到医护人员的手上或是床上。然后你就会听到宝宝的第一次哭声！

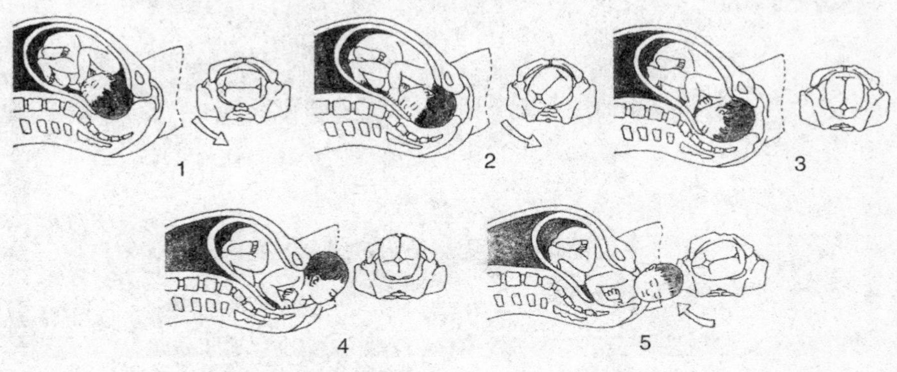

第二产程：从宫口开全到胎儿娩出

3. 第三产程（胎盘娩出期）

胎儿娩出后，子宫继续收缩，随之胎盘剥离并娩出。此期需5～15分钟，一般不超过30分钟。

在子宫轻微收缩娩出胎盘的时候，可能会有抽筋的感觉，或是微弱的排出东西的感觉。如果做了会阴切开术，或是有裂伤，医生可能还有缝合的工作要完成。为了方便缝合，医生会注射局部麻醉药，所以可能会有一点刺刺的感觉。

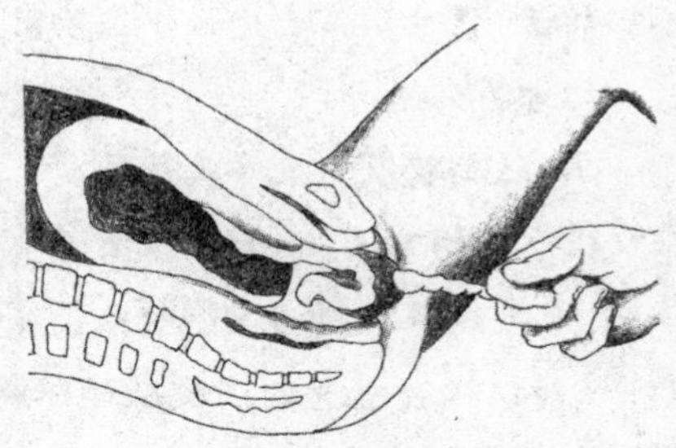

第三产程：胎盘娩出

第37周

就要相见了

第37周记：我的乳罩上湿了一小块。我已经开始漏出少量的乳汁了。宝宝的头位置很低，让我总觉得两腿间像有一只西瓜。我感觉到下腹有阵阵刺痛，是她压迫着我的神经。不过好在我的呼吸现在要顺畅些了。

我还在长胖。但是大夫说这是正常的，因为体重还包括到胎盘和羊水等等的重量。

胎宝宝状况 身长50厘米左右，重量约3000克。有的小宝贝会相对瘦些，但一般只要超过2500克就算正常。胎宝贝的头现在已经完全进入骨盆，如果此时胎位不正的话，医生通常会建议孕妈咪采取剖宫产的方法分娩。

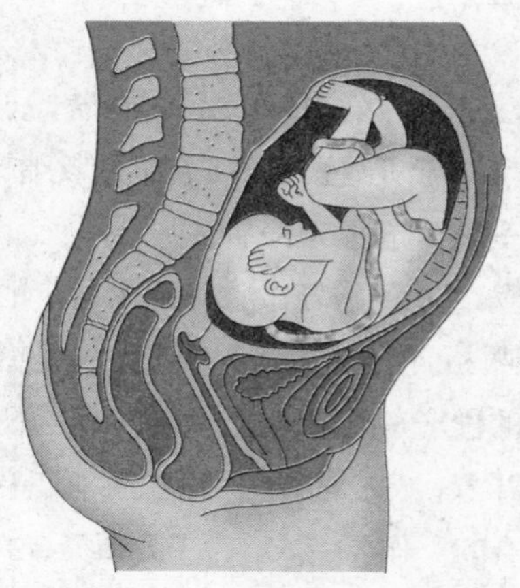

第37周（10月胎宝宝）

孕妈妈状况 乳房高高隆起，开始分泌出少量的乳汁。因为小家伙的头位置很低，你会觉得两腿间下坠的感觉沉甸甸的；可能偶尔会感觉到下腹有阵阵刺痛，不用紧张，那是胎宝贝在压迫你的神经。临近分娩时孕妈咪可能会紧张不安，这时要注意防止失眠了。

分娩前保持良好心理状态十分重要，它关系到分娩时能否顺利。孕妈咪可多了解分娩的事，以免盲目担心。丈夫及家人也要作好心理准备，尤其是给产妇开始阵痛时，不要惊慌失措，免得给产妇增加不安和无用的担忧，各项“后勤”工作更要准备充分。孕后期，家中应有人时刻看护，或保证孕妇随时能与丈夫或亲友取得联系，使孕妇心中有所依托。

孕 10 月专家提示（第 37～40 周）

1. 若发生不正常出血或早期破水宜马上去医院待产,切莫拖延。

2. 将可能需要联络的电话，粘贴在电话机上，以方便及时联络。

3. 宜充分补充营养及睡眠，保持身体清洁，建议剪个方便又容易清理的短发。

4. 不宜和先生性交，以免过度刺激造成子宫收缩或早期破水的情形。

5. 在预产期的前后 1 周内出生的宝宝，皆是“足月生产”，若预产期 2 星期后仍无产兆，宜马上就医检查，以免“过期”。

6. 夜间睡眠宜左侧卧姿。不论坐下或躺卧要起身时，先用双手支撑上身，动作和缓不宜太快，且分段进行，以免引起眩晕而受伤。

7. 用粉饼修饰肤色，并更注意口红及眉形的整体搭配。

8. 穿传统孕妇装，以舒适为原则，布料最好是素面不要有花色。

9. 与先生一起练习生产时的呼吸方法及如何用力的方法。

安心在家待产

孕妇临产时身在医院是最保险的。但在正常情况下，不提倡孕妇提早入院待产。

首先，医院的医疗设备有限，不可能像家里那样舒适、方便；其次，产科病房发生的每件事都可能影响住院者的情绪，入院后较长时间不临产的孕妇，通常会在大环境影响下产生紧迫、焦虑感，尤其是当看到后入院者已经分娩时。所以，没有特殊情况，安心在家待产才是孕妈咪最好的选择。

感到“快了”

到了临产的月份，由于不知道什么时候分娩，出门也安不下心来。一般来说，分娩并不是突然开始的，母体和胎儿在一步步地做好分娩的准备，并送出信号。下面所列举的就是通知临产的代表性征兆，但并不一定所有的人都出现这些征兆，出现的程度也不同。出现了这些征兆，并不意味着马上就要分娩，只是感到“快了”，没有必要立即住院。

1. 胃部的压迫感消失

妊娠中随着胎儿的成长而变大的子宫底，在怀孕35～36周时最高，以后逐渐下降，这是因为随着分娩的临近，子宫口和产道变软，胎儿下降到骨盆所发生的变化。

由于一直压迫胃部和胸部的子宫下降，胃部的不舒畅感消失，消化不良、烧心等现象消失，吃饭也吃得痛快了，呼吸也舒畅了。

2. 下腹部疼痛、腹胀

到妊娠后期，一天会有几次感到腹部间断性发硬、发胀，也有人会感到轻微疼痛。这是由于子宫不规则收缩所致，应与临产后的宫缩相区别。这称作前驱宫缩或前阵痛，是临近分娩的征兆之一。

这种子宫收缩如以15分钟的间隔有规律地进行，那么就是临产的信号——真正的宫缩。也有的经产妇没有感觉到前驱宫缩，就开始了真正的宫缩。

3. 尿频

由于下降的胎儿头部压迫膀胱，多出现尿频。稍微有点尿就想去厕所，即使去了厕所有时也尿不出来，有时刚出厕所又立即想去。

4. 腰痛

腰痛也是临产的征兆，有时步履艰难，耻骨部分疼痛。这是因为胎儿的头部下降，压迫骨盆内神经而表现出的症状。

5. 分泌物增多

为准备分娩，子宫颈管张开，阴道分泌物（带下）增多，呈透明的或白色粘性分泌物。如出现茶色的血性分泌物，就应住院了。因此，在妊娠后期有必要经常注意带下的性状。

6. 胎动变化

一直活跃着的胎动，渐渐变得迟缓了，这是由于子宫经常收缩使胎儿难以活动，同时也是由于胎儿在临产前位置固定的缘故。

在胎动感觉方面，每个人都不一样，但没有突然停止的。

分辨"假临产"

有一点你必须知道的就是"假临产"。在分娩前2～3周，孕妈咪会自觉轻微腰酸，有较频繁的不规律宫缩——其特点是收缩力弱、持续时间短，常少于30秒且不规则，强度也不会逐渐增加；常常在夜间出现，清晨消失；子宫颈不随宫缩而扩张，不伴有血性粘液及流水。由于假临产多在夜间出现，最大的不利因素在于影响休息，使孕妈咪彻夜难眠、疲劳不堪，增加不安或焦虑。所以辨别假临产迹象是很有必要的。那么怎样分辨假临产或者说真假宫缩呢？请看下面真假宫缩的对比情况。

1. 分娩前宫缩（假性宫缩）

（1）不规则；连续几个小时都没有明显的规律出现。

（2）没有进展；强度、持续时间、频率都没有增加。

（3）大部分出现在前面、腹部下方。

（4）从无痛到轻微的不舒服，比较像是压力，而不是痛。

（5）如果你改变姿势、走动、躺下、泡个热水澡或淋浴，反应就不那么剧烈，也不那么难过。

（6）感觉子宫好像一个很硬的球。

2. 分娩宫缩（也称为真的宫缩或真实宫缩）

（1）有规律（虽然不至于分秒不差）。

（2）有进展；越来越强、持续更久、次数更多。宫缩的时间变长（持续20～30秒），间隔则缩短（5～6分钟）。

（3）大部分出现在腹部下方，但是会扩散到背部下方。

（4）从不舒服的压力到紧绷、拉扯的痛。但是通过有意义地放松其他部分的肌肉，这种痛是可以克服，甚至可以减轻的。

（5）如果你是躺着的，维持这个姿势；如果不是，就改变姿势。走动可能会更痛。

（6）通常会见红。

第38周

已是"足月儿"

第38周记：离预产期只有两周了。宝宝已是"足月儿"了，现在出世也属正常，她已经发育完全，而且有50厘米长。

过了多日的慵懒生活之后，我忽然有了力量，疯了一样把屋子打扫得干干净净，令老公激动不已。

胎宝宝状况 身长约50厘米，体重已经长到3200克左右了。当你活动时，小家伙的脑袋会在你的骨盆腔内摇动，但尽管放心，有骨盆的骨架保护，很安全；而且骨盆里也有一定空间让小宝贝的小胳膊、小腿、小屁股继续生长。

孕妈妈状况 这段时期，孕妈咪常常会感到腰痛、脊背痛，有时甚至肋间也痛。沉重的身体加重了腿部的负担，时常出现抽筋和疼痛。尽管你的身体越发沉重，但是一定要记住，产前经常做力所能及的活动对即将到来的分娩会大有帮助。这时的孕妈咪最适宜的运动莫过于散步了，这给她们带来很多益处：肌肉力量得到锻炼加强，可帮助骨盆运动，有助于分娩时减轻疼痛；改善脚部血液循环，刺激足下穴位，调理脏腑功能，进而促进全身血液循环，使胎宝贝血液供应更充足；还能安定神经系统，增加肺部换气功能，促进孕妈咪的消化、吸收及排泄功能。

分娩可能随时发生，现在你应该再确认一次住院的必需品有没有准备好，以及与家人联系的方法、交通工具等。外出时，一定要有人陪同。每天要清洁身体，做好母乳喂养的准备，继续对乳房、乳头进行清洁、按摩、矫正。尽可能地多休息，养精蓄锐，为分娩做好充分的心理、精神与体力准备。

第38周，别忘了到医院做例行产检、盆腔检查。

什么时候该到医院

怀孕进入 37 周以后，就进入了待产阶段。如果你有预兆，家人就得快速反应，马上带你到医院。但到底什么时候该去医院，要视你个人情况而定。

1. 第九个月产检时，询问一下什么情况下该到医院的清楚指示。医生会给你一些数据，让你可以掌握打电话的时机，如宫缩的间隔时间，以及每次宫缩持续多久。医生也会告诉你真正分娩的产兆。

2. 区别分娩前宫缩和分娩宫缩的不同，以确定你的确处在分娩进行的状态。如果是分娩宫缩，就必须到医院。

3. 如果出现下面一些问题，要立刻就医：

(1) 见红：阴道大量出血（血色鲜红而且比平时月经的量还多）。

(2) 破水，而且发现阴道流出浓稠绿色的液体，这是胎便（宝宝第一次大便），这表示宝宝可能发生窘迫。

(3) 出现规律性的阵痛时。

(4) 胎儿突然停止活动时。

(5) 直觉告诉你有情况发生，虽然你实在没有具体的证据来证明所有问题，还是相信母性的本能吧。

破水提前

还未临产，羊水却已经迫不及待地涌出来。这时候，千万不要考虑是否要先冲个澡，要马上通知家人直奔医院。

1. 怎么发现早期破水？

所谓早期破水就是产痛还没有开始，准妈妈突然感觉到有较多的液体从阴道排出，然后会持续有少量液体不断流出。但情况因人而异，有的准妈妈在咳嗽、打喷嚏等腹压增加时，阴道有较多液体流出；有的则可能阴道流液排出一段时间后就终断；也有人会感觉到腹部子宫略为变小，胎儿变得比原先清楚。据统计，有 35% 的早产儿都是因为早期破水而出生的。

2. 为什么会发生早期破水？

导致早期破水的原因很多，通常与感染有关，其他的原因包括羊水过多、胎位异常、子宫颈闭锁不合、多胎妊娠、胎膜发育不良等。但多数早期破水的准妈妈没有办法查出原因。另外，有些研究表明:准妈妈如果营养不良，特别是缺乏维生素C，也比较容易发生早期破水。

3. 早期破水为什么很危险?

羊水的主要成份是胎儿的尿液，其中还含有非常少量的矿物质、稀有元素和生长激素，它的主要功能是防止胎儿在母体跌倒、撞伤时受到激烈的震荡，就好比汽车中的防撞气囊一样，只不过是胎儿"减震设备"罢了。

早期破水给胎儿带来的最主要的危险因素是发生脐带脱出、感染、引发早产、胎盘剥离等并发症。

4. 发生早期破水该如何处理?

(1)无论什么时候感觉破水，都要赶快到医院做检查，确定是不是破水。

(2)在发现有破水迹象之后，务必要躺下休息，不能再起来活动。为了避免羊水流出过多和脐带脱垂，应该用垫子将臀部垫高一些。

(3)不要洗澡。

5. 如何预防早期破水的发生?

(1)定期到医院接受产前检查。

(2)注意孕期卫生，保持膳食平衡，保证充足的维生素C和维生素D的摄入，保持胎膜的韧度。

(3)怀孕期间如果分泌物比较多，有感染的现象，应该及时到医院就诊。

(4)如果是多胎，要多注意休息。

(5)怀孕最后一个月不宜同房。

(6)避免过度劳累和对腹部的冲撞。

(7)如果怀疑自己是破水，应该立刻去医院就诊。

真实故事——剖宫产的感受

一位妈妈讲叙了她的生产过程——

本来预产期是6月7日，但超过了两天，宝宝依然没有一点要出来的意思，经医院检查和动员，我们决定选择剖宫产，原因是脐带绕颈，羊水又太少了。

6月9日上午9点

我被推进了手术室。手术室的中间摆放着一张小手术台，房间开了凉气，一大群护士医生摆弄着手术刀啊什么的，这样的氛围让人想不紧张都不行。在护士们的指点下，我挪动着怀孕四十周过两天的笨重身体爬上了手术台，接着我的手指上、胳膊上就连接上了各种仪器，记得麻醉师看了血压器后还问我：你紧张吗？我说当然很紧张了。麻醉师说：那怎么办，你总得想办法让宝宝出来吧。想想也是，于是就努力让自己放松。也不知用了多长时间，麻醉师才在两个护士的帮助下（帮我把头和腿使劲往一起靠，方便麻醉师找腰椎打麻药）打完了麻醉药。剩下的就是等麻药起作用了。刚过了大约两分钟，麻醉师就问我的脚还能动吗？我一听怕他们动刀，便立即动了动脚指头，还好麻醉师让再等一会。刚过了一会，麻醉师又问，这回可能是麻药上来了，腰部好像有些涨，我告诉麻醉师说。于是，医生用针头挑了挑肚皮，怎么回事，好像还有感觉，有些疼，我赶紧告诉医生，麻醉师可不吃我这一套，一声令下：开始吧！好疼啊！他们可不管这些，于是手术便在我一声惨叫声中开始了！

麻醉师告诉我，不能太麻了，否则对宝宝不好。还好，往下就不怎么疼了，但意识非常清晰，我明显感觉到他们先用刀划了一下，然后用剪刀剪，一层一层的。接着医生告诉我张嘴哈气，然后就感到医生用手从腰部把宝宝往刀口那里推，然后就感到一个东西塞进了我的肚子（后来才知道是医生的手），接着医生使劲把孩子往外拉。“哇！……”

6月9日9点40分

一声嘹亮的哭声传了出来。一阵惊喜，是我的宝宝吗？我激动地问医生。麻醉师告诉我是的，是你的孩子，太棒了！是个男孩，他很棒！我要求看看我的宝宝，麻醉师说要等护士把他弄干净，并告诉我要往点滴里加药了，可能一会就睡着了。于是，慢慢地，我的意识些模糊，隐约听见她们说6斤9两，一听心中窃喜：6月9日，6斤9两！也不知过了多久，我被护士拍醒，让我看看孩子，朦胧中我看见我的宝宝，我刚出生的儿子满面春光（小脸粉红粉红的），正咧着大嘴哭着呢！而且小手指还塞在嘴里，太可爱了，太高兴了，太激动了！潜藏的母性一下子全涌了出来，噢，我的儿子，我的宝贝！

接下来就什么也不知道了，只是迷迷糊糊中好像感觉有人拍我的脸，让我自己挪回推床上去，要回病房了。天哪，那时候哪里还动得了！等我醒来时已经在病房里了，老公坐在一旁笑咪咪地告诉我：生了个儿子！

真实故事——顺产的历程

这是一位顺产妈妈的故事，故事如产程，要长一些——

我的预产期是5月29日，但我的直觉告诉我肯定会提前，而且提前不少。因此，从五一长假过后，我就做好随时分娩的准备了。到医院要用的证件、物品和现金早都已经打包备用。虽然每天都能感觉到他在我肚子里的"运动"，但这个时候，我还说不上对他有什么感情，只是希望这个漫长的孕期快快结束。

老公大胆预测宝宝出生的日期不是在5月21日就是在5月26日（其实我自己认为会更早），但21日悄悄过去了，还是没有动静。急脾气的我有些着急了，怎么还不出来呢？老公决定无论我生不生，他都从26日开始请假在家陪我。

26日早晨，好像预感到什么，还是肚子里的宝宝给我的"信息"，我破天荒地吃了一人份的早餐。要知道在整个怀孕期间，因为反应，早餐一般只是一杯牛奶了事的。

八点半开始，腹部隐隐有些作痛，我知道，最后那一刻终于要来了。所有有关分娩的知识全部来自于书本，知道这个时候还不用去医院。我躺在床上，一边再看一遍有关分娩的书，一边忍受着大约半小时一次的疼痛。

下午两三点钟的时候，我和老公来到医院，这时候我的阵痛已是在十五分钟左右一次。医生告诉我可能要直接住院，不能再回家了。之后就是做胎心监护、B超等一系列的检查。在做胎心的时候，我几乎无法完整做完整个监护，疼得我几次中断。

下午四五点钟，医院没有病房，我被安排在急诊室。急诊室共有六张病床，我进去的时候已经有两个羊水先破了的待产孕妇静静地躺在床上，和守在床边的家属聊着天。只有我，每隔几分钟就疼得从床上坐起来，捂着肚子轻轻地"哎哟"几声。

我从书上了解到初产妇从频繁阵痛到最后分娩，需要12～16个小时，因

此我想最早也要在第二天上午宝宝才能出生。这个时候安排老公去接我妈妈和弟弟来，妈妈和老公负责轮流看护我，弟弟负责开着车随时待命。

这个时候阵痛已是十分钟一次，护士偶尔会进来问问我的感受，给听听胎心什么的。老公不在，就我一个人，真觉得有些孤单。这时候有个做了十年助产士的朋友打我手机来安慰我，告诉我正确的呼吸方法，还没说几句，又一阵阵痛袭来，痛得我无法说出话来……

我就这样一边疼着，一边等着老公他们回来。心里想，这要是明天上午生，我这一夜得怎么过呀！实际上因为太疼，我中饭、晚饭一口也没吃，老公也曾数次问我吃不吃东西，都被我拒绝了。

晚上快八点的时候，妈妈他们终于到了，看到我疼成这样都有些不知所措。我让老公和弟弟先回家睡觉，半夜三四点钟再来换妈妈的班，反正我认为最早第二天才会生嘛，也没必要让他们全陪在这儿。可老公他们才走，我的阵痛就频繁起来，五分钟一次。妈妈去叫护士来看看，护士来看了一眼说没关系的，宫口还没开，还需要一段时间呢，没那么快。

可随着越来越频繁的疼痛，我有些受不了了，大叫着让妈妈去叫护士来。妈妈慌忙跑去回来的结果是让我自己走到护士间去检查。护士间和我待的急诊室隔了两个门，我晃晃悠悠走进去，艰难地躺到了检查床上，护士过来看了看，惊叫了一声：“已经开了两指半了，快去产房。”这个时候是八点半钟。妈妈慌忙给刚刚走了半小时的老公打电话，让他们快回来，我就要生了。可她不会用手机，着急地乱按，我接过手机，自己给老公打了电话。虽然这个时候很疼，也有些慌乱，但自己比我预想的要镇静，心想该来的总会来，慌也于事无补。我相信，别人能，自己也一定顺利地生下宝宝。

在走去产房之前，一阵剧烈地恶心感袭来，我冲到洗手间，把估计还是早晨吃的那一点点食物吐了个干干净净，这下肚子里是彻底空了。

像我这样开到两指半还不能上产床，只能在产房的“待产室”里。刚刚在急诊室做检查的时候我已经见红了，待产室的护士又给检查了一遍，并给我做了人工破水。我问她大约需要多长时间才能生，被告之每开一指大约需要两到三小时。我暗自在心里算了算，天哪，那开到十指岂不是还要十几二十个小时。我又一次绝望地想着，这漫漫长夜该怎么渡过呀。同时我又在心里对老公说：这下你的预测全部不灵了吧，说我26日生，现在看来肯定是生不了的了，现在已经是晚上九点半了嘛。

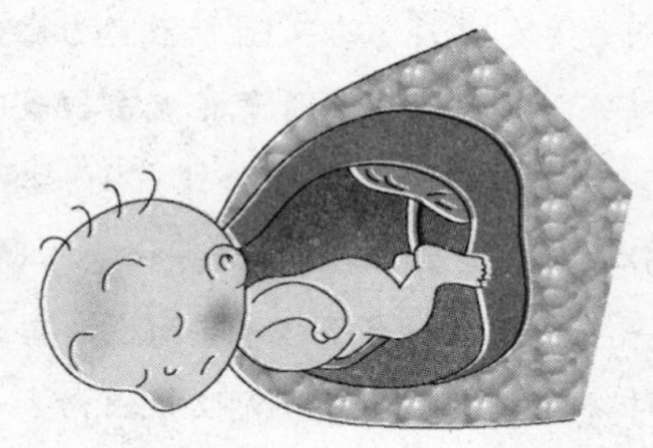

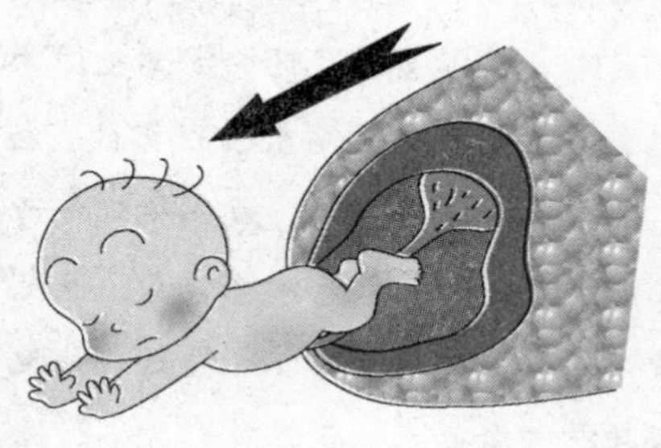

待产室里是不能有家属陪着的，我"孤独"地疼着。就在我觉得疼得实在受不了的时候，我曾大叫护士再给我检查检查，被护士拒绝了，告诉我频繁检查也不好，容易感染，而且她们的规定是四个小时检查一次。我问护士能不能做无痛分娩，护士说无痛也并非完全不痛，最疼的那段还是要自己忍受，她们不鼓励做无痛。回头想想，我好像从来没动过做剖宫产的念头，就算再疼，也是一直想着要自己生。

我不记得在待产室躺了多长时间，觉得每分钟都过得很漫长。就在我第二次疼得实在不行，大叫护士的时候，护士才好像勉为其难地来看看，结果又是一声惊呼："快上产床，都开到八指了，这么快！"

产床是要自己走去上的。下了待产室的床，再走到十几米远的产房，上产床之前还要换上生产的衣服和鞋子，这些都是在"剧烈"的疼痛之下完成的，之后真的是"爬"上产床的，没有人帮你，也没有人扶你。后来我想，要不然怎么说做了妈妈的人伟大呢，经历过这些真的是会勇敢很多。

上了产床，周围的医生护士就多了起来，各有分工，有人听胎心，有人看宫口。还有个护士问我需不需要老公陪产，我说要。这是我们早就商量好了的，能陪产肯定要陪。一会儿老公也穿着医院的衣服进来了，看到他，这下我心里有底了。没有看表，这个时候应该是夜里十一点左右了，我依然以为孩子还要很长时间才会出来。倒是老公，为了让我放轻松，还在我耳边悄悄地开玩笑说："你一定要争取在26日生出来。""这是我能决定的吗？"我有些啼笑皆非地想，"况且现在马上就要到27号了，看来是不可能了。"

之后的过程超乎想象的快。我在医生的指导下呼吸、使劲，我只是觉得剧痛，痛得我没有一点儿精力去想别的，我甚至都不知道我的宝宝已经缓缓地出来了，只是不由自主地使劲、使劲……随着医生一句：“好了，出来了！”

“哇” 的一声，我的宝宝哭了出来，我就觉得肚子突然瘪了下去，一下子轻松了，没那么疼了。我知道，一切都结束了，终于结束了，我的眼泪也不由自言地涌了出来。

“男孩，50厘米，2900克，出生时间是5月26日23点52分。” 我的宝宝，真的是如他爸爸所预测的，赶在26日，还差八分钟就要到27日的时候，来和我们见面了。在医生给宝宝称完体重，擦干身体，放在我胸口上的时候，在我第一次和他这样肌肤接触，第一眼看到他的时候，我就开始深深地爱上他了。

第39周

离宝宝越来越近

第39周记： 我的腹部忽然平静下来，感觉不到大的动作了。大夫说是因为我的身体里没有足够的空间了。而我把小宝宝想象成一个运动员，正在短暂的平静中积聚力量，准备着最后的冲刺。我觉得很不舒服，好像我的身体已经负担不起两个人了。想到孩子的出世，我忐忑不安。

胎宝宝状况　小宝贝身体各部份器官都已发育完毕，而肺是最后一个成熟的器官——直至小家伙出生后的几个小时里，正常的呼吸模式才能建立起。小家伙的动作似乎安静了很多，主要是因为头部已经固定在骨盆中。随着头部位置的不断下降，与小宝贝见面的时刻越来越近了。

孕妈妈状况　你常常会觉得很不舒服，好像你的身体已经负担不起两个人了。想到孩子的出世你也许会忐忑不安，甚至是焦躁、急迫的。在这个阶段尽量夫妻双方多谈些轻松的话题如，如何将来和宝宝在一起玩耍等。生活中的各种活动都要小心，比如避免长时间站立、洗澡时要避免滑倒等等。总之，要充分休息，密切注意自身变化，随时做好临产的准备。

检查一下，还有什么事没有安排好？入院和出院所需的所有衣物、卫生用品、产前检查记录、可以随时取出以备急用的钱等必需品是否已经整理妥当。如果住高层住宅楼，了解清楚电梯夜间运行情况，以保证夜间使用电梯。甚至应该计划一下妻子一旦临产时乘什么车、选什么路线去医院，尽可能把所有的问题都想到。

第39周，别忘了到医院做例行产检。

紧急分娩

有时宝宝不会按部就班地给你信息，告诉你分娩进行得怎么样了。这时候，你会突然意识到："糟糕！要生了！"于是你知道上医院是来不及了。为了胎儿安全，一定要到医院分娩，如果确实因各种原因来不及到医院，也一定要在分娩的同时，做好随时去医院的准备。万不得已，不要在家中分娩。

遇到这种情况时，要注意：

1．立刻打电话给医院或打急救电话。

2．准备一个分娩床。为了不弄脏床垫，在床垫和床单之间铺一层防水垫（几层厚厚的纸或塑胶桌布等），然后再铺上一层干净的床单。

3．调整临时产房的室温到23～26℃。

4．叫丈夫或其他什么人烧两盆热水，其中一盆用来消毒各种用具，另一盆让它凉到微温的程度，让妈妈分娩完后可以清洗一下。

用一盆热水消毒1把剪刀、两条脚掌长度的线（用来扎脐带）。

还要准备几样东西：一个洗碗盆可以用来装胎盘，至少3条干净的大毛巾，温暖、干净的毯子或毛巾可以用来包裹宝宝。

5．想办法用最舒适的姿势来躺：仰着、侧躺等。

6．接生人事先用酒精或消毒肥皂把手洗干净。如果只有你一个人在家，必须靠自己把孩子生下来，记得事先把手洗干净。

7．在宝宝的头先露出之后，不要再用力，也不要把它拉出来，要让宝宝的头自己慢慢滑出来，掉到接生人的手上，落到床上。然后，轻轻地把脐带绕过宝宝的头拿开来。

8．随着宝宝的头突然转向，接着出现的就是宝宝的肩膀了。宝宝的头已经出来，肩膀还没有出来的时候，用双手在肛门开口上方以毛巾按住的方式来保护会阴，以防它在宝宝露出肩膀的时候被撕裂。

9．让接生的人帮宝宝把黏液从鼻子里吸出来，然后把宝宝倒举起来维持几秒，好让宝宝喉咙里的黏液流出来。

10．宝宝分娩出来后，立刻把宝宝腹部朝下，让他趴在你的胸前。接着把宝宝身上多余的液体清理干净。至于宝宝身上干酪状的覆膜就不用急着清理掉。然后用温暖的毛巾把宝宝的背部和头盖起来。

11．如果宝宝看起来好像没在呼吸，摩擦宝宝的背部，以刺激他呼吸。如果宝宝的嘴唇发紫，就轻轻地对宝宝进行五六次口对口的人工呼吸。记得你的嘴要同时盖住宝宝的鼻子和嘴巴。

12．如果家中无消毒物品，建议不要在家中处理脐带。

13．让宝宝吸吮乳头，刺激胎盘的娩出。通常胎盘在宝宝娩出后的5～30分钟内就会排出来。

14．让宝宝持续吸吮你的乳房。

15．胎盘娩出以后，在骨盆上方的位置轻轻地按摩子宫，以帮助子宫继续收缩，同时适度地压缩血管。

16.产后并非完事大吉，如有可能,仍要到医院进一步检查产妇和孩子，并注射破伤风抗毒素。切记:此种情况容易出现在偏远山区，尽量避免。

去医院的路上

面对突发情况如果没有经验，将会很被动。在去医院的路上，如果紧急分娩发生，往往令人焦急无措。出现这情况，要注意以下几点：

1．开车要注意安全，越急越容易出问题，一定要稳。

2．电话通知医院，产妇已在路上，情况紧急，以便医院作好接生准备。

3．产妇应安排在后座休息，尽量躺着，有人陪护。座位铺上床单、毛巾等，防止车座椅套不卫生。

4．如果临产，要减速稳行或干脆停车，等宝宝生出来再继续赶往医院处理、医护。

第40周

结束所有的辛苦等待

第40周记：我全身发热，我厌倦了等待。准备在医院用的东西已经收拾好，装进一个大包里。宝宝的摇篮也准备好了。我不停的搓着手指，焦躁不安。老公说，听听音乐吧。哦，等等，好像是，是宫缩吗？我想不是。15分钟后，又是一次。我想她要来了，老公赶忙去叫车。梦终于要实现了。

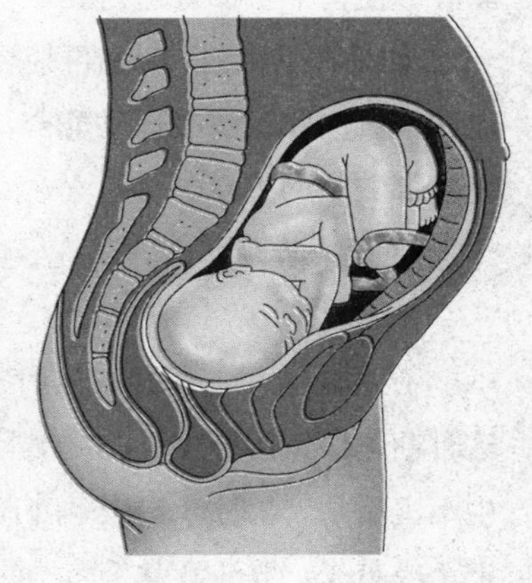

第40周（成熟胎宝宝）

生命诞生 宝宝成熟了，妈妈时刻面临分娩，生命中的重大时刻即将来临。十月怀胎，一朝分娩，期待已久的小生命很快就要投入你温暖的怀抱中。

现在医生可根据胎儿和你的情况确定分娩方式。大多数妈妈都能自己生下宝宝，即阴道分娩，这是最自然、最健康的方式，也有利于宝宝的身心健康。不要因为怕疼或保持体形而选择剖宫产。大多数的胎儿都将在本周诞生，但准确地在预产日出生的只有5%。预产日期的推算包括合理误差，提前或推迟两周都是正常的。但如果推迟两周后还没有临产迹象，特别是胎动明显减少时，就应该尽快去医院，尽快娩出胎儿，否则对胎儿也不利。

要注意避免胎膜早破，即还未真正开始分娩就破水，羊水大量流出，阴道中的细菌会乘机侵入子宫，给胎儿带来危险。丈夫应该随时处于待命状态，保证妻子随时可以找到你，妻子身边随时应有亲友陪伴。

当宫缩时间间隔越来越短，疼痛时间越来越长的时候，就应该考虑马上去医院，特别是在距离医院路程较远的情况下，一定要把时间安排好。

配合接生

生孩子固然需要医生或接生员的帮助和指导，更需要产妇的正确配合。如果产妇在分娩时不合作，就容易发生意外。

1. 第一产程的配合

临产后进入第一阶段，产妇一定要保持安静，养精蓄力，不要乱喊乱叫或乱用劲而消耗体力（这时宫口尚未开全，过度用劲是徒劳的），以免到后来需要用劲时反而没劲了。为了减轻痛楚，产妇应集中注意力做深、慢、均匀的深呼吸，即每次宫缩时，深吸气渐渐鼓起腹部，呼气时缓慢下降。深呼吸运动可以增加氧气的吸入，提高产妇血液内氧的含量，有利于补充胎儿在子宫内需要的氧气和消除子宫肌肉的疲劳，并且可以使产妇转移注意力，保持镇静，使宫缩协调地进行。

如果在宫缩时，产妇再轻轻地按摩自己的小腹部，或者紧紧地用拳头压迫腰部肌肉和深呼吸运动配合，更可以减轻子宫收缩对大脑的刺激，从而减轻腹部酸胀的感觉。

在这一阶段，产妇还应尽量补充营养和水分，并利用一切机会休息。

2. 第二产程的配合

产程进入第二阶段，这时宫缩痛已减轻，主要有下坠感，想使用腹压。这时期是保障母子安全的关键时刻，产妇必须和接生人员密切配合，防止发生不良后果。此时产妇应平卧在产床上，两腿屈膝分开，两手分别握住床边把手或带子。要注意掌握每次宫缩，有劲要用在宫缩上。当宫缩时，先深吸一口气，憋住；接着随宫缩如解大便样向下用力屏气；当宫缩间隙时不要用力，全身肌肉放松，安静休息。如用力不当，徒然消耗体力，反而造成宫缩乏力，影响产程进展。

当胎头即将娩出阴道口时，必须听从助产人员指导，宫缩时不要再使猛劲。而要张开嘴“哈气”，这样可使会阴肌肉充分扩张，然后再让胎头缓慢娩出，防止胎头娩出过快，撕裂会阴。

3. 第三产程的配合

胎儿娩出后，进入第三产程。此时产妇已非常疲劳，产妇可以抓紧时间休息一下，约过5～15分钟，产妇又感到有宫缩，子宫底上升，阴道有少量

血液流出，此时只须稍用腹压，就可协助胎盘很快娩出；若超过30分钟胎盘不下，应听从医生指导，在医生帮助下娩出胎盘。

分娩时吃点什么

医生过去都希望产妇分娩时不要进食或是喝饮料，但现在还是建议分娩中的妇女进食少量容易消化的食物。

1. 早一点进食：在分娩初期进食以储存能量。

2. 进食次数多一点：以小吃代替正餐（少量多餐或吃零食）。

3. 吃高热量食物：分娩初期，尽量往肚子里填些复合碳水化合物（谷类、面食）；分娩后期，小口吃或喝一些简单的碳水化合物，如果汁、蜂蜜等。

4. 吃容易消化的食物，避免脂肪太多或是油炸、油腻的食物。

5. 适当多喝水：分娩初期，每小时可补充些水，有利于分娩。

贴心·提醒

产妇在临产前吃一两块巧克力，能在分娩过程中产生更多热量。巧克力最好是黑色的。

留住宝宝的第一次

1. 胎毛

每个人一生之中只有一次机会可以将胎毛留下，建议你可以将胎毛制作成胎毛笔，留下永恒的记忆。

2. 脐带血

脐带血贮存是为以后应用，这需要一定条件，需要事先与脐血库联系。

3. 摄像

从宝宝出生后的每一时、每一刻，都是令人欢天喜地的，同时也让整个家庭充满了生命力。建议你可以从宝宝出生后的每一个重点阶段，用摄像机留下宝宝最可爱的的一举一动。

宝宝生出的那一刻是红着屁股还是闭着眼睛呢？你可以和医生协调，捕捉宝宝瓜瓜坠地的一瞬间。

4. 录音

宝宝的第一个声音是什么样的，是哇哇大哭还是伊伊呀呀。建议你进行录音，以保存宝宝独一无二、意义非凡的第一个声音。

5. 脚、手印

小宝宝的小手、小脚是最惹人怜爱的，宝宝的一小步是妈妈的一大步；建议你可以用红色或是紫色的印泥，印画出最可爱的小手印和小脚印。

产后护理

1．正常分娩后约6小时即可下床用餐和排尿。若顺利约3天左右即可出院。

2．产后应以卫生棉遮护会阴以吸收恶露。并随时更换，且排便后应用温开水或消毒水由前往后冲洗。

3．满月前宜采用淋浴，切勿使用盆浴，以防细菌进入子宫引起发炎。

4．洗发后迅速吹干即可。

5．产后常口渴，可多饮开水、牛奶及热的易消化食物。

6．恶露干净、子宫完全恢复才可开始性生活。通常在产后7周后，否则易感染或出血。

7．产后6周即需做产后检查，可以按一般就医程序办理，以检查生殖器官是否已完全恢复。

8．产后进行适宜运动可增强腹肌收缩、促进子宫收缩，快速恢复身材。

母乳喂养

1. 促进乳汁分泌的方法

（1）分娩后尽早喂哺母乳。

（2）除喂母乳外，避免以牛奶补充。

（3）依婴儿的需要采用弹性时间喂哺母乳。

(4) 当宝宝不在身边时，可用手或挤奶器将乳汁挤出。并将乳汁冰存起来留给宝宝吃。

(5) 正确的吸吮方式及喂奶姿势。

(6) 喂奶前按摩乳房。

(7) 每天保持充足的睡眠及愉快的心情。

(8) 多喝牛奶、汤水或吃一些能促进乳汁分泌的食物，例如猪蹄。

2. 奶胀的预防与处理

(1) 新生儿出生后即让其吸吮母乳，并经常喂奶，不另添加牛奶。不让新生儿口含奶嘴。

(2) 按摩乳房，挤出一些奶水，使乳房柔软后再让婴儿吸吮。

(3) 避免让婴儿采用同一个姿势吸奶。

(4) 母亲穿戴合适的胸罩支托。

最后的叮咛

终于迎来了这个小小人，一切都不一样了。也许尿布脏了、也许肚子饿了，婴儿一旦不舒服，马上就啼哭起来。不管怎么说，生活规律打乱了，做妈妈的常常会感到很疲劳，这时候要请丈夫帮忙。正常生活秩序将会在等待身体复原过程中渐渐地恢复。

新妈妈的精神不安、休息不好是产后恢复的大敌，所以必须好好调养，注意休息。白天婴儿睡觉的时候自己也可睡一会儿，以保证睡眠充足。

最后的叮咛

1. 出院后直到产后第2周，以在床上休息为主。最初的第1周可躺躺、起起，适度下床。从第2周的后半周开始，起床的时间长一点。第3周开始下床，逐渐使身体恢复以前的习惯。

产后1月后才能外出，但不能去很远的地方，从到附近买东西开始，再渐渐走远。6周过后，就可以骑自行车或开车，也可以带婴儿一起散步了。四处参观、步行观光这样的旅行及海外旅行，至少要在出院2个月以后。

2. 每次大小便后，从阴部由前往后冲洗会阴部，再用卫生纸将会阴周围的水吸干，随时保持会阴部清洁，以免受细菌感染。

3. 产后3天可以开始淋浴，恶露消失以后得到医生许可也可以盆浴。要注意室内温度和保持空气流通，洗澡后要立即擦干身体，头发也要立即吹干以免受寒。

4. 第7天后可逐渐从事日常轻微的工作，但要避免过度疲劳及提重物。

5. 为促进身体的复原和乳汁分泌，产妇要多摄取高蛋白食物，如鱼类、肉类、蛋、蔬菜及水果。也要多喝开水，以补充足够的水份和减少便秘的机会。

6. 发烧38℃以上、乳房出现红肿现象、突发性的大量出血、恶露出现恶臭味、会阴部伤口越来越痛、剖宫产伤口化脓时，应立即到医院检查。

7. 产后6星期应回医院接受产后检查，以了解身体及其他部位是否已恢复正常。

8. 产后约6星期，身体状况已恢复，无不适状况，可过性生活。

新生活又开始了！

历经了孕期40周，是辛苦的，更是幸福的！人生已翻开了新的一页，让我们怀着眷恋和憧憬，自信地迈向新的生活！

The
WILEY
advantage

Dear Valued Customer,

We realize you're a busy professional with deadlines to hit. Whether your goal is to learn a new technology or solve a critical problem, we want to be there to lend you a hand. Our primary objective is to provide you with the insight and knowledge you need to stay atop the highly competitive and ever-changing technology industry.

Wiley Publishing, Inc., offers books on a wide variety of technical categories, including security, data warehousing, software development tools, and networking — everything you need to reach your peak. Regardless of your level of expertise, the Wiley family of books has you covered.

- For Dummies – The ***fun*** and ***easy*** way to learn
- The Weekend Crash Course –The ***fastest*** way to learn a new tool or technology
- Visual – For those who prefer to learn a new topic ***visually***
- The Bible – The ***100% comprehensive*** tutorial and reference
- The Wiley Professional list – ***Practical*** and ***reliable*** resources for IT professionals

The book you hold now, *Mastering Tomcat Development,* is a code-intensive guide to developing J2EE applications using the Tomcat server. This book takes a developer's perspective on Tomcat, showing you how to use Tomcat with related tools such as JDBC, Struts, Jakarta Taglibs, and Velocity. The result is a comprehensive approach to developing sophisticated and secure Java Web applications. All of the source code used in the real-world examples throughout the book is available for you to download from the book's companion Web site at www.wiley.com/compbooks/harrison.

Our commitment to you does not end at the last page of this book. We'd want to open a dialog with you to see what other solutions we can provide. Please be sure to visit us at www.wiley.com/compbooks to review our complete title list and explore the other resources we offer. If you have a comment, suggestion, or any other inquiry, please locate the "contact us" link at www.wiley.com.

Thank you for your support and we look forward to hearing from you and serving your needs again in the future.

Sincerely,

Richard K Swadley

Richard K. Swadley
Vice President & Executive Group Publisher
Wiley Technology Publishing

15 HOUR WEEKEND CRASH COURSE

Bible

FOR DUMMIES

more information on related titles

Mastering Tomcat Development

Ian McFarland
Peter Harrison

Wiley Publishing, Inc.

Publisher: Robert Ipsen
Editor: Robert M. Elliott
Managing Editor: John Atkins
Book Packaging: Ryan Publishing Group, Inc.
Copyeditor: Elizabeth Welch
Proofreader: Nancy Sixsmith
Compositor: Gina Rexrode

This book is printed on acid-free paper. ∞

Published by Wiley Publishing, Inc., Indianapolis, Indiana

Published simultaneously in Canada.

Library of Congress Cataloging-in-Publication Data:

ISBN: 0-471-23764-7

Printed in the United States of America

10 9 8 7 6 5 4 3 2 1

This book is dedicated to The Apache Software Foundation, to the Tomcat team, and to the spirit of the open source movement, which has created such wonderful tools and made them freely available to the world.

Acknowledgments

Thanks first to Tim Ryan of Ryan Publishing for contacting me in the first place and enticing me to work on this book. Thanks also for all his support and encouragement during the whole writing, rewriting, and production process.

Thanks to Rick Hightower, who contributed two excellent chapters—the one on Ant and the one on Struts. They significantly improve the book, and his writing them ensured that I was able to see the sun a couple of times during the two weeks he was working on them.

Thanks to Liz Welch, my copyeditor, whose suggestions were always insightful and informed, and whose input greatly improved the quality of this book.

Thanks to all my friends, who understood that I didn't have much time to see them during the two-month marathon that the production of this book entailed.

Thanks also to my colleagues at LocalLogic and inkchaser for understanding the deadlines, which often took me away from working on their projects.

Thanks to my downstairs neighbor Said, his restaurant Zaré, and his fine staff, Adel and the others, who let me sit for hours in the afternoon on the patio and work on this book. Such a pleasant change from sitting at my desk in the same room hour after hour!

Contents

About the Author

Ian McFarland is president of Neo Ventures, Ltd., a San Francisco–based consulting firm. His articles on Java and Mac OS X appear monthly in *Java Developer's Journal*. He has been developing client-server Java applications since Java version 1.0 alpha 2, and with his team wrote the first client-server application ever written in Java: a demo seating-reservation application used for the Java product announcement at SunWorld in 1995. He first started working on networked hypertext publishing working with Ted Nelson at Autodesk, Inc., in 1989, and was on the launch team of HotWired. He subsequently served as Java Evangelist for Symantec's Visual Café before returning to consulting. He is the author of a number of articles for various publications, including the Sun Microsystems developer site Java Developer Connection and Developer.com.

He is also published in the anthology *Drama in the Desert.*

About the Contributors

Peter Harrison is senior developer and technical team leader for Customer Information Technologies, located in New Zealand. At CIT he leads a team of Java Web application developers who primarily use servlets and JSP. He is responsible for writing and maintaining all standards and procedures; he has implemented the XP methodology of project development; and he manages all testing, including setting up automated unit testing, source-code control, peer-review systems, and planning procedures.

Applications that Peter has developed using servlet/JSP include a digital rights management system, a mailing list server, a security product called Eproxy, and the dynamic content-delivery application that powers www.devcentre.org.

Peter is Webmaster for DevCentre.org, a resource for open source developers that includes articles he has written. He has been a software developer for 11 years, and also teaches a Java class at Glenfield College in Auckland, New Zealand.

Richard Hightower is CTO of Trivera Technologies, a leading Java education company that offers online and classroom training, as well as consulting on enterprise Java application development. Rick is a software engineer by training who specializes in software development tools and processes; and developing enterprise applications using J2EE, XML, UML, JDBC, SQL, and open source technologies. Formerly, he was the Senior Software Engineer for Java Architecture at Intel's Enterprise Architecture Lab. At Intel he led a team of developers, designing and implementing three-tier client-server applications; introduced OO CASE tools; and created several frameworks using a variety of Java, COM, CORBA, and middleware technologies. Rick also created ICBeans and authored the patent application for this technology, which was awarded to Intel.

Rick is the co-author of the popular *Java Tools for Extreme Programming*, writes frequently for *Java Developer's Journal*, speaks at Java industry conferences, and teaches a variety of enterprise Java development classes at Trivera.

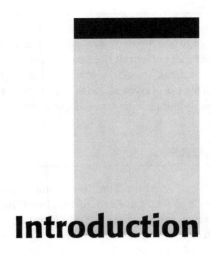

Introduction

This is a book about Tomcat 4.1. It covers installation and configuration, and also a wide variety of development topics. It will teach you how to develop Web applications on Tomcat, and how to configure Tomcat to support those applications. It won't teach you Java, so if you're going to be writing code, you should already know Java or have a good basic Java text on hand.

There are two detailed appendices covering the complete syntax of both the server.xml configuration file and the Servlet 2.3 deployment descriptor file. Our experience has shown these to be two key areas of difficulty for people new to Tomcat and servlets. Both topics are discussed extensively in their own chapters as well.

Who Should Read This Book

This book is intended to give complete coverage of Tomcat from both a development and an administration perspective. It is primarily oriented toward servlet and JSP developers who inevitably have a need to administer their own development installation of Tomcat. Depending on the size of the organization in which readers find themselves, they may also have responsibility for some server configuration and administration, or may wish to provide guidance to the systems administration staff.

Another important audience for this book is the person whose job it is to administer Tomcat. The first half of the book focuses extensively on configuration and management of the Tomcat server. Not all of the development chapters will be necessary reading for these folks, but a greater understanding of the development process will help them make informed configuration and administration decisions.

The third important audience consists of those responsible for quality assurance. By understanding the whole development process, these readers can better anticipate the issues, improve testing strategies, and ensure that the development and quality assurance platforms closely match the production environment.

Development, quality assurance, and systems administration are three parts of the same whole. This book gives all sides of the team a common vocabulary and a greater understanding of the development, testing, and deployment process.

Versions

This book covers both Tomcat 4.1 and Tomcat 4.0. There are significant new features in Tomcat 4.1 (see Chapter 1 for more information) that we cover in detail. If you are working with Tomcat 4.0, you may notice some slight differences from the examples and figures in this book, and we are confident that you will find the coverage here quite instructive and useful.

Tomcat 4.x implements version 2.3 of the Servlet Specification and version 1.2 of the JSP Specification. We provide chapters on both of these platforms and their accompanying specifications.

Companion Web Site

This book's companion Web site (www.wiley.com/compbooks/harrison) contains all the code listings from the book. It also contains a bonus chapter (Chapter 21, "Source Code Management with CVS") that describes the range of tools available to help you manage your source code. This chapter focuses on CVS and explains how to set up the tool and use it to manage your software projects.

Roadmap

This book is divided into two parts, the first concentrating on server configuration issues and the second on servlet development issues. The chapters are arranged in such a way that you can choose to read the book straight through, with later chapters building on topics covered in earlier chapters. However, it is generally quite possible to skip ahead to topics of particular interest to you. If you're not using HTTP Authentication, for instance, there's no particular need for you to read Chapter 8, "Managing Authentication with Realms." This section is intended to help you understand how the book is laid out so that you can quickly find the information you want.

Part I: Tomcat Configuration and Management

Chapter 1, "Introduction to Tomcat," gives you the nickel tour of what Tomcat is, where Tomcat came from, and what's new in Tomcat 4.1.

Chapter 2, "Installing Tomcat," gets you up and running with the latest version of the Tomcat server.

Chapter 3, "Configuring Tomcat," covers the basics of Tomcat configuration. You'll learn how to configure Tomcat for most applications, without spending time on less-used or more esoteric features.

Chapter 4, "Hello World Wide Web," discusses the fundamentals of servlet development, with an emphasis on HTTP servlets. This chapter also explains how Tomcat calls the doGet(), doPost(), and init() methods in response to client requests.

Chapter 5, "Anatomy and Life Cycle of a Servlet," walks you through the structure of a servlet and explains how the container goes about instantiating and managing servlets.

Chapter 6, "Configuring Web Applications," goes into depth on the configuration and file structure of a Web application and examines the structure of the deployment descriptor file. It also talks about how to build Web Archive (WAR) files, which are designed to simplify Webapp deployment.

Chapter 7, "The server.xml File in Depth," takes you through the nitty-gritty of the server.xml file, covering the material in Chapter 3 in more detail and also explaining anything we left out.

Chapter 8, "Managing Authentication with Realms," describes how to configure Tomcat to manage HTTP user authentication.

Chapter 9, "The Manager Application," explains the Tomcat manager servlet, which can be used to deploy and manage servlets.

Part II: Tomcat Development

Chapter 10, "The Model-View-Controller Architecture," gives you some background on a key development paradigm used extensively through the technologies in the four chapters that follow.

Chapter 11, "JavaServer Pages," covers the basics of JSP development.

Chapter 12, "Tag Libraries," explains how to create and use tag libraries.

Chapter 13, "MVC with Struts," covers how to use Struts, a Web application development framework based on the Model-View-Controller paradigm.

Chapter 14, "Template Systems," examines template systems generally, and then discusses Velocity, a template system developed by the ASF to further abstract page layout from code development.

Chapter 15, "Session Management," shows you how to use the excellent support for session management that is a part of the servlet platform.

Chapter 16, "Databases, Connection Pools, and JDBC," covers how to integrate databases into your servlets.

In Chapter 17, "Database-Aware Objects," we develop a reusable framework for object persistence that uses a database for the underlying datastore.

In Chapter 18, "Security," we discuss security considerations, both from a software configuration and a development perspective.

Chapter 19, "The Development Cycle," focuses on using the techniques in this book on a day-to-day basis.

Chapter 20, "Developing Web Applications with Ant and XDoclet," is a detailed discussion of using Ant and XDoclet to automate the build and deploy process of your server-side Java Web components for Tomcat.

Appendixes A and B are references for the server.xml file and web.xml file, respectively.

CHAPTER

1

Introduction to Tomcat

Many of you picking up this book have developed Java Web applications and want to learn the details of Tomcat configuration, management, and development. Some of you may be new to Tomcat and are considering whether to deploy it. Others may be new to servlet programming. In this chapter, we create a common frame of reference for all readers, and put Tomcat in both a technical and an historical context.

The Apache Software Foundation

Tomcat is a servlet and JavaServer Pages (JSP) container developed under the auspices of The Apache Software Foundation (ASF). This foundation is an outgrowth of the Apache Project, an initiative that led to the creation of Apache, the most successful Web server platform in the still-short history of the World Wide Web. Apache itself began as a series of patches to the NCSA HTTPd, which we started at HotWired to support the huge (at the time) user load we experienced on the site from the moment we launched. Apache, in fact, derives its name from those patches. (The server was so named because it was a "patchy" version of the NCSA HTTPd.) Brian Behlendorf—who was responsible for some of the first patches and on whose desktop SGI Indy, one of the first two instances of the patched NCSA HTTPds, ran—developed the ASF to promote open source development of key technologies and has become an icon of the whole open source movement. (By the way, the other instance ran on the desktop Indy belonging to one of your authors, Ian McFarland.)

The ASF has a number of larger subdivisions, called projects, each focused around a different technology area. Perhaps the three key projects of interest to the Java developer are the HTTP Server Project, which maintains the Apache Web server we just talked about; the Jakarta Project, which has a Java focus; and the Apache XML Project, which, as the name implies, focuses on XML tools.

The Jakarta Project's mission statement contains a concise summary of the Project's goals: "Jakarta is a Project of The Apache Software Foundation, charged with the creation and maintenance of commercial-quality, open source, server-side solutions for the Java Platform, based on software licensed to the Foundation, for distribution at no charge to the public."

The Jakarta Project is responsible for many significant and award-winning Java tools, and Tomcat is one of them. Another very significant project, one that has gained substantial momentum, is Ant, a portable build management system written in Java but applicable to development in any language (see Chapter 20 for in-depth coverage of Ant). Nearly half of the remaining subprojects are related in some way to servlets. A number are template systems or application toolkits. We'll look at two of them, Struts and Velocity, in this book. Other subprojects include the following:

- Turbine is a framework for developing secure Web applications.
- JMeter is a performance testing tool you can use to load test your servlets.
- Log4J is a very highly regarded logging package, originally developed elsewhere, substantially improved by IBM, and then transferred to the Jakarta Project.
- ORO and Regexp are two regular expression packages, also donated to the foundation.
- Jetspeed is a portal platform built on servlets.

Although the Apache XML Project focuses on XML, not Java, there are a large number of Java-based projects there as well, many of particular interest to developers of Web applications. The Xerces parser library has long been a staple of XML development. Xalan is a fine Extensible Stylesheet Language Transformations (XSLT) engine. Axis, and its predecessor, Apache SOAP, are implementations of the Simple Object Access Protocol, which is at the root of the current Web services craze. Cocoon is an XML- and XSLT-based publishing framework. Batik is a Java library for working with Scalable Vector Graphics (SVG) files. And so on.

All of this software has the dual advantages of being open source and, at the same time, commercial-application friendly. If you are developing a commercial application, you can safely use the libraries provided, and the Apache License allows you to embed and redistribute those libraries. In a few cases, third-party libraries with redistribution restrictions are required, notably the security libraries that are part of the Java platform. But for the most part, if you build software using the Apache tools, you can redistribute it as you see fit.

Tomcat

Tomcat is the principal servlet engine developed under the auspices of the ASF. Tomcat is not, however, the first servlet engine developed by the foundation. The JServ Project predates it by a substantial interval. The key reason for Tomcat's success was that it included a JSP engine, whereas JServ did not. Over the years, as Tomcat gained momentum, support for JServ died off or users migrated to Tomcat.

Tomcat got a huge boost when Sun and Apache announced that Tomcat would be the official reference implementation of both the Servlet and JSP specifications. Sun also dedicated engineers to working on the project, keeping it freely available, modifiable, embeddable, and distributable. It is this openness and the nonproprietary nature of the Apache License—which makes it free for all commercial and noncommercial use—that allows so many other tools and platforms to include and embed the Tomcat engine. One result is that when you develop servlets in a number of major IDEs, both open source and commercial, from JBuilder to NetBeans, your servlets can be run and debugged inside Tomcat.

It's a big win for developers, as is the fact that the source code is there to be used, understood, and modified if necessary. Bugs get fixed by users and incorporated back into the main distribution. If there's a critical patch you need in order to make your application work, you don't have to wait for the vendor to make it available; you can just make the change yourself. If you've ever been caught in a release cycle waiting for some company to fix its product for you, as we have, we're sure you'll appreciate this.

The ASF has a great history of working with major commercial technology vendors, such as IBM, Sun, and Hewlett-Packard, to collaborate on open source development, and is the chosen organization for a number of collaborative projects. In fact, IBM has transferred a lot of Java technology it developed to the foundation for ongoing development and support, and all of the companies mentioned have full-time engineers devoted to working on these open source projects.

In short, Tomcat is a robust, scalable, production-quality servlet engine, in extensive deployment worldwide. It leverages a long legacy of experience within the Apache community, creating enterprise-grade network servers and libraries, and the support of all the major commercial Java technology vendors.

Tomcat Versions

Tomcat is currently in its fourth major release, Tomcat 4.1. The core of Tomcat 4.x is the Catalina servlet container, which is based on a new architecture and completely rewritten in order to make it more component-oriented and flexible. The other key component is Jasper, the JSP compiler, which is what initially gave Tomcat its edge.

Tomcat 4.x is the reference implementation for both the Servlet Specification, version 2.3, and the JSP Specification, version 1.2. As a result, Tomcat requires a Java 2 runtime, with Java Development Kit (JDK) 1.3.1 or later recommended. It also has excellent support for JDK 1.4.

Tomcat 4.1 improves upon Tomcat 4.0.x in several other areas, the most noticeable being the enhanced management tools. Tomcat 4.1 includes a new Struts- and JSP-based administration tool, and a much improved management servlet, also with a Struts- and JSP-based user interface. There is a JMX interface for administering the server, and the manager Web application also has improved tool support, including features enabling better integration with development tools, and a set of Ant tasks that leverage those tools. There is a new and improved connector class, which implements HTTP 1.0 and

1.1, HTTPS, and AJP 1.3. The Jasper JSP engine has also been rewritten, and there are a number of memory usage and performance improvements throughout.

Tomcat 3.x is the reference implementation for both the Servlet Specification, version 2.2, and the JSP Specification, version 1.1. Tomcat 3 will also run on JDK 1.1, so if you need to run a servlet engine on a platform that still doesn't support Java 2, this is the place to turn.

Servlets

We've already talked about servlets indirectly, but it's worth taking a moment to give an overview of servlet technology and talk about some of its advantages. Servlets are simply Java classes that are used to handle incoming requests to a server, providing a response. Using the intrinsic ability of Java to bind objects at runtime, the servlet container can dynamically load instances of these classes to handle requests. Since Java is platform-neutral, the same compiled servlets, usually packaged in the form of a Web application, can be deployed on any machine with a compliant servlet container, like Tomcat.

Servlets have some key advantages over other technologies when it comes to delivering dynamic content. Since servlets are loaded into the core server to execute, they run in a smaller footprint and use fewer resources than do systems, such as traditional Perl CGI, that create new processes to handle requests. This makes servlets very well suited to the job.

Beyond this, because they're Java objects, they give the developer access to a huge library of functionality to handle XML parsing, server-to-server communication, database access, encryption, image manipulation, email—almost anything you can think of. Java has a very rich core runtime library, and a vast amount of code has been written to the platform over the seven years since it was introduced.

One of the main differences, however, is that the servlet specification requires all servers to manage session state. This is harder than it sounds, given that HTTP is intrinsically a stateless protocol. If you're writing servlets or JSPs, you never have to worry about managing sessions. Sessions are automatically created and maintained for you by the runtime system. If you want to store some information specific to a given session, you can store a full-fledged Java object right in the session object itself, and go and retrieve it at any point while the session is still valid. This has been a notable source of brittleness for other platforms.

Servlets are also highly reliable, and scale well to very large applications. As a result, they have been very widely adopted for large, mission-critical applications, often when other technologies have fallen short and have had to be abandoned. Java has also done very well in enterprise integration settings, providing excellent access to legacy data. Further, because servlets are part of the larger Java 2 Enterprise Edition (J2EE) platform, there is an upward migration path to Enterprise JavaBeans (EJB), Java Message Service (JMS), and Java Transaction API (JTA) for applications that are highly transactional, require robust messaging, or need to be run on distributed systems.

Servlets are used so often to handle HTTP requests to produce HTML pages that people often think of them only in that context. They can in fact be used to handle other request-response-oriented protocols, and serve other datatypes beyond HTML as well. In practice, so many communication protocols are using HTTP now that the ability to handle other protocols seldom comes into play; however, the ability of servlets to produce other datatypes is used quite often. Images can be generated on the fly; documents can be converted from one type—say, XML—to one or more other types—say, HTML and Website Meta Language (WML). Files can be compressed on the fly, or encrypted, or otherwise manipulated. Servlets are often used to fulfill these functions. Further, new protocols like SOAP are leveraging HTTP as their low-level communication protocol, and communicating by sending XML messages back and forth. Coupled with the dynamism of Java as a language and platform, this makes servlets a compelling platform for developing custom protocols, and for serving this new wave of backend-to-backend communication.

We cover servlet technology extensively throughout this book, starting with Chapter 4, "Hello World Wide Web."

What's New in the Servlet 2.3 Specification

The Servlet 2.3 Specification adds a few new features to an already extensive and full-featured standard. Since many of you are already experienced servlet engineers, let's take a moment to highlight the new features introduced in 2.3.

Life Cycle Events

The new specification adds support for event notification for a number of events relating to two major subcategories: context events and session events. Context events provide notification when contexts are created or destroyed; and when attributes on those contexts are added, removed, or modified. Similarly, session events provide notifications when sessions are created or destroyed, and when attributes are added, removed, or modified on those sessions. We talk more about life cycle events at the end of Chapter 5, "Anatomy and Life Cycle of a Servlet."

Filters

Filters are used to modify the behavior of the servlets they are applied to. They can intercept and modify the request or the response, which allows for a wide range of possible behavior. Functionally, filters are similar to the Tomcat Valves construct, which we discuss in Chapter 7, "The server.xml File in Depth." Filters can also be chained together, which makes it easy to factor their functionality into handy reusable classes. Some things you can do with filters include:

- Managing authentication and access control
- Logging and auditing
- Converting documents to other formats, for example, via XSLT
- Converting image formats
- Compressing or encrypting data on the fly
- Using filters to trigger notifications when resources are accessed

You could even use filters to attach headers and footers, or use them to proxy requests off to an entirely different server, or translate the requested page into Swedish Chef or Pig Latin, if you were so inclined. Filters have the freedom to modify both the incoming request and the outgoing response, so they can really do almost anything you want them to do.

Platform Requirement Changes

The Servlet 2.3 Specification now leverages features of Java 2 Standard Edition (J2SE), particularly in the area of security, and as such requires a J2SE-compliant platform on which to run. If you need a servlet engine that can run on JDK 1.1, you can use Tomcat 3, but of course you won't have access to the new features mentioned earlier.

The Servlet 2.3 Specification also leverages some of the optional J2SE packages, notably the Java Naming and Directory Interface (JNDI), and various Java security extensions. You will notice that Tomcat 4.1 includes jndi.jar, among others, and you'll also notice a number of references to JNDI as you read through this book.

This specification is also a subset of J2EE version 1.3, so any 1.3-compliant J2EE platform is required to support the Servlet 2.3 Specification.

Finally, 2.3 is a superset of 2.2, so Servlet 2.2-compliant Web applications should run fine in a 2.3-compliant container like Tomcat 4.1.

JavaServer Pages

JSP is a technology for embedding executable Java code into HTML pages or other text-based documents, such as XML documents. It is quite easy to use JSP to create interactive forms. Coupled with the session management features of the underlying platform and the JavaBeans model for constructing self-describing data components, JSP provides an effective way of encapsulating functionality into reusable objects, allowing Web pages to be created by Web designers rather than by engineers. This typically results both in decreased cost and more attractive Web pages. Of particular advantage to the engineers involved, this type of encapsulation also means that Web designers are not prone to break the functional parts of the code.

There are even design tools, most notably Macromedia Dreamweaver, that will allow the components to execute at design time, so that designers can look at real data in their design view and avoid nasty surprises at integration time.

Functionality can be further abstracted out into tag libraries, also known as taglibs. This mechanism allows the engineer to create new custom tags that designers can use just like the standard built-in tags that are part of HTML. These tags are interpreted on the server and can do pretty much anything that Java can do. What gets rendered out in place of the tag is up to the tag developer. The tag could encapsulate anything from a login box, to a system status message, to a mechanism for managing ad banners, to a system for managing user preferences, to smart form components. The server interprets the tag as defined in the tag library, and renders out whatever HTML is appropriate. The client just sees regular HTML, so there is no client compatibility issue.

We provide a more detailed exploration of JSP in Chapter 11, "JavaServer Pages," and Chapter 12, "Tag Libraries."

What's New in the JSP 1.2 Specification

The biggest change in JSP 1.2 is simply that it sits on top of the Servlet 2.3 platform. Beyond this, it has enhanced support for internationalization; better support for tool-based generation; and a number of refinements providing for better syntax validation, a more stringent contract for tag handling, and a newly completed XML Document Type Definition (DTD) that allows JSP pages to conform to XML validation rules.

Summary

In this chapter, we put Tomcat into both a technical and an historical context. You should now have a better idea of what Tomcat is, how it came to be, and its relationship to both the Servlet and JSP standards. We covered the major changes in Tomcat 4.1, and in the current versions of the Servlet and JSP specifications, versions 2.3 and 1.2, respectively. We also laid out a roadmap to the chapters ahead, so you should have a good sense of what this book covers, and where to go from here.

We wish you a good read, and hope the information you find here will make you more productive and help you get the most out of a very powerful platform.

CHAPTER

2

Installing Tomcat

In this chapter, we show you how to install Tomcat. We look at three platforms: Linux, Windows, and Mac OS X. The instructions for Linux and OS X are similar to those for other Unix-based operating systems, including Solaris and Tru64.

Installing Tomcat is very easy. First, you need a copy of the Java Development Kit (JDK) installed on your machine. Then, simply download Tomcat, unpack it, configure the environment, and run it. It's really that simple. Let's get into a little more detail.

Installing the Java SDK

You can use any Java Virtual Machine implementation to run Tomcat that is version 1.2, Standard Edition (J2SE) or higher, although version 1.4 has been released for most platforms and is fully supported. Sun provides the Java Standard Edition free for Solaris, Linux, and Windows users; and OS X users have JDK 1.3.1 preinstalled (with JDK 1.4 coming soon). You can download the Java SDK from Sun directly.

For Solaris, Linux, and Windows, download the J2SE SDK here:

```
http://java.sun.com/downloads.html
```

For Compaq Tru64 Unix, OpenVMS Alpha, and Linux Alpha machines, you can download a copy of the Java SDK here:

```
http://www.compaq.com/java/download/
```

For HP-UX, you can download a copy of the Java SDK here:

```
http://www.hp.com/products1/unix/java/
```

And again, if you're using Mac OS X, the Java 2 SDK is already installed.

You need to download and install the Java SDK before attempting to install Tomcat. If you're a Windows user, you'll be using a standard and straightforward installer. Linux and Solaris users must download and execute a text-based installer script. After accepting the license and answering a few questions about your preferred install location, you'll be ready to proceed to the next step.

Installing the Tomcat Files

Installation of Tomcat is reasonably easy for most platforms and does not require a special installation application. Tomcat usually comes in a compressed archive file. For Windows, it will come in a ZIP file; while Unix, Linux, and OS X users will typically use the .tar.gz distribution. You can obtain the latest binary distribution of Tomcat by visiting the Tomcat site:

```
http://jakarta.apache.org/tomcat
```

This book covers Tomcat 4.x, and in particular Tomcat 4.1.

Windows Installation

You perform the installation by uncompressing the contents of the compressed file into a directory of your choice. For Windows machines, you can uncompress the file into a directory directly off the root directory, such as c:\jakarta-tomcat-4.1.10. You can use the WinZip application to accomplish this. Since there is no install application and no changes to the Windows Registry, installation really is as easy as uncompressing the ZIP file. Throughout this book, we refer to this Tomcat directory as *<$CATALINA_HOME>*.

Linux, OS X, and Other Unix Installations

On Unix and Linux machines, you can install Tomcat under any publicly accessible directory. The most popular place to install it is under the /usr/local directory. This will mean that your Tomcat home directory will usually be the /usr/local/jakarta-tomcat-4.1.10 directory or something similar, depending on the version of Tomcat you are installing. You may find it convenient to create a symbolic link to the current Tomcat version and name it /usr/local/tomcat. This makes it easier to update to new versions as they become available, since you normally don't have to modify startup scripts.

On OS X systems, another good alternative is to create a symbolic link to your install base, named /Library/Tomcat. This makes the distribution more accessible from the Finder.

If you're using OS X Server, Tomcat is already installed. You can turn it on from the Server Settings application. Select the Internet tab, and click on Configure Web Service. Select the General tab, and then check the Start Tomcat on system startup checkbox (see Figure 2.1).

To install the Tomcat binary distribution, download it (for example, into your home directory), change directories to the location in which you want to install, and

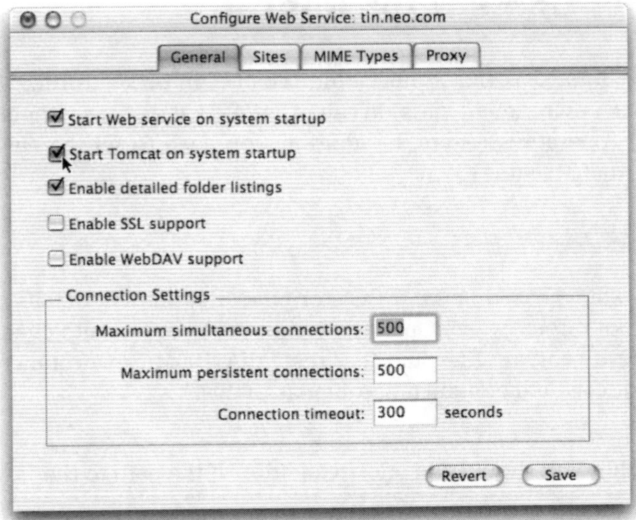

Figure 2.1 Configuring Tomcat on OS X Server.

then extract the distribution. On Linux and most Unix distributions, use the following commands:

```
# cd /usr/local
# tar xzvf ~/jakarta-tomcat-4.1.10.tar.gz
# ln -s jakarta-tomcat-4.1.10 tomcat
```

Note that if you are using an older version of tar, you may have to uncompress the archive manually before extracting from it:

```
# gunzip jakarta-tomcat-4.1.10.tar.gz
```

On Mac OS X, you should make it a habit to use gnutar in place of tar, since there are a few semantic differences between the GNU version of tar and the Apple version, and the Apache Project uses the GNU version to create its archives. (Note that you'll have to install the free developer tools in order to get gnutar installed.) You should also avoid using StuffIt Expander, because it is currently not capable of handling long filenames. If StuffIt Expander automatically extracted the distribution when you downloaded it, delete the files and directories created before extracting and installing. Also, since the /usr/local/ directory is owned by root, you need to use sudo to run some of the commands with root privileges. You will be prompted for your password when you do this, and you must be an administrator on the system to do this. (If you're not an administrator on the system, you can also install Tomcat in your home directory, substituting ~/Library for /usr/local, and omitting sudo in the following instructions.) Issue these commands:

```
$ cd /usr/local$ sudo gnutar xzvf ~/jakarta-tomcat-4.1.10.tar.gz
$ cd /Library
$ sudo ln -s /usr/local/jakarta-tomcat-4.1.10 Tomcat
```

In order to run Tomcat, you first have to set up the environment variables.

Setting Up the Environment for Tomcat

The primary requirement for Tomcat is that it must find the JDK in order to run. To ensure this, you must set up an environment variable called JAVA_HOME. This variable is the same, regardless of the operating system. In addition, you need to set the environment path to find Java Virtual Machine (JVM).

Windows 95/98/ME

All the Windows operating systems based on MS-DOS store the environment details in the autoexec.bat file in the root directory, c:\. Open the c:\autoexec.bat file, and check that the path is set to find Java program files and that the JAVA_HOME environment variable is set correctly. The file should contain a line similar to this:

```
SET PATH=c:\windows;c:\windows\command;c:\jdk1.4\bin
```

If you don't see a line like this, you should add one. In addition, if the path to the Java SDK is not included, as in:

```
SET PATH=c:\windows;c:\windows\command
```

you should alter it to point to the Java program files, as shown here:

```
SET PATH=c:\windows;c:\windows\command;c:\jdk1.4\bin
```

The file should contain another line that sets the JAVA_HOME environment variable. If there is no line defining JAVA_HOME, you should add one at the bottom of the file. The line should look something like this:

```
SET JAVA_HOME=c:\jdk1.4
```

Note that this directory is the top directory of the Java install, not the directory that contains the Java programs, which we used in the path earlier. Remember to restart Windows for the new autoexec.bat file to take effect.

Windows NT/2000

Windows NT stores the environment variable in the Registry rather than in editable text files. To change your environment variable, you need to access the System properties sheet from Control Panel. Then, choose the Environment tab. You will need to have administrator access to be able to make any changes.

First, check that the path is set correctly. You should see an item called PATH, which will contain a string of directories separated by semicolons. If the Java program directory is not included on this line, you must add it manually. Usually, this directory will be something like c:\jdk1.3\bin. The path tells the operating system where to look for executables. By adding the Java SDK binary directory, we can run the JVM without specifying the directory.

Second, you must ensure there is an environment variable called JAVA_HOME, and that it points to the Java directory. This directory (for example, c:\jdk1) is the one shown above the program directory. Tomcat uses the environment variable to establish the location of the Java 2 SDK in order to use it. Windows NT does not require a reboot for the environment variables changes to take effect.

Linux

To change the environment of Linux, you can alter the .profile or .cshrc file, depending on which shell you use. The .profile file is a script used by Linux to set up the environment when starting the shell you will use to start and stop Tomcat. You'll find the profile file under the /etc directory. The /etc directory is used for most of the configuration files in Linux applications. Listing 2.1 contains a sample .profile file that has been altered from the default provided with Red Hat Linux 7.1.

```
# /etc/profile
# System wide environment and startup programs
# Functions and aliases go in /etc/bashrc

if ! echo $PATH | /bin/grep -q "/usr/X11R6/bin" ; then
 PATH="$PATH:/usr/X11R6/bin"
fi

PATH="$PATH:/usr/java/jdk1.4/bin"
JAVA_HOME="/usr/java/jdk1.4"
CVSROOT="/usr/local/cvsroot"

ulimit -S -c 1000000 > /dev/null 2>&1
if [ `id -gn` = `id -un` -a `id -u` -gt 14 ]; then
    umask 002
else
    umask 022
fi

USER=`id -un`
LOGNAME=$USER
MAIL="/var/spool/mail/$USER"

HOSTNAME=`/bin/hostname`
HISTSIZE=1000

if [ -z "$INPUTRC" -a ! -f "$HOME/.inputrc" ]; then
    INPUTRC=/etc/inputrc
fi

export PATH USER LOGNAME MAIL HOSTNAME HISTSIZE INPUTRC
 JAVA_HOME CVSROOT

for i in /etc/profile.d/*.sh ; do
    if [ -x $i ]; then
```

Listing 2.1 The profile file settings. (continues)

```
        . $i
    fi
done

unset i
```

Listing 2.1 The profile file settings. (continued)

In order for your profile settings to take effect, you will need to log out and then log in again, or simply open a new shell. You do not, however, have to reboot your Linux system.

Mac OS X

Under Mac OS X, *$JAVA_HOME* should be set to /Library/Java/Home. This is a symbolic link to the current Java version, and is automatically updated to point to the current version as new versions of the JDK are released. <*$CATALINA_HOME*> will point to /Library/Tomcat or /usr/local/tomcat, depending on where you installed Tomcat; however, the startup script is smart enough to set that variable up for you, so you won't need to declare it explicitly.

By default, the user shell is tcsh on Mac OS X, so the environment variable setup should be done in the .cshrc file in your home directory. Open this file with your favorite text editor (or create the file, if it doesn't exist already), and add the following line:

```
setenv JAVA_HOME=/Library/Java/Home
```

Java is already on your path by default, so this is all the setup you need to do to get started.

Starting Up Tomcat for the First Time

Starting and stopping Tomcat is usually performed through two scripts, called startup and shutdown. They can be found under Tomcat's <*$CATALINA_HOME* >/bin directory. Each operating system has slightly different startup and shutdown syntax.

Windows

Enter the MS-DOS Prompt. If you are operating under an MS-DOS-based Windows OS, ensure that the MS-DOS Prompt has an environment space as large as possible, which should be 4096. To check this, open the properties of the MS-DOS icon and select the Memory tab, as shown in Figure 2.2.

First, enter Tomcat's binary directory:

```
c:> cd \jakarta-tomcat-4.0.1/bin
```

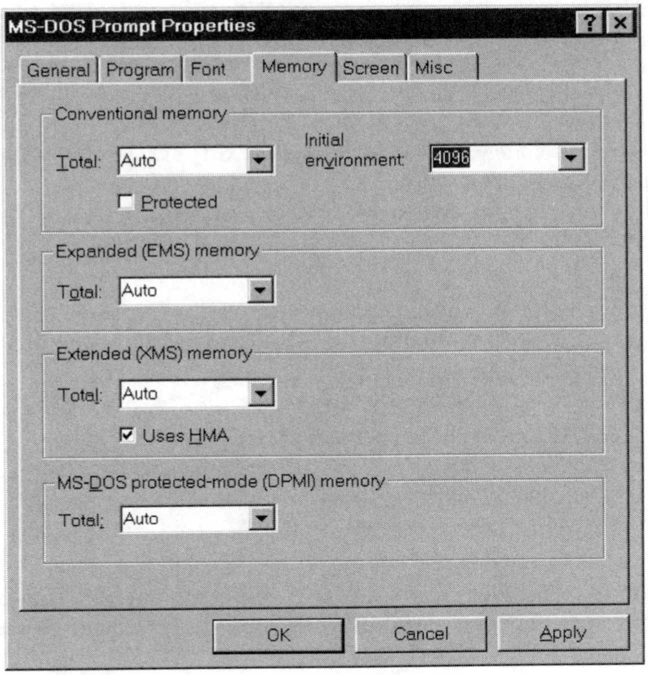

Figure 2.2 MS-DOS Prompt properties.

Once in the Tomcat binary directory, you can start Tomcat by running startup.bat:

```
c:> startup
```

To shut down Tomcat, run shutdown.bat:

```
c:> shutdown
```

Linux, OS X, and other Unix

Start a command-line terminal in Linux and enter the <*$CATALINA_HOME*>/bin:

```
# cd $CATALINA_HOME/bin
```

To start Tomcat, run the script startup.sh:

```
# ./startup.sh
```

To shut down Tomcat, run the script shutdown.sh:

```
# ./shutdown.sh
```

If you need to restart Tomcat, simply run the shutdown script, and then run the startup script.

Note that the shutdown script just sends a request to the server to shut down; occasionally, the shutdown will not be complete when you execute the startup script again. If this happens, the old Tomcat process will not have given up the ports it was using yet, and you'll get error output like this in the logs:

```
java.net.BindException: Address already in use:8080
        at org.apache.tomcat.util.net.PoolTcpEndpoint.initEndpoint
  (PoolTcpEndpoint.java:268)
        at org.apache.coyote.http11.Http11Protocol.init
  (Http11Protocol.java:150)
        at org.apache.coyote.tomcat4.CoyoteConnector.initialize
  (CoyoteConnector.java:1002)
        at org.apache.catalina.core.StandardService.initialize
  (StandardService.java:579)
        at org.apache.catalina.core.StandardServer.initialize
  (StandardServer.java:2241)
        at org.apache.catalina.startup.Catalina.start
  (Catalina.java:509)
        at org.apache.catalina.startup.Catalina.execute
  (Catalina.java:400)
        at org.apache.catalina.startup.Catalina.process
  (Catalina.java:180)
        at java.lang.reflect.Method.invoke(Native Method)
        at org.apache.catalina.startup.Bootstrap.main
  (Bootstrap.java:203)
```

If this happens to you, run the shutdown script again. It will complain that Tomcat wasn't running, but it will also close the open ports, allowing you to make a clean restart using the startup script.

Sometimes when Tomcat does not start some of its services due to incorrect configuration, the shutdown command will not work. The startup will also be blocked by the crashed Tomcat still in memory. When this occurs, you need to kill the Tomcat process. To do this, execute the following command from the shell:

```
# ps aewwx | grep tomcat  | more
```

This command will list all the current Tomcat processes and will return a list of the current processes. (You may need to tune the flags you pass to ps for your system; for example, awwx works better for Linux, and aewx works better for OS X.) Identify the first Tomcat process, which will look something like this:

```
3502 ?        S      0:09 /usr/local/jdk1.3/bin/i386/
  native_threads/java -Djava.endorsed.dirs=/opt/tomcat/bin:/opt/
  tomcat/common/lib -classpath /usr/local/jdk1.3/lib/tools.jar:/
  opt/tomcat/bin/bootstrap.jar -Dcatalina.base=/opt/tomcat
  -Dcatalina.home=/opt/tomcat -Djava.io.tmpdir=/opt/tomcat/temp
  org.apache.catalina.startup.Bootstrap start
```

Then kill that thread with the kill command:

```
kill 3502
```

Tailing the Log

It is often quite useful (and instructive) to watch the startup process as it happens. You can do this by "tailing the log," or using the tail command with the -f modifier to "follow" the log output as it is written to the log. To do this, execute the following command:

On OS X:

```
tail -f /Library/Tomcat/logs/catalina.out &
```

On other Unix flavors:

```
tail -f /usr/local/tomcat/logs/catalina.out &
```

If you're using Cygwin (http://www.cygwin.com/), you can do this on Windows, too:

```
tail -f /cygdrive/c/jakarta-tomcat-4.0.1/logs/catalina.out &
```

Starting Tomcat on Boot

Now that Tomcat has been installed, you'll probably want to have it start automatically when your machine reboots. How this is done varies from platform to platform.

Windows

If you want to start Tomcat on boot for an MS-DOS-based Windows machine, you should add a link to the startup.bat file in the Tomcat bin directory from the Startup directory. However, MS-DOS-based Windows machines are not considered stable enough for a true server. It also means that a user must be logged on, and therefore will not start until someone has manually logged on. It is a good idea to run a live system on Windows NT, Windows 2000, Linux, or another Unix system rather than operating systems designed for desktop applications.

Jakarta Tomcat has a service wrapper in order to turn Tomcat into an NT Service. (Note that when we use the term *NT* it also means Windows 2000.) The service wrapper can usually be found at the same location as the binary distribution of Tomcat, under the win32/i386 directory. The file you need to download is jk_nt_service.exe.

Next, you must alter the wrapper.properties file, which is found in the <*$CATALINA_HOME*>/conf directory. Change the wrapper.java_home property to point to your Java SDK home directory, and change the wrapper.CATALINA_HOME property to point to your Tomcat installation. Once this is complete, you are ready to install the service by executing the jk_nt_service.exe. Simply type the following:

```
jk_nt_service -l tomcat c:/jakarta-tomcat/conf/wrapper.properties
```

Tomcat is now installed as a service. To start and stop the service, you can use the NT Services Control Panel application, as shown in Figure 2.3.

Linux

There is no one way to set up Tomcat to autoboot under Linux because there are many distributions, and each handles this setup differently. However, Red Hat and other major Linux distributions are beginning to standardize. The script in Listing 2.2 should work on any Red Hat install of Linux version 7.1 or later, as well as on other versions with some modifications. In every case, you'll need to make sure the paths that you export at the beginning of the script—JAVA_HOME and CATALINA_HOME—specifically, match the paths that you use on your system. Note also that we're running Tomcat as user nobody, for security reasons. You may also want to set up a Tomcat user with minimal privileges and run as that user instead.

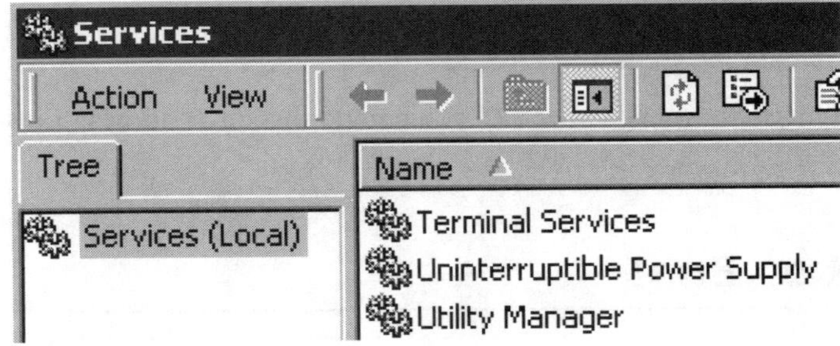

Figure 2.3 The NT Services Control Panel.

```
#!/bin/sh
# Tomcat daemon start/stop script.
# tomcat      This shell script takes care of starting and stopping
#             Tomcat.
#
# chkconfig: 2345 87 15
# description: Tomcat is a servlet container.
# processname: tomcat

mode=$1

export TOMCAT_HOME=/usr/local/tomcat
export CATALINA_HOME=$TOMCAT_HOME
export JAVA_HOME=/usr/local/jdk1.4

case "$mode" in
  'start')
    # Start daemon
    echo Starting Tomcat.
    su -c "$TOMCAT_HOME/bin/startup.sh" nobody
    ;;

  'stop')
    # Stop daemon. We use a signal here to avoid having to know the
    # root password.
    echo Stopping Tomcat.
    $TOMCAT_HOME/bin/shutdown.sh
    ;;

  'restart')
    $TOMCAT_HOME/bin/shutdown.sh
    sleep 10
```

Listing 2.2 A script for starting Tomcat on boot. (continues)

```
    $TOMCAT_HOME/bin/startup.sh
    ;;

  *)
    # usage
    echo "usage: $0 start|stop|restart"
    exit 1
    ;;
esac
```

Listing 2.2 A script for starting Tomcat on boot. (continued)

Once this file is in place, you must make it executable. As root, run this command:

```
# chmod 755 /etc/rc.d/init.d/tomcat
```

You also have to create a symbolic link to the script from the runlevels that you want Tomcat to start from. The easiest way to do this is to run chkconfig. If this is available on your system—which it is by default on RedHat and a number of other Linux distributions—execute this command:

```
# /sbin/chkconfig -add tomcat
```

This command creates symbolic links in the appropriate run control directories for the different Unix runlevels.

If your OS doesn't have chkconfig, you can always create symbolic links in the appropriate run control directories for your system, or append the commands to start Tomcat to your rc.local file.

Mac OS X Server

As we mentioned previously, OS X Server comes with Tomcat preloaded, ready to be turned on and run behind Apache. If you're running OS X Server, just use the Server Settings app to have Apache launch on startup, and configure Tomcat to start with it, as shown in the section "Installing the Tomcat Files" at the beginning of this chapter.

Mac OS X

The way OS X manages services is similar to other flavors of Unix; however, there are a few enhancements that accommodate loading precedence and internationalization. As with the Linux install earlier, the startup script is simply a shell script. OS X uses NetInfo to store user information, so setting up an unprivileged user is a little different from what you'd find on a typical Linux environment. It's all very straightforward, but as with almost any Unix flavor, some of the filenames and conventions are a little different. Let's cover that now.

Services are managed by startup scripts that can potentially be stored in few locations. In every case, the scripts live inside a /Library directory; however, there are five different relevant /Library directories on the system, each set aside for software installed by different users. This is quite similar to the typical Unix convention of having several /bin directories—for example, /bin, /usr/bin, /usr/local/bin, /sbin, /usr/sbin, /usr/local/sbin, ~/bin, and so on.

The Library directories—/Library, /System/Library, ~/Library, and /Network/Library—are all examined at boot time for any modules in the /StartupItems subdirectory. The /System/Library directory is reserved for software that is part of the official release. This is where startup scripts for key daemons—for instance, Apache, Cron, NetInfo, NFS, SSH, and Sendmail—are located. The root level /Library folder is for globally available third-party software, and if you have administrator access to the server, this is the best place to install Tomcat and the Tomcat startup script. (We assume this location in the examples that follow.) The /Library folder in each user's home directory is also consulted, so if you don't have administrator privileges and want to set up a development server (with the administrator's permission, of course), you can set it up here. Of course, Tomcat will run with your privileges, not the privileges of the Tomcat user we set up next. (You won't be able to create new users without administrative privileges, or open port 8080 on the firewall if it's configured.)

Creating the Tomcat User

Let's start by creating a user. You can do this through the NetInfo Manager application (in /Applications/Utilities), but the easiest way to do it is to execute the commands shown in Listing 2.3.

```
sudo nicl . -create /users/tomcat uid 8080
sudo nicl . -create /users/tomcat gid -2
sudo nicl . -create /users/tomcat passwd '*'
sudo nicl . -create /users/tomcat realname "Tomcat Role Account"
sudo nicl . -create /users/tomcat home /dev/null
sudo nicl . -create /users/tomcat shell /dev/null
sudo nicl . -create /users/tomcat change 0
sudo nicl . -create /users/tomcat expire 0
sudo nicl . -resync
```

Listing 2.3 Commands for creating an unprivileged user.

We've chosen to make the UID for the user 8080, since that's the port Tomcat will be running on, but you can use any UID you like, as long as it's not already taken. (Consult the NetInfo Manager to see what UIDs are already taken.) Let's run through what those commands did:

1. Created a new user tomcat (implicitly) and assigned it UID 8080.
2. Set the GID for tomcat to group nobody. (-2)
3. "Starred out" the password. (The string * doesn't match any hashed password, so this is shorthand for saying that this account will have no valid password.)
4. Set the *realname* to Tomcat Role Account. (This is the human-readable name for the account.)

5. Set the user's home directory to /dev/null, the bit bucket, which will prevent the user from logging in.
6. Set the user's shell to /dev/null, so that the user will have no login shell to shell out to.
7. Set the amount of time before the password must be changed to 0, the magic value for "Do not require this password to be changed."
8. Set the amount of time before the password expires to 0, which has the same meaning.
9. Told NetInfo to resync the database, making this user live.

It is important when running Web servers on Internet-connected hosts to make sure that they don't run with excessive privileges, so that if they are ever compromised, the damage the intruder will be able to do will be as severely limited as we can manage.

Next we need to change the ownership of everything under /Library/Tomcat (where we have installed the Tomcat server and all its required directories). Do this by executing the following command:

```
sudo chown -R tomcat /Library/Tomcat/*
```

We have to make sure Tomcat can read its configuration and library files and write to its working directories. They should by default. If somehow the permissions on your files do not grant read permission to the owner, you should also run the following commands:

```
sudo chmod -R o+r /Library/Tomcat/*
sudo chmod -R o+w /Library/Tomcat/work
```

And for more security, you should make sure that the user tomcat cannot write the configuration files, since this would open you to an intruder modifying the configuration of the server over the Web. Note of course that this also means you won't be able to do legitimate administration of the site over the Web, so, for example, the new administration tools in 4.1 will probably not work correctly. You can make the choice between flexibility and security. If you want more security, also execute this command:

```
sudo chmod o-wx /Library/Tomcat/conf/*
```

The Startup Items Package

Next we must create the startup module. Again, we're assuming you have administrative privileges. First, create the StartupItems directory under /Library/, if it doesn't exist already:

```
$ sudo mkdir /Library/StartupItems
```

Then create a directory that will hold the startup module:

```
$ sudo mkdir /Library/StartupItems/Tomcat/
```

Into this directory, place the startup script, which must have the same name as your module directory. Create the Tomcat script with your favorite editor. (If you are using TextEdit, please remember to save as plain text, and without an extension. You can't save shell scripts in Rich Text Format, the default, and expect them to run!)

The startup script appears in Listing 2.4.

```
#!/bin/sh

. /etc/rc.common
export JAVA_HOME=/Library/Java/Home

if [ "$1" = "start" ]; then
   if [ "${TOMCAT}" = "-YES-" ]; then
      ConsoleMessage "Starting Tomcat Servlet/JSP Server"
      sudo -u tomcat /Library/Tomcat/bin/startup.sh
   fi
elif [ "$1" = "stop" ]; then
   ConsoleMessage "Stopping Tomcat Servlet/JSP Server"
   sudo -u tomcat /Library/Tomcat/bin/shutdown.sh
elif [ "$1" = "restart" ]; then
   if [ "${TOMCAT}" = "-YES-" ]; then
      ConsoleMessage "Restarting Tomcat Servlet/JSP Server"
      sudo -u tomcat /Library/Tomcat/bin/shutdown.sh
      sleep 5
      sudo -u tomcat /Library/Tomcat/bin/startup.sh
   fi
fi
```

Listing 2.4 The OS X Tomcat startup script: /Library/StartupItems/Tomcat/Tomcat.

There are a couple of things to note in Listing 2.4. First, we're executing /etc/rc.common. This loads a number of variables, some coming from /etc/hostconfig, which acts as a central switching station for specifying which services are to be run. rc.common also loads in some useful functions for us. /etc/hostconfig is where we set the value of the variable *${TOMCAT}*, which we use to specify whether to start Tomcat on boot.

We test to see what argument we were given—start, stop, or restart—and then run the appropriate script or scripts if Tomcat is turned on in /etc/hostconfig. The ConsoleMessage function is used to log output to syslog, and also flashes the service startup messages you see when OS X is booting.

This is also where we configure under which permissions the server will run. We use sudo -u tomcat to make the server run with the effective permissions of the user tomcat. Note that this does mean we won't be able to bind Tomcat to low-numbered ports (anything below 1024), so if you want to run Tomcat on port 80, your best bet is to run it behind Apache, using the Webapp connector, or JK2. You can also run it stand-alone as root, but this is not necessarily a good idea on a live, publicly accessible server.

The StartupParameters.plist File

The next file we must create is the StartupParameters.plist file. OS X uses property lists, or .plist files, to control all sorts of things. In this case, it provides a description of the service used by the startup manager to determine any dependencies it may have. Listing 2.5 contains our StartupParameters.plist file.

```
{
  Description    = "Tomcat Servlet/JSP Server";
  Provides       = ("Tomcat Servlet/JSP Server");
  Requires       = ("Resolver");
  OrderPreference = "None";
  Messages =
  {
    start   = "Starting Tomcat Servlet/JSP Server";
    stop    = "Stopping Tomcat Servlet/JSP Server";
    restart = "Restarting Tomcat Servlet/JSP Server";
  };
}
```

Listing 2.5 /Library/StartupItems/Tomcat/StartupParameters.plist.

In Listing 2.5, we declare a description, the name of the service we provide, and any services we depend on. We want Tomcat to be started after the Resolver has been started, so we list Resolver in the Requires line. The OrderPreference provides hints to the startup manager about the order to load Tomcat relative to the other services with the same dependencies. We also list the messages we want displayed to the user. These can be localized as well through the addition of a /Resources directory and an appropriate set of /.lproj directories, one per language, containing a Localizable.strings file with the translations. (See http://www.javaosx.com/ for more details.)

Turning On Tomcat in /etc/hostconfig

Once those files are set up, we need to do one last thing: add one line to the end of /etc/hostconfig:

```
TOMCAT=-YES-
```

That's the line that sets up the ${TOMCAT} variable. It's also responsible for managing the startup of all the other services on boot.

As of this writing, Ian is also working on a Tomcat installer for OS X. By the time this book hits shelves, it should be available. This and other OS X software (including an Ant installer) can be found at http://www.javaosx.com/.

Other Unix Flavors

Startup on other flavors of Unix is similar to the configuration for Linux, although in general chkconfig is not supported. Follow the Linux previous example, adapting it to local conditions. Typically this will involve installing the startup script in the various run control directories on your system, specifically rc3.d and rc5.d at a minimum (call the script S87tomcat or something similar), or simply adding commands to start Tomcat to your rc.local file or equivalent.

First Look at Tomcat

You have now started Tomcat. Start your browser, and type the following URL on the same computer on which you are running Tomcat:

```
http://localhost:8080/
```

When Tomcat runs using the default configuration, it sets up two connectors. One of the connectors allows Apache to connect to Tomcat. The other connector is an HTTP 1.1 interface, which allows Tomcat to operate just like any other Web server. Initially this is configured to listen to port 8080 by default. Connecting to this interface is as easy as using your browser to connect to port 8080, as described earlier. You should see the Tomcat welcome screen; from here you can verify that Tomcat is fully operational. First, check that the servlets are running by looking at the servlet examples. These examples show many of the useful features of servlets and provide some example source code.

Once you have tested the servlets, return to the main page and select the JSP examples. The JSP examples will need to be compiled, which may take up to about 10 seconds, depending on the performance of your server. This is because JSP files need to be first compiled into servlets before they can be run. This is a once-off process, and once loaded into memory, JSP files are just as fast in operation as normal servlets.

If servlets are working but the JSP examples are returning a 500 server error, most likely Tomcat is not able to access tools.jar. Find this file and add it to the classpath to rectify this problem.

Running the examples will give you an idea of some of the functionality Tomcat has built in. By accessing this page, you can view all the documentation for Tomcat, including the Servlet API, a valuable resource when developing servlets.

Summary

In this chapter, we took our first look at installing Tomcat, and showed you how to run it as a service under Windows, Linux, and OS X. We also took our first look at Tomcat. Now that Tomcat is installed, it's time to start looking at configuring it. Over the next few chapters, we walk you through the basics of Tomcat configuration and servlet configuration. In subsequent chapters, we go into more detail on the particulars of configuring Tomcat to do the things you'd like it to do.

CHAPTER

3

Configuring Tomcat

In this chapter, we explain how to configure Tomcat and two of the most popular Web servers that work with Tomcat. Tomcat comes configured ready to go, and you need make no changes to the configuration files supplied with it to get started. You install and configure many Web applications simply by placing a Web Archive (WAR) file in the *<$CATALINA_HOME>*/webapps directory. However, Tomcat is also very flexible, with a rich configuration system.

We start by giving you an overview of the file structure inside the installation directory, so that you know where to find everything and what controls what. As installed, the top-level directory contains the subdirectories shown in Listing 3.1.

```
<$CATALINA_HOME>/
    /bin
    /classes
    /common
        /classes
        /lib
    /conf
    /lib
    /logs
    /server
```

Listing 3.1 The Tomcat install directory structure. (continues)

```
        /classes
        /lib
    /webapps
        /examples
        /manager
        /ROOT
        /tomcat-docs
        /webdav
    /work
        /localhost
```

Listing 3.1 The Tomcat install directory structure. (continued)

There are additional subdirectories under the /webapps and /work directories, which we discuss later in this chapter. The /webapps directory in particular is where you will spend the bulk of your development life.

One thing you probably have already noticed is that there are a number of pairs of classes and lib directories at various levels of the hierarchy. (And beyond those shown in the listing above, there is an additional such pair under each of the directories in the /webapps directory.) These contain classes loaded by the Tomcat server in various contexts, which are handled by different class loaders. This is an important concept in the way Tomcat operates: different Web applications, and the Tomcat server itself, have discrete class loaders and, as a result, do not conflict with each other. This is intended to provide some security, and to prevent brittleness resulting from the use of otherwise incompatible class and library versions between different Web applications and the server itself.

To illustrate such a problem and the way we solve it, let's assume that Webapp A was built against the API of vendor A's CORBA implementation, and that Webapp B uses either a different version of the same implementation or a CORBA implementation from a different vendor. Both define objects with the same names in the OMG.CORBA package hierarchy.

On the security side, this separation of class loaders also prevents a different implementation of a library loaded by one Webapp from compromising the functionality and security of another Webapp, or of the server itself. Another effect is to keep discrete the data space of separate Webapps and the server itself. This prevents one Webapp from manipulating the data space of another Webapp, providing further security and the removal of unexpected interactions. This separation is also part of the servlet specification, and any specification-compliant servlet container must enforce it. If you do need Webapps to cooperate with each other, there is a mechanism to allow this. You can communicate through the servlet context by calling getServletContext() on the ServletConfig passed into init(). This will make more sense after you read more about servlets.

Each of the classes directories, and all of the JAR files in each of the lib directories, are automatically added to the classpath for the given context. This saves a lot of administrative hassle in manually manipulating classpaths, which has traditionally remained one of the fussy bits of Java application management. Note also that most of the classes directories (all of them as shipped) are empty. This is simply because the classes needed for each of the preinstalled contexts are contained in the JAR files in each of the lib directories instead.

Aside from the several classes and lib directories, the other directories contain the following:

bin—The actual executable files used to run the server. This includes shell scripts and batch files to start and stop the server on the various supported platforms.

conf—This contains the master configuration files for the server itself, which we cover in more depth in the next section.

logs—This directory contains the various log files generated by Tomcat. Note that they are automatically rotated daily at midnight, and are named with a date-stamp, in YYYY-MM-DD format, for the day to which they pertain. The logs break down into three basic types: server-wide, Webapp-specific, and hostname-specific. If you are having issues with the starting and stopping of your server, you'll want to examine catalina.out, the current catalina_log.txt file; and determine whether you are running Tomcat behind Apache, the current apache_log.txt file. If you're on a Unix platform, you can best handle this by tailing the log in question. For example, to watch what happens when Tomcat shuts down and starts up, issue the following commands:

```
cd <$CATALINA_HOME>
tail -f logs/catalina.out &
bin/shutdown.sh
bin/startup.sh
```

You should see a number of console messages as Tomcat shuts down the various services, and then several messages as Tomcat starts them up again. (The example assumes that Tomcat is already running from when you set it up in the last chapter, so execute the steps in this order. Otherwise, reverse the startup and shutdown steps.)

The second set consists of standard access logs, named for the primary interface that the given connector is serving. As installed, this will typically be *localhost*, so you'll see logs named localhost_access_log.<*date*>.txt. These are pretty standard access logs, similar to the logs generated by Apache, Microsoft Internet Information Server (IIS), and most other Web servers; and consist of these fields: the IP address the request came from, the time of the request, the first line of the HTTP request, the result code served by Tomcat, and the length in bytes of the object returned. Here's an example:

```
127.0.0.1 - - [06/May/2002:15:10:44 -0800] "GET / HTTP/1.1" 302 654
127.0.0.1 - - [06/May/2002:15:10:44 -0800] "GET /index.html HTTP/1.1"
  200 6836
```

The third set of log files are generated one per Webapp and have names to match. These files will be important when you're debugging your Webapps because these files are where log output from your Webapps is written. After reading any error message, the server returns to the browser; this is the next place you can turn if your Webapp is misbehaving. The files are likewise named for the primary interface for the connector the Webapp was served from, but in this case with the name of the Webapp appended—for example, localhost_examples_log.<*date*>.txt. Logs for the ROOT Webapp (which is associated with the URI "/") are stored simply in localhost_log.<*date*>.txt.

The /webapps directory contains subdirectories for each Webapp installed on the server. We cover this directory in depth after we discuss the configuration files in the conf directory.

NOTE It is possible to reference Web applications that don't live under the /webapps directory, but this must be done explicitly in the conf/server.xml file, and should typically be avoided unless you have a compelling reason to do so.

Finally, the work directory is where Tomcat stores interim results, particularly during JSP compilation. This means two things to you as a developer. First, it is essential that Tomcat be provided sufficient permissions to write to this directory. We did this when we installed the server in the previous chapter, but if at some point Tomcat is complaining about not being able to compile your JSPs, try to remember to have this on your checklist for problem resolution.

The second thing that it means is that you can find the servlet code that was generated by the Jasper JSP compiler in this directory. This is particularly useful when you're trying to debug JSP pages, because the line numbers referenced in tracebacks refer to the lines in these source files, which are subsequently compiled into the servlets that actually handle the requests. We talk more about how all this works in Chapter 11, "JavaServer Pages."

Tomcat Configuration Files

The conf directory contains four key files that manage the Tomcat server as a whole: catalina.policy, tomcat-users.xml, the main web.xml file, and server.xml.

The catalina.policy file is a Java security policy file, which we discuss in Chapter 18, "Security."

The tomcat-users.xml file sets up users and roles to be used for user-auth authentication by Tomcat. We modify it at the end of this chapter to enable the manager application, and we discuss users and roles in more depth in Chapter 18 as well.

The web.xml configuration file is used to set up base parameters for each Web application, and each application has its own web.xml file. The web.xml file in the conf directory controls global initialization parameters and is read before any Webapp-specific configuration is performed. We cover the web.xml file in more detail in the next section when we discuss the webapp directory hierarchy.

The primary configuration file for Tomcat is server.xml. This file controls the details of the operation of Tomcat as a whole. You will note that it is heavily commented. It's worth reading the comments in addition to reading our description.

As we said at the beginning of this chapter, the configuration that comes in a default Tomcat install is ready to go. You should not need to alter it at all unless you wish to add or modify connectors such as the WARP, IIS, or HTTPS connector; set up virtual hosts or modify port numbers; or point to Webapps outside the *<$CATALINA_HOME>*/ webapp directory.

The HTTP 1.1 Connector

The HTTP 1.1 is pre-configured in the server.xml file to listen on port 8080. This is why you had to specify http://localhost:8080 when accessing Tomcat directly from a browser.

If you want Tomcat to act as a standard Web server, serving the standard HTTP port 80, you need to change the port parameter in the following code to 80 and restart Tomcat. Note, however, that on Unix systems, ports below 1024 are reserved and can be opened only as root. Unfortunately, Java doesn't provide a means for switching to a less-privileged user, so if you wish to use Tomcat to handle requests on port 80 (or port 443 for HTTPS), it's advisable to run it behind Apache using the WARP connector, or to otherwise proxy the handling of the privileged ports, so that Tomcat can continue to run as an unprivileged user. Since the Windows security model doesn't provide the same security mechanism or protection for low-numbered ports, this is not an issue if you're running Tomcat under Windows.

The default attributes should work well for most applications:

```
    <!-- Define a non-SSL HTTP/1.1 Connector on port 8080 -->
    <Connector
className="org.apache.coyote.tomcat4.CoyoteConnector"
               port="8080" minProcessors="5" maxProcessors="75"
               enableLookups="true" redirectPort="8443"
               acceptCount="10" debug="0" connectionTimeout="60000"/>
```

The <Connector/> node takes a number of attributes. Here we enumerate the main ones and describe their function. For complete coverage, see Chapter 7, "The server.xml File in Depth." We specify the classname (required) of the underlying implementation we wish to use. We use the standard implementation for Tomcat 4: org.apache.coyote.tomcat4.CoyoteConnector.

The address attribute specifies which IP address to listen on. This is relevant for multihomed servers on which you want to run multiple separate server instances. If we don't specify it, Tomcat binds to all available IP addresses.

The port attribute, which is required, specifies the port on which the connector should listen.

The enableLookups attribute (optional,) which must be either true or false, specifies whether the server should look up the hostname associated with the IP address of each inbound connection. If the attribute is set to true, hostnames are logged instead of just IP addresses. In a production environment, enableLookups should typically be set to false, since name lookups are expensive. You can always convert the IP addresses to hostnames later by postprocessing the logs. The default value for this attribute is true.

The redirectPort attribute (optional) has somewhat intricate semantics. If this connector is not configured to provide a secure communication method, and a request comes in for a resource requiring a secure connection (as specified in a security constraint), then the connector redirects the request to the port specified in this attribute. Typically, this means that if you are configuring an HTTP connector on port 80, you specify port 443, the standard HTTPS port, as the redirect port. You then need to configure another connector to handle HTTPS connections on port 443.

The scheme attribute (optional) specifies the name of the protocol the connector will handle. This sets the string that the getScheme() method on the request object (passed into a servlet's service() method) will return (we see this again in Chapter 18, "Security"). If, for example, you are configuring a connector to support HTTP, this should be set to "http". This is also the default value.

The secure attribute (optional) specifies whether the protocol this connector is configured for should be considered secure. The value set here is the value returned by the isSecure() method on the request object. (Again, we see how to use this in your servlets in Chapter 18.) The default value is false.

The minProcessors and maxProcessors attributes (both optional) control the number of instances of the connector in the instance pool. On startup, Tomcat creates the number of instances specified in minProcessors and keeps them ready to handle inbound requests. If all of the instances are in use at any time and a new request comes in, new instances are created for each additional request until the number of processors specified in maxProcessors is reached. At that point, additional requests are kept in a queue until a processor becomes available. The default values are 5 and 20, respectively.

The acceptCount attribute (optional) specifies the maximum number of requests to keep in that queue. If additional requests are received when all the processors are busy, and the queue is also full, they will be refused. The default value is 10.

The connectionTimeout attribute sets how many milliseconds the connector will wait from the time the connection is initiated until the time the line of the request containing the requested URI is received. This is to prevent the server becoming bogged down by requests from clients on very slow connections, and to free up resources from connections that stall. Requests that take longer than this timeout to process will be terminated. The default is 60000 (one minute).

The optional debug attribute allows you to turn on additional logging in the connector class.

The WARP Connector

The WARP connector uses the WARP protocol to communicate with another Web connector. Typically this will be an extension for Apache or IIS. It enables Tomcat to serve dynamic data from behind an Apache, IIS, or any other WARP-enabled HTTP server.

You can find the configuration in the server.xml file in its own service close to the bottom of the file. By default it runs on port 8008. None of the defaults normally need to be changed. Listing 3.2 contains the default WARP connector configuration. Although the WARP connector is installed by default, you need to follow further instructions we give later to install a WARP connector into Apache or IIS.

```
<Service name="Tomcat-Apache">

  <Connector className="org.apache.catalina.connector.warp.
WarpConnector"
```

Listing 3.2 server.xml—WARP connector. (continues)

```
    port="8008" minProcessors="5" maxProcessors="75"
    enableLookups="true"
    acceptCount="10" debug="0"/>

   <!-- Replace "localhost" with what your Apache "ServerName" is
set to -->
   <Engine className="org.apache.catalina.connector.warp.WarpEngine"
    name="Apache" debug="0" appBase="webapps">

     <!-- Global logger unless overridden at lower levels -->
     <Logger className="org.apache.catalina.logger.FileLogger"
             prefix="apache_log." suffix=".txt"
             timestamp="true"/>

     <!-- Because this Realm is here, an instance will be shared
globally -->
     <Realm className="org.apache.catalina.realm.MemoryRealm" />

   </Engine>

  </Service>
```

Listing 3.2 server.xml—WARP connector. (continued)

Other Connectors

There are other types of connectors for various other purposes. There is an Apache Java Protocol (AJP) connector that has been used in previous versions of Tomcat to connect to Apache and IIS. There is also a Secure Sockets Layer (SSL) implementation to enable Tomcat to be used as a secure server directly without running it through Apache or IIS. Disabled entries for these connectors are built into the default server.xml file.

Webapp Contexts

A <context/> entry in the server.xml file establishes a relationship between a URI and a Webapp, establishes the Webapp's relationship to its log file, can pass initialization parameters to the Webapp, and can establish other relationships between the Webapp and services provided by the Tomcat servlet container—for example, persistent session state. However, Webapp contexts can more conveniently and portably be established in the web.xml file associated with each Webapp. If you install your Webapps in the /webapps directory, you won't need to make any changes to the server.xml file. This is by far the easiest way to add Web applications. In the next section, we explain how to do this.

In addition to adding the directory, you need to create a directory structure under it like this:

```
/webapps
    /mywebapp
        /WEB-INF
            /classes
```

Under the WEB-INF directory, you also need to copy in a web.xml file from one of the other Web applications. The file you need to copy in should resemble the one shown in Listing 3.3. This web.xml file can be found in the *<$CATALINA_HOME>*/webapps/ROOT/WEB-INF directory, and is the most simple web.xml possible. It is the configuration file for a Web application, for which we provide further details in the next section.

```
<?xml version="1.0" encoding="ISO-8859-1"?>

<!DOCTYPE web-app
   PUBLIC "-//Sun Microsystems, Inc.//DTD Web Application 2.3//EN"
   "http://java.sun.com/dtd/web-app_2_3.dtd">

<web-app>
</web-app>
```

Listing 3.3 The web.xml from webapps/ROOT/WEB-INF.

The next easiest way of adding a context is to use the manager, as we described in the previous section. Finally, you have the option of directly adding a context to the server.xml file. A context entry is needed only when the Web application you are adding is located somewhere on the local hard drive other than under Tomcat.

To add a context, stop Tomcat and edit the server.xml file. Find the existing context elements and add one directly after them. A context need contain only a few attributes to enable it, such as this:

```
<!-- Tomcat Manager Context -->
<Context path="/manager" docBase="manager" debug="0"
  privileged="true"/>
```

The important attributes for a context is its path and its docBase. The path is the unique path that will be used via HTTP to access the Web application. The docBase is the filesystem path used to find the Web application's root directory. This is a relative path from the /webapps directory under Tomcat, unless otherwise specified with a slash. Let's describe all the possible attributes you can use with a context.

The path attribute (required) specifies the base URI relative to which all contained servlet paths will be constructed. Again, you need to have exactly one <Context/> container with the empty string specified as its path in order to form the default context.

The docBase attribute (required) specifies where the Webapp specified in the context is to be found. The path specified here can either be the path to a directory containing the Webapp or a path including a Web Archive (WAR) file. In the latter case, the Webapp will be run directly from the WAR file without expanding it. If the path specified is a relative path, it will be appended to the path specified in the appBase attribute of the containing <Host/> element.

For this container, the className attribute (optional) need not be defined. We're using the default implementation, org.apache.catalina.core.StandardContext.

The reloadable attribute (optional) specifies whether you want the servlet engine to monitor the WEB-INF/lib and WEB-INF/classes directories under the configured docBase and reload the Webapp when they change. This is set to true by default. This setting does not affect whether the context can be reloaded by the manager application (see Chapter 9, "The Manager Application").

The cookies attribute (optional) specifies whether you wish to allow Tomcat to use cookies for session management. If you want to force Tomcat to rely only on URL rewriting (for security reasons or otherwise), you should set this attribute to false. It is true by default.

The crossContext attribute (optional) specifies whether objects in this context are allowed to communicate with the objects in other contexts on the same host. Specifically, this attribute specifies whether calls to ServletContext.getContext() return a valid context. If set to false, ServletContext.getContext() will always return null. Unless you have a specific reason to allow intercontext communication, this should be left set to false (the default) for security reasons.

The privileged attribute (optional) specifies whether servlets in this context should be allowed to use special container servlets, such as the manager servlet. The default is false.

The wrapperClass attribute (optional) specifies the wrapper class to be used to manage any servlets contained in the context. This class is responsible for managing the life cycle of the servlets in the context, including keeping track of the configuration specified in the deployment descriptor, calling the servlet's init() and destroy() methods, and otherwise managing communication between the container and the servlet. Classes specified in this attribute must implement the org.apache.catalina.Wrapper interface. The default value is org.apache.catalina.core.StandardWrapper.

The useNaming attribute (optional) specifies whether the servlet engine should create a Java Naming and Directory Interface (JNDI) InitialContext for this Webapp. The InitialContext Tomcat will create is compatible with Java 2 Enterprise Edition (J2EE) conventions. It is set to true by default.

The workDir attribute (optional) specifies a writable directory for use by servlets contained in this context. The path to this working directory will be passed into the servlet as the javax.servlet.context.tempdir attribute on the ServletContext. That attribute will be an instance of java.io.File. If it's not configured manually, Tomcat will assign a suitable directory inside the work directory assigned to the host. By default, this is a subdirectory of the *<$CATALINA_HOME>*/work directory.

And as with the other Tomcat components, a debug attribute (optional) is provided for configuring additional logging.

Once you have created your context, restart Tomcat. The startup of each context is stored in the log files, so it's a good idea when installing a new Web application to check the log files for exceptions on startup.

Web Application Configuration

Each Web application has its own configuration file, a web.xml file located under the WEB-INF directory of the application. This file is called the Web application deployment descriptor. We cover this file in depth in Chapter 6, "Configuring Web Applications," so this is just a taste to get you started.

Listing 3.4 contains a simple web.xml file that is configured to run the init() method of the ConnectionPoolServlet on startup of the Web application. In this example, the Web application is calling this servlet to create database connections so that they are ready to use when a request from a client is made.

```
<?xml version="1.0" encoding="ISO-8859-1"?>
<!DOCTYPE web-app
  PUBLIC "-//Sun Microsystems, Inc.//DTD Web Application 2.3//EN"
  "http://java.sun.com/dtd/web-app_2_3.dtd">

<web-app>
  <servlet>
    <servlet-name>ConnectionPoolServlet</servlet-name>
    <servlet-class>ConnectionPoolServlet</servlet-class>
    <load-on-startup>1</load-on-startup>
  </servlet>
</web-app>
```

Listing 3.4 The web.xml file for the connection pool servlet.

Configuring Tomcat with Apache

A connector is simply a means to connect a Web server to a servlet engine such as Tomcat. Tomcat 4.x has introduced the WARP connector to replace the older AJP connector. The WARP connector is configured by default in Tomcat 4.1. WARP is much easier to configure than the older AJP connector used with Tomcat 3.

Before we get into configuring Tomcat to work with Apache, make sure that both have been installed and are working. You should be able to access Tomcat through http://localhost:8080 and the Apache Server through http://localhost. If you have not installed both Tomcat and Apache, go back and ensure both are running.

Once you have both Apache and Tomcat running, shut down Apache (since you will now need to alter its configuration files). You should also download the binary connector from the Jakarta Apache Web site. Note that there is a different distribution for each operating system.

After downloading the binary files, uncompress them into a directory. The compressed file will contain the binary files required for Apache to connect to Tomcat.

Changes to Apache

The best way to set up Apache with Tomcat is to use dynamically loaded modules. Most binary distributions of Apache today use dynamically loaded modules, and the best bet is to download and install a clean Apache distribution from http://apache.org if you are in doubt about whether dynamically loaded modules are supported by your install of Apache. From this point on, we assume you have Apache installed and working. If you're using Mac OS X, Apache is already installed with dynamic module support.

Start by downloading mod_webapp. There are precompiled binaries for most platforms under http://jakarta.apache.org/builds/jakarta-tomcat-4.0/archives/v4.0.1/bin/<*os name*>. Download and uncompress the binary for your platform.

Now you'll need to move the mod_webapp shared library into the directory where your install of Apache keeps its extensions. This is in /usr/libexec/httpd on OS X and /usr/httpd/libexec on several other Unix flavors. If you are installing on Windows, copy the mod_webapp.so and the libapr.dll files to Apache's modules directory. Note that under OS X, you'll most likely need to move the module into place using the terminal, since by default Unix system directories like /usr and /etc are hidden from the Finder.

At this point, you have to add a few lines to the Apache configuration. You must include a line that adds a module into Apache so that it is loaded when Apache is run. On most Linux or Unix machines, you make the changes in the httpd.conf file found under /etc/httpd/conf.

We first need to add the WARP connector module to the Apache configuration. Look for a series of lines that begin with LoadModule. Add the following line to your httpd.conf file directly after the last LoadModule line:

- Windows: LoadModule webapp_module modules/mod_webapp.so
- Linux/Unix: LoadModule webapp_module libexec/mod_webapp.so
- Mac OS X: LoadModule webapp_module libexec/httpd/mod_webapp.so

Next, look for a series of lines under the LoadModule lines that start with AddModule. Add the following line directly after all the AddModule lines:

```
AddModule mod_webapp.c
```

Finally, you need to add some lines to the end of your Apache configuration file to map Apache directories to Tomcat Web applications. Add the following lines at the very end of your httpd.conf file:

```
<IfModule mod_webapp.c>
WebAppConnection conn warp localhost:8008
WebAppDeploy examples conn /examples
WebAppInfo /webapp-info
</IfModule>
```

Save the httpd.conf file and restart Apache. You should now be able to access the Tomcat examples Web application from within Apache. Tomcat itself does not need any additional configuration, since the connector is configured to start up the default Tomcat installation. You should also be able to access the Web connectors information page with the following URL:

```
http://localhost/webapp-info
```

The syntax for the WebAppConnection line in the httpd.conf file is:

```
WebAppConnection <name> <provider> <host:port>
```

<name>—A unique name for the connection created between Apache and Tomcat. It is referred to in the WebAppDeploy lines.

<provider>—The name of the provider used to connect to the servlet container. There is currently only one provider, which is called WARP.

<host:port>—The hostname and port where the connection is to be made. The default Tomcat configuration is set up to listen on port 8008. The localhost name specifies that Tomcat is operating on the same machine.

```
WebAppDeploy <application name> <name> <url path>
```

<application name>—The application name, which must map to a Web application name or context that is already established in Tomcat.

<name>—The name of the connection, as specified in the WebAppConnection.

<url path>—The URL path where this application will be deployed.

```
WebAppInfo <url path>
```

<url path>—The URL path where you can access the information page about the connections.

Configuring Tomcat with Microsoft IIS

Configuring Tomcat 4 .x with IIS is a little more involved than with Apache, primarily because the WARP connector available for Apache is not yet available for IIS. Therefore, we must use the older AJP connector used by Tomcat 3 to connect to Tomcat 4.x.

Before we get into configuring Tomcat to work with Microsoft IIS, make sure that both have been installed and are working. You should be able to access Tomcat through http://localhost:8080 and the IIS Server through http://localhost. If you have not installed both Tomcat and IIS, go back and ensure both are running.

Once you have both IIS and Tomcat running, shut down IIS because you will now need to alter its configuration. You should also download from the Jakarta Apache Web site the binary connector you require. The connector is called isapi_redirect.dll. Download and save the file into the *<$CATALINA_HOME>*/bin directory. You can obtain a copy of the connector from:

```
http://jakarta.apache.org/builds/jakarta-tomcat/release/v3.3/bin/
win32/i386
```

You will also require two configuration files, which are provided with Tomcat 3, but not with Tomcat 4.1. Download and uncompress Tomcat 3 in order to obtain these files, which are called workers.properties and uriworkermap.properties. Once you have downloaded Tomcat 3, you can copy them from *<tomcat_3_home>*/conf/jk into your Tomcat 4.1 configuration directory *<$CATALINA_HOME>*/conf.

Adding Registry Entries

Configuring the redirector requires you to edit the Registry and add some entries. Open the Registry by running the RegEdit application. You can usually do this by selecting Run from the Start menu and then entering

```
regedit
```

into the Run box.

Open HKEY_LOCAL_MACHINE\SOFTWARE. Add a new key to SOFTWARE called

```
Apache Software Foundation
```

Under this new key, add another key called

```
Jakarta Isapi Redirector
```

and finally add another key called

```
1.0
```

Your RegEdit program should now look something like the one shown in Figure 3.1.

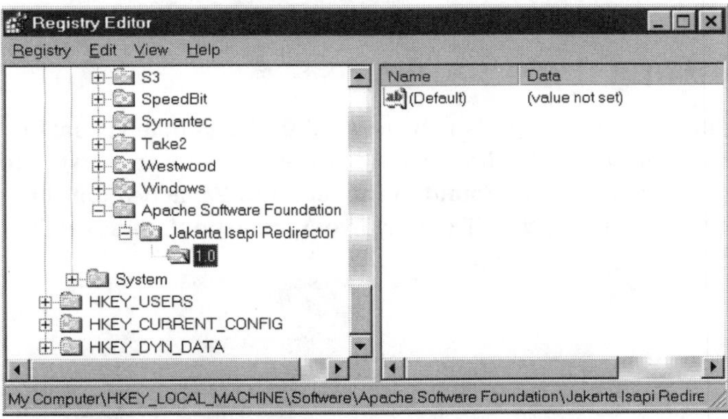

Figure 3.1 Your RegEdit after you've added keys.

You now need to add the following String values under the 1.0 key:

- extension_uri - /jakarta/isapi_redirect.dll
- log_file—This is the path and filename pointing to a location in which Tomcat should store the log files. A good idea is to point this to your Tomcat logs directory at <*$CATALINA_HOME*>/logs/isapi.log.
- log_level—The logging level. It can be debug, info, error, or emerg.
- worker_file—The path and filename of your workers.properties file. You should have already downloaded a copy of this file and copied it to your Tomcat 4.1 configuration directory. The path here should therefore be <*$CATALINA_HOME*>/conf/workers.properties.
- worker_mount_file—The path and filename of your uriworkermap.properties file. As with workers.properties, you should already have this in your Tomcat 4.1 configuration directory.

Once these changes have been made in the Registry, you should start the IIS Management console and add isapi_redirect.dll as a filter to your Web site. Then, restart the World Wide Web Publishing Service using the Services Control Panel. You should now be able to access the examples Web application via IIS.

Virtual Host Configuration

Added in HTTP 1.1, support for virtual hosts allows a single Web server to host multiple Web sites from a single IP address. The server uses information supplied by the clients request to determine which Web site to deliver. There are two ways in which you can provide virtual hosting.

The traditional way has been to use Tomcat through Apache. Apache built-in virtual hosting is used for a huge number of Web sites. The new way of providing virtual hosting (introduced in Tomcat 4) is through Tomcat directly.

Which method you choose will depend on whether you intend to use Tomcat as a stand-alone server or via the WARP connector and a traditional Web server.

Apache Virtual Hosting

Setting up virtual hosting in Apache is easy. Usually you will find a sample virtual host entry in the httpd.conf configuration file that describes how to add an entry. The httpd.conf configuration file can usually be found in the /etc/httpd/apache/conf directory. Listing 3.5 shows the virtual host section from my live Apache configuration file.

```
NameVirtualHost 192.168.1.2

<VirtualHost 192.168.1.2>
ServerName devcentre.org
DocumentRoot /home/devcentre
ServerAlias www.devcentre.org *.devcentre.org
TransferLog /var/log/httpd/apache/dc_access_log
LogFormat "%{Referer}i -> %U" referer
CustomLog /var/log/httpd/apache/dc_referer_log referer
</VirtualHost>

<VirtualHost 192.168.1.2>
ServerName nothingbutnet.co.nz
DocumentRoot /home/nbn
ServerAlias www.nothingbutnet.co.nz *.nothingbutnet.co.nz
TransferLog /var/log/httpd/apache/nbn_access_log
LogFormat "%{Referer}i -> %U" referer
CustomLog /var/log/httpd/apache/nbn_referer_log referer
</VirtualHost>
```

Listing 3.5 httpd.conf—the virtual hosting section.

The first entry is the NameVirtualHost, which should be set to the external IP address of the server. Then comes the VirtualHost entries. The VirtualHost element specifies the IP address it should be connected to. This allows a remarkable flexibility when more than one Ethernet card is installed; however, usually this will be the same IP as in the NameVirtualHost.

- ServerName—The name for this virtual host.
- DocumentRoot—The physical location on disk for this Web site.
- ServerAlias—A list of other domains this site is known by. Wildcard names using asterisks are allowed. This field is optional.
- TransferLog—The location of the transfer log. This field is optional. If omitted, the log details will be included in the main log file rather than a separate one.
- LogFormat—Specifies the format of a log. In this example, it is defining the format of the referrer log. You need to define only log formats that you will be using in CustomLogs.
- CustomLog—Specifies the location and nature of a log for this site. This field is optional.

The Apache configuration is very powerful. For every virtual host, you can use the same configuration command as in the main Apache configuration to customize the behavior of a single virtual host. The basic configuration we've shown should provide a basic virtual hosting setup, however.

Once you have altered your Apache configuration, restart Apache in order for your changes to take effect. If you have previously set up Tomcat with Apache, all the contexts will be available for all your sites. If this is not desirable, move the context definitions within each VirtualHost section, thus limiting the scope of that context to a single site.

Tomcat Virtual Hosting

Tomcat 4.x has introduced hosts as part of the server.xml configuration file. Tomcat 4.1 comes with a single default host already configured. It is within the scope of this default host that all the contexts are configured. You can now add hosts. Each host section has its own contexts and Web applications. Listing 3.6 shows a very basic host entry.

```
    <Host name="developer.mycompany.com" debug="0" appBase=
"devcentre" unpackWARs="true">
     <Valve className="org.apache.catalina.valves.AccessLogValve"
          directory="logs"  prefix="devcentre_access_log."
suffix=".txt"
          pattern="common"/>

     <Logger className="org.apache.catalina.logger.FileLogger"
          directory="logs"  prefix="devcentre_log."
```

Listing 3.6 server.xml—an example of a virtual host configuration. (continues)

```
suffix=".txt"
        timestamp="true"/>

    </Host>
```

Listing 3.6 server.xml—an example of a virtual host configuration. (continued)

Summary

In this chapter, we looked at the file structure and configuration of Tomcat in enough depth to get you a little more grounded in the basics. After reading this chapter, you should have a good feel for where files are and where to look to configure your server to suit your needs. Most of the remaining chapters in Part I of this book build on the knowledge you gained in this chapter.

In the next chapter, we step through the proc of writing a servlet. If you're a servlet guru and are reading this book just to get a better handle on Tomcat, you may want to skip this chapter.

CHAPTER

4

Hello World Wide Web

We have now installed Tomcat and have seen the front page in our browser. You've probably also looked at the example servlets and JSPs in http://localhost:8080/examples. (If not, you may want to take a moment to do that now.) At this point, we begin our discussion of how to write code for Tomcat by creating a Java servlet. A *servlet* is simply a class that descends from the GenericServlet class. Usually your class will extend HttpServlet, which itself is a descendant of GenericServlet. HttpServlet has a substantial amount of machinery to deal specifically with HTTP requests, including parameter parsing, cookie management, and session support.

Listing 4.1 is just about the simplest servlet that can be written—when executed, the servlet returns an HTML page with "Don't Panic" in large, friendly letters. It will serve as our Hello World servlet.

```
import java.io.*;
import javax.servlet.*;
import javax.servlet.http.*;

public class DontPanic extends HttpServlet {

    public void doGet(
      HttpServletRequest request,
      HttpServletResponse response
```

Listing 4.1 A simple servlet (DontPanic.java). (continues)

```
    ) throws IOException, ServletException
    {

      response.setContentType("text/html");
      PrintWriter out = response.getWriter();

      out.println("<html>");
      out.println("<head>");
      out.println("<title>Dont Panic</title>");
      out.println("</head>");
      out.println("<body>");
      out.println("<h1>Don't Panic</h1>");
      out.println("</body>");
      out.println("</html>");
    }
}
```

Listing 4.1 A simple servlet (DontPanic.java). (continued)

In this first example servlet, we are introduced to the two packages required to run servlets that handle HTTP requests: javax.servlet and javax.servlet.http. These packages include all the base classes required for servlets. Also imported is java.io, which includes the PrintWriter class (used to handle text streams) and IOException.

An HttpServlet has several methods that you can override to implement functionality. The four most commonly implemented methods are:

doGet()

doPost()

init()

service()

The doGet() method handles a simple GET request for a page. The doPost() method handles forms being posted back to the server using the HTTP method POST. The init() method is called by the servlet container (i.e., Tomcat) when an instance of the servlet is created, and information about the servlet context is passed in as a parameter in the form of the ServletConfig object. The init() method is where you do any expensive setup operations, such as establishing a connection to a database. It is guaranteed to be called by the servlet container before the container sends the first request to any of the request handler methods—for example, doGet() or doPost(). The service() method is responsible for dispatching requests to the specific request handler methods, and the doGet() and doPost() methods are actually called by it; you will see examples that intercept the request at this point rather than implementing doGet() or doPost(). We don't recommend this approach because it has a tendency to limit reusability and can cause confusion for other developers who must maintain your code. The request handler methods are there for a reason—we recommend you use them. (We cover all of this in greater detail in Chapter 5, "Anatomy and Life Cycle of a Servlet.")

The Don't Panic example simply implements the doGet() method. All the other methods are there, but are inherited from its base class, HttpServlet. Servlets, even HttpServlets, can return more than HTML; they can return any type of data, such as images, sounds, or even Java applets. However, the majority of servlets will return HTML, and we concentrate on that for now. In this example, our first two statements deal with setting up an HTML response:

```
response.setContentType("text/html");
PrintWriter out = response.getWriter();
```

The first statement sets the MIME type of the response to text/html, which is of course the MIME type for HTML. This is sent to the client with the response so that the client knows how to handle the incoming data. The second statement gets the PrintWriter on the HttpResponse object the server passed us, so that we can write data back to the client. When you're writing text-based output, a PrintWriter is usually the most sensible class to use. However, other data types will require the use of different types of Writers or Streams.

The remaining statements are all println() statements, which send text directly to the response. The text sent out is an HTML document that will display the words "Don't Panic" in large, friendly letters in your browser. To run this Java servlet, you can place it into the *<$CATALINA_HOME>*/webapps/examples/WEB-INF/classes directory and then compile it using the standard command-line method:

```
javac -classpath <$CATALINA_HOME>/common/lib/servlet.jar DontPanic.java
```

Since we're using javax.servlet.* and javax.servlet.http.*, we need to tell the compiler where to find those packages. They are included in servlet.jar, which in turn can be found in *<$CATALINA_HOME>*/common/lib. If you are using an IDE, such as JBuilder or NetBeans, you will be able to compile by the click of a button, although you may need to explicitly add servlet.jar to your classpath.

Of course, this isn't how we're going to handle development on an ongoing basis, but rather than let you struggle with configuring a deployment descriptor, we'll piggy-back off the example's servlet context and just build our first servlet inside a context that's already registered.

You can test the servlet by starting Tomcat (or restarting it if it was already running) and taking a look at the servlet through your browser. Once Tomcat has started, type the following into your browser:

```
http://localhost:8080/examples/servlet/DontPanic
```

With any luck you should see the screen shown in Figure 4.1.

The servlet will be loaded into memory and then run. Once loaded into memory, it will stay there ready for the next request. It is possible to change the server.xml configuration file to reload servlets when they have been changed. However, complex Web applications will have many classes that are not servlets, and these will not reload automatically even if they are changed. The safest way to be sure you're using the latest classes is to restart Tomcat every time a change is made. With the new management system, however, you can restart a specific Web application at any time simply by passing in the right URL. (See Chapter 9, "The Manager Application," for more details.)

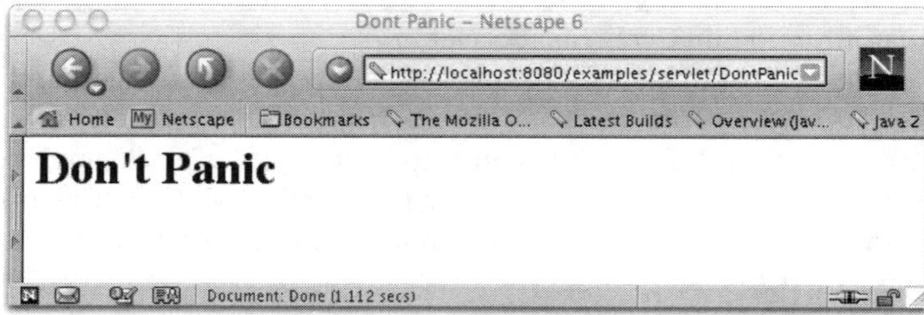

Figure 4.1 http://localhost:8080/examples/DontPanic.

Handling a Request

When a client sends a request, all the data included with the request is packaged into an HttpServletRequest object and passed to the servlet. The request is used primarily to hold parameters returned from the client to the server. In Listing 4.2, the user must guess a number the computer has in memory. Each guess tells the user if he or she is too high or too low. The guess is entered in an HTML form and is accessed in code as a parameter.

```
import java.io.*;
import java.util.*;
import javax.servlet.*;
import javax.servlet.http.*;

public class NumberGuess extends HttpServlet {

   public void doPost(HttpServletRequest request, HttpServletResponse
  response) throws IOException, ServletException {

     response.setContentType("text/html");
     PrintWriter out = response.getWriter();

     out.println("<html>");
     out.println("<head>");
     out.println("<title>Number Guess</title>");
     out.println("</head>");
     out.println("<body>");
```

Listing 4.2 The number-guessing servlet (NumberGuess.java). (continues)

```
        int number = 45;
        String guessText = request.getParameter( "guess" );
        int guess = new Integer( guessText ).intValue();

        if( guess > number ) {
          out.println("<H2>Guess too High</H2>");
        }

        if( guess < number ) {
          out.println("<H2>Guess too Low</H2>");
        }

        if( guess == number ) {
          out.println("<H2>Guess CORRECT</H2>");
        }

        out.println("</body>");
        out.println("</html>");

      }
  }
```

Listing 4.2 The number-guessing servlet (NumberGuess.java). (continued)

There are a few differences between the number guess example and the Don't Panic example. The first difference is that the number guess example implements a doPost() method rather than a doGet() method. The doPost() method is called when an HTML form is posted by the client. This example makes use of the request by extracting a value named *guess* from the parameters within the request. Since an HTTP parameter must always be text, it must be converted to a numeric value prior to being evaluated.

In order to call this servlet, you'll have to have an HTML form. A *form* is an HTML page that includes form tags. Forms provide the basic mechanism for users to send information back to a server. Listing 4.3 contains the HTML form that calls the number guess servlet. You should place it in the root directory of your Web application—in this case, <*$CATALINA_HOME*>/webapps/examples.

```
<html>
<head>
<title>Number Guess Form</title>
</head>
<body>
```

Listing 4.3 The number-guessing form (numberguess.html). (continues)

```
<h1>Number Guessing Form</h1>
<form method="post" action="servlet/NumberGuess">
<p>Guess Number: <input type="text" name="guess"></p>
<p><input type="submit"></p>
</form>
</body>
</html>
```

Listing 4.3 The number-guessing form (numberguess.html). (continued)

The HTML specifies the servlet servlet/NumberGuess to process the form and to use the post action. The input elements specify where input boxes and buttons should appear, as well as their names. In this example, we have only one input box—called guess—and a submit button that users click to post the data back to the server.

Parameters can also be sent to a doGet() method, although through a different mechanism. If you replace doPost() in Listing 4.3 with a doGet() method, you can call the servlet directly without a form at all. Instead, you would type the following into your browser:

```
http://localhost:8080/examples/NumberGuess?guess=23
```

The parameter is tacked on to the end of the URL after a question mark. The name and value is separated by an equal sign. If you wish to send more than one parameter, you can use an ampersand sign, like this:

```
http://localhost:8080/examples/NumberGuess?guess=23&name=peter
```

The request also contains a method for retrieving the header information in a request, which can identify the browser being used, what page pointed to the servlet, the IP address of the client, and many other details. You can also interrogate cookies that are included with the request.

What's In a Response

The HttpServletResponse class allows you to do more than simply send an HTML response. Usually, you will simply set the content type to text/html and then create a PrintWriter to output your HTML. However, you can send any kind of data, including images.

Listing 4.4 shows how you might handle sending an image. To indicate we are sending a GIF image from this servlet, we use the MIME type image/gif. Rather than getting a PrintWriter from the response, we get an OutputStream instead, since the data will be in binary form. We then open a file on the file input stream *in*. We then use a buffer to extract the data from the input file and push it out to the response.

While this example is about as useful as the Don't Panic example by itself, you could easily modify it to return different images at random, for example, and thus use it to rotate the banner on a Web page. You might also create your own graphical images using the Java Graphics libraries to return to the user. Servlet technology is generally used for standard HTML, but is capable of delivering many types of data.

```
import java.io.*;
import javax.servlet.*;
import javax.servlet.http.*;

public class ViewImage extends HttpServlet {

  public void doGet(HttpServletRequest request, HttpServletResponse
 response)
  throws IOException, ServletException{

    response.setContentType("image/gif");
    OutputStream out = response.getOutputStream();

    FileInputStream in = new FileInputStream( "/usr/local/
 tomcat/webapps/examples/images/code.gif" ); // Replace /usr/
 local/tomcat with the correct value for <$CATALINA_HOME>

    byte[] buffer = new byte[1024];
    int bytesRead = 0;

    while( in.available() > 0 ) {
      bytesRead = in.read( buffer );
      out.write( buffer, 0, bytesRead );
    }

  }
}
```

Listing 4.4 Sending an image (ViewImage.java).

Summary

In this chapter, we examined servlets for the first time. We saw how the basic mechanisms work within servlets. We also saw how Tomcat calls the doGet(), doPost(), and init() methods in response to client requests, and learned that the service() method is responsible for calling the doGet() and doPost() methods. We learned how the doGet() and doPost() methods receive request and response parameters, and how to use mechanisms to extract data from requests and post data to the response.

In the next chapter, we discuss in depth the API through which servlets communicate with the servlet container, and learn what actually happens at runtime.

CHAPTER

5

Anatomy and Life Cycle of a Servlet

No, this is not a diversion into the world of biology. In the previous chapter, we introduced the servlet programming model and touched briefly on some key features of the HttpServlet class. In this chapter, we provide you with a more complete treatment of the servlet interface and examine the servlet life cycle. The servlet container is responsible for creating individual servlet instances, and manages all communication with the servlet, in addition to the instantiation and destruction of individual instances of the servlet. Beyond this, the Servlet 2.3 Specification adds an API that enables the servlet container to notify the servlet of events taking place outside it.

The Servlet Life Cycle

Let's begin by looking at the life cycle of a servlet. We focus on the life cycle of an HttpServlet since in the vast majority of cases, you'll be using servlets to handle HTTP or HTTPS requests. The concepts are similar when you're writing servlets for custom protocols, but by the time you're doing that kind of development—if in fact you ever decide you need to—you will probably be pretty comfortable with the information in this chapter.

At startup time, the servlet container examines its configuration files, as well as the configuration files of the Web applications contained in the /webapps directory. The container then determines:

- Which URIs to associate with servlet contexts
- Which servlet classes to instantiate in order to handle requests

For example, let's assume that we have a Web application called sample, residing in the /webapps directory, that contains the servlet class com.wiley.tomcatbook.SampleServlet. In the deployment descriptor file for our application (the *web.xml file*, which we will look at in depth in the next chapter), we see that it is to be associated with the /sampleservlet URI. Tomcat creates a ServletContext instance for this Web application, and records that any inbound requests for /sample/sampleservlet are to be redirected to an instance of com.wiley.tomcatbook.SampleServlet. (The servlet container constructs the URI from the Webapp name and the URI described in the deployment descriptor—this prevents namespace collisions between Webapps.)

Depending on the configuration of the server, it may instantiate one or more instances of the servlet then, or wait for the first request for the resource before instantiating the servlet. In either case, at the time the servlet is instantiated, the public no argument constructor for the class is called to instantiate the servlet. Then the init() method is called, and a ServletConfig object is passed to it. This ServletConfig object contains information about the ServletContext it's running in, including any initialization parameters stored in the deployment descriptor or explicitly written to the server.xml. Note that there is one and only one instance of ServletContext for each Web application, and that it is used to manage all instances of all servlets that are part of that Web application.

Let's assume that our SampleServlet opens a JDBC connection to a database server, and that one of the initialization parameters is the JDBC URL that will be used to open this connection. The servlet should then perform any initialization needed. In our case, the init() method will open a connection to the database server and store a reference to it in an instance variable. That way, all subsequent calls to the various request handler methods will have access to the resource. The servlet container also signals the servlet that its context is ready and available to provide services. Prior to init() being called, the servlet should not assume that the servlet container is ready to handle requests from it or that its containing context is valid.

If the initialization is successful, the init() method will return, and the servlet will be considered available to handle requests. If there is a failure during initialization—for example, if our SampleServlet fails to connect to the database—the method should throw an exception (either a ServletException or an UnavailableException) to signal to the servlet container that it will not be able to handle requests. The servlet engine will then remove the mapping and mark the resource as unavailable.

At some point, a request comes in via HTTP, be it a GET request, a POST request, or one using any of the other request methods supported by the servlet specification (HEAD, PUT, DELETE, TRACE, or OPTIONS). Note that *request method* refers to the method specified in the first line of an HTTP request; for instance:

```
GET /sample/sampleservlet HTTP/1.1
```

This results in the servlet container creating the following:

- An HttpRequest object that contains information about the request; for example, all headers and query parameters
- An HttpResponse object, with methods for getting the OutputStream the request handler should write to, for setting headers and the like

These objects are passed to the service() method on our servlet, which in our case, as is typical, is inherited from the HttpServlet base class. The service() method duly passes the request to one of the special-purpose request handler methods: doGet(), doPost(), doHead(), doPut(), doDelete(), doTrace(), or doOptions().

That request handler is then responsible for examining the request object and determining what to write to the OutputStream associated with the response. The handler can set headers—such as the Content-type header, which we saw being set in the previous chapter with response.setContentType()—send cookies, or attach any arbitrary header it chooses to.

When the method returns, the servlet container takes the data written to the OutputStream and flushes it to the client that requested it. Depending on the parameters associated with the request, it may close the connection or keep it alive for subsequent requests, but the container has now finished working with our servlet until the next request comes in. It may then destroy the instance or keep it around for the next request—again, depending on the server configuration.

If for any reason the servlet is unable to complete the request, it should throw an exception, either a ServletException or an UnavailableException. A ServletException signals that the servlet is functioning correctly, but that there was something wrong with the request or something happened that caused the request to fail (such as an IOException). In our example, let's assume that the request came in with an incorrect request parameter. The client sent the parameter *datasource=bardata*; however, we only know about the datasource *foodata*. We then signal this by throwing a ServletException, preferably one with a sensible message about what failed.

An UnavailableException, on the other hand, signals that the request was valid, but that some required resource was unavailable, or some other intermittent or permanent problem caused the servlet to fail. In our example, let's assume that the request came in with a valid request for *datasource=foodata*, but that the database connection has failed and we weren't able to re-establish it. Let's assume that the database server is no longer available due to a server crash. Our servlet should signal this by throwing an UnavailableException, again preferably with a sensible error message. The UnavailableException provides a mechanism for indicating whether the failure is intermittent or permanent. If the failure is indicated to be intermittent, the server will respond to the requesting client with a 503 Service Unavailable exception, indicating that the client should retry in the future. If the failure is permanent, the servlet container will remove the servlet from service, call its destroy() method, and release it for garbage collection.

On destruction of the servlet instance, the servlet container calls the servlet's destroy() method. At this point, the servlet should release any resources it is holding. In our example, the destroy() method would close the database connection opened in the init() method. When the servlet container decides to release the servlet instance, it will wait for all threads to complete their access of the service() method (and by extension, to the other request handler methods) and then call destroy() before releasing the instance for garbage collection.

Note that the servlet container may send multiple concurrent requests to the request handler methods of your servlet, and as a result, you should make sure that your servlet code is re-entrant. Or, if for some reason you can't or don't wish to ensure this, your servlet can implement the SingleThreadModel interface or add the synchronized keyword to its implementation of the service() method. However, because this forces the servlet containter to serialize requests to the servlet, performance can *severely* degrade under load. Remember, under normal circumstances, a lot of the time spent handling a request is spent waiting for network I/O to be completed, so a servlet based on the SingleThreadModel can really bog down if, for instance, even a single client is connected over a slow link. This is preferable to a servlet mishandling data as a result of thread-safety issues, but it is reasonable to request that you, as a servlet developer, write thread-safe code.

Note also that, as we stated at the beginning of this section, one or more servlet instances may be created. Typically, for efficiency, the servlet container will pool instances of the servlet to save on the servlet-creation overhead. All instances of a servlet will share a single ServletContext, but they will be separate instances of their class. When designing your servlet, be sure to consider whether this has any side effects in your application. Don't assume, for example, that an individual servlet instance will have handled all previous requests. If there's some information you need to remain persistent, you should store it in the ServletContext, in a Session object, or in some other accessible place.

Servlet Anatomy

From the previous section, you saw that the servlet container uses a number of methods to interface with your servlet. In this section, we'll look at the method signatures by way of some sample code and see how we handle the requests we discussed in the previous section.

Let's start with the simplest possible HTTP servlet, shown in Listing 5.1.

```
import javax.servlet.*;
import javax.servlet.http.*;

public class SampleServlet extends HttpServlet
{
}
```

Listing 5.1 The simplest possible HTTP servlet.

Yes, that's really all you have to do. The parent class, HttpServlet, is a fully functional (if somewhat uninteresting) servlet. It will compile and run, but it won't return anything to any requests it receives because its request handler methods don't do anything. Just like java.applet.Applet, the base class is a complete, functional implementation and not an abstract base class. This lets you implement only the life cycle methods you're interested in. For instance, our DontPanic servlet didn't need to do any special initialization, so we didn't include an init() method. The servlet was just supposed to handle GET method requests, and so we simply implemented the doGet() method.

Of course, the sample in Listing 5.1 isn't very interesting. Let's go through and add each of the methods we mentioned earlier. We start by adding an import statement and writing a doGet() method, as shown in Listing 5.2.

```
import java.io.*;
...
public void doGet(HttpRequest request, HttpResponse response)
        throws ServletException, IOException
{
        String bgcolor;
        PrintWriter out;
        response.setContentType("text/html");
        response.setHeader("X-My-Header", "From SampleServlet");
        bgcolor = request.getParameter("bgcolor");
        if (bgcolor == null) bgcolor = "FFFFFF";
        out = response.getWriter();

out.println("<html>\n<head>\n<title>SampleServlet</title>\n</head>");
        out.println("<body bgcolor=\"#" + bgcolor + "\">);
        out.println("<h1 align=\"center\">Set the Background Color
  </h1>");
        out.println("<p>Set the background color by passing in the bgcolor");
        out.println("parameter with a 6 digit hexadecimal number.
  </p>");
        out.println("</body>\n</html>");
}
```

Listing 5.2 The doGet() method.

This should be fairly familiar from the previous chapter. We set the content type to text/html, as we did previously. Then we set our own header on the response. Sometimes this is useful when you want to pass metadata about the response to a client that knows about the header in question—for example, if you're writing both the client and the servlet. Other clients are supposed to just ignore headers they don't understand.

We then look for a parameter, *bgcolor*, and if it exists, we use it to set the background color of the page we're generating. If it doesn't (in which case getParameter() returns null), we set it to a default color of white, or 0xFFFFFF. If, for example, the request were for /sample/sampleservlet?bgcolor=FF00FF, you'd get a bright purple page. It's a baby step toward customizing a site based on user preference.

What we've done in Listing 5.3 is something you will see fairly often in servlet code. We're simply passing the request and the response to the doGet() method for processing. It is often the case that you want the behavior of a servlet to be the same, whether the query is sent using the GET or the POST method. Even when this is not the case, it is often useful to do this during development time so that you can type parameters into a browser, and therefore use GET, rather than having to build a form to pass the parameters in using POST.

```
public void doPost(HttpRequest request, HttpResponse response)
        throws ServletException, IOException
{
        doGet(request, response);
}
```

Listing 5.3 The doPost() method.

The doHead() method in Listing 5.4 responds to HEAD requests. HTTP HEAD is intended to serve back only the metadata about the document pointed to by the URI in the request. It is often used in building indexes of sites, testing for validity of a URL, checking for modifications, and performing similar tasks when it's used at all. It can also be used over a slow link to allow the client to determine whether it wants to download the whole document. Ideally, it should return all the same metadata as would be returned from a GET request. According to the RFC 2616, which defines HTTP, the response to a HEAD request *must not* include a body element.

```
public void doHead(HttpRequest request, HttpResponse response)
        throws ServletException, IOException
{
        PrintWriter out;
        response.setContentType("text/html");
        response.setHeader("X-My-Header", "From SampleServlet");
}
```

Listing 5.4 The doHead() method.

In these examples, we'll let the base class handle the remaining request types. PUT and DELETE are used for manipulating content on the server. You can implement custom handlers for these rather more specialized tasks if you wish; however, handling these methods is outside the scope of this overview. OPTIONS is used to negotiate what types of communication the client and server can both handle. The session transcript shown in Listing 5.5 indicates what the server returns when it receives an OPTIONS request. You can try this yourself to get a feel for what the server is actually doing. The parts you enter appear in boldface.

```
[titanium:~] imf% telnet localhost 8080
Trying 127.0.0.1...
Connected to localhost.
Escape character is '^]'.
OPTIONS * HTTP/1.0
```

Listing 5.5 A typical OPTIONS request session. (continues)

```
HTTP/1.1 200 OK
Content-Length: 0
Allow: GET, HEAD, POST, PUT, DELETE, TRACE, OPTIONS
Date: Fri, 14 Jun 2002 22:59:41 GMT
Server: Apache Tomcat/4.0.3 (HTTP/1.1 Connector)

Connection closed by foreign host.
```

Listing 5.5 A typical OPTIONS request session. (continued)

Listing 5.5 tells the client (in this case, you and your telnet client) that this server knows about GET, HEAD, POST, PUT, DELETE, TRACE, and OPTIONS.

The TRACE command tells the server to send back the actual request received rather than the requested URI. This can be useful in debugging an application because you can verify that the request received matched the request you think you sent.

In our sample, we want to connect to a JDBC data source, so we'll set that up in our init() method, as shown in Listing 5.6. We'll need to import java.sql.*, of course.

```
import java.sql.*;
...

private Connection con;

public void init(ServletConfig config) throws ServletException
{
   String driver = config.getInitParameter("database-driver-class");
   String jdbcurl = config.getInitParameter("database-url");
   String login = config.getInitParameter("database-login");
   String password = config.getInitParameter("database-password");
   try
   {
      Class.forName(driver); // Load the driver
      con = DriverManager.getConnection(jdbcurl,
         login, password);
   }
   catch (Exception e)
   {
      throw new UnavailableException(e.getMessage());
   }
}
```

Listing 5.6 The init() method.

In Listing 5.6, we get four init parameters—database-driver-class, database-url, database-login, and database-password—passed in from the deployment descriptor. (We cover the deployment descriptor in detail in the next chapter.) We then use the parameters to load the driver and connect to the database. If we are unable to make the connection, we signal the container that things didn't work out by throwing an UnavailableException. Note that in a production-quality application, we would want to use connection pooling (and probably would want to have a little more granularity on the exception handling as well), retrying the connection and perhaps passing information in the exception message about the actual parameters passed in.

There are also, of course, a number of methods on the HttpRequest and HttpResponse objects. We'll see many of them throughout the rest of this book, and it's worth exploring the JavaDoc to find out more about them. One helpful method we want to touch on here is the sendError() method on the Response object. This method basically encapsulates the sending of an error back to the client, and interrupts the execution of the method from which it is called. You could handle this by throwing a ServletException, but the sendError() method gives you a little more control over the error message returned.

In Listing 5.7, we've enhanced our doGet() method from Listing 5.2 to validate the passed-in parameter.

```
public void doGet(HttpRequest request, HttpResponse response)
        throws ServletException, IOException
{
        String bgcolor;
        PrintWriter out;
        response.setContentType("text/html");
        response.setHeader("X-My-Header", "From SampleServlet");
        bgcolor = request.getParameter("bgcolor");
        if (bgcolor == null) bgcolor = "FFFFFF";
        if (bgcolor.length != 6)
response.sendError(400, "Parameter bgcolor \""
+ bgcolor + "\" is the wrong length.");
        out = response.getWriter();
        out.println("<html>\n<head>\n<title>SampleServlet</title>\n</head>");
        out.println("<body bgcolor=\"#" + bgcolor + "\">);
        out.println("<h1 align=\"center\">Set the Background
  Color</h1>");
        out.println("<p>Set the background color by passing in the
  bgcolor");
        out.println("parameter with a 6 digit hexadecimal number.
  </p>");
        out.println("</body>\n</html>");
}
```

Listing 5.7 The doGet() method, with validation.

Note that we've included a descriptive message and set the error code to 400: Bad Request. (You can also use Response.SC_BAD_REQUEST to make your code more readable. Many developers are already quite familiar with a number of the HTTP result codes, however.) You can find a listing of the HTTP result codes, and the static final variables for them, in the JavaDoc for the Response object.

Life Cycle Events

The events in the life cycle we've covered so far all explicitly affect our servlet, because they call methods on it. However, a lot of other things happen in the servlet container, and some of them are potentially things we might be interested in knowing about. To help out with this, servlet containers also generate a few life cycle events we can listen for. This is a new feature in the current servlet specification, version 2.3, and as a result, since Tomcat 4.0 is the first release to implement the Servlet 2.3 Specification, it's also the first to support these events.

The basic model should be familiar if you've been using Java for a while—it's based on the Java 1.1 event model. If we're interested in an event, we create a class that implements the listener interface for the events we're interested in, and we register it with the servlet engine. The servlet engine then delivers events by calling the appropriate interface method on our class. We'll look at some basic examples that implement each of the four interfaces and show how to register them with Tomcat. The interfaces are standard, as is the mechanism for registering them. Both are part of the Servlet 2.3 Specification, so they should work fine with any 2.3-compliant servlet engine.

There are four event listener interfaces in the 2.3 specification, which we examine here in turn. Two relate to events occurring in the servlet context, and two relate to events occurring in connection with sessions. Which interface or interfaces you need to implement depends entirely on which events you're interested in being notified about, and typically you may not be interested in every event notification defined in the interface. If you're not, you can just stub out the method and discard the event. The interfaces are quite simple, and none requires you to implement more than three methods, as we'll see in the following examples. When we're done with the examples, we'll show you how to add them to the deployment descriptor (which we cover in depth in the next chapter) so that they are registered with the servlet container and will start getting events.

javax.servlet.ServletContextListener

The ServletContextListener listens for either of two things to happen to the context: for the context to be created, or for the context to be destroyed. The interface has two methods: contextInitialized() and contextDestroyed(). Each takes a ServletContext Event as its only parameter, and this event has a reference to the context in question. Our sample listener will listen for these events and then enumerate the names of the attributes on the affected context. You can, of course, use it to do whatever you want, but an excellent use for such a listener is to manage initialization and shutdown of underlying services—for example, database connections—which are shared by all of the servlets in your Web application. Listing 5.8 contains our SampleLifecycleListener.

```
package com.wiley.tomcatbook;

import java.util.*;
import javax.servlet.*;

public class SampleLifecycleListener implements
  ServletContextListener
{
    public void contextInitialized(ServletContextEvent event)
    {
        System.out.println("Servlet context initialized! " + event);
        enumerateContextAttributes(event.getServletContext());
    }

    public void contextDestroyed(ServletContextEvent event)
    {
        System.out.println("Servlet context destroyed! " + event);
        enumerateContextAttributes(event.getServletContext());
    }

    public final void enumerateContextAttributes
  (ServletContext context)
    {
        Enumeration e = context.getAttributeNames();
        while(e.hasMoreElements())
        {
            System.out.println("\tAttribute: " + e.nextElement());
        }
    }
}
```

Listing 5.8 The SampleLifecycleListener.

As you can see, the interface is very straightforward. Each method gets called when the specified event occurs, and an event object is passed in that contains a reference to the context. In our class, we then iterate over the attributes that happen to appear on the context, and print out the name of each.

When we install this listener (which we show you how to do in a moment) and then restart Tomcat, our listener prints the following to the log:

```
Servlet context initialized! javax.servlet.ServletContextEvent[source=org.apache.catalina.core.
 ApplicationContext@28d6ab]
    Attribute: javax.servlet.context.tempdir
    Attribute: org.apache.catalina.resources
    Attribute: org.apache.catalina.WELCOME_FILES
    Attribute: org.apache.catalina.jsp_classpath
```

Listing 5.9 Log output from SampleLifecycleListener.

When we shut down the server, we see very similar output since our two event handler methods are so similar.

javax.servlet.ServletContextAttributeListener

The ServletContextAttributeListener lets us know when context attributes are added, removed, or replaced. The interface declares three methods: attributeAdded(), attributeRemoved(), and attributeReplaced(). Each takes a ServletContextAttributeEvent as its only argument, which has a getName() and a getValue() method, returning the name of the attribute and the new value, respectively.

Our sample listener class, shown in Listing 5.10, implements each of these, and again simply prints out the key attributes.

```
package com.wiley.tomcatbook;

import javax.servlet.*;

public class SampleAttributeChangeListener
   implements ServletContextAttributeListener
{
   public void attributeAdded(ServletContextAttributeEvent event)
   {
      System.out.println("Servlet context attribute \"" +
         event.getName() + "\" added with value " +
         event.getValue()
      );
   }

   public void attributeRemoved(ServletContextAttributeEvent event)
   {
```

Listing 5.10 The SampleAttributeChangeListener. (continues)

```
        System.out.println("Servlet context attribute \"" +
            event.getName() + "\" removed with value " +
            event.getValue()
        );
    }

    public void attributeReplaced(ServletContextAttributeEvent event)
    {
        System.out.println("Servlet context attribute \"" +
            event.getName() + "\" replaced with value " +
            event.getValue()
        );
    }
}
```

Listing 5.10 The SampleAttributeChangeListener. (continued)

Again, the class is fairly self-explanatory. Each method is called when an event of the appropriate type occurs.

The other two listener interfaces listen for events related to session management, and are quite analogous to the two interfaces related to context management that we just saw.

javax.servlet.http.HttpSessionListener

The HttpSessionListener interface, much like the ServletContextListener, listens for the creation or destruction events. Of course, these events relate to the creation or destruction of sessions. The two methods declared in the interface are sessionCreated() and sessionDestroyed(), both taking an HttpSessionEvent as an argument. The HttpSessionEvent has a getSession() method, which will return the session in question.

```
package com.wiley.tomcatbook;

import javax.servlet.http.*;
import java.util.*;

public class SampleHttpSessionListener implements HttpSessionListener
{
    public void sessionCreated(HttpSessionEvent event)
    {
        HttpSession s = event.getSession();
        System.out.println("Session created: " + s);
        enumerateSessionAttributes(s);
```

Listing 5.11 The SampleHttpSessionListener. (continues)

```
    }

    public void sessionDestroyed(HttpSessionEvent event)
    {
        HttpSession s = event.getSession();
        System.out.println("Session destroyed: " + s);
        enumerateSessionAttributes(s);
    }

    public final void enumerateSessionAttributes(HttpSession session)
    {
        Enumeration e = session.getAttributeNames();
        while(e.hasMoreElements())
        {
            System.out.println("\tAttribute: " + e.nextElement());
        }
    }
}
```

Listing 5.11 The SampleHttpSessionListener. (continued)

In SampleHttpSessionListener, shown in Listing 5.11, we simply print a message stating which event occurred, and then iterate over the set of attributes on the session, much like we did in the ServletContextListener.

javax.servlet.http.HttpSessionAttributeListener

The HttpSessionAttributeListener interface, much like the ServletContextAttibuteListener, listens for the addition, removal, or modification of a session attibute. The methods declared in the interface are attributeAdded(), attributeRemoved(), and attributeReplaced(). Each takes an instance of HttpSessionBindingEvent as its only parameter. Like ServletContextAttributeEvent, HttpSessionBindingEvent has methods for returning the name of the modified attribute and the new value. Again, in Listing 5.12 we simply print out the name and value of the modified attribute.

```
package com.wiley.tomcatbook;

import javax.servlet.http.*;

public class SampleHttpSessionAttributeListener implements HttpSessionAttributeListener
{
    public void attributeAdded(HttpSessionBindingEvent event)
```

Listing 5.12 The SampleHttpSessionAttributeListener. (continues)

```
    {
        System.out.println("Session attribute \"" + event.getName()
  + "\" added with value " + event.getValue());
    }

    public void attributeRemoved(HttpSessionBindingEvent event)
    {
        System.out.println("Session attribute \"" + event.getName()
  + "\" removed with value " + event.getValue());
    }

    public void attributeReplaced(HttpSessionBindingEvent event)
    {
        System.out.println("Session attribute \"" + event.getName()
  + "\" replaced with value " + event.getValue());
    }
}
```

Listing 5.12 The SampleHttpSessionAttributeListener. (continued)

Since the listener definitions are all interfaces, it's up to you whether you implement these methods on separate helper objects, directly on one of your servlets, or elsewhere in your application.

Configuring Life Cycle Listeners

Now that we have some listener classes, let's register them with the Tomcat servlet engine. We do this in the deployment descriptor, or web.xml file, for a Web application. We start by creating the appropriate file structure in our /webapps directory. Let's call the Webapp *lifecycle*, so the file hierarchy looks like this:

```
<$CATALINA_HOME>/webapps/lifecycle
    /WEB-INF
        /web.xml
            /classes
                /com
                    /wiley
                        /tomcatbook
                            SampleLifecycleListener.class
                            SampleAttributeChangeListener.class
                            SampleHttpSessionListener.class
                            SampleHttpSessionAttributeListener.class
```

Compile the classes above and put them in your classes directory, as we indicated earlier. (You can also put them in a JAR file and place them in <*$CATALINA_HOME*>/webapps/lifecycle/WEB-INF/lib instead, if you prefer.)

Then we need to create the deployment descriptor, or web.xml file. It should look like the one shown in Listing 5.13.

```
<?xml version="1.0" encoding="UTF-8"?>
<!DOCTYPE web-app
  PUBLIC "-//Sun Microsystems, Inc.//DTD Web Application 2.3//EN"
  "http://java.sun.com/dtd/web-app_2_3.dtd">
<web-app>
  <listener>
     <listener-class>com.wiley.tomcatbook.SampleLifecycleListener
 </listener-class>
  </listener>
  <listener>
     <listener-class>com.wiley.tomcatbook.
 SampleAttributeChangeListener </listener-class>
  </listener>
  <listener>
     <listener-class>com.wiley.tomcatbook.SampleHttpSessionListener
 </listener-class>
  </listener>
  <listener>
     <listener-class>com.wiley.tomcatbook.
 SampleHttpSessionAttributeListener </listener-class>
  </listener>
</web-app>
```

Listing 5.13 The life-cycle Webapp deployment descriptor.

The XML file shown in Listing 5.13 tells the servlet container to create a new context and to load our four listener classes, connecting them to the event delivery mechanism. As you can see, we simply declare the classname of each listener in a separate <listener-class/> element, each contained in a single <listener/> element. If this doesn't make sense for any reason, don't worry. We talk a lot more about the deployment descriptor in the next chapter.

Once this file is in place, the next time Tomcat is restarted, you should start seeing log output similar to what we saw in Listing 5.9. Try tailing the logs (see Chapter 3, "Configuring Tomcat") and restarting Tomcat.

If you want to see what's going on with the servlet container in your own Webapps, or in other Webapps you've installed, you can always add these listeners to another Webapp simply by adding all the <listener/> nodes here to that Webapp and throwing a JAR containing the listener classes into the /WEB-INF/lib/ directory of the Webapp you want to add the listeners to.

Try adding the listeners to the example Webapp. Copy your class files into *<$CATALINA_HOME>*/webapps/examples/WEB-INF/classes/com/wiley/tomcatbook/. (You'll have to create the /com, /wiley, and /tomcatbook directories.) Then add all the

<listener/> and <listener-class/> lines to *<$CATALINA_HOME>*/webapps/ examples/ WEB-INF/web.xml, inserting them after the last </listener> line in that file. (Node order is important in the web.xml file, so the nodes have to go there.)

Next, restart Tomcat again, still tailing the logs. You'll see the context get created. Then poke around in some of the sample apps, particularly ones that create session objects, like http://localhost:8080/examples/jsp/num/numguess.jsp, and watch the logs. You'll see a session get created, and the attribute(s) that get added to that session. Try other example servlets and JSPs that create session information. The logs can be quite interesting; you can see some of what the servlets are doing under the covers.

Here is some sample output after restarting tomcat, visiting http://localhost:8080/ examples/jsp/num/numguess.jsp, and visiting http://localhost:8080/examples/jsp/sessions/carts.jsp:

```
Servlet context initialized!
  javax.servlet.ServletContextEvent[source=org.apache.catalina.core.
  ApplicationContext@2eea84]
        Attribute: javax.servlet.context.tempdir
        Attribute: org.apache.catalina.resources
        Attribute: org.apache.catalina.WELCOME_FILES
        Attribute: org.apache.catalina.jsp_classpath
Session created: org.apache.catalina.session.
  StandardSessionFacade@6d65b
Session attribute "numguess" added with value num.
  NumberGuessBean@3a818f
```

Summary

In this chapter, we gave you an overview of the structure of a servlet, and explained how the various methods are called at various times in the life cycle of the servlet. You should now have a better understanding of what actually happens to your servlet as it is instantiated and handles requests inside the servlet container. You may wish to refer back to this chapter as we explore more complex topics relating to servlet development throughout the rest of the book.

In the next chapter, we see how to configure the servlet and set up your Web applications.

CHAPTER

6

Configuring Web Applications

In this chapter, we discuss installing and configuring Web applications under Tomcat. You can do this in a few different ways, but in all cases the process includes two primary tasks: telling Tomcat about your application, and making accessible to Tomcat the files your Webapp needs. The first task is typically a matter of writing a deployment descriptor, or web.xml file. The second is a matter of knowing where to place your JAR files, class files, JSPs, and so forth.

The three cases we'll examine are:

- Installing a Web application in the /webapps/ directory
- Creating and deploying a WAR file
- Registering a Web application from the server.xml configuration file

Appendix B, "Deployment Descriptor (web.xml) Reference," explains the syntax of the deployment descriptor.

Installing in /webapps

In Chapter 3, "Configuring Tomcat," we gave you an overview of the Tomcat file structure. In this section, we discuss the /webapps directory in depth. The /webapps directory contains separate subdirectories for each Web application project, or Webapp. Each Webapp can contain static pages and JSPs, with the document root for the application being the main subdirectory (see Listing 6.1).

In addition to these regular content files, there is a special directory called /WEB-INF (note that the filename is case-sensitive and should be in all caps). This directory contains subdirectories for class files and JAR files associated with the Webapp, along with the all-important deployment descriptor file: web.xml. Its function is similar to the function of the manifest file inside a JAR file: It describes the Web application in a machine-readable way so that its environment—in this case, Tomcat—knows what to do with it. Listing 6.1 is a directory listing of a Webapp containing only static content, and a single applet, stored in myapplet.jar.

```
<$CATALINA_HOME>
  /webapps
    /mywebapp
      index.html
      mystylesheet.css
      myapplet.jar
      /images
        mylogo.gif
        illustration.jpeg
      /articles
        an_article.html
        another_article.html
      /WEB-INF
        web.xml
        classes/
        lib/
```

Listing 6.1 Directory listing of a hypothetical Webapp.

By default, Tomcat will establish a context for our Webapp based on the name of the directory containing our Webapp, in this case */mywebapp*. If we were to go to the URL http://localhost:8080*/mywebapp/*, the server would redirect us to the index.html file indicated in Listing 6.1. In turn, index.html would load any referenced objects, which might include the style sheet mystylesheet.css, the logo image mylogo.gif, and the applet in myapplet.jar.

Of course, it's probably more interesting for us to include some servlets and JSPs in our Web application.

You can include JSPs as easily as you can HTML files. In fact, we could simply rename index.html to index.jsp (valid HTML files are also valid JSP files), and the next time the object was requested, the servlet engine would compile the JSP using the Jasper parser, and the compiled JSP would handle the request. (We talk more about JSPs in Chapter 11, "JavaServer Pages.") This gives you a lot of flexibility in deciding where you locate your JSPs, and makes it easy to integrate JSP-based pages with static HTML pages, images, and other static content.

Servlet classes and other library files are kept in one of two places under the /WEB-INF directory. If they are packaged in JAR files, they are kept in the /lib directory. If they are class files, they are kept in a directory hierarchy under the /classes directory, based on the Java package they belong to. For example, our hypothetical SampleServlet from Chapter 5, "Anatomy and Life Cycle of a Servlet," was part of the com.wiley.tomcatbook package and the /sample Webapp, so the class file would live in <*$CATALINA_HOME*>/webapps/sample/WEB-INF/classes/com/wiley/tomcatbook/SampleServlet.class.

Both sets of classes are automatically placed on the classpath used by the class loader assigned to our Webapp, so all the classes in both hierarchies are available for use in your servlets and JSPs. It's important to include library files here when they're needed. In our example in the previous chapter, we loaded a JDBC driver from our servlet's init() method. That driver needs to be available to the class loader for our servlet. If we configured our servlet to use the MySQL driver, we would need to include mysql.jar in the /WEB-INF/lib directory for our Webapp. If we chose to use Oracle, we would use an appropriate Oracle driver library, such as oracle-jdbc-1.2.jar.

In addition to the previous directories, the class loader for our servlet has access to <*$CATALINA_HOME*>/common/classes/ and common/lib; however, remember that each Webapp has a separate class loader, so even if you use the same class file, loaded from the same library, in two different Webapp contexts, they will have separate namespaces. This has implications if you intend to share data between Webapps (and very good implications if you *don't* intend to share data between Webapps, but might otherwise do so inadvertently). If you need to communicate between Webapps, there are other mechanisms for doing so—through the Session object, for example.

As you may remember from the previous chapter, our sample servlet chose a database at runtime, based on the ServletConfig passed into the init() method. This means that different deployments of our application might end up using different drivers. Because selection of the database is left until runtime, the user of our Webapp has a lot of flexibility about how to configure it. With a couple of changes to the deployment descriptor, and the inclusion of the appropriate JAR file in our /WEB-INF/lib directory, we can use the same servlet to connect to an entirely different database. By factoring out deployment time decisions into a configuration file, we can drastically increase the reusability of our Webapps. Of course, developing portable database code is not trivial, but there are several good books on JDBC that can help you with this.

The file hierarchy is fairly straightforward. With this, we've satisfied our second requirement in deploying a Web application: making the resources available to the server. Now, let's tackle the first: telling the server about our Web application.

The Deployment Descriptor: web.xml

Each Web application has its own configuration file, a web.xml file located under the /WEB-INF directory of the Web application. This file is called the Web application deployment descriptor. Let's start by looking at how we might write the deployment descriptor for our SampleServlet introduced in Chapter 5.

The web.xml file in Listing 6.2 is probably pretty familiar to you already, since we've been discussing this sample application. One of the advantages of using XML for configuration files is that XML files have a tendency to be self-describing. However, let's go through this file in detail to make sure everything is clear.

```
<?xml version="1.0" encoding="ISO-8859-1"?>
<!DOCTYPE web-app
  PUBLIC "-//Sun Microsystems, Inc.//DTD Web Application 2.3//EN"
  "http://java.sun.com/dtd/web-app_2.3.dtd">

<web-app>
    <servlet>
        <servlet-name>SampleServlet</servlet-name>
        <servlet-class>com.wiley.tomcatbook.SampleServlet
  </servlet-class>
    </servlet>
    <servlet-mapping>
        <servlet-name>SampleServlet</servlet-name>
        <url-pattern>/sampleservlet</url-pattern>
    </servlet-mapping>
    <init-param>
        <param-name>database-driver-class</param-name>
        <param-value>org.gjt.mm.mysql.Driver</param-value>
    </init-param>
    <init-param>
        <param-name>database-url</param-name>
        <param-value>jdbc:mysql://localhost/sampledb
  </param-value>
    </init-param>
    <init-param>
        <param-name>database-login</param-name>
        <param-value>sample</param-value>
    </init-param>
    <init-param>
        <param-name>database-password</param-name>
        <param-value>badpassword</param-value>
    </init-param>
</web-app>
```

Listing 6.2 The web.xml file for the sample Webapp in Chapter 5.

The web.xml file starts off by declaring its encoding and its DOCTYPE. All web.xml files will start with this text (though perhaps with a different encoding, depending on the local requirements) and have a root node named <web-app/>. In fact, that is a sufficient web.xml for the static site in Listing 6.1. Tomcat (and any other Servlet 2.3-compliant servlet engine) will be smart enough to figure out the rest. However, this wouldn't be a very useful chapter if we only showed you that. So let's configure our servlet.

Inside the <web-app/> root node, we have a <servlet/> node, a <servlet-mapping/> node, and four <init-param/> nodes.

The <servlet/> node declares that there will be a servlet known as SampleServlet. Its implementation can be found in the class com.wiley.tomcatbook.SampleServlet.

The <servlet-mapping/> node tells the server what URI to map to our servlet, and so determines at what URL users will get to our servlet through the Web server. It states that the servlet known as SampleServlet (which we declared in the previous node) should be found under the URI /sampleservlet. The servlet engine then prepends the name of our Webapp onto this URI. Therefore, since our Webapp lives in a directory named <*$CATALINA_HOME*>/webapps/sample, the complete URI will be /sample/sampleservlet. When combined with the hostname and port, we get a full URL; for example: http://localhost:8080/sample/sampleservlet.

The <init-param/> nodes create the parameters that will be passed to the init() method in the ServletConfig object. You probably recall from our previous chapter that we loaded four parameters to set up our database connection. (You may want to compare Listing 5.6 with Listing 6.2.) One such line in the init() method was:

```
String driver = config.getInitParameter("database-driver-class");
```

Based on the deployment descriptor in Listing 6.2, this would result in the string variable *driver* containing the string “org.gjt.mm.mysql.Driver”.

With the deployment descriptor in place, the Tomcat server will know how to associate your class with the right URI, and will know what parameters to pass into it on initialization. This is enough information for the vast majority of Web applications. If you need to do something more complex, refer to Appendix B for more information about the other directives available in your deployment descriptor. We'll also talk more about additional configuration, where relevant, as we discuss other topics, most notably in Chapter 12, “Tag Libraries,” and Chapter 18, “Security.” But for now, you should have everything you need to deploy your first servlets. Once you install or modify a Webapp, you have to restart the servlet engine, or load or reload the context using the manager application, which we discuss in Chapter 9, “The Manager Application.”

WAR Files

Once you've configured a Web application, in most cases you'll want to deploy it from your development server to one or more live servers. You could do this simply by copying the file hierarchy from your development server to your live server, but Java provides a nicer mechanism for doing this: the Web Archive, or WAR, file.

Basically, a WAR file is just a JAR file whose contents conform to the file hierarchy we just discussed. You can create a WAR file of your Webapp by changing directories to the root of your Webapp (in our example, <*$CATALINA_HOME*>/webapps/sample) and jarring the contents:

```
jar -cvf sample.war *
```

You can then deploy this WAR file to any compliant container (such as Tomcat) either by placing it in the /webapps directory manually or by using a deployment tool such as the Tomcat manager application. Tomcat will automatically extract and install any WAR files it finds in the /webapps directory on launch.

This is also a very nice way to distribute servlets. You can find a number of useful servlets and JSP applications packaged this way on the Web.

Configuring Servlets from the server.xml File

It is also possible to configure servlets directly from the system-wide server.xml file. This is generally not a good way to go, so unless you have a compelling reason to do so, you're probably better off simply using the methods we've already described to configure your Webapp.

One reason that a servlet might be configured here is if it's part of the core Tomcat application. The ROOT Webapp is a good example of this. This Webapp is the default handler for all requests not handled by any other application. Its configuration is very simple:

```
<Context path="" docBase="ROOT" debug="0"/>
```

Remember that XML is case-sensitive. The <Context/> tag must start with an initial capital and the remaining letters must be lowercase. Keeping this rule in mind when modifying the server.xml file will save you some time wondering why this or that modification didn't seem to work.

Another reason for configuring an application in server.xml is if you want to set up a URI mapping that is not based on the name of your Webapp. For example, if we wanted our SampleServlet to handle requests to the URI /myapp instead of the longer URI /sample/sampleservlet, we could do this by adding the following line to server.xml:

```
<Context path="/myapp" docBase="sample" debug="0"/>
```

Another reason you may want to resort to configuring an application in server.xml is if you want it to be available only to certain virtual hosts. By default, when you install a Webapp, it is available at the same URI on all configured virtual hosts. In the server.xml file, you can add a <Context/> node as a child of a <Host/> node, and it will be valid only for the host specified.

And if you want to refer to a Webapp for which the files reside outside the *<$CATALINA_HOME>*/webapps directory, you can use the server.xml file to specify a servlet context with a doc base outside the *<$CATALINA_HOME>* directory. You may want to do this if, for example, your servlet code lives on a shared volume, as shown here:

```
<Context path="/myapp" docBase="/Volumes/RemoveServer/webapps"/>
```

On your development machine, it may make sense to configure a servlet path that is connected to your build directory. That way, you can quickly test servlets without moving them to the /webapps directory. We describe ways to make development and testing easier in Chapter 19, "The Development Cycle."

There are other reasons why you may want to do your configuration in the server.xml file. When it's relevant to the topics we're covering, we point out the required configuration information. Beyond that, take a look at Appendix A, "Server Configuration (server.xml) Reference." If there's something you need to do that we haven't covered in sufficient detail, you may wish to peruse the documentation at http://jakarta.apache.org/tomcat. It's hardly a tutorial, but with the background you get from this book, you will find it quite useful.

Summary

In this chapter, we explained how to configure a Webapp for use with Tomcat. After reading this chapter, you should be able to manage configuration for the Webapps you write. Appendix B, "Deployment Descriptor (web.xml) Reference," lays out every attribute for you in table form, so take a look there if you have any unanswered questions.

In the next chapter, we cover the server.xml file to the same level of detail, although if you're itching to start writing code, you might want to jump ahead to the portion of this book focusing on development, which starts in Chapter 10, "Model-View-Controller Architecture." You can always come back and read more about the server.xml file and other configuration issues when you have more questions or a specific problem to solve.

CHAPTER

7

The server.xml File in Depth

In Chapter 3, we covered the basics of Tomcat configuration, which is plenty to get you up and running. In this chapter, we delve more deeply into the details of the server.xml file. As you recall, this is the main configurtion file for Tomcat. It tells Tomcat everything it needs to know about how to run, what ports to listen on, what virtual hosts to recognize, how many instances of the HttpConnectionHandler to keep in the instance pool for each connection, and even what classes to use to handle incoming connections. Java is a very dynamic language, and Tomcat leverages that dynamism to great effect, yielding a platform that is very flexible and tuneable.

The server.xml file, found in *<$CATALINA_HOME>*/conf/, is, of course, an XML file. As we've noted elsewhere, XML is case-sensitive, and the server.xml file has the convention of using tags that start with an initial capital, followed by lowercase characters. The sample server.xml file that is distributed with Tomcat as of this writing is not, strictly speaking, a valid XML file; it is missing the *<?xml version="1.0" encoding="ISO-8859-1"?>* preamble. It is not based on a DTD, so it can be extended *ad hoc* if new implementations of the Tomcat sever interfaces (developed by the Jakarta team or by you the developer) are used to implement various features. As a result, the server.xml file also does not have a DOCTYPE line. Otherwise, it basically conforms to the XML guidelines.

This model makes it legal to extend the built-in tag attributes in new classes you implement yourself. This just means that you can't use a validating parser to confirm validity of your document. Future versions of this file may use XML Schema for validation. This would preserve the flexibility of the current model while allowing for third-party tools to handle structural validation. Tomcat will tell you on startup (or on shutdown) if the file is structurally invalid in any way. If you later want to edit the file in a strict XML editor, you can always add the <?xml?> tag yourself, but again because there is no Document Type Definition (DTD), attempts at structural validation will fail, so you'll want to turn validation off.

New Features in Tomcat 4.1

Tomcat 4.1 adds a much wider range of features than its small product number increment would indicate. In this chapter, we'll focus on the new Web-based Web Server Administration Tool, which you can use to configure the server.xml file. This application is an enormous improvement on editing the server.xml file by hand. Even if you're planning to deploy on Tomcat 4.0, you may want to set up a 4.1 install to experiment with while you're getting a feel for Tomcat configuration. You can then look at the modifications that the Web Server Administration Tool makes to the server.xml file, and get some hands-on experience with what you can configure Tomcat to do.

Editing the server.xml file by hand can be a trying experience at first. It's easy to break your server if you're not familiar with how this all-important configuration file works. We're going to start by explaining the server.xml file itself, and then at the end of this chapter, we'll walk you through the basics of the new admin tool. Armed with the details in the first part of this chapter, you should be able to use the tool very effectively, even if the final UI ends up being slightly different from the one available to us as we're writing this book.

The Basic Model

Tomcat consists of one main process, the server, which contains a number of subcomponents. These subcomponents collaborate in order to process requests. The core components are a set of containers and a set of connectors. Containers are the glue that holds the other components together, and they also provide a common set of parameters for some portion of the server. The main container is the engine, which is really the core of Tomcat. In a lot of ways, this object is what we think of when we think of a server. It handles the dispatching of all requests, and it functions as the interface between each connector and the rest of the system, including your servlets.

The other containers are host containers and contexts. Contexts establish an environment in which servlets can run, and facilitate such tasks as establishing a runtime configuration (including authentication requirements, for example). You use host containers when you want one server to serve multiple virtual hosts or separate interfaces. They hold configuration for a single host. Inside these containers you configure loggers, authentication realms, and resources available to the container—for example, a database connection pool.

Connectors are protocol handlers that convert input and output in a given network protocol into Java method calls. At the end of this chapter, we discuss various connectors you may want to configure.

Even the servlets you write yourself are in fact components that are part of this larger model.

The core components are configured in the server.xml file. (Servlets you write can be configured in the server.xml file as well, but it is usually simpler to configure them in their own web.xml files.) Since XML documents are hierarchical, in this chapter we start at the top-level node and work our way in. Each node has a set of required attributes, as well as a set of optional attributes. We tell you which is which as we introduce them.

Most nodes also can contain child nodes that further affect their configuration, principally by configuring a component to handle some function and associating it with the object configured in the parent node. While we touch on all the potential child nodes at each level, we focus on the most commonly used elements first. We then offer a detailed examination of the less-used elements. The intent is to give you a good grounding in the fundamentals first, without neglecting the complete details.

The <Server/> Node

The root node is the <Server/> node. It contains all of the other nodes that control the server, and it supports three attributes.

The first attribute (which is optional) is className. This is the fully qualified name of the class to be used as the Tomcat server itself. Typically, you'll just omit this attribute and let Tomcat use the default implementation, but you can, if you're so inclined, write a whole different implementation of the servlet engine. The class you specify here has to implement the org.apache.catalina.Server interface, but you could implement a replacement for the Tomcat Catalina server. Of course, unless you have a really good reason to do that, just omit this attribute.

The other two attributes—port and shutdown—control the service Tomcat uses to listen for shutdown commands. Both these attributes are required. The port attribute specifies the port to listen on. The shutdown attribute contains the string that this port looks for. When an inbound connection on the specified port comes in, and that connection sends the string specified in the shutdown attribute, Tomcat will shut down. Tomcat listens on the loopback port only, so this is not as dangerous as it might seem, but it's a good idea to change the shutdown string (at least) to prevent users on the system from accidentally (or intentionally) shutting down the server without permission. The shutdown script reads the same configuration file to see which port to connect to and what string to send, so configuration is pretty easy. As we mentioned, these attributes are listed as required elements in the current implementation; if you don't configure them, they will default to 8005 and SHUTDOWN, respectively.

If you implement your own server, you can have it read additional attributes if you so desire. The default server implementation, org.apache.catalina.core.StandardServer, like many of the components we'll see, also takes a debug attribute (optional), which sets a log level. The default is *0*, which means "Turn debug logging off."

The <Server/> node contains one or more <Service/> nodes, which we look at next.

The <Service/> Container

The <Service/> nodes are basically containers grouping together resources that cooperate to handle requests. They contain one or more <Connector/> nodes that specify protocol handlers that listen for requests, and they share a single <Engine/> node that dispatches the requests. The <Connector/> nodes should precede the <Engine/> node.

The <Service/> node has two principal attributes. The name attribute (required) assigns a name to the service, which will be printed in log messages generated by standard Tomcat components. The className attribute (optional) specifies the class that will be instantiated for this node. This class must implement the org.apache.catalina.Service interface. As with the <Server/> node, this attribute is usually omitted, and the class used is the default, org.apache.catalina.core.StandardService.

Of course there's more to the Service container than that. The important service configuration takes place in the nodes inside of the <Service/> node, as we'll see below.

The <Engine/> Container

As we mentioned earlier, the engine component is responsible for dispatching all requests. Requests come in through one of the connectors and are processed by the engine, which passes them off to further appropriate handlers—for instance, one of your servlets, depending on the URI requested and the nature of the request. The output from the handler is then passed back to the appropriate connector.

The name attribute (required) specifies the logical name of the engine. This attribute is included in any log output generated by the engine at runtime.

The defaultHost attribute (required) specifies which <Host/> container Tomcat should pass incoming requests to if the hostname in the request doesn't match any of the configured hosts (perhaps the request came to an alias for your server, for which you haven't configured an alias) or if a request comes in that doesn't specify a host. (HTTP 1.0 did not include a mechanism for specifying the hostname for which a request was intended. As a result, users connecting with older browsers may not get directed to the intended host and will fall through to the default host.) There must be a <Host/> container configured with a name attribute that matches the domain name specified in this attribute. (See the following section for details.)

The className attribute (optional) specifies the implementation class that should be used to implement this feature. The class specified must implement the org.apache.catalina.Engine interface. The default value of this attribute is org.apache.catalina.core.StandardEngine.

The jvmRoute attribute (optional) is used in clustering to identify which server is handling a given request. It is appended to the session identifier to ensure that requests from a given client can be consistently routed to the first server contacted.

The default implementation, org.apache.catalina.core.StandardEngine, adds the debug attribute (optional), which functions as it does with the other Tomcat components.

As we will see in Chapter 8, "Managing Authentication with Realms," the <Engine/> container can also be configured by the addition of a <Realm/> node for

HTTP authentication. The <Engine/> container can be configured further by the addition of a child <Logger/> node and zero or more <Valve/> nodes (we discuss both of these a little later).

The <Realm/> Node

The <Realm/> node may appear as a child of an <Engine/> container, a <Host/> container, or a <Context/> container. There must be no more than one <Realm/> node per container, although a <Host/> and its containing <Engine/> may each have a <Realm/> node, as can a <Context/> and its containing <Host/>. In these cases, the realm with narrower scope—that is, the realm configured in the inner container—overrides the realm with broader scope—that is, the realm configured in the outer container.

For instance, you may want to set up in your <Engine/> container a global realm to be used by most of the configured hosts. Perhaps this realm is a Java Database Connectivity (JDBC) realm, with general customer login information stored in a database. However, for one specific host, you may want to use a different realm. Perhaps for your intranet site, you want to use a Java Naming and Directory Interface (JNDI) realm, tied to your corporate Lightweight Directory Access Protocol (LDAP) server, to provide access. This realm you would configure inside the relevant <Host/> container; it would replace the realm with the broader scope defined in your <Engine/> container.

Configuration of realms is a large topic, so we'll defer detailed discussion of the topic, and the coverage of class-specific attributes, to the next chapter. The realm node itself is quite simple, having only a single attribute, the class attribute (required). This attribute must be the classname of a class that implements the org.apache.catalina.Realm interface. Each of the three main implementations—org.apache.catalina.realm.MemoryRealm, org.apache.catalina.realm.JDBCRealm, and org.apache.catalina.realm.JNDIRealm—has substantially different attributes, which we also cover in the next chapter.

The <Logger/> Node

Loggers are configured in <Logger/> nodes, which, like <Realm/> nodes, may be configured as a child of an <Engine/> container, a <Host/> container, or a <Context/> container. Note also that there must be no more than one <Logger/> node per container, although the same scoping rules apply as for the <Realm/> node.

The <Logger/> node has only two attributes common across all implementations. The first, the className attribute (required), specifies a class implementing the org.apache.catalina.Logger interface. (We examine the three standard logger classes later.)

The second attribute, verbosity (optional), specifies the types of messages Tomcat should log. The standard log levels are 0, for fatal messages only; 1, which includes error messages; 2, which includes warnings; 3, which includes informational messages; and 4, for verbose debugging output. The default value is 1.

Two of the implementation classes—org.apache.catalina.logger.SystemOutLogger and org.apache.catalina.logger.SystemErrLogger—simply write to standard out and standard error, respectively (by way of System.out and System.err, as you may have guessed). The default startup script redirects both of these streams to *<$CATALINA_HOME>* /logs/catalina.out. If you don't configure a logger, this is where your log output (along with anything your servlets or referenced classes write to System.out or System.err) will show up.

A better logger to use is org.apache.catalina.logger.FileLogger, which lets you configure a filename and directory to log to, and also will include a timestamp in the filename for you.

Attributes for the FileLogger are:

directory (optional)—Specifies the directory to log to. Relative paths are treated as being relative to *<$CATALINA_HOME>*, and the default value is "logs", pointing to *<$CATALINA_HOME>*/logs/.

timestamp (optional)—Specifies whether or not to include a timestamp in the filename of the log file created. The default is *false*.

prefix (optional)—Specifies the portion of the log name that precedes the timestamp (if timestamp is set to true) or simply precedes the suffix (if timestamp is set to false). The default value is catalina.

suffix (optional)—Specifies the extension to add to the log name. It follows the timestamp (if timestamp is set to true) or simply follows the prefix (if timestamp is set to false). The default value is .log. If you don't want a prefix, or don't want a suffix, just set them to be an empty string: "".

Tomcat rotates log files automatically at midnight and timestamps the old logs.

The <Host/> Container

The <Host/> container is used to configure attributes to be associated with a single host, whether that host is a virtual host or one with a separate IP address on a multihomed server. In many cases, you may want to have a single-server instance service requests for more than one domain name or hostname. An obvious example is where multiple companies share hosting services. Another example is where you want separate Web sites to serve separate functions—such as your principal public Web site (www.mycompany.com) and a second Web site for your developer community (developer.mycompany.com). Perhaps you have one fast reliable box at a co-location facility, and you want to consolidate maintenance of your entire public Web presence on that single box. The ability to configure one machine to serve multiple hosts gives you a lot of flexibility.

NOTE It is never advisable to share a single-server instance between production and development. (See Chapter 19, "The Development Cycle," for information on setting up your development environment.) One of the reasons to separate your development server from your live server is to ensure that your live server is as stable as possible. Running untested code on your live server is not a good way to promote this, to say the least! Beyond this, however, you

will want to be able to bring your development server down in order to make configuration changes. You probably won't want to wait for a maintenance window on your live server to do this.

You probably also don't want to put your intranet server on the same box as your public Web site. Why expose yourself to the risk of a security hole in your code and risk revealing confidential information to the world? Hardware is cheap, and you'll save yourself a lot of headaches—and most likely also expense in the long run—by setting up a separate server when a service has substantially different requirements, particularly when they are requirements for availability, access, or security.

Each <Engine/> container must have at least one <Host/> element, configured with its name attribute (required) matching the engine's defaultHost setting. This name must be a valid hostname, and one that points to the server the Tomcat instance is running on. In the example server.xml file that ships with Tomcat, these are both set to localhost. A typical setting for this attribute is www.*yourcompany.com*. Again, this must be a valid DNS name for the machine the Tomcat instance is running on, and it must map to the IP address of an interface Tomcat can bind to.

If you want to map more than one domain name to a single set of content—for instance, you want Tomcat to respond both to www.yourcompany.com and just plain yourcompany.com, or even youroldcompanyname.com—don't configure separate <Host/> containers. This results in extra threads being created to handle the incoming requests, and can significantly increase the footprint of Tomcat without providing any extra value. If you have multiple hostnames that are all supposed to serve identical content, handle this with an <Alias/> node inside your <Host/> container:

```
<Host name="www.mycompany.com">
    <Alias>mycompany.com</Alias>
    <Alias>myoldcompanyname.com</Alias>
    <Alias>www.myoldcompanyname.com</Alias>
</Host>
```

The appBase attribute (required) specifies where this host will look for Web applications. In the sample configuration file that comes with Tomcat, this is set to *<$CATALINA_HOME>* /webapps, which is a good default choice. (All the examples in this book are based on the assumption that this is your application base. If you decide to change it, you'll need to modify the examples to match.) So why would you change it? The main reason is if you are serving different Webapps on different virtual hosts. You may want to have a special application—a bug reporter, for instance—running on your developer Web site but not accessible from your general public Web site. Conversely, if they all share the same application base, each virtual host will get its own copy of each Webapp loaded into memory. Unless your Webapps provide some generally useful function, this is probably not what you want. Of course, you may want to maintain a different file structure than the default, based on local standards, or to facilitate development, for example. (You might want to set up a development host with your build directory as the appBase directory, although usually having a good build system that can deploy your apps to the appropriate application base is a better solution.)

You can specify either an absolute path or a relative path. If you specify a relative path, it will be taken as being relative to *<$CATALINA_HOME>*.

The className attribute (optional) must specify a class that implements the org.apache.catalina.Host interface. The default class is org.apache.catalina.core.StandardHost.

The autoDeploy attribute (optional) specifies whether Tomcat should automatically update the running server to include new or modified Web application files in the appBase directory. The default value for this attribute is true. This is very handy on a development server, since for most changes you don't have to do anything special to get the servlet to reload. When autoDeploy is enabled, dropping a new version of a JAR file into the /WEB-INF/lib directory causes the classes to be reloaded. Tomcat looks for modified files intermittently as it's running, and updates the Webapps when it finds new files.

You may not want to have this attribute enabled in a production environment, however. It's usually better to get your files in place and manually reload the application. Also, using this and other auto-reload features increases the processing overhead of the server, which can negatively affect performance. You can do this by restarting the server, or by using the Manager Webapp (see Chapter 9, "The Manager Application"). By making this explicit, you have more control over what's deployed on the running server.

That class also uses the following attributes:

unpackWARs (optional)—Specifies whether Web Archive (WAR) files in the appBase directory should be unpacked when the server starts. When this is set to true, the host will check the appBase directory for any WAR files that may not have been unpacked yet, and will unjar them into a directory with the same name as the WAR file, minus the extension. (For example, foo.war gets unpacked into the foo/ subdirectory of the appBase directory.) The server then constructs a context matching the directory name and loads the Webapps contained within. The server will not unpack the WAR file if there is already a matching directory. If you want to redeploy a Webapp from a WAR file, you will have to delete that directory. The default value of this attribute is true. The same considerations regarding production systems apply to this attribute, as we mentioned for autoDeploy.

liveDeploy (optional)—Is similar in function, but specifies whether a new unpacked Webapp being added to the appBase directory should be automatically loaded when it is detected. It is also true by default, and should typically be set to false on a production server.

deployXML (optional)—Specifies whether runtime deployment based on a context XML file shall be allowed. Context XML files are new in Tomcat 4. They allow you to keep context information in a separate XML file. (We discuss what these are and what they look like in the next section, "The <Context/> Container.") The default value is true.

workDir (optional)—Specifies where Tomcat should write temporary files, such as the source code and compiled servlets it generates from JSPs. If it is not specified, Tomcat will create working directories under the *<$CATALINA_HOME>*/work/ directory, and make sure each has a unique name so that different Webapps don't interfere with each other. You may want to change this attribute—particularly if you want to run your Tomcat server from a read-only filesystem for security reasons, or if you're running it from a read-only shared volume. In this case, you'll need to change this attribute to point to a directory that can be written to by the Tomcat server (that is, written to by the user with whose permissions Tomcat is executed). You might also want to write to a different partition or volume, such as /var, to prevent Tomcat output from filling up a given partition. Typically, however, this is not much of an issue.

errorReportValveClass (optional)—Specifies a Valve class (see our discussion in the section "The <Valve/> Node" later in this chapter) to be used to control how error reports served by Tomcat are formatted. The class specified must implement the org.apache.catalina.Valve interface, and the default value is org.apache.catalina.valves.ErrorReportValve. (There are a few other special valve classes that are relevant to the <Host/> container, which we'll see later.)

debug (optional)—Functions as it does with the other Tomcat components.

Like the <Engine/> container, the <Host/> container can be configured further by the addition of <Realm/>, <Logger/> and <Valve/> nodes. Beyond these, there are two additional components that are configured as children of <Host/> elements: <Alias/> nodes and <Context/> containers.

We've already discussed the <Alias/> node. As shown in the example, it doesn't have any attributes, and a <Host/> may contain zero or more of them. Each <Alias/> node contains an additional hostname to associate with this host container.

The <Context/> Container

Each <Host/> node can contain one or more <Context/> nodes. The <Context/> container is the one we've been exposed to the most so far. A context relates a URI to a Web application.

Every host must have one context with an empty context path, as specified by the path attribute. This context represents the default context for the host, and is used when no other context matches. The default context also provides configuration information that is used (unless you specify otherwise) by the other contexts configured within the containing host.

Beyond this default context, you can add as many other contexts as you need. Context paths are matched to incoming requests at runtime. When a request comes in, the server compares the URI to each of the context paths, until it finds the longest one that matches. The reason for this rule will become clear if you imagine an application where you want to have nested contexts handled by different servlets. Perhaps you want to have the /intranet URI served by one context, but the /intranet/stockplan URI served by a different context, with different authentication requirements and a different set of servlets. A request coming in for /intranet/stockplan/login.jsp would be handed to the second context, whereas a request for /intranet/news/index.jsp would be passed to the first context. A request for /index.jsp would be passed to the default context, since neither of the other two contexts matches the URI pattern.

We configured contexts in the deployment descriptors we looked at in Chapter 6, "Configuring Web Applications," so as you can tell already, the server.xml file is not the only place where you can configure a context. In fact, in addition to the server.xml file and your various web.xml files, you can now configure a context from a separate XML file. These files will have the same structure as that used in context nodes inside the server.xml file, so that's what we focus on here. If you want to configure contexts separately, though, simply put the context container XML into a separate file and place it in the appropriately configured place—your <*$CATALINA_HOME*>/webapps directory by default or the appBase attribute you specified in a <Host/> container entry. (You can also associate a context stored in an external XML file with a specified host by simply specifying a separate appBase for each <Host/> container.)

The path attribute mentioned earlier (required) specifies the base URI relative to which all contained servlet paths will be constructed. Again, you need to have exactly one <Context/> container with the empty string specified as its path in order to form the default context.

The docBase attribute (required) indicates where the Webapp specified in the context is to be found. The path specified here can be either the path to a directory containing the Webapp or a path including a WAR file. In the latter case, the Webapp will be run directly from the WAR file without expanding it. If the path specified is a relative path, it will be appended to the path specified in the appBase attribute of the containing <Host/> element.

For this container, the className attribute (optional) need not be defined. In most cases, you can configure the default implementation, org.apache.catalina.core. StandardContext, to do anything you might need. If you do choose to specify a different class, the class specified here must implement the org.apache.catalina.Context interface.

As mentioned previously, optional attributes specified in the default context will be propagated to the other contexts configured within the same <Host/> container. These settings will supercede the matching attributes found in the other <Context/> nodes. You can override this behavior by setting the override attribute (optional) to true. It is set to false by default.

The reloadable attribute (optional) specifies whether you want the servlet engine to monitor the WEB-INF/lib and WEB-INF/classes directories under the configured docBase and reload the Webapps when they change. The attribute is set to true by default. This setting does not affect whether the context can be reloaded by the manager application (see Chapter 9 for more information).

The cookies attribute (optional) specifies whether you want to allow Tomcat to use cookies for session management. If you want to force Tomcat to rely only on URL rewriting (for security reasons or otherwise), you should set this attribute to false. It is true by default.

The crossContext attribute (optional) specifies whether objects in this context are allowed to communicate with the objects in other contexts on the same host. Specifically, this attribute specifies whether calls to ServletContext.getContext() return a valid context. If this attribute is set to false, ServletContext.getContext() will always return null. Unless you have a specific reason to allow intercontext communication, leave this attribute set at the default (false) for security reasons.

The privileged attribute (optional) specifies whether servlets in this context should be allowed to use special container servlets, such as the manager servlet. The default is false.

The wrapperClass attribute (optional) specifies the wrapper class Tomcat should use to manage any servlets contained in the context. This class is responsible for managing the life cycle of the servlets in the context, including keeping track of the configuration specified in the deployment descriptor, calling the servlet's init() and destroy() methods, and otherwise managing communication between the container and the servlet. Classes specified in this attribute must implement the org.apache.catalina.Wrapper interface. The default value is org.apache.catalina.core.StandardWrapper.

The useNaming attribute (optional) specifies whether the servlet engine should create a JNDI InitialContext for this Webapp. The InitialContext Tomcat will create is compatible with J2EE conventions. It is set to true by default.

In addition to these general attributes, the default class, org.apache.catalina.core.StandardContext, provides two more attributes. The workDir attribute (optional) specifies a writable directory for use by servlets contained in this context. The path to this working directory will be passed into the servlet as the javax.servlet.context.tempdir attribute on the ServletContext. That attribute will be an instance of java.io.File. If this attribute is not configured manually, Tomcat will assign a suitable directory inside the work directory assigned to the host. By default, this is a subdirectory of the <*$CATALINA_HOME*>/work directory.

And as with the other Tomcat components, a debug attribute (also optional) is provided to configure additional logging.

Like the <Engine/> and <Host/> containers, <Context/> containers can contain <Realm/>, <Logger/>, and <Valve/> nodes. In addition, <Context/> nodes can contain <Resources/>, <Loader/>, and <Manager/> nodes. The node types we haven't already covered are discussed in the sections that follow.

The <Valve/> Node

A *valve* is a component that is added to the processing pipeline. Valves can manipulate the request or response, limit access, format output, or do a variety of other tasks. They are very flexible and provide a wide range of functionality. Rather than trying to explain the general case here, we begin by showing you some examples. They have only one required attribute in common: The className attribute specifies a class implementing the org.apache.catalina.Valve interface.

Access Log Valve

The Access Log Valve (org.apache.catalina.valves.AccessLogValve) is used to format the contents of the logs produced by loggers configured in <Logger/> nodes. It can be used to conform your logs to Common Log Format or Combined Log Format (both sadly abbreviated and commonly referred to as CLF) or any other log format you choose to configure.

The directory, prefix, and suffix attributes (all optional) function in the same way as the <Logger/> attributes (see the section "The <Logger/> Node" earlier in this chapter).

The resolveHosts attribute (optional) specifies whether a hostname lookup should be performed for each incoming IP address. As discussed elsewhere, setting resolveHosts to *true* increases latency, particularly for the first request, because of the time it takes to resolve the DNS names. In a high-performance production system, this attribute should be set to *false* unless you need to have this information logged in real time for some reason. You can always post-process your logs to add this information.

The pattern attribute (optional) provides a pattern string that is used to specify the formatting of the log output. It is composed of literal text and a series of escapes that will be replaced in the log output with various pieces of information from the request. Those escape sequences include the following:

- %A—Specifies the local IP address
- %a— Specifies the remote IP address
- %B—Specifies the number of bytes sent, excluding HTTP headers
- %b—Specifies the number of bytes sent, excluding HTTP headers, or '-' if zero
- %H—Specifies the protocol used in the request (e.g., HTTP/1.1)
- %h—Specifies the remote hostname (or the remote IP address, if resolveHosts is false)
- %l—Specifies the remote logical username from identd (always returns '-')
- %m—Specifies the request method (GET, POST, etc.)
- %p—Specifies the local port on which this request was received
- %q—Contains any query string sent (prepended with a '?' if it exists)
- %r—Contains the complete first line of the request (this includes the method and request URI, e.g., "GET /index.html")
- %S—Specifies the user session ID
- %s—Specifies the HTTP status code of the response (200 for ok, 404 for resource not found, etc.)
- %t—Specifies the date and time, expressed in Common Log Format
- %U—Specifies the requested URL path
- %u—If HTTP authentication was used, specifies the user who was authenticated, or "-" if there was none
- %v—Specifies the local server name
- %{<header>}—Specifies that the header matching <header> should be included in the output
- %{<header>}I—Specifies that the header matching <header> should be included in the output, regardless of case

There are two special pattern names for the two CLR formats. The pattern "common" specifies the common log format, which maps to %h %l %u %t "%r" %s %b. The pattern "combined" adds the values of the Referer (*sic*) and User-Agent headers, and is equivalent to the pattern * %h %l %u %t "%r" %s %b "%{Referer}i" "%{User-Agent}i".

The default value is *common*.

Remote Host Filter and Remote Address Filter

The Remote Host Filter and Remote Address Filter (org.apache.catalina.valves.RemoteHostValve and org.apache.catalina.valves.RemoteAddrValve, respectively) are used to restrict access to certain hosts based on their domain names or IP addresses. They function very similarly to each other—the only difference is whether they match based on hostnames or IP addresses, as you probably have worked out for yourself.

They each have an allow attribute and a deny attribute (both optional), which are used to limit access. Each take a comma-separated list of regular expressions to be used as matching criteria. If allow criteria are specified, access will be granted only to hosts that match one or more of the regular expressions specified in the parameter. Anyone coming in from a non-matching host will receive a 403 Forbidden response from the server. If, on the other hand, a deny attribute is used, anyone coming in from a host that *doesn't* match any of the regular expressions will be allowed access. Those coming from hosts matching the deny criteria will receive a 403 Forbidden response. If both are set, the deny attribute is checked first, and anyone who doesn't match the deny list is passed on to the accept filter. Anyone coming from a host that passes both tests is allowed to see the content.

Request Dumper Valve

The Request Dumper Valve (org.apache.catalina.valves.RequestDumperValve) can be extremely useful for debugging unexpected client interactions. It logs a dump of each incoming request to the configured logger. This is particularly useful when you are working with custom clients, or are having problems with a specific client or set of clients, because it lets you see exactly what is being sent to the server. It has no attributes beyond the globally required className attribute.

Single Sign On Valve

The Single Sign On Valve is used within a <Host/> container to share realm credentials across applications. We cover this topic further in Chapter 8, "Managing Authentication with Realms."

Additional Valves

There are other valves beyond those documented here. Some are part of the Apache project, and some aren't. And of course, you can always write your own. We'll mention one briefly to give you some ideas. Valves not included with the core distribution will need to be added to the *<$CATALINA_HOME>*/server/lib directory (if they are packaged as JAR files) or to the *<$CATALINA_HOME>*/server/classes directory in subdirectories appropriate to their package hierarchy (if they are class files).

The JDBC Access Log Valve

The JDBC Access Log Valve (org.apache.catalina.valves.JDBCAccessLogValve) is a good example of an add-on Valve. It allows you to log output to a database instead of to a filesystem. Its attributes are similar to those found in the logger class, and it provides two additional attributes for specifying a JDBC driver class and a JDBC URL for the database that contains the log table. You can read more about this Valve in the JavaDoc for Tomcat. If you do use it, don't forget to put the JAR containing the JDBC driver in <*$CATALINA_HOME*>/server/lib or <*$CATALINA_HOME*>/common/lib as well.

The <Resources/> Node

The <Resources/> node is used to specify other resources available to the Webapp specified in the containing <Context/> container, and it allows the servlet access to resources other than those stored in a filesystem, whether they be resources contained in a JAR or WAR file, data in a database, elements in a JNDI directory, or objects in some other form of repository. If a given <Context/> container does not have a <Resources/> element specified, a default filesystem-based instance will be created for the context.

Note that resources contained in non-filesystem-based data stores must be accessed through methods on the ServletContext. The servlet engine doesn't intercept calls that operate on files and magically translate them; rather, the ServletContext will return a JNDI-style initial context, and you can use its methods to look up and retrieve objects stored in repositories made available through the <Resources/> node.

As a result, the className attribute (optional) must specify a class implementing the javax.naming.directory.DirContext interface. This is the only attribute that is global across all implementations. Note that some base classes are available as part of the Tomcat framework that simplify the implementing of classes to be configured in a <Resources/> node. It is recommended that you base any of your own classes on org.apache.naming.resources.BaseDirContext and that you use the objects in org.apache.naming.resources for return types. This will ease interoperability and provide some performance benefits. The default value for this attribute is org.apache.naming.resources.FileDirContext. We'll look at the additional attributes provided with this class next.

The cached attribute (optional) indicates whether the implementation should use caching. It defaults to true.

The caseSensitive attribute (optional) is used on non-case-sensitive operating systems, principally Microsoft Windows, to specify whether strict case sensitivity should be observed in looking up objects. The default value is true.

The docBase attribute (optional) specifies the root directory under which the named resources are to be found in the filesystem. It has the same semantics and rules as the docBase attribute of a context, and is constructed relative to the document base of the containing context if a relative path is used.

The <Loader/> Node

You use the <Loader/> node when you want to configure a class loader other than the default one provided with Tomcat, or if you want to constrain the behavior of the default class loader. It must appear as the child of a <Context/> container if it is used. If it's omitted, an instance of the default class loader implementation, org.apache.catalina. loader.WebappLoader, will be used. You should consider at least setting the delegate and reloadable attributes, discussed next, in security-sensitive environments.

The className attribute must specify a class that implements the org.apache. catalina.Loader interface. This attribute is optional.

Use the delegate attribute (also optional) if you want the class loader to follow the standard Java 2 delegation model and attempt to load classes from parent class loaders before looking inside the Web application. This prevents classes contained in the Web application from overriding the behavior of classes with the same names in the runtime environment, and therefore provides some security advantages. If this attribute is set to false (the default), the class loader will load classes from inside the Web application first, before asking parent class loaders to find requested classes or resources. This will give the Web applications a bit more flexibility and may simplify configuration, but if your first concern is security—as it should be in a production environment—you should set delegate to true, particularly if you allow untrusted code to run inside your server. There are other ways to constrain access to resources, but unless you need to override the behavior of the globally available classes, it's probably not worth leaving this attribute set to false.

The reloadable attribute (optional), like the reloadable attribute on the <Context/> container discussed earlier, specifies whether you want the servlet engine to monitor the WEB-INF/lib and WEB-INF/classes directories under the configured docBase and reload the Webapp when they change. As with that attribute, this setting does not affect whether the context can be reloaded by the manager application. The reloadable attribute is set to true by default.

NOTE **The reloadable attribute will be overridden by any value you set in the parent context.**

In addition to the standard attributes, the org.apache.catalina.loader.WebappLoader class supports the following additional attributes:

checkInterval (optional)—Specifies (in seconds) how frequently Tomcat should check to see if the libraries in WEB-INF/lib/ and WEB-INF/classes/ have been changed. This attribute is ignored if the reloadable attribute is set to false. The default value is 15 seconds.

loaderClass (optional)—Can be used to specify any class implementing the java.lang.ClassLoader interface that Tomcat should use to do the actual class loading. In this way, you don't need to implement your own wrapper class to support another class loader you may want to use. The default value is org.apache.catalina.loader.WebappClassLoader.

workDir (optional)—Functions identically to the workDir attribute on the <Context/> container.

debug (optional)—Functions as it does on the other core classes.

The <Manager/> Node

You use the <Manager/> node to configure the session manager used in the containing context. The session manager is responsible for creating and managing session objects as well as the session key used to look up the session. The <Manager/> node must be nested inside a <Context/> container if it is used. As with the <Loader/> and <Resources/> nodes, there can be at most one instance of this node inside a single <Context/> container. If it is omitted, the default implementation, org.apache.catalina. session.StandardManager, will be used.

A second implementation is supplied with Tomcat that might be of interest: the org.apache.catalina.session.PersistentManager class. This class stores session information on disk and enables sessions to survive a Tomcat restart. Note that as of this writing, this class had not yet been thoroughly tested. If you want to make use of this class in a production environment, you should plan on testing it thoroughly, and you may have to make some changes. If you do make changes or discover shortcomings during your testing (with this or with any other component), you are encouraged to share your findings with the Tomcat community.

All implementations share the following attributes:

className (optional)—Must be the name of a class that implements the org.apache.catalina.Manager interface. The default is org.apache.catalina.session.StandardManager.

distributable (optional)—Specifies whether the manager should be required to conform to the servlet specification standards for distributable sessions. This is important if you are using Tomcat in a clustered environment and will be sharing session state across a pool of Tomcat instances. The main constraint this imposes is that the session object be serializable (i.e., that it implement java.io.Serializable, which further requires that all objects stored in it likewise be serializable). If distributable is set to false (the default), Tomcat will allow non-serializable sessions to be constructed. (Note that this attribute will be inherited from the Webapp deployment descriptor if it is not specified here. This is managed in the deployment descriptor by including—or not including—a <distributable/> node.)

maxInactiveInterval (optional)—Specifies how long sessions can remain inactive before they will be timed out. As with the distributable attribute, you can specify this attribute in the deployment descriptor of the Webapp—in this case, in <session-timeout/> node. The default value is 60 minutes.

The standard implementation, org.apache.catalina.session.StandardManager, has the following additional attributes:

checkInterval (optional)—Specifies (in seconds) how frequently to check whether sessions need to be expired. The default value is 60.

maxActiveSessions (optional)—Specifies the maximum number of active sessions this manager should be allowed to create. If set to -1, the manager will not limit the number of sessions. -1 is the default value.

algorithm (optional)—Specifies which digest algorithm Tomcat should use to generate a session key. The value specified here must be supported by java.security.MessageDigest. This includes MD5, MD2, and SHA-1. (You can load additional algorithms by including and loading the appropriate provider library.) The default is MD5.

randomClass (optional)—Specifies which class Tomcat should use to generate the random numbers needed to seed the digest algorithm. This attribute must specify a class that implements java.util.Random. The default value is java.security.SecureRandom.

entropy (optional)—Specifies a seed string used to seed the random number generator specified in the randomClass attribute. If none is specified, Tomcat will try to generate a useful seed value, but in environments where security is a priority, it is safer to set this attribute to a very long string. The default is to allow Tomcat to generate one.

pathname (optional)—Specifies a filename and path into which the session state is to be serialized during a restart. Relative paths are constructed relative to the working directory of the context (specified in the workDir attribute of the context, among other possible places). Tomcat will attempt to serialize the session state out to disk during a restart. In order for it to succeed, all contained objects must be serializable. (See the distributable attribute described earlier for more information.) The default value is SESSIONS.ser.

debug (optional)—Functions as it does on the other core classes.

You can find attributes for the experimental org.apache.catalina.session.PersistentManager class on the Tomcat Web site at http://jakarta.apache.org/tomcat/tomcat-4.1-doc/config/manager.html.

The <Connector/> Node

<Connector/> nodes connect protocol handlers to IP addresses and ports. A number of different connectors come with Tomcat, and we'll look at them in turn. Let's start with the parameters they share in common.

The <Connector/> node has five standard attributes shared across all connector classes. Again, we can specify a className (required) for our connector. This is the fully qualified classname of a class that implements the org.apache.catalina.Connector interface. Of course, since there are a variety of connector types, you must specify an appropriate class.

The enableLookups attribute (optional) specifies whether Tomcat should look up the hostname associated with the IP address of each inbound connection. If enableLookups is set to true, hostnames are logged instead of just IP addresses. In a production environment, you should set this attribute to false because name lookups are expensive. You can always convert the IP addresses to hostnames later by postprocessing the logs. The default value for this attribute is true.

The redirectPort attribute (optional) has somewhat intricate semantics. If you don't conifgure this connector to provide a secure communication method and a request comes in for a resource requiring a secure connection (as specified in a security constraint), then the connector redirects the request to the port specified in this attribute. Typically, this means that if you are configuring an HTTP connector on port 80, you will specify port 443, the standard HTTPS port, as the redirect port. You'll then have to configure another connector to handle HTTPS connections on port 443.

The scheme attribute (optional) specifies the name of the protocol the connector will handle. This sets the string that the getScheme() method on the request object (passed into a servlet's service() method) will return (we'll see this again in Chapter 18, "Security.") If, for example, you are configuring a connector to support HTTP, this should be set to *http*, which is also the default value.

The secure attribute (optional) specifies whether the protocol this connector is configured for should be considered secure. The value you set here is the value returned by the isSecure() method on the request object (this is also covered in more detail in Chapter 18). The default value is *false*.

Aside from the standard attributes, a few attributes are left to the individual implementation. These attributes are still common across several connector implementations, however, so let's discuss them here before proceeding on to the specifics of the principal connector types.

The most obvious and important of these is the port attribute. This attribute, which is required, specifies the port on which the connector should listen.

As with the other Tomcat classes, there is a debug attribute. This attribute is optional.

The minProcessors and maxProcessors attributes (both optional) control the number of instances of the connector in the instance pool. On startup, Tomcat creates the number of instances specified in minProcessors, and keeps them ready to handle inbound requests. If all of the instances are in use at any time and a new request comes in, new instances are created for each additional request until the number of processors specified in maxProcessors is reached. At that point, additional requests are kept in a queue until a processor becomes available. The default values are 5 and 20, respectively.

The acceptCount attribute (optional) specifies the maximum number of requests that should be kept in that queue. If additional requests are received when all the processors are busy and the queue is also full, those requests will be refused. The default value is *10*.

Some attributes are appropriate only to some connectors. We'll talk about the main connector classes now, and as we go through, we'll cover the semantics of the additional attributes.

The Coyote HTTP/1.1 Connector

First, let's look at the Coyote HTTP/1.1 connector, org.apache.coyote.tomcat4.CoyoteConnector. This is a versatile connector, capable of handling HTTP 1.1, HTTP 1.0, and HTTPS connections. Let's start with the parameters required to configure it to support HTTP. You'll want to set the className attribute to *org.apache.coyote.tomcat4.CoyoteConnector*. In addition, you should leave the secure attribute set to its default value of *false*.

The address attribute specifies which IP address to listen on. This is relevant for multi-homed servers on which you want to run multiple separate server instances. You could, for example, bind Tomcat to port 80 on one interface and Apache to port 80 on another. You can also use the address attribute to bind a service only to 127.0.0.1, the loopback port. You might want to configure a specific application to be available only from the local machine. Using this mechanism in connection with an appropriate context configuration (which we discuss later) is one way to accomplish this. The default is to bind to all interfaces.

The connectionTimeout attribute sets how many milliseconds the connector will wait from the time the connection is initiated until the time the request containing the requested URI is received. This is to prevent the server from becoming bogged down by requests from clients on very slow connections, and to free up resources from connections that stall. Requests that take longer than this timeout to process will be terminated. The default is 60000, or one minute.

The bufferSize attribute specifies the size (in bytes) of the buffer that should be created to buffer the connection. This can be tuned based on available memory and performance requirements, although the optimal tuning parameters will vary, depending on the typical request size, among other factors. The default value is 2048.

The tcpNoDelay attribute specifies whether the TCP_NO_DELAY option should be set on the server socket. Under most circumstances, enabling this attribute improves performance. The default is true.

The proxyName and proxyPort attributes are used to configure a connector that is running behind a proxy server. These methods set the values returned by the Response.getServerName() and Response.getServerPort() methods, respectively. These methods are used to construct some redirect URLs. By default, they return the hostname and port number the connector is configured on. In the case of a server operating behind a proxy, the methods will not render the correct URL, so these attributes are provided to let you set the name and port number to the name and port number of the proxy server clients are connecting to.

When configuring the Coyote HTTP/1.1 connector to support an HTTPS connection, you'll want to set the secure attribute to true. The default port for HTTPS is 443. Another common port is 8443, particularly when you're running Tomcat as an unprivileged user. You'll also need to add a <Factory/> node inside the <Service/> node in order to configure the SSLSocketFactory that will handle creation of the secure connections. We cover the attributes of the <Factory/> node in the section "The <Factory/> Node," later in this chapter.

Server Proxy Connectors

There are several connectors that can be used to communicate with another Web server. You may want to configure Tomcat to use such a connector, and let another Web server proxy incoming requests. The main reasons to do this are security, performance, and functionality.

For example, as far as security is concerned, you may use this approach to allow Apache to bind to ports 80 and 443, and permit the Tomcat instance to run with restricted privileges. On Unix systems, only the root user can bind to ports 1024 and below. Apache uses system calls to allow it to run as root long enough to gain access to the ports, and then switches the effective permissions under which it is running to those of a lesser-privileged user. Unfortunately, as of this writing, Java does not have a mechanism for doing this, so Tomcat is unable to lower its privileges in a similar way. You either run as root in order to secure the ports and then continue to run as root (with your servlet code executing as root, an unscrupulous user could gain total access to your system, assuming the other security provisions you've set up can be subverted), or you run as a lesser-privileged user (and thus be restricted from running on the standard ports for HTTP and HTTPS: 80 and 443, respectively). The other advantage is simply that Apache has been much more rigorously tested, having been the leading Web server for many years now. Such security flaws as remain are discovered quickly, and patches are developed even more quickly.

If you are running on Windows, where such security measures haven't been designed into the system, the security argument is blunted significantly. This is particularly true if you are choosing between running Tomcat stand-alone or behind Microsoft IIS, which has proven to be a rich vein of security flaws without any help from the underlying OS.

The performance argument is particularly strong if you are serving large numbers of static pages in addition to the content served by servlets and JSPs, or if you are using HTTPS. In the former case, Apache is just faster at serving static content than is Tomcat. In the latter case, Apache's implementation of Secure Sockets Layer (SSL) is also faster, which results in lower latency when users connect over HTTPS. Of course, the best way to determine if there is a performance benefit is to test your own application. Sometimes, particulars of an application can change the performance profile, and you may find you are getting better performance out of a stand-alone Tomcat configuration.

The functionality argument comes into play if you want to use other technologies to serve dynamic Web content on the same server—for example PHP, ColdFusion, or various Common Gateway Interface (CGI) technologies. Tomcat does provide libraries to support CGI and server-side includes natively. The libraries are located in the *<$CATALINA_HOME>* /server/lib directory, and are called servlets-cgi.renametojar and servlets-ssi.renametojar. As the "renamed to .jar" filenames imply, once loaded these libraries will add CGI SSI functionality; however, you won't be able to run C CGI code, ACGI, and FastCGI style PERL processes in the same process space as Tomcat.

These connectors will require you to install a library in your Web server in order to provide support for the protocol.

So now that we've covered some of the reasons, let's look at the two main connectors that are used to support server-to-server communication.

The JK 2 Connector

The JK 2 connector communicates with the principal Web server using the AJP protocol, and supports versions 1.3 and 1.4 of that protocol. The class that implements this connector is org.apache.coyote.tomcat4.CoyoteConnector; you need to specify this in the className attribute for the connector. In addition, you must specify the correct protocol handler in the protocolHandlerClassName attribute.

The protocolHandlerClassName attribute (required) must be set to org.apache.jk.server.JkCoyoteHandler. This is the only attribute specific to the JK 2 connector.

The Webapp Connector

The Webapp connector communicates with the principal Web server over the WARP protocol. The WARP protocol has some advantages when you are using Apache merely to proxy Tomcat services (if, for example, you are using Apache for the security and performance reasons outlined earlier). WARP, supported by the mod_webapp.so library, allows you to drive the VirtualHost configuration of Tomcat from the httpd.conf file used to configure Apache. If you want to do this, you'll need to run the Webapp connector in its own service and configure that service to use the WarpEngine engine instead of the default engine. The class that defines WarpEngine is org.apache.catalina.connector.warp.WarpEngine; specify this name in the className attribute of the <Engine/> context for this service. The default server.xml file that comes with Tomcat has a section with this configuration included.

The class that implements the Webapp connector is org.apache.catalina.connector.warp.WarpConnector. Specify this in the className attribute of the <Connector/> node.

The appBase attribute (optional) specifies the application base to use for hosts created based on the information brought in from the Apache configuration. It functions similarly to the appBase attribute in the <Host/> container. Of course, all hosts created in this way will share the same appBase attribute. The default value is webapps, which (unless the base path has been configured differently elsewhere) will point to the *<$CATALINA_HOME>*/webapps directory.

The <Factory/> Node

Some connectors, specifically those that use SSL to provide encryption, are further configured with a contained <Factory/> node that specifies which factory class Tomcat should use to construct the underlying socket. The native implementation of SSL provided by Java uses the Factory design pattern (We explore this pattern in Chapter 17, "Database-Aware Objects") to provide a standard interface to a heterogeneous set of underlying socket implementation classes. This node is used to configure that factory class to give us properly configured SSLSocket instances.

In this section, we focus on the requirements for the Coyote HTTP/1.1 connector, since that's the only currently endorsed connector supplied with Tomcat that uses the

<Factory/> node, and because other current uses of the <Factory/> node are very similar. If you're using a third-party connector that is configured through a <Factory/> node, the vendor should provide adequate documentation to fill in any gaps left by this section.

The className attribute (required) specifies the factory class. In the current implementation, according to the Tomcat documentation, this attribute must be set to org.apache.coyote.tomcat4.CoyoteServerSocketFactory.

The algorithm attribute (optional) specifies what type of certificates Tomcat should use in the exchange of credentials at the start of the session. Since X.509 certificates are the most widely supported, leaving this set to the default of SunX509 is a good choice. If you have other requirements, you are probably already aware of them.

The clientAuth attribute (optional) is a true or false attribute that specifies whether you want to require users of the connector to authenticate with a client certificate. Be advised that it is quite rare for end users to have a client certificate installed in their browser. This feature is primarily useful for developing intranet applications, where the IT department has control of the configuration of the machines used to access the service. If clientAuth is set to true, every request to the containing connector will require client authentication via client-side certificate. If clientAuth is set to false, you can still configure a specific resource to require a client certificate by adding a security constraint of CLIENT-CERT. The default is false.

The following attributes are all optional and are used to configure access to the keystore file:

- keystoreFile—The default value is the keystore file in the home directory of the user Tomcat is running as.
- keystoreType—The default value is JKS, the standard Java keystore.
- keystorePass—The default value is changeit.

The protocol attribute (optional) configures the protocol version that Tomcat should use for the containing connector. The default is TLS.

The Tomcat Web Server Administration Tool

As we mentioned in the introduction to this chapter, Tomcat 4.1 has a new administration tool that makes server configuration much simpler, particularly for first-time Tomcat administrators. Armed with the knowledge you've gained already in this chapter, and with Appendix A as a reference, you should be able to make full use of this powerful tool.

Setup

The administration utility is turned off by default (see the next section entitled "Security" to learn why). To turn the administration utility on, you'll need to do a little bit of security realm configuration. In this section, we provide enough information for you to get up and running using the administration tool. For information on customizing your realm setup further (for example, by storing log information in a database or on an LDAP server), please see Chapter 8 for complete details.

First, you will need to edit <*$CATALINA_HOME*>/conf/tomcat-users.xml, which contains the configuration information for the memory-based access realm. That file, as shipped, already includes a node specifying an admin role:

```
<role rolename="admin" description="Administration Tool users"/>
```

By default, however, there are no users configured to be members of that role. Simply add a user in among the other <user/> nodes in that file:

```
<user username="admin" password="badpassword" fullName="Administrator
  Role Account" roles="admin"/>
```

Of course, you'll want to replace *badpassword* with a good password. (We'll use *badpassword* throughout this book when you are to make up a more secure password.)

You can also configure the same user to be able to use the Manager application, which controls webapp deployment (further described in Chapter 9. To do this, simply add the manager role to the roles attribute of the <user/> node you just created:

```
<user username="admin" password="badpassword" fullName="Administrator

  Role Account" roles="admin,manager"/>
```

Once you've configured the tomcat-users.xml file, restart Tomcat. You should find the administration tool configured and available at http://localhost:8080/admin, as illustrated in Figure 7.1.

Security

Of course, providing full access to configure the server from anywhere on the Internet isn't necessarily a great recipe for security success. You'll need to be very judicious about how you deploy this tool. You will almost definitely want to provide access to it only from behind your firewall, and you may choose not to run it at all. Some of the techniques we discuss for protecting Tomcat from attack in Chapter 18 will prevent the administration tool from running. In particular, changing the permissions on the server.xml file so it is not writable by the Tomcat user will preclude you from using Tomcat to configure itself, *a priori*. And this is exactly why we suggest doing this: so someone doesn't compromise Tomcat and coerce it to allow them to configure it to further compromise your network.

However, just because you may not want to enable the administration tool on a production server, that doesn't mean you won't find some good uses for it. On a development machine, you can use it to tune your configuration, and to learn about Tomcat configuration generally. Then you can manually transfer the server.xml file, making any necessary modifications, to your live server.

Using the Administration Tool

Once you've logged in to the administration tool, you will be presented with a tree view of the various nodes in your server.xml file, as pictured in Figure 7.2.

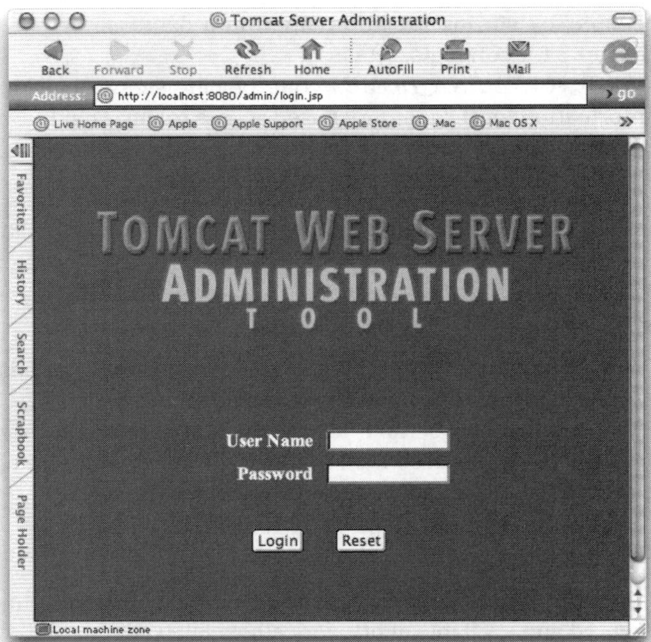

Figure 7.1 The Tomcat Administration Tool login screen.

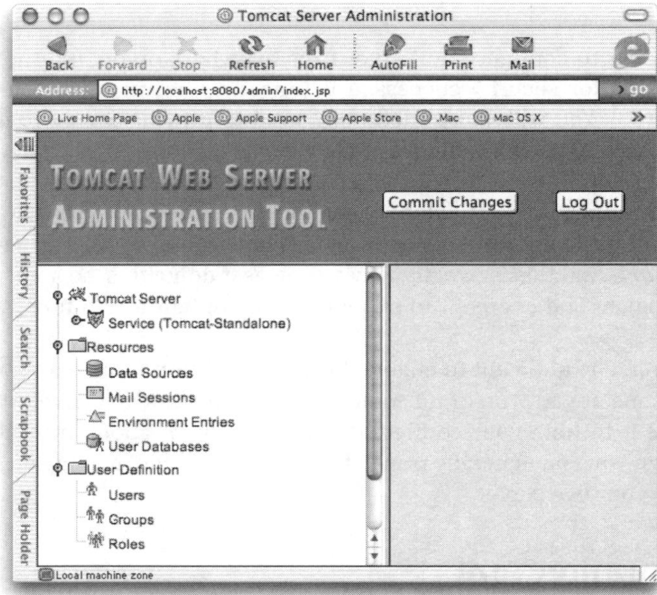

Figure 7.2 The Main Administration screen.

If you've read the material earlier in this chapter, you should find most of the information presented in the administration tool's tree view very familiar. Drilling down into the Service node, you will find each of the connectors configured for that service, along with the various host entries configured on your server. From this tree view, you can configure, add, and remove nodes simply by clicking on the node you wish to modify. You will then be presented with a set of actions appropriate to that pane in the right half of the window.

For example, let's take a look at the configuration information for our main HTTP connector, on port 8080 (see Figure 7.3).

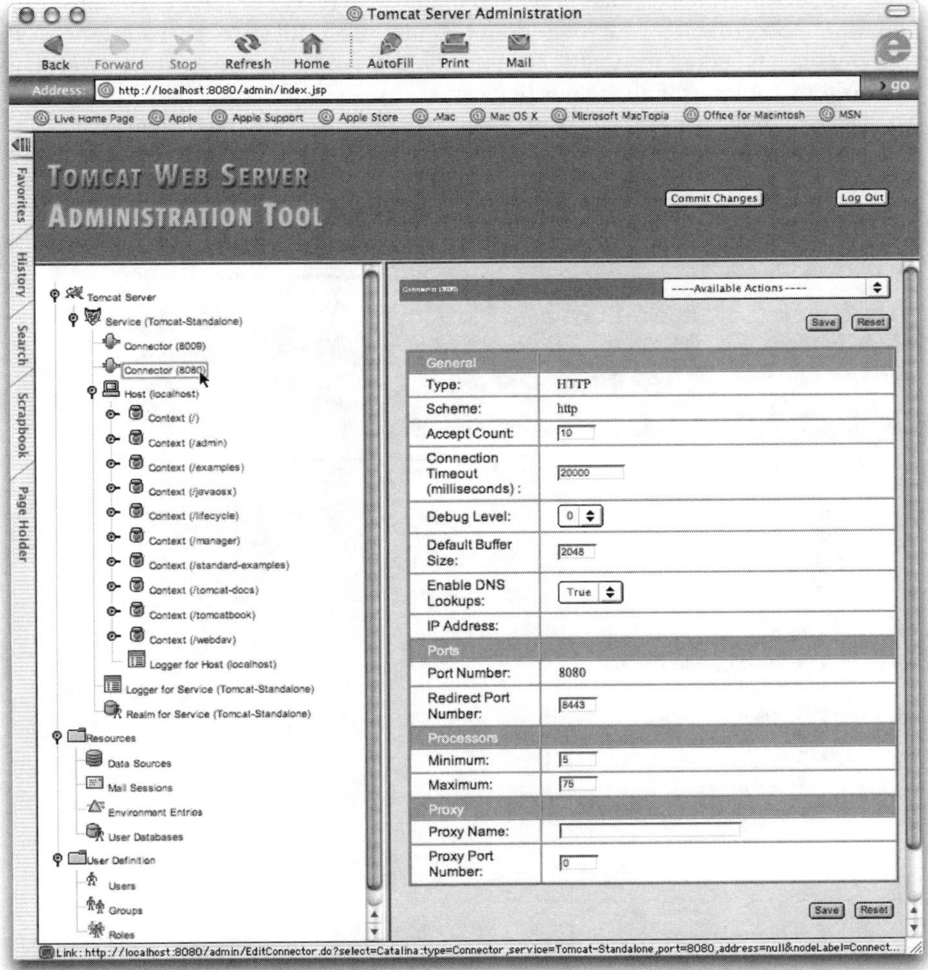

Figure 7.3 Looking at the configuration of the connector on port 8080.

As you can see, all of the attributes we discussed previously in this chapter can be easily accessed and modified. The first thing you'll probably want to do is turn off Enable DNS Lookups. Don't forget to save and to commit changes by pressing the respective buttons. If you don't like your changes, you can just hit *Reset*. Changes are flushed to disk (and to the running configuration) only when you click the *Commit Changes* button.

Operations to create or remove nodes can be found in the *Available Actions* menu for the parent node. For example, to create a new connector, you would simply select the Service node in the tree view at left, and then select *Create New Connector* from the *Available Actions* menu. You are limited (at least at the time of this writing) to using the Coyote connector, which enables you to configure HTTP, HTTPS, and AJP connections. If you want to configure your own connections, you'll need to go back out to the server.xml file, and edit it manually. For most typical configuration issues, however, the administration tool puts it all at your fingertips.

The last example we'll show is configuring a connection pool (see Figure 7.4).

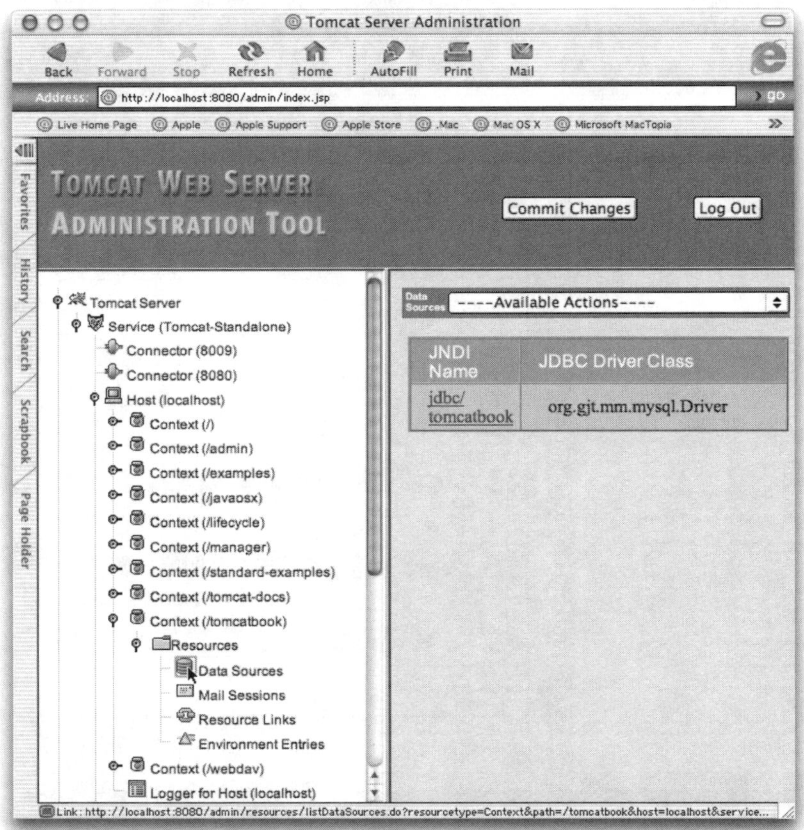

Figure 7.4 Configuring a connection pool.

Here, we see the configuration of the connection pool from the database in Chapter 16. Originally, we entered all this information manually, but the administration application displays it correctly and in a form that we can edit it. In this respect, the administration application is an excellent tool for trying to figure out how to configure a new technology that you may not be very familiar with, and it prevents you from entering improperly formatted information into your server configuration.

Summary

In this chapter, we examined all the gory details of the server.xml file. You should be much more familiar with the contents of that file, and have a firm grasp on how to configure Tomcat to do the things you want it to do. We also hopefully showed you enough of the new administration tool in Tomcat 4.1 to whet your appetite. We didn't cover configuration or HTTP authentication yet; we tackle those topics in the next chapter. Tomcat is massively configurable, as you can see from the material presented here. In fact, if there's something you want it to do that it doesn't do already, you probably have a good idea at this point where you could add that support.

CHAPTER

8

Managing Authentication with Realms

Now that you know how to configure your Web application, it is time to discuss user authentication and the mechanisms in Tomcat you use to enable and manage this authentication. Almost all Web servers have tools for managing HTTP-based authentication, and Tomcat is no exception.

HTTP Authorization Schemes

HTTP includes a basic request-response protocol for requesting user credentials and granting access to resources based on those credentials. When a request comes in for a protected resource, the Web server checks to see if the browser has sent authentication credentials. If it hasn't, the server sends a 401 error code back to the browser, specifying in the response header the type of credential it's looking for. The browser is then responsible for requesting the information from the user, or providing it from its local cache if it already has the information from a previous request. In the former case, this typically results in a dialog box being presented to the user that includes text boxes for entering the information needed to authenticate the user and the authorization realm for which the request was generated. Servlets and JSPs also give you a mechanism for redirecting the request to a different page, allowing you to handle login through the use of a form. On subsequent requests to the same server, this authentication information is sent in each request as a set of headers.

The simplest of the HTTP authorization schemes is Basic Authorization, or *Basic Auth* for short. This scheme consists simply of using a login and a cleartext password.

The first time the user visits a set of resources protected by Basic Auth, he or she will be presented with a dialog box similar to the one in Figure 8.1 below. Both the login and password are sent in the clear by the browser with each request to the server. This is a simple way to handle user authentication. Unfortunately, since the authorization credentials are sent in the clear, and sent with every request, it is pretty easy for someone snooping on the network to get hold of these credentials and use them for nefarious purposes.

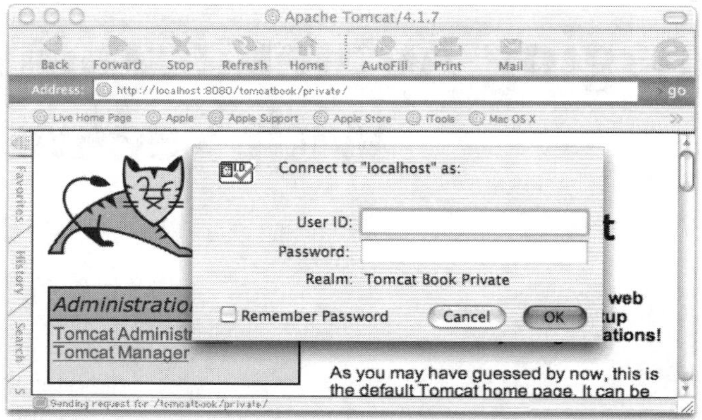

Figure 8.1 The Basic Auth password dialog box

For that reason, a new authorization scheme, called Digest Auth, was added. In this scheme, the user still enters a cleartext password, but before it is transmitted over the wire, it is combined with a string (the *nonce*) provided by the server and encrypted using a one-way hashing algorithm, such as SHA or MD5. Because the nonce can be (and should be) updated by the server for subsequent requests, this prevents the nefarious snooper from simply reusing the digested string to gain access through a replay attack—the encrypted string is different each time the nonce changes. And, since the cleartext password is never transmitted and the credential presented is based on a strong encryption algorithm, there is little risk of the snooper getting access to the original password and being able to generate his or her own credentials.

The third principal authorization scheme is certificate-based. In this scheme, a user must have a client-side certificate in order to access the server. This approach is more secure because certificates can be centrally managed and granted, and additional real-world credentials can also be required by the granting authority (be it your company's human resources department or a third party such as VeriSign or Thawte).

Unfortunately, not all schemes are supported by all browsers, or all servers. It is only recently that even Digest Auth has been widely supported in browsers. You can get around browser limitations by handling authentication directly in your application, or by allowing Basic Auth only over an HTTPS connection. In this chapter, however, we focus on server-managed authorization and the two most widely available authentication protocols: Basic Auth and Digest Auth.

HTTP has a notion of authorization realms. What they boil down to is a realm name, a user or set of users authorized to access that realm, and a required authorization scheme. These are typically associated with directory nodes or partial URIs so as to limit access to what amounts to a subtree of the documents available on a given server. They allow the browser to identify which credential to present in order to access the resource requested.

Setting Up Realms on Tomcat

On Apache and other similar servers, you typically set up realms by including an .htaccess file in the base directory of the area that you wanted to secure. User and role information was stored in text files, or, with the appropriate mod files installed, sometimes in .gdb or .ndb files, or in a proper database. Different servlet containers configure realms in different ways.

Tomcat has a flexible built-in mechanism for managing realms, users, and roles. You configure them in the server.xml file, which we introduced in Chapter 3, "Configuring Tomcat." You can configure users and roles in an XML file, store them in a database, or read them out of a Lightweight Directory Access Protocol (LDAP) server or other Java Naming and Directory Interface (JNDI) accessible source. Default providers are available for each of these three cases, and if they don't provide enough flexibility for your application, you can even write your own provider. What they all have in common is that they provide a way of authenticating a user, and a way of associating users with roles. Keep in mind these rules:

- Any user can be a member of zero or more roles.
- Any role can contain zero or more users.
- Realms specify which users may access them by providing a list of one or more roles that have access. A user that is a member of one or more of those roles will be granted access to the realm.

The MemoryRealm

We'll start by looking at the file-based realm that comes installed and configured for use with the examples. The file with the actual user and role information is called <*$CATALINA_HOME*>/conf/tomcat-users.xml (see Listing 8.1).

```
<!--
  NOTE:  By default, no user is included in the "manager" role
  required to operate the "/manager" web application.  If you wish
  to use this app, you must define such a user - the username and
```

Listing 8.1 The tomcat-users.xml file. (continues)

```
  password are arbitrary.
-->
<tomcat-users>
  <user name="tomcat" password="tomcat" roles="tomcat" />
  <user name="role1"  password="tomcat" roles="role1" />
  <user name="both"   password="tomcat" roles="tomcat,role1" />
</tomcat-users>
```

Listing 8.1 The tomcat-users.xml file. (continued)

Thanks to the implicit clarity of XML, you've probably already guessed that there are three users in this system: tomcat, role1, and both. There are also two roles: tomcat and role1. The user both is a member of both roles. Of course, so far, this file is just a text file. In order to create a realm, you must configure it in the server.xml file. Here is the location in the default servlet.xml file where you configure this realm:

```
<Realm className="org.apache.catalina.realm.MemoryRealm" />
```

This line, which appears as a child of the <Engine/> tag that sets up your stand-alone server, sets up a MemoryRealm (as opposed to a JDBCRealm or JNDIRealm), and loads in the users and roles defined in tomcat-users.xml.

So now Tomcat knows about the users and roles. The next thing that needs to happen is to turn on authorization for a given resource. Then, we'll turn to the examples webapp and its deployment descriptor, *<$CATALINA_HOME>*/webapps/examples/WEB-INF/web.xml, the relevant portion of which is shown in Listing 8.2.

```
<security-constraint>
    <display-name>Example Security Constraint</display-name>
    <web-resource-collection>
      <web-resource-name>Protected Area</web-resource-name>
      <!-- Define the context-relative URL(s) to be protected -->
      <url-pattern>/jsp/security/protected/*</url-pattern>
      <!-- If you list http methods, only those methods are
 protected -->
      <http-method>DELETE</http-method>
      <http-method>GET</http-method>
      <http-method>POST</http-method>
      <http-method>PUT</http-method>
    </web-resource-collection>
    <auth-constraint>
      <!-- Anyone with one of the listed roles may access this
 area -->
```

Listing 8.2 Fragment of examples web.xml where a realm is mapped to a URI. (continues)

```
        <role-name>tomcat</role-name>
        <role-name>role1</role-name>
      </auth-constraint>
    </security-constraint>
```

Listing 8.2 Fragment of examples web.xml where a realm is mapped to a URI. (continued)

The <security-constraint/> node shown in Listing 8.2 is a top-level element inside the <webapp/> root node. As you can see, this mapping protects all accesses to pages within this Webapp under /jsp/security/protected/, requiring users to be members of the role tomcat and/or the role role1.

As you can also see from this fragment, we must list explicitly which access methods are subjected to this security constraint. In this case, we limit GET, POST, PUT, and DELETE. The reason for this is to allow different constraints for different access methods. As an example, consider a Web site that uses PUT and DELETE methods to manage content. You could use a security constraint like this to limit access only to PUT and DELETE, to allow only registered users to process forms with POST, and to allow anyone to see the static content of your site served via GET.

Immediately following this <security-constraint/> is a <login-config/> node (see Listing 8.3) that further configures our Webapp to use forms-based login, rather than having the browser present an authorization dialog box.

```
<!-- Default login configuration uses form-based authentication -->
  <login-config>
    <auth-method>FORM</auth-method>
    <realm-name>Example Form-Based Authentication Area</realm-name>
    <form-login-config>
      <form-login-page>/jsp/security/protected/login.jsp</form-
 login-page>
      <form-error-page>/jsp/security/protected/error.jsp</form-
 error-page>
    </form-login-config>
  </login-config>
```

Listing 8.3 Fragment of examples web.xml where form-based login is configured.

This fragment configures two pages that the browser should be redirected to, and the name of the realm. The name of the access realm is *Example Form-Based Authentication Area*, which is also the name that will be presented to the browser.

The first file, specified in <form-login-page/>, is the page the server should send in place of the requested page, when the user has not yet authenticated (i.e., in circumstances where the server would otherwise be sending a 401 response requesting login).

The /jsp/security/protected/login.jsp file (see Listing 8.4) is the form the user will submit in order to log in.

The second file, specified in <form-error-page/>, is the page users will be served if they submit an invalid credential (i.e., when the server would otherwise be returning a 403 Unauthorized response error).

To see these users in action, start up Tomcat if it isn't running already, and go to http://localhost:8080/examples/jsp/security/protected/index.jsp (or any page under this directory). Because you haven't logged in yet, you will be presented with the login page.

To configure the same application to use dialog box-based login, simply change the <auth-method/> from FORM to BASIC. Legal auth-methods are FORM, BASIC, DIGEST, and CLIENT-CERT. (But remember, not all browsers support all authorization methods. Form-based and Basic Auth are the only ones pretty much guaranteed to work across browsers, and both send passwords in the clear, unless the authorization is sent over HTTPS. For more on security, see the section "Security and Identity," later in this chapter.)

```
<html>
<head>
<title>Login Page for Examples</title>
<body bgcolor="white">
<form method="POST" action='<%= response.encodeURL("j_security_
  check") %>' >
  <table border="0" cellspacing="5">
    <tr>
      <th align="right">Username:</th>
      <td align="left"><input type="text" name="j_username"></td>
    </tr>
    <tr>
      <th align="right">Password:</th>
      <td align="left"><input type="password" name="j_password"></td>
    </tr>
    <tr>
      <td align="right"><input type="submit" value="Log In"></td>
      <td align="left"><input type="reset"></td>
    </tr>
  </table>
</form>
</body>
</html>
```

Listing 8.4 login.jsp.

As you can see in Listing 8.4, login.jsp is a very simple form. It has only one JSP directive in it, which appears in bold. (We cover JSPs more fully in Chapter 11, "JavaServer Pages.") The encodeURL() method on HttpServletResponse is used to encode session information, including redirect targets, into a URL. j_security_check is a magic URI set up by the realm that processes authorization requests.

JDBC Realms

Using a flat file to configure security is easy, but this approach leaves a lot to be desired in terms of security and management. You certainly don't want some Webapp writing a systemwide security configuration file (and possibly corrupting it or compromising it) every time your Webapp wants to add a new user. You also don't want cleartext passwords lying around in a file readable by an unprivileged user. It's just not safe.

Two built-in adapters avoid these problems. First, let's look at JDBCRealm. As the name implies, this realm stores user and role information in a database, and accesses it via Java Database Connectivity (JDBC). We talk a lot more about JDBC and how to use databases in your servlets in Chapter 16, "Databases, Connection Pools, and JDBC." If you're already familiar with databases, you should find everything you need here to connect your security system to a database. Actually setting up a database is beyond the scope of this chapter, but you can find some pointers to get you started in Chapter 16.

The JDBCRealm object is very flexible. You can set up special-purpose tables to handle users and roles, but you can also access user and role information in an existing database. Let's start by setting up a new database, and then explain what you need to do if you want to connect to an existing database instead.

For this example, we are using MySQL as our database, although you can connect to any database with a JDBC driver available. (Again, for database setup information and more detail, see Chapter 16.) If you choose to use a different database, the specific steps will vary slightly from those we cover here, but you should get the idea.

We start by creating a new database to contain our usernames. Assuming MySQL is already installed, you create a new database by using the mysqladmin command:

```
mysqladmin -u root -p create tomcatbook
```

If you have set up a password for the root database account, you will be prompted for it. (Note that this is *not* the root password for the machine the database is running on, but the password for the root user of MySQL.)

We also want to create a user with privileges to access the database so that the Tomcat server can read the user and role information from it. We need to log into the mysql shell to create the user we'll use to access this information and grant it complete access permissions to the tomcatbook database. (Note that in a real application, you will in most cases want this user to have more restricted read-only permissions, and set up a different user to modify the values stored in the database.)

We launch the MySQL shell to edit the system tables (stored in the database called *mysql*) as follows:

```
mysql -u root -p mysql
```

Again, you will be prompted for the root MySQL password. Listing 8.5 shows the commands you'll need to enter to set up the user Tomcat will employ to access the realm data.

```
Reading table information for completion of table and column names
You can turn off this feature to get a quicker startup with -A

Welcome to the MySQL monitor.  Commands end with ; or \g.
Your MySQL connection id is 41 to server version: 3.23.51-entropy.ch

Type 'help;' or '\h' for help. Type '\c' to clear the buffer.

mysql> GRANT ALL PRIVILEGES ON tomcatbook.* TO tomcat@localhost
 IDENTIFIED BY 'badpassword' WITH GRANT OPTION;
Query OK, 0 rows affected (0.06 sec)

mysql> quit;
Bye
```

Listing 8.5 Creating the tomcat user.

You have now created a user tomcat with a password *badpassword* that has permissions to access all the tables in the tomcatbook database. (You should substitute a better password everywhere *badpassword* appears.)

Next, we log in using this newly created user, create our user and role tables, and then populate them with a few sample users:

```
mysql -u tomcat -p tomcatbook
```

This time you will be prompted for the password you set up in the previous step. Listing 8.6 shows the commands you'll need to enter to establish the users and roles used by the JDBCRealm we're creating.

```
Welcome to the MySQL monitor.  Commands end with ; or \g.
Your MySQL connection id is 42 to server version: 3.23.51-entropy.ch

Type 'help;' or '\h' for help. Type '\c' to clear the buffer.

mysql> CREATE TABLE user (
    -> login VARCHAR(40) NOT NULL,
    -> password VARCHAR(40) NOT NULL,
    -> PRIMARY KEY (login)
    -> );
Query OK, 0 rows affected (0.02 sec)

mysql> CREATE TABLE role (
    -> name VARCHAR(40) NOT NULL,
```

Listing 8.6 Creating the user and role tables and populating them. (continues)

```
    -> login VARCHAR(40) NOT NULL
    -> );
Query OK, 0 rows affected (0.01 sec)

mysql> INSERT INTO user VALUES ('tomcat', 'tomcat');
Query OK, 1 row affected (0.00 sec)

mysql> INSERT INTO user VALUES ('ian', 'javarules');
Query OK, 1 row affected (0.00 sec)

mysql> INSERT INTO user VALUES ('peter', 'kiwipower');
Query OK, 1 row affected (0.00 sec)

mysql> INSERT INTO role VALUES ('tomcat', 'tomcat');
Query OK, 1 row affected (0.00 sec)

mysql> INSERT INTO role VALUES ('tomcat', 'ian');
Query OK, 1 row affected (0.00 sec)

mysql> INSERT INTO role VALUES ('tomcat', 'peter');
Query OK, 1 row affected (0.00 sec)

mysql> INSERT INTO role VALUES ('special', 'ian');
Query OK, 1 row affected (0.00 sec)

mysql> INSERT INTO role VALUES ('special', 'peter');
Query OK, 1 row affected (0.00 sec)

mysql> SELECT * FROM user;
+--------+-----------+
| login  | password  |
+--------+-----------+
| tomcat | tomcat    |
| ian    | javarules |
| peter  | kiwipower |
+--------+-----------+
3 rows in set (0.02 sec)

mysql> SELECT * FROM role;
+---------+--------+
| name    | login  |
+---------+--------+
| tomcat  | tomcat |
```

Listing 8.6 Creating the user and role tables and populating them. (continues)

```
| tomcat | ian    |
| tomcat | peter  |
| special | ian   |
| special | peter |
+---------+--------+
5 rows in set (0.00 sec)

mysql> quit;
Bye
```

Listing 8.6 Creating the user and role tables and populating them. (continued)

The Tomcat JDBCRealm requires two tables, the first containing a username-to-password mapping, and the second mapping users to the roles to which they belong. It doesn't matter what the columns are called, or if there are other columns in the tables or other tables in the database. If you have an existing application that already contains this type of mapping, you can configure Tomcat to use the existing tables instead. You just need to have the requisite data in two tables in your database, and the column name of the column containing the login name needs to be the same in both tables.

Now that we have the database tables in place, we can configure the realm in our server.xml file by adding a new <Realm/> node. In its simplest form, this will look like Listing 8.7.

```
<Realm className="org.apache.catalina.realm.JDBCRealm"
   connectionName="tomcat"
   connectionPassword="badpassword"
   connectionURL="jdbc:mysql://localhost/tomcatbook"
   driverName="org.gjt.mm.mysql.Driver"
   userTable="user"
   userNameCol="login"
   userCredCol="password"
   userRoleTable="role"
   roleNameCol="name"
/>
```

Listing 8.7 The <Realm/> node we want to add to *<$CATALINA_HOME>*/conf/server.xml.

Insert the <Realm/> node from Listing 8.7 into your server.xml file after the MemoryRealm that came preinstalled. You also need to place a JAR file containing the JDBC driver for your database on the server classpath by placing it either in *<$CATALINA_HOME>*/server/lib or in *<$CATALINA_HOME>*/common/lib. (If you place the JAR file in /common/lib, it will also be available to your Webapps.)

Once everything is in place, you need to restart Tomcat before the new realm will be available. Once you've done that, you can go back to http://localhost:8080/examples/jsp/security/protected/index.jsp and log in as one of the users you created.

There are two things you should note about the life cycle (excerpted from the Tomcat Realms readme file):

- When a user attempts to access a protected resource for the first time, Tomcat will call the authenticate() method of this realm. Thus, any changes you have made to the database directly (new users, changed passwords or roles, etc.) will be immediately reflected.
- Once a user has been authenticated, the user (and his or her associated roles) are cached within Tomcat for the duration of the user's login. (For FORM-based authentication, that means until the session times out or is invalidated; for BASIC authentication, that means until the user closes their browser). Any changes to the database information for an already authenticated user will *not* be reflected until the next time that user logs on again.

Tomcat doesn't provide any tools for manipulating the data in your database, although it's simple enough to write a servlet or JSP to handle that. Chapter 16 should give you the tools you need to write your own password-management system.

JNDI Realms

An elaborate discussion of directory services, and in particular the setting up of an LDAP server, are beyond the scope of this book, so we assume in the following examples that you already have a directory service running somewhere, and that you want to access it to get user and role information. If you aren't already using an LDAP server or some other JNDI source for user management, you'll probably find that the JDBCRealm is adequate for your purposes. If at a later date, you do start to use directory services, then these examples will begin to make more sense. If you're not interested in JNDI, you can safely skip ahead to the next section.

Each directory server represents manages creation of its schema in different ways, so you'll need to refer to the documentation for your particular server in order to get the schema set up appropriately. The schema will need to conform to the following rules in order for it to be compatible with the JNDIRealm provided with Tomcat (summarized from the Tomcat Realms readme file):

- Each user that can be authenticated is represented by an individual element in the top-level DirContext that is accessed via the connectionURL attribute.
- The user element must have the following characteristics:
    - The distinguished name (dn) attribute of this element contains the username that is presented for authentication.
    - There must be an attribute (identified by the userPassword attribute of our Realm element) that contains the user's password, either in cleartext or digested.

- Each group of users that has been assigned a particular role is represented by an individual element in the top-level DirContext that is accessed via the connectionURL attribute.
- The user group element must have the following characteristics:
    - The set of all possible groups of interest can be selected by an LDAP search pattern configured by the roleSearch attribute of the Realm element.
    - The roleSearch pattern optionally includes pattern replacements "{0}" for the distinguished name and/or "{1} for the username of the authenticated user for which roles will be retrieved.
    - The roleBase attribute can be set to the element that is the base of the search for matching roles. If not specified, the entire directory context will be searched.
    - The roleSubtree attribute can be set to true if you wish to search the entire subtree of the directory context. The default value of false requests a search of only the current level.
    - The element includes an attribute (whose name is configured by the roleName attribute of the Realm element) containing the name of the role represented by this element.
- There must be an administrator username and password that Tomcat can use to establish a connection to the directory server, with at least read-only access to the information described earlier. A future version of Tomcat will support an option to use the user's username and password to attempt this connection.

As was the case with the JDBCRealm, we need to install a JAR file with the JNDI provider or providers needed to access the directory service, in either the <*$CATALINA_HOME*>/server/lib directory or the <*$CATALINA_HOME*>/common/lib directory.

We then need to configure the realm, establishing which fields we will use for each of the elements, as shown in Listing 8.8.

```
<Realm className="org.apache.catalina.realm.JNDIRealm"
   connectionName="cn=Manager,dc=mycompany,dc=com"
   connectionPassword="secret"
   connectionURL="ldap://localhost:389"
   roleBase="dc=roles,dc=mcclan,dc=net"
   roleName="cn"
   roleSearch="(uniqueMember={0})"
   roleSubtree="false"
   userPassword="userPassword"
   userPattern="cn={0},dc=mycompany,dc=com"
/>
```

Listing 8.8 The <Realm/> node for a JNDIRealm.

Custom Realms

What do you do if your database or directory server doesn't conform to the schema requirements we've described, or if you manage users in some other way? In that case, you can always write your own Realm class simply by implementing the org.apache.catalina.Realm interface. The details are beyond the scope of this book, but you can find substantial examples in the implementations of the three realms provided. You need to download a source distribution to get the source code for these classes, but that's one of the advantages of an open source server: If there's something that doesn't quite do what you need it to do, you have everything you need to fix it. And in this case, all you need to do to extend Tomcat's capabilities is to implement a new Realm class, put it on the trusted classpath, and restart.

Scope of Realms

Where you place a <Realm/> node in your server.xml file determines the scope in which the realm is valid. If you want your realm to be visible globally, then place the <Realm/> node inside the <Engine/> node, as we have in the examples. However, if you want to operate multiple realms that are more narrowly scoped, you have a couple of other options. You can also associate a realm with a specific connector, context, or host by placing the <Realm/> node inside the <Connector/> node, <Context/> node, or <Host/> node, respectively. This is particularly important when you are using Tomcat in a multi-homed environment—where different hosts may be running different applications with different authorization requirements—or when you have two Webapps (running in two different contexts) that likewise have different authorization requirements. Generally, the <Realm/> node is valid within the scope of its containing node in the server.xml file.

Single Sign-On

By default, each Webapp has a separate authentication scope. This prevents users from unintentionally gaining access to different applications, and more important, prevents the server from inadvertently presenting the credentials from one application to another. However, in many contexts, it is desirable for the user to be allowed to log in once and gain access to all of the Webapps on a given host. Fortunately, Tomcat provides an easy mechanism to accommodate this. Inside the <Host/> node for which you want to enable this feature, simply add the following <Valve/> node:

```
<Valve className="org.apache.catalina.authenticator.SingleSignOn"
  debug="0"/>
```

Here are a few additional requirements you need to be aware of:

- All of the Webapps sharing the single sign-on have to use the same realm. That means that the realm will have to be configured in a shared context, either the Engine context (which is global) or the Host context for the host in question.

Configuring the realm in each of the <Context/> nodes for the individual Webapps won't work, since this will create separate instances of the realm.

- Once the user accesses a protected resource in any application, he or she will be presented with the specified login mechanism. He or she will remain logged in for all Web applications on the configured host, and his or her credentials will automatically be presented for all roles of which that user is a member.
- Logging out from one application logs you out from all of the other applications, too.
- Single sign-on uses cookies to share a session token between Web applications (see Chapter 15, "Session Management," for a description), and as a result, it will function only if the browser accepts cookies.

Security and Identity

Now that we've discussed how to configure Tomcat to manage access to resources, it's time to review some security considerations. Security is an important area, and one that continues to grow in importance as more and more business is conducted over the Internet and by computers in general. We've mentioned a few pitfalls already, and now is a good time to review them in a little more depth. We've examined one common way to secure Web applications, but it's important for you to realize that this level of security is not adequate to protect important resources.

First, let's examine the fundamental security of password-based authentication. Its biggest advantage is its ease of implementation. Users understand the notion of needing a login and password in order to access a resource, so it's easy for them to understand and adopt. However, a password-based system is only as secure as the passwords themselves, and there are a number of ways in which a password can be compromised. Bad passwords can be guessed, and bad password habits can lead to their being compromised in other ways as well. It's all but impossible to prevent users from writing them down, sending them in email, or even sharing them with friends or colleagues. If identity is determined solely on the basis of a login and password, there is no way to distinguish between the actual authorized user and someone else who just happens to use the same login and password to access a resource.

Even if users keep passwords secure, unencrypted network traffic can easily be compromised by anyone connected to the same physical networks between the user and the server. A nefarious hacker can snoop on network traffic and look for authentication headers being sent in the clear. Using Basic Auth or Form-based Auth is not fundamentally secure when the traffic is sent over HTTP, since HTTP is not encrypted.

Using HTTPS can help you work around this shortcoming, since it uses Secure Sockets Layer (SSL) encryption to protect the data transmitted by encrypting each packet before sending it over the wire. This makes it much more difficult (although not impossible) to gain access to the transmitted logins and passwords. Because 128-bit encryption makes it extremely expensive to decrypt network traffic—to the point where days or weeks of CPU time is required to get access to the packets—this level of protection is adequate for all but the most secure communications. Most banks, for instance, require this level of encryption when handling online customer transactions.

However, here too are ways in which the password can be compromised. One of the most insidious is the case where a browser sends authentication information in the clear on a subsequent request. Most browsers are smart enough not to do this, but it's something to be aware of. Perhaps more common is for the file or system containing the passwords itself to be compromised. If our nefarious hacker gets access to the flat file or database that contains the passwords, he or she can easily pick and choose which password to use to authenticate his or her false identity.

Securing password files is actually quite difficult. Because of the underlying complexity of software and operating systems, even if the obvious means of attack are cut off, it is often possible to gain access to resources by exploiting bugs in the software protecting them, whether that software is the operating system, a database, a directory server, or some other system. A vast amount has been written about this topic, so we won't go into detail here. Suffice it to say that it is all but impossible to create truly secure, uncrackable systems; and it is always to assume that it is possible for any file or resource to be compromised, if enough effort is exerted on the part of the hacker.

A safer way to handle password authentication is not to send or store cleartext passwords at all. By using secure one-way hashing algorithms, we can create a representation of a password that cannot be reverse-engineered into the original password by means short of guessing every possible password until the matching one is discovered.

The way these are used is as follows: On the server, the password is digested using a one-way hashing algorithm—for example, MD5. In the case of MD5, the result is a 33-byte-long string that bears no resemblance to the string from which it was generated, but that will always be generated by the algorithm if the same string is fed into it. On the client, the same algorithm is used to process the password with which the client is attempting to log in, and the digested string is sent to the server for comparison. If the strings match, then it is assumed that the passwords were identical.

Note also that the authorization data stored on the server doesn't have to contain a cleartext password. Each of the realm implementations provide for the passwords contained to be stored encrypted. Tomcat comes with tools for generating encrypted passwords, either manually from the command line, or dynamically.

To generate a digested password from the command line, execute the following:

```
java -classpath <$CATALINA_HOME>/server/lib/catalina.jar
  org.apache.catalina.realm.RealmBase -a <algorithm> <password>
```

There are three supported algorithms in this implementation: SHA, MD2, or MD5. So in order to generate an MD5 hash of our password *badpassword*, you would run:

```
java -classpath <$CATALINA_HOME>/server/lib/catalina.jar
  org.apache.catalina.realm.RealmBase -a  MD5 badpassword
```

with the following result:

```
badpassword:31edaffbaba455bc30c52681ceb1ea9d
```

The part in bold is the MD5 hash of our password.

In order to generate the MD5 hash dynamically, you need to call the static method Digest() on org.apache.catalina.realm.RealmBase, and pass in the cleartext password and the algorithm name, as shown in Listing 8.9.

```
import org.apache.catalina.realm.RealmBase;
...
String cleartextPassword = "badpassword";
String digestedPassword = RealmBase.Digest(cleartextPassword, "MD5");
...
```

Listing 8.9 Dynamically digesting a cleartext password.

If your application generates new user accounts on the fly, this is how you might go about generating the digested passwords to store in your database.

To use this password in any of our realm implementations, you have to store this MD5 hash in the password field, whether that field is a database field or part of a <user/> node in tomcat-users.xml, or a password in the appropriate context on your directory server. Then, when configuring the realm, add a digest attribute specifying the algorithm used to digest the password, as shown in Listing 8.10.

```
<Realm className="org.apache.catalina.realm.JDBCRealm"
   digest="MD5"
   connectionName="tomcat"
   connectionPassword="badpassword"
   connectionURL="jdbc:mysql://localhost/tomcatbook"
   driverName="org.gjt.mm.mysql.Driver"
   userTable="user"
   userNameCol="login"
   userCredCol="password"
   userRoleTable="role"
   roleNameCol="name"
/>
```

Listing 8.10 Configuring the JDBCRealm to use digested passwords.

Digest Auth has its downsides as well. As we mentioned earlier, not all browsers support this authentication. In fact, very few do as of this writing. This means that you have to constrain your users to use one of the few supported browsers in order to connect to your site. In an intranet application, this can be a viable solution. This is less viable if your application is an Internet service, such as a banking application.

Also as we mentioned previously, certificate-based authentication adds the advantage of using cryptographically strong client-side certificates for authentication. Alas, client-side certificates are likewise inconsistently supported, so again you have to stipulate a limited number of browser choices if you go this route.

Beyond the standard authentication methods, there are some other options, too. Particularly secure is the use of time-based and onetime password (OTP)-based login systems, such as SecurID. SecurID uses a very small integrated circuit to generate a new number every 15 seconds. This number is not guessable, but is predictable. The server-side component knows what particular number is valid during any 15-second interval, and can authenticate the validity of that number for you. These systems typically consist of an entry field for a login and password, and another field for this magic number. By combining a password (something the user has to know) with the number generated by the device (something the user has to have), a very strong form of identification is created. This system is used by a number of major corporations to provide access to their corporate networks, and is considered to be very secure.

One step beyond this is the use of biometric devices for authentication. These devices consist of a component that examines some feature of the actual person, typically a fingerprint (occasionally the configuration of blood vessels in the retina of the person), and compares that information with a stored model of the biometric data. This is clearly a very secure form of identification, since the would-be hacker has to have access to the actual physical person in order to log into the system (and get the user to interface with the biometric device, to boot). The obvious downside is that every computer the user wants to connect from must be outfitted with the biometric scanner device, but for very secure applications, this is often an acceptable trade-off.

Both of these stronger identity systems will require you to write code to handle the establishment of the validity of the credential in your application. Once a session is authenticated, be it through a password or through more secure means, it is safer simply to use a cryptographically secure token to identify a session, and not to pass credential information again until the next session commences. Fortunately, Tomcat provides a whole set of features to manage sessions, which we will discuss fully in Chapter 15.

There are no easy answers to security questions. Security is always a matter of determining how much security is *good enough*. And unfortunately, security also almost always comes at the expense of ease of use. Use common sense to determine what is safe enough, and ask yourself what would happen to you and your company or client if the data in your system were compromised. If you answered "Not much," then Basic Auth over HTTP is probably plenty. If, however, your application handles sensitive data—for example, banking transactions, medical records, or corporate or state secrets—it's probably in your best interest to think long and hard about the security implications of what you're doing.

We'll talk more about security in Chapter 18. The security-related content in this book is intended to provide an overview of some of the security tools available to you and to get you started. A number of excellent books on security and cryptography are available.

Summary

In this chapter, we discussed how to manage access to resources on your Tomcat server; and how to configure Tomcat to get its access control information from a flat file, a database, or a directory service such as an LDAP server. We examined trade-offs between the different authorization protocols, both in terms of security and availability.

Security is a very important topic, and we examine it further in Chapter 18. It is important for you as an application developer or server administrator to understand how passwords are handled and what the trade-offs are between the various security systems, and to decide whether HTTP authentication is adequate for your application. Consider using HTTPS to secure otherwise non-secure authentication protocols. Unless the information you're serving isn't very important or private, it pays to spend some time working out the security requirements of your application, and making sure that your application is as secure as you think it needs to be.

The next chapter, Chapter 9, "The Manager Application," completes the section on server configuration by introducing a utility you can use to manage the Web applications running on Tomcat.

CHAPTER

9

The Manager Application

Tomcat 4.0 added a new Web application that you can use to deploy, configure, and manage other Webapps running on the server. Specifically, the manager application allows you to use your browser to start and stop Webapps, deploy new Webapps, and restart existing Webapps. The plaintext interface is not pretty, but it does make managing applications remotely a lot easier. A friendlier HTML-based interface has been added in Tomcat 4.1, which we discuss at the end of this chapter. The bulk of this chapter is based on Tomcat 4.0 since most features are common to both versions). The point is that it works, and it lets you manage what's running on your server explicitly. For maximum security, though, you should typically disable the manager application and use other means to control what's running on your server.

Tomcat is shipped with the manager application disabled so that it cannot be used by people with malicious intent who happen to know the default settings. To enable the manager application, you simply create a realm that contains one or more users with the "manager" role. You can configure this any way you wish; complete instructions for managing authorization realms are included in Chapter 8, "Managing Authentication with Realms." For simplicity, however, we use the preconfigured MemoryRealm found in the sample server.xml file included in the distribution.

In this chapter, we take you through the principal features of the manager application. In addition, we list some of the error messages you may get at each step and describe some troubleshooting tips.

Adding a Management User to the Default MemoryRealm

Tomcat comes configured to use a MemoryRealm to authenticate users. This realm reads the tomcat-users.xml file in the configuration directory, *<$CATALINA_HOME>*/conf/. The tomcat-users.xml file is a simple XML file consisting of <user/> nodes, each with a name attribute, a password attribute (containing the cleartext password you'll use when you log in), and a list of roles the user is allowed to participate in, separated by commas. Roles are created implicitly: The set of all available roles is the set of all roles named in the roles attribute of any <user/> node.

You need to restart Tomcat in order for modifications to the realm to take effect. Once there is at least one member of the manager role, the manager application will be activated, and you can use the application by authenticating as that user.

You should also comment out (or at least change passwords for) the users that came preconfigured. They provide access only to the basic auth example pages included in the examples Webapp; however, you may forget at some point that the tomcat and role1 roles were predefined in the file, and find that someone using the default account has gained access to some system setup that uses a role of the same name. In general, it's always a good idea to turn off default accounts.

Modifications to the file appear in bold in Listing 9.1.

```
<!--
 NOTE:  By default, no user is included in the "manager" role
 required to operate the "/manager" web application.  If you wish
 to use this app, you must define such a user - the username and
 password are arbitrary.
-->
<tomcat-users>
 <!-- Comment out the sample roles
 <user name="tomcat" password="tomcat" roles="tomcat" />
 <user name="role1"  password="tomcat" roles="role1"  />
 <user name="both"   password="tomcat" roles="tomcat,role1" />
 -->
 <user name="admin"  password="badpassword"
roles="tomcat,manager" />
</tomcat-users>
```

Listing 9.1 The tomcat-users.xml file with a user added for management.

It's goes without saying that you should change the password specified here to something better than *badpassword.* If you actually use this password for your system and it gets hacked, the fault lies entirely with you.

Once you have set up the appropriate user and role, we can start reviewing the commands available in the manager application. All of the commands to the manager take this form:

```
http://hostname[:port]/manager/command[?parameter-list]
```

Listing Installed Web Applications

To list all Web applications currently installed, type the following URL at the local browser:

```
http://localhost:8080/manager/list
```

The first time you access the manager application, you will be asked to authenticate. Use the username and password you created in tomcat-users.xml (or by other means if you used another technique from the previous chapter to configure the security realm).

If everything is configured correctly, you should see a response listing all the installed contexts, each indicating the path under which it is configured; followed by a colon and the current state of the context, followed by another colon and the current number of active sessions connected to the indicated context. If you're running Tomcat 4.1, this will be followed by another colon and the local path to each Webapp relative to the location of the manager application. The root context is the last line here, specified by the path "/". Figure 9.1 shows a typical output from http://localhost:8080/manager/list.

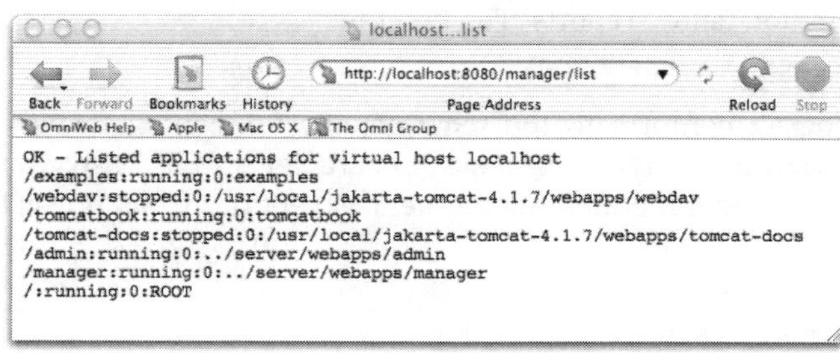

Figure 9.1 Typical output from http://localhost:8080/manager/list.

Starting and Stopping a Web Application

You can use the manager application to control whether a given context is running. To illustrate, let's use the manager to turn off the examples Webapp.

To stop the examples Webapp, load the following URL in your browser:

```
http://localhost:8080/manager/stop?path=/examples
```

The server will respond with:

```
OK - Stopped application at context path /examples
```

Now, if you list the applications again, you should see something like this:

```
OK - Listed applications for virtual host localhost
/examples:stopped:0
/webdav:running:0
/tomcat-docs:running:0
/manager:running:0
/:running:0
```

More important, if you now go to http://localhost:8080/examples, you will get a 404 error because the context has, for all intents and purposes, ceased to exist.

To bring back the context, simply load the following URL in your browser:

```
http://localhost:8080/manager/start?path=/examples
```

Note that if you made any changes to the Webapp's classes, they will be reloaded when the context starts again.

As we're sure you have worked out, you can start or stop any context by using:

```
http://localhost:8080/manager/start?path=context-path
```

or

```
http://localhost:8080/manager/stop?path=context-path
```

where *context-path* represents the path specified in the given context node and listed by the list command in the manager application.

There isn't too much that can go wrong when starting and stopping existing contexts. Usually, exceptions relate to simple pilot error: forgetting or misspelling the context, stopping or starting contexts that are already stopped or started, and things of that nature. Let's look at some common failure reports. The first one:

```
FAIL - Invalid context path was specified
```

means the path specified doesn't conform to the requirements for context names. Remember that the context path must start with a slash character. In this case, you probably mistyped the path. Follow directions for the next exception if this doesn't clear things up.

If you see this:

```
FAIL - No context exists for path /foo
```

it means the context name you specified does not exist on this server. Make sure you spelled the path correctly and didn't introduce any spaces or other extraneous characters. Use the list command (/manager/list) to get a list of valid paths for this server.

If you see this:

```
FAIL - No context path was specified
```

it means you forgot to specify the path parameter. Again, you probably mistyped the path. Perhaps you misspelled "path," or introduced an extraneous character.

One last word of caution: Don't stop the manager application and expect to be able to restart it. After all, if you stop it, you won't be able to use it to issue the commands to start it up again.

Reloading a Web Application

The reload function allows you to reload a context after you've made changes to it. While by default Tomcat will reload an application when it detects that the underlying libraries have changed, there are a few circumstances in which this may not be adequate.

The first, and most obvious, case is where automatic reloading is turned off. Perhaps the server in question is a production server and you don't want the overhead of automatically reloading code, or you want to manually control when reloads take place. In this case, you can use the manager application to reload the app once all your changes have been made.

A less-obvious case is one in which the changes are not to libraries contained in the Webapp itself, but rather changes made when you updated libraries stored in <*$CATALINA_HOME*>/common/. This may be the case when you update a JDBC driver, for instance.

There are a few other cases where a reload may not occur, or may not occur with the results you expect. If these occur, or you want to prevent them from occurring, you can restart the context manually by way of the manager application. You can also restart every context by stopping Tomcat and then restarting it, but this has the disadvantage of introducing some downtime for your users.

To reload a context, load the following URL:

```
http://localhost:8080/manager/reload?path=context-path
```

The server will respond with a message that the context path has been loaded, or indicate if there was a problem. The problems you will encounter here are similar to those outlined in the previous section, with similar resolutions.

Displaying Statistics

The Session statistics show information about the timeout for sessions, and details how many sessions are active in each time range. To display this information, type the following in the local browser:

```
http://localhost:8080/manager/sessions?path=/examples
```

You should see a result something like this:

```
OK - Session information for application at context path /examples
Default maximum session inactive interval 30 minutes
30 - <40 minutes:1 sessions
```

If not, the server will indicate if there was a problem. Again, the problems you will encounter here are similar to those outlined previously, with similar resolutions.

Installing a Web Application

You can also use the manager application to install new contexts at runtime, either from the local filesystem or over the network.

To install a Web application that is already uncompressed on the local hard drive, you need to specify the name of the context you want to create and the path to the directory containing the Webapp:

```
http://localhost:8080/manager/install?path=context-
path&war=file:/path/to/base/directory
```

Similarly, you can install a Webapp from a Web Archive (WAR) file by specifying the full pathname to the WAR file containing the Webapp. Note that since the URL is a JAR-based URL, you need to include the path to the root of the virtual filesystem included in the JAR, following an exclamation point, which is used to delimit the real file path from the virtual file path. WAR files always contain their WEB-INF directories at the root of the virtual filesystem, so this path will always be "!/", as shown here:

```
http://localhost:8080/manager/install?path=context-
path&war=jar:file:/path/to/war/file!/
```

You load a WAR file over the network in the same way. All that differs is the URL you use to specify the location of that file. The syntax, then, is as follows:

```
http://localhost:8080/manager/install?path=context-path&war=jar:url-
of-war-file!/
```

For example, if you want to load a Webapp called *myapp* into the context /myapp from a WAR file found at http://www.mycompany.com/warfiles/myapp.war, you load it using the following URL:

```
http://localhost:8080/manager/install?path=/myapp&war=jar:http://
www.mycompany.com/myapp.war!/
```

Assuming that the installation worked as expected, you will receive an acknowledgement similar to this:

```
OK - Installed application at context path /myapp
```

However, what this command does is potentially a little more error-prone than the other commands, so let's take a moment to go over some of the exceptions that may occur. The four main classes of problems are:

- Conflicts with pre-existing context names
- Incorrect paths and URLs
- URLs referencing directories that are inaccessible to the user under which Tomcat is running
- Improperly structured Web applications and WAR files

As we saw earlier, if Tomcat fails in completing a command, it will report the failure by sending back an appropriate message. Let's look at the most common failures for the install command. First:

```
FAIL - Application already exists at path /foo
```

means the context name you chose is already in use. Context names must be unique on a given host. Either choose a different context path for this application, or undeploy the existing Web application currently using this context path first and then reattempt the deployment of the new application.

If you see this:

```
FAIL - Document base does not exist or is not a readable directory
```

it means the WAR attribute you specified is not readable or does not contain a valid Web application. To fix this problem, confirm that the path is in fact correct. Then confirm that the directory, and all the parent directories, are readable by the user under whose permissions Tomcat is running. Finally, confirm that the directory is in fact structured correctly as a Web application. (See Chapter 6, "Configuring Web Applications," for more details.) If you aren't sure that the Webapp is structured correctly, try installing it manually. You can do this by placing it in the webapps directory (or another directory that you have configured to contain Webapps) and restarting the server.

If you see:

```
FAIL - Encountered exception
```

it means that something *bad* happened. You can usually determine what that is by looking at the logs. If the logs don't contain enough information, consider increasing the log level for the host in question.

Often, this exception is the result of the Webapp being incorrectly configured in some way. Perhaps the deployment descriptor is incorrectly structured, or some class dependency failed. (Did you remember to install any library files your application relies on, either in the /WEB-INF/lib directory of the Webapp or in the /common/lib directory of the server?) The range of possible causes is quite large. If these suggestions don't help, check your work, view the logs, and make sure that the Webapp can be installed manually.

If you see this exception:

```
FAIL - Invalid application URL was specified
```

it means that the URL you specified does not conform to structural requirements. The protocol may not match what was expected. If you specified a WAR file, check to ensure that you included the "!/" at the end. Also, does the URL start with jar:file: or jar:http:? If you specified an unpacked Webapp, does the URL start with file:?

If you see this:

```
FAIL - Invalid context path was specified
```

it means the path you specified isn't a legal context name. Remember that the context path must start with a slash character.

Finally, if you see this exception:

```
FAIL - No context path was specified
```

you forgot to specify the path parameter. Did you perhaps misspell "path," or include a space that you shouldn't have?

Removing a Web Application

If you want to permanently remove a context, you can do so by using the remove command. The command stops the context, and then removes it and any directories that were created for it. It has the following syntax:

```
http://localhost:8080/manager/remove?path=context-path
```

Be careful with this one—it can be quite destructive. Make sure you specify the right path, and don't remove the manager application and expect to be able to restore it without a bit of manual configuration work.

If you do encounter any exceptions here, the resolutions are similar to those outlined in the previous section.

The HTML Interface in Tomcat 4.1

As we mentioned at the beginning of this chapter, Tomcat 4.1 adds a new, HTML-based interface that allows you to more easily manage applications through a browser. You can access this interface, shown in Figure 9.2, at http://localhost:8080/manager/html/list.

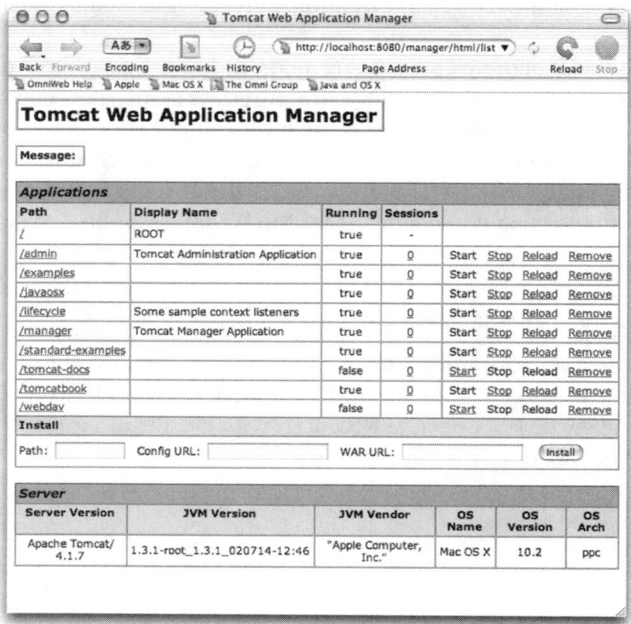

Figure 9.2 The HTML interface in Tomcat 4.1.

The functionality is the same as that you've seen in this chapter, so it should be easy for you to apply the information you've learned here to operate the 4.1 HTML interface. You just don't have to remember how to construct the URLs. This is particularly a plus when it comes to deploying new Webapps because getting the URLs right is sometimes not the easiest thing. You simply enter the path, the context path, and the URL for the WAR file into the appropriate boxes; and click the Install button.

The Ant Interface in Tomcat 4.1

There is also new Ant support in 4.1 that takes the form of an optional task library. You can find the appropriate JAR file in <*$CATALINA_HOME*>/server/lib/catalina-ant.jar (see Chapter 20, "Developing Web Applications with Ant and XDoclet," for more information). If you want to use it in your Ant build files, you need to copy catalina-ant.jar to your ant /lib directory (typically /usr/local/ant/lib) and add the appropriate <taskdef/>

nodes to your build.xml file for the tasks you want to use. You'll insert something like the code shown in Listing 9.2 in your build.xml file. Then, you can use the tasks in your build targets to execute the matching commands in the manager application.

```
<taskdef name="deploy"    classname="org.apache.catalina.ant.
DeployTask"/>
  <taskdef name="install"   classname="org.apache.catalina.ant.
InstallTask"/>
  <taskdef name="list"      classname="org.apache.catalina.ant.
ListTask"/>
  <taskdef name="reload"    classname="org.apache.catalina.ant.
ReloadTask"/>
  <taskdef name="remove"    classname="org.apache.catalina.ant.
RemoveTask"/>
  <taskdef name="resources" classname="org.apache.catalina.ant.
ResourcesTask"/>
  <taskdef name="roles"     classname="org.apache.catalina.ant.
RolesTask"/>
  <taskdef name="start"     classname="org.apache.catalina.ant.
StartTask"/>
  <taskdef name="stop"      classname="org.apache.catalina.ant.
StopTask"/>
  <taskdef name="undeploy"  classname="org.apache.catalina.ant.
UndeployTask"/>
```

Listing 9.2 The <taskdef/> nodes for loading the Tomcat Ant tasks.

Generally, these tasks take the form of:

```
<command url="http://localhost:8080/manager"
     username="<login>"
     password="<password>"
     path="<the context path>"/>
```

For example:

```
<reload url="http://localhost:8080/manager"
     username="admin"
     password="badpassword"
     path="/examples"/>
```

If you use Ant (and you should!), using these tasks can greatly simplify your write–compile–deploy–test cycle, since compile and deploy can effectively be reduced to a single step: typing "ant" at the command line. Note also that you don't have to include your login or password in the build.xml file. You can simply define a new property at runtime with the -D option, and then reference it as you would any other Ant property: ant -Dusername=*mylogin* -Dpassword=*goodpassword*.

Summary

In this chapter, we examined the manager application, which is used to manage and deploy contexts on the server. We also looked at two of the great new features in the upcoming Tomcat 4.1 release.

Remember to consider the security implications before enabling the manager application, particularly since Tomcat will allow anyone with access to the application to install arbitrary WAR files over the Internet. Be sure to look for new expanded features and better usability in upcoming releases.

Starting with Chapter 10, "Model-View-Controller Architecuture," we'll shift our focus to development-oriented topics. Chapter 10 gives you a concise overview of the MVC development pattern, which we'll be using extensively in Chapters 11-14.

CHAPTER

10

The Model-View-Controller Architecture

The Model-View-Controller (MVC) architecture helps promote a clean separation of business logic from display logic. It's a simplifying abstraction that resolves several problems that make developing complex dynamic Web applications difficult. The overarching design principle is that the objects containing the logical representation of the data should be separate from the objects manipulating that data, and that both should be separate from the display components responsible for presenting those components to the user. This abstraction makes each component simple and, at the same time, reusable. In this chapter, we see how to model problems using this paradigm, and describe some of the benefits this technique provides.

What Is MVC Architecture?

The purpose of MVC is to free the core business logic of an application from the display logic. It separates an application into three sections: a Model, Views, and a Controller. MVC is not a new design paradigm; it dates back at least to the early days of Smalltalk 80. The principles of MVC saw early expression at the Xerox Palo Alto Research Center in the Alto operating system, which was subsequently cloned by the team at Apple to create the original Mac OS, and then again by the folks at Microsoft when they developed Windows. Most of the user interface (UI) objects in Smalltalk 80 used this paradigm to enforce a clean separation between Model and View, and to allow extensive reuse and modification of UI classes and model classes, independently of each other.

Model Objects

Using object-oriented programming techniques, we can create whole class structures that model real-world problems. We break down complex systems first into Model components, each representing some data-containing element of our system. Each model class is typically named so that it relates to real-world objects within the problem domain so that there is a close correlation between the real world and the Model. Typical model classnames might be Invoice, Customer, or Order. Each would contain data members to describe the data we need to associate with the real-world object—for instance, let's say that our Invoice may contain references to zero or more Order instances, and a Customer may have references to zero or more Invoice objects, as shown in Figure 10.1.

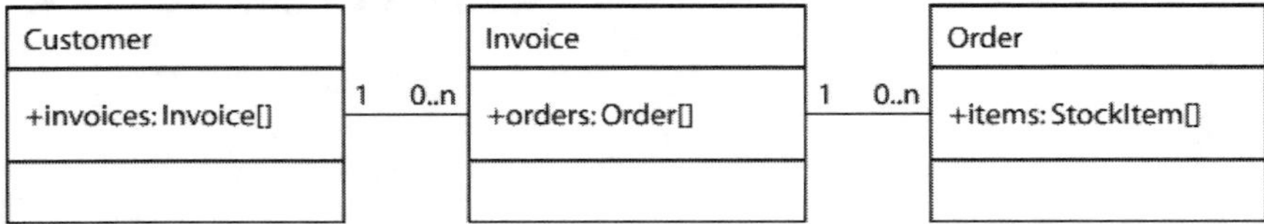

Figure 10.1 Example Model object relationships.

Without abstracting out separate Model objects, you might be tempted to spread code relating to Invoices through several classes, perhaps creating code to do almost the same thing in different classes. Modeling your data in conceptually simple Model objects—particularly ones with clear real-world counterparts—makes your code conceptually simple, with the result that your code will be easier to understand and implement, and unintended consequences can more readily be avoided. Also, by keeping all of the data associated with a conceptual object, we make it easy to control the integrity of the object and ensure the validity of the data it contains.

View Objects

An application can't be all Model; it must be able to communicate with the outside world. The first thing we want to do is to let the user see what's in the object. We do this by implementing a View object. In a stand-alone application, we might do this with a Swing component, such as a JList or a JTree. On the server side, we might implement a View component to render this object as HTML, perhaps another to render it as XML, and another to render it as WML. The power of this abstraction is that we can keep our data model very simple and attach the appropriate View object to it when we want to render it out. And we can even attach different Views to the same Model object, and because the Model object always contains the canonical data representation, the Views stay in sync automatically.

Communication between Controller and View

The way the Views stay in sync with the Model is through event notification. The Model fires an event when a property changes, and the View, which has previously registered interest in the event, updates itself, querying the Model for state information. This event-notification model is the same as that found in the AWT 1.1 event model, the JavaBeans event model, and the Swing event model. When the View is first attached to the Model, it registers itself as an event listener, and the Model then notifies its listeners whenever there is a state change.

Controller Objects

The Controller objects are responsible for causing state changes in the Model, whether it be as a result of user input or other events. They are responsible for handling user input—for example, a button click in the UI and the translation of that input into an action on the data. The Controllers are where business rules are implemented, and in general, this is where the action takes place in a given application. There are methods on the View and Model objects, but they are primarily there to handle basic plumbing, such as the event notifications mentioned earlier.

Advantages of MVC

The MVC architecture has several key advantages, including clean code design, the encapsulation of data and functions within well-defined classes, and a code base that is easier to refactor and reuse. Let's take a look at each advantage.

Clean Design

Clean design means easy-to-understand, maintainable code. By segmenting the objects along the MVC lines, we ensure that each individual object is much simpler, and it is much more obvious to the developer and subsequent maintainers how the objects in the system are supposed to interact.

When writing small applications, you can get away with even complete spaghetti code. It's when those small applications grow without a framework that you start to run into problems. The MVC approach encourages good design of your applications from the very start. By keeping to a clean, clear design and framework, you can avoid the "big ball of mud" syndrome so common in software development.

Encapsulation

Java itself encourages encapsulation of data, and functions within well-defined classes. MVC takes this one step further by enforcing encapsulation of the data model, keeping it separate from the UI. This isolation allows changes in the models and application logic to be isolated from changes in the UI, and vice versa. For example, different clients can be written by attaching different View objects to the same Model. The business logic is also kept isolated from the data model and from the UI, so if business rules change, the changes can be implemented in many cases without having to modify the Models or the Views.

Extensibility

Having a separate Model means that various UIs can be developed for the same Model. For example, an online store may have a Web interface for the Internet customers and a Java application for staff to administer the store. While the interface code would be dramatically different between the two applications, the Model code would be shared.

Reuse and Refactoring

Clean code also encourages coding efficiency and smart code reuse. When there is one and only one object responsible for a given duty, it is more obvious when duties are being handled in the wrong place. With MVC, there is a natural tendency to reduce duplication of code between modules because it is obvious where the code is supposed to be. That way, confusion about how to handle a given manipulation of the data is less likely to arise.

A few months ago, Peter had to rework an ASP application into JSP. There were about 50 pages with ASP script embedded in them. It looked like it was going to be a nightmare; however, on further analysis it turned out that 90 percent of the code had been duplicated between the pages. One specific piece of code (which checks that the user has logged on, and redirects the user if they haven't) was repeated on virtually every page! Once Peter had converted this application to use JSP and servlets, the method was called in only one place to check the user's logon. One call to one method replaced over 50 separate copies of the same code.

As you can see, one of the main points of MVC architecture is to encourage good design, reuse, and refactoring from the earliest phases, rather than letting bad design run rampant.

Using MVC on the Web

MVC was originally developed for use in some of the earliest graphical user interfaces. With this in mind, you may be wondering how all of this is applicable to you as a developer of Web applications. Quite simply, separating Model from View is something equally applicable to a Web-based UI as it is to a graphical UI running in the same process as the Model objects it renders. In fact, in Web-based applications, there is a greater likelihood that the same Model components will be referenced by multiple View objects. Let's look at a simple example: a contact list.

There will be two Model objects for our simple contact list. One, a Contact object, encapsulates the information we want to keep for a given contact: name, address, phone number, and email address. The other, a ContactGroup, contains a set of contacts. (In a real application, you'd probably want to break the Contact object down further to contain separate Model objects for addresses, phone numbers, and email addresses, but our oversimplified example will get the idea across just as well.)

We provide two different front ends to our contact list, one HTML-based and the other applet-based. Each of these front ends will have three separate Views: one for displaying a contact, one for editing a contact, and one for displaying the whole list of contacts. We want each of these Views to stay in sync when the underlying data changes, and we don't want to try to keep multiple copies of the data. That's really just asking for trouble when you're attempting to keep a canonical representation straight. Instead, because we're following the MVC development paradigm, we'll let our Model objects contain the canonical representation of the data and have our View objects request that data when they want to display themselves. When the Model changes, we'll have it send a notification to all attached view objects so they know they need to redraw themselves.

In the case of our applet front end, this means messaging the View components. We can handle this either by keeping an active connection open from the applet to the server, or by having the applet poll the server for Model-changed events. Both mechanisms are quite straightforward. In the case of the HTML front end, the situation is slightly complicated by the fact that HTML pages are not typically refreshed once they are served. Here again, we can have the Web page poll the server (by using a meta refresh header, for instance, or by using a bit of JavaScript or dynamic HTML). This again works out to be relatively simple: if there is a state change, we simply reload the data by reloading the whole page and letting the servlet or JSP responsible for view generation get the current data from the Model object. (Our servlet or JSP is implicitly a View object. The key notion to bring into development of the servlet or JSP is that it should be a client of some Model object and request the appropriate data from that object, rather than assembling the data for presentation on an ad hoc basis or through extensive custom code.)

In this example, we also have a Controller object, which is responsible for updating the Model (and controlling access to the Model) when a user edits the data through the edit view. The Controller object will be responsible for validating that the user has permission to update the object, and will also be responsible for manipulating the values on the Model object and causing the Model object to be saved to persistent storage if necessary.

Since even our simple application has six different Views connected to the same Model objects, we're already starting to see some of the benefits of this separation. Because the Model contains the canonical representation of the data for each object, we don't have to worry about sync issues. Whatever data is stored in the Model object is the correct state of the object. When that state is updated, we notify all View objects referencing the Model object that they need to be redrawn, and they are dutifully updated. Of course, on a multiuser system there is the possibility for a race condition to occur if someone attempts to write to the object in the interval between a previous write and the completion of the subsequent View updates, so we need to evaluate what the right thing to do is in such an instance.

Our Controller object should be responsible for enforcing whatever policy we choose. It could check to see that the View knew about the most current state and, if not, notify the user that the object state had changed, and verify that the second update is still desired. Or if object locking is not a priority, it could simply allow the write. It all depends on how critical concurrency management is for your particular application. In any case, by using MVC we have reduced the complexity of handling this race condition by putting state in a single object and control over manipulating the state in another single object. This is a lot simpler to manage than having to query a set of combined

Model/View objects to find out which has the most current state and verifying cache consistency at every step.

We hope this simple example has helped to make the concepts a bit more concrete for you. We'll be looking at a lot more examples of the MVC development paradigm in the coming chapters, and we'll put the concepts in this short overview to work in a number of ways.

Summary

In this chapter, we've given you a brief overview of the design principles behind the Model-View-Controller architecture. We've discussed how to separate an application into Model, View, and Controller components, and the value of doing this. Over the next few chapters, we examine various development paradigms that leverage MVC to a varying extent. This background should give you an understanding of the design goals and implementation choices made in the various systems, and help you make smarter choices about how to approach the design of your own applications.

CHAPTER

11

JavaServer Pages

JavaServer Pages enable you to add server-side Java code directly into your HTML pages. In this chapter, we discuss writing JSP pages, and we show you how to move your business logic into external classes rather than including it inside the JSP files.

Tomcat takes your JSP files, compiles them into servlets when first requested, and then executes the code in the compiled servlets. In previous chapters, HTML had to be manually entered into println statements. If you used this approach in a text-heavy production system, maintaining the pages would become a nightmare. Every time you had to make a change to the HTML, you'd have to manually change the Java code. As a result, using HTML editor tools to maintain the pages would be impossible.

JSP comes to the rescue, allowing HTML coders to develop the look and feel of Web pages while the Java code takes care of implementing business logic. JSP is one way of making servlet development much easier.

What Does a JSP Page Look Like?

JSP looks exactly like HTML, except for the special tags that give instructions to the JSP compiler. The first time a JSP file is requested, the file is compiled into a servlet. The JSP-derived servlet is then loaded and run like any other servlet.

Listing 11.1 shows two kinds of tags that can be included in JSP files. The <% and %> tags indicate where Java code is being included. To start coding in Java, simply insert a <% tag into your code and add a %> tag at the end of your Java.

The second type of tag is the same, except that the opening tag includes an equals sign. The <%= tag means that the value returned by the expression in this tag should be converted to text for display. In our example, integer values of variables are automatically converted to text in the HTML.

```
<html>
<head>
<title>Adding Numbers</title></head>
<body>

<%
int a = 5;
int b = 10;
%>

<h1>Number Adding Example</h1>

<p>
<%= a %> + <%= b %> = <%= a+b %>
</p>

</body>
</html>
```

Listing 11.1 numberadd.jsp.

Save numberadd.jsp in the <*$CATALINA_HOME*>/webapps/tomcatbook directory and access the page via your browser with the following URL:

`http://localhost:8080/tomcatbook/numberadd.jsp`

Depending on how fast your machine is, it may take a few seconds to go through the process of turning the JSP file into a servlet and then compiling the first time you load it. Figure 11.1 shows the result.

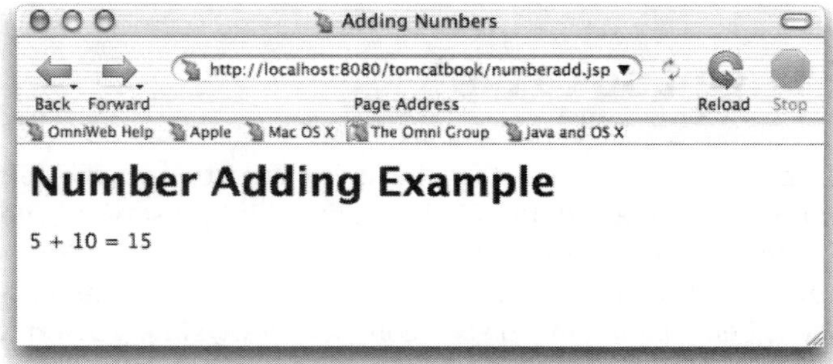

Figure 11.1 numberadd.jsp in a browser.

The HTML served back to the user is indistinguishable from any other HTML, since the JSP tags are all processed on the server. Listing 11.2 contains the HTML that was generated by our JSP.

```
<html>
<head>
<title>Adding Numbers</title></head>
<body>



<h1>Number Adding Example</h1>

<p>
5 + 10 = 15
</p>

</body>
</html>
```

Listing 11.2 The HTML source generated by numberadd.jsp.

In practice, the HTML generated from JSP pages often has a lot of extra whitespace in it. That's because page developers often include hard returns between their JSP tags. Like other JSP engines, Tomcat's Jasper parser faithfully reproduces those hard returns in the page output, just like all other content not enclosed in JSP tags. If you want to avoid this, you can always run your JSP tags together. Whitespace inside JSP tags is included as whitespace in the source code, but extra whitespace in Java source code doesn't affect the class file that's generated, and so does not get passed back in the response.

JSPs Are Really Servlets

So how does all this work? What happens at runtime when a JSP page is requested? The first time a JSP page is requested, the Jasper compiler (which we cover later in this chapter) translates the JSP source file you wrote into Java source code. This source code is then compiled into a servlet, and that compiled servlet is what actually handles the request. Subsequent requests skip this compilation process (unless the JSP source file changes), making subsequent request handling very efficient.

Tomcat handles this by checking the modification date on the JSP file each time the page is requested; if the JSP page changes, Tomcat recompiles it automatically. This facilitates page maintenance without sacrificing efficient request handling—the page content is almost always generated by compiled, in-memory code.

And what does the generated servlet look like? Listing 11.3 shows the actual source code generated by Jasper for the numberadd.jsp file we saw in Listing 11.1.

```
package org.apache.jsp;

import javax.servlet.*;
import javax.servlet.http.*;
import javax.servlet.jsp.*;
import org.apache.jasper.runtime.*;

public class numberadd$jsp extends HttpJspBase {


  private static java.util.Vector _jspx_includes;

  public java.util.List getIncludes() {
    return _jspx_includes;
  }

  public void _jspService(HttpServletRequest request, HttpServletResponse response)
        throws java.io.IOException, ServletException {

    JspFactory _jspxFactory = null;
    javax.servlet.jsp.PageContext pageContext = null;
    HttpSession session = null;
    ServletContext application = null;
    ServletConfig config = null;
    JspWriter out = null;
    Object page = this;
    JspWriter _jspx_out = null;


    try {
      _jspxFactory = JspFactory.getDefaultFactory();
      response.setContentType("text/html;ISO-8859-1");
      pageContext = _jspxFactory.getPageContext(
        this, request, response,
            null, true, 8192, true
      );
      application = pageContext.getServletContext();
      config = pageContext.getServletConfig();
      session = pageContext.getSession();
      out = pageContext.getOut();
      _jspx_out = out;
```

Listing 11.3 The source generated for numberadd.jsp. (continues)

```
      out.write("<html>\n");
      out.write("<head>\n");
      out.write("<title>Adding Numbers");
      out.write("</title>");
      out.write("</head>\n");
      out.write("<body>\n\n");

   int a = 5;
   int b = 10;
      out.write("\n\n");
      out.write("<h1>Number Adding Example");
      out.write("</h1>\n\n");
      out.write("<p>\n");
      out.print( a );
      out.write(" + ");
      out.print( b );
      out.write(" = ");
      out.print( a+b );
      out.write("\n");
      out.write("</p>\n\n");
      out.write("</body>\n");
      out.write("</html>\n\n");
    } catch (Throwable t) {
      out = _jspx_out;
      if (out != null && out.getBufferSize() != 0)
        out.clearBuffer();
      if (pageContext != null) pageContext.handlePageException(t);
    } finally {
      if (_jspxFactory != null) _jspxFactory.releasePageContext(pageContext);
    }
  }
}
```

Listing 11.3 The source generated for numberadd.jsp. (continued)

We've highlighted in bold the code snippets taken from the JSP tags in Listing 11.1 so that you can see exactly how those snippets are rendered in the generated code. It all looks remarkably similar to a servlet you might write yourself. That's important when it comes time to debug JSPs because it's at that point that you need to start looking at the generated source code to understand what's happening.

Tomcat writes these source files, and the class files generated from them, into the work directory. The work directory is further divided into subdirectories with names based on the context hierarchy you establish through your server.xml and deployment descriptors. You can find Listing 11.3 in <*$CATALINA_HOME*>/work/Standalone/localhost/tomcatbook/numberadd$jsp.java. Different versions of Jasper have slightly different naming conventions, so filenames on your system may differ slightly. They should be fairly intuitive, though, so browsing around under the work directory should give you a good feel for what gets generated where. We talk more about debugging JSPs later in this chapter.

There are some constructs in JSP that may not be immediately intuitive, even though the behavior falls out of the relatively simple rules for JSP compilation. We think the interaction between loops and the HTML contained in them is one of these cases. Just to make this all a little clearer, let's look at another example; Listing 11.4 demonstrates how we'd create a few rows in a table.

```
<html>
<head>
<title>Loop Example</title></head>
<body>



<h1>A Simple Loop</h1>

<table>
<tr bgcolor="#cccccc">
<th>Factors</th>
<th>Product</th>
</tr>

<%

String rowcolor;
boolean oddRow = true;

for (int a = 1; a <= 4; a++)
{
   for (int b = a; b <= 4; b++)
   {
      if (oddRow) rowcolor = "#eeeeee";
      else rowcolor = "#dddddd";
      oddRow = ! oddRow;

%>
<tr bgcolor="<%= rowcolor %>">
<td><%= a %> x <%= b %></td>
<td><%= a * b %></td>
</tr>
```

Listing 11.4 loopexample.jsp. (continues)

```
<%
    }
}

%>

</table>

</body>
</html>
```

Listing 11.4 loopexample.jsp. (continued)

We've set up our JSP to iterate through two nested loops, each incrementing one of the two variables, *a* and *b*, which represent the factors we'd like to show in our table. The goal is to generate what was my elementary school teachers referred to as a times table. (In this case, we show the products that result from multiplying all of the values from 1 to 4.)

To make the table easy to read, we also employ a simple trick to alternate the background color of each row. We simply use a boolean to keep track of whether we're on an odd- or an even-numbered row, and set the *rowcolor* variable to the desired background color, represented as an HTML hexadecimal RGB value.

When we install this JSP in our tomcatbook webapp (by copying the file to <*$CATALINA_HOME*>/webapps/tomcatbook/) and load it (from the URL http://localhost:8080/tomcatbook/loopexample.jsp), we see a page that looks like the one shown in Figure 11.2.

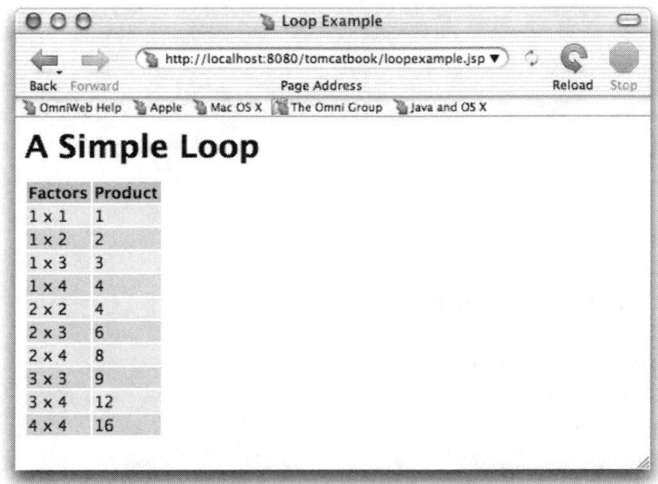

Figure 11.2 loopexample.jsp in a browser.

Note how the formatting inside the inner loop was reapplied for each iteration through the loop. This may be obvious to some readers, but we've found that it confuses a lot of people. Remember, the JSP is basically translated line by line into a piece of servlet source code. The servlet source code generated for this JSP appears in Listing 11.5.

```
package org.apache.jsp;

import javax.servlet.*;
import javax.servlet.http.*;
import javax.servlet.jsp.*;
import org.apache.jasper.runtime.*;

public class loopexample$jsp extends HttpJspBase {


  private static java.util.Vector _jspx_includes;

  public java.util.List getIncludes() {
    return _jspx_includes;
  }

  public void _jspService(HttpServletRequest request, HttpServletResponse response)
      throws java.io.IOException, ServletException {

    JspFactory _jspxFactory = null;
    javax.servlet.jsp.PageContext pageContext = null;
    HttpSession session = null;
    ServletContext application = null;
    ServletConfig config = null;
    JspWriter out = null;
    Object page = this;
    JspWriter _jspx_out = null;


    try {
      _jspxFactory = JspFactory.getDefaultFactory();
      response.setContentType("text/html;ISO-8859-1");
      pageContext = _jspxFactory.getPageContext(this, request, response,
                  null, true, 8192, true);
      application = pageContext.getServletContext();
      config = pageContext.getServletConfig();
      session = pageContext.getSession();
      out = pageContext.getOut();
```

Listing 11.5 loopexample$jsp.java. (continues)

```
    _jspx_out = out;

    out.write("<html>\n");
    out.write("<head>\n");
    out.write("<title>Loop Example");
    out.write("</title>");
    out.write("</head>\n");
    out.write("<body>\n\n\n\n");
    out.write("<h1>A Simple Loop");
    out.write("</h1>\n\n");
    out.write("<table>\n");
    out.write("<tr bgcolor=\"#cccccc\">\n");
    out.write("<th>Factors");
    out.write("</th>\n");
    out.write("<th>Product");
    out.write("</th>\n");
    out.write("</tr>\n\n");


String rowcolor;
boolean oddRow = true;

for (int a = 1; a <= 4; a++)
{
  for (int b = a; b <= 4; b++)
  {
    if (oddRow) rowcolor = "#eeeeee";
    else rowcolor = "#dddddd";
    oddRow = ! oddRow;

   out.write("\n");
   out.write("<tr bgcolor=\"");
   out.print( rowcolor );
   out.write("\">\n");
   out.write("<td>");
   out.print( a );
   out.write(" x ");
   out.print( b );
   out.write("</td>\n");
   out.write("<td>");
   out.print( a * b );
   out.write("</td>\n");
   out.write("</tr>\n\n");
```

Listing 11.5 loopexample$jsp.java. (continues)

```
      }
    }

        out.write("\n\n");
        out.write("</table>\n\n");
        out.write("</body>\n");
        out.write("</html>\n");
      } catch (Throwable t) {
        out = _jspx_out;
        if (out != null && out.getBufferSize() != 0)
          out.clearBuffer();
        if (pageContext != null) pageContext.handlePageException(t);
      } finally {
        if (_jspxFactory != null) _jspxFactory.releasePageContext(pageContext);
      }
    }
  }
```

Listing 11.5 loopexample$jsp.java. (continued)

Note how the HTML embedded in the middle of the two for loops is translated into Java. There is really no surprise here, but how Jasper would render these loops is not necessarily immediately obvious.

Jasper: The Tomcat JSP Compiler

We've mentioned Jasper a couple of times, so we thought it only fair to give you a little more background. Jasper is the JSP framework inside Tomcat. (This is analogous to Catalina's role as the core servlet engine.) The main components are:

- The Generator, which generates source code like that we saw earlier
- The Compiler
- An array of runtime support classes
- Tools used by the Generator to handle the linking in of such things as tag libraries, which we learn about in the next chapter

As a developer, you will most likely never have to deal too directly with Jasper, but you'll hear it mentioned quite often. And if you're tracking down some pernicious bug, you may have cause to venture into the Jasper source code to see exactly what's happening. We hope this brief overview gives you some context for that exploration.

One of the big improvements in Tomcat 4.1 is a rewrite of Jasper. This has resulted in massive performance improvements, particularly in applications making extensive use of custom tags (which we discuss in the next chapter, "Tag Libraries") and by extension, applications using Struts (which we cover in Chapter 13, "MVC with Struts"). Informal testing shows an eight- to tenfold increase in some applications, including the HTML front-end to the manager Webapp (see Chapter 9, "The Manager Application") and the Administration Tool, both new in 4.1.

Another improvement reduces the impact of a Java limitation. The jspService() method of some JSPs can grow quite large, since they translate HTML into the body of a single method call. The Java Virtual Machine specification does not allow for a single method to be larger than 64K, so this can become an issue, particularly when the number of custom tags in a single page gets up into the low hundreds. The new version of Jasper is smarter about how it handles this situation, so you should run into this limitation less frequently under Tomcat 4.1.

Expressions

Expressions are used to insert values directly into HTML. For example, we used them in Listing 11.1 to display integer values. Expressions are converted automatically to text, so there is no need to convert integers or other types to text manually. The syntax for an expression is very simple:

```
<%= expression %>
```

In order to simplify expressions, you can use predefined variables in your expressions: request for the HttpServletRequest, response for the HttpServletResponse, session for the HttpSession, and out for the PrintWriter used to send the response to the client. Here is an example of how to display the remote hostname of the client making a request:

```
<%= request.getRemoteHost() %>
```

Scriptlets and Declarations

Scriptlets and declarations are very similar to each other in that they both allow you to insert Java code directly into the compiled servlet. They differ, though, in where you place the code. Scriptlets are sections of code that are included within the service method of the generated servlet. Declarations, on the other hand, include the code in the main body of the servlet class.

Within a scriptlet, you can write any Java you like that would normally be included in a servlet's service method. As with expressions, you have available to you the request, response, session, and out variables, which you can reference in your code. Here is an example of a simple scriptlet that determines whether the request method was a POST; and if so, loads the name parameter:

```
<%
String theName = "";
if( request.getMethod().equals("POST") ) {
  theName = request.getParameter( "name" );
}
%>

<%= theName %>
```

Within a declaration tag, you can write any Java code you would normally include in the body of a servlet class, such as an instance variable or method declarations. You might use a declaration to load parameters or database connection pools into memory. You begin a declaration with a <%! tag. In Listing 11.6, we declare a method that can be called later to establish database access through a connection pool. (We discuss the details of connection pools in Chapter 16, "Databases, Connection Pools, and JDBC.")

```
<%@ page import="javax.sql.*"%>
<%@ page import="javax.naming.*"%>
<%!
private DataSource ds;

public void initdb()
   throws ServletException
{
   try
   {
      Context initCtx = new InitialContext();
      Context envCtx = (Context) initCtx.lookup("java:comp/env");
      ds = (DataSource) envCtx.lookup("jdbc/tomcatbook");
   }
   catch (Exception e)
   {
      throw new ServletException(e.getMessage());
   }
}
%>
```

Listing 11.6 An example of a declaration tag.

Although it is quite possible to write complex Java code directly into JSP, doing so is not usually a good idea. If you have some complex functionality, it is best to remove that Java code from the JSP and then create a separate class that can be called from the JSP. You can call these objects either by instantiating them within a scriptlet and calling their methods, or you can create JavaBeans and use them using some special features of JSP designed to facilitate their use (which we describe later in this chapter).

Removing complex business code from JSP files is important for a number of reasons. It allows the Java coders to be somewhat independent of the HTML coders. Java classes that do the real work can be modified without any changes to JSP files. It also allows the same Java classes to be used in many JSPs.

Page Directives

The page directives in JSP affect the structure of the compiled servlet classes that are generated from your JSP. A page directive has the following syntax:

```
<%@ page attribute="value" %>
```

The import Attribute

The import attribute is used to import other packages into the servlet. A number of packages are automatically included, such as javax.servlet and javax.servlet.http. However, if you want to include other packages, they must be specifically imported. For example, if you want to import the org.devcentre.utils package, you would include the following directive:

```
<%@ page import="org.devcentre.utils.*" %>
```

The contentType Attribute

The default content type of a JSP will be text/html. If you are returning an HTML page, you do not have to include a specific directive to set the content type. If you are returning something other than HTML, however, you have to change the content type by using the contentType directive. For example, if you are returning an XML document rather than an HTML document, use the following directive:

```
<%@ page contentType="text/xml" %>
```

Note that, as this implies, JSPs do not have to return HTML, but can in fact be used to return any kind of data. You can just as easily use JSP to return XML, WML, or some other file format simply by embedding JSP tags into these files, setting the output type to the proper MIME type, and changing the extension of the files to .jsp. You could even go so far as to configure the servlet engine to treat all HTML, XML, or WML files as JSPs, and leave the file extensions as they are.

The threadSafe Attribute

Thread safe means that multiple requests can be handled by the same instance of the servlet. The default is to have this attribute set to true. Therefore, you should set threadSafe to false when you are writing a JSP that contains code that is not thread safe:

```
<%@ page threadSafe="false" %>
```

The session Attribute

The session attribute defaults to true to indicate that the predefined session variable should be bound to an existing session if one is included in the request, and that a new session should be created if no session already exists. If you do not want to make use of sessions, you can turn off the session functionality with the following directive:

```
<%@ page session="false" %>
```

The buffer Attribute

The buffer page directive specifies the size in kilobytes of the output buffer. The original size of the buffer depends on the implementation of the JSP compiler being used. The value must be at least 8 kilobytes. This directive is not normally required in a JSP. Here is an example of how you might set the buffer size to 32 kilobytes:

```
<%@ page buffer="32" %>
```

The autoflush Attribute

This attribute's default value of true indicates that the buffer should be flushed when it becomes full. A value of false indicates that an exception should be thrown when the buffer becomes full. A false value is rarely used.

```
<%@ page autoflush="false" %>
```

The extends Attribute

The extends attribute specifies the class from which the generated servlet will descend from. You will not normally need to change this attribute from its default setting of HttpJspBase. The class you specify in the extends attribute should be a child class of the HttpJspBase class:

```
<%@ page extends="org.devcentre.servlets.MySpecialJspBase" %>
```

The info Attribute

The info attribute allows you to define a single string that describes the servlet:

```
<%@ page info="This servlet eats apple pie for breakfast" %>
```

The errorPage Attribute

The errorPage attribute is used to define a page that will handle any errors that are not caught manually in the servlet. The value supplied is a URL, which can either be a relative URL (as in the following example) or a fully qualified URL including the hostname and path. This attribute has no default value, and so the server will return a plain error page if an error page is not specified. Setting up an appropriate error page with helpful navigation and human-friendly error message handling is an excellent way to improve the user experience at your Web site. You use the errorPage attribute to redirect error output to that page:

```
<%@ page errorPage="error.jsp" %>
```

The isErrorPage Attribute

The isErrorPage attribute specifies whether the JSP page is an error page. The default is false. However, when you are writing an error page, such as error.jsp, you must set the isErrorPage attribute to true:

```
<%@ page isErrorPage="true" %>
```

The language Attribute

The language attribute specifies the programming language used for the JSP file. Currently, there is only one option for this—Java—and so there is no need to change this attribute.

Including Pages

One of the more useful features of JSP is the ability to import other files. Typically, you include headers and footers, login boxes, navigation, and other formatting content that is common between a large number of pages. The contents of the included files are compiled directly into the generated servlet, so there is no runtime penalty other than the negligible added overhead when the JSP is first compiled. The alternative to using this mechanism is to simply copy and paste between documents; however, in terms of maintainability, that approach leaves a lot to be desired. The file to be included is treated the same as the rest of the text of your JSP, just as if the contents of the included JSP were inserted into the main JSP. This means that all expressions, scriptlets, and directives that are in the included files are also processed by the JSP compiler, and everything lives within the same Java source file. Listing 11.7 contains an example of a JSP that includes the header shown in Listing 11.8.

```
<% String title = "Include Example"; %>
<%@ include file="header.jsp" %>

<%
int a = 5;
int b = 10;
%>

<p>
<%= a %> + <%= b %> = <%= a+b %>
</p>

</body>
</html>
```

Listing 11.7 includeexample.jsp.

```
<html>
<head>
<title><%= title %></title></head>
<body>

<h1><%= title %></h1>
```

Listing 11.8 header.jsp.

The include functionality introduces a little wrinkle in the area of dependency checking: Tomcat only checks the modification date of the actual JSP requested to see if it needs recompilation. (The overhead of checking for dependencies on each request would be significantly more than the overhead of checking the single file.) This means that if you change an included file, Tomcat won't notice, and so the servlet won't get recompiled.

Consequently, you must manually force all the pages that refer to the included file to be rebuilt. You can do this by deleting the Java and class files out of the *<$CATALINA_HOME>*/work/ directory, or by changing the modification time of the containing JSP files, either by resaving them or, on Unix platforms, by using the touch command:

```
touch *.jsp
```

An alternative to including a file at compile time is to use the <jsp:include/> tag. Unlike the include functionality discussed earlier, this results in the parent JSP calling into the included JSP at *runtime*. The results are similar to the previous model, but execution is quite different. There are a couple of implications:

- You get a small increase in runtime overhead as the result of the additional servlet being instantiated and of the additional message passing.
- Since the included page is an instance of a different class, you can't readily share instance variables between pages.

In some situations, of course, this separation is exactly what you want; in these cases, you should use <jsp:include/>. The syntax for including a file using this mechanism is quite similar:

```
<jsp:include page="header.jsp" flush="true" />
```

Working with Beans

You can use any Java class from within a JSP simply by using it in the Java you write inside a scriptlet. But JSP also gives you some handy tools to use and reuse JavaBeans within your JSPs without even writing any scriptlet code. This enables you to move your business logic outside your JSPs, and makes it easy for HTML people to maintain JSPs without interfering with the business logic. JavaBeans are simply classes with various get and set methods for controlling properties of the bean; that have a no-argument constructor; and implement the java.io.Serializable marker interface. You can access the get and set methods within JSP to perform various functions without having to embed the Java code in the JSP itself. Listing 11.9 shows how to use beans in a JSP.

```
<%@ page import="com.wiley.tomcatbook.*"%>
<% String title = "Bean Example"; %>
<%@ include file="header.jsp" %>

<jsp:useBean id="mybean" class="ClientBean" />
<jsp:setProperty name="mybean" property="firstname" value="Henry" />
<jsp:setProperty name="mybean" property="lastname" value="Smith" />
<jsp:setProperty name="mybean" property="phone" value="763-7462" />

<p>Client First Name is <jsp:getProperty name="mybean" property=
    "firstname" /></p>
<p>Client Last Name is <jsp:getProperty name="mybean" property=
    "lastname" /></p>
<p>Client Phone is <jsp:getProperty name="mybean" property="phone" />
    </p>

</body>
</html>
```

Listing 11.9 beanexample.jsp.

The first thing you must do is tell the JSP that you want to use the bean. You use the <jsp:useBean/> tag to create an instance of the bean. You have to supply the classname of the bean and an identifier. If the identifier matches an instance that has already been created, the existing instance is used instead of a new instance being created. The bean we're using appears in Listing 11.10.

```
package com.wiley.tomcatbook;

import java.io.*;

public class ClientBean implements Serializable
{
   private String firstName = "";
   private String lastName = "";
   private String phone = "";

   public void setFirstName(String name)
   {
      firstName = name;
   }

   public String getFirstName()
   {
      return firstName;
   }

   public void setLastName(String name)
   {
      lastName = name;
   }

   public String getLastName()
   {
      return lastName;
   }

   public void setPhone(String number)
   {
      phone = number;
   }

   public String getPhone()
   {
      return phone;
   }

}
```

Listing 11.10 ClientBean.java.

Scope

In addition, you can specify a scope for the bean, which affects its visibility to other parts of the system. The four different scopes are page, request, session, and application. Bean scope provides a convenient and logically simple way of managing and sharing state in your Web application:

```
<jsp:useBean id="mybean" class="com.wiley.tomcatbook.Client"
  scope="session"/>
```

Beans with a page scope are visible only on the current page. Beans with a request scope are visible for the current request, which may include other pages. The session scope will keep a bean visible to the current request and to any other requests within the same session. An application scope will make the bean visible to the entire Web application, JSPs and servlets alike. These simple semantics allow you to manage session state quite effortlessly. If you've ever had to develop your own session management tools, you'll appreciate how much time this saves you. Aside from the time savings, because the semantics are so clear and simple it's also much easier to develop higher-quality code. Plus, since all the session state management happens in the servlet engine, it's much cheaper than using session management systems that require roundtrips to the database for each page request.

Once this is complete, you can access the properties of the bean with the jsp:setProperty and jsp:getProperty directives. In both setProperty and getProperty, you must specify the name (which is the id in useBean) and the property.

When using setProperty, you have the option of setting the property to a specific value or setting it to the value of a parameter supplied in the request. The parameters can come from fields filled in by users or passed in the URL:

```
<%-- example of setting property by value --%>
<jsp:setProperty name="mybean" property="firstName" value="Henry" />

<%-- example of setting property by referring to parameter --%>
<jsp:setProperty name="mybean" property="firstName" valueparam="fname"
/>
```

You can even let the JSP do all the work of matching up the parameters with the attributes on your bean:

```
<jsp:setProperty name="mybean" property="*"/>
```

When you use this mechanism, any parameters passed in the request are automatically matched up with properties on the JavaBean with the same name.

Debugging JSPs

JSP debugging is a little more complicated than servlet debugging, simply because the JSP source file goes through a couple of translation steps before it turns into the code that executes on the server. JSPs can fail in a couple of ways. Like servlets, they can fail when they are executing—for example, if some object they try to load is invalid. Unlike servlets, they can also fail if there is a syntax error in the JSP that causes compilation to fail.

In the first case, JSP debugging is a lot like servlet debugging because you'll be working with the generated source file to do your analysis. Debugging information you'll get in error output includes the line numbers from the generated Java source file, not from the JSP itself, so it's important to look at that generated source when you're trying to figure out what went wrong in the execution of a JSP page. If you're using a debugging tool, perhaps in an IDE, you can take this source and compile and run it, just as if it were a servlet you had written yourself. You will need to have the Jasper runtime library, jasper-runtime.jar, in your classpath, however, since the generated servlets extend HttpJspBase and rely on a number of classes in the org.apache.jasper.runtime package. You can find this library in <*$CATALINA_HOME*>/common/lib/.

In the second case, unless your IDE supports direct JSP debugging, you'll have to read the error output as you would normally read compiler output.

In both cases, the error page you receive will start with an HTTP status message, 500, and a massive and somewhat daunting stack trace, as shown in Figure 11.3.

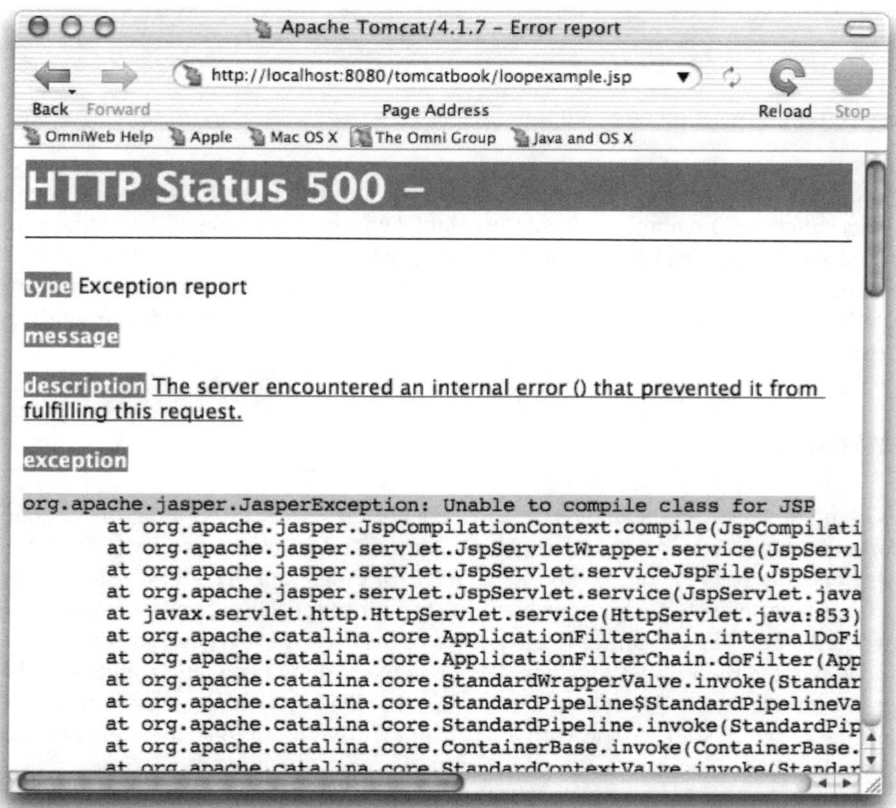

Figure 11.3 Typical JSP error output.

The exception being reported tells you more or less which class this exception falls into, but is otherwise of little interest:

```
org.apache.jasper.JasperException: Unable to compile class for JSP
```

The part you typically need to concern yourself with is at the very end, in the section labeled *root cause*, an example of which is shown in Listing 11.11.

```
root cause

An error occurred at line: 15 in the jsp file: /loopexample.jsp

Generated servlet error:
   [javac] Compiling 1 source file
/usr/local/jakarta-tomcat-4.1.7/work/Standalone/localhost/tomcatbook/loopexample$jsp.java:
65: ';' expected
        if (oddRow) rowcolor = "#eeeeee"
                                        ^
1 error
```

Listing 11.11 Compilation error output.

This output—which is from a compilation error and therefore falls into the second case—*does* include line numbers from the original source JSP, along with the line in the generated source that caused the specific compilation error. In this case, we left the semicolon out at the end of line 15 of our JSP. Sometimes the error messages are a little less obvious than this, but once you know where to look, it's a lot easier to work out what exactly went wrong.

Summary

In this chapter, we gave you an overview of Java Server Pages. JSP is a flexible technology for embedding server-side Java logic into pages, and allows you to write arbitrarily complex code directly in your HTML, XML, WML, or other source code. We showed you how to use JavaBeans to factor your business logic into reusable external Java classes, and explained how JSP simplifies management of the life cycle of these objects. We also pointed you in the right direction when it comes time to debug your JSPs, and described the great performance improvements in Tomcat 4.1. We barely had a chance to scratch the surface of what can be done with JSPs. You can find a number of excellent books dedicated to that subject for further reading.

In the next chapter, we see how to implement our own custom JSP tags, and talk a little about the JSP Standard Tag Library. Custom tags allow you to further separate presentation from business logic and give more power to the page designer, while also protecting the underlying code from accidental modification.

CHAPTER

12

Tag Libraries

So far, we have discussed the standard tags used in JSP. However, you can add your own tags to JSP by defining your own tag library. A tag library, or *taglib*, consists of a set of classes that implement the javax.servlet.jsp.tagext.Tag and BodyTag interfaces and a tag library descriptor, or TLD file. This API enables you to create your own custom tags for use in JSP files.

The tag library system is generally used for two purposes. It can be used to provide additional global functionality to JSP in general, allowing the JSP to do more than the standard JSP would allow. However, perhaps more important, it enables Java developers to move business logic code out of JSP and into Java classes. We explore this concept more fully in Chapter 10, "Model-View-Controller Architecture," where we explore how a framework can make use of the tag library functionality to separate business logic from JSP files.

The tag library development model also fosters reuse. Because the separation between logic and application of that logic is so clean, and because the model allows for tag libraries to be packaged and distributed, there are a number of tag libraries available on the Web that you can use in your own projects without any modification. There's even a standard tag library, the JSP Standard Tag Library (JSTL), that implements a variety of useful tags. We talk about those after we show you how to write your own. Of course, by now it will come as no surprise to you that the reference implementation of JSTL is maintained by the Apache Jakarta Project. You can download it and read more about it at http://jakarta.apache.org/taglibs/.

Writing a Basic Tag Library

In Listing 12.1, we show you how to create a simple tag extension. The first thing we need to do is write a tag library descriptor file. This TLD describes each custom tag and what Java class those tags are handled by. In this case, we are going to create a new tag library called tomcatbooktags. Let's start by writing only one trivial tag, called tagexample. We attach this example tag to the new class ExampleTag. The tag library descriptor file, which has a .tld extension, should be placed in the WEB-INF/tlds/ directory of the Webapp in which it is defined. You'll have to add the tlds directory to your WEB-INF directory, unless your project already has one.

```
<?xml version="1.0" encoding="ISO-8859-1" ?>
<!DOCTYPE taglib PUBLIC
     "-//Sun Microsystems, Inc.//DTD JSP Tag Library 1.1//EN"
     "http://java.sun.com/j2ee/dtds/web-jsptaglibrary_1_1.dtd">

<taglib>
   <tlibversion>1.0</tlibversion>
   <jspversion>1.1</jspversion>
   <shortname>tomcatbooktags</shortname>
   <info>Example Tag Library from Mastering Tomcat Development</info>

   <tag>
      <name>tagexample</name>
      <tagclass>com.wiley.tomcatbook.ExampleTag</tagclass>
      <bodycontent>empty</bodycontent>
   </tag>

</taglib>
```

Listing 12.1 Simple tag extension (/WEB-INF/tlds/tomcatbook.tld).

This tag handler is a class that extends the TagSupport class. All tag-handling classes must implement javax.servlet.jsp.tagext.Tag. The easiest way to do this is to subclass TagSupport or BodyTagSupport. (we discuss BodyTagSupport in the "Tags with Bodies" section later in this chapter). In the simple tag example shown in Listing 12.2, we insert the text "Hello!" with a little formatting into a JSP where the tag occurs.

```
package com.wiley.tomcatbook;

import javax.servlet.jsp.*;
```

Listing 12.2 ExampleTag.java. (continues)

```
import javax.servlet.jsp.tagext.*;

public class ExampleTag extends TagSupport {

    public int doStartTag() throws JspException {

        try {
            JspWriter out = pageContext.getOut();
            out.print("<b>Hello!</b>");
        }
        catch (Exception ex) {
            throw new JspTagException("ExampleTag: " +
        ex.getMessage() );
        }
        return SKIP_BODY;
    }

    public int doEndTag() {
        return EVAL_PAGE;
    }

    public void release() {
    }

}
```

Listing 12.2 ExampleTag.java. (continued)

Packaging the Tag

The JAR file containing your tag library is quite an ordinary JAR file. You can deploy it into the /WEB-INF/lib directory of your /tomcatbook Webapp. If you haven't stored your class file in a JAR, you can simply include it in the proper directory hierarchy under /WEB-INF/classes. Your taglib definition file, tomcatbook.tld, should already be safely ensconced in the /WEB-INF/tlds directory. All that remains is to add a taglib binding to your deployment descriptor. Remember, the web.xml file is a validated XML document, so tag order is important and enforced. You need to add a taglib entry after all of your <servlet-mapping/> nodes and before any <resource-ref/> or <security-constraint/> nodes. If your web.xml is more complicated than the examples in this book so far, you should check the order in Appendix B to make sure you're inserting the entry in the right place.

Listing 12.3 contains the <taglib/> node we must insert to load the tag library we just created.

```
...
<web-app>
...
  <taglib>
    <taglib-uri>
      /WEB-INF/tlds/tomcatbook.tld
    </taglib-uri>
    <taglib-location>
      /WEB-INF/tlds/tomcatbook.tld
    </taglib-location>
  </taglib>
...
</web-app>
```

Listing 12.3 The <taglib/> node for our tag library.

The URI we specify in <taglib-uri/> can be absolute or relative, and defines a globally unique identifier for the taglib library it refers to. We specify this URI to identify the tag library we want when we load the taglib into a JSP. The location specified in <taglib-location/> tells the Tomcat runtime where to find the TLD file that describes the tag library we want to load. We don't have to specify the location of the JAR file; it just has to be on the classpath so that the runtime can load the class(es) specified in the TLD file when it needs them.

Using the Tag

Using the new tag in a JSP is very simple. The <%@ taglib %> directive tells the JSP runtime to make the tag library available, specifying the URI we included in the deployment descriptor that uniquely identifies the taglib to load. It also specifies, in the prefix attribute, the namespace we'll use to refer to tags in this particular taglib.

In our first example, shown in Listing 12.4, our tag is just an empty one, with no attributes and no body. Wherever the tag is included in the JSP file, it will be replaced at runtime with the text "Hello!" in bold (see Figure 12.1).

```
<%@ page language="java" %>
<%@ taglib uri="/WEB-INF/tlds/tomcatbook.tld" prefix="tomcatbook" %>

<html>
<head>
<title>Trivial Tag</title></head>
<body>
```

Listing 12.4 tagexample.jsp. (continues)

```
Here is our example tag: <tomcatbook:tagexample />

</body>
</html>
```

Listing 12.4 tagexample.jsp. (continued)

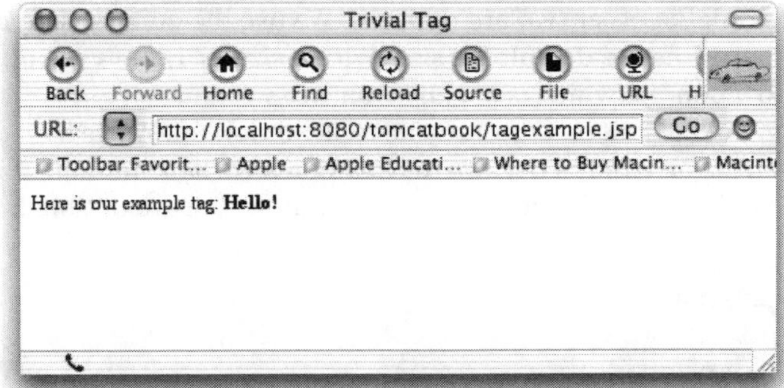

Figure 12.1 tagexample.jsp at runtime.

A Word about Namespaces

In our previous example, we specified a prefix of *tomcatbook*, which specifies the namespace in which the tags in the taglib appear. We can then refer to any tag in the taglib by prepending *tomcatbook:* to the tag name defined in the TLD file. The reason for this is to allow us to use multiple taglibs in a single document. The string we specified is arbitrary, and is not specified anywhere in the tag library. If, for example, you want to use two taglibs in the same document, but the examples for each taglib use the same namespace, you simply change the prefix for one of them. Then you can refer to each independently by prepending the prefix you specified.

In this example, where we have one taglib containing a single tag, it may seem like overkill. But then, you probably weren't planning to deploy the tagexample tag given here, and once you've started using taglibs, we think you may find yourself using lots of custom tags from several different libraries in your JSPs.

A Practical Tag Example

We've seen a trivial use of a tag library. So what is a *practical* use of a tag library? Let's take a look. The tag we create in this section creates a set of three pop-up menus to be used for date entry, and automatically sets them to show the current date by default. If you've had to code this sort of thing by hand, you know that while it's not all that difficult to do, it's quite tedious and easy to mess up. That makes it a perfect candidate for inclusion in a tag library.

Our tag will take a few attributes:

- *name*, the name to prefix to each of the three input names, used to identify the input fields
- *defaultdate*, the date to display by default
- *size*, which tells the control how many rows to display

The name attribute is required; the other two are optional. We use the current date if no defaultdate is set, and we use 1 as the default for size. With a size of 1, the <select> tag changes from a list box to a pop-up, which is usually what we want.

Listing 12.5 contains the updated version of the TLD file tomcatbook.tld. We've added a new tag entry, called dateselect. We need to declare the attributes we'll be defining for our tag, and specify in the descriptor which ones are required and which are optional.

```
<?xml version="1.0" encoding="ISO-8859-1" ?>
<!DOCTYPE taglib PUBLIC
    "-//Sun Microsystems, Inc.//DTD JSP Tag Library 1.1//EN"
    "http://java.sun.com/j2ee/dtds/web-jsptaglibrary_1_1.dtd">

<taglib>
  <tlibversion>1.0</tlibversion>
  <jspversion>1.1</jspversion>
  <shortname>example</shortname>
  <info>Example Tag Library from Mastering Tomcat Development</info>

  <tag>
    <name>tagexample</name>
    <tagclass>com.wiley.tomcatbook.ExampleTag</tagclass>
  <bodycontent>empty</bodycontent>
  </tag>

  <tag>
    <name>dateselect</name>
    <tagclass>com.wiley.tomcatbook.DateSelectTag</tagclass>
    <bodycontent>empty</bodycontent>

    <attribute>
      <name>name</name>
      <required>true</required>
    </attribute>

    <attribute>
```

Listing 12.5 Modified /WEB-INF/example.tld. (continues)

```
            <name>defaultdate</name>
            <required>false</required>
        </attribute>

        <attribute>
            <name>size</name>
            <required>false</required>
        </attribute>

    </tag>

</taglib>
```

Listing 12.5 Modified /WEB-INF/example.tld. (continued)

Now that we've declared the tag, we have to implement it (see Listing 12.6).

```
package com.wiley.tomcatbook;

import java.util.*;
import java.text.*;
import javax.servlet.jsp.*;
import javax.servlet.jsp.tagext.*;

public class DateSelectTag extends TagSupport
{
    protected String name = null;
    protected String defaultdate = null;
    protected String size = "1";

    public int doStartTag() throws JspException
    {
        try
        {
            JspWriter out = pageContext.getOut();

            // If default date is supplied, use that date
            // otherwise use todays date.

            GregorianCalendar calendar = new GregorianCalendar();
            if(defaultdate!=null)
            {
                SimpleDateFormat dateFormat
```

Listing 12.6 DateSelectTag.java. (continues)

```
            = new SimpleDateFormat("MM/dd/yyyy");
        dateFormat.setCalendar(calendar);
        dateFormat.parse(defaultdate);
    }

    int day = calendar.get( calendar.DAY_OF_MONTH );
    int month = calendar.get( calendar.MONTH ) + 1;
    int year = calendar.get( calendar.YEAR );

    out.println( "<select name=\""
            + name
            + "_month\" size=\""
            + size
            + "\" >" );

    String aString = null;
    String selectedMarker = null;

    for(int m=1; m<=12; m++)
    {
        if( m==month )
        {
            selectedMarker = " SELECTED";
        }
        else
        {
            selectedMarker = "";
        }

        out.println("<option value=\""
                + m
                + "\"" + selectedMarker + ">"
                + m
                + "</option>");
    }

    out.println("</select>");

    out.println("<select name=\""
            + name
            + "_day\" size=\""
            + size
            + "\" >" );

    for(int d=1; d<=31; d++)
```

Listing 12.6 DateSelectTag.java. (continues)

```
{
   if( d==day )
   {
      selectedMarker = " SELECTED";
   }
   else
   {
      selectedMarker = "";
   }

   out.println("<option value=\""
            + d
            + "\"" + selectedMarker + ">"
            + d
            + "</option>" );
}

out.println("</select>");

out.println("<select name=\""
         + name
         + "_year\" size=\""
         + size
         + "\" >" );


for( int y=year - 2; y <= year + 2; y++ )
{
   if( y==year )
   {
      selectedMarker = " SELECTED";
   }
   else
   {
      selectedMarker = "";
   }

   out.println( "<option value=\""
            + y
            + "\"" + selectedMarker + ">"
            + y
            + "</option>" );
}

out.println( "</select>" );
```

Listing 12.6 DateSelectTag.java. (continues)

```
        }
        catch (Exception ex)
        {
            throw new JspTagException("DateSelectTag: "
                + ex.getMessage() );
        }
        return SKIP_BODY;
    }

    public int doEndTag()
    {
        return EVAL_PAGE;
    }

    public String getName()
    {
        return (this.name);
    }

    public void setName(String parameter)
    {
        this.name = parameter;
    }

    public String getDefaultdate()
    {
        return (this.defaultdate);
    }

    public void setDefaultdate(String parameter)
    {
        this.defaultdate = parameter;
    }

    public String getSize()
    {
        return (this.size);
    }

    public void setSize(String parameter)
    {
        this.size = parameter;
    }

}
```

Listing 12.6 DateSelectTag.java. (continued)

The doStartTag() method generates the HTML for the three selection inputs. The name of each input uses the name supplied as an attribute, and each adds a suffix of _day, _month, or _year to differentiate it from the other two. We start by creating a new Calendar object, which defaults to contain the current date. We then check to see whether the defaultdate attribute was set; if it was, we parse the date string, in MM/DD/YYYY format, and reset the Calendar object accordingly. We then pull out the day, month, and year values for use when constructing our <select> form elements.

We then construct the individual <select> elements, iterating inside for loops through the range of possible values we may want to display. We render an <option> tag for each, with a value attribute set to the current value of the iterator. We also place the current value of the iterator after the <option> tag (so it will be displayed on the control that the browser renders). Each time through the loop, we check to see whether the current value matches the appropriate value from our Calendar object; if it does, we add the SELECTED attribute to the <option> tag. This attribute sets the default value for the <select> control.

Note that in the year control, we set the range of dates to be the current year, plus or minus two years. Depending on the application, you may have other requirements, but it's nice to base this value on the date you configure so that the control will continue to be usable for many years to come. If, for instance, this control were to be used for a credit card expiration date, you would probably want to set the range from the current year forward 5 to 8 years instead.

At the end of the doStartTag() method, we return SKIP_BODY to signal the JSP runtime to ignore anything contained in the body of this tag.

As we discussed earlier, this tag also takes three attributes. All we have to do to connect these attributes up to our code is to implement getters and setters for each, following standard JavaBeans naming conventions. (That is, they must follow JavaBeans naming conventions, with the exception that boolean attributes follow the pattern of get*Foo*() instead of is*Foo*(), which is standard for JavaBeans.) The runtime takes care of calling these methods and passing in the attribute values specified in the JSP source.

Now all that remains is to try out our new tag. Using this tag, you can easily insert a handy date selection widget into your JSPs with a single simple tag. Since we've already configured our deployment descriptor to load this tag library, all we have to do is make sure the context has been reloaded; then deploy a JSP that uses the tag, as shown in Listing 12.7.

```
<%@ page language="java" %>
<%@ taglib uri="/WEB-INF/tomcatbook.tld" prefix="tomcatbook" %>

<html>
<head>
<title>Transaction Report</title></head>
<body>

<h1>Transaction Report</h1>
```

Listing 12.7 transreport.jsp. (continues)

```
<form action="/examples/jsp/snp/snoop.jsp">
<table width=600 border=1>

<tr>
<td>Report Start Date</td>
<td><tomcatbook:dateselect name="startdate" defaultdate="1/4/2001"/>
    </td>
</tr>

<tr>
<td>Report End Date</td>
<td><tomcatbook:dateselect name="enddate"/></td>
</tr>

<tr>
<td></td>
<td><input type="submit" value="Process"></td>
</tr>

</table>
</form>
</body>
</html>
```

Listing 12.7 transreport.jsp. (continued)

And what does this look like? Figure 12.2 shows the date selector in action.

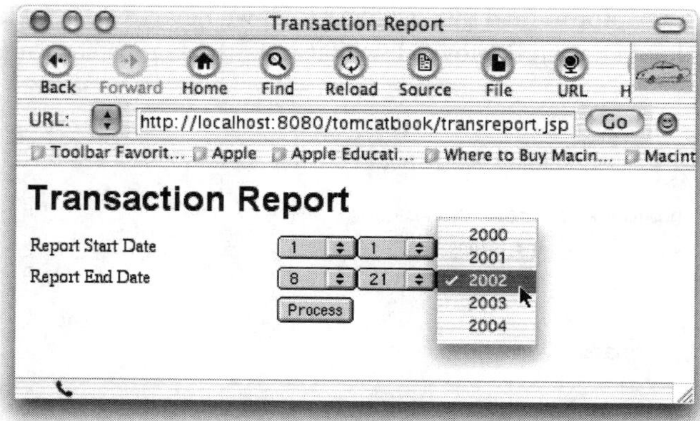

Figure 12.2 transreport.jsp in action.

So you see that by writing a fairly simple object, we end up with a very reusable component that can readily be embedded into any number of Web pages. You probably already have ideas about where you could use tag libraries to promote reuse and simplify page development, but we have one more kind of tag to show you before we discuss the JSP Standard Tag Library. Not all tags are empty tags; some have content between the start and end tag. Using taglibs, you can manipulate the content of your tags.

Tags with Bodies

Sometimes you want to use custom tags just to insert an element into a Web page, as we did in our earlier examples. Other times you want to use tags to format content—in this case, you simply place a start tag and an end tag around the content to be formatted. You can also use the techniques we described earlier and simply include the formatting instructions you want in the doStartTag() and doEndTag() methods. The formatting you specify in the doStartTag() method will be included before the text between the tags, and the formatting you specify in the doEndTag() will be included after the tags. This is a nice way to handle fancy table formatting; that's how Ian generates the formatted tables on javaosx.com, for example.

Sometimes, however, you want to manipulate the text between the tags before sending it to the client. That is what this section is about. In our next example, we write a simple tag that encrypts the contents using one of a few different algorithms. We also show you an example that parses the contents to generate a pop-up menu from the values listed in the tag. You could also use it to convert the contents to anything else you can think of—from generating a table from comma-separated values, to looking up localized versions of the text, to inserting image references for each of the characters to support exotic languages, to parsing the contents as a script using an embedded scheme or TCL interpreter...or anything else you might wish to do with the contents before sending them.

When you want to manipulate the contents of your tag, you need to implement the javax.servlet.jsp.tagext.BodTag interface. The easiest way is to subclass the BodyTagSupport class. The tag we create is called *encrypt*, and we have it accept an *algorithm* attribute. We implement three algorithms:

- *reverse*, which reverses the order of the characters
- *rot13*, which shifts ASCII alphabetic characters forward by 13 characters
- *MD5*, which returns an MD5 hash of the string, represented as hexadecimal digits

In addition, we give our tag an *returnoriginal* attribute, which tells the tag whether we want to include the raw, unencrypted text as well.

Aside from MD5, our encryption algorithms are far from secure, but they have the advantage that you can look at them and see if they're working correctly, since they're so easy to "crack." They also have the advantage that they're both symmetric: applying them twice gets you the original back. That's also nice for demonstrating how they work.

First, let's run through our algorithms very quickly. The methods that implement them will be included as methods on our EncryptTag class. The simplest is the reverse() method, shown in Listing 12.8.

```
public static String reverse(String cleartext)
  {
    StringBuffer sb = new StringBuffer(cleartext);
    sb.reverse();
    return sb.toString();
  }
```

Listing 12.8 The reverse() method.

The reverse() method simply returns the string in the reverse order. The rot13() method is not much more complicated, as you can see in Listing 12.9.

```
public static String rot13(String cleartext)
  {
    StringBuffer sb = new StringBuffer(cleartext);
    for (int i = 0; i < sb.length(); i++)
    {
      char ch = sb.charAt(i);
      if (ch >= 'a' && ch <= 'z')
      {
        ch += 13;
        if (ch > 'z') ch -= 26;
      }
      else if (ch >= 'A' && ch <= 'Z')
      {
        ch += 13;
        if (ch > 'Z') ch -= 26;
      }
      sb.setCharAt(i, ch);
    }
    return sb.toString();
  }
```

Listing 12.9 The rot13() method

The rot13() method checks each character to see whether it's an ASCII alphabetic character (the characters A–Z and a–z), and if so, it adds 13 to the value. If this pushes it past the end of the alphabet, we subtract 26 to make it wrap around to the beginning of the alphabet.

The md5hash() method (see Listing 12.10) uses java.security.MessageDigest to generate an MD5 hash of the string passed in, and then converts the byte array returned into a human-readable string of hexadecimal numbers.

```
public static final String md5hash(String cleartext)
  {
    try
    {
      MessageDigest md = MessageDigest.getInstance("MD5");
      byte[] digest = md.digest(cleartext.getBytes());
      StringBuffer sb = new StringBuffer();
      for (int i = 0; i < digest.length; i++)
      {
        int hiNybble = digest[i] >> (byte) 0x04;
        int loNybble = digest[i] & (byte) 0x0F;
        sb.append(nybbleToUnsignedNybbleString(hiNybble));
        sb.append(nybbleToUnsignedNybbleString(loNybble));
        sb.append(":");
      }
      sb.deleteCharAt(sb.length() - 1);
      return sb.toString();
    }
    catch (NoSuchAlgorithmException nsae)
    {
      System.err.println("Couldn't get MD5 MessageDigest
 instance: " + nsae);
      nsae.printStackTrace(System.err);
      return null;
    }

  }

  public static final String nybbleToUnsignedNybbleString(int
 nybble)
  {
    int value = 0;
    if ((nybble & 0x01) != 0) value += 1;
    if ((nybble & 0x02) != 0) value += 2;
    if ((nybble & 0x04) != 0) value += 4;
    if ((nybble & 0x08) != 0) value += 8;
    return Integer.toString(value, 16);
  }
```

Listing 12.10 md5hash() and a helper method.

The first two lines in the try block handle creation of the MD5 digest. We then iterate over each byte in the byte array we get back, passing each nybble to a string conversion helper method, nybbleToUnsignedNybbleString(). (This is one way to get around the fact that Java treats all bytes as signed values, and we want to treat the bytes as unsigned values.) We then string all the nybbles together, putting colons between bytes to make the whole thing easier to read.

The rest of the code for our tag isn't much more complicated. First, we have the setters and getters for the attributes, shown in Listing 12.11.

```
public void setAlgorithm(String parameter)
  {
    this.algorithm = parameter;
  }

  public String getAlgorithm()
  {
    return (this.algorithm);
  }

  public void setReturnoriginal(boolean parameter)
  {
    this.returnOriginal = parameter;
  }

  public boolean getReturnoriginal()
  {
    return (this.returnOriginal);
  }
```

Listing 12.11 Accessors for the algorithm and return original attributes.

We then can use these attribute values to determine which method to call in order to encrypt the body of our tag. See Listing 12.12 four our encrypt() method.

```
public String encrypt(String cleartext, String method)
  {
    if ("MD5".equalsIgnoreCase(method))
      return md5hash(cleartext);
    else if ("ROT13".equalsIgnoreCase(method))
      return rot13(cleartext);
    else if ("Reverse".equalsIgnoreCase(method))
      return reverse(cleartext);
    else
      return "<blink>Unsupported encryption method: " + method + "</blink>";
  }
```

Listing 12.12 The encrypt() method.

All that remains is to write the implementations of the tag method we're interested in, doAfterBody(). Listing 12.13 contains the EncryptTag class and the doAfterBody() method.

```
package com.wiley.tomcatbook;

import java.util.*;
import java.text.*;
import java.security.*;
import javax.servlet.jsp.*;
import javax.servlet.jsp.tagext.*;

public class EncryptTag extends BodyTagSupport {

    protected String algorithm = "MD5";
    protected boolean addDelimiters = false;
    protected boolean returnOriginal = false;

    public int doAfterBody() throws JspTagException {

        try
        {
            BodyContent bodyContent = getBodyContent();
            String body = bodyContent.getString();

            bodyContent.clearBody();
            JspWriter writer = bodyContent.getEnclosingWriter();
            if (returnOriginal)
            {
                writer.println("<hr>");
                writer.println(body);
                writer.println("<hr>");
                writer.println("Algorithm: " + algorithm + " =&gt; ");
            }
            writer.print(encrypt(body, algorithm));
        }
        catch (Exception ex)
        {
            throw new JspTagException("EncryptTag: "
                + ex.getMessage() );
        }

        return SKIP_BODY;

    }
    ...
    // Previously listed methods here.
}
```

Listing 12.13 The EncryptTag class and doAfterBody() method.

The doAfterBody() method is called once the contents of the tag have been read but before they are returned to the client. We get the body content with a call to getBodyContent() and get the actual string with a call to getString(). We then use getEnclosingWriter() to grab a writer from the body content object; we can use this writer to write directly into the body that will be returned to the client. We test to see whether returnOriginal is set; and if it is, we print back the original, with a little formatting and a message telling the user which algorithm was used.

We then print back the encrypted version of the body content, with a call to the encrypt() method we saw in Listing 12.12. If no exception was thrown, we return SKIP_BODY, which tells the runtime not to render back the body content itself.

The additions to tomcatbook.tld are shown in Listing 12.14.

```
<tag>
   <name>encrypt</name>
   <tagclass>com.wiley.tomcatbook.EncryptTag</tagclass>
   <bodycontent>tagdependent</bodycontent>

   <attribute>
      <name>algorithm</name>
      <required>false</required>
   </attribute>

   <attribute>
      <name>returnoriginal</name>
      <required>false</required>
   </attribute>
</tag>
```

Listing 12.14 Additions to tomcatbook.tld.

An example of using the tag is shown in the JSP in Listing 12.15; Figure 12.3 shows the results.

```
<html>
<head>
<title>Encrypt Tag Example</title>
<%@ taglib uri="/WEB-INF/tlds/tomcatbook.tld" prefix="tomcatbook" %>
</head>

<body>
<tomcatbook:encrypt algorithm="rot13">Uryyb Frperg
Jbeyq!</tomcatbook:encrypt>
<br>
```

Listing 12.15 crypto.jsp. (continues)

```
<tomcatbook:encrypt algorithm="reverse">.desrever saw txet
sihT</tomcatbook:encrypt>
<br>
<tomcatbook:encrypt returnoriginal="true">This text has the following
 MD5 hash:</tomcatbook:encrypt>
</body>
</html>
```

Listing 12.15 crypto.jsp. (continued)

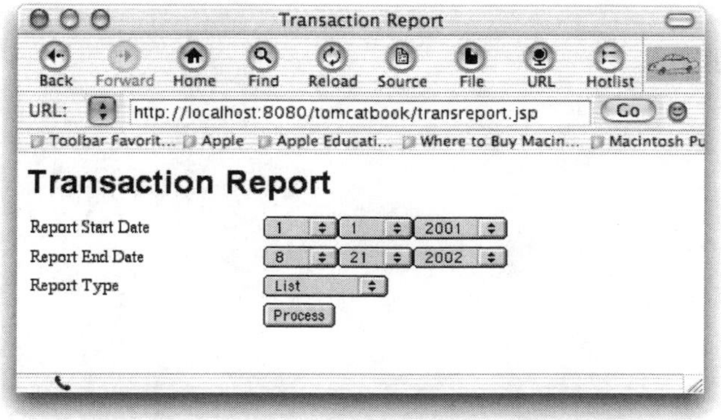

Figure 12.3 Output from crypto.jsp.

From the fun and mysterious world of lightweight cryptography, we turn now to another example. In this one, we use the body of the tag to configure values for a pop-up menu. The body contains a comma-separated list of menu item names, which we convert into an HTML <select> element:

```
<tomcatbook:select name="type"
  default="List">List,Report,Dissection</tomcatbook:select>
```

Figure 12.4 The <select> tag pop-up.

We'd like our tag to have a few attributes, a name, a default selection, and a size attribute. The size attribute is used to control the number of rows our <select> element will have. As mentioned earlier, a <select> element with a size of 1 shows up as a pop-up menu. We use this as our default.

This time, let's start with the additions to the TLD file, shown in Listing 12.16.

```
<tag>

   <name>select</name>
   <tagclass>com.wiley.tomcatbook.SelectTag</tagclass>
   <bodycontent>tagdependent</bodycontent>

   <attribute>
      <name>name</name>
      <required>true</required>
   </attribute>

   <attribute>
      <name>default</name>
      <required>false</required>
   </attribute>

   <attribute>
      <name>size</name>
      <required>false</required>
   </attribute>

</tag>
```

Listing 12.16 Additions to tomcatbook.tld for the <select> tag.

Next, let's take a look at the implementation of this tag (see Listing 12.17).

```
package com.wiley.tomcatbook;

import javax.servlet.jsp.*;
import javax.servlet.jsp.tagext.*;
import java.util.*;
import java.text.*;

public class SelectTag extends BodyTagSupport
{

   protected String name = null;
   protected String defaultvalue = null;
   protected String size = "1";

   public int doStartTag() throws JspException
   {
```

Listing 12.17 SelectTag.java. (continues)

```
        try
        {
            JspWriter out = pageContext.getOut();

            out.println("<select name=\""
            + name
            + "\" size=\""
            + size
            + "\" >");

        }
        catch (Exception ex)
        {
            throw new JspTagException("SelectTag: " +
                ex.getMessage() );
        }
        return EVAL_BODY_TAG;
    }

    public int doEndTag() throws JspTagException {

        try
        {
            JspWriter out = pageContext.getOut();
            out.println("</select>");
        }
        catch (Exception ex)
        {
            throw new JspTagException("SelectTag: " +
                ex.getMessage());
        }

        return EVAL_PAGE;
    }

    public int doAfterBody() throws JspTagException
    {

        try {

            BodyContent bodyContent = getBodyContent();
            String options = bodyContent.getString();
            String nextOption = null;
```

Listing 12.17 SelectTag.java. (continues)

```
            bodyContent.clearBody();
            JspWriter writer = bodyContent.getEnclosingWriter();

            int offset = 0;
            int next = 0;

            while( next != -1 )
            {

               next = options.indexOf( ",", offset );
               nextOption = options.substring( offset, next );
               writer.print( "<option value=\""
               + nextOption
               + "\">"
               + nextOption
               + "</option>" );
               offset = next + 1;

            }

        }
        catch (Exception ex) {
           throw new JspTagException("SelectTag: " +
      ex.getMessage() );
        }

        return SKIP_BODY;
    }

    public String getName() {
        return (this.name);
    }

    public void setName( String parameter ) {
        this.name = parameter;
    }

    public String getDefault() {
        return (this.defaultvalue);
    }

    public void setDefault( String parameter ) {
        this.defaultvalue = parameter;
```

Listing 12.17 SelectTag.java. (continues)

```
    }

    public String getSize() {
        return (this.size);
    }

    public void setSize( String parameter ) {
        this.size = parameter;
    }

}
```

Listing 12.17 SelectTag.java. (continued)

We can then use the tag in transreport.jsp by adding the HTML fragment in Listing 12.18. Figure 12.5 shows the result of all this work.

```
<tr>
<td>Report Type</td>
<td><tomcatbook:select name="type" default="List"
    >List,Report,Dissection</tomcatbook:select></td>
</tr>
```

Listing 12.18 An HTML fragment using the <select> tag.

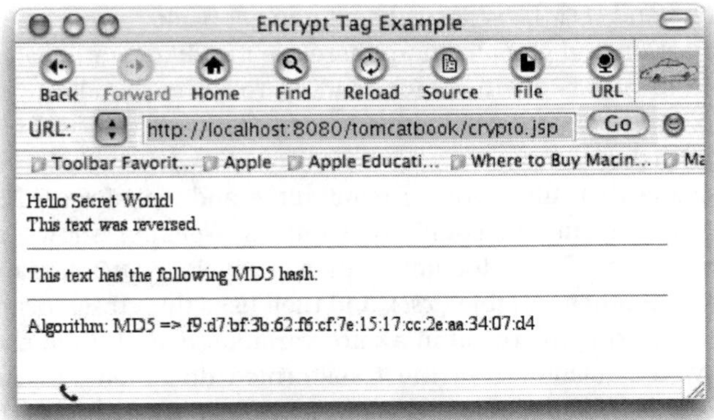

Figure 12.5 transreport.jsp in transaction report form.

So now you know the basics of writing tag libraries. For more information, see *Mastering JSP Custom Tags and Tag Libraries*, written by James Goodwill and also published by Wiley.

One of the best things about tag libraries, however, is that, for a lot of things, you don't even need to write one. There are a lot of taglibs out there already that do many of the things you might want to write one to do. In the next section, we give you a quick overview of the official standard base tag library, the JSP Standard Tag Library. Quite a number of other tag libraries are maintained by the Jakarta Project (24 at this writing), and many others are available elsewhere as well. As a result, chances are awfully good that a tag library already exists for doing the things you might be thinking of doing with this API—so it pays to search the Web a little before embarking on a big taglibs project.

JSTL: The JSP Standard Tag Library

The JSP Standard Tag Library (JSTL) was developed under the Java Community Process (it is JSR 52). JSTL is based on the Servlet 2.3 and JSP 1.2 specifications, so you need a container that supports those APIs (which, of course, Tomcat 4 does). The Jakarta Project is responsible for maintaining the reference implementation of the JSTL, and you can read more about it and download it at this URL: http://jakarta.apache.org /taglibs/doc/standard-doc/intro.html.

The JSTL includes tags that fall into a few different categories: tags that support iteration and flow control, importing text via HTTP or FTP, text manipulation and internationalization, XML processing, database access, and a couple of general-purpose tags.

The general tags <set/> and <out/> let you store values in variables, and then get them back out.

The flow control tags include conditional tags, such as <if/> or <choose/>, that allow your JSPs to control what is displayed based on runtime criteria. They also include iterators like <forEach/> and <forTokens/>, which let you iterate over sets of values.

The text import tag <import/> lets you grab text from a remote location over HTTP or FTP. There are also utility tags like <param/> and <escapeHtml/> that allow you to URL-encode text for parameters and HTML-escape the text you get back.

In the area of internationalization and globalization, there are tags like <setLocale/> that facilitate use of multiple locales, <bundle/> for loading resource bundles, and <message/> and <param/> to support parametric replacement to insert values determined at runtime into localized strings.

A number of tags are available that allow you to manipulate and transform XML. Listing 12.19, which we've taken from the standard-examples Webapp, shows an example that creates and stores an XML document in a variable (*xml*); creates and stores an XSL style sheet in another variable (*xsl*); and then uses the <transform/> tag to apply the transformation, storing the result in a third variable (*doc*). It then uses an XPath expression to show the header from the transformed document. It uses another XPath expression to subset the document stored in *xml*, and then applies the transformation rules stored in *xsl* to the minidocument created by the XPath query. Finally, it performs a transformation on an XML fragment declared inline inside a <transform/> tag.

```
<%@ taglib prefix="c" uri="http://java.sun.com/jstl/core" %>
<%@ taglib prefix="x" uri="http://java.sun.com/jstl/xml" %>

<html>
<head>
  <title>JSTL: XML Support -- Transform</title>
</head>
<body bgcolor="#FFFFFF">
<h3>Parse / Expr</h3>

<c:set var="xml">
  <a><b>header!</b></a>
</c:set>

<c:set var="xsl">
  <?xml version="1.0"?>
  <xsl:stylesheet
    xmlns:xsl="http://www.w3.org/1999/XSL/Transform" version="1.0">

  <xsl:template match="text()">
    <h1><xsl:value-of select="."/></h1>
  </xsl:template>

  </xsl:stylesheet>
</c:set>

Prints "header" as a header:<br />
<x:transform xml="${xml}" xslt="${xsl}"/>

<hr />

Prints "header" in normal size:<br />
<x:transform xml="${xml}" xslt="${xsl}" var="doc"/>
<x:out select="$doc//h1"/>

<hr size="5" />

<hr />
<h3>Transformations using output from XPath expressions</h3>

<x:parse var="xml" xml="${xml}" />
```

Listing 12.19 Transform.jsp, from the standard-examples Webapp. (continues)

```
<x:set var="miniDoc" select="$xml//b" />
<x:transform xslt="${xsl}" xml="${miniDoc}" />
<hr />

<h3>Inline transformations</h3>

<x:transform xslt="${xsl}">
  <a>
   <b>
    <c>Paragraph one!</c>
    <c>Paragraph foo!</c>
   </b>
  </a>
</x:transform>

</body>
</html>
```

Listing 12.19 Transform.jsp, from the standard-examples Webapp. (continued)

The SQL tags include <setDataSource/> (to manage establishing a connection), tags like <query/> and <update/> (for sending queries and updates), and <transaction/> (which allows you to group commands into a single transaction). The objects returned have attributes, such as rowsByIndex, that can be used with <forEach/> to iterate over result sets.

If you are interested in getting a better feel for what it does, the sample application that comes with the distribution, standard-examples.war, is an excellent way to get your feet wet, since it walks you through each tag, with examples of the tags in action.

Other Tag Libraries from the ASF

As we mentioned earlier, a huge number of tags are available from The Apache Foundation. To see them all, just go to the Taglibs Web page (http://jakarta.apache.org/taglibs/). To give you an idea of what is available, Table 12.1 contains a quick overview of the libraries they support.

Table 12.1 The Apache Software Foundation Tag Libraries (continues)

LIBRARY	DESCRIPTION
Application	Contains tools for accessing objects with application scope.
Benchmark	Provides tools for performance-testing taglibs and JSPs.

Table 12.1 The Apache Software Foundation Tag Libraries (continued)

LIBRARY	DESCRIPTION
BSF	Bean Scripting Framework: Contains tools that let you embed scripting in JavaScript/ECMAScript, VBScript, Perl, Tcl, Python, NetRexx, and Rexx.
Cache	Supports granular caching of JSP content to improve performance.
DateTime	Provides input and formatting tools for dates and times.
DBTags	Contains tags supporting database interaction.
I18n	Provides tags supporting internationalization.
Input	Contains tags that make it easy to keep form fields populated with user-entered data from page to page.
IO	Contains tags that facilitate executing requests over HTTP, HTTPS, FTP, XML-RPC, and SOAP.
JMS	Provides tags that support JMS-based messaging from inside a JSP. Based on the Messenger object in Jakarta Commons.
JNDI	Lets you do JNDI lookups from a JSP.
Log	Lets you embed explicit logging calls in your JSPs. Based on log4j.
Mailer	Contains tags that let you send email from a JSP.
Page	Contains tags that let you access objects with page scope.
Random	Provides tags for creating random number and string generators.
Regexp	Contains tags for doing Perl 5-style regular expression operations: s///, split(), /pattern/.
Request	Gives you complete access to the request object from tags.
Response	Gives you complete access to the response object from tags.
Scrape	Contains tag-based tools for extracting content from Web pages.
Session	Lets you store and retrieve information on the session.
String	Provides string-manipulation tools based on the Lang object in Jakarta Commons.
Utility	Contains examples of basic tag development techniques.
XSL	Contains example tags showing how to handle XSL from a tag library.
XTags	Contains tags for transforming XML in an XSLT-like way with XPath semantics. Based on dom4j.

As you can see, there is no shortage of tag libraries to choose from, and Table 12.1 includes just the ones currently maintained by the Jakarta Project. They're all open source, of course, so they're also a good resource if you get stuck when writing your own tag libraries.

Summary

Tag libraries are a powerful tool for streamlining JSP development and encapsulating functionality into easy-to-use (and hard-to-break) reusable components. They can be used for anything from simplifying repetitive tasks (such as creating form widgets) to encapsulating complex functionality (such as accessing a database, scraping content from a remote Web page, and sending email). In this chapter, we've shown you the basics of how to write your own tag libraries, and we've shown you some of the rich variety of custom tags that are already out there, waiting for you to use them. Tags are a good way to abstract away coding complexity, and help you to achieve a deeper model/view separation than JSP alone. In the next chapter, we go further in our quest to separate our app into discrete MVC components.

CHAPTER

13

MVC with Struts

Generally speaking, developers create ugly HTML, and Web designers are allergic to Java. Sure, there are exceptions to these rules, but how do you get these two groups of people working together on the same project? Struts—with its set of custom tags and emphasis on getting scriptlets out of JSP—allows both sides to live in harmony.

Struts is an open source, Model-View-Controller (MVC) framework developed by The Apache Software Foundation as part of its Jakarta project. Struts is built on top of JSP, servlets, and tag libraries. While Sun was printing up the J2EE Blueprints, Apache was making them come to life. After reading the first J2EE Blueprints from Sun with their explanation of MVC and how to accomplish it with custom tags, servlets, and JSP, one can clearly see that Struts is the incarnation of Sun's J2EE MVC vision.

In many ways, Struts has led to the further development of J2EE with regard to the J2EE Web presentation tier. It's clear that Struts and Apache's TagLib project have influenced JavaServer Pages Standard Tag Library (JSTL) and JavaServer Faces. Struts pushed the MVC vision to its limits and discovered issues not covered by JSP and servlets. JSTL and JavaServer Faces were created to address the issues Struts discovered by pushing the limits of JSP/servlet-based MVC. Struts is another example of the powerhouse Jakarta projects like Tomcat, Ant, and many others.

Struts is a growing, evolving project. It would be impossible to cover all of Struts in one chapter, so this chapter focuses on giving you a solid foundation and practical code examples for using Struts. If you need more information, we suggest James Goodwill's *Mastering Jakarta Struts*, also published by John Wiley & Sons.

WHERE TO GET STRUTS **Struts 1.1 was developed by the Apache Software Foundation as part of its Jakarta project. Struts is distributed with the Apache Software License version 1.1, and you can download it at http://jakarta.apache.org/ant/index.html.**

This chapter starts out with a brief description of Struts. Then, we present a common Model 1-style JSP application. Throughout most of this chapter, we reshape the Model 1 into a Model 2 and an MVC application, using and explaining Struts along the way.

Note that the code for the Model 1 and the MVC application is focused on showing the concepts; it is not robust code. For example, the exception handling is kept short to make it easier to follow. To get the most out of this chapter, you should have a background with JavaBeans, JSP, and Java Database Connectivity (JDBC). You can utilize your knowledge of JSP to learn Struts in a Rosetta Stone fashion, as we compare the Model 1 versus the MVC way of writing the sample application.

Overview of Struts

Applications written using the Struts framework provide JSP pages for the View and custom actions and configuration files for the Controller. They endeavor to separate the Model so that the Model is not aware that it is being used for a Web application. In other words, the Model code is divorced from the presentation code. A typical Struts application has JSPs with very few and relatively small JSP scriptlets.

Many control features are provided by the Struts framework and are highly configurable. The Struts Controller servlet dispatches and coordinates interaction between Actions and JSPs. Actions are subclasses of org.apache.struts.action.Action. The Struts Controller uses a configuration file that specifies ActionMappings. An ActionMapping maps path information to Actions, and specifies interaction between the Action and other resources and properties (such as forwarding information). Typically, an Action (as part of the Controller) interacts with the Model and then forwards to a JSP to display and get further user input. The Action will typically map domain objects (JavaBeans) into request, session, or application scope, and the JSP uses these objects to display information and collect user input.

Common areas of concern, such as form validation, are handled by the framework. Applications use ActionForms to validate data and populate HTML forms. ActionForms are a special type of JavaBean that subclasses org.apache.struts.action.ActionForm. Struts automatically stores the data for HTML form data in these strongly typed form beans. You can even nest form properties by having composite beans. Actions are mapped to ActionForms. Actions receive the results of form submissions via ActionForms that have been validated by the framework. Action can use ActionForms to populate HTML forms with data. The life cycle of ActionForms is managed by the Struts framework, and ActionForms are notified when to do form validation.

The Struts framework comes with a set of custom tags that manages the interaction between the View and the Contoller. One custom tag manages the ActionForm population from the HTML forms.

Just as you can write non-object-oriented code using Java if you try hard enough, you can write non-MVC code with Struts. Generally speaking, Struts should be used only for managing the View and the Controller. The Actions are like a glue between the presentation logic and your business logic and domain objects—that is, your Model. Actions should typically invoke your API set, which may consist of JavaBeans or Enterprise JavaBeans (EJBs). The JavaBeans that the Action uses should not refer to classes under the javax.servlet or the org.apache.struts package. For example, you would not expect to see JDBC calls in an Action, but the Action may call a bean that in turns calls JDBC (refer to Chapter 10 for more details). You may have additional mediator classes between your true Model facade and your Actions.

Now I must confess that I am not a purist. I believe in the simplest possible solution that will work. There are times when you must use MVC, and there are times when you can avoid it. If your project is not a prototype or a one-off solution, then you should use MVC. If you need to get Web designers and developers working together, then you should use MVC. Struts is a good vehicle for getting things done fairly quickly and still using MVC. We've worked on large projects using Struts, and we've found Struts to be very useful, as well as a good vehicle for learning a lot about JSP and custom tags.

A Typical Model 1-Style JSP Application

JSP was originally Sun's answer to the success of Microsoft's Active Server Pages (ASP). Much of the syntax and style is the same as those found in ASP. In fact, this was intentional; tools suited for Web designers could already recognize the special ASP tags, and JSP copied them so it could also work with these tools. Along with ASP's success, JSP also inherited ASP's biggest "flaw": It allows, in fact almost encourages, developers to write sloppy code. JSP scriptlets are quick-and-dirty, but always rough-and- ready.

You can still get a lot of mileage out of Model 1-style development, but it can be a hindrance. For example, there is a lot of mixing of Java code and HTML, which makes the HTML harder for Web designers to change, not to mention harder to maintain as the logic gets spread over many pages.

In this section, we present a simple application created in Model 1-style JSP development. The domain will be separated from the JSP pages, but there will be a lot of scriptlets in the JSP.

The application lists all of the departments in a fictional company. When the user clicks on a department, the browser shows all of the employees in that department in the Employee Listing view. The Employee Listing view allows the user to add, edit, or delete employees for the given department.

The Department Model

First, let's cover the domain objects for this application. There are only two domain objects for this example: Dept (which represents a department) and Employee (which represents an employee). Both the Dept and the Employee objects can read themselves out of the database. The Employee object can also, update, add, and remove itself.

Listing 13.1 shows the class for the Dept domain object, and Listing 13.2 shows the class for the Employee domain object. These classes will be used unchanged in both the Model 1 and MVC versions of the application. Skim Listings 10.1 and 10.2 before we go into the Model 1 application's JSP.

```
package bean;
import java.sql.*;
import java.util.*;
import javax.naming.*;
import javax.sql.DataSource;

public class Dept implements java.io.Serializable {

  private String name;
  private int id;

  private static final String select = "select deptid, name " +
                       "from dept";
   private static final String selectEmployee =
          "select empid, fname, lname, phone, deptid" +
          " from employee where deptid=? " +
          " order by lname";

  public Dept() {
  }

  public Dept(ResultSet rs) throws SQLException{
    init(rs);
  }

  public void init(ResultSet rs) throws SQLException{
    this.name = rs.getString("name");
    this.id = rs.getInt("deptid");
  }

  public String getName() {
    return this.name;
  }

  public void setName(String name) {
    this.name = name;
  }

  public int getId() {
    return this.id;
```

Listing 13.1 The Dept domain object. (continues)

```
    }

    public void setId(int id) {
        this.id = id;
    }

    static Connection getConnection(){
        try {
            Context initCtx = new InitialContext();
            Context envCtx = (Context) initCtx.
            lookup("java:comp/env");
            DataSource ds = (DataSource) envCtx.lookup("jdbc/emp");
            return ds.getConnection();
        }catch (Exception e){
            e.printStackTrace();
        }

...
        }
        catch (Exception e){
...
        }
    }

    public static Dept [] getDepartments()throws SQLException{

        Connection connection = null;
        Statement statement = null;
        ResultSet resultSet = null;
        ArrayList depts = new ArrayList();

        try{

            connection = getConnection();
            statement = connection.createStatement();
            resultSet = statement.executeQuery(select);

            while(resultSet.next()){
                Dept dept = new Dept(resultSet);
                depts.add(dept);
            }
        }finally {
            if (resultSet!=null) resultSet.close();
            if (statement!=null) statement.close();
```

Listing 13.1 The Dept domain object. (continues)

```
            if (connection!=null) connection.close();
        }

        Dept [] arrayDepts = new Dept[depts.size()];
        return (Dept []) depts.toArray(arrayDepts);

    }


    public Employee [] getEmployees() throws SQLException{

        Connection connection = null;
        PreparedStatement statement = null;
        ResultSet resultSet = null;
        ArrayList emps = new ArrayList();

        try{

            connection = getConnection();
            statement = connection.prepareStatement(selectEmployee);
            statement.setInt(1, this.id);

            resultSet = statement.executeQuery();


            while(resultSet.next()){
                Employee emp = new Employee(resultSet);
                emps.add(emp);
            }

        }finally {
            if (resultSet!=null) resultSet.close();
            if (statement!=null) statement.close();
            if (connection!=null) connection.close();
        }

        Employee [] arrayEmps = new Employee[emps.size()];
        return (Employee []) emps.toArray(arrayEmps);

    }

}
```

Listing 13.1 The Dept domain object. (continued)

As you can see in Listing 13.1, the Dept class has a static method called getDepartments(), which returns a Dept array that contains every department in the company. The Dept class also has a method called getEmployees(), which returns an array of all the employees in the department. The getConnection() helper method gets access to a JDBC connection pool using JNDI to access the component's naming context. The Employee class also uses getConnection() to get its JDBC connection.

```
package bean;
import java.sql.*;

public class Employee implements java.io.Serializable{

   private String firstName;
   private String lastName;
   private String phone;
   private int id;
   private int deptId;

   private static final String insert =
      "insert into employee (fname, lname, phone, deptid) values "
                                          +(?,?,?,?)";

   private static final String delete =
      "delete from employee where empid=";

   private static final String select =
    "select empid, fname, lname, phone, deptid " +
    " from employee where empid=";



   public Employee() {
   }

   public Employee(ResultSet rs) throws SQLException{
      init(rs);
   }

   public void init(ResultSet rs) throws SQLException{
      this.firstName = rs.getString("fname");
      this.lastName = rs.getString("lname");
      this.phone = rs.getString("phone");
```

Listing 13.2 The Employee domain object. (continues)

```
        this.id = rs.getInt("empid");
        this.deptId = rs.getInt("deptid");
    }


    public Employee(int id) throws SQLException{
        load(id);
    }

    public String getFirstName() {
        return this.firstName;
    }

    public void setFirstName(String firstName) {
        this.firstName = firstName;
    }

    public String getLastName() {
        return this.lastName;
    }

    public void setLastName(String lastName) {
        this.lastName = lastName;
    }

    public String getPhone() {
        return this.phone;
    }

    public void setPhone(String phone) {
        this.phone = phone;
    }

    public int getId() {
        return this.id;
    }

    public void setId(int id) {
        this.id = id;
    }

    public int getDeptId() {
        return this.deptId;
    }
```

Listing 13.2 The Employee domain object. (continues)

```
public void setDeptId(int deptId) {
    this.deptId = deptId;
}

public void remove() throws Exception{
    Connection connection = null;
    Statement statement = null;


    try{

        connection = Dept.getConnection();
        statement = connection.createStatement();

        System.out.println(delete+id);
        int worked = statement.executeUpdate(delete+id);
        if (worked != 1)
          throw new RuntimeException
                ("Unable to delete the employee");


    }finally {
        if (statement!=null) statement.close();
        if (connection!=null) connection.close();
    }
}

public void add() throws SQLException{
    Connection connection = null;
    PreparedStatement statement = null;


    try{

        connection = Dept.getConnection();
        statement = connection.prepareStatement(insert);

        //fname, lname, phone, deptid
        statement.setString(1, this.firstName);
        statement.setString(2, this.lastName);
        statement.setString(3, this.phone);
        statement.setInt(4, this.deptId);
```

Listing 13.2 The Employee domain object. (continues)

```
            int worked = statement.executeUpdate();
            if (worked != 1)
                throw new RuntimeException("Unable to add employee");

        }finally {
            if (statement!=null) statement.close();
            if (connection!=null) connection.close();
        }

    }

    public void load() throws SQLException{
        load(this.id);

    }
    public void load(int id) throws SQLException{

        Connection connection = null;
        Statement statement = null;
        ResultSet resultSet = null;

        try{

            connection = Dept.getConnection();
            statement = connection.createStatement();

            resultSet = statement.executeQuery(select+id);

            if(resultSet.next()){
                init(resultSet);
            }else{
                throw new RuntimeException("Unable to load " +
                          employee id=" + id);

            }

        }finally {
            if (resultSet!=null) resultSet.close();
            if (statement!=null) statement.close();
            if (connection!=null) connection.close();
        }
```

Listing 13.2 The Employee domain object. (continues)

```
    }

    public void edit() throws Exception{
        remove();
        add();

    }

    public String toString(){
        StringBuffer buf = new StringBuffer(100);
        buf.append("firstName=");
        buf.append(this.firstName);
        buf.append(", lastName=");
        buf.append(this.lastName);
        buf.append(", phone=");
        buf.append(this.phone);
        buf.append(", deptid=");
        buf.append(this.deptId);
        return buf.toString();
        }
}
```

Listing 13.2 The Employee domain object. (continued)

Listing 13.2 shows the Employee class. This class can create, load or remove an employee from the database, or update an employee's record in the database. The code is standard JDBC, and it is assumed you have some JDBC experience. Even if you don't, however, the sample code is straightforward enough for you to follow along.

The Employee class has three constructors: One constructor takes a result set and is used by the Dept class to load a whole department at a time. Another constructor takes an employee ID, which is used to load an employee. The empty Employee constructor is used for serialization.

The Department Database Schema

Listing 13.3 shows the database schema that the Dept and Employee can access. This code is taken from the build script included with this sample application. The build script is similar in form and function to the build scripts described in Chapter 20, "Developing Web Applications with Ant and XDoclet."

```
CREATE TABLE DEPT (
   DEPTID    INT      IDENTITY   PRIMARY KEY,
   NAME      VARCHAR (80)
);
```

Listing 13.3 The Dept application schema. (continues)

```
CREATE TABLE EMPLOYEE (
  EMPID     INT      IDENTITY    PRIMARY KEY,
  FNAME     VARCHAR (80),
  LNAME     VARCHAR (80),
  PHONE     VARCHAR (80),
  DEPTID    INT,
  CONSTRAINT  DEPTFK FOREIGN KEY (DEPTID)
            REFERENCES DEPT (DEPTID)
);
```

Listing 13.3 The Dept application schema. (continued)

The Dept and Employee classes make up the model for this application. Neither the model nor the database schema will change when we switch to using Struts and MVC.

The JSPs for the Model 1 Department Application

The Model 1 consists of the following JSPs:

- DeptListing.jsp
- EmployeeUpdate.jsp
- EmployeeDelete.jsp
- EmployeeForm.jsp
- EmployeeListing.jsp
- Footer.jsp
- Header.jsp

DeptListing.jsp lists all the departments in the company. DeptListing.jsp includes Header.jsp and Footer.jsp, as shown here:

```
...
<jsp:include page="Header.jsp">
       <jsp:param name="header" value="Dept Listing"/>
</jsp:include>

...

<%@include file="/Footer.jsp" %>
```

Header.jsp and Footer.jsp provide a common header and footer for all the main pages. Note that the HTML is kept as simple as possible so you can focus on the concepts.

DeptListing.jsp uses the Dept class to load all the departments in the system:

```
<%@page import="bean.*" %>

...
<%    Dept[] depts = Dept.getDepartments(); %>
```

DeptListing creates an HTML table of departments. Each row in the table contains the Dept name in one column and a link to the employees in that department in the other column. DeptListing iterates over the array of departments with JSP scriptlets, as shown here:

```
<%
    for (int index=0; index < depts.length; index++){
%>
        <tr>
            <td>
            <%=depts[index].getName()%>
            </td>

            <td>
                <a href="EmployeeListing.jsp?deptid=<%=depts[index].
  getId()%>">
                   show
                </a>
            </td>

        </tr>
<%}%>
```

For each iteration, DeptListing creates a link to EmployeeListing.jsp and passes the deptid as a parameter on the link's query string. So far, you will notice that this solution uses a lot of JSP scriptlets. When a user clicks on the Employee listing link, EmployeeListing.jsp lists all the employees for that department. Listing 13.4 shows the complete listing for DeptListing.jsp. As you can see in Listing 13.5, EmployeeListing.jsp is similar to DeptListing.jsp in both structure and content.

```
<%@page import="bean.*" %>

<jsp:include page="Header.jsp">
   <jsp:param name="header" value="Dept Listing"/>
</jsp:include>

<%   Dept[] depts = Dept.getDepartments(); %>

   <table>
```

Listing 13.4 DeptListing.jsp. (continues)

```
<%
   for (int index=0; index < depts.length; index++){
%>
      <tr>
         <td>
         <%=depts[index].getName()%>
         </td>

         <td>
            <a href="EmployeeListing.jsp?deptid=<%=depts[index].getId()%>">show</a>
         </td>

      </tr>
<%}%>

   </table>

<%@include file="/Footer.jsp" %>
```

Listing 13.4 DeptListing.jsp. (continued)

```
<%@page contentType="text/html"%>
<%@page import="bean.*" %>

<jsp:include page="Header.jsp">
   <jsp:param name="header" value="Employee Listing"/>
</jsp:include>


<jsp:useBean id="dept" scope="page" class="bean.Dept" />

<jsp:setProperty name="dept" property="id" param="deptid"/>

<a href="EmployeeForm.jsp?add=true&deptid=<%=dept.getId()%>">add</a>

<%   Employee[] emps = dept.getEmployees(); %>

   <table>

<%
   for (int index=0; index < emps.length; index++){
%>
```

Listing 13.5 EmployeeListing.jsp. (continues)

```
    <tr>
      <td>
        <%=emps[index].getFirstName()%>
      </td>

      <td>
        <%=emps[index].getLastName()%>
      </td>

      <td>
        <%=emps[index].getPhone()%>
      </td>

      <td>
        <a href="EmployeeForm.jsp?id=<%=emps[index].
getId()%>&edit=true">
          edit
        </a>
      </td>

      <td>
        <a href="EmployeeDelete.jsp?id=<%=emps[index].
getId()%>">
          delete
        </a>
      </td>

    </tr>
  <%}%>

  </table>

  <%@include file="/Footer.jsp" %>
```

Listing 13.5 EmployeeListing.jsp. (continued)

EmployeeListing.jsp uses the Dept JavaBean by using the jsp:useBean action:

```
<jsp:useBean id="dept" scope="page" class="bean.Dept"  />
```

The Employee listing features an add link at the top of the page so that a user can add more employees to this department:

```
<a href="EmployeeForm.jsp?add=true&deptid=<%=dept.getId()%>">add</a>
```

EmployeeListing.jsp then calls the getEmployees() method of the Dept JavaBean. It iterates over the employees and fills out columns in the table. Each row represents another employee. Each column represents a different property of the employee bean—except for the last two columns, which are links for editing and deleting the employee associated with that row. These last two action columns are defined as follows:

```
<td>
     <a href="EmployeeForm.jsp?id=<%=emps[index].
     getId()%>&edit=true">
        edit
     </a>
</td>

<td>
     <a href="EmployeeDelete.jsp?id=<%=emps[index].getId()%>">
        delete
     </a>
</td>
```

Notice that both the edit link and the add link point to EmployeeForm.jsp. The add link passes the dept ID on the query string, while the edit link passes the employee ID. Also notice that the edit link passes the edit parameter, which is set to true. This means EmployeeForm.jsp will have to keep track of whether it is in add mode or edit mode, and it will have to populate the HTML form fields if it is in edit mode. Listing 13.6 shows the amount of Java code EmployeeForm.jsp needs to perform its tasks. It is scriptlet overkill. Later, when we switch to Struts, it will handle add and edit modes transparently.

```
<%@page contentType="text/html"%>
<jsp:useBean id="employee" scope="page" class="bean.Employee" />
<jsp:setProperty name="employee" property="id" param="id" />

<jsp:include page="Header.jsp">
   <jsp:param name="header" value="Employee Form"/>
</jsp:include>

<%
  String firstName = "";
  String lastName = "";
  String phone = "";
  String sEdit = request.getParameter("edit");
  String deptID = "0";
  String mode = "";
```

Listing 13.6 EmployeeForm.jsp. (continues)

```
  boolean edit  = sEdit!=null;
  if (edit == true){
    mode = "edit";
    out.println("<h1> edit mode </h1>");
    employee.load();
    firstName = employee.getFirstName();
    lastName = employee.getLastName();
    phone = employee.getPhone();
    deptID = ""+employee.getDeptId();

  }
  else{
    mode="add";
    out.println("<h1> add mode </h1>");

    deptID=request.getParameter("deptid");
  }

%>


<form action="EmployeeUpdate.jsp" method="POST" >
    First Name <input type="TEXT" name="firstName" value="<%=
  firstName%>"/>
    Last Name <input type="TEXT" name="lastName" value="<%=
  lastName%>"/>
    Phone <input type="TEXT" name="phone" value="<%=phone%>"/>
    <input type="HIDDEN" name="deptId" value="<%=deptID%>"/>
    <input type="HIDDEN" name="id" value="<jsp:getProperty name=
  "employee" property="id"/>"/>
    <input type="HIDDEN" name="mode" value="<%=mode%>"/>
    <input type="SUBMIT" />
</form>

<%@include file="/Footer.jsp" %>
```

Listing 13.6 EmployeeForm.jsp. (continued)

EmployeeForm.jsp has an HTML form that posts to EmployeeUpdate.jsp, shown in Listing 13.7. EmployeeUpdate.jsp could be written as a servlet since it is essentially non-graphical. Most of the logic for managing mode was done by EmployeeForm.jsp, so EmployeeUpdate.jsp is fairly simple. It maps the HTML form parameters to the Employee bean and then calls add() or edit(), depending on what mode the form was in.

```
<%@page contentType="text/html"%>
<html>
<head><title>Employee Add/Edit</title></head>
<body>

<jsp:useBean id="employee" scope="page" class="bean.Employee" />
<jsp:setProperty name="employee"  property="*" />

<%
String mode=request.getParameter("mode");

if (mode.equals("add")){
   employee.add();

}else{
   employee.edit();
}
%>


Employee <%=employee.getLastName()%>

<a href="EmployeeListing.jsp?deptid=<%=employee.getDeptId()%>">
 back to listing </a>

</body>
</html>
```

Listing 13.7 EmployeeUpdate.jsp.

That's it. As you can see, it is a fairly simple application, but it proves how powerful JSP is. With a minimal amount of code, we implemented add, edit, list, and delete functionality for Employees. However, we have not done a good job of separating the presentation logic from the HTML. This code base would be difficult to maintain, and it would be hard to solicit the help of a Web designer. In the next section, we learn how to use Struts to get the Java out of our JSPs so that we can live in peace and harmony with our Web designer friends.

The MVC Struts Version of the Application

The Dept and Employee classes make up the Model for this application, too. The Model is unchanged from our previous example.

The MVC version consists of the following JSPs:

- DeptListing.jsp
- EmployeeForm.jsp
- EmployeeListing.jsp
- Footer.jsp
- Header.jsp

The MVC version also includes the following Actions:

- DeleteEmployeeAction.java
- EditEmployeeAction.java
- ListDepartmentsAction.java
- ListEmployeesAction.java
- UpdateEmployeeAction.java

And the following ActionForm:

- EmployeeForm.java

At first, this seems like a lot of extra components—and it is—but it isn't as bad as you think. The Actions separate the Java code from the JSPs and are relatively small.

List Department Action

ListDepartmentsAction.java works in conjunction with DeptListing.jsp to list all the departments in the company. We moved all the necessary Java code out of DeptListing.jsp and put it into ListDepartmentsAction.java.

An action mapping binds ListDepartmentsAction.java and DeptListing.jsp to a path /listDepartments.do, as follows:

```
<action path="/listDepartments"
        type="action.ListDepartmentsAction"
        scope="request"
        validate="true">
  <forward name="listing"
                path="/DeptListing.jsp">
  </forward>
</action>
```

Actions interact with the Model classes and then delegate the display to JSP. In this case, action.ListDepartmentsAction will get the departments out of the Model and pass them to the DeptListing.jsp to display.

You may wonder why the link ends in *.do*. This identifies the action so that the Action Servlet (org.apache.struts.action.ActionServlet) can handle these requests. The configuration is stored in /WEB-INF/struts-config.xml as specified by the config parameter in the Action Servlet declaration in the deployment descriptor (/WEB-INF/web.xml), as shown here:

```
    <servlet>
      <servlet-name>action</servlet-name>
      <servlet-class>org.apache.struts.action.ActionServlet</servlet-
  class>
      <init-param>
        <param-name>application</param-name>
        <param-value>ApplicationResources</param-value>
      </init-param>
        <init-param>
          <param-name>config</param-name>
          <param-value>/WEB-INF/struts-config.xml</param-value>
        </init-param>
...
        <load-on-startup>2</load-on-startup>
    </servlet>
```

There is an servlet mapping entry in the deployment descriptor so that the Action Servlet handles all requests that end in *.do, as follows:

```
 <!-- Standard Action Servlet Mapping -->
    <servlet-mapping>
        <servlet-name>action</servlet-name>
        <url-pattern>*.do</url-pattern>
    </servlet-mapping>
```

The ListDepartmentsActionclass is particularly short. It gets all of the departments in the system, maps the departments into request scope, and then forwards *listing*. From the action mapping above, you can see that *listing* is mapped to DeptListing.jsp.

The implementation of this Action has only two lines of code in the execute() method:

```
package action;
...

import bean.Dept;
...
public class ListDepartmentsAction extends Action {

...
    public ActionForward execute(
        ActionMapping mapping, ActionForm form,
        HttpServletRequest request, HttpServletResponse response)
                          throws Exception {

        request.setAttribute("departments",Dept.getDepartments());
        return mapping.findForward("listing");

    }

}
```

Action Details

Notice that the ListDepartmentAction subclasses the Action class. The Action class defines an execute() method, as follows:

```
public ActionForward execute(ActionMapping mapping,
                             ActionForm form,
                             HttpServletRequest request,
                             HttpServletResponse response)
  throws Exception;
```

Action classes process requests via their execute() method and return an ActionForward object. The ActionForward object identifies where control should be forwarded (in our case, DeptListing). Most of your interaction with the Model classes will occur in the Actions. The Model will in turn do things such as add rows to database tables.

When the Action has finished interacting with the Model, it returns an appropriate ActionForward object, which identifies the JSP page to be used to generate the View. The Action and the View (forward) are defined in the configuration file so that they can be changed without modifying any code. The findForward() method of the action mapping is used to look up the View. For example, if you wanted to add steps in a user registration system, you could do so without affecting your current code base. Just add the new Actions and JSP, and wire them into the application using the Struts configuration file.

The Struts DeptListing View

Notice that the Struts DeptListing in Listing 13.8 is considerably different from the DeptListing in Listing 13.4. First, the Struts DeptListing has no JSP scriptlet and no import page directives; instead, it uses the custom tags that come with Struts.

```
<%@ taglib uri="strutslogic" prefix="logic" %>
<%@ taglib uri="strutsbean" prefix="bean" %>
<%@ taglib uri="strutshtml" prefix="html" %>


<jsp:include page="Header.jsp">
   <jsp:param name="header" value="Dept Listing"/>
</jsp:include>


   <table>

      <logic:iterate id="dept" name="departments">
```

Listing 13.8 Struts DeptListing.jsp. (continues)

```
            <tr>
                <td>
                    <bean:write name="dept" property="name" />
                </td>

                <td>
                  <html:link  page="/listEmployees.do"
                          paramId="deptid" paramName="dept"
                          paramProperty="id">
                  show
                  </html:link>

                </td>

            </tr>
        </logic:iterate>

    </table>

  <%@include file="/Footer.jsp" %>
```

Listing 13.8 Struts DeptListing.jsp. (continued)

The structure of the JSP is similar to our previous example. For instance, we still use the include action to dynamically include Header.jsp:

```
<jsp:include page="Header.jsp">
    <jsp:param name="header" value="Dept Listing"/>
</jsp:include>
```

The Struts Custom Tags

One way the Struts DeptListing gets rid of the JSP scriptlets is by using these Struts tag libraries: bean, logic, and html. We use these taglibs throughout this chapter to remove Java code from our JSPs.

The Struts DeptListing uses the taglib directive to import three taglibs, as follows:

```
<%@ taglib uri="strutslogic" prefix="logic" %>
<%@ taglib uri="strutsbean" prefix="bean" %>
<%@ taglib uri="strutshtml" prefix="html" %>
```

The tag library descriptor files are stored in /WEB-INF/tlds. Then, a reference to the tag libraries is defined in the Web application deployment descriptor (/WEB-INF/web.xml) as follows:

```
      <!-- Struts Tag Library Descriptor -->
    <taglib>
        <taglib-uri>
```

```
            strutsbean
        </taglib-uri>
        <taglib-location>
            /WEB-INF/tlds/struts-bean.tld
        </taglib-location>
    </taglib>
    <taglib>
        <taglib-uri>
            strutshtml
        </taglib-uri>
        <taglib-location>
            /WEB-INF/tlds/struts-html.tld
        </taglib-location>
    </taglib>
    <taglib>
        <taglib-uri>
            strutslogic
        </taglib-uri>
        <taglib-location>
            /WEB-INF/tlds/struts-logic.tld
        </taglib-location>
    </taglib>
...
```

Logic Iterate Struts Custom Tag

Remember that the ListDepartmens action mapped the departments to our request object. Instead of using a JSP scriptlet to iterate over each entry in the department list in order to build an HTML table, this version of DeptListing.jsp uses the Struts iterate tag:

```
        <logic:iterate id="dept" name="departments">
            <tr>

...
            </tr>
        </logic:iterate>
```

Compare this to the first version of DeptListing, which used a scriptlet:

```
<%
    for (int index=0; index < depts.length; index++){
%>
```

If you are a Web designer, the Struts version looks less intimidating.

Note that the iterate tag specifies that it is going to iterate over the departments array with the name attribute—that is, *name="departments"*. Each iteration extracts a department and maps to a dept mapped to the page scope of our JSP, as specified by the id attribute—that is, *id="dept"*.

Bean Write Struts Custom Tag

The dept that is mapped to our page scope is an instance of bean.Dept. You may recall that bean.Dept has a property called name. Each iteration defines another row in the HTML table with the dept name and a link to the listing of employees in the dept. The dept name is extracted with the bean:write custom tag:

```
<td>
    <bean:write name="dept" property="name" />
</td>
```

Note that the name attribute specifies the bean we wish to write out, and the property specifies which field of the beans we wish to write out. Compare this to the last version of DeptListing:

```
<td>
    <%=depts[index].getName()%>
</td>
```

This Struts version seems to be a little more verbose, but the former version requires knowledge of Java arrays and indexing.

HTML Link Struts Custom Tag

Next, we need to add a link to the employee listing using the html:link tag:

```
<td>
   <html:link  page="/listEmployees.do"
               paramId="deptid"
               paramName="dept" paramProperty="id">
   show
   </html:link>
</td>
```

Notice that we do not link directly to EmployeeListing.jsp. This is because we've divided what was in EmployeeListing into two components: the ListEmployeesAction class and EmployeeListing.jsp (more on this later in this section). The html:link tag specifies the page to link with the page attribute—/listEmployees.do, in this case. The link tag also lets you specify the name of the parameter that you wish to pass using the paramId attribute—*paramId="deptid"*. The link tag will automatically build the correct query string and encode it if necessary. The html:link tag uses paramName and paramProperty to specify the name of the bean and the name of the property it will use to set the deptid parameter of the query string. The above html:link is equivalent to this code in the first non-Struts DeptListing.jsp, as follows:

```
<td>
     <a href="EmployeeListing.jsp?deptid=<%=depts[index].
     getId()%>">
         show
     </a>
</td>
```

The problem with the first sample solution for adding the EmployeeListing link is that it will not automatically encode the jsessionid; if users have cookies turned off, the application will lose their session information when they click on the EmployeeListing link. The html:link takes care of encoding the URL for us so the link will not lose the session information if the user has cookies turned off.

The html:link for the Struts employee listing points to /listEmployees.do. The list Employees action is defined with the following action mapping in the configuration file:

```
<action path="/listEmployees"
        type="action.ListEmployeesAction"
        scope="request"
        validate="true">
  <forward name="listing"
           path="/EmployeeListing.jsp">
  </forward>
</action>
```

EmployeeListing: Action and View

Thus, the Action Servlet directs the request specified by /listEmployees.do to the action.ListEmployeeAction class, shown in Listing 13.9.

```
package action;

import javax.servlet.http.HttpServletRequest;
import javax.servlet.http.HttpServletResponse;

import org.apache.struts.action.Action;
import org.apache.struts.action.ActionForm;
import org.apache.struts.action.ActionForward;
import org.apache.struts.action.ActionMapping;
import bean.Dept;

/**
 * @author Rick Hightower
 * @struts:action
 *          path="/listEmployees"
 *
 *
 * @struts:action-forward name="listing" path="/EmployeeListing.jsp"
 */
public class ListEmployeesAction extends Action {


/**
 * @see org.apache.struts.action.Action#execute(ActionMapping,
```

Listing 13.9 ListEmployeesAction.java. (continues)

```
ActionForm,
                 HttpServletRequest, HttpServletResponse)
*/
   public ActionForward execute(
        ActionMapping mapping,
        ActionForm form,
        HttpServletRequest request,
        HttpServletResponse response)
                throws Exception {

      Dept dept = new Dept();

      int deptid = Integer.parseInt(
                  request.getParameter("deptid"));

      dept.setId(deptid);

      request.setAttribute("dept",dept);
      return mapping.findForward("listing");
   }
}
```

Listing 13.9 ListEmployeesAction.java. (continued)

The ListEmployeesAction creates a new Dept domain object called dept:

```
Dept dept = new Dept();
```

Then, it gets the deptid from the request—that is, from the query string parameter deptid, as shown here:

```
int deptid = Integer.parseInt(request.getParameter("deptid"));
```

It passes the deptid to the Dept domain object, and then maps the dept to the request so that the Dept domain object can use the ID to load the employees for the department and the JSP can use the Dept instance to display department information of the end user:

```
dept.setId(deptid);
request.setAttribute("dept",dept);
```

Finally, it forwards this request to the View—that is, the listing, which is mapped to EmployeeListing.jsp in the Struts configuration file:

```
return mapping.findForward("listing");
```

The View, EmployeeListing.jsp, uses the dept object to iterate over a list of employees:

```
<logic:iterate id="employee" name="dept" property="employees">
    <tr>
...
    </tr>
</logic:iterate>
```

Notice that this time we use the property parameter to specify that we want the employees property from the dept object. The previous code is functionally equivalent to the following non-Struts code in the original EmployeeListing.jsp:

```
<%    Employee[] emps = dept.getEmployees(); %>

...

<%
    for (int index=0; index < emps.length; index++){
%>
        <tr>
...
        </tr>
<%}%>
```

Here we can see that using custom tags and Struts really pays off--our code is much simpler and relies a lot less on the Web designer's knowledge of Java. The complete listing for the Struts version of EmployeeListing appears in Listing 13.10. Please take some time and compare this to Listing 13.5 (the original Model 1 EmployeeListing.jsp).

```
<%@ taglib uri="strutslogic" prefix="logic" %>
<%@ taglib uri="strutsbean" prefix="bean" %>
<%@ taglib uri="strutshtml" prefix="html" %>


<jsp:include page="Header.jsp">
   <jsp:param name="header" value="Employee Listing"/>
</jsp:include>

<html:link    page="/EmployeeForm.jsp"
          paramId="deptid"
          paramName="dept"    paramProperty="id">
   add
</html:link>


   <table>

   <logic:iterate id="employee" name="dept" property="employees">
      <tr>
         <td>
```

Listing 13.10 Struts EmployeeListing.jsp. (continues)

```
            <bean:write name="employee" property="firstName" />
        </td>

        <td>
            <bean:write name="employee" property="lastName" />
        </td>

        <td>
            <bean:write name="employee" property="phone" />
        </td>

        <td>
            <html:link   page="/editEmployee.do"
                         paramId="id"
                         paramName="employee" paramProperty="id">
            edit
            </html:link>
        </td>

        <td>
            <html:link   page="/deleteEmployee.do"
                         paramId="id"
                         paramName="employee" paramProperty="id">
            delete
            </html:link>
        </td>

    </tr>
  </logic:iterate>

  </table>

<%@include file="/Footer.jsp" %>
```

Listing 13.10 Struts EmployeeListing.jsp. (continued)

The Struts EmployeeListing has an add link just as before, and for each employee there is also an edit link and a delete link. Notice that the edit link points to /editEmployee.do while the add link point to /EmployeeForm.jsp. The add link passes the dept ID on the query string, while the edit link passes the employee ID just as before.

Managing Form Data with Struts

In our previous non-Struts example, EmployeeForm.jsp had to keep track of whether it was in add or edit mode, and it populated the HTML form fields if it was in edit mode.

Look back to Listing 13.5 to see the amount of Java code EmployeeForm.jsp needed to perform its tasks; as we mentioned then, it was scriptlet overkill. This time, EditEmployeeAction will (with some help from the Struts framework) handle the population of the form fields. Listing 13.11 shows EditEmployeeAction.java.

```
package action;

import javax.servlet.http.HttpServletRequest;
import javax.servlet.http.HttpServletResponse;

import org.apache.struts.action.Action;
import org.apache.struts.action.ActionForm;
import org.apache.struts.action.ActionForward;
import org.apache.struts.action.ActionMapping;
import bean.Employee;
import form.EmployeeForm;

/**
 * @author Rick Hightower
 * @struts:action path="/editEmployee"
 *           attribute="employeeForm"
 *
 * @struts:action-forward name="form" path="/EmployeeForm.jsp"
 */
public class EditEmployeeAction extends Action {

   /**
    * @see org.apache.struts.action.Action#execute(ActionMapping,
    */
   public ActionForward execute(
         ActionMapping mapping,
         ActionForm form,
         HttpServletRequest request,
         HttpServletResponse response)
                        throws Exception {

     int empid = Integer.parseInt(request.getParameter("id"));


           /* Populate the employee form */
     if (form == null) {
           form = new EmployeeForm();
           if ("request".equals(mapping.getScope())) {
```

Listing 13.11 Struts EditEmployeeAction.java. (continues)

```
            request.setAttribute(mapping.getAttribute(),
form);
        } else {
            request.getSession()
                .setAttribute(mapping.getAttribute(), form);
        }
    }



        /* Load the employee information */
    EmployeeForm eform = (EmployeeForm) form;
    eform.getEmployee().load(empid);

        /* Set the mode attributes */
    eform.setAction(EmployeeForm.EDIT_MODE);

    return mapping.findForward("form");

  }
}
```

Listing 13.11 Struts EditEmployeeAction.java. (continued)

The action mapping for EditEmployeeAction is defined in the Struts configuration file as follows:

```
<action path="/editEmployee"
        type="action.EditEmployeeAction"
        attribute="employeeForm"
        scope="request"
        validate="true">
  <forward name="form"
           path="/EmployeeForm.jsp">
  </forward>
</action>
```

Notice that the attribute refers to the name that the EmployeeForm bean will be mapped to in the request (more on this later in this section).

EditEmployeeAction looks up the employee ID passed on the query string:

```
int empid = Integer.parseInt(request.getParameter("id"));
```

EditEmployeeAction then creates a new EmployeeForm (which is defined in Listing 13.12) and maps the employee form to the session object or the request object, depending on how the scope was defined in the ActionMapping:

```
        /* Populate the employee form */
    if (form == null) {
```

```
            form = new EmployeeForm();
            if ("request".equals(mapping.getScope())) {
                request.setAttribute(mapping.getAttribute(), form);
            } else {
                request.getSession()
                    .setAttribute(mapping.getAttribute(), form);
            }
        }
```

EmployeeForm has a property that refers to a bean.Employee—in our case, the Employee domain object. EditEmployeeAction passes the empid to the nested bean.Employee instance via the load() method. You may recall that the load() method loads the Employee information that is stored in the database. The code that loads the nested employee property in EmployeeForm is defined as follows:

```
        /* Load the employee information */
EmployeeForm eform = (EmployeeForm) form;
eform.getEmployee().load(empid);
```

EmployeeForm has a property called action, which specifies whether EmployeeForm should be in add, edit, or delete mode. EditEmployeeAction sets the Action to edit mode, as shown here:

```
        /* Set the mode attributes */
eform.setAction(EmployeeForm.EDIT_MODE);
```

Finally, EditEmployeeAction forwards this request to the View:

```
return mapping.findForward("form");
```

The form forward is mapped to EmployeeForm.jsp in the Struts configuration file—*<forward name="form" path="/EmployeeForm.jsp">*. The EmployeeForm.java extends ActionForm and is used to populate the HTML form in EmployeeForm.jsp, and validate form data from Employee.jsp (see Listings 13.12 and 13.13 for the complete code for EmployeeForm.java and EmployeeForm.jsp). Before we delve into the details of how EmployeeForm.jsp is implemented, let's cover some background on form beans.

```
package form;

import javax.servlet.http.HttpServletRequest;

import org.apache.struts.action.ActionErrors;
import org.apache.struts.action.ActionError;
import org.apache.struts.action.ActionForm;
import org.apache.struts.action.ActionMapping;

import bean.Employee;

/**
```

Listing 13.12 Struts form bean EmployeeForm.java. (continues)

```
 * @author Rick Hightower
 *
 * @struts:form name="employeeForm"
 */
public class EmployeeForm extends ActionForm {

public static final String EDIT_MODE = "edit";
   public static final String DELETE_MODE = "delete";
   public static final String ADD_MODE = "add";

   String action;

   Employee employee;

   public EmployeeForm() {
      employee = new Employee();
      action = EmployeeForm.ADD_MODE;
   }

   public Employee getEmployee() {
      return employee;
   }
   public void setEmployee(Employee employee) {
      this.employee = employee;
   }

   /**
    * Returns the action.
    * @return String
    */
   public String getAction() {
      return action;
   }

   /**
    * Sets the action.
    * @param action The action to set
    */
   public void setAction(String action) {
      this.action = action;
   }

   /**
```

Listing 13.12 Struts form bean EmployeeForm.java. (continues)

```
     * @see org.apache.struts.action.ActionForm#reset(ActionMapping,
                                          HttpServletRequest)
     */
    public void reset(ActionMapping mapping,
                HttpServletRequest request) {


        this.employee = new Employee();
        this.action = ADD_MODE;
    }

    /**
     * @see org.apache.struts.action.ActionForm#validate(ActionMapping,
     *                                        HttpServletRequest)
     **/
    public ActionErrors validate(ActionMapping arg0,
                        HttpServletRequest arg1) {
        ActionErrors errors = new ActionErrors();
        if ((employee.getFirstName() == null)
            || (employee.getFirstName().length() < 3)) {

            errors.add("FirstName", new ActionError("error.employee.
            firstname"));

        }
        return errors;
    }

}
```

Listing 13.12 Struts form bean EmployeeForm.java. (continued)

```
<%@ taglib uri="strutsbean"  prefix="bean" %>
<%@ taglib uri="strutshtml"  prefix="html" %>
<%@ taglib uri="strutslogic"  prefix="logic" %>


<jsp:include page="Header.jsp">
   <jsp:param name="header" value="Employee Form"/>
</jsp:include>
```

Listing 13.13 Struts EmployeeForm.jsp. (continues)

```
<logic:equal name="employeeForm" property="action"
        scope="request" value="edit">
  <h3>Editing employee</h3>
</logic:equal>

<logic:equal name="employeeForm" property="action"
        scope="request" value="delete">
  <h3>Are you sure you want to delete the following employee?</h3>
</logic:equal>

<logic:equal name="employeeForm" property="action"
        scope="request" value="add">
  <h3>Adding a new employee</h3>
</logic:equal>



<html:errors/>

<html:form action="/updateEmployee.do" method="POST">

   First Name <html:text property="employee.firstName" />

   Last Name <html:text property="employee.lastName" />
   Phone <html:text property="employee.phone" />
   <html:hidden property="employee.id" />
   <html:hidden property="employee.deptId" />

   <html:hidden property="action"/>
   <html:submit property="submit"/>
   <input type="hidden" name="deptid" value="<%=request.
  getParameter("deptid")%>" />

</html:form>

<%@include file="/Footer.jsp" %>
```

Listing 13.13 Struts EmployeeForm.jsp. (continued)

Background Information on ActionForms

ActionForm beans allow you to create a bridge between HTML forms in the View and domain objects in the Model. EmployeeForm.java defines an ActionForm bean. EmployeeForm, which extends the ActionForm class, represents the HTML input form parameters used in the Struts version of EmployeeForm.jsp (which we define in detail later in this section). We declare the EmployeeForm form bean in the Struts configuration file, as follows:

```
<form-beans>
  <form-bean name="employeeForm"
             type="form.EmployeeForm" />
</form-beans>
```

The Struts Action Servlet, the Controller servlet, will use EmployeeForm to automatically map a new EmployeeForm bean into the request or session if it does not exist. Then, it will use EmployeeForm to map any HTML form request parameter whose name corresponds to the name of a property in the bean or in the nested bean properties. This is similar to the standard JSP action <jsp:setProperty> when you use the asterisk wildcard to select all properties; this is more powerful, however, since it can work with nested beans, and it features support for validation.

Form Validation and Application Resources

The EmployeeForm bean overrides the validate() method and provides error messages in the standard application resource. The Struts framework uses this validate() method to notify you when in the life cycle of the form bean to do the validation. EmployeeForm defines the validate() method as follows:

```
   public ActionErrors validate(ActionMapping arg0,
 HttpServletRequest arg1) {
       ActionErrors errors = new ActionErrors();
       if ((employee.getFirstName() == null)
           || (employee.getFirstName().length() < 3)) {

           errors.add("FirstName",
           new ActionError("error.employee.firstname"));
      }
       return errors;
   }
```

This is a simple example of some possible validation. It just checks if the employee's first name is present and, if it is, whether it is greater than three characters. If it is not valid, the validate() method creates a new ActionError and adds it to the list of errors. The ActionError refers to an error message (error.employee.firstname) defined in ApplicationResources.properties, which is located in the classes directory of the Web application. The ApplicationResources defines String constants used by the application, and can be used to help create an internationalized version of our application. ApplicationResources.properties defines the following properties for validating this form:

```
error.employee.firstname=<li>First name must be set and greater than
  three characters</li>

errors.header=<h3><font color="red">There were problems processing
  your form: <ul>

errors.footer=</ul></font><hr>
```

The errors.header and errors.footer are used to define the boundaries of the error block. The error.employee.firstname is the message that will be used for this applicaiton. If we want to provide a German-language version of ApplicationResources, we could also define an ApplicationResource_dn.properties file, for Japanese an ApplicationResource_jp.properties file, and on.

View: Forms and Displaying Validation Errors to Users

The EmployeeForm.jsp file uses the html:errors tag to inform the user of any errors that were created by our validate() method:

```
<html:errors/>
```

The EmployeeForm form bean has a nested property reference to bean.Employee, the employee domain object. This "employee" property will be used to map properties of the employee to form parameters in EmployeeForm.jsp:

```
<html:form action="/updateEmployee.do" method="POST">

    First Name <html:text property="employee.firstName" />

    Last Name <html:text property="employee.lastName" />
    Phone <html:text property="employee.phone" />
    <html:hidden property="employee.id" />
    <html:hidden property="employee.deptId" />

    <html:hidden property="action"/>
    <html:submit property="submit"/>
    <bean:parameter id="deptid" name="deptid"/>
    <input type="hidden" name="deptid" value="<bean:write
  name="deptid" />" />

</html:form>
```

Notice that all of the properties are passed back as either fields the user can modify or as hidden fields. The mode is sent via the action property.

EmployeeForm.jsp's HTML form posts its form data to the /updateEmployee.do action. The updateEmployee action mapping is defined as follows:

```
<action path="/updateEmployee"
        type="action.UpdateEmployeeAction"
        name="employeeForm"
        attribute="employeeForm"
        scope="request"
        input="/EmployeeForm.jsp"
        validate="true">
  <forward name="listing"
                  path="/EmployeeListing.jsp">
  </forward>
</action>
```

Updating the Employee

Thus, the path updateEmployee.do is mapped to UpdateEmployeeAction, which is shown in Listing 13.14. Note that the name attribute specifies the form that will be used—in this case, it refers to employeeForm, which is mapped to the EmployeeForm form bean. UpdateEmployeeAction does one of the following—adds an employee, updates an employee, or deletes an employee—based on what the EmployeeForms action property is set to. Then, it shows the listing of employees by forwarding it back to EmployeeListing.jsp.

```
package action;

import org.apache.struts.action.*;
import javax.servlet.http.*;
import form.EmployeeForm;
import bean.Dept;
import bean.Employee;


/**
 * @author Rick Hightower
 * @struts:action name="employeeForm"
 *            path="/updateEmployee"
 *            input="/EmployeeForm.jsp"
 *            attribute="employeeForm"
 *
 * @struts:action-forward name="listing" path="/EmployeeListing.jsp"
 */
public class UpdateEmployeeAction extends Action {

    public ActionForward execute(
            ActionMapping mapping,
            ActionForm form,
            HttpServletRequest request,
            HttpServletResponse response)
                    throws Exception {

            /* Cast the ActionForm into EmployeeForm */
        EmployeeForm eform = (EmployeeForm) form;

            /* Add, edit or delete this employee */

            /* ADD */
```

Listing 13.14 Struts UpdateEmployeeAction.java. (continues)

```
        if (EmployeeForm.ADD_MODE.equals(eform.getAction())) {

            Employee employee = eform.getEmployee();
            int deptid = Integer.parseInt(
                        request.getParameter("deptid"));

           employee.setDeptId(deptid);
            eform.getEmployee().add();

            /* EDIT */
        } else if (EmployeeForm.EDIT_MODE.equals(eform.getAction())) {
           eform.getEmployee().edit();

            /* DELETE */
        } else if (EmployeeForm.DELETE_MODE.equals(eform.getAction())){
           eform.getEmployee().remove();

            /* ILLEGAL STATE */
        } else {
           throw new java.lang.IllegalStateException("invalid " +
                        "action");
        }

        Dept dept = new Dept();
        int deptid = eform.getEmployee().getDeptId();
        dept.setId(deptid);
        request.setAttribute("dept",dept);


        return mapping.findForward("listing");
    }

}
```

Listing 13.14 Struts UpdateEmployeeAction.java. (continued)

Let's walk through UpdateEmployeeAction step-by-step since it is by far the most complicated action. Struts will instantiate an EmployeeForm and populate its properties and nested bean properties. Then it will allow EmployeeForm to validate itself. If the validation fails, the user will be shown the error message and given a chance to change things; if the validation passes, the execute() method of UpdateEmployeeAction will be called. Therefore, for all intents and purposes the form bean passed to the execute() method is a valid one. This means that the first thing the execute() method does is cast the ActionForm form to an EmployeeForm, as shown here:

```
         /* Cast the ActionForm into EmployeeForm */
      EmployeeForm eform = (EmployeeForm) form;
```

You may recall that the employee form has an action property. The action property specifies what mode the form was submitted in—add, edit, or delete. We check to see if the form is in add mode:

```
          /* ADD */
      if (EmployeeForm.ADD_MODE.equals(eform.getAction())) {

          Employee employee = eform.getEmployee();
          int deptid = Integer.parseInt(
                           request.getParameter("deptid"));

         employee.setDeptId(deptid);
         employee().add();

      }
```

If the form was in add mode, then we get the nested employee from the form, set the employee dept id, and then call the employee.add() method to store the employee in the database. The EmployeeForm form bean default action mode is add. If the employee form's mode is set to edit, as shown here:

```
          /* EDIT */
     } else if
(EmployeeForm.EDIT_MODE.equals(eform.getAction())) {
          eform.getEmployee().edit();
     }
```

then we get the nested employee domain object and call its edit() method to update the employee in the database. You may recall that EditEmployeeAction populated the form bean and set its action mode to edit. If the employee form's mode is set to delete, as shown here:

```
          /* DELETE */
     } else if (EmployeeForm.DELETE_MODE.equals(eform.getAction())){
         eform.getEmployee().remove();
     }
```

then we get the nested employee domain object and call its remove() method to remove the employee from the database. DeleteEmployeeAction is similar to EditEmployeeAction in that it sets the mode to delete (they are so similar that we do not cover both actions, just EditEmployeeAction).

Now we need to prepare the employee listing view, as shown here:

```
Dept dept = new Dept();
int deptid = eform.getEmployee().getDeptId();
dept.setId(deptid);
request.setAttribute("dept",dept);
```

This code prepares the dept so that the view can use the dept to get the list of current employees. Finally, we forward this request to EmployeeListing:

```
return mapping.findForward("listing");
```

That's it. It is still a fairly simple application, and it is a lot more functional than before. You can see again the power of Struts. With just a little more code, we implemented add, edit, list, and delete functionality for Employees, with the added benefits of validation, encoded URLs, and more. Unlike with the Model 1 version of the application, we have done a good job of separating the presentation logic from the HTML. This code base will be easier to maintain and change. We have removed our Java code from our JSPs, and we can live in peace and harmony with our Web designer friends just as promised.

Templates

The Struts template custom tags are used to create templates for groups of pages that share a common format. The functionality of these templates is similar to the JSP include directive or the JSP include action, but more dynamic than the include directive and more flexible than the include action.

Previously, we used the JSP include action to dynamically include the header and footer files as runtime resources:

```
<jsp:include page="Header.jsp">

    <jsp:param name="header" value="Dept Listing"/>
</jsp:include>
...
<%@include file="/Footer.jsp" %>
```

This is okay, but what if we want the copyright information somewhere other than the footer? This approach is not very flexible. A more flexible approach would let us define a template, and the individual pages would insert their components into the template. You can think of templates as the reverse of dynamic includes.

The template taglib contains three custom tags: put, get, and insert. Put tags put content into request scope, and this content is used by the template JSP to fill itself in using the get tag. Templates are included with the insert tag.

The first step is to define a template JSP (Template.jsp) as follows:

```
<%@ taglib uri='strutstemplate' prefix='template' %>
<%@ taglib uri="strutshtml"  prefix="html" %>

<html:html>
<head>
    <html:base/>
    <title>
        <template:get name='header'/>
    </title>
</head>

<body>
<h1><template:get name='header'/></h1>

<table border='1'>
    <tr>
        <td>
```

```
          <template:get name='navigation'/>
        </td>
        <td>
          <template:get name='content'/>
        </td>
    </tr>
</table>

<template:get name='footer'/>
</body>

</html:html>
```

This code would specify the layout for our pages; it is saved in a file called Template.jsp. The template:get custom tag gets content from the pages that are using this template. The template expects the pages to fill out the navigation, header, content, and footer. Here is an example of DeptListing redone to use templates:

```
<%@ taglib uri="strutslogic" prefix="logic" %>
<%@ taglib uri="strutsbean" prefix="bean" %>
<%@ taglib uri="strutshtml" prefix="html" %>
<%@ taglib uri="strutstemplate" prefix="template" %>

<template:insert template="/Template.jsp">
    <template:put name='header' direct='true' content='Department
Listing'/>
    <template:put name='footer' content='/CopyLeft.jsp' />
    <template:put name='navigation' content='/Navigation.jsp' />
    <template:put name='content' >
    <table>
        <logic:iterate id="dept" name="departments">
            <tr>
                <td>
                    <bean:write name="dept" property="name" />
                </td>
                <td>
                    <html:link  page="/listEmployees.do"
                                paramId="deptid"
                                paramName="dept" paramProperty="id">
                    show
                    </html:link>
                </td>
            </tr>
        </logic:iterate>
    </table>
    </template:put >
</template:insert>
```

You'll notice how much shorter this listing is than the last version of DeptListing.jsp. Also notice that there is almost no code that specifies the layout of the page. Let's step through the template version of DeptLising.jsp.

The first step is to import the Struts template taglib:

```
<%@ taglib uri="strutstemplate" prefix="template" %>
```

Then, we use the template:insert custom tag to insert the template:

```
<template:insert template="/Template.jsp">
</template:insert>
```

The template parameter specifies the page we are going to use as a template, which was shown earlier. Although we insert the template, we still have to fill in the missing pieces using the template:put custom tag:

```
<template:put name='footer' content='/CopyLeft.jsp' />
```

The line of code *<template:put name='footer' content='/CopyLeft.jsp' />* inserts the full output of CopyLeft.jsp in the location defined in the template as *<template:get name='footer'/>*. The name attribute of the put in this page will be put where the corresponding name attribute is used with a template:get in template jsp.

In addition to inserting the full output of JSP pages, you can include just the contents of a String. This is really useful for elements such as page titles:

```
<template:put name='header' direct='true' content='Department
Listing'/>
```

This code snippet uses template:put to replace the header get in the template with the String “Department Listing”. The direct parameter specifies that this will be a simple String in the content. If the direct parameter is false (the default), then the content parameter is assumed to be a resource, such as a JSP page.

You can also insert the body of the template:put custom tag, as shown here:

```
<template:put name='content' >
<table>
    <logic:iterate id="dept" name="departments">
        <tr>
            <td>
                <bean:write name="dept" property="name" />
            </td>
            <td>
                <html:link  page="/listEmployees.do"
                            paramId="deptid"
                            paramName="dept" paramProperty="id">
                show
                </html:link>
            </td>
        </tr>
    </logic:iterate>
</table>
```

Notice here that we do not have a content attribute; instead, template:put has a body.

Struts and XDoclet

In Chapter 20, we use XDoclet for servlets to keep the mapping and parameters in sync with the deployment descriptor, and we use XDoclet to keep the variables and attributes in sync with our custom tags. Well, we can also use XDoclet to keep our Action and form beans in sync with our Struts configuration file. In this chapter, we've used XDoclets to generate the Struts configuration file.

Each action defines an action mapping with JavaDoc tags—for example, UpdateEmployeeAction uses the @struts:action tag to define an action mapping:

```
/**
 * @author Rick Hightower
 * @struts:action name="employeeForm"
 *                path="/updateEmployee"
 *                input="/EmployeeForm.jsp"
 *                attribute="employeeForm"
 *
 * @struts:action-forward name="listing" path="/EmployeeListing.jsp"
 */
public class UpdateEmployeeAction extends Action {
```

In addition, you can create entries in the Struts configuration file for form beans. Here, EmployeeForm uses the @struts:form to define a form entry:

```
/**
 * @author Rick Hightower
 *
 * @struts:form name="employeeForm"
 */
public class EmployeeForm extends ActionForm {
```

The Struts configuration file generated appears in Listing 13.15. We find it much easier to generate this file rather than to create it by hand.

```
<?xml version="1.0" encoding="ISO-8859-1" ?>

<!DOCTYPE struts-config PUBLIC "-//Apache Software Foundation//DTD
 Struts Configuration 1.0//EN" http://jakarta.apache.org/struts/
 dtds/struts-config_1_0.dtd">

<struts-config>

 <!-- ========== Form Bean Definitions =========================== -->
 <form-beans>
  <form-bean name="employeeForm"
        type="form.EmployeeForm" />

  <!-- If you have non XDoclet forms, define them in a file called
 struts-forms.xml and place it in your merge directory. -->
 </form-beans>

 <!-- ========== Global Forward Definitions ====================== -->
```

Listing 13.15 Struts configuration file. (continues)

```
<!--
 Define your forwards in a file called global-forwards.xml and
 place it in your merge directory.
-->

<!-- ========== Action Mapping Definitions =================== -->
<action-mappings>
 <action path="/deleteEmployee"
       type="action.DeleteEmployeeAction"
       attribute="employeeForm"
       scope="request"
       validate="true">
   <forward name="form"
         path="/EmployeeForm.jsp">
   </forward>
 </action>
 <action path="/editEmployee"
       type="action.EditEmployeeAction"
       attribute="employeeForm"
       scope="request"
       validate="true">
   <forward name="form"
         path="/EmployeeForm.jsp">
   </forward>
 </action>
 <action path="/listDepartments"
       type="action.ListDepartmentsAction"
       scope="request"
       validate="true">
   <forward name="listing"
            path="/DeptListing.jsp">
   </forward>
 </action>
 <action path="/listEmployees"
       type="action.ListEmployeesAction"
       scope="request"
       validate="true">
   <forward name="listing"
         path="/EmployeeListing.jsp">
   </forward>
 </action>
 <action path="/updateEmployee"
       type="action.UpdateEmployeeAction"
       name="employeeForm"
```

Listing 13.15 Struts configuration file. (continues)

```
            attribute="employeeForm"
            scope="request"
            input="/EmployeeForm.jsp"
            validate="true">
        <forward name="listing"
                path="/EmployeeListing.jsp">
        </forward>
      </action>

      <!-- If you have non XDoclet actions, define them in a file
    called struts-actions.xml and place it in your merge directory. -->
    </action-mappings>

  </struts-config>
```

Listing 13.15 Struts configuration file. (continued)

The build script for this example has the following target to generate the Struts configuration:

```
<target name="actions">
  <delete file="${WEBINF}/struts-config.xml" />

  <taskdef name="webdoclet"
           classname="xdoclet.web.WebDocletTask"
           classpath="${xdocpath}"
  />
  <echo message="${xdocpath}" />

  <webdoclet
     sourcepath="${src}"
     destdir="${dest}">

     <classpath refid="cpath"/>

     <fileset dir="${src}">
        <include name="**/*.java" />
     </fileset>

     <strutsconfigxml destdir="${WEBINF}" />

  </webdoclet>


</target>
```

This code is similar to the targets for generating Web application deployment descriptors, except it uses the strutsconfigxml subtask to generate the Struts configuration file.

Summary

Struts is an MVC framework built on top of JSP, servlets, and taglibs. Struts is a growing, evolving project. It would be impossible to cover all of Struts in one chapter, but we did examine the fundamentals. We did not cover the Struts template mechanism or its new validation framework. The book *Mastering Jakarta Struts*, by James Goodwill, covers those topics in detail.

This chapter started out with a brief description of Struts. Then, we presented a common Model 1-style JSP application, which we later compared to a Struts/MVC version. With Struts, we were able to get our Java code out of our JSPs and create a flexible, easily maintained version of our application.

CHAPTER

14

Template Systems

Template technologies have the same goal as JSP. The aim is to be able to maintain the HTML used in dynamic responses by using standard tools and to keep the business logic separate from the display logic. Tag libraries have advantages similar to those of template systems, and their creation was driven by similar design goals; however, they do not enforce the separation of display logic and business logic because they are deployed inside JSP pages.

A number of technologies are available for templating. In this chapter, we take a look at one such system, Velocity. Which of these technologies you choose depends on your specific needs and on the skills of the people on your development and Web team. Before choosing a particular template system, it's worth evaluating several for yourself, and seeing which has the best match for your particular requirements.

Velocity is an open-source template system that is maintained as part of the Jakarta project. Data is provided to the Velocity engine by way of a context object. The engine then fills in the data. Velocity templates are based on a simple scripting language.

Why Templates Rather than JSP?

Templates and JSP are technologies that are used to allow the separation of HTML coding from Java coding. While templates and JSP are used for similar purposes, they work in totally different ways. The primary difference between templates and JSP is that JSP allows the use of Java code directly in its HTML. This makes JSP comparable to PHP or the Microsoft Active Server Pages system in many respects.

Unfortunately, the ability to include Java directly in JSP means that it is possible to write business logic directly in the HTML. You should resist putting business logic into your JSPs: the ability to insert Java is a temptation that is best avoided. Putting business logic into a JSP makes it difficult to test the logic with unit tests. It reduces the ability to reuse the code later, and it can lead to repetitive code that is difficult to maintain. It also means that HTML coders can accidentally break the Java code when they make changes to the pages.

Template systems typically do not allow the developer to place code in HTML at all. This way, it is impossible to confuse business rules with the display. This separation means that the HTML coders cannot get in the way of the Java coders, and each can go about doing what they are good at without stepping on one another's toes and messing up one another's work.

Templates also typically do not require a compilation process, and you can easily change them without worrying about ensuring that they and their linked components have been recompiled. Templating also encourages good system design—there is less temptation to mix the business logic of the system with the display logic. Separation of business logic from display logic is of course a theme we keep coming back to. However, keep in mind that it is still possible to misuse templates—for example, by including explicit HTML in a servlet rather than including it in the template.

What Is Velocity?

Velocity is a Java Template Engine maintained by the Apache Foundation. Velocity is not tied specifically to delivery of Web pages only; however, that is one of its primary uses. Velocity loads template files from disk directly rather than having them compiled into servlets like JSP.

The Velocity engine takes a template and a context, and merges the two to generate the output. The context contains all the data required for the template, usually in the form of data objects and lists. The Velocity Servlet provides a framework for working with the Velocity engine. As a result, you'll find that working with the Velocity engine is easy.

Installing Velocity

You can find a distribution of Velocity at http://jakarta.apache.org. The binary distribution comes with two JAR files: one that has the Velocity-related classes but none of the classes Velocity depends on, and a second JAR file that contains Velocity and all the other classes required for Velocity to work.

The binary distribution also contains instructions on how to build Velocity using another Jakarta project called Ant (see Chapter 20, "Developing Web Applications with Ant and XDoclet"). Unless you want to start maintaining and building Velocity yourself, you can just use the prebuilt JAR files. However, it can be worthwhile to have the source for development in an integrated development environment (IDE). This is because IDEs can look at the source and discover the parameter names, and thus give you good parameter names instead of nondescriptive ones.

Installing Velocity is simply a matter of copying the Velocity JAR file (called velocity-dep-1.2.jar) from the distribution into the *<$CATALINA_HOME>*/common/lib directory.

An Example of Using Velocity

In our first example (see Listing 14.1), we add two integers together and display the result. The HTML uses the dollar sign (a part of Velocity syntax) to indicate that the following string is to be interpreted as a variable. If you want to use a literal dollar-sign character in a Velocity template, you need to escape it by inserting a slash prior to the dollar sign.

```
<html>
<head><title>Velocity Example</title></head>
<body>

<h1>Velocity Example</h1>

<p>$a + $b = $c</p>

</center>
</html>
```

Listing 14.1 velocity.vm.

To manage the Velocity engine and make life generally easier for Velocity Web developers, a class called VelocityServlet is available that descends from HttpServlet. This new class replaces the normal doGet(), doPost(), and init() methods with handleRequest() and loadConfiguration() methods.

The handleRequest() method is similar to doGet() and doPost(), except that a template context is provided as a parameter. The context is used to store all the data you want to display in the HTML. The handleRequest() method expects to receive a valid template as the return value of the method. The VelocityServlet calls handleRequest(); then parses the template with the data supplied in the context before sending it to the user.

The loadConfiguration() method is similar in function to the servlet init() method and takes the same parameter as init(). It expects a return value, however—a Properties object with all of the values for the template set. In Listing 14.2, we've set up the path to the templates and added a path and filename for storing the Velocity engine log.

```
import java.io.*;
import java.util.*;
import javax.servlet.*;
```

Listing 14.2 VelocityAdd.java. (continues)

```
import javax.servlet.http.*;
import org.apache.velocity.*;
import org.apache.velocity.context.*;
import org.apache.velocity.servlet.*;
import org.apache.velocity.app.*;
import org.apache.velocity.exception.*;

public class VelocityAdd extends VelocityServlet
{

  protected Properties loadConfiguration( ServletConfig config )
    throws IOException, FileNotFoundException {

   Properties p = new Properties();

   String path = config.getServletContext().getRealPath("/");

   if (path == null) {
    System.out.println("VelocityAdd.loadConfiguration() : " +
       "unable to get the current webapp root.  Using '/'. " +
       "Please fix.");
"
    path = "/";
   }

   p.setProperty( Velocity.FILE_RESOURCE_LOADER_PATH,  path );
   p.setProperty( "runtime.log", path + "velocity.log" );

   return p;
  }

  public Template handleRequest( HttpServletRequest request,
     HttpServletResponse response, Context ctx )
  {

   Template outty = null;

   try {

    int a = 10;
    int b = 5;
    int c = a + b;

    ctx.put( "a", new Integer( a ) );
```

Listing 14.2 VelocityAdd.java. (continues)

```
        ctx.put( "b", new Integer( b ) );
        ctx.put( "c", new Integer( c ) );
        outty =  getTemplate("velocityadd.vm");
      }
      catch( ParseErrorException pee ) {

        System.out.println("VelocityAdd : parse error for template
   " + pee);
      }
      catch( ResourceNotFoundException rnfe ) {
        System.out.println("SampleServlet : template not
   found " + rnfe);
      }
      catch( Exception e ) {
        System.out.println("Error " + e);
      }

      return outty;
    }
  }
```

Listing 14.2 VelocityAdd.java. (continued)

To get the example in Listing 14.2 going, you need to have the VelocityAdd.class file in the classes directory of a Web application; for example, <*$CATALINA_HOME*>/webapps/examples/WEB-INF/classes. Copy the velocityadd.vm file to the <*$CATALINA_HOME*>/webapps/examples directory. Then, compile the VelocityAdd.java file and start Tomcat. You should now be able to access the example VelocityServlet.

The Velocity Template Language

Velocity incorporates the *Velocity Template Language*. Listing 14.1 shows a trivial example of that language, in which a field is replaced. The template language enables us to develop complex templates.

References

References are essentially field markers; they are replaced with the real data when the template is processed. Every reference starts with a dollar sign, and has a name that follows naming rules similar to those you'd use for Java. You must start the name with a letter, and subsequent characters must be letters, numeric, an underscore, or a hyphen. There are three kinds of references: variables, properties, and methods.

Variables

We used variables in Listing 14.1; we used a Java method to place a reference and value pair into a context, which is later inserted into the template in the appropriate place. In the Java code, inserting a reference into a context looks like this:

```
context.put( "reference", "myvalue" );
```

The second parameter can be any kind of object, not just a String. The template engine will render the object by calling the toString() method of that object when it is inserted in the HTML.

The second way of defining a variable is within the HTML itself. You can do this with the set directive. In Listing 14.3, we altered the template file to include three directives to set the variables rather than having the Java code do it. In this example, the variables *$a* and *$b* are set to integer values. Velocity can do basic math, but only on integers.

```
<html>
<head><title>Velocity Example</title></head>
<body>

<h1>Velocity Example</h1>

#set( $a = 10 )
#set( $b = 5 )
#set( $c = $a+$b )

<p>$a + $b = $c</p>

</center>
</html>
```

Listing 14.3 Our modified velocityadd.vm sets its own variables.

Properties

Properties take the form of an identifier of the item in the context, followed by a second identifier (the name of the property). The identifiers are separated by a period. Here are some examples of properties:

```
$user.alias
$invoice.issuedate
```

There are two ways in which you can set up properties. The first way is to create a Hashtable and add the Hashtable to the template context. Listing 14.4 contains a template to display a client with a first name, a last name, and a phone number. We can store all the information about the specific client in a Hashtable. The Hashtable itself is referenced by the left identifier, and the value returned is the value in the Hashtable with a key matching the right identifier. The code that handles this template, and that creates the Hashtable we've been discussing, is shown in Listing 14.5.

```
<html>
<head><title>Velocity Example</title></head>
<body>

<h1>Velocity Properties</h1>

<p>In this example we see how we can access properties through
 a hash table.</p>

<p>Clients First Name: $client.firstname</p>
<p>Clients Last Name: $client.lastname</p>
<p>Clients Phone Number: $client.phone</p>

</center>
</html>
```

Listing 14.4 velocityproperties.vm.

```
  public Template handleRequest( HttpServletRequest request,
HttpServletResponse response, Context ctx )
  {

    Template outty = null;

    try {

      Hashtable client = new Hashtable();
      client.put( "firstname", "Harry" );
      client.put( "lastname", "Potter" );
      client.put( "phone", "479-0875" );

      ctx.put( "client", client );

      outty =  getTemplate("velocityproperties.vm");
    }
    catch( ParseErrorException pee ) {
      System.out.println("SampleServlet : parse error for
template " + pee);
    }
    catch( ResourceNotFoundException rnfe ) {
      System.out.println("SampleServlet : template not
found " + rnfe);
    }
```

Listing 14.5 The handleRequest() method of VelocityProperties.java. (continues)

```
    catch( Exception e ) {
      System.out.println("Error " + e);
    }

    return outty;
  }
```

Listing 14.5 The handleRequest() method of VelocityProperties.java. (continued)

The second way to use properties is to reference properties of a Java class based on the calling conventions of a JavaBean. In this case, the left identifier maps to the instance of the class in question, and the right identifier designates which getter or setter to call on the bean when a value is read or stored. This allows you easy access to data objects from within your templates. All the Java code needs to do is add the data classes to the template context. In Listing 14.6, we use the same template, but change the mechanism of storing the data to a class called Client, which appears in Listing 14.7.

```
  public Template handleRequest( HttpServletRequest request,
HttpServletResponse response, Context ctx )
  {

    Template outty = null;
    try {

      Client client = new Client();
      client.setFirstname( "Henry" );
      client.setLastname( "Ford" );
      client.setPhone( "345-2345" );

      ctx.put( "client", client );

      outty =  getTemplate("velocityproperties.vm");
    }
    catch( ParseErrorException pee ) {
      System.out.println("SampleServlet : parse error for
template " + pee);
    }
    catch( ResourceNotFoundException rnfe ) {
      System.out.println("SampleServlet : template not
found " + rnfe);
    }
```

Listing 14.6 The handleRequest() method of VelocityProperties2.java. (continues)

```
    catch( Exception e ) {
      System.out.println("Error " + e);
    }

    return outty;
  }
```

Listing 14.6 The handleRequest() method of VelocityProperties2.java. (continued)

```
public class Client {

  String firstName = "";
  String lastName = "";
  String phone = "";

  public String getFirstname() {
    return firstName;
  }

  public String getLastname() {
    return lastName;
  }

  public String getPhone() {
    return phone;
  }

  public void setFirstname( String value ) {
    firstName = value;
  }

  public void setLastname( String value ) {
    lastName = value;
  }

  public void setPhone( String value ) {
    phone = value;
  }

}
```

Listing 14.7 Client.java.

Methods

The final type of reference is a reference to an arbitrary method on an object. You use this in essentially the same way you access a property that is the method of an object in our previous example. The syntax is similar to what you'd use to access properties, except that you add a set of brackets to the end to enclose parameters that are sent to the method.

In Listing 14.8, we have modified the HTML in the velocityproperties.vm file to first set the properties to a new value and then to display those values. We are still using the same VelocityProperties2 Servlet to process the template.

```
<html>
<head><title>Velocity Example</title></head>
<body>

<h1>Velocity Properties</h1>

<p>In this example we see how we can access properties through
 a hash table.</p>

$client.setFirstname( "Bill" )
$client.setLastname( "Gates" )
$client.setPhone( "567-1234" )

<p>Clients First Name: $client.getFirstname()</p>
<p>Clients Last Name: $client.getLastname()</p>
<p>Clients Phone Number: $client.getPhone()</p>

</center>
</html>
```

Listing 14.8 Our modified velocityproperties.vm calling methods.

Directives

Directives give the template engine commands. We have already taken a brief look at one—the set directive—in the section "Variables." Other directives are the conditional if, elseif, and else directives; the foreach directive (for implementing loops); an include directive (for including the contents of other files); and a parse directive (for loading and processing other files), among others. Directives always start with a hash sign, followed immediately by the name of the directive.

Setting Variables

The set directive allows you to set variables within a template—Listing 14.8 shows an example of using the set directive to set three variables. In this example, the directives are setting some integers; however, several variable data types are available. Let's take a look.

String

There are two ways to set a String variable. The first method uses double quote marks. If you use double quote marks, the string you provide will be parsed. This means that if you include a reference inside the string, it will be replaced as if it were part of the template. For example:

```
#set( $firstname = "henry" )
#set( $greeting = "hello $firstname" )
$greeting
```

results in the following:

```
hello henry
```

On the other hand, if you enclose your string in single quote marks, the string is simply inserted into the response without being parsed at all—which means this

```
#set( $firstname = "henry" )
#set( $greeting = 'hello $firstname' )
$greeting
```

results in this:

```
hello $firstname
```

Integer

As we mentioned earlier, the Velocity template engine can handle basic math. Listing 14.3 contains an example: the variable named *$c* is set equal to *$a* + *$b*, where *$a* and *$b* were previously set to be integer values. The template engine can perform addition, subtraction, multiplication, and division:

```
#set( $a = $b + 4 )        ## example of addition
#set( $a = $b - 4 )        ## example of subtraction
#set( $a = $b * 4 )        ## example of multiplication
#set( $a = $b / 4 )        ## example of division
#set( $a = $b % 5 )        ## example of finding remainder in division
```

When you use division, the result returned is always an integer. To find the remainder of a division operation, you should use the percent symbol in place of the division symbol. Velocity will also handle your division-by-zero errors by simply setting the result value to *null*, as if it had not been set at all.

Boolean

A *boolean* is simply a true or false value. Booleans are generally used in conditional operations. You set them using the following syntax:

```
#set( $doit = true )        ## set doit to a boolean value of true
#set( $doit = false )       ## set doit to a boolean value of false
```

Reference

You can also set a variable by reference. All three types of references—variable, property, and method—are supported:

```
#set( $myclient = $client )            ## example of variable reference
#set( $myclient.name = $client.name ) ## example of property reference
#set( $money = $client.getBalance() ) ## example of method reference
```

ArrayList

An ArrayList can hold an array of values. For example, the following stores an array list:

```
#set( $money.countries = [ "Africa", "Australia", "United States" ] )
```

To access each individual element of the ArrayList object, you would use the syntax like the following:

```
$money.countries.get(0)     ## returns "Africa"
$money.countries.get(1)     ## returns "Australia"
$money.countries.get(2)     ## returns "United States"
```

Conditionals

The classic if-elseif-else-end construct is supported in the template language and enables us to to support conditional sections of HTML. The basic syntax resembles that of many languages, including Java. Here's an example:

```
#if( $expression1 )
<p>Display something if first expression1 is true.</p>
#elseif( $expression2 )
<p>Display something if second expression is true.</p>
#else
<p>Display something if none of the previous expressions are true.</p>
#end
```

In this example, the expressions used are both simple booleans: They are either true or not true. There are three other forms of comparision: string, object, and integer.

String Comparisons

You can compare one String to another by using the double-equal signs. This comparison is case-sensitive:

```
#if( $mycountry == "United States" )
```

Object Comparisons

You can also compare one object to another. In this comparison, it is important to know that the comparison is true only if both references are pointing to the same object. If the two objects have the same values in their properties but are different instances of a class, the comparison will be false. For example, you can compare whether the client being processed is the same as the one requesting data:

```
#if( $myclient == $remoteclient )
```

Integer Comparisons

Finally, you can perform three kinds of integer comparison within an if directive:

```
#if( $a == 10 )      ## example of testing for equal to 10
#if( $a > 10 )       ## example of testing for value is greater than 10
#if( $a < 10 )       ## example of testing for value is less than 10
```

Loops

The loop construct allows you to repeat a specific section of HTML but replace the fields in each iteration with different data. This construct is mostly used in lists and reports. The directive for a loop is called *foreach*. In order to loop, you need to provide the context with a Vector, Hashtable, or Array. In Listing 14.9, we show you how to loop using a Hashtable.

```
<html>
<head><title>Velocity Example</title></head>
<body>

<h1>Velocity Loop Example</h1>

<table border=1>

<tr>
<td>First Name</td>
<td>Last Name</td>
<td>Phone</td>
</tr>

#foreach( $client in $clientlist )

<tr>
<td>$client.firstname</td>
<td>$client.lastname</td>
<td>$client.phone</td>
</tr>

#end

</table>
</center>
</html>
```

Listing 14.9 A looping example with velocityloop.vm.

Listing 14.9 shows how to build a table using the foreach directive. The *$client* is the Client class we created previously. The *$clientlist* is a Hashtable filled with Client instances. The foreach directive specifies that every client in the clientlist should have the HTML repeated between the foreach and the next end. Listing 14.10 shows a trivial way of filling the Hashtable. Usually, this will be done in a loop with access to a data source, such as a SQL database.

```
 public Template handleRequest( HttpServletRequest request,
HttpServletResponse response, Context ctx )
 {

  Template outty = null;

  try {

    Hashtable clientlist = new Hashtable();

    Client client = new Client();
    client.setFirstname( "Henry" );
    client.setLastname( "Ford" );
    client.setPhone( "345-2345" );
    clientlist.put( client.getLastname(), client );

    client = new Client();
    client.setFirstname( "Jim" );
    client.setLastname( "Smith" );
    client.setPhone( "789-2345" );
    clientlist.put( client.getLastname(), client );

    client = new Client();
    client.setFirstname( "Shane" );
    client.setLastname( "Taylor" );
    client.setPhone( "765-3456" );
    clientlist.put( client.getLastname(), client );

    ctx.put( "clientlist", clientlist );

    outty =  getTemplate("velocityloop.vm");
  }
  catch( ParseErrorException pee ) {
    System.out.println("SampleServlet : parse error for
template " + pee);
   }
```

Listing 14.10 The handleRequest() method of VelocityLoop.java. (continues)

```
    catch( ResourceNotFoundException rnfe ) {
      System.out.println("SampleServlet : template not
found " + rnfe);
    }
    catch( Exception e ) {
      System.out.println("Error " + e);
    }

    return outty;
  }
```

Listing 14.10 The handleRequest() method of VelocityLoop.java. (continued)

Including Files

One of the biggest advantages of developing Web pages using templates is the ability to reuse elements of pages by including them rather than by copying and pasting directly into the HTML. This means that when you need to change a common portion of HTML, such as a header, you do not need to change the header on every HTML document--you change it in only one place.

The Velocity template engine has two methods of including separate files into a template: the include and parse directives. The include directive allows you to include files as-is, and does not parse the included file. This directive is typically used for HTML that does not change for each request. The parse directive is used to load a file and parse it, treating it as a template, just as the current template is treated.

The Include Directive

The include directive can take a series of filenames and include all of them in the order specified. Each filename can also be a literal string, or a variable that you can set using conditional blocks to create different effects on the same page. In the following code snippet, we've defined a page name in a conditional block, and then by using the include directive, we've included the HTML appropriate for the client's balance:

```
#if( $client.balance > 1000 )
#set( $page = "wealthy.html" )
#else
#set( $page = "value.html" )
#end
#include( "header.html", $page, "footer.html" )
```

It is important to remember that the template engine does not process the documents included with this directive; it only transmits them to the client. The engine passes all references and directives in these files unmodified to the client.

The Parse Directive

The parse directive is similar to include, except that the file specified is actually parsed in the same manner as the current template file. The parse directive is also limited to a single file. You can use this directive with headers, for example, which have references built in, so that the title will be changed from document to document. Like the include directive, parse can take a variable as its parameter. Here are some examples:

```
#parse( "header.vm" )    ## load and parse the header.vm file
#parse( $mypage )        ## load and parse the file specified by $mypage
```

Macros

A *macro* is a segment of script that can be called throughout a template. You can use a macro to replace repetitive HTML. Using a macro reduces the amount of code required, and therefore makes maintenance of HTML easier. Using a macro is similar to using the parse directive in that it allows you to insert some code, perhaps repetitively, into your template. The difference is that instead of coming from another file, the macro is defined within the template itself.

The downside of using macros is that HTML editors such as Macromedia's Dreamweaver do not understand this syntax and so will not be able to edit files that use macros. If you are using an HTML editing tool, it might be a good idea to wait until this syntax is supported by your tool before you begin using macros.

In Listing 14.11, we've modified our velocityloop.vm file, which uses a table for formatting the output. A table requires repetitive use of the <td> and <tr> tags. To make this easier to format, we can use a macro to format the table instead.

```
<html>
<head><title>Velocity Example</title></head>
<body>

<h1>Velocity Loop Example</h1>
<table border=1>

#line( "First Name" "Last Name" "Phone" )
#foreach( $client in $clientlist )
#line( $client.firstname $client.lastname $client.phone )
#end

</table>
</center>
</html>

#macro( line $fn $ln $ph )
<tr>
```

Listing 14.11 Our modified velocityloop.vm now uses macros. (continues)

```
<td>$fn</td>
<td>$ln</td>
<td>$ph</td>
</tr>
#end
```

Listing 14.11 Our modified velocityloop.vm now uses macros. (continued)

Summary

A number of template type systems are now available for developing Web applications. They all address the problem of how to separate the HTML code from the Java code, and each one has its own approach. Velocity enforces separation of HTML and code to a large degree. It enables you to use conditional and looping constructs directly in HTML, and it provides other methods of pulling information directly out of data objects. This means that Session objects and other data objects can simply be passed to the Velocity context in order to be available within HTML.

Velocity requires you to learn a simple scripting language, and you're restricted to doing only things that the template engine can do. One of the problems with template languages is balancing the benefits of a restricted feature set against the limitations. While the looping and conditional structures in the Velocity language are not as complex as arbitrary source code, they do require some understanding of programming principles.

In the next few chapters, we shift focus away from content presentation, and on to data management. We start by examining the features the servlet platform provides to facilitate session management.

CHAPTER

15

Session Management

In this chapter, we discuss the session management features of Tomcat and of the Servlet 2.3 Specification in general. Session management is one of the areas in which servlet technology stands out from the other dynamic page-generation platforms available because the Servlet API very elegantly and effectively hides the complexities of session management—which lets you focus on the more interesting programming tasks specific to your application.

State Management and HTTP

If you have not worked extensively in Web application development at this point, you might be wondering why session management is so complex. The fundamental problem is that HTTP is a *stateless* protocol. This means that each request is logically discrete from every other request, and as a result, every request needs to provide all the information required to establish any continuity with previous requests.

HTTP was designed to be stateless for one simple reason: It dramatically reduces the overhead required per remote user. Other protocols available when HTTP was developed typically were connection-oriented protocols. A good example is FTP. With FTP, when you first connect to a server, you open a single connection, which is maintained until you explicitly close it by logging out or the server decides to boot you off. This means that system resources are being kept open for you, even when you're just sitting there idle, deciding what command to send next. Under traditional HTTP, the connection is closed after the response is sent. The next request is a completely discrete transaction. This means the server doesn't need to remember anything about you, and it doesn't need to keep a socket open for you. As a result, Web servers can be smaller and much lighter weight than connection-oriented servers, and they can handle significantly more requests for a given amount of memory and maximum number of file descriptors. Think about how often you've gone to an FTP server and been told that the maximum number of users had been reached. You probably can't remember the last time you ran into a Web server that wouldn't let you in because it was overloaded.

NOTE **HTTP 1.1 added support for keep-alive, which actually does keep a connection open in order to reduce the overhead of creating new connections. However, because the underlying protocol is stateless, these connections can readily be dropped if the demand on the server grows to the point where the resource is required.**

From a user perspective, there is little difference because some state is stored in the Web browser, in the form of the page that was just requested. Because URLs absolutely identify resources, and Web pages contain links to URLs, the user has the perception of always being connected, and can readily browse from page to page in a coherent way. URLs and HTTP cooperate to make the user experience seem stateful while preserving the efficiencies of a stateless protocol. That's a big part of why URLs were developed. If you can absolutely identify the location of the object you want to request by using a URL, you don't need to keep state on the server; users can just request the next object they want directly, without the server needing to know anything about the previous request or the context from which the request is coming.

This does create some limitations, of course, and most Web applications of any complexity do in fact require the server to keep track of session state, which implies a requirement for some form of session management. The classic example of a feature that requires session state is the shopping cart. (This is also historically where the need for session management first started to make its presence felt in a big way.) When users come to the site, they want to be able to browse through the available items and place the ones that interest them into a shopping cart rather than having to purchase each item separately. There are a few ways we could handle this.

We could require users to log in first and then pass their login information with each subsequent page request. This could be accomplished by appending a query string to each request, which would require rewriting every URL we serve (known as *mangling* the URLs, or URL rewriting, and yes, mangling is actually the technical term for it); or we could make every page into a form and pass the information in a hidden field. Both approaches are rather clunky and require a lot of work to implement. They also require the user to log in, which is not a great way to encourage browsing.

We could just make up an identifier for the session, and pass it as part of a query string. This has the advantage of not requiring a login, but also requires URL mangling or lots of clunky form processing.

We could also store login information in a cookie. A cookie is a token passed back to the browser, which the browser then sends on subsequent requests as part of the HTTP header. This essentially makes the client responsible for providing an identifier to help manage session state, which, like the humble URL, gives us the dual advantages of apparent statefulness and actual statelessness. Cookies were in fact developed at Netscape to solve this very problem, and were subsequently added as an official part of the HTTP 1.1 standard. Of course, cookies have some disadvantages as well, mostly relating in some way to abuses in the past. Cookies are typically stored unencrypted on the client machine, and some sites were thoughtlessly or even negligently sending back logins and passwords, or even credit card numbers, which would sometimes get scavenged, particularly from lab computers or terminals in Internet cafés. Some sites also used cookies to gather user-tracking information and usage patterns on customers, particularly to target ad banners, which a lot of people objected to. As a result, many people turn cookie support off in their browsers, so it's not always a mechanism that we can rely on as application developers. To be safe, we need a hybrid approach to reach the most customers.

Of course, once we have a session identifier, we still need to do some work in our Web application to take that session information and turn it into something meaningful inside our app. We could store a list of all the items the user has selected in a cookie or a series of query parameters, but this is unwieldy and may be objectionable to privacy-concerned users: It's far better to generate an opaque token and use it as a key into either an in-memory data structure or a database, and then store the session state information that way.

And we also need a mechanism to create unique session identifiers and to expire sessions that have been idle for too long.

However, if you remember, we said that the Servlet API hides these complexities, and of complexities, as you will now appreciate, there is no shortage. Servlets can generate and maintain an HttpSession object automatically, and on this session object, you can store just about any object you want. Your shopping cart can be an arbitrary class, with methods for adding and removing items, getting lists of the items; or even sorting them, grouping them, suggesting related items, totaling prices, or more. In two lines, as illustrated below, you can store a shopping cart instance on the session object, and you can let Tomcat manage the session cookie generation and expiration. Tomcat will also make sure you get the right session object for each request. And best of all, it will do it reliably, whether users have cookies turned on or not, with very little work from you.

```
HttpSession session = request.getSession(true);
session.setAttribute("shoppingcart", cart);
```

In this chapter, we examine the session mechanism, and also show you how you can manage cookies directly—which you need to do if you want to maintain continuity between sessions (for example, if you want to automate login or store customization preferences between sessions).

Using HttpSession

The HttpSession object can be treated pretty much like a Hashtable, into which you can store any arbitrary Java object. Once a session is created, it is accessible from the HttpRequest object passed into the service() method, and by extension into the various handler methods—doGet(), doPost(), and so forth. Behind the scenes, Tomcat manages the session state by using cookies, if cookies are available; and if not, it will fall back automatically to use URL mangling instead. Tomcat generates a session token based on an MD5 hash by default and times out sessions after 15 minutes, unless you specify otherwise. All the details of how this is done are highly configurable, and we discuss them in Chapter 6, "Configuring Web Applications"; Chapter 7, "The servlet.xml File in Depth"; Appendix A, "Server Configuration (server.xml) Reference"; and Appendix B, "Deployment Descriptor (web.xml) Reference." If you don't want to store session information in a cookie—for example, if you have unusually high security requirements or want to change or eliminate the session timeout length—you can do that all declaratively, either in the deployment descriptor or on a global level in the server.xml file.

NOTE If you intend to serve hardcoded URLs in the HTML you output from a servlet, you'll have to wrap the strings containing the URL in a response.encodeURL() call. That lets Tomcat mangle the URL to include the session ID.

A session is created implicitly by calling getSession() on the request object and passing in true to signal that the session should be created if it doesn't already exist. (If you only want to grab an existing session object, simply pass in false as the only parameter.) From there, it's simply a matter of storing the objects you'd like to store and retrieving them when you want to use them. We look at a couple of simple examples in a moment. Fortunately with servlets, the implementation is as simple to use as the conceptual model.

Let's start with a shopping cart example, since this is where it all started. We define three relatively simple objects: an Item object, which will describe the objects we make available for sale; an ItemHolder, which will associate an item with a unit count for this order and which we'll let the user select; and a ShoppingCart object, which will include a list of item holders and give us a convenient subtotal on the cost of the items selected. These classes are illustrated in Figure 15.1.

You can see the implementation for each of these classes in Listings 15.1, 15.2, and 15.3.

```
package com.wiley.tomcatbook.shopping;

public class Item implements java.io.Serializable
{
   private String name;
   private transient int unitPrice;

   public String getName()
   {
      return name;
   }
```

Listing 15.1 Item.java. (continues)

```
    public int getUnitPrice()
    {
        return unitPrice;
    }

    protected void setName(String name)
    {
        this.name = name;
    }

    protected void setUnitPrice(int price)
    {
        this.unitPrice = price;
    }

}
```

Listing 15.1 Item.java. (continued)

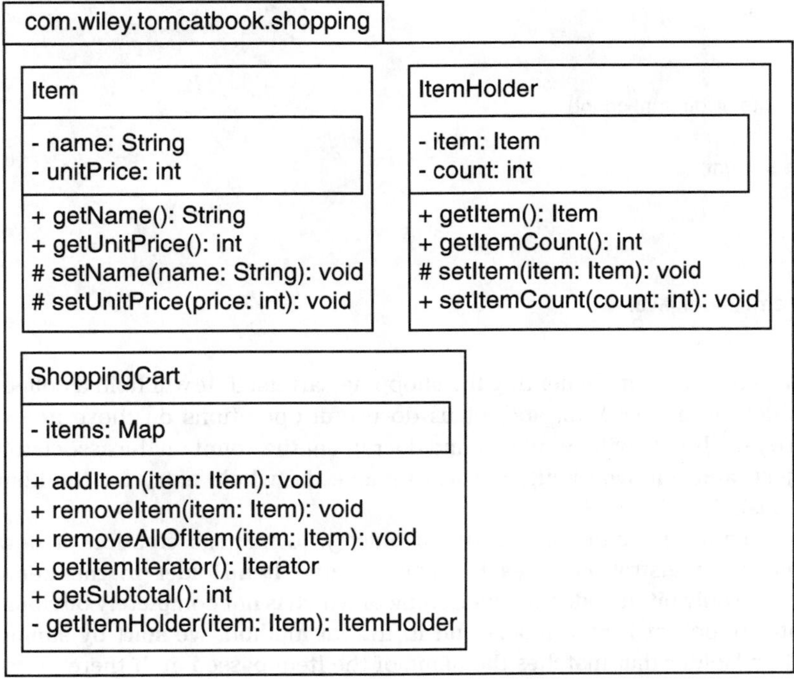

Figure 15.1 The objects for our shopping cart example.

Item objects contain very basic information about the stock item they describe: just a name and a unit price. ItemHolder objects will keep track of how many of a given item the user wants to buy.

```
package com.wiley.tomcatbook.shopping;

public class ItemHolder implements java.io.Serializable
{
   private Item item;
   private int count;

   public Item getItem()
   {
      return item;
   }

   public int getItemCount()
   {
      return count;
   }

   protected void setItem(Item item)
   {
      this.item = item;
   }

   public void setItemCount(int count)
   {
      this.count = count;
   }
}
```

Listing 15.2 ItemHolder.java.

Next, let's write the class implementing the shopping cart itself. It will hold a collection of ItemHolders in a HashMap, and let us do useful operations on those items. addItem() and removeItem() will increment and decrement the count on the associated ItemHolder object, and removeAllOfItem() will remove the whole entry for the item from the items HashMap.

Note how we use a helper method, getItemHolder(), to manage creation of new ItemHolders and the registration of each newly created ItemHolder in the items HashMap. That's the only bit of code the functioning of which is not completely obvious, so take a minute to look at it and understand it. In that method, we start by simply requesting the ItemHolder that matches the name of the Item passed in. If there previously was none (that is, if *holder* == null), then we create a new instance, set its item property to the item passed in, and set the item count to zero. We then store the ItemHolder in items before passing the newly created holder back to the caller.

Note that in removeItem() we do a little management of items as well. Once we've decremented the count, we check to see if we have any left; and if not, we simply remove the entry in the HashMap for the removed item. These two blocks of code, in removeItem() and in getItemHolder(), serve to make sure *items* always only has entries for items with positive item counts. We let the garbage collector deal with items with zero or negative item counts.

```
package com.wiley.tomcatbook.shopping;

import java.util.*;

public class ShoppingCart implements java.io.Serializable
{
   private Map items = new HashMap();

   private ItemHolder getItemHolder(Item item)
   {
      ItemHolder holder = (ItemHolder) items.get(item.getName());
      if (holder == null)
      {
         holder = new ItemHolder();
         holder.setItem(item);
         // The following line isn't necessary, since the new
         // holder will have an itemCount of zero by default,
         // but is included for readability.
         holder.setItemCount(0);
         items.put(item.getName(), holder);
      }
      return holder;
   }

   public void addItem(Item item)
   {
      ItemHolder holder = getItemHolder(item);
      holder.setItemCount(holder.getItemCount() + 1);
   }

   public void removeItem(Item item)
   {
      ItemHolder holder = getItemHolder(item);
      holder.setItemCount(holder.getItemCount() - 1);
      if (holder.getItemCount() <= 0)
```

Listing 15.3 ShoppingCart.java. (continues)

```
        {
            items.remove(item.getName());
        }
    }

    public void removeAllOfItem(Item item)
    {
        items.remove(item.getName());
    }

    public Iterator getItemIterator()
    {
        return items.values().iterator();
    }

    public int getSubtotal()
    {
        int subtotal = 0;
        Iterator i = getItemIterator();
        while (i.hasNext())
        {
            ItemHolder holder = (ItemHolder) i.next();
            subtotal += holder.getItemCount()
                * holder.getItem().getUnitPrice();
        }
        return subtotal;
    }
}
```

Listing 15.3 ShoppingCart.java. (continued)

Note that we declared all of these classes as being serializable. This is because Tomcat will write the HttpSession object out to disk on a restart so that the sessions will survive a restart. As a result, take care to ensure that objects you store on the HttpSession are serializable, and that variables containing items that cannot be serialized are marked as transient.

Now that we have the objects that we'll use to keep track of items being purchased, we need to write a servlet that will let our user select items and add them to the cart. We'll also dummy up some items for the user to purchase. In a real application, you would most likely load the items you're selling out of a database. We cover that in depth in the next two chapters, so for now, let's just hardcode in three sample items.

We start by taking a look at the finished product. Figures 15.2 and 15.3 show what the servlet looks like: Figure 15.2 with no items in the shopping cart and Figure 15.3 with a few of each item in the shopping cart.

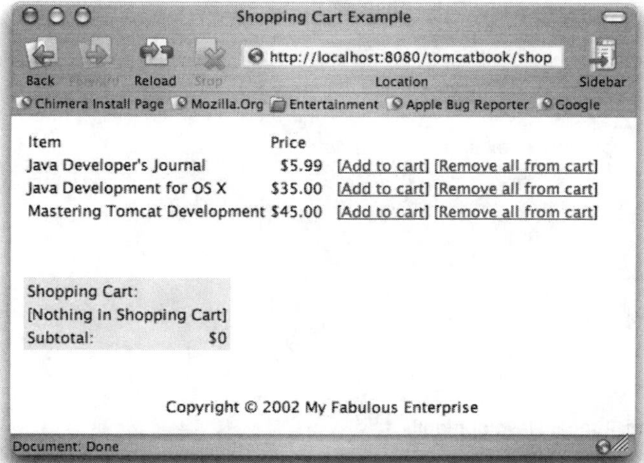

Figure 15.2 An empty shopping cart.

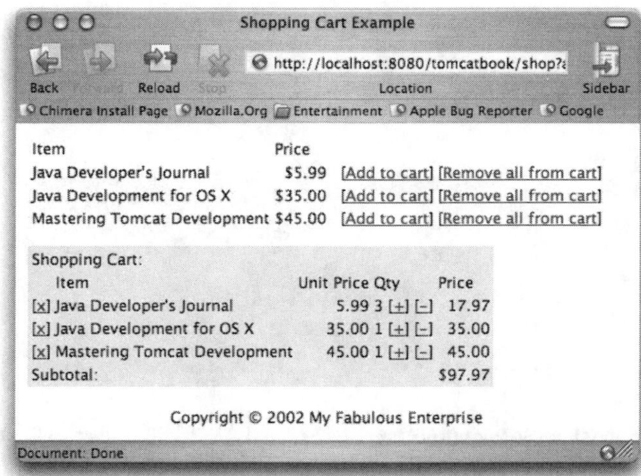

Figure 15.3 A shopping cart with items in it.

The code that generated these figures appears in Listing 15.4. Like many servlets, this one is quite verbose. Let's break it apart into more digestible chunks.

```
package com.wiley.tomcatbook.shopping;

import java.io.*;
```

Listing 15.4 ShoppingCartExampleServlet.java. (continues)

```
import java.util.*;
import javax.servlet.*;
import javax.servlet.http.*;

public class ShoppingCartExampleServlet extends HttpServlet
{
  Map items = new HashMap();

  public void init(ServletConfig conf)
    throws ServletException
  {
    super.init(conf);
    Item item = new Item();
    item.setName("Mastering Tomcat Development");
    item.setUnitPrice(4500);
    items.put(item.getName(), item);
    item = new Item();
    item.setName("Java Development for OS X");
    item.setUnitPrice(3500);
    items.put(item.getName(), item);
    item = new Item();
    item.setName("Java Developer's Journal");
    item.setUnitPrice(599);
    items.put(item.getName(), item);
  }

  public void doGet(
    HttpServletRequest request,
    HttpServletResponse response
  )
    throws ServletException, IOException
  {
    HttpSession session = request.getSession(true);
    ShoppingCart cart = (ShoppingCart)
      session.getAttribute("example.shopping.cart");
    if (cart == null)
    // i.e. there was no previous cart
    // associated with the session
    {
      cart = new ShoppingCart();
      session.setAttribute("example.shopping.cart", cart);
    }
    // Handle any requests
```

Listing 15.4 ShoppingCartExampleServlet.java. (continues)

```
String action = request.getParameter("action");
String itemName = request.getParameter("name");
Item targetItem = (Item) items.get(itemName);
if (targetItem != null)
{
   if ("add".equals(action))
   {
      cart.addItem(targetItem);
   }
   else if ("remove".equals(action))
   {
      cart.removeItem(targetItem);
   }
   else if ("remove-all".equals(action))
   {
      cart.removeAllOfItem(targetItem);
   }
}

ServletOutputStream out = response.getOutputStream();

out.println("<html>");
out.println("<head>");
out.println("<title>Shopping Cart Example");
out.println("</title>");
out.println("</head>\n");
out.println("<body>");
out.println("<table width=\"100%\" height=\"100%\">");
out.println("<tr valign=\"top\">\n");
out.println("<!-- Body Content -->");
out.println("<td>");
out.println("<table>\n");

Iterator i = items.values().iterator();
if (i.hasNext())
{
   out.println("<tr>");
   out.println("<td>Item");
   out.println("</td>");
   out.println("<td>Price");
   out.println("</td>");
   out.println("<td> </td>");
   out.println("<td> </td>");
```

Listing 15.4 ShoppingCartExampleServlet.java. (continues)

```
        out.println("</tr>\n");
        while(i.hasNext())
        {
            Item item = (Item) i.next();
            out.println("<tr>");
            out.println("<td>" + item.getName());
            out.println("</td>");
            out.println("<td align=\"right\">$"
                + toCurrency(item.getUnitPrice()));
            out.println("</td>");
            out.println("<td>");
            out.print("<td>[<a href=\"");
            out.print(response.encodeURL("?action=add&name="
                + item.getName()));
            out.println("\">Add to cart</a>]</td>");
            out.print("<td>[<a href=\"");
            out.print(response.encodeURL(
                "?action=remove-all&name="
                + item.getName()));
            out.println("\">Remove all from cart</a>]</td>");
            out.println("</td>");
            out.println("</tr>");
        }
    }
    out.println("</table>");
    out.println("</td>");
    out.println("</tr>\n");
    out.println("<tr valign=\"top\">\n");
    out.println("<!-- Shopping Cart -->");
    out.println("<td>");
    out.println("<table bgcolor=\"#eeeeee\">");
    out.println("<tr>");
    out.println("<td colspan=\"7\">Shopping Cart:");
    out.println("</td>");
    out.println("</tr>");
    i = cart.getItemIterator();
    if (i.hasNext())
    {
        out.println("<tr>");
        out.println("<td> </td>");
        out.println("<td>Item</td>");
        out.println("<td>Unit Price</td>");
        out.println("<td colspan=\"3\">Qty</td>");
```

Listing 15.4 ShoppingCartExampleServlet.java. (continues)

```
        out.println("<td>Price</td>");
        out.println("</tr>\n\n");
        while(i.hasNext())
        {
          ItemHolder holder = (ItemHolder) i.next();
          out.println("<tr>");
          out.print("<td>[<a href=\"");
          out.print(response.encodeURL(
            "?action=remove-all&name="
            + holder.getItem().getName()));
          out.println("\">x</a>]</td>");
          out.println("<td>" + holder.getItem().getName());
          out.println("</td>");
          out.println("<td align=\"right\">" +
            toCurrency(holder.getItem().getUnitPrice())
          );
          out.println("</td>");
          out.println("<td>" + holder.getItemCount());
          out.println("</td>");
          out.print("<td>[<a href=\"");
          out.print(response.encodeURL("?action=add&name="
            + holder.getItem().getName()));
          out.println("\">+</a>]</td>");
          out.print("<td>[<a href=\"");
          out.print(response.encodeURL("?action=remove&name="
            + holder.getItem().getName()));
          out.println("\">-</a>]</td>");
          out.println("<td align=\"right\">");
          out.println(
            toCurrency(holder.getItem().getUnitPrice()
            * holder.getItemCount())
          );
          out.println("</td>");
          out.println("</tr>\n\n");
        }
      }
      else
      {
        out.println("<tr>");
        out.print("<td colspan=\"7\">[Nothing in Shopping
Cart]");
        out.println("</td>");
        out.println("</tr>");
```

Listing 15.4 ShoppingCartExampleServlet.java. (continues)

```
        }
        out.println("<tr>");
        out.println("<td colspan=\"6\">Subtotal:</td>");
        out.println("<td align=\"right\">$"
            + toCurrency(cart.getSubtotal()));
        out.println("</td>");
        out.println("</tr>");
        out.println("</table>");
        out.println("</td>\n");
        out.println("</tr>\n");
        out.println("<tr>\n");
        out.println("<td colspan=\"4\">");
        out.println("<center>Copyright &copy; ");
        out.print((new Date()).getYear() + 1900);
        out.println(" My Fabulous Enterprise");
        out.println("</center>");
        out.println("</td>");
        out.println("</tr>");
        out.println("</table>");
        out.println("</body>");
        out.println("</html>");
    }

    /**
     * Takes an integer and returns a string representing
     * a value in cents, and returns a string with a decimal
     * inserted at the right place to render the integer
     * as a matching dollar amount.
    */
    public static final String toCurrency(int anInt)
    {
        StringBuffer sb = new StringBuffer("" + anInt);
        if (sb.length() > 2)
            sb.insert(sb.length() - 2, '.');
            // This will work for the example, but you probably
            // want something more robust for a real deployment.
        return sb.toString();
    }

}
```

Listing 15.4 ShoppingCartExampleServlet.java. (continued)

Like most servlets, this is a lot of code, although most of it consists of println() commands to send all the HTML back to the Web client.

The init() method sets up three Item objects, with names and unit prices in cents, and stores them off into the items HashMap. We iterate over them later when it comes time to show the items we have for sale.

The doGet() method contains most of the remaining code. The most interesting bit is right at the beginning, so let's reproduce a small portion of it in Listing 15.5 to facilitate the discussion.

```
public void doGet(
      HttpServletRequest request,
      HttpServletResponse response
   )
      throws ServletException, IOException
   {
      HttpSession session = request.getSession(true);
      ShoppingCart cart = (ShoppingCart)
         session.getAttribute("example.shopping.cart");
      if (cart == null)
      // i.e. there was no previous cart
      // associated with the session
      {
         cart = new ShoppingCart();
         session.setAttribute("example.shopping.cart", cart);
      }
      ...
```

Listing 15.5 Detail from ShoppingCartExampleServlet.java showing creation of the session and the shopping cart.

In Listing 15.5, we see the session being loaded. Because we have passed in true to request.getSession(), if no session object previously existed, a new one will be created for us.

Next, we look up the attribute example.shopping.cart on the session we just loaded, and store the result in cart. Of course, if this session were newly created, there would be no such attribute, and as a result, cart would now contain null. So we next check to see if cart == null, and if so, we create a new instance of ShoppingCart, store it in the cart, and also store it as an attribute on the session, so it will be there for us next time.

The code fragment in Listing 15.6 handles the commands we'll be sending as query parameters. First, we store the parameters action and name into string variables to make it easier to work with them. We then look up the item named in the name parameter, and store it in targetItem. If either the name parameter is absent or it specifies a name we don't know about, targetItem will now contain null. (If the string we used to look up the item was null, it won't match anything, and the HashMap will return null. This is also true if there is no key in the HashMap matching a valid string.) We test to see whether targetItem contains null before proceeding; and if so, we simply skip the rest of the block responsible for checking which action was specified.

```
...
// Handle any requests
String action = request.getParameter("action");
String itemName = request.getParameter("name");
Item targetItem = (Item) items.get(itemName);
if (targetItem != null)
{
   if ("add".equals(action))
   {
      cart.addItem(targetItem);
   }
   else if ("remove".equals(action))
   {
      cart.removeItem(targetItem);
   }
   else if ("remove-all".equals(action))
   {
      cart.removeAllOfItem(targetItem);
   }
}
...
```

Listing 15.6 Detail from ShoppingCartExampleServlet.java showing command handling.

We then test to see if the action is equal to any of the three verbs we know about: add, remove, and remove-all. Note that by placing the literal string, we want to compare against on the left side of the equals() expression; we don't have to test to see whether the parameter exists. If the parameter doesn't exist, action will equal null, which will simply fail the equals() test.

Then depending on which verb we got, we add an item to the cart, remove a single item from the cart, or remove all items matching targetItem from the cart.

From there, we simply start sending back HTML, until we get to the first iteration block, as shown in Listing 15.7.

```
...
Iterator i = items.values().iterator();
if (i.hasNext())
{
   out.println("<tr>");
   out.println("<td>Item");
```

Listing 15.7 Detail from ShoppingCartExampleServlet.java showing iteration over the Items in items. (continues)

```
        out.println("</td>");
        out.println("<td>Price");
        out.println("</td>");
        out.println("<td> </td>");
        out.println("<td> </td>");
        out.println("</tr>\n");
        while(i.hasNext())
        {
            Item item = (Item) i.next();
            out.println("<tr>");
            out.println("<td>" + item.getName());
            out.println("</td>");
            out.println("<td align=\"right\">$"
                + toCurrency(item.getUnitPrice()));
            out.println("</td>");
            out.println("<td>");
            out.print("<td>[<a href=\"");
            out.print(response.encodeURL("?action=add&name="
                + item.getName()));
            out.println("\">Add to cart</a>]</td>");
            out.print("<td>[<a href=\"");
            out.print(response.encodeURL(
                "?action=remove-all&name="
                + item.getName()));
            out.println("\">Remove all from cart</a>]</td>");
            out.println("</td>");
            out.println("</tr>");
        }
    }
    ...
```

Listing 15.7 Detail from ShoppingCartExampleServlet.java showing iteration over the Items in items. (continued)

The block of code in Listing 15.7 is where we iterate over each of the items in the items HashMap. First, we get an Iterator to iterate over the values in the HashMap, which we store in *i*. We then check to see if there are any items to iterate over, and only print the column headings if there are in fact items that we're going to display.

We then iterate over the items, printing out the name and unit price, and we include two hyperlinks to let the user add or remove the given item from the shopping cart. In the hyperlinks, we pass the action command and the name of the item as the query portion of the URL. We omit any URI. When the URI is omitted, browsers will construct the URL to point back at the document containing the link, which is what we want. We want each subsequent request to be handled by exactly the same servlet.

Note that we use response.encodeURL() to give Tomcat an opportunity to write out a session cookie as part of the URL, so it can be passed as one of the query parameters.

Next, in Listing 15.8, we examine the portion of the doGet() method that renders the shopping cart table, which is the whole point of the exercise.

```
...
out.println("<table bgcolor=\"#eeeeee\">");
out.println("<tr>");
out.println("<td colspan=\"7\">Shopping Cart:");
out.println("</td>");
out.println("</tr>");
i = cart.getItemIterator();
if (i.hasNext())
{
  out.println("<tr>");
  out.println("<td> </td>");
  out.println("<td>Item</td>");
  out.println("<td>Unit Price</td>");
  out.println("<td colspan=\"3\">Qty</td>");
  out.println("<td>Price</td>");
  out.println("</tr>\n\n");
  while(i.hasNext())
  {
    ItemHolder holder = (ItemHolder) i.next();
    out.println("<tr>");
    out.print("<td>[<a href=\"");
    out.print(response.encodeURL(
      "?action=remove-all&name="
      + holder.getItem().getName()));
    out.println("\">x</a>]</td>");
    out.println("<td>" + holder.getItem().getName());
    out.println("</td>");
    out.println("<td align=\"right\">" +
      toCurrency(holder.getItem().getUnitPrice())
    );
    out.println("</td>");
    out.println("<td>" + holder.getItemCount());
    out.println("</td>");
    out.print("<td>[<a href=\"");
    out.print(response.encodeURL("?action=add&name="
      + holder.getItem().getName()));
    out.println("\">+</a>]</td>");
    out.print("<td>[<a href=\"");
```

Listing 15.8 Detail from ShoppingCartExampleServlet.java rendering the shopping cart. (continues)

```
            out.print(response.encodeURL("?action=remove&name="
               + holder.getItem().getName()));
            out.println("\">-</a>]</td>");
            out.println("<td align=\"right\">");
            out.println(
               toCurrency(holder.getItem().getUnitPrice()
               * holder.getItemCount())
            );
            out.println("</td>");
            out.println("</tr>\n\n");
         }
      }
      else
      {
         out.println("<tr>");
         out.print("<td colspan=\"7\">[Nothing in Shopping
            Cart]");
         out.println("</td>");
         out.println("</tr>");
      }
      out.println("<tr>");
      out.println("<td colspan=\"6\">Subtotal:</td>");
      out.println("<td align=\"right\">$"
         + toCurrency(cart.getSubtotal()));
      out.println("</td>");
      out.println("</tr>");
      out.println("</table>");
      ...
```

Listing 15.8 Detail from ShoppingCartExampleServlet.java rendering the shopping cart. (continued)

Here again, we get an Iterator, which we will use to iterate over each item in the shopping cart, and again we test to see whether there are in fact any items in the shopping cart with the initial i.hasNext() statement. (If not, we don't show the headers and instead show a message stating that there is nothing in the shopping cart.) As in the previously discussed code segment, we again iterate over a set of elements—this time the ItemHolders contained in the shopping cart—and for each of these, we show the item name, the unit price, the number of units in the cart, and the subtotal for the item, along with three hyperlinks allowing the user to increase or decrease the quantity of each item or remove an item entirely.

In both code blocks, we make use of a helper method to convert the prices from integer values to currency values. We simply store the value in cents, then use the toCurrency() method shown in Listing 15.9 to convert that integer value to a decimal value in dollars.

```
/**
  * Takes an integer and returns a string representing
  * a value in cents, and returns a string with a decimal
  * inserted at the right place to render the integer
  * as a matching dollar amount.
 */
 public static final String toCurrency(int anInt)
 {
    StringBuffer sb = new StringBuffer("" + anInt);
    if (sb.length() > 2)
       sb.insert(sb.length() - 2, '.');
       // This will work for the example, but you probably
       // want something more robust for a real deployment.
    return sb.toString();
 }

}
```

Listing 15.9 ShoppingCartExampleServlet.java's toCurrency() method.

In real production code, you'd want to extend this a little to pad values below 100 and above 0 with extra zeros. Or you could use the text formatting tools in java.text.* to do more elaborate currency handling, particularly if you need to internationalize the Web site to show other currency values. For simplicity, though, since we know from the items we create that no value will ever be between 1 and 99, this simple method got us the behavior we needed.

Finally, to tie it all together, we must add a couple of entries to our deployment descriptor and copy the classes into the *<$CATALINA_HOME>*/webapps/tomcatbook/WEB-INF/lib or /classes directory (depending on whether you've packaged your classes as a JAR or as a directory hierarchy of class files).

The changes to the deployment descriptor are minimal. Among the other <servlet/> nodes, add:

```
<servlet>
    <servlet-name>shopping</servlet-name>
    <servlet-class>
        com.wiley.tomcatbook.shopping.ShoppingCartExampleServlet
    </servlet-class>
</servlet>
```

Among the <servlet-mapping/> nodes, add:

```
<servlet-mapping>
    <servlet-name>shopping</servlet-name>
    <url-pattern>/shop</url-pattern>
</servlet-mapping>
```

With that, your servlet should be available at http://localhost:8080/tomcatbook/shop.

Expiring Sessions

Aside from letting sessions time out on their own, you can manually expire any session simply by calling invalidate() on the session object. You could then turn around and create a new session by calling request.getSession(true) again. You may want to do this with an active session (storing off all the attributes so you can attach them to the new session, of course) if you're concerned that a session may be compromised. (Perhaps you're charging for access, and you want to make sure people aren't sharing their session keys with others.) By creating new sessions on a more frequent basis, you make it harder for people to misappropriate a session token and use it to access services they're not authorized for. Using this rollover technique of setting up a new session in the same request as you invalidate an old session, you still maintain the illusion of a single continuous session.

Setting Your Own Cookies

Sometimes, you want to maintain state not just during a single session, but also across visits from a given user. Probably the most prevalent case is where you want to allow users to automate login. Of course, you want to make this optional. Not everyone is connecting from a machine securely ensconced in a private office or home. And for very sensitive information (like banking records or services), you may not want to allow automated login at all, or at the very least may want to require a password (with the login name automatically supplied). The easiest way (and just about the only way) to do this is through the use of cookies.

It is important when setting up something like automated login that you spend some effort considering the security implications of what you are doing. Don't store passwords or sensitive information in cookies on the client machine, and don't send sensitive information in the clear. You can instead simply store an opaque token that will be used to look up the user information when presented back to the server, and you should probably expire the tokens on a regular basis, replacing them with new, valid tokens when you do. Secure tokens can be generated by generating an MD5 hash off some value, the variations in which the server can predict in order to validate the token. We talk a bit more about this, and about security concepts in general, in Chapter 18, "Security."

You can store noncritical information (for instance, a user's color preferences or similar nonsensitive information) in a cookie on the client, but it is much nicer for your users if you can just look this information up on the server, again based on an opaque token. Clients have limited storage for cookies, so storing their entire life history back in their machine is hardly going to ingratiate you with your users, particularly if they find that you're keeping more information about them than they might like.

Once you've decided to set a cookie on the client machine, it's quite easy to do so from any servlet or JSP. The HttpResponse object has methods for setting cookies, and the HttpRequest object has methods for getting them. Cookies contain pairs of strings, arranged into name-value pairs. The names are used to look up the value, much as parameter names are used to look up the string values passed in as parameters.

To set a cookie, simply call addCookie() on the response object, and pass in a Cookie object that contains the information you want to store on the client:

```
response.addCookie(new Cookie("color.favorite", "blue"));
```

Once you've set the cookie, until it expires it will be passed along with each request, so you can read it again at any time. Unfortunately, it's a little harder to find the cookie you want on the request object, since there is no method to allow you to get a single cookie. Instead, there is a getCookies() method that returns an array of all the Cookie objects associated with the request. You then have to iterate over the cookies to look for the one you want (or null, if there weren't any cookies). So the code to look up the color.favorite cookie we set before is typically something like this:

```
String favoriteColor;
Cookie[] cookies = request.getCookies();
for(i=0; i < cookies.length; i++)
{
    Cookie thisCookie = cookie[i];
    if (cookies[i].getName().equals("color.favorite")
        favoriteColor = cookies[i].getValue;
}
```

It's a little clunky, but certainly not hard to use, and you can always wrap up the code to do this into a utility method to keep your code simple and readable.

What you do with the cookie once you get it back is entirely up to you, but again one of the most common uses of cookies, aside from managing session state, is to automate login. Let's say you have a cookie named login.token, which contains an arbitrary string used to allow a user to log in. Once you receive the cookie, you can look up this token in a database or other persistent store, and if it's valid, log in the user with which the token is associated, establish a session, or do whatever other housekeeping you may choose to.

Additional Cookie Attributes

Aside from a name and a value, cookies have a few other attributes you should know about. The first we'll talk about is age. Cookies expire after a certain period, the duration of which you can set when you initially create and set the cookie by calling setMaxAge(). The single integer parameter is the interval, in seconds, between when the cookie was created and when the browser should destroy it. (-1 is a special value that means "Destroy the cookie at the end of the session.") Note that browsers may destroy cookies before the maximum age is reached as well, in particular if they run out of space to store cookies or if the user explicitly deletes the cookie.

The next key attribute is domain. The domain attribute instructs the browser on which requests to include the cookie we're defining. setDomain() takes a string specifying a full or partial domain name to use to restrict access to the cookie we create. If we set the domain to foo.com, then the cookie will be sent along with requests to www.foo.com, or intranet.foo.com, or to any other machine within the zone specified. Note, however, that further subdomains will not be matched. If, for example, you have subdomains sf.foo.com and ny.foo.com, foo.com will *not* match www.sf.foo.com or www.ny.foo.com. If this attribute is not specified, the cookie will be sent only to the domain name of the machine that set the cookie.

You can also specify that the cookie is supposed to be supplied only when specific URIs are requested by specifying a path attribute. Like the domain attribute, the path attribute specifies a pattern. Unlike a domain attribute, however, the URI pattern will match any subdirectory or path that starts with the pattern. This means that if you set the path for your cookie to /tomcatbook, then requests for URIs below /tomcatbook—for example, /tomcatbook/cookie-examples—would also receive the cookie.

The secure attribute specifies whether it's okay to send the cookie over a transport that is not secure. Calling setSecure() on your cookie with a parameter of true prevents it from being sent over any transport that does not specify that it's secure. Typically, this means the cookie won't be sent over HTTP, but can be sent over HTTPS. This is not an absolute guarantee, however, because you are relying on the browser to determine what it considers a secure transport. Still, if your security requirements are low enough that you can allow automated login, if you are sending a login cookie, it's worth forcing it to go over a secure channel. Remember, just because you may have logged in over a secure connection, that doesn't mean any subsequent traffic sent in the clear can't be hijacked. If part of that information is a session token, there's really nothing preventing a nefarious individual from hijacking the token and using it to gain access to information and services you might not want them getting into. Keep your logins and session management information secure by sending it over a secure channel, if you want to try to prevent such a man-in-the-middle attack from leaving you vulnerable.

The two remaining attributes are version and comment. The version attribute specifies the cookie protocol version that the cookie supports. The two currently supported versions are 0 and 1. Version 0 is the original Netscape specification, and version 1 is codified in RFC 2109. The comment attribute can be used (with RFC 2109-compliant cookies) to attach a human-readable comment to a cookie.

Summary

In this chapter, we covered how you can leverage the Servlet API to manage state information in your Web applications, and we discussed how the Servlet API supports direct manipulation of cookies. The support provided in the Servlet API makes it so easy to handle session management that you'll probably want to use it in more of your applications. In the introduction to this chapter, we tried to impress upon you just how much trouble this saves you, although until you've tried to do session management on your own (and tried in particular to debug weird session state problems), we doubt you'll be able to fully appreciate just how much value this support adds to the servlet platform. If you've ever used an ASP or PHP site and ended up with strange session-related behavior, perhaps you do have an inkling of the value this adds to the servlet platform.

In the next two chapters, we look at how to connect servlets with databases. By combining the techniques in this chapter with the techniques in the next two chapters, you can create highly functional Web applications that are easy to maintain.

CHAPTER

16

Databases, Connection Pools, and JDBC

Most serious Web applications built with servlets use a database. In this chapter, we explain how to connect to databases and how to organize data access classes. There are a number of flavors of database architecture. Peter first learned database programming on dBASE-type file-based databases. When Ian was a kid, it was all about writing out text files. For smaller systems, using the filesystem for persistence still makes sense sometimes, especially now that XML is starting to help developers standardize file formats. For the most part, though, file-based systems have given way to client-server databases and multitier databases for data-management needs.

Most databases now available are client-server and use the SQL standard as a means of manipulating the data they contain. Essentially this means that the interface between application and database has been standardized in such a way that in theory you can choose your database to meet your needs and (in theory) can move between databases easily. In Java, the Java Database Connector (JDBC) has been developed to give you a standard API for communicating with a SQL client-server-based database.

JDBC Drivers

The JDBC is a Java API that is part of the J2EE platform. JDBC enables Java applications to talk to SQL databases. This facility allows you to interoperate with the products of all major database vendors. The JDBC makes use of drivers developed specifically for each database product or, in some cases, generic drivers to attach to other abstraction layers. Four types of JDBC drivers are available:

Type 1: ODBC middleware driver: The ODBC system was developed for Windows-based operating systems. Like the JDBC, it is an abstraction layer with its own API, so that an application may use a variety of different databases.

The JDBC-ODBC bridge, the standard Type 1 driver, was originally implemented to give developers ready access to the enormous number of databases for which vendors had implemented ODBC drivers. Since JDBC calls are translated into ODBC calls before being passed to the database, it is not terribly efficient, and can mask features that may be available in a native Type 4 driver. In addition, using the JDBC-ODBC bridge requires you to configure an ODBC datasource, which typically requires a Windows server be in the equation somewhere. (There are Unix implementations of ODBC middleware, but on the whole they are not well supported.) If another type of driver is available, particularly a Type 4 driver, you should use it instead. These days, this is almost always the case.

Type 2: Native middleware driver: Some databases include special software designed to connect to a JDBC driver. This software, called *middleware*, is written for a specific platform, such as Windows or Unix. With this type of driver, the native API must reside on the client side for the JDBC to connect to. This approach limits configuration options (for example, client code cannot be downloaded in an applet or a WebStart application), requires additional client-side configuration, and can in some cases incur performance penalties because the middleware is still sitting between the database and the JDBC. Further, you may not be able to locate a version of the drivers for all the platforms you want to support, so using a native driver further limits your options.

Type 3: Java middleware driver: This approach is similar to the native middleware driver, except that the software that runs between the JDBC and the database is a Java application. Since this driver is pure Java (like the Type 4 driver, which we describe next), it runs anywhere Java runs. This also means that the driver can in most cases be downloaded and run on the fly, without any user configuration.

Type 4: Pure Java native driver: A Type 4 JDBC driver connects directly to the database. As with the Type 3 driver, this driver has the portability benefits of Java. The advantage of this type of driver is that it talks directly to the database server with no translation, which usually means that this driver will deliver the best performance. Most major database vendors and most open source databases alike now provide Type 4 JDBC drivers for their databases. This includes Oracle, MS SQL, Informix, Sybase, DB2, MySQL, PostgreSQL, InterBase, and mSQL; along with the various databases written in Java, such as OpenBase, Cloudbase, CocoBase, and HSQL.

SQL Database Products

The database you choose will depend on many factors. At least four open source databases and a number of Java databases are available, and several major database vendors offer commercial products. The following is a brief rundown on some of the most popular SQL databases you have to choose from. All these databases have Type 4 JDBC drivers available for them.

Although several databases are implemented in Java—with new ones appearing fairly regularly—we aren't going to give too much information on these because most sites and developers are using more traditional databases. Some of the databases implemented in Java, such as HSQL (http://hsqldb.sourceforge.net/), are open source and are particularly interesting to look at if you want to see how a database is implemented and how a query interpreter works, or if you just want to learn the gory details of a JDBC driver.

MySQL

Ian has been using MySQL for about five years, and it's the first place he turns when he needs a lightweight persistence layer, and often for larger database tasks as well. A wide range of open source tools is available to support it, and a lot of the JDBC example code you find out there uses MySQL in its examples.

MySQL is an open source database developed and supported by a company called MySQL AB. MySQL is licensed under the GNU General Public License (GPL). You can also purchase MySQL under a non-GPL license if you prefer not to be under GPL restrictions. While this database still lacks some enterprise-level features, MySQL is a robust platform used by complex Web sites such as Yahoo! MySQL prides itself on excellent performance, and is available for a wide variety of hardware platforms and operating systems. The principal trade-off is between advanced database features and performance. If you need stored procedures, extensive referential integrity checking, or transactions, you should probably look at PostgreSQL or one of the commercial databases. If, however, you want to use the database as a backing store for your data objects (as is often the case with servlet projects) and are planning to handle your business logic in the Java layer, the raw performance of this server will serve you very well.

Native Type 4 JDBC drivers are available for MySQL, making this database a good choice for any Java-based Web site. MySQL comes with some Linux installations out of the box; however, the best place to pick up your copy of MySQL is to visit the Web site at www.mysql.com.

PostgreSQL

PostgreSQL is another popular open source database. It is available for all major modern operating systems, including Linux, Windows, OS X, and Solaris. PostgreSQL originated from state-of-the-art database research at the University of California at Berkeley, and is now maintained by a stable global development group and various other contributors around the world. It is licensed under the BSD license, which means that the restrictions for using it as part of an integrated commercial solution are not as great as with GNU GPL databases. PostgreSQL is supplied in some Linux distributions; you can also obtain a copy from www.postgresql.org. The native Java JDBC driver for PostgreSQL can be found at http://jdbc.postgresql.org.

InterBase/Firebird

Peter has been using InterBase for five years, and for a mid-range database it holds up very well. A few years ago, Borland released InterBase's code as open source. As a result, the open source community has continued to develop and maintain the code—under the name Firebird—as open source. Borland has continued to develop a commercial, non-open source version of InterBase. Consequently, there has been a code fork between the open source version of InterBase (Firebird) and Borland's closed source version.

InterBase/Firebird has a JDBC driver called InterClient, and includes a middleware application with a Type 2 driver called InterServer. The open source community has also developed a Type 4 driver that communicates directly with InterBase. You can purchase an official licensed copy of InterBase from Borland at its Web site (www.borland. com). The purchase price depends on the number of development seats. You can also download a copy of the open source version of InterBase (Firebird) from www.ibphoenix.com, which is free. InterClient is supplied as a separate download on both sites. Supported operating systems include Windows, Linux, and various Unix flavors.

Oracle

Oracle and DB2 are the two biggest commercial database products in the world. Oracle has many features not found in any other database product. It even includes the ability to embed Java code into its stored procedures. Oracle is certainly the Rolls Royce of databases. As you may have guessed, Oracle runs on most of the major hardware platforms and operating systems. It has a Type 4 JDBC driver available for work with Java applications. To learn more about Oracle, take a look at its site at www.oracle.com.

Being one of the major database suppliers worldwide with a significant market share means that Oracle is indeed a solid, high-performance solution. For mission-critical systems in a business that can't afford downtime, and that demands excellent performance and advanced database technologies as well as a wide range of support options, Oracle is worth serious consideration. However, there are two downsides: high license costs and, more important perhaps, the fact that Oracle databases are quite complex and tend to need professional, full-time database administrators to configure and maintain them.

DB2

DB2 is a commercial database aimed at high-end servers with heavy workloads. It is typically used in government and corporate environments that require big iron databases, and is not usually found serving smaller Web sites. As with all the previous databases, DB2 can operate on most of the modern hardware platforms and operating systems, including Linux, Windows, and many forms of Unix; plus a number of IBM platforms where database server options may be limited.

DB2 shares many of the same advantages and downsides as Oracle. It is a solid, high-performing database, with many features in addition to the standard SQL specifications. You can download a trial version of DB2 from www.ibm.com, or you can order a trial CD from the same site. Naturally, a Type 4 JDBC driver is available for DB2.

MS SQL

Microsoft has not been very supportive of Java; there have been public spats with Sun over including Java in Microsoft's latest operating system, XP. For some time, this also extended to Java connectivity with Microsoft's database product (Microsoft SQL Server). The good news is that Microsoft has released a Microsoft SQL Server native JDBC driver for MS SQL. Prior to this, there had been only rather costly commercial JDBC drivers, which we suspect were extracting some considerable money from Java developers wanting to access MS SQL without going through the painfully slow ODBC.

Microsoft bought one of these companies and released the product for free in order to encourage the thousands of Java developers to use Microsoft SQL Server on Windows. Unfortunately, MS SQL is a viable alternative only if you wish to restrict your database server to a Microsoft operating system. It also means you have to put up with the occasional annoying problem, such as the inability to hold more than one result set open on a single connection at the same time, and the occasional system reboot or crash. As licenses go, it is probably cheaper than Oracle or DB2; however, MS SQL has neither the track record nor the market share of these two competitors. In comparison with the other two major database products, it is also relatively feature-poor. In fact, MS SQL does not really hold any significant advantage over the free open source alternatives.

Others

Three more products rate a mention here. Informix (www.informix.com) and Sybase (www.sybase.com) are both enterprise-class products. There's also FrontBase (www.frontbase.com), which is inexpensive, has some very nice management tools, and is supported on a wide range of platforms.

Building a Database Servlet

In this section, we assume that you have chosen a database, installed it, and installed the JDBC driver into the appropriate library directory in Tomcat (usually either the *<$CATALINA_HOME>*/common/lib directory or the /WEB-INF/lib directory of your Webapp). The detailed install for each database is different and beyond the scope of this book. In this first example, we use MySQL; and in the second example, we use generic SQL so that it will work no matter what database you are using.

Before we can do anything, we have to create a database to run our example. To do so, we'll use the command-line tools. A number of GUI tools are available for Unix, Windows, OS X, and Linux that you can use to create and modify databases, but the simplest and most ubiquitous is the good old command line. The command to create the database we'll be using is:

```
mysqladmin -u root -p create tomcatbook
```

You will be prompted for the root password you set up for your database. Enter it to let MySQL set up the table for you. Note that the mysql root password is not related in any way to the system root password, but is simply the password you set up when you installed MySQL.

Once the database is created, we add the Client table. This table will be simple. It consists of four fields:

- An ID field, which is an integer that will act as a unique identifier for each row
- A 40-character first name field
- A 40-character last name field
- A 20-character phone number field

Connect to the database by entering

```
mysql -u tomcatbook -p tomcatbook
```

Then enter the SQL shown in Listing 16.1 into the MySQL shell.

```
CREATE TABLE client (
ID INT AUTO_INCREMENT,
first_name CHAR(40),
last_name CHAR(40),
phone CHAR(20),
PRIMARY KEY(ID)
);
```

Listing 16.1 The SQL for creating our Client table.

Once you've created the table, add some rows to it (see Listing 16.2) so that there's something for our servlet to display. Feel free to substitute different values if you'd like.

```
INSERT INTO client VALUES(null, 'Ian', 'McFarland', '+1 415 555
1515');
INSERT INTO client VALUES(null, 'Peter', 'Harrison', '+64 9 555
1551');
INSERT INTO client VALUES(null, 'Tim', 'Ryan', '+1 718 555 5151');
```

Listing 16.2 The SQL that adds rows to our Client table.

A Simple Database Servlet

In this first example database servlet, we list all the records in the Client table. To keep this example as simple as possible, we are using a basic servlet with no other technology beyond JDBC to create the text for the response. The basic procedure when working with databases is to open a connection, use the connection to create a statement, execute the statement, and then close the connection. If the command was a SELECT, this process returns a result set, which you interrogate to get access to the data. Listing 16.3 shows ClientList.java.

```
package com.wiley.tomcatbook;

import java.io.*;
import javax.servlet.*;
import javax.servlet.http.*;
import java.sql.*;
import java.util.*;

public class ClientListServlet extends HttpServlet
{

    private Connection con;

    public void init(ServletConfig config) throws ServletException
    {
        super.init(config);
        String driver = config.getInitParameter("database-
driver-class");
        String jdbcurl = config.getInitParameter("database-
url");
        String login = config.getInitParameter("database-
login");
        String password = config.getInitParameter("database-
password");
        try
        {
        Class.forName(driver); // Load the driver
        con = DriverManager.getConnection(jdbcurl,
            login, password);
        }
        catch (Exception e)
        {
            throw new UnavailableException(e.getMessage());
        }
    }

    public void doGet (HttpServletRequest request,
HttpServletResponse
  response)
   throws ServletException, IOException
  {
        response.setContentType("text/html");
```

Listing 16.3 ClientList.java. (continues)

```
        PrintWriter out = response.getWriter();

        out.println("<html>");
        out.println("<head>");
        out.println("<title>Client List</title>");
        out.println("</head>");
        out.println("<body>");

        out.println("<h1>Contacts</h1>");
        out.println("<table border=\"1\">");
        out.println("<tr>");
        out.println("<th>First Name</th>");
        out.println("<th>Last Name</th>");
        out.println("<th>Phone</th>");
        out.println("</tr>");
        try
        {
            Statement s = con.createStatement();
            ResultSet rs = s.executeQuery("SELECT *
  FROM client");

                while(rs.next())
            {
                out.println("<tr>");
                out.println("<td>" + rs.getString("first_
  name") + "</td>");
                out.println("<td>" + rs.getString("last_
  name") + "</td>");
                out.println("<td>" + rs.getString("phone") +
"</td>");
                out.println("</tr>");
                }

            rs.close();
                s.close();

            }
            catch (SQLException sqle) {
                response.sendError(500, "Exception
  communicating with the database: " + sqle);
            }
        out.println("</table>");
        out.println("</body>");
        out.println("</html>");
```

Listing 16.3 ClientList.java. (continues)

```
    }

    public void destroy()
    {
        try
        {
            con.close();
        }
        catch (Exception e)
        {
            // Noop.
        }
        super.destroy();
    }

}
```

Listing 16.3 ClientList.java. (continued)

The first thing we need to do when dealing with a database is open a connection. This is an expensive operation, so we do it in the servlet init() method and keep the connection around. First, we need to load the appropriate database driver. We do this with the Class.forName(driver) line. The actual driver to be used should be specified in the deployment descriptor for the Webapp. We then open a connection with the getConnection() method of DriverManager (part of the javax.sql package) and pass in the JDBC URL of the database, the login name, and the password. All of these parameters are also specified in the deployment descriptor.

You will have to include the JAR with the javax.servlet libraries (servlet.jar) on your classpath to get the servlet to compile: javac -classpath <*$CATALINA_HOME*>/common/lib/servlet.jar ClientListServlet.java.

The deployment descriptor, with the configuration information for the database, is shown in Listing 16.4.

```
<?xml version="1.0" encoding="ISO-8859-1"?>
<!DOCTYPE web-app
  PUBLIC "-//Sun Microsystems, Inc.//DTD Web Application 2.2//EN"
  "http://java.sun.com/j2ee/dtds/web-app_2.2.dtd">

<web-app>
  <servlet>
    <servlet-name>ClientList</servlet-name>
    <servlet-class>com.wiley.tomcatbook.
```

Listing 16.4 The deployment descriptor for our Webapp. (continues)

```
ClientListServlet</servlet-class>
      <init-param>
         <param-name>database-driver-class</param-name>
         <param-value>org.gjt.mm.mysql.Driver</param-value>
      </init-param>
      <init-param>
         <param-name>database-url</param-name>
         <param-value>jdbc:mysql://localhost/tomcatbook</param-
value>
      </init-param>
      <init-param>
         <param-name>database-login</param-name>
         <param-value>tomcatbook</param-value>
      </init-param>
      <init-param>
         <param-name>database-password</param-name>
         <param-value>badpassword</param-value>
      </init-param>
   </servlet>
   <servlet-mapping>
      <servlet-name>ClientList</servlet-name>
      <url-pattern>/client-list</url-pattern>
   </servlet-mapping>
</web-app>
```

Listing 16.4 The deployment descriptor for our Webapp. (continued)

At this point, you've done the following:

1. Installed and configured your database.
2. Put the deployment descriptor in place.
3. Compiled the servlet source.
4. Placed the ClientListServlet.class file in the <*$CATALINA_HOME*>/webapps/tomcatbook/WEB-INF/classes/com/wiley/tomcatbook directory.
5. Installed the MySQL driver library (mysql.jar) in either the <*$CATALINA_HOME*>/common/lib or <*$CATALINA_HOME*>/webapps/tomcatbook/WEB-INF/lib directory.

Now, a servlet engine restart should have our servlet working at http://localhost:8080/tomcatbook/client-list. You've now created a simple but functional three-tier enterprise application. You can build some fairly complex applications by simply recombining the techniques we've used so far.

Let's look at what we've written in a little more detail. Once our database connection is established in the init() method, our doGet() method is free to utilize it to handle requests. We start by calling con.createStatement() to get a Statement object on which to execute our query. Executing the query

```
SELECT * FROM client
```

returns a ResultSet containing all of the fields in the database, row by row. We iterate over the rows by calling rs.next(), and request the fields we want to display with statements like

```
rs.getString("first_name");
```

We're not going to teach you everything about SQL in this book. There are plenty of books out there that can give you more background on SQL, JDBC, and databases in general. But before we move on, you can try modifying the SELECT statement to do more interesting things that leverage the database engine more heavily. Try queries like

```
SELECT * FROM client ORDER BY last_name
```

or

```
SELECT * FROM client WHERE ID > 1
```

or

```
SELECT * FROM client WHERE last_name LIKE '%an%'
```

You can start to see how SQL can be used to produce interesting results in your servlets. And since the queries are just simple strings passed to the database engine for parsing, you can even let the user have some influence on what gets sent to the database. Be careful with this, however. You don't want to give end users the ability to send arbitrary queries to the database if you want your data to be safe. If you let them send statements like

```
DELETE FROM client
```

or

```
DROP TABLE client
```

you may not be happy with the results.

Using Connection Pools

Creating and freeing a connection for every servlet requires a certain amount of time to allocate resources, negotiate the connection with the database, authenticate the connection, and finally close the connection and free the resources. It also uses up connections to the database, which are usually a fairly scarce resource. It would be good if there were a pool of connections already open that a servlet could use as required. This is exactly what a connection pool allows you to do.

Prior to Tomcat 4, there was no connection pooling functionality within Tomcat, and you had to make a choice about the connection pooling technology to use. With Tomcat 4.x, you get an easy-to-use connection pooling library to work with, built into the server.

Connection Pools for JDBC Datasources

The standard way to access connection pools in Tomcat 4.x is to use a J2EE DataSource. This also has the benefit of making it easier for applications written for Tomcat to be run on other commercial J2EE servers. It moves the configuration information for the database drivers out of your code and into a server configuration file, either the server.xml file or optionally in a separate context XML file if you're running Tomcat 4.1 or later.

Note that a few little differences exist between Tomcat 4.0 and 4.1 when it comes to configuring datasources. Some rough edges in the 4.0 configuration model have been smoothed out in 4.1. Unfortunately, that improvement came at the cost of configuration portability, so you'll want to pay particular attention if you're porting a 4.0 configuration to 4.1, or vice versa.

Tomcat 4.1 also added some flexibility regarding where you can configure contexts, which we alluded to a few sentences ago. In this section, we talk about your context configuration file. If you're running 4.0, this file will be your server-wide configuration file: server.xml. If you're running 4.1, you can make these configuration changes either in the server.xml file or in a context-specific configuration file (a file named for the context it represents, stored in your /webapps directory). Specifically, if you are writing a configuration for your foo context, you would create a file called foo.xml, and into it you would write just the <Context/> node you would otherwise write into the server.xml file. The admin.xml and manager.xml files that come with the 4.1 distribution are good examples to check to see how this works.

To configure a connection pool, you have to add configuration lines to both your Web application and the server. You must add a resource to your context configuration file, and you must make the JAR file containing the database driver available to the server. This is because the server will be making the connection pool available as a service, and our Webapp will be a client of that service. What this means to you is that if you previously installed the driver in the webapps/tomcatbook/WEB-INF/lib/ directory, you have to move or copy it to the *<$CATALINA_HOME>*/common/lib directory in order for this to work.

Listing 16.5 shows how we configured Tomcat 4.0 to create a connection pool attached to the MySQL database we configured earlier and make it available to the /tomcatbook context.

```
<Context path="/tomcatbook" docBase="tomcatbook" debug="0"
 reloadable="true">

  <Resource name="jdbc/tomcatbook" auth="Container"
 type="javax.sql.DataSource"/>

  <ResourceParams name="jdbc/tomcatbook">

     <parameter>
```

Listing 16.5 The tomcatbook context definition for 4.0 in server.xml. (continues)

```
        <name>user</name>
        <value>tomcatbook</value>
      </parameter>

      <parameter>
        <name>password</name>
        <value>badpassword</value>
      </parameter>

      <parameter>
        <name>driverClassName</name>
        <value>org.gjt.mm.mysql.Driver</value>
      </parameter>

      <parameter>
        <name>driverName</name>
        <value>jdbc:mysql://localhost/tomcatbook</value>
      </parameter>

    </ResourceParams>
  </Context>
```

Listing 16.5 The tomcatbook context definition for 4.0 in server.xml. (continued)

If you're configuring a Tomcat 4.1 server, the syntax is slightly different. Instead of using the poorly named driverName parameter, you put the JDBC URL in the more appropriately named URL parameter, as shown in Listing 16.6.

```
<Context path="/tomcatbook"
  docBase="tomcatbook"
  debug="0"
  reloadable="true">

  <Resource
    name="jdbc/tomcatbook"
    auth="Container"
    type="javax.sql.DataSource"/>

  <ResourceParams name="jdbc/tomcatbook">

    <parameter>
       <name>user</name>
```

Listing 16.6 The tomcatbook context definition for 4.1 in tomcatbook.xml. (continues)

```
            <value>tomcatbook</value>
        </parameter>

        <parameter>
            <name>password</name>
            <value>badpassword</value>
        </parameter>

        <parameter>
            <name>driverClassName</name>
            <value>org.gjt.mm.mysql.Driver</value>
        </parameter>

        <parameter>
            <name>url</name>
            <value>jdbc:mysql://localhost/tomcatbook</value>
        </parameter>

    </ResourceParams>
</Context>
```

Listing 16.6 The tomcatbook context definition for 4.1 in tomcatbook.xml. (continued)

Once you have added these elements to your configuration files, you can make a copy of the original ClientListServlet.java servlet and modify it to create ClientListPooledServlet.java. In this example, we revised the init() method to look up the DataSource we set up in the server.xml file. The purpose of the DataSource is to provide a source of database connections for your Web application. The DataSource in Tomcat has an implementation for connection pooling built in, so you do not need to worry about the details of the connection pooling. You simply need to look up the DataSource and then call getConnection() to get a connection. To return the connection to the pool after use, simply call close() on the connection. Because getting a connection is very inexpensive now, we no longer have to keep the Connection object in an instance variable set up at init time, but can request a connection from the DataSource object each time we need one. Otherwise, the code is similar to our previous example. All that has changed is how we obtain the connection we use, and what we do with it when we've finished using it.

Note also that we're using more J2EE frameworks here: javax.naming.* (the Java Naming and Directory Interface, or JNDI) and javax.sql.* (the J2EE JDBC 2.0 extensions). Don't worry too much about the specifics for now. It should suffice for you to understand that we are looking up the DataSource we declared in the server.xml earlier.

You will have to include the right JARs on your classpath to get the new servlet to compile:

```
javac -classpath <$CATALINA_HOME>/common/lib/servlet.
jar:<$CATALINA_HOME>/common/lib/jdbc2_0-stdext.jar
ClientListPooledServlet.java
```

Remember to replace the *:* with a *;* if you're using Windows. Listing 16.7 shows ClientListPooledServlet.java.

```
package com.wiley.tomcatbook;

import java.io.*;
import javax.servlet.*;
import javax.servlet.http.*;
import java.sql.*;
import java.util.*;
import javax.naming.*;
import javax.sql.*;

public class ClientListPooledServlet extends HttpServlet
{

  private DataSource ds;

  public void init(ServletConfig config) throws ServletException
  {
    super.init(config);
    try
    {
      Context initCtx = new InitialContext();
      Context envCtx = (Context) initCtx.
 lookup("java:comp/env");
      ds = (DataSource) envCtx.lookup("jdbc/tomcatbook");
    }
    catch (Exception e)
    {
      throw new UnavailableException(e.getMessage());
    }
  }

  public void doGet (HttpServletRequest request,
 HttpServletResponse response)
    throws ServletException, IOException
  {
    response.setContentType("text/html");
    PrintWriter out = response.getWriter();

    out.println("<html>");
    out.println("<head>");
    out.println("<title>Client List</title>");
```

Listing 16.7 ClientListPooledServlet.java. (continues)

```
    out.println("</head>");
    out.println("<body>");

    out.println("<h1>Contacts</h1>");
    out.println("<table border=\"1\">");
    out.println("<tr>");
    out.println("<th>First Name</th>");
    out.println("<th>Last Name</th>");
    out.println("<th>Phone</th>");
    out.println("</tr>");
    try
    {
      Connection con = ds.getConnection();
      Statement s = con.createStatement();
      ResultSet rs = s.executeQuery("SELECT * FROM CLIENT");

      while(rs.next())
      {
        out.println("<tr>");
        out.println("<td>" + rs.getString("first_name") +
"</td>");
        out.println("<td>" + rs.getString("last_name") +
"</td>");
        out.println("<td>" + rs.getString("phone") + "</td>");
        out.println("</tr>");
      }

      rs.close();
      s.close();
      con.close();

      }
      catch (SQLException sqle) {
        response.sendError(500, "Exception communicating
with the database: " + sqle);
      }
     out.println("</table>");
     out.println("</body>");
     out.println("</html>");
  }


}
```

Listing 16.7 ClientListPooledServlet.java. (continued)

We also need to add the new servlet to our deployment descriptor, and a declaration of the dependency on the datasource we're relying on, as highlighted in Listing 16.8. Note again that, since this is a validated XML document, the order of the elements counts.

```
<?xml version="1.0" encoding="ISO-8859-1"?>
<!DOCTYPE web-app
  PUBLIC "-//Sun Microsystems, Inc.//DTD Web Application 2.2//EN"
  "http://java.sun.com/j2ee/dtds/web-app_2.2.dtd">

<web-app>
  <servlet>
    <servlet-name>ClientListPooled</servlet-name>
    <servlet-class>com.wiley.tomcatbook.
 ClientListPooledServlet</servlet-class>
  </servlet>
  <servlet>
    <servlet-name>ClientList</servlet-name>
    <servlet-class>com.wiley.tomcatbook.
 ClientListServlet</servlet-class>
    <init-param>
      <param-name>database-driver-class</param-name>
      <param-value>org.gjt.mm.mysql.Driver</param-value>
    </init-param>
    <init-param>
      <param-name>database-url</param-name>
      <param-value>jdbc:mysql://localhost/tomcatbook</
param-value>
    </init-param>
    <init-param>
      <param-name>database-login</param-name>
      <param-value>tomcatbook</param-value>
    </init-param>
    <init-param>
      <param-name>database-password</param-name>
      <param-value>badpassword</param-value>
    </init-param>
  </servlet>
  <servlet-mapping>
    <servlet-name>ClientList</servlet-name>
    <url-pattern>/client-list</url-pattern>
  </servlet-mapping>
  <servlet-mapping>
```

Listing 16.8 The revised web.xml file. (continues)

```
      <servlet-name>ClientListPooled</servlet-name>
      <url-pattern>/client-list-pooled</url-pattern>
    </servlet-mapping>
    <resource-ref>
      <description>
        This is a reference to the data source we use
        to talk to the database configured in the
        server.xml file.
      </description>
      <res-ref-name>jdbc/tomcatbook</res-ref-name>
      <res-type>javax.sql.DataSource</res-type>
      <res-auth>Container</res-auth>
    </resource-ref>
  </web-app>
```

Listing 16.8 The revised web.xml file. (continued)

Restart Tomcat, and you should now be able to view both servlets: the old one (at http://localhost:8080/tomcatbook/client-list) and the new one (at http://localhost:8080/tomcatbook/client-list-pooled).

If for some reason it didn't work, make sure you have included the driver for your database in the <*$CATALINA_HOME*>/common/lib directory, and look at the logs to make sure that Tomcat isn't complaining about some other misconfiguration.

Summary

In this chapter, we covered the basics of how to access databases from your Web applications. We also examined the connection pooling tools provided in Tomcat 4. These tools give you everything you need in order to build efficient and scalable database-driven Web applications.

In the next chapter, we look at a more object-oriented approach to database use. We build an object-oriented framework that lets us easily create new data object classes in a few lines of code, and that takes care of object persistence for us.

CHAPTER

17

Database-Aware Objects

In our previous chapter, we covered the basics of using databases with servlets. In this chapter, we build some lightweight, reusable JavaBeans that know how to store themselves in databases; this will enable us to get back to working with objects rather than having to write bunches of SQL throughout our code.

This is not to say that SQL doesn't have its place. Clearly it does. And we barely scratched the surface of what a database engine can do for an application: we've used it simply as a persistent data store. When we're building object-based systems, that's often all we need the database for anyway, and it's these situations that this chapter is meant to address.

Wouldn't it be nice if we could use just a few different types of JavaBeans to hold our data, and then let the beans deal with object persistence for us? Well, we can do that. We need to write a simple reusable framework to handle the object persistence for us, but once we're done with it, we can return our focus to manipulating first-class objects rather than figuring out what SQL we need to write in order to get the results we want. Java development is supposed to be object-oriented, after all, and traditional SQL is anything but object-oriented.

However, the goal of this chapter is not to show you an object framework, nor to suggest this is *the* way to accomplish object persistence. What we create here is simply a lightweight framework for handling object persistence. It's not very high-performance, and it doesn't do much to guarantee that transactions are Atomic, Consistent, Isolated or Durable. (These are the so-called ACID properties that transactional systems are supposed to ensure.) If you want a framework to do that for you, there's always Enterprise JavaBeans (EJBs).

In this chapter, we show you how to build your own frameworks and integrate them with the various servlet technologies in order to simplify your work. The two main things we're trying to achieve here are *abstraction* and *reuse*.

By letting the framework deal with persistence, we achieve abstraction from the underlying SQL layer. This allows us to modify the behavior of the system if we so choose—for instance, by changing the database we use (which typically involves tweaking the SQL a bit so it will work on the new dialect we get with a different RDBMS) or by getting rid of the database altogether, perhaps by persisting the objects out as XML documents or into some other type of persistent store.

By keeping our sample framework simple and flexible, we allow for future reuse. Once we've finished with the framework, we can create new database-aware JavaBeans simply by subclassing a single base class. We've chosen to use inheritance rather than delegation for ease of implementation. This approach has trade-offs. We save ourselves writing some code at the expense of requiring our beans to derive from a single base class; however, the beans we construct can simply proxy other objects with other base classes where necessary, thus giving us back a large portion of that flexibility. And if you don't like this implementation, you can always implement your framework in a different way.

The Factory and Modified Singleton Design Patterns

To achieve our goal of flexibility (particularly with regard to datatypes) while at the same time encapsulating housekeeping functions, we have chosen to follow the Factory Design pattern for the core of our persistence framework. We also want to tie the database-aware objects tightly to their data representations, and so we use ideas from the Modified Singleton pattern.

The normal way to get instances of objects in Java is to call a constructor on a class by using the new operator—for example:

```
Object o = new Object();
```

In the Factory Design pattern, however, we create objects only indirectly: by requesting them from the factory class. Assume we create a class named ObjectFactory, which is responsible for doling out new instances of Object when we request them. In this case, the syntax would likely be something like:

```
Object o = ObjectFactory.getInstance();
```

The Modified Singleton pattern is based on the Singleton pattern, so let's start by explaining that pattern. A *singleton* is an instance of a class that is implemented to ensure that only one instance of that class exists. There are many cases where you want exactly one of something. A good example involves an object responsible for controlling access to a resource; say we choose to implement a singleton in order to handle locking or synchronization. There's no point in telling a lock object that you want to lock a resource if someone else is just going to ask their own lock object (with its own separate state) whether the resource is locked. Or to put it another way, you want to prevent the situation in which Johnny asks Mom if he can have money for the movies, and when she says no, he can just ask Dad and get a different answer.

A modified singleton is a class that allows a *finite number* of instances to be created. According to the pattern, that number is known in advance, and the instances are typically created during class initialization. Here's an example of why you might want to use this: Suppose you want to pass in one of a finite number of parameters to another method. Typically, you do this by assigning static final int variables with names that match the parameter types. This has a distinct disadvantage, however; there is no type safety in doing this. Just because your code expects values from one to five, nothing is preventing another piece of code from sending you the integer 6, or -65534.

Furthermore, nothing is making the developers use the symbolic name, so they may get sloppy and start passing just the integers. That's okay unless the API changes, or unless they mistake one integer for another. Also, when you're debugging it's hard to tell what that *3* you passed in represents. If we use a modified singleton as a parameter, we eliminate all these problems, and implicitly get compile-time type safety and range-checking as well.

However, what we want to do is a little different. We want to make sure that the objects we create are kept in sync with the database representation of those objects, and we also want to control what objects get created. We also want to keep a pool of objects around, and we may not want to create a new instance of Object at every request. We desire more control over object creation, and we want to manage the construction of the objects.

To illustrate, let's consider another more concrete example. Suppose we wish to create a set of objects containing logins and usernames. We want to keep the login and username as two separate strings in String variables inside the objects we create. We call our objects *User objects*. Our User class will look roughly like the one shown in Listing 17.1.

```
package com.wiley.tomcatbook.user;

public class User
{
        private String login;
        private String fullName;

        public User(String login, String name)
        {
                this.login = login;
                this.fullName = name;
}

public String getLogin()
{
                return login;
```

Listing 17.1 The User class. (continues)

```
    }

    public String getFullName()
    {
        return fullName;
    }
}
```

Listing 17.1 The User class. (continued)

So far, so good. Whenever we want to create a new user, we just use some code like this:

```
User u = new User("jdoe", "John Doe");
```

In so doing, we may end up creating a new User object when there already was a perfectly good one lying around in memory. And what's to prevent some piece of code from creating a new instance of User with the matching login (accidentally or intentionally) and thereby circumventing our security procedures? What if we want one and only one instance of User for any given username?

This is where our factory object comes in. At this point, let's create a new class, called UserFactory, shown in Listing 17.2.

```
package com.wiley.tomcatbook.user;

import java.util.*;

public class UserFactory
{
    private static Hashtable users = new Hashtable();

            public static User getUser(String login)
            {
                return (User) users.get(login);
            }

            public static User newUser(String login, String name)
            {
                if (users.containsKey(login)) return getUser(login);
                // implied else
                User theUser = new User(login, name);
                users.put(login, theUser);
                return theUser;
            }
}
```

Listing 17.2 The UserFactory class.

We should also make one modification to the User object in order to prevent other code from creating new users without going through the factory. We do this by changing the visibility of the constructor from public to protected, as shown in Listing 17.3.

```
protected User(String login, String name)
{
        this.login = login;
        this.fullName = name;
            }
```

Listing 17.3 The revised constructor for the User class.

This way, the only way classes outside the com.wiley.tomcatbook.user package can create a User object is indirectly, by talking to the UserFactory class.

Our factory is a little simplistic: in particular, our getUser() method should probably be smart enough to throw an exception if the requested user isn't in the Hashtable rather than just returning null. But even with this oversimplified example, you can see that it is impossible from outside the com.wiley.tomcatbook.user package to create more than one instance of User with the same login. If you're not sure this is true, see the simple test shown in Listing 17.4.

```
import com.wiley.tomcatbook.user.*;

public class UserTest
{
        public static void main(String[] args)
        {
                User a, b, c;
                a = UserFactory.newUser("jdoe", "John Doe");
                b = UserFactory.newUser("jdoe", "Jane Doe");
                c = UserFactory.newUser("jdonne", "John Donne");
                System.out.println("User a = User b? " + (a == b));
                System.out.println("User a = User c? " + (a == c));
                System.out.println("User b's full name: " + b.getFullName());
}
}
```

Listing 17.4 The UserTest class.

If you compile and run the classes shown in Listings 17.1 through 17.4, you will see the following output:

```
User a = User b? true
User a = User c? false
User b's full name: John Doe
```

We hope that's what you expected to see. Our test code created two instances of User from three newUser() calls to UserFactory, where only two unique logins were passed in. This is exactly the behavior we wanted under these circumstances.

But as we mentioned before, there are a few reasons—beyond simply limiting the number of instances of a class—why we might choose to create our instances indirectly. Another reason is to allow us to do a little more behind the scenes when an object is requested, or even before. Let's consider our user factory again. Imagine that we want our User objects to be stored off in a database and that most of the time we would just be grabbing existing users, using UserFactory.getUser(). We could handle this in a couple of ways: One, we could load all of the users into the Hashtable at startup time to improve performance. Then, every request for a user would simply grab an instance out of the Hashtable-based cache we created. Two, we could lazily populate the cache: we would still look in the Hashtable-based cache first to see if we have a matching user. If we do have a matching user, we simply return it. If we don't, we go to the database and see if it contains a matching record. If it does, we create a new instance of User, based on that record, and store it off in our Hashtable before returning it to the requestor.

Perhaps the main reason to use factories is as a means of handling polymorphism. Factories are often used to manage returning heterogeneous datatypes that conform to some overriding pattern. A good example is the MessageDigest factory, which is used to create MessageDigest instances. In this case, the same class fulfills the roles of both factory and base class for the created objects. Depending on what string you pass into MessageDigest.getInstance()—for example, MD5 or SHA—you will get back an instance of a different subclass of MessageDigest, one that implements the algorithm specified in the parameter. This pattern is followed in many places in the JDK, many of them in java.security, which contains a number of Service Provider Interface-based mechanisms for constructing heterogeneous objects that conform to the same or similar API. The SSLSocketFactory is another good example; it is used to create instances of various subclasses of SSLSocket, which implement different transport-layer security protocols.

This mechanism is often used to create instances of classes implementing an interface or one of several subclasses of an abstract base class. Neither interfaces nor abstract classes may be directly instantiated, so factory methods—either on a factory class or on the abstract base class itself—are used to create the instances instead.

But enough theory. With this background, let's start developing a framework that handles object persistence for us.

The Design

The principal design goal we've set for ourselves is ease of development. What we really want to be able to do is write what more or less amounts to simple JavaBeans, with simple accessor methods and little else, and let the framework handle the persistence. We don't want to have to write any SQL when we create new beans; we want the framework to *figure out* how to write the data. We also want to be able to configure the framework to commit the object with each change (autocommit) or wait for an explicit commit. Finally, we want our framework to be able to handle heterogeneous datatypes contained in arbitrary packages and be extensible without requiring any changes to the framework.

To achieve all of this, we've opted to focus on a factory class (which will be responsible for most of the operations on the objects) and an abstract base class (which will contain the variables and methods we need in order to handle the persistence and state management requirements we set for ourselves). We've also opted to use introspection and reflection to discover the attributes on our database-aware beans so that we don't have to write any SQL in our beans.

We've called our object framework *smartobjects*, and we've put it into the com.neo.smartobjects package. When we're done, we plan to create an object or two inside the com.wiley.tomcatbook package that will leverage this framework and rework the database examples in the last chapter to use them.

Setting Up the Project

For simplicity's sake, let's look at setting up our working directory for this project and using Ant to build the project. As you'll see, the directory structure we've chosen is quite similar to the directory structure of the Tomcat source and a number of other open source projects. We like it and think it's a good way to structure projects, but you're free to structure your workspace however it suits you. If you structure your files differently, it will be up to you to adapt our instructions to the specifics of your file layout.

In our home directory, we have a project directory, which we refer to as *<project-root>*. We create a directory inside it called smartobjects. Inside that directory, we create an /src directory and a /lib directory. Inside the /src directory, we set up a file hierarchy that matches the package hierarchy for our project. We're going to be working with two packages—com.neo.smartobject and com.wiley.tomcatbook. As a result, our final file hierarchy looks like the one shown in Listing 17.5.

```
<project-root>/
  /smartobjects
    /src
      /com/
        /neo
          /smartobjects
        /wiley
          /tomcatbook
    /lib
```

Listing 17.5 The file structure for our project.

Once we've established the file hierarchy, we can start implementing the objects we need.

SmartObject.java

Let's start by defining the abstract base class from which we derive all child objects. This class will be called <project-root>/smartobjects/src/com/neo/smartobjects/

SmartObject.java, and it will be responsible for managing the attributes we'll use to maintain state and the uniqueness of the object. The principal attributes are shown in Table 17.1.

Table 17.1 Attributes of a SmartObject

ATTRIBUTE	DESCRIPTION
TableName	Contains the name of the table in the database containing the persistent data for a given class implementing the SmartObject interface.
ID	Contains the object ID for the individual instance; unique per class.
autocommit	Specifies whether or not changes to the state of this object should be commited whenever a property is changed.
clean	Indicates whether any changes have taken place since the last commit.

The object is simple enough. Although it does not have any abstract methods, we declare it as abstract because it would be meaningless to instantiate an instance of this base class. (It wouldn't have any data values other than the ones we use internally.) Our implementation is shown in Listing 17.6.

```
package com.neo.smartobjects;

public abstract class SmartObject
{
   private boolean autocommit;
   private boolean clean;
   private int id;
   String tableName = "<none>";

   protected void setTableName(String tableName)
   {
      this.tableName = tableName;
   }

   protected String getTableName()
   {
      return this.tableName;
   }

   public boolean isAutoCommit()
```

Listing 17.6 SmartObject.java. (continues)

```
    {
        return autocommit;
    }

    public void setAutoCommit(boolean state)
    {
        autocommit = state;
    }

    public boolean isClean()
    {
        return clean;
    }

    protected void setClean(boolean state)
    {
        clean = state;
    }

    protected void setID(int id)
    {
        this.id = id;
    }

    public int getID()
    {
        return id;
    }

    protected void propertyChanged()
        throws SmartObjectException
    {
        ObjectFactory.notifyPropertyChanged(this);
    }

}
```

Listing 17.6 SmartObject.java. (continued)

Note in particular the visibility modifiers we've chosen. The methods that we've protected are the ones we want only our factory object to have access to. This includes all of the setters for the state properties. We've made the getters public so that other objects can look at the state if they're interested. The only method that isn't a simple getter or setter is the propertyChanged() method, which we call from child classes to notify the factory that our state has changed. We talk about what propertyChanged() does in the section.

Before we jump into the ObjectFactory, let's define SmartObjectException, a fairly straightforward exception class. We use this class, shown in Listing 17.7, to report any problems that occur at runtime.

```
package com.neo.smartobjects;

public class SmartObjectException extends Exception
{
   private Throwable nestedException;

   SmartObjectException()
   {
      super();
   }

   SmartObjectException(Throwable nestedException)
   {
      this();
      this.nestedException = nestedException;
   }

   SmartObjectException(String message)
   {
      super(message);
   }

   SmartObjectException(String message, Throwable nestedException)
   {
      this(message + " Nested exception: " + nestedException);
      this.nestedException = nestedException;
   }

   public Throwable getNestedException()
   {
      return nestedException;
   }
}
```

Listing 17.7 SmartObjectException.java.

Note that we've added constructors that take a Throwable; this is so that we can pass along any nested exceptions to the caller. This can be quite useful—for logging purposes, for example. (As you'll see toward the end of the chapter, we'll have the calling servlet print to the log the stack trace from the nested exception.)

ObjectFactory.java

From this point forward, what we're doing gets a little more complicated, so let's go method by method through the factory object. We begin with the initialize() method, which takes as parameters the name of a JNDI initial context and the name of a data-source. Let's use the Tomcat connection pooling features we touched on in our previous chapter. Listing 17.8 shows how we implement this method.

```
package com.neo.smartobjects;

import java.util.*;
import java.beans.*;
import java.lang.reflect.*;
import java.sql.*;
import javax.sql.*;
import javax.naming.*;

public class ObjectFactory
{
    private static boolean initialized = false;
    private static DataSource ds;
    private static Hashtable cache = new Hashtable();

    public static void initialize(String context, String sourceName)
        throws SmartObjectException
    {
        if (! initialized)
        {
            try
            {
                Context initCtx = new InitialContext();
                Context envCtx = (Context)
initCtx.lookup(context);
                ds = (DataSource) envCtx.lookup(sourceName);
                initialized = true;
            }
            catch (NamingException ne)
            {
                throw new SmartObjectException("Could not initialize
factory.", ne);
            }
```

Listing 17.8 The ObjectFactory class declaration and initialize(). (continues)

```
        }
    }
   .
   .
   .
}
```

Listing 17.8 The ObjectFactory class declaration and initialize(). (continued)

The first things we see in Listing 17.8 are the package statement and some imports. Since we'll be using introspection and reflection, we need to pull in java.beans.* and java.lang.reflect.*, respectively. We're also using JDBC with the JDBC 2.0 extensions (DataSource is a JDBC 2.0 object), so let's pull in java.sql.* and javax.sql.*. And we're using JNDI to look up the datasource, so we need to pull in javax.naming.*.

Those last two are standard extensions (and part of J2EE). Therefore, we need to make sure that we've included the JAR files for them in our project and that they are included on the classpath when we compile. Both JARs are part of the Tomcat distribution, so we can simply copy them from <*$CATALINA_HOME*>/common/lib. We copy the files—called jdbc2_0-stdext.jar and jndi.jar, respectively—to the /lib directory inside our /project directory (<*project-root*>/smartobjects/lib). Our initialize() method is static, as all of our methods will be. The factory we're implementing is effectively a singleton. (Although we don't instantiate a single instance of the class, as we would in a true singleton, this class conforms to the so-called Static Singleton design pattern: A class always exists as a single instance within the namespace of the class loader that loaded it, and we take advantage of that to create a single, globally accessible code object in the form of the ObjectFactory class.)

We use a Hashtable to contain a set of object caches, one per registered class. We declare it here as a static variable, and initialize it inline with an empty Hashtable instance.

The initialization method itself is pretty straightforward. A String representing the root context and a String representing the name of a JDBC 2.0 DataSource are passed in. We look up the datasource and store it in a static variable: *ds*. If everything goes well, we set the static boolean variable initialized to true so that this code cannot be called again. If things don't go so well (if for instance we can't find the datasource in the JNDI InitialContext, or the InitialContext can't be created), we throw a SmartObjectException and pass in the NamingException that was thrown. That way, the caller knows that we aren't able to be initialized and can take appropriate action.

Getting Existing Objects

The next method we look at is the getObject() method. It takes the fully qualified name of a class that extends SmartObject and the ID of the object we want it to get for us. Listing 17.9 contains the ObjectFactory getObject() method.

```
public static SmartObject getObject(String classname, int id)
    throws SmartObjectException
  {
    try
    {
      SmartObject so;
      Class theClass = Class.forName(classname);
      if (! (isSubclass(SmartObject.class, theClass)))
        throw new SmartObjectException("Invalid class. Class
" + theClass + " does not implement com.neo.smartobjects.SmartObject.");
      so = getCachedObject(theClass, id);
      if (so != null) return so;
      // implied else
      so = newObject(theClass);
      so.setID(id);
      load(so);
      cacheObject(theClass, so);
      return so;
    }
    catch (SmartObjectException soe)
    {
      throw soe;
    }
    catch (ClassNotFoundException cnfe)
    {
      throw new SmartObjectException("Exception occurred getting
instance of " + classname + " with object id: " + id + ".", cnfe);
    }
  }
```

Listing 17.9 The ObjectFactory getObject() method.

There are four methods in Listing 17.9 that hide a good deal of complexity: getCachedObject(), newObject(), load(), and cacheObject(). Before we look at these methods, let's concentrate on the flow of the getObject() method. First, we load the class for the name passed in. We check to see that it's a legitimate subclass of SmartObject; if it is, we pass the class and the ID to the getCachedObject() method, which checks the cache to see if it contains an instance of the class with a matching ID. If for some reason the classname passed in is invalid, we throw a SmartObjectException.

The getCachedObject() method returns the object matching the ID, or null if there is no such object in the cache. If we get the object back, we simply return it to the caller. If, however, we get back a null, we have to load the object.

First, we pass the class to the newObject, from which we get back a new, uninitialized instance of that class. We then store the uninitialized (or hollow) SmartObject in the variable *so*.

We then set the ID on the hollow SmartObject and pass it to the load() method on the factory. The load() method then pulls the values out of the database (assuming that the ID is valid), and we then have a fully initialized object. Otherwise, load() will throw a SmartObject exception, which we will likewise throw.

We store the fully initialized object in the cache by calling cacheObject(). We then return the object to the caller.

Now let's take a look at those methods we just glossed over. First off, the isSubclass() method we saw here is in fact our own method. Surprisingly, there is no easy way to ask a class if it is a subclass of another class. It's easy enough to know if an *instance* of a class is a subclass of some other class—that's what the instanceof operator does. However, we don't have an instance of the class, so we have to roll our own test. The closest we get is the Class.getSuperclass() method, which returns the immediate superclass of the class it's called on, or returns null if the class has no parent class (for example, Object.getSuperclass() returns null). Let's use that in a recursive method to determine inheritance, as shown in Listing 17.10.

```
public static final boolean isSubclass(Class parentClass, Class
childClass)
   {
      if (parentClass == childClass) return true;
      if (childClass == null) return false;
      return isSubclass(parentClass, childClass.getSuperclass());
   }
```

Listing 17.10 The ObjectFactory isSubclass() method.

The method shown in Listing 17.10 simply checks to see whether the classes passed in are the same. If so, it returns true. If not, it calls itself, asking if the parent class of the subclass we're testing is the same as the parent class we initially passed in. It keeps going this way until it finds a match, or until it runs out of parent classes, in which case it returns false. We declare it final so that the compiler has a chance to optimize it.

The getCachedObject() method checks to see whether we already have the object requested in the cache, and returns it if we do. It returns null if we don't. Listing 17.11 shows the ObjectFactory getCachedObject() method. Here we also see the beginnings of the cache structure.

```
private static SmartObject getCachedObject(Class aClass, int id)
{
      WeakHashMap cachePage = (WeakHashMap) cache.get(aClass);
      if (cachePage == null)
      {
            return null;
      }
      return (SmartObject) cachePage.get(new Integer(id));
}
```

Listing 17.11 The ObjectFactory getCachedObject() method.

The cache, as we saw before, is simply a Hashtable. Inside the cache, we use a set of WeakHashMaps—one for each class registered with the factory—as the basis for a cache. Every time a new class is registered, we create an instance of WeakHashMap and store it in the Hasthable *cache*, using the class as the key. We store it in the static variable *cache* when the class is loaded. For those of you who are not familiar with the WeakHashMap (added in JDK 1.2), it uses weak references to store values so that when they are no longer needed they can be garbage collected. To quote from the JavaDoc:

A hashtable-based Map implementation with weak keys. An entry in a WeakHashMap will automatically be removed when its key is no longer in ordinary use. More precisely, the presence of a mapping for a given key will not prevent the key from being discarded by the garbage collector, that is, made finalizable, finalized, and then reclaimed. When a key has been discarded its entry is effectively removed from the map, so this class behaves somewhat differently than other Map implementations.

So our cache simply consists of a set of WeakHashMaps, one per registered Smart Object subclass, to contain the individual instances of the class. When we want an object from the cache, we look up the WeakHashMap for the class in question and store it in cachePage. If there is no cache page for the class in question, then by definition we cannot have the instance in cache—if we did, then the cache page would exist. As a result, we can simply return false if the cache page doesn't exist. If it does exist, we next look up the individual instance of the class. We can just return the result, since WeakHashMap.get() will simply return null if the item doesn't exist. That's what we'd return anyway if we knew about it.

Of course, when the factory is first started, there are no cache pages at all in the Hashtable *cache*; we create the cache pages as we load objects. This technique (creating instance of objects only as they're needed) is called lazy instantiation. We'll see that in a moment when we look at the cacheObject() method.

The newObject() and load() methods are probably the most interesting methods in our factory class, since we're using reflection and introspection to figure out what constructor to call and what the properties on the object are, respectively. Next we take a look at the newObject() method, shown in Listing 17.12.

```
private static SmartObject newObject(Class aClass)
        throws SmartObjectException
    {
        try
        {
            SmartObject so;
            Class[] argTypes = new Class[0];
            Object[] args = new Object[0];
            Constructor c = aClass.getConstructor(argTypes);
            so = (SmartObject) c.newInstance(args);
            return so;
        }
        catch (Exception e) // Can be ClassCastException, NoSuchMethodException, or
```

Listing 17.12 The ObjectFactory newObject() method. (continues)

```
InstantiationException.
    {
        throw new SmartObjectException("Requested class " +
aClass + " is malformed or does not inherit from
com.neo.smartobjects.SmartObject. ", e);
    }
  }
```

Listing 17.12 The ObjectFactory newObject() method. (continued)

If you're not familiar with reflection, the newObject() method may be a little confusing at first. (If you *are* familiar with reflection, it will be pretty obvious what's going on here, but it's a feature not used terribly often, so there's a good chance you're not.)

Since we don't know until runtime what class is going to be passed in, we need to use the objects in the java.lang.reflect package to handle the dynamic invocation of the constructor on the class in question. Because we do know the class passed in is a subclass of SmartObject, and we have control over the subclasses we create, we can enforce a rule that all children of SmartObject will have a no-argument constructor. This will be one of the rules we set for ourselves in creating our database-aware objects.

Once we know that there will be a no-arg constructor, we can go about invoking it. We call getConstructor on the class passed in, passing in an array of the argument types for that constructor—an array of Class objects. Since this is the no-arg consructor, we pass in a zero-length array of Class objects and are handed back the no-arg constructor, if it exists. Since we made an agreement with ourselves that our SmartObjects would all have no-arg constructors, we should be okay. (If we forget, a NoSuchMethod exception will be thrown, which we'll catch and wrap in a SmartObjectException.) Next, we call newInstance() on the constructor returned. Again, we pass in an array, this time an Object array containing the arguments. And again, it's a zero-length array. (We could in fact have passed in argTypes, since an array of Class is also an array of Object, but for readability, we'll keep these separate.) The newInstance() method then returns to us a new instance of the class, which we return to the caller.

Back in the getObject() method, the next thing we do is set the ID of the object we just created to the ID passed to the request. This hollow object (which now has what we hope is a valid ID) now gets passed to the load() method. We've simplified this example a bit by requiring all of the attributes of our SmartObjects to be Strings. That way, we don't have to look up the correct return type for each property before figuring out which method on ResultSet to call. The resulting code is shown in Listing 17.3.

```
public static void load(SmartObject so)
        throws SmartObjectException
{
try
{
```

Listing 17.13 The ObjectFactory load() method. (continues)

```
String query = "SELECT * FROM " + so.getTableName() + " WHERE ID = "
+ so.getID();
Connection con = ds.getConnection();
Statement s = con.createStatement();
ResultSet rs = s.executeQuery(query);
if (! rs.next()) throw new SmartObjectException("No " + so.getClass()
+ " instance matching ID " + so.getID() + ".");
PropertyDescriptor[] props = Introspector.getBeanInfo(so.getClass()).getPropertyDescriptors();
for (int i = 0; i < props.length; i++)
{
String prop = getPropertyName(props[i]);
String methodName = getReadMethodName(props[i]);
if (! methodName.startsWith("java.") && !
methodName.startsWith("com.neo.smartobjects.SmartObject"))
{
Object[] args = new Object[1];
args[0] = rs.getString(prop);
props[i].getWriteMethod().invoke(so, args);

}
}
closeAll(rs, s, con);
}
catch (Exception e)
{
throw new SmartObjectException("Exception loading " + so.getClass() + " ID " + so.getID() + ".",
e);
}

}
```

Listing 17.13 The ObjectFactory load() method. (continued)

In Listing 17.13, we use introspection to determine the JavaBean properties that our SmartObject subclasses expose. Introspection relies on reflection, along with some rules, to determine at runtime what properties a JavaBean has. Properties are simply values with a setter and/or getter that conform to the JavaBeans standard. We further constrain our SmartObject subclasses by agreeing that only properties that use Java Beans-style accessor conventions will be persisted out to the database by our framework.

Let's go through this method in depth. This is, after all, the most complex method in the whole class. Take your time to work through it if you find it confusing.

The first thing we do is create a query string to load in the persisted data for this object. It takes the form:

```
SELECT * FROM <table-name> WHERE ID = <id>
```

The *table-name* we get from the SmartObject itself. The *ID* is the ID passed in.

We then get a connection from the datasource and use it to execute the query; we store the results in the result set *rs*. We next make sure that we got back a row from the database—that is, that the requested ID does in fact exist in the database. We do this by calling rs.next(). This also has the side effect of advancing us to the first row of the result set. If there is no first row—in other words, rs.next() returns false—then we know that the ID was invalid and we throw an exception. Otherwise, we continue.

Now that we have a result set, and it's on the first row (there should be only one row, since the ID is in effect the primary key and will be declared as such), we're ready to read in the properties from the database. Of course, we need to know which properties to look for; that's where introspection comes in.

We use the Introspector to get us back an array of property descriptors. We then iterate over the property descriptors, storing the property name and one of the method names in two temporary Strings. We then use the method name (which includes the full classname of the class on which it's defined) to determine which properties we're interested in. We don't want any of the properties inherited from Object (or any other built-in class), nor do we want the properties defined on the SmartObject base class, so we check to see if the method names start with either *java.* or *com.neo.smartobjects.SmartObject.*

If the property doesn't start with either String, then we know that the current property is one that we want. We then construct an array of Objects to pass in as a set of arguments to the write method on the property. We then call getString() on the result set and pass in the name of the property. The database will have a column for each of these properties, with the same name. We then invoke the write method on our SmartObject instance and pass in the value we got from the database.

We keep iterating over the properties until we've gone through them all. At the end, our object has all its values set, and we're ready to return it to the caller. All we need to do is to close all of the database resources we used, and we can return the object. We have a helper method, closeAll(), to handle this; see Listing 17.14.

NOTE **Note that this framework does not handle non-String properties. For most HTML-oriented data, that's not a huge issue, and we don't want to lose you in the details. The framework is complex enough already! If you would like the framework to handle non-String values as well (and we could see why you would want it to), by all means take what you find here and extend it to do that. You'll find that the property descriptors will help you determine the underlying type. You'll just need to add some conditionals to call the right ResultSet methods and decide whether or not to quote the values you're passing in. Many SQL variants don't even mind if you pass in a quoted integer for storage in a field of type INT, so it's really not that much harder. The proof, however, is still left to the reader.**

```
public static final void closeAll(ResultSet rs, Statement s,
Connection con)
    {
```

Listing 17.14 The ObjectFactory closeAll() method. (continues)

```
        if (rs != null)  try { rs.close(); }  catch(SQLException e)  {}
        if (s != null)   try { s.close(); }   catch(SQLException e2) {}
        if (con != null) try { con.close(); } catch(SQLException e3) {}
    }
```

Listing 17.14 The ObjectFactory closeAll() method. (continued)

The closeAll() method is there to make it easy for us to be good about closing connections. Unfortunately, JDBC leaves a lot of the responsibility for connection hygiene to the developer, which often leads to nasty bugs caused by connections being left open. If you've seen a lot of JDBC code, we're sure you've seen code like this more than a few times:

```
try
{
        // execute some SQL code, then...
        rs.close();
        s.close();
        con.close();
}
catch (SqlException e)
{
        // exception code
}
```

It's not really safe to call rs.close(), s.close(), and con.close() in the same try block (any of the calls could fail, leaving the rest of the block unexecuted), but it's a big hassle to type out code to handle this correctly every time. Therefore, much of the time we developers don't bother with it. Usually, we promise ourselves we'll go back and fix it when we get a moment. We don't know about you, but we can't remember the last time we "got a moment" to go fix things like this.

Instead, we like to write a helper method just once, and then call it whenever we have SQL objects that need closing. The way we've written it, you can just pass in null if you don't have a result set to close. It's easy, and it saves *lots* of typing. Declaring it final lets the compiler inline it, so the object code looks a lot like it would if you'd typed the whole thing out each time.

So now that we've returned the new, fully populated instance to the getObject() method, that method needs to make sure it gets added to the cache before returning it to its caller. We do that in the cacheObject() method, shown in Listing 17.15.

```
private static void cacheObject(Class aClass, SmartObject anObject)
    {
        WeakHashMap cachePage = (WeakHashMap) cache.get(aClass);
        if (cachePage == null)
```

Listing 17.15 The ObjectFactory cacheObject() method. (continues)

```
        {
            cachePage = new WeakHashMap();
            cache.put(aClass, cachePage);
        }
        cachePage.put(new Integer(anObject.getID()), anObject);
    }
```

Listing 17.15 The ObjectFactory cacheObject() method. (continued)

The method shown in Listing 17.15 simply stores our object in the appropriate cache page (it creates that cache page if it doesn't exist already). We start by looking up the appropriate cache page in the main cache Hashtable. If it doesn't exist, we create it and store it back into the main cache Hashtable. We then simply put our object in the cache, storing it at a key value based on its ID.

With that, we have completed the mechanism for getting existing instances of an arbitrary subclass of SmartObject out of a database. It wasn't completely trivial to implement, certainly, but it really wasn't all that much code to write. As a result, we have a good chunk of our persistence framework done.

This would be a good time to get up, stretch, and get a cup of coffee before we dive into the other half of the process, storing our arbitrary data objects into the database. We still have a lot of ground to cover, but the good news is, all the conceptually difficult stuff is out of the way, and the remaining code will reinforce the concepts we've covered already.

Storing the Data

So we've created a factory class that knows how to pull data in from a database and store it in an instance of an arbitrary subclass of SmartObject. That's pretty useful, but it's not *that* useful unless we can store new data in the database as well. Our SmartObjects are supposed to deal with this appropriately when new values are set for any of their properties. This is a lot simpler than loading a new arbitrary instance, since we don't have to worry about creating an object or getting it out of the cache, loading a class, or determining whether it's even a valid object request. All we have to do is iterate over its values and store them in the database—and we already know how to iterate over the values. Listing 17.16 shows our store() method.

```
public static void store(SmartObject so)
    throws SmartObjectException
  {
    try
```

Listing 17.16 The ObjectFactory store() method. (continues)

```
    {
        boolean addedProperty = false;
        StringBuffer sb = new StringBuffer("UPDATE ");
        sb.append(so.getTableName());
        sb.append(" SET ");
        PropertyDescriptor[] props =
Introspector.getBeanInfo(so.getClass()).getPropertyDescriptors();
        for (int i = 0; i < props.length; i++)
        {
            String prop = getPropertyName(props[i]);
            String methodName = getReadMethodName(props[i]);
            if (! methodName.startsWith("java.") && !
methodName.startsWith("com.neo.smartobjects.SmartObject"))
            {
                sb.append(prop + "=\'" + sqlEscape(props[i].getReadMethod().invoke(so, null)) + "\',
");
                addedProperty = true;
            }
        }
        sb.deleteCharAt(sb.length() - 2);
        sb.append("WHERE id = " + so.getID());
        if (addedProperty)
        {
            executeUpdate(sb.toString());
            so.setClean(true);
        }
    }
    catch (Exception e)
    {
        throw new SmartObjectException("Exception storing object:
" + so, e);
    }
  }
```

Listing 17.16 The ObjectFactory store() method. (continued)

The store() method, like the load() method, has a big loop in the middle where we iterate over the properties on the object. The store() method also has a lot of nasty string handling in it to generate the SQL query because the query we're generating is a lot more complex. (This is why we wanted to factor it out of the data objects we create using this framework, remember?) For efficiency, we use a StringBuffer to handle the assembly of our string. Note that strings are not as big of a resource drain as they once were since the advent of HotSpot with its generational garbage collector. Short-lived objects, such as strings that we declare and then discard, are allocated on the stack in HotSpot-based VMs.

We start by setting a boolean flag, addedProperty, to specify whether we have actually added any properties to our query. (We'll need this in a moment, as you'll see.) We then set up a StringBuffer containing the string

```
UPDATE <table-name> SET
```

To this we append name/value pairs for each of the properties on the SmartObject we were handed. We use the identical logic we used in the load() method to figure out which properties we want. (It's important that these properties be identical so we don't end up with any mismatches between what we load and what we store.) If, for instance, we had a property Foo with a value Bar, we would then add

```
Foo='Bar',
```

to the end of our string. That's a comma-space at the end, and we quote the value because it is a string, although usually SQL will let you quote numerical values as well. Note that we SQL-escape the string we pass in, so it won't break our request and the value will be recorded correctly. We then set our boolean flag addedProperty to true.

When we've finished iterating over the properties, we need to remove the last comma we added to the string. That comma should be the next-to-last character in the StringBuffer, so we delete it.

If there were no properties on our object (which is possible if, for example, the child object were just an empty subclass), then deleting the next-to-last character from our StringBuffer would delete the *T* in *SET*, which is not what we want. If there were no properties to added, however, then our query would be invalid anyway. So we use the boolean flag addedProperty to prevent us from sending the update on classes that don't have any properties of their own.

Another approach, equally valid, would be to agree that SmartObjects with no properties are invalid and then simply to throw an exception if the query failed. We followed the first approach primarily to make explicit in the code what was supposed to happen. If you follow this second approach, we strongly advise that you include a note in a JavaDoc comment that explains the described behavior and clearly states that this is the *desired* behavior.

So assuming that the object passed in did in fact have some properties on it (which it would in all cases but the degenerate case we mentioned earlier), we then execute the query and set the clean flag on the object to true. If something bad happens along the way, we throw a SmartObjectException.

You'll notice that our design automatically persists every property when store() is called. You might want to extend the framework to update only the specific properties that were changed. We've made the operation fairly cheap, though, by making store() execute just a single update to persist the entire object, and in the process simplified our design significantly.

Our store() method used two new helper methods: sqlEscape() and executeUpdate(). Let's look at these now, beginning with sqlEscape(), shown in Listing 17.17.

```
public static String sqlEscape(String aString)
   {
```

Listing 17.17 The ObjectFactory sqlEscape() method. (continues)

```
        if (aString == null) return "";
        if (aString.indexOf("'") == -1) return aString;
        StringBuffer aBuffer = new StringBuffer(aString);
        int insertOffset = 0;
        for (int i = 0; i < aString.length(); i++)
            {
            if (aString.charAt(i) == '\'')
                aBuffer.insert(i + insertOffset ++, "'");
            }
        return aBuffer.toString();
    }
```

Listing 17.17 The ObjectFactory sqlEscape() method. (continued)

In SQL, the apostrophe is a reserved character used to quote strings. As a result, any apostrophe characters in a string you want to store in the database need to be escaped. Usually, this is done by inserting a second apostrophe next to the first. In the interest of robustness and convenience, in our application we return an empty string if we are passed in a null. (This may not always be the right thing to do. It might be better to return null or to throw an exception. In our application, we treat null as equivalent to an empty string, so this is a reasonable return value.) Next, we check to see if there are in fact any apostrophes in the string passed in. There's no sense in creating an extra StringBuffer, iterating over the string, and then creating a new String if the result is going to be identical.

If we've gotten this far, then we know we have apostrophes to deal with, so we copy the string into a StringBuffer, iterate over the string, and when we find an apostrophe, insert a second one. We then return the result as a String, and we're done. It's as simple as that. If we want it to be even more efficient (although slightly less readable), we can even start at the end of the string and work our way to the beginning. That way, we wouldn't have to keep incrementing the insertOffset. But remember, readability is good! You can optimize this if it's actually becoming a performance issue for you, but it's not likely the extra clock cycle will be noticed.

Listing 17.18 contains our executeUpdate() method. (This code will be familiar from the previous chapter.) Here, we factored out a section of code to make the calling code more readable. We get a valid Connection object from the datasource we configured in the initialize() method, create a statement on it, and then use the statement to execute the query we created in the store() method. Then we call closeAll() to close the connection for us.

```
public static final void executeUpdate(String query)
        throws SmartObjectException
    {
```

Listing 17.18 The executeUpdate() method of ObjectFactory.java. (continues)

```
        try
        {
            Connection con = ds.getConnection();
            Statement s = con.createStatement();
            s.executeUpdate(query);
            closeAll(null, s, con);
        }
        catch (SQLException sqle)
        {
            throw new SmartObjectException("Store failed.", sqle);
        }
    }
```

Listing 17.18 The executeUpdate() method of ObjectFactory.java. (continued)

Automated Commits

Our framework is starting to be useful. We can load and store data, and the groundwork is there to handle automated commits to the database. Now we're at the point where it starts making sense to look at an object based on this framework and how it delegates management of its state to the ObjectFactory.

We start with an object with only one property in order to keep things as simple as possible. We call our class the NamedObject class, and the one property will be the name property. We name it into com.wiley.tomcatbook, as shown in Listing 17.19.

```
package com.wiley.tomcatbook;

import com.neo.smartobjects.*;

public class NamedObject extends SmartObject
{
    private String name;

    public NamedObject()
    {
        setTableName("so_named_object");
    }

    public synchronized void setName(String aName)
        throws SmartObjectException
```

Listing 17.19 NamedObject.java. (continues)

```
    {
        name = aName;
        propertyChanged();
    }

    public String getName()
    {
        return name;
    }

}
```

Listing 17.19 NamedObject.java. (continued)

This class couldn't be much simpler, so in that respect, our strategy would seem to be quite a success. The class contains just three methods: a setter and a getter for the one property, and a one-line constructor that sets the name of the table. The only special conventions we have to keep in mind when writing the class are:

- All properties must be Strings.
- All setters must call propertyChanged() after they set their value.
- As a result of the previous rule, all setters must also throw SmartObjectException.

Instances of this simple class will be able to persist temselves to the database once the framework is finished, and the factory will know how to create and manage them. Not bad for a framework that's less than 500 lines of code.

Incidentally, we decided to use a naming convention for the tables so that we could have them in the same table space as the other database examples without any collisions. We simply prepend *so_* to the name and convert intercaps to underscores. In a more complete framework, we could even have the factory handle this for us and convert the fully qualified classname to our table name.

So how does this little object, as simple as it is, manage to ensure that its data is stored out to the database? Through the propertyChanged() method, of course! You may remember that we defined a propertyChanged() method in the base class, Smart Object. Listing 17.20 contains that method.

```
protected void propertyChanged()
        throws SmartObjectException
    {
        ObjectFactory.notifyPropertyChanged(this);
    }
```

Listing 17.20 The SmartObject propertyChanged() method.

The propertyChanged() method simply passes a message to the ObjectFactory, notifying it which object has been updated, and as a result which object needs to be updated. It calls the notifyPropertyChanged() method (see Listing 17.21). This method is protected, so our NamedObject class would not have been able to call it directly. We want to protect the inner workings of the framework from developers inadvertently affecting the state of the objects, and we use this mechanism to accomplish that.

```
protected static void notifyPropertyChanged(SmartObject so)
    throws SmartObjectException
  {
    if (so.isAutoCommit())
    {
      store(so);
    }
    else
    {
      so.setClean(false);
    }
  }
```

Listing 17.21 The ObjectFactory notifyPropertyChanged() method.

The notifyPropertyChanged() method is effectively an event handler. It is called whenever a property on any SmartObject changes. What happens next depends on whether or not the object is configured to autocommit. If autocommit is enabled for the object passed in, then the store() method is called and passes in that object. If autocommit is not enabled, it the object is simply marked as having new information, and not yet synced to the database. We set autocommit to be on by default; this means that if you were to enter all the code you've seen so far and manually set up a table in the database called so_named_object with an ID column and a name column, and put some appropriate records in it, the framework would now work.

All that's left to make the storage side of our framework commit is to implement a commit() method so that we can persist objects that have autocommit set to false. Listing 17.22 contains our ObjectFactory commit() method.

```
protected static void commit(SmartObject so)
  throws SmartObjectException
{
  if (! so.isClean())
  {
    store(so);
  }
}
```

Listing 17.22 The ObjectFactory commit() method.

The commit() method is very simple. All we do is check first to see if the object needs committing. There's no sense in generating the overhead if the object is already in sync, and it's nice to make the operation cheap enough that we can sprinkle commits through the code every place we need to be sure the database state is consistent with the object state. On the other hand, if the object does need to be committed, then we store it with our store() method. Remember that store() handles setting the clean flag for us, so we don't (and shouldn't) do that ourselves.

The other thing we need is a rollback() method, so that if there are changes we don't want to commit, we can get the object back to its last saved state. We could just call load() again (which is what we do in the rollback() method), but it's nice to save the overhead for the same reasons mentioned earlier. Listing 17.23 contains our rollback() method.

```
protected static void rollback(SmartObject so)
   throws SmartObjectException
{
   if (! so.isClean())
   {
      load(so);
   }
}
```

Listing 17.23 The ObjectFactory rollback() method.

The public API to these methods will be to call rollback() and commit() directly on the object in question, so we need to add those methods to SmartObject, as shown in Listing 17.24.

```
public void rollback()
   throws SmartObjectException
{
   ObjectFactory.rollback(this);
}

public void commit()
   throws SmartObjectException
{
   ObjectFactory.commit(this);
}
```

Listing 17.24 The SmartObject rollback() and commit() methods.

Now we have a pretty sophisticated rollback and commit interface to our objects, considering the few lines of code it took to implement. You can even turn autocommit off on a single object if you know you're going to make a lot of changes you might not want to persist, and then turn it back on after you're done.

You might like to enhance your framework by making the objects more aware of their initial state (so that you can clear the dirty flag if the properties, after being modified, get set back to their initial state; or to protect other holders of the instance from the interim state). For our purposes, though, this is plenty. Note also that our code assumes the database itself is configured to autocommit.

Creating New Objects

Okay, we now have a framework that will load and store objects and that even has reasonably sophisticated commit semantics. That's great, but we still don't have a way to create new objects, which obviously we need. We need a public method that lets us create a new instance of any SmartObject subclass and hands it back to us connected up to the database with a valid ID. Our public newObject() method appears in Listing 17.25.

```
public static SmartObject newObject(String classname)
      throws SmartObjectException
   {
      try
      {
         SmartObject so = newObject(Class.forName(classname));
         prepare(so);
         load(so);
         return so;
      }
      catch (ClassNotFoundException cnfe)
      {
         throw new SmartObjectException(cnfe);
      }
   }
```

Listing 17.25 The public newObject() method of ObjectFactory.java.

This variant of newObject() loads the class specified, creates an instance of the class, and then passes that instance off to the prepare() method, which creates a new row in the database for it and sets its ID. The method then loads the object, so that all of its fields are initialized with the default values (we initialize each property to the empty string in the prepare() method), and returns the fully initialized object to the caller. Listing 17.26 shows our prepare() method (the Java 1.4 variant).

```
public static SmartObject prepare(SmartObject so)
      throws SmartObjectException
```

Listing 17.26 The ObjectFactory prepare() method (Java 1.4 variant). (continues)

```
{
    try
    {
        StringBuffer sb = new StringBuffer("INSERT INTO ");
        sb.append(so.getTableName());
        sb.append(" VALUES (NULL, ");
        PropertyDescriptor[] props =
Introspector.getBeanInfo(so.getClass()).getPropertyDescriptors();
        synchronized(so)
        {
            for (int i = 0; i < props.length; i++)
            {
                String prop = getPropertyName(props[i]);
                String methodName = getReadMethodName(props[i]);
                if (! methodName.startsWith("java.") && !
methodName.startsWith("com.neo.smartobjects.SmartObject"))
                {
                // pad with the right number of empty values.
                    sb.append("\'\', ");
                }
            }
            sb.deleteCharAt(sb.length() - 2);
            sb.append(")");
            try
            {
                String[] keyFields = {"id"};
                Connection con = ds.getConnection();
                Statement s = con.createStatement();
                s.execute(sb.toString(), keyFields);
                ResultSet rs = s.getResultSet();
                rs.next();
                so.setID(rs.getInt("id"));
                so.setClean(true);
                closeAll(rs, s, con);
                return so;
            }
            catch (SQLException sqle)
            {
                throw new SmartObjectException("Object creation
failed when trying to insert into database.", sqle);
            }
        }
    }
    catch (Exception e)
```

Listing 17.26 The ObjectFactory prepare() method (Java 1.4 variant). (continues)

```
    {
        throw new SmartObjectException("Exception creating
object: " + so, e);
    }
  }
```

Listing 17.26 The ObjectFactory prepare() method (Java 1.4 variant). (continued)

The prepare() method shares a lot conceptually with the load() and store() methods, not surprisingly, since we need to create and execute a query. The query string we're trying to create looks like this:

```
INSERT INTO <table-name> VALUES (null, '' [,'' ...])
```

The null is for the ID field; we'll let the database automatically increment that. Then, we need an empty string for each of the properties, so we iterate over them, and append '', once per property.

Once we have built our query string, we want to execute it; however, in this case we have one last trick to perform. We need to get back from the database the ID value it created for the new row.

There is a new way to do this, introduced in version 1.4 of the J2SDK, which is what you see in Listing 17.26. Not everyone has moved to 1.4 yet, and not all drivers will support it, so in a moment we'll show you a variant that works with JDK 1.3.

The new feature we're using makes it much easier to work with automatically generated keys. Statement.execute() now has a variant that accepts an array of column IDs (either integers or Strings), and creates a result set behind the scenes populated with these values. The relevant lines of code are set in bold in Listing 17.27. If you need to do the same on a 1.3 platform, this code (which replaces the contents of the try block in Listing 17.26) is slightly less efficient, but accomplishes the same thing.

```
// String[] keyFields = {"id"};
System.out.println("Create -> " + sb);
Connection con = ds.getConnection();
Statement s = con.createStatement();
s.execute(sb.toString());//, keyFields);
s.executeQuery(SELECT MAX(id) AS id FROM "
   + so.getTableName());
ResultSet rs = s.getResultSet();
rs.next();
so.setID(rs.getInt("id"));
so.setClean(true);
closeAll(rs, s, con);
return so;
```

Listing 17.27 The revised code section of prepare() method (Java 1.3 variant).

Our framework is almost done. All we really need now is a delete() method. Fortunately, after the complexities of the last method, it is quite simple, as shown in Listing 17.28.

```
public static void delete(SmartObject so)
        throws SmartObjectException
    {
        try
        {
            StringBuffer sb = new StringBuffer("DELETE FROM ");
            sb.append(so.getTableName());
            sb.append("WHERE id = " + so.getID());
            executeUpdate(sb.toString());
        }
        catch (Exception e)
        {
            throw new SmartObjectException("Exception deleting object:
" + so, e);
        }
    }
```

Listing 17.28 The ObjectFactory delete() method.

Now for the first time the framework can be said to be fully functional, so let's stop working on it for a little while and start using it.

Using the Framework

We begin by writing a new SmartObject, a Client, that contains the same data we used in our previous example. See Listing 17.29.

```
package com.wiley.tomcatbook;

import com.neo.smartobjects.*;

public class Client extends SmartObject
{
    private String firstName;
    private String lastName;
    private String phone;
```

Listing 17.29 Client.java. (continues)

```
    public Client()
    {
        setTableName("so_client");
    }

    public synchronized void setFirstName(String aName)
        throws SmartObjectException
    {
        firstName = aName;
        propertyChanged();
    }

    public String getFirstName()
    {
        return firstName;
    }

    public synchronized void setLastName(String aName)
        throws SmartObjectException
    {
        lastName = aName;
        propertyChanged();
    }

    public String getLastName()
    {
        return lastName;
    }

    public synchronized void setPhone(String aNumber)
        throws SmartObjectException
    {
        phone = aNumber;
        propertyChanged();
    }

    public String getPhone()
    {
        return phone;
    }

}
```

Listing 17.29 Client.java. (continued)

There really shouldn't be any surprises here, so we won't waste your time explaining what Client does. If you want more explanation, take a look at the discussion of Named Object after Listing 17.19.

Let's start by setting up the so_client table in the database. Here again, we assume you're using MySQL, although other database engines should allow similar, if not identical, syntax for table declarations. How you declare ID to be an auto-incrementing ID field in particular is likely to be different on another RDBMS.

The table we want to create looks like the one shown in Table 17.2.

Table 17.2 Attributes of the Client SmartObject

NAME	TYPE	ATTRIBUTES
id	int	auto_increment, primary key
firstName	varchar(255)	
lastName	varchar(255)	
phone	varchar(255)	

To create the table, we use the following commands with the MySQL command-line client:

```
CREATE TABLE so_client (
id INT AUTO_INCREMENT,
firstName VARCHAR(255),
lastName VARCHAR(255),
phone VARCHAR(255),
PRIMARY KEY(id)
);
```

We also need to install the JAR or JARs containing the framework classes and com.wiley.tomcatbook.Client into the /lib directory of the tomcatbook Webapp. In addition, we want to write a simple servlet that handles initializing the ObjectFactory for us. This servlet appears in Listing 17.30.

```
package com.neo.smartobjects;

import java.io.*;
import javax.servlet.*;
import javax.servlet.http.*;

public class ObjectFactoryInitializer extends HttpServlet
{
   private String status;
```

Listing 17.30 The ObjectFactoryInitializer servlet. (continues)

```
    public void init(ServletConfig conf)
        throws ServletException
    {
        super.init(conf);
        String context = conf.getInitParameter("context");
        String source = conf.getInitParameter("datasource");
        try
        {
            ObjectFactory.initialize(context, source);
            status = "Object Factory initialized.";
        }
        catch (SmartObjectException soe)
        {
            status = "Object Factory initialization failed. " + soe;
        }
    }

    public void doGet(HttpServletRequest request, HttpServletResponse
response)
        throws IOException, ServletException
    {
        response.setContentType("text/plain");
        ServletOutputStream out = response.getOutputStream();
        out.print(status);
    }

}
```

Listing 17.30 The ObjectFactoryInitializer servlet. (continued)

The important method in Listing 17.30 is the init() method, in which we initialize the ObjectFactory. We simply read in the relevant JNDI reference information from the deployment descriptor (which we modify in a moment) and pass it to the initialize() method on ObjectFactory. We also store a status message in the String variable *status*, which we use in our doGet() method to report whether the object factory was satisfactorily initialized. This is a handy thing to do for debugging purposes.

As we mentioned, we must modify the deployment descriptor for our project to include this new servlet, as shown in Listing 17.31.

```
<?xml version="1.0" encoding="ISO-8859-1"?>
<!DOCTYPE web-app
    PUBLIC "-//Sun Microsystems, Inc.//DTD Web Application 2.2//EN"
    "http://java.sun.com/j2ee/dtds/web-app_2.2.dtd">
```

Listing 17.31 The revised web.xml file. (continues)

```
<web-app>
  <servlet>
    <servlet-name>initializer</servlet-name>
    <servlet-class>
      com.neo.smartobjects.ObjectFactoryInitializer
    </servlet-class>
    <init-param>
      <param-name>context</param-name>
      <param-value>java:comp/env</param-value>
    </init-param>
    <init-param>
      <param-name>datasource</param-name>
      <param-value>jdbc/tomcatbook</param-value>
     </init-param>
    <load-on-startup>1</load-on-startup>
   </servlet>
   <servlet>
    <servlet-name>ClientListPooled</servlet-name>
    <servlet-class>
      com.wiley.tomcatbook.ClientListPooledServlet
    </servlet-class>
  </servlet>
  <servlet>
    <servlet-name>ClientList</servlet-name>
    <servlet-class>com.wiley.tomcatbook.
ClientListServlet</servlet-class>
    <init-param>
      <param-name>database-driver-class</param-name>
      <param-value>org.gjt.mm.mysql.Driver</param-value>
    </init-param>
    <init-param>
      <param-name>database-url</param-name>
      <param-value>jdbc:mysql://localhost/tomcatbook</
param-value>
    </init-param>
    <init-param>
      <param-name>database-login</param-name>
      <param-value>tomcatbook</param-value>
    </init-param>
    <init-param>
      <param-name>database-password</param-name>
      <param-value>badpassword</param-value>
```

Listing 17.31 The revised web.xml file. (continues)

```
    </init-param>
  </servlet>
  <servlet-mapping>
    <servlet-name>ClientList</servlet-name>
    <url-pattern>/client-list</url-pattern>
  </servlet-mapping>
  <servlet-mapping>
    <servlet-name>ClientListPooled</servlet-name>
    <url-pattern>/client-list-pooled</url-pattern>
  </servlet-mapping>
  <servlet-mapping>
    <servlet-name>initializer</servlet-name>
    <url-pattern>/init-status</url-pattern>
  </servlet-mapping>
  <resource-ref>
    <description>
      This is a reference to the data source we use
      to talk to the database configured in the
      server.xml file.
    </description>
    <res-ref-name>jdbc/tomcatbook</res-ref-name>
    <res-type>javax.sql.DataSource</res-type>
    <res-auth>Container</res-auth>
  </resource-ref>
</web-app>
```

Listing 17.31 The revised web.xml file. (continued)

We configure the servlet with the initialization parameters of the JNDI context and resource names for the datasource we configured in our previous chapter, and we instruct the servlet container to load this servlet with priority 1. Note that we have to set the <load-on-startup/> parameter on our servlet to ensure that the servlet gets initialized before our JSP (which we defined next) gets loaded. Otherwise, the ObjectFactory may not get initialized. We then set up a mapping to our servlet, so we can check to make sure the ObjectFactory was initialized if we run into any trouble later. Next, we'll write our simple edit form, which we'll lay out in a JSP, as shown in Listing 17.32.

```
<%@page import="com.wiley.tomcatbook.*"%>
<%@page import="com.neo.smartobjects.*"%>
<%

Client myClient;
```

Listing 17.32 edit.jsp. (continues)

```
try
{
        int id = Integer.parseInt(request.getParameter("id"));

myClient = (Client) ObjectFactory.getObject("com.wiley.tomcatbook.
Client", id);
}
catch (Exception e)
{
        myClient = (Client) ObjectFactory.newObject("com.wiley.tomcatbook.Client");
}

String firstName = request.getParameter("firstName");
if (firstName != null) myClient.setFirstName(firstName);
String lastName = request.getParameter("lastName");
if (lastName != null) myClient.setLastName(lastName);
String phone = request.getParameter("phone");
if (phone != null) myClient.setPhone(phone);

%>
<html>
<head>
        <title>Edit: <%= myClient.getFirstName() %> <%= myClient.getLastName() %></title>
</head>
<body>
<p>
Editing record for <%= myClient.getFirstName() %> <%= myClient.getLastName() %>

<form method="GET">
<input type="hidden" name="id" value="<%= myClient.getID() %>">
<table>
<tr>
<td>First Name:</td>
<td><input name="firstName" value ="<%= myClient.getFirstName() %>">
</td>
</tr>
<tr>
<td>Last Name:</td>
<td><input name="lastName" value ="<%= myClient.getLastName() %>">
</td>
</tr>
<tr>
<td>Phone:</td>
```

Listing 17.32 edit.jsp. (continues)

```
<td><input name="phone" value ="<%= myClient.getPhone() %>"></td>
</tr>
<tr>
<td colspan="2">
<center><input type="submit" value ="Update Client <%=
myClient.getID() %>"></center>
</td>
</tr>
</table>
</form>
</body>
</html>
```

Listing 17.32 edit.jsp. (continued)

This page is a simple editing interface for one of our Client objects. It displays each attribute in a separate text box, where we can edit it to contain whatever String we like. When we click the Submit button, we are redirected to the same page, which duly assigns the new Strings to the appropriate variable.

This JSP takes up to four parameters, with *id* being the most important. The *id* parameter specifies which client we want to edit. If it's not a valid ID, or if it is omitted, the JSP creates a new Client object. (In a real application, you'd probably want to have it create an error page instead, but here we're concentrating on the framework we just wrote.) The other three parameters—firstName, lastName, and phone—correspond to the three properties on the Client class.

We start out with a couple of imports: we need to bring in the smartobjects framework and our Client class. We then request the appropriate object from the ObjectFactory, based on the ID. If an exception occurs, we request a new object.

We then work our way through the other three parameters, checking to see if any of them were supplied. Since autocommit is on by default, we simply pass in the values and they're updated in the database. Note that in a JSP, the *request* variable is always automatically initialized to the request passed in to the service() method on the servlet that will be created from the page.

Once we've initialized our Client object, we can use it in the page itself. We set the title to be

```
Edit: <client.firstName> <client-lastName>
```

and we lay out a form. Note that we have to include client.ID as a hidden parameter so that the next page will know for which instance of Client the changes are intended. We then prepopulate a set of form fields with the appropriate property values from our Client object. And just to make it more obvious which client we're editing, we include the ID in the text of our Submit button.

Since we don't specify an action for the form, it defaults to redirecting to itself. This means that when we click Submit, the values we specified in the form are passed in, and the next time we process the parameters, they have the new values in them. In this way, our Client object is updated appropriately.

One other thing we could do to increase the efficiency of our JSP would be to use the support we added for explicit commits. The way it is now, there are actually three separate writes to the database every time we update a record; one every time we set a parameter. If we modify our JSP to have the block of code shown in Listing 17.33 (with the new lines in bold), we reduce the database traffic to a single transaction.

```
myClient.setAutoCommit(false);
String firstName = request.getParameter("firstName");
if (firstName != null) myClient.setFirstName(firstName);
String lastName = request.getParameter("lastName");
if (lastName != null) myClient.setLastName(lastName);
String phone = request.getParameter("phone");
if (phone != null) myClient.setPhone(phone);
myClient.commit();
myClient.setAutoCommit(true);
```

Listing 17.33 Using explicit commits to improve efficiency.

So there you have it: efficient, object-oriented data persistence, courtesy of a framework we wrote in a few hundred lines of code.

Next, let's create a JSP to list all of the clients we've entered.

Adding the getObjects() Method

When it comes time to re-create the functionality of the servlets we built in the previous chapter, we find that we don't yet have an easy method of getting all of the instances of our Client object. So far, we have to know the ID in order to load the instance. So now we have to extend our framework to give us a mechanism for loading a whole set of instances.

There are two different strategies we could take here: we could either write a new method that does a single select, and then creates all the objects and stores them off in the cache, or we could let the framework do more of the work. In this second approach, we simply get all of the valid object IDs from the database and then let the methods we created already do the work for us. Listing 17.34 shows our getObjects() method.

```
public static SmartObject[] getObjects(String classname)
    throws SmartObjectException
  {
    try
    {
      Vector smartObjects = new Vector();
```

Listing 17.34 The ObjectFactory getObjects() method. (continues)

```
        Class theClass = Class.forName(classname);
        SmartObject so = newObject(theClass);
        String query = "SELECT id FROM " + so.getTableName();
        Connection con = ds.getConnection();
        Statement s = con.createStatement();
        s.executeQuery(query);
        ResultSet rs = s.getResultSet();
        while (rs.next())
        {
          smartObjects.add(getObject(classname,
rs.getInt("id")));
        }
        closeAll(rs, s, con);
        return (SmartObject[]) smartObjects.toArray(new SmartObject[0]);
      }
      catch (ClassNotFoundException cnfe)
      {
        throw new SmartObjectException("The " + classname + "
class could not be loaded.", cnfe);
      }
      catch (SQLException sqle)
      {
        throw new SmartObjectException("Exception geting object
IDs for " + classname + ".", sqle);
      }
    }
```

Listing 17.34 The ObjectFactory getObjects() method. (continued)

The getObjects() method returns an array of SmartObjects, but since we don't know how many we'll have, we start out by declaring a Vector to store the objects as we collect them.

We then load the class passed in and create a new, hollow instance of the class. (This is the protected newInstance() method we're calling, the one we use internally, not the one client code uses to create a new fully initialized object.) We need this in order to get the table name, which we use when creating our SELECT query in the next line. (We simply discard the hollow object we created when we're done.) Our SELECT returns each of the object IDs for the class passed in, and we iterate through the result set.

We use the ID in each row of the result set as the second parameter for a getObject() call, and let getObject() load all the data and manage the cache for us. We store the result in the Vector (*smartObjects*) we created at the beginning of the method. We close our database objects; then convert our Vector to an array of SmartObjects with a toArray() call and return the result. If anything goes wrong along the way, we throw an appropriate exception.

Now that we have a new factory method, we can use it in a second JSP in order to display all the client records. Listing 17.35 contains our client-list.jsp.

```
<%@page import="com.wiley.tomcatbook.*"%>
<%@page import="com.neo.smartobjects.*"%>
<html>
<head>
        <title>Client List</title>
</head>
<body>
<p>
Contacts
<%

try
{
   SmartObject[] clients = ObjectFactory.getObjects("com.wiley.tomcatbook.Client");
%>

<table cellpadding="2">
<tr bgcolor="#D0D0D0">
<td>First Name</td>
<td>Last Name</td>
<td colspan="2">Phone</td>
</tr>

<%
boolean oddRow = true;
for (int i = 0; i < clients.length; i++)
{
   Client aClient = (Client) clients[i];
   String rowColor = "#E0E0E0";
   if (oddRow) rowColor = "#F0F0F0";
   oddRow = ! oddRow;
%>
<tr bgcolor="<%= rowColor %>">
<td><%= aClient.getFirstName() %></td>
<td><%= aClient.getLastName() %></td>
<td><%= aClient.getPhone() %></td>
<td>[<a href="edit.jsp?id=<%= aClient.getID() %>">edit</a>]</td>
</tr>
<%
}
%>
```

Listing 17.35 client-list.jsp. (continues)

```
</table>
[<a href="edit.jsp">Create a new record</a>]
<%
}
catch (SmartObjectException soe)
{
%>
<br>
<b>Unable to load contacts!</b> <%= soe %>
<%
}
%>
</body>
</html>
```

Listing 17.35 client-list.jsp. (continued)

In Listing 17.35, we initialize a variable *clients* to contain the result of the getObjects() call. (Note that we have to store it in an array of type SmartObject[], since we can't cast an array in Java. In a moment, we do a class cast when we iterate over the objects.) We then set up our table and column titles in an HTML segment of the JSP.

In the next code block, we set up a variable, oddRow, which we use to keep track of what row we're on. We use this to alternate background colors for the rows in order to make the page easier to read.

Then, we set up a for loop to iterate over the clients array. We set up a variable, *aClient*, which we can reference in the HTML, and we store in it the Client at the current index. Again, we have to cast the SmartObject in the array to a Client at this point. Next, we set up a String with the row color in the form of an HTML hex string. If we're in an odd-numbered row, we then immediately change the value to a string representing a lighter shade of gray.

We then have another HTML block, in which we lay out what each row will look like. We set the background color of the row, and then create cells for each of the attributes we're displaying. We also add a cell with a link to the edit page. Note how we embed *<%= aClient.getID() %>* at the end of the link href in order to specify the ID of the record to edit. We then close the for loop code block after the *</tr> with <% } %>*.

Note that the whole table is inside the try block, we set up the first code segment. If an exception is thrown, we then execute the catch block instead, printing out a helpful error message: "Unable to load contacts!" followed by the exception itself, converted (implicitly) to a String. (Remember, the <%= %> construct calls toString() on the contained expression.)

One last thing: we add a link to our edit.jsp back to this list:

```
<a href="clientlist.jsp">Back to List</a>
```

With that, we have a small but complete application.

One interesting thing to note here is the advantage of extending the framework rather than just writing custom code to do this for us. That advantage is in reuse, and it's a special kind of reuse. By extending the framework, we ensure that all of the classes that use it get the new functionality for free. That includes any pre-existing instances as well. If you had been using this framework in an application that managed a collection of NamedObjects, for example (or perhaps even more interesting objects), you would now be able to use this new functionality in that application.

The other side of the coin is that you have to be careful when you extend the framework to make sure you don't do things in a way that's incompatible with those existing objects and uses. Designing for reuse means *designing*, above all else. The extra power you get with a good design more than makes up for the additional effort, though. You'll end up saving a lot of time in the end by thinking through things at the start—and keeping thinking through things as you go.

Some Remaining Issues

The framework we've shown you here isn't thread-safe. If you're in the middle of deleting an object in one thread and someone else loads the same object, it is possible for the cache state to get out of sync. Thread safety is an important issue, but beyond the scope of this book. There are a number of excellent texts on concurrent programming in Java, and we encourage you to seek out one of those.

We'd like to add a few other things, such as a utility method (and associated command-line tool) to set up the table for a newly registered class, as well as methods to return all instances of a class matching a certain set of criteria. We're sure you have some ideas of your own as well. However, at this point we think we've given you a good start. Now it's time to take these concepts and apply them to your own projects.

Summary

In this chapter, we've drawn the outline of a framework you might implement to handle object persistence, and we hope we've given you some food for thought as to how you can go about creating some reusable libraries of your own. Keep in mind that this level of abstraction is not always appropriate: if your application heavily leverages the underlying RDBMS, this is probably not the way to go, at least not without a lot of modification. And if you want the framework to give you strong transactional integrity, you should probably consider making the leap to EJB. For a lot of smaller apps, though, a simple object persistence library can be quite helpful (and you can always use it to prototype and then do your optimizations later).

In the next chapter, we look at what is perhaps the most important area of software development, particularly in a networked world: security. This is an important topic, so don't skip it, even if you may be tempted to read about more fun stuff instead. It's definitely an area worth your most careful consideration.

CHAPTER

18

Security

Security is an important and wide-ranging topic. In this chapter, we attempt to give you a good grounding in security concepts, discuss how to configure Tomcat to run more securely, and provide an overview of how to write servlets that use some of the cryptography features of the Java platform.

You may have noticed that we used the phrase "more securely." You will find this phrase over and over again in texts on computer security. There is a reason for this: It is simply impossible to devise a system that is *truly* secure. The best we can do is develop a system that thwarts the widest range of threats and that does not have any known security holes. If you wanted to make a computer truly secure, you'd have to disconnect it from the Internet and then not turn it on!

But all is not lost. Security is about risk management, and for most applications it is quite possible to make systems "secure enough." For systems with no particularly sensitive information, "secure enough" may mean simply requiring a password, even one sent in the clear (which means it could be intercepted by anyone on any network between the user and the server). Of course, if you opt for this level of security, don't be surprised to find one day that your data has been compromised. If you can live with that and don't mind if some "script kiddie" sees your holiday snaps or Weblog, then maybe basic auth is sufficient (see Chapter 8, "Managing Authentication with Realms," for more information on access control mechanisms). If, however, you cringed when you read about passwords being intercepted, then you probably should read on.

Always keep in mind, though, that any system will have holes and may at some point in the future be compromised. Just because you think you developed the most secure application ever, don't think you're done when you deploy your code. A big part of security is *monitoring* your application and employing intrusion detection. You will have to evolve your code as new security bugs are discovered and as new threat models appear.

And of course, your application is only as secure as the environment it runs in. If you just developed a super secure servlet, don't expect it to stay secure if you're running on Windows behind IIS. If your operating system or Web server is compromised, the nefarious individual who compromised the system can probably also replace your secure code with code that does what he or she wants. To keep up-to-date on known security risks for various platforms, you should monitor the CERT Coordination Center at www.cert.org to see reports of new vulnerabilities.

The goal of this chapter is to get you thinking about security and show you some techniques that can make your application more secure. We hope these techniques will help reduce your security risks. If for some reason you find that these techniques don't work for you, or that your application is less secure in some way because of following them, please remember that you are responsible for the security of your own application. We disclaim any liability. There is no way for us to know what threats your specific applications face, and it is up to you to access potential threats and design your security to match those threats.

Configuring Tomcat

We'll begin by looking at how you can configure Tomcat to run more securely. Tomcat 4, unlike previous versions, supports HTTPS out of the box. Tomcat also is designed to work with a security manager to limit access from servlets to system services, reducing the opportunity for ill-behaved or malicious servlets to compromise your system.

SSL, HTTPS, and TLS

Secure Sockets Layer (SSL) is a mechanism for encrypting communication between two endpoints on a network. It was developed by Netscape specifically for use underneath HTTPS (also developed by Netscape) to provide connection layer security to HTTP connections. Prior to the development of HTTPS, there was no real way to secure communication between client and server, since HTTP by design sends all communications in the clear. At roughly the same time, there was an initiative to develop a standard secure version of HTTP, called SHTTP; however, Netscape's HTTPS won out, primarily because they had both a working protocol and a working browser, one that at the time had close to 90 percent market share.

HTTPS is quite simply HTTP over SSL. The communication protocol is ostensibly the same, aside from the fact that the actual protocol name (which is sent in the messages) has an "S" at the end and a different default port is used. (HTTPS defaults to port 443, whereas HTTP defaults to port 80.) SSL, on the other hand, can be used to secure any type of network traffic and has been widely used to secure other protocols, such as Secure Internet Messaging Application Protocol (IMAP). (Secure IMAP is just IMAP running over SSL; it also uses a different default port.)

Transport Layer Security (TLS) is a layer similar to SSL in design and function, and was developed as an official RFC (2246) by the Internet Engineering Task Force (IETF), the principal standards body for the core Internet protocols. In fact, TLS is based on SSL 3.0. Both use an asymmetric, public-key algorithm to negotiate a secure session in order to exchange a shared secret value, which in turn is used as the key for the symmetric encryption algorithm used to encrypt the actual traffic. The reason for this approach is that symmetric algorithms are less computationally expensive than asymmetric algorithms; however, asymmetric algorithms are required to establish a secure communication channel on a non-secure medium. None of this need concern you—it all happens transparently from a user and developer perspective—but you may find it interesting nonetheless.

Using Tomcat Behind Another Server to Provide HTTPS

One of the safest and most efficient ways to set up Tomcat to handle HTTPS connections is to use Apache to handle the actual HTTPS connection and let it proxy the servlet handling to Tomcat. (See Chapter 3, "Configuring Tomcat," for details on configuring the WARP connector to accept connections from Apache and IIS.) There are a few reasons why this is a good way to go in a production environment. On Unix, the first and most important reason is because Apache can be started as root and run as root long enough to gain access to low-numbered ports, but will then downgrade its own access credentials to that of an unprivileged user, with minimal permissions. You can then run Tomcat as an unprivileged user, thus limiting your risk exposure should an unscrupulous cracker manage to gain control of your Web server.

The other reason to do this in a production system is that the native Apache implementation of HTTPS is faster and more efficient than the Java implementation used by Tomcat. This will speed up response times for your users.

In a firewalled development environment, or if you're running on a high-numbered port, there can be some advantages to running Tomcat stand-alone and to letting Tomcat handle the HTTPS connections itself. We'll take a look at how to do that next.

Setting Up the HTTPS Connector

Starting with version 4.0, Tomcat comes with an HTTPS connector ready to configure. If you're using JDK 1.3 or earlier, you'll need to download the Java Secure Socket Extension version 1.0.2 or later from Sun (http://java.sun.com/products/jsse), but the connector class is precompiled and ready to go. JDK 1.4 includes JSSE by default. (The Apache Foundation can't include the libraries because of export restrictions. Remember, cryptographic software is considered an armament by the U.S. federal government.) Prior to 4.0, you had to recompile Tomcat with a few libraries in place in order to build the HTTPS connector.

If you're using an older JDK, download jsse.jar and install it in the extensions directory for your Java runtime—*$JAVA_HOME*/jre/lib/ext on most platforms, and /Library/Java/Extensions/ or one of the other valid locations on OS X. (See the 10.1 Java release notes for more information: http://developer.apple.com/techpubs/macosx/ReleaseNotes/java10.1.html#JavaExtensions.)

Installing the connector is as simple as installing a certificate to identify your server and configuring the connector in your server.xml file. Let's take a look.

Digital Certificates

Digital certificates provide a cryptographically strong way of identifying an entity, whether it be a user, a Web server, or a company. Certificates can be based on any of a number of asymmetric or public-key algorithms. The public key can be used to verify the validity of the private key, and vice versa. Furthermore, public keys can be used to sign other digital certificates, effectively allowing other entities to vouch for the validity of a given certificate and in effect creating a circle of trust. If you trust the owner of the certificate that signed the certificate you're examining, then you can trust the validity of the certificate.

Anyone can generate a certificate. In fact, we're going to generate a certificate now and use that certificate to sign itself. This so-called self-signed certificate is what we'll use to get our HTTPS connector going. HTTPS uses this certificate to authenticate the endpoint of the communication. To understand why this is so, let's look at a threat model.

Suppose user Andy wants to connect to a server at Behemoth.com. He connects to the server at Behemoth.com, which presents a certificate identifying the server as belonging to them, and identifies its hostname and IP address. Andy, trusting the certificate, allows his browser to set up a secure connection to the Behemoth.com server. The communication between the endpoints is encrypted so that only the client Andy is using and the server identified by the certificate as belonging to Behemoth.com have access to the data being sent over the wire.

Let's assume that nefarious hacker Cindy has managed to get access to the network to listen to the traffic between Andy and Behemoth.com. Because the communication is encrypted, it would require an enormous amount of computing power to decrypt (in proportion to the size of the key used to encrypt), and so the communication is relatively quite secure.

Now let's assume that Cindy has managed to intercept the communication to Behemoth.com by convincing Andy's browser, proxy server, or some router along the way to send the traffic to her instead. Cindy could then decrypt the traffic, read it, and re-encrypt it before sending it on to the real server at Behemoth.com. Without no certificate required, there would be no way for Andy or Behemoth.com to know that they weren't talking to the endpoint they thought they were.

Of course, since anyone can create a certificate, Cindy could just create a self-signed certificate stating that her machine was actually the Behemoth.com machine and send it to Andy when his client connected. She could also create a client certificate stating that her machine belonged to Andy, and use that to connect to the server at Behemoth.com.

So how do certificates help to prevent this sort of thing? This is where certificate signing comes into play. Let's now assume that in place of a self-signed certificate, Behemoth.com has a certificate issued by (and signed by) a well-known certificate authority (CA)—for example, VeriSign or Thawte. Andy's browser has a copy of the public key from the root certificates from these CAs and can therefore verify the validity of the signature on the certificate being presented by the Behemoth.com server. Because Andy trusts the certificate in his browser, he can also trust the validity of certificates signed by that certificate. He can be reasonably assured that the Behemoth.com server does in fact belong to Behemoth.com.

Now when Cindy tries to convince Andy that her server is really the Behemoth.com server, he checks the validity of the certificate presented and finds that it was not signed by an authority he trusts. He can then reject the creation of a session between his client and that server. He should also contact Behemoth.com and tell them that a questionable certificate was presented to him. Behemoth.com can then use the information in the forged credential to help track down Cindy's nefarious activities.

So, what have we learned from this scenario? We've learned that even a self-signed certificate can be used to initiate a secure connection between two endpoints, but that a self-signed certificate is not much good for validating that the endpoint is the one we think it is. The practical application of this information is as follows: Self-signed certificates used with HTTPS provide you with a little more security than just plain HTTP, but not really enough to be considered secure. Self-signed certificates are great for setting up development servers, where the concern is not the security of the data but getting a working HTTPS connection going. They have a few advantages over properly signed certificates in these environments, particularly their (lack of) cost, and the fact that they can be generated on the spot. Certificates are valid only for a single hostname and IP address, so if your development environment changes a lot or includes a lot of hostnames, buying a trusted certificate from a trusted CA every time a configuration changes or for a large number of machines can take time and be expensive. If, however, you're intending to send sensitive data over HTTPS, you really need a certificate from a trusted CA.

Generating a Certificate

Generating your own certificate is easy. Java includes a tool called keytool that will generate certificates for you. (We use this functionality again to generate client certificates for our application in the second half of this chapter.) All you have to do to generate a self-signed certificate for Tomcat is to run $JAVA_HOME/bin/keytool -genkey -alias tomcat -keyalg RSA (on Unix) or %JAVA_HOME%\bin\keytool -genkey -alias tomcat -keyalg RSA (on Windows). You will be prompted for some information about yourself and your company, and asked for a password for the keystore and for the certificate. Tomcat by default expects this password to be *changeit*, so for now enter this when prompted. Once you see how to manage the connector, you can (and should) change the password to something else.

Here's how you'd generate a key on OS X or another Unix system:

```
[carbon:~] imf% $JAVA_HOME/bin/keytool -genkey -alias tomcat
-keyalg RSA
Enter keystore password:  changeit
What is your first and last name?
  [Unknown]:  Ian McFarland
What is the name of your organizational unit?
  [Unknown]:  San Francisco Office
What is the name of your organization?
  [Unknown]:  Neo Ventures, Ltd.
What is the name of your City or Locality?
  [Unknown]:  San Francisco
What is the name of your State or Province?
```

```
  [Unknown]:  California
What is the two-letter country code for this unit?
  [Unknown]:  US
Is <CN=Ian McFarland, OU=San Francisco Office, O="Neo Ventures,
Ltd.", L=San Francisco, ST=California, C=US> correct?
  [no]:  yes

Enter key password for <tomcat>
        (RETURN if same as keystore password):  changeit
[carbon:~] imf%
```

The interaction with keytool is the same on Windows or any other system with a Java runtime.

Getting a Real Certificate

The two largest providers of certificates in the world are VeriSign (www.verisign.com) and Thawte (www.thawte.com). There are others, but keep in mind that it is important to be sure that the certificate you use for your server is one that will be trusted by the browsers out there. There is no point in getting a certificate from a CA if the browsers your customers are using don't trust that CA. It pays to do a little research before selecting a CA.

Applying for a server certificate typically consists of presenting credentials to the CA verifying your identity and paying some money. Exact requirements and costs vary by provider; as of this writing, Thawte charges $125 for one year and $225 for two years, for an SSL Server Certificate, and VeriSign's fees start at $349.

As we mentioned earlier, using a CA can get somewhat price-prohibitive when you're just doing development or changing configurations frequently. In a production environment, the cost of *not* having a signed certificate can get very high indeed.

Configuring the Connector

You'll need to decide what port you want to run your HTTPS connector on. The default is port 443; however, as we mentioned earlier, on Unix systems access to these ports is restricted to the root user. Again, you don't really want to run your Tomcat server instance as root on a production server, since this may make you more vulnerable to attack. By default, Tomcat likes to use port 8443 for the SSL connector.

Here's how you'd configure the SSL connector:

```
<!-- Define an SSL HTTP/1.1 Connector on port 8443 -->
    <Connector
className="org.apache.catalina.connector.http.HttpConnector"
               port="8443" minProcessors="5" maxProcessors="75"
               enableLookups="true"
               acceptCount="10" debug="0" scheme="https"
secure="true">
      <Factory className="org.apache.catalina.net.
SSLServerSocketFactory"
               clientAuth="false" protocol="TLS"/>
    </Connector>
```

As you can see, once you've installed the certificate, configuring the connector is easy. All the HTTPS-specific stuff is in the <Factory/> node. First, we specify the SSLServerSocketFactory as the class Tomcat should use to get the socket. Second, we specify that we don't need the client to authenticate itself with a certificate. (Set this attribute to true to require client-side certificates.) Third, we specify whether we want Tomcat to use TLS or SSL. That's it. This example already exists in the default server.xml; it's just commented out. As with other connectors, you can configure an HTTPS connector on any port, have it bind only to a specific IP address, and otherwise configure it to your liking.

The Security Manager

Now that our communication channel is more secure, it's time to turn our attention to the servlet container. Tomcat makes use of a security manager to restrict access to various features of the environment.

As you are probably aware, Java has long had a place in its architecture for code security. Since the earliest days, Java was designed to prevent mobile code from doing damage to the systems it runs on. You are probably familiar with the concept of the *applet sandbox*, the container in which downloaded applets run with restricted rights. Clearly in the case of an applet, it is desirable to limit what this executable code can do on and to your machine. This is, after all, a piece of code being downloaded to your Web browser on the fly from some remote server. You don't want some cute stock-ticker applet secretly vacuuming up your financial information to send back to the server or deleting files from your hard drive. Typically you won't even know that a page has an applet on it until it downloads and starts. With this in mind, the designers of the Java runtime included in it the concept of a sandbox, a container that limits access to the underlying system resources. Over the years, the mechanisms that control this access have been refined to allow smaller grained control over access and to allow signed and trusted code more access. In JDK 1.2, the designers gave us a new SecurityManager class and policy file as mechanisms to control this access.

This makes lots of sense for applets, but why is it important for a servlet container like Tomcat? One of the main reasons is to protect the Tomcat runtime from badly behaved servlet code. Let's consider a servlet that calls System.exit(). Without any external protection, this call would result in the containing JVM exiting and taking the whole Tomcat server instance with it. Tomcat servlets do, after all, execute within the same VM as the server itself. Worse than this, of course, would be a bug in a servlet that deletes or overwrites key files on the system. Particularly pernicious would be one that overwrites key security files on the system, especially ones controlling our Tomcat instance. We'll look at such a threat model in a moment.

There are three major categories of threat that the Security Manager helps to protect us from: bad code; pernicious code; and attacks designed to exploit weak, dangerous, badly written, or misconfigured code. Let's examine these in turn.

Bad Code

We've already seen a couple of examples of how badly written servlet or JSP code could damage the server it's running in. This threat model is perhaps the most common, since this threat can be a problem simply because of carelessness on the part of the developer.

Pernicious Code

There are a lot of useful servlets out there packaged up as handy, ready-to-install Web Archive (WAR) files. Let's say you (ill-advisedly) decide to install a blogger servlet from Cindy Hacker's Dangerous Servlet and Warez Site to run your local Weblog. Let us further assume that blogger.war includes a servlet with some undocumented features, like the ability to install new servlets remotely, and Cindy Hacker's Peer-to-Peer Warez Warehouse Server, which she uses to distribute pirated software. She's also included her Distributed Denial-of-Service Server Death Servlet. And let's also assume that she's included a handy telnet server in her WAR file that lets her telnet in to poke around on your server and create more mayhem. Suddenly, you're running a piece of code that has compromised your system, has gotten a bunch of customer data stolen, and has gotten you in trouble with both the Business Software Alliance and the FBI. We're exaggerating, of course—but only slightly. Once your system is compromised, all of these problems and even more are just a few keystrokes away.

Weak, Dangerous, Badly Written, or Misconfigured Code

Let's say we've written a file download/upload servlet and haven't adequately thought through how we'll handle URLs. Our design intends to limit the file hierarchy the servlet can manipulate by prepending a path to our working directory—say, /usr/local/tomcat /uploadspace/—to the path sent by the Web client. Let's assume that we forgot to range-check to see if the path included .. elements in it and merely constructs the path by combining our base path with whatever string is sent. Now the pernicious hacker uses our servlet to download "../../../../etc/passwd" to her hard drive. She can now run *crack* or some other password-cracking utility against the passwords in that file at her leisure, or worse, upload a revised version with the root password set to something to her liking. This would be a bad thing. A very bad thing.

Let's take another badly designed Webapp, one that accesses a database. Let's assume that for the purpose of flexibility, the application stores the SQL query to be sent to the database in a hidden field in one of the forms. In addition, to make development easier, the servlet is connecting to the database as the root user. Everything seems to work great. (If you're cringing, you should. If you're saying to yourself that this never happens, don't. We've seen it more times than we'd like to think about in production code we've been asked to fix.) Discovering this, our nefarious hacker grabs the source to one of our pages and rewrites it to include a query like:

```
GRANT ALL ON *.* TO cracker@'%' IDENTIFIED BY 'ha><0r' WITH GRANT OPTION
```

She submits the form, and suddenly she gains the ability to read or write any record in our database from anywhere in the world.

Now let's assume that you've configured the manager application (see Chapter 9, "The Manager Application") but have given it a particularly weak password, or that a snooping hacker on your network has sniffed the cleartext password you're using to talk to the server. Now she can log in and use the manager application to upload and install a dangerous WAR file directly from the browser. Part of the danger here derives from the flexibility of the servlet model.

Tomcat and the Security Manager

Okay, now that you're sufficiently afraid of the consequences of doing nothing, it's time to look at how you can limit access to resources by configuring the Security Manager used by Tomcat. We'll start by going over some of the basic properties you can configure. Most of these (the ones in the various java.* packages) are the standard permissions from the Java runtime. Tomcat also adds one of its own, JndiPermission.

java.util.PropertyPermission: Controls read and write access to JVM system properties like java.home.

java.lang.RuntimePermission: Controls access to system and runtime functions like exit(), exec(), and halt().

java.io.FilePermission: Controls read, write, and execute permissions on files and directories.

java.net.SocketPermission: Controls access to network sockets.

java.net.NetPermission: Controls the use of multicast network connections.

java.lang.reflect.ReflectPermission: Controls the use of the reflection API.

java.security.SecurityPermission: Controls access to security methods.

java.security.AllPermission: When granted, allows access to all permissions, just as if you were running Tomcat without the Security Manager.

org.apache.naming.JndiPermission: Controls read access to JNDI named file-based resources.

These properties are controlled by the *<$CATALINA_HOME>*/conf/catalina.policy file, which completely replaces any policies set in your system java.policy file. You can edit this file manually or use policytool, part of the JDK, to edit it. By default, the policy file looks like the one shown in Listing 18.1.

```
// ============================================================================
// catalina.corepolicy - Security Policy Permissions for Tomcat 4.0
//
// This file contains a default set of security policies to be
// enforced (by the JVM) when Catalina is executed with the
// "-security" option.  In addition to the permissions granted here,
// the following additional permissions are granted to the codebase
// specific to each Web application:
//
// * Read access to the document root directory
//
```

Listing 18.1 *<$CATALINA_HOME>*/conf/catalina.policy. (continues)

```
// $Id: catalina.policy,v 1.14.2.1 2001/10/06 18:51:03 remm Exp $
// ============================================================================

// ========== SYSTEM CODE PERMISSIONS
=============================================

// These permissions apply to javac
grant codeBase "file:${java.home}/lib/-" {
      permission java.security.AllPermission;
};

// These permissions apply to all shared system extensions
grant codeBase "file:${java.home}/jre/lib/ext/-" {
      permission java.security.AllPermission;
};

// These permissions apply to javac when ${java.home] points at
$JAVA_HOME/jre
grant codeBase "file:${java.home}/../lib/-" {
      permission java.security.AllPermission;
};

// These permissions apply to all shared system extensions when
// ${java.home} points at $JAVA_HOME/jre
grant codeBase "file:${java.home}/lib/ext/-" {
      permission java.security.AllPermission;
};

// ========== CATALINA CODE PERMISSIONS =======================

// These permissions apply to the server startup code
grant codeBase "file:${catalina.home}/bin/bootstrap.jar" {
      permission java.security.AllPermission;
};

// These permissions apply to the servlet API classes
// and those that are shared across all class loaders
// located in the "common" directory
grant codeBase "file:${catalina.home}/common/-" {
      permission java.security.AllPermission;
```

Listing 18.1 *<$CATALINA_HOME>*/conf/catalina.policy. (continues)

```
};

// These permissions apply to the container's core code, plus any
// additional libraries installed in the "server" directory
grant codeBase "file:${catalina.home}/server/-" {
      permission java.security.AllPermission;
};

// These permissions apply to shared web application libraries
// including the Jasper page compiler in the "lib" directory
grant codeBase "file:${catalina.home}/lib/-" {
      permission java.security.AllPermission;
};

// These permissions apply to shared web application classes
// located in the "classes" directory
grant codeBase "file:${catalina.home}/classes/-" {
      permission java.security.AllPermission;
};

// ========== WEB APPLICATION PERMISSIONS ===========================


// These permissions are granted by default to all web applications
// In addition, a web application will be given a read FilePermission
// and JndiPermission for all files and directories in its document
// root.
grant {
   // Required for JNDI lookup of named JDBC DataSource's and
   // javamail named MimePart DataSource used to send mail
   permission java.util.PropertyPermission "java.home", "read";
   permission java.util.PropertyPermission "java.naming.*", "read";
   permission java.util.PropertyPermission "javax.sql.*", "read";

   // OS Specific properties to allow read access
   permission java.util.PropertyPermission "os.name", "read";
   permission java.util.PropertyPermission "os.version", "read";
   permission java.util.PropertyPermission "os.arch", "read";
   permission java.util.PropertyPermission "file.separator", "read";
   permission java.util.PropertyPermission "path.separator", "read";
   permission java.util.PropertyPermission "line.separator", "read";

   // JVM properties to allow read access
   permission java.util.PropertyPermission "java.version", "read";
```

Listing 18.1 *<$CATALINA_HOME>*/conf/catalina.policy. (continues)

```
    permission java.util.PropertyPermission "java.vendor", "read";
    permission java.util.PropertyPermission "java.vendor.url", "read";
    permission java.util.PropertyPermission "java.class.version",
"read";
    permission java.util.PropertyPermission "java.specification.
version", "read";
        permission java.util.PropertyPermission "java.specification.
vendor", "read";
        permission java.util.PropertyPermission "java.specification.
name", "read";

        permission java.util.PropertyPermission "java.vm.
specification.version", "read";
        permission java.util.PropertyPermission "java.vm.
specification.vendor", "read";
        permission java.util.PropertyPermission "java.vm.
specification.name", "read";
        permission java.util.PropertyPermission "java.vm.version",
"read";
        permission java.util.PropertyPermission "java.vm.vendor",
"read";
        permission java.util.PropertyPermission "java.vm.name",
"read";

        // Required for getting BeanInfo
        permission java.lang.RuntimePermission "accessClassInPackage.sun.beans.*";

        // Allow read of JAXP compliant XML parser debug
        permission java.util.PropertyPermission "jaxp.debug", "read";
};
```

Listing 18.1 *<$CATALINA_HOME>*/conf/catalina.policy. (continued)

Each entry consists of a grant of one or more permissions, which can be applied either globally or based on a specified scope in the form of a codeBase argument (consisting of a path to the classes for which the grant applies). For example, the following entry grants global access to all of the JAR files in the *<$CATALINA_HOME>*/classes directory (so keep that in mind when you're throwing in third-party libraries):

```
grant codeBase "file:${catalina.home}/classes/-" {
        permission java.security.AllPermission;
};
```

You can also grant permissions to files signed by a specific certificate. The generalized form is as follows:

```
grant [signedBy <signer>,] [codeBase <code source>] {
             permission  <class>  [<name> [, <action list>]];
             [permission  <class>  [<name> [, <action list>]];]
```

```
            .
            .
            .
            [permission  <class>  [<name> [, <action list>]];]
};
```

Using the Security Manager with Tomcat

By default, Tomcat doesn't use the Security Manager. Once you have configured permissions to your liking, you will need to tell Tomcat explicitly to use the Security Manager by passing in the *-security* parameter to the startup script (for example, <*$CATALINA_HOME*>/bin/startup.sh -security). Don't forget to add this parameter to any automated startup script you may use to launch the server on boot.

Debugging Permissions Issues

If one of your Webapps start dying mysteriously and is throwing AccessControlExceptions or SecurityExceptions, this means your application is trying to do something prohibited by the Security Manager. It may not always be obvious exactly what this is, but start by looking at the line in your servlet where the exception is thrown and comparing this to the policies you've set. One other thing you can do is to turn on security decision logging by setting *java.security.debug=all*. You can do this by setting the environment variable *CATALINA_OPTS=-Djava.security.debug=all* prior to starting Tomcat. Be advised, however, that this logging is extremely verbose. You will have to wade through megabytes of data to find what you're looking for. If you're not having any luck working it out for yourself, though, looking at the logged decision criteria can be helpful.

Permissions

Having sensible permissions on your files in the filesystem helps a lot, too. In particular, make sure that your configuration files are not writable by the user under whose permissions Tomcat is running, and be very discriminating regarding other users who have access to that file. You'll also want to make any directories to which you've granted AllPermissions non-world-writable and non-writable by that user. In general, you want to limit access as much as you can and still have your programs work. If your programs need to do things that might compromise the security of your server, rewrite them so they don't. It's that simple. Any security hole you leave open will most likely be exploited at some time during the life of your application. So don't leave any.

Of course, we know that this is not a simple proposition. Security is hard. It's probably the hardest part of application development in a networked environment. If you're new to writing code for networked applications, it will serve you well to be cautious and to find someone in your organization, or an outside security consultant, who has more experience in these matters. This stuff is extremely dangerous. If you feel like it's not worth the effort, picture what your day would be like if you came in to find that you had to explain why (a) your entire server farm has been down for the last 12 hours; (b) why all the sensitive data in your database has been stolen and customer information has been used for, say, identity theft purposes; or (c) all the data in the database (or worse yet, 20 percent of the data, but it's not clear which 20 percent) may have been replaced with incorrect information. The last thing developers want is to get their name on the cover of their favorite computer magazine because their app destroyed a company.

Don't think these things don't happen—they do. A reader survey of network administrators in a prominent IT magazine showed over half of those surveyed admitted that their systems had at least one point in the past been compromised. (Since this is just about the last thing a network administrator would want to admit, you can draw your own conclusions about what the real percentage might be.)

We have heard a lot of regrets about choices made in security. They are never regrets that the approach taken was too conservative or that the system implemented was too secure.

Running as an Unprivileged User

Changing the permissions on files won't protect you much if Tomcat is running as root. Even compromising a server running under normal user privileges can lead to significant security problems. Servers should be run using the permissions of an unprivileged user. The easiest way to do this is to create a Tomcat account on your system, make it a member of an unprivileged group like nobody or daemon, and take away its login shell and home directory. You'll need to make sure that some working directories are writable by the Tomcat user, particularly the *<$CATALINA_HOME>*/work directory, as well as any directory your servlets need to write to. If you want Tomcat to automatically unpack WAR files, then you'll need to make the *<$CATALINA_HOME>*/webapps directory writable by the Tomcat user as well. A handy solution on a development machine is to have the /webapps directory owned by Tomcat, with group ownership by a group that your development team belongs to, and make it both owner- and group-writable. That way, both Tomcat and the developers can write the files they need to.

Of course, if you want to make your system more secure, you may not want to let Tomcat write to the /webapps directory at all. You can always unpack WAR files manually simply by unjarring them in the /webapps directory. (Remember, WAR files are just JAR files with a different file structure and a different extension.) It's a good idea to do installs manually on a production server, anyway. Reserve your Tomcat-writable /webapps directory for a development machine safely secured behind a firewall.

Servlet Development

Now that we've gone over some threat models and examined some steps you can take to protect the server, it's time to discuss what you can do when writing code to make the applications themselves more secure.

Using Onetime Passwords

We'll start by showing an example of how secret information can be verified over a nonsecure network without allowing it to be compromised. In practice, you will most likely use other methods to handle logins; however, we felt that this example would help you understand a little more about cryptography, and thereby help you make more informed decisions about security.

The technique we'll be using is called a onetime password (OTP). It is the basis of the S/Key authentication scheme, developed by Bellcore.

The basic idea is a relatively simple one—once you understand and accept that there are such things as secure hashing algorithms—which produce hashes that have no predictable relationship to the string passed in other than that any string passed in will always produce the same hash.

Here's how an OTP algorithm works. The user knows his or her password, but doesn't want to transmit it in the clear. The server also knows this password. The server needs to know that the user knows the password, but must verify it without the user sending the actual password across the network.

For our example, let's assume that the password is *badpassword*. The MD5 hash of this password is the hexadecimal value *31edaffbaba455bc30c52681ceb1ea9d*.

We don't want to just hash the password and send it because this would leave us vulnerable to a replay attack; if the hashed password remains the same between sessions, it's just as good as knowing the secret password that was used to create it. But because a secure hash bears no predictable resemblance to the string that created it but the result of hashing the string always is the same, both sides can combine the secret string with some arbitrary second string they agree on and then hash the combined string instead. This arbitrary string, which changes over time, is called a *nonce*.

To see how this works, let's see what happens when our client and server agree to use the word "happy" as the nonce for our first iteration. Both sides combine the nonce with the secret password and compute the MD5 hash. The MD5 hash of *badpasswordhappy* is *a49e1fb0f208281f1d1efbff3aa3e91c*. The client computes this value and sends it to the server, which compares it to the value it computed. Since it matches, we know that the password was the same (at least to the same extremely high degree of likelihood we mentioned in Chapter 8).

On the next iteration, the nonce is "sad". Again, both sides combine the nonce with the password to produce *badpasswordsad*, with an MD5 hash of *435538c0455a 090b901645aac5a694ae*.

Let's examine what our nefarious hacker friend sees when she snoops our network. We use some pseudocode to show what the client and server are transmitting. The exact protocol here is not important.

```
Server: 401 Request Authentication using OTP. Nonce: happy
Client: Hashed password with nonce: a49e1fb0f208281f1d1efbff3aa3e91c
Server: 200 Authentication successful.
```

On the next communication, the handshake looks like this:

```
Server: 401 Request Authentication using OTP. Nonce: sad
Client: Hashed password with nonce: 435538c0455a090b901645aac5a694ae
Server: 200 Authentication successful.
```

There is just no way our hacker is going to be able to predict what hash code to send. The odds against guessing the right hash are astronomical. The trick is that the client has to have a way to calculate an OTP without communicating with the server, but that's pretty easy to accomplish. In fact, you can find a simple OTP calculator applet, with full source code, at www.cs.umd.edu/~harry/jotp/. On the server side, we can calculate the MD5 hash using the same code or by using the java.security.MessageDigest.

The actual OTP protocol (as specified by the IETF and which is compatible with S/Key) combines a number and a string to create a nonce, and then converts the hash from a hexadecimal number to a series of six short (four-letter or shorter) English language words to simplify transmission and reduce errors. A real nonce might be *22 happy*. When combined with our secret password, this generates the OTP *LAP WHO GALT NINA BLUM LET*, and *22 sad* yields *SWAY WOVE IO YARN LIP BEEF*. There are 2048 words that make up the set used to transmit the values, so you can think of those six words as a six-digit base 2048 number. That is, in fact, exactly how it's treated. To see the actual words, take a look at the words array at the end of this file: http://www.cs.umd.edu/~harry/jotp/src/otp.java.

Discovering the Protocol of Your Connection

The previous exercise was merely intended to give you an example of how cryptography works. Now that you have a little more background, let's see how some of the libraries can work for us. The best way we have readily available to us to secure our client server communication is to use HTTPS. Of course, we may want to verify that our servlet is really being accessed via HTTPS, and even determine the key strength being used for the connection. Then we can politely refuse to do anything dangerous if we're not satisfied with the security of the connection. Fortunately, the servlet API and Tomcat work together to give us access to the information we need in order to do this.

If we just want to know what protocol is being used to connect to our servlet, there are a few methods on the Request object we can use to find this out: getProtocol(), getScheme(), and isSecure().

By far the simplest of these is isSecure(), which returns true if the connection was over HTTPS and false if it was over HTTP. The getScheme() method will return the protocol portion of the requested URL—http, https, ftp, etc. The getProtocol() method will return the scheme and the protocol version—for example, HTTPS/1.1.

If we want to actually verify the key strength, we have a little more work to do. Unfortunately, this bit is not standardized in the servlet specification, so we will have to rely on vendor-specific attributes to determine the key strength. Since we know we'll be running on Tomcat, we can look up the attributes *javax.servlet.request.cipher_suite* and *javax.servlet.request.key_size* on the request object passed into our service(), doGet(), or doPost() method, as shown in Listing 18.2.

```
package com.wiley.tomcatbook

import java.io.*;
import java.util.*;
import javax.servlet.*;
import javax.servlet.http.*;
```

Listing 18.2 A simple servlet that demonstrates testing key strength. (continues)

```
public class SecurityTestServlet extends HttpServlet
{
public void doGet(HttpServletRequest req, HttpServletResponse resp)
throws ServletException, IOException
{
            resp.setContentType("text/plain");
ServletOutputStream out = resp.getOutputStream();
if (! req.isSecure())
{
       out.println("Not secure!");
       return;
}
String cypherSuite = (String) req.getAttribute("javax.servlet.request.cipher_suite");
int keySize = ((Integer) req.getAttribute("javax.servlet.request.key_size")).intValue();
out.println("Connected using cypher suite " + cypherSuite);
out.println("Key Size: " + keySize);
if (keySize >= 128)
out.println("That's a good strong key.");
else
{
       out.println("That key is not strong enough.");
}
}
}
```

Listing 18.2 A simple servlet that demonstrates testing key strength. (continued)

We need to compile this servlet and add the code in Listing 18.3 to the deployment descriptor for our tomcatbook Webapp.

```
<servlet>
<servlet-name>SecurityTestServlet</servlet-name>
<servlet-class>com.wiley.tomcatbook.SecurityTestServlet</servlet-class>
</servlet>
<servlet-mapping>
<servlet-name>SecurityTestServlet</servlet-name>
<url-pattern>/securitytestservlet</url-pattern>
</servlet-mapping>
```

Listing 18.3 Deployment descriptor additions for SecurityTestServlet.

When we connect to this servlet over HTTP, to http://localhost:8080/tomcatbook/securitytestservlet, we get the following result:

```
Not secure!
```

When we connect to it over HTTPS, to https://localhost:8443/tomcatbook/securitytestservlet using the U.S. version of Internet Explorer 5.1, we get this result:

```
Connected using cypher suite SSL_RSA_WITH_RC4_128_MD5
Key Size: 128
That's a good strong key.
```

As you can see from this method, we can find out a lot about the connection the request came in on. We can use this information to determine whether we're willing to talk to the connected client. If you're writing a banking application, for example, then you should probably insist on a 128-bit key. That's what Wells Fargo and Bank of America do. If you connect to either of those banks with a browser that supports only 40-bit keys, they will simply refuse to let you log in.

Using Certificates as User Credentials

Okay, now that we're satisfied that the connection is secure, what's the best way to determine whom we're talking to? Well, at this point, we may decide it's safe enough just to ask for a login and password. Using certificates is a stronger way to authenticate users, though, particularly when combined with a password. The procedure for configuring a browser to present a client certificate varies from browser to browser, as does the extent to which each browser supports client-side certificates. Let's start by examining how an organization might create and use certificates to secure access to Web-based services.

A good place to start is with an application developed for a human resources (HR) department to create the certificates used at a company. This application is one that creates certificates and signs them by a trusted root certificate (which is kept secure). This could be either a self-signed certificate or a server certificate issued by a trusted CA. In doing this, the company is effectively creating its own CA. Since you can trust a certificate you generated yourself and verify that the user certificates you generate were signed by that certificate, this is a secure solution for creating credentials—as long as the root certificate remains secure. Of course, this solution as a whole is only as secure as the means you use to determine how to issue the credentials. If all someone has to do to get a certificate is fill out a form on a Website, and nobody in the organization is responsible for verifying the identity of the people involved, then you really don't know any more about who is using this credential than you would about someone coming in without any credentials at all.

It is important that the HR department understand that these certificates are key pieces of identification that provide access to resources your applications will make available. In our scenario, access to this application is secured by requiring a trusted officer of the company to sign in using such a trusted certificate to access the forms that generate the new user certificates, and access requires strong identification of the users to whom the certificates are being issued. (Requiring a driver's license, national identity card, and employee identity card is a good place to start.) Remember, once you trust a certificate, you're effectively trusting all the actions taken by the holder of that certificate. This needs to be the most secure part of the whole operation.

Once the certificates are generated, they must be checked to verify their authenticity by verifying that the signature from the root certificate is valid. Certificates will also need to be revoked when they are compromised, or when employees leave the company.

When the user logs in, his or her browser, if so configured, will present the certificate for authentication. The server then verifies the signature on the certificate and, if it is valid, creates a session with the validated user information. Access control within the application is then up to the application logic to determine, but this can now be done with the confidence that the user is in fact the person we think he or she is.

Other Techniques for Validating Identity

Beyond what you've seen here, you can also use systems such as SecurID from RSA and other cryptographically strong server-based solutions. Configuring these systems is beyond the scope of this book, since it has little to do with Tomcat per se. If you're interested, there is a wealth of information on the RSA Website, www.rsasecurity.com/products/securid/. Like the OTP scheme we saw earlier in this chapter, SecurID combines a piece of information that varies over time with a password you know to provide an OTP that is fundamentally unguessable. The difference with these systems is that the nonce is typically supplied by a little device that cycles through numbers in a deterministic but unguessable sequence, one number every 60 seconds. The server knows what the sequence is, and therefore knows what number the device will be displaying at any given time. These two pieces of information can likewise be combined to provide a secure OTP, with the added security of requiring access to the device itself.

Summary

Security is perhaps the most important topic you need to understand when developing networked systems. Servlets are by their very nature networked. It is the nature of security that the risk a system faces can remain hidden. Developing secure systems is a matter of managing that risk.

In this chapter, we reviewed some techniques for configuring Tomcat to run as a more secure environment. We looked at how you can configure Tomcat to run as a specific user, how you can configure an HTTPS connector, and how to use the Security Manager to control servlet access to system resources. We then discussed techniques you can use to authenticate users more securely, and how you can determine the security of your session.

Remember, there is no such thing as "secure," only "more secure" and (one hopes) "secure enough." This is not a book on security: lots of those are available. Security is not a trivial matter. Our hope is that this chapter has served to make you more aware of the basic issues and shown you the Tomcat-specific tools available to deal with them.

Now go out and buy a good book or two on security, and make sure your apps are safe!

CHAPTER

19

The Development Cycle

At this point, you're already familiar with the fine points of Tomcat management and servlet development. In this chapter, we walk you through a typical development process to help you put all the pieces together. We discuss a number of best practices designed to encourage good development habits and to ease the development process generally.

The focus of this chapter is on good development hygiene. Being productive (and more significant, *staying* productive) depends on good development habits. In this chapter, we examine areas where developers can make their own lives easier through the use of relatively simple techniques and principles during development. Using these techniques may take a few more minutes to set up, and a little bit more time to maintain; however, they will save you hours of anguished hair-pulling later and increase the quality of your software. This leads to very good things, like high customer satisfaction, better reviews, and praise from managers; not to mention a much lower stress level. Don't believe us? Get back to us after you just accidentally delete 1,500 lines of hard-won code without a backup, or when a code change subtly breaks some other part of your application in a way that you don't discover until weeks later. The techniques in this chapter will show you how to check out the last version of the code you worked on to recover those deleted lines. We'll also show you how to use regression tests that will identify broken code the very next time you build it. Discovering your mistakes quickly is important because you probably still remember what change you made. Most likely you will even have the typical "doh!" reaction and know exactly what to do to fix it. How often is this the case weeks later?

In the examples in this chapter, we use some of the leading open source tools for build management, version control, testing, and the like. You can, of course, substitute your own tools as appropriate. While we recommend the tools in this chapter for most development processes, what is really important is the methodology behind the use of the tool. It is vital that you have a way to check in working versions of your code, and to roll back when something goes wrong, or check out older versions when you need to issue a patch for a customer who hasn't upgraded to your latest and greatest. The tools we use are all well established, used by major development teams in large companies and small, and in the open source movement as well. With the exception of some of the load testing tools we discuss, they are also all free, so even if you're reading this book on your own and setting up your own development environment, or you're working in a department that is strapped for cash, as long as you have an Internet connection, you'll be able to get everything you need.

Structuring Your Workspace

The first thing to do when setting up any development environment is to decide how to structure the filesystem where you're going to work. There isn't one magic correct way to do this, but what good techniques have in common is that they are organized and that it is easy to find the files you need and easy to configure build management software to compile the files correctly. This usually means segregating your source code from library files, configuration files from resource files, and so on. The file structure we provide here is tried and true, and has worked great for us. It also maps well onto the file structures a lot of development tools use and to guidelines developed by various people and companies. Some development tools may have different requirements, and you may have do adapt them to local requirements, but the principles here should give you some guidance, and will also help out when we get further along into version control and build management.

Follow these steps:

1. Decide where you will keep your development projects. Ian likes to keep all of his projects in a /projects directory under his home directory. Under Linux, this is /home/imf/projects. Under OS X, he uses /Users/imf/Projects. Wherever you choose to set up your development directory, it's good to have it someplace readily accessible and separate from your other directories.
2. Each project should have its own subdirectory. Name the directory based on the name of the project—for example, ~/projects/tomcatbook. It may be tempting to get some reuse of common elements by doing all of your development in a single directory, but experience has shown that this can cause more problems than it's worth. Invariably, you end up in a situation where two projects depend on different versions of some file or other, and you find work on one project breaking the work you do on another. Beyond this, it makes version control all but impossible to manage, and you end up with huge amounts of old irrelevant code being packaged up with what would otherwise be simple new code. Achieve reuse by packaging code you intend to reuse into libraries and managing those library projects as separate projects, with their own subdirectories, in your development directory.

3. Inside the projects directory, set up separate directories for your source code, libraries, configuration files, documentation, binary resource files, and HTML and JSP files.
4. Inside of your source directory, keep Java source files in directories that match the package hierarchy.
5. Copy any library files your project will need (for example, servlet.jar) into your library directory. This will result in a file hierarchy like the one shown in Listing 19.1.

```
~/
 /projects
   /tomcatbook
      /conf
         web.xml
      /doc
         notes.txt
      /lib
         servlet.jar
      /resources
         logo.jpeg
      /src
        /com
          /wiley
            /tomcatbook
                    ClientServlet.java
      /webroot
         /images
            logo.jpeg
            navbar.gif
index.jsp
login.jsp
```

Listing 19.1 A typical file hierarchy for a development directory.

Once your development directory is set up like this, it will be much easier to build your project from build scripts and to manage your project in a version-control system.

Version Control

The next thing a well-run development environment needs is a version-control system. You have several choices, and in many ways it doesn't matter which you choose. The Concurrent Version System (CVS) is one the most broadly used in Java development. Many open source projects also use CVS to provide a publicly accessible repository. In fact, you can use CVS to check out the latest version of Tomcat, or any previous version, for that matter. CVS itself can be found at http://www.cvshome.org.

A few platforms, OS X and most Linux distributions in particular, come with CVS preinstalled. For the rest of this section, we assume that you have access to a CVS repository. For details on how to install your own CVS repository, and for a reference, please see the bonus chapter on this book's companion Web site (www.wiley.com/compbooks/harrison).

The purpose of a version-control system is to provide a safe repository for your code. By allowing you to check in your work at various intervals (typically, when you've added a new piece of functionality and gotten it working), you free yourself to be more aggressive in reworking your code. Once it's checked in, you don't have to worry so much about breaking things because you know you can always go back to the way you had it before. This is surprisingly liberating the first time you experience it. This, coupled with testing, makes it much easier and safer to rewrite problematic parts of your code base, and as a result can help you write better code.

As we pointed out earlier, the C in CVS stands for concurrent. One of the advantages of CVS over some other version-control systems is the way it handles locking. Most version-control systems require a developer to get an exclusive lock on a section of code before he or she can modify it. This is in principle not such a bad idea, since it means that developers won't collide with each other and end up writing incompatible revisions to the same piece of code. This approach has its problems, however. One of the more frequently encountered is the problem of the piece of code that gets left checked out. Let's say developer A checks out B.java, works on it for a bit, and then goes to lunch. Developer C then needs to work on it, but it's still locked by developer A, and so she has to track him down and get him to check it back in.

There is a larger problem here, however. Let's say that A has the code checked out for a long while because he is having difficulty getting his revisions to work, but C has to make changes to the same code in order to get a new feature working and is on a deadline. Should A check in nonworking code? No. That would break the build, and in particular not help C with her development problem, since she'd be making revisions to A's nonworking code. What's the alternative? A can back out his changes and check it back in, or simply revert his code, but then he loses the work he's done so far. Also not optimal, but C needs to get her project done to keep someone in marketing at bay. A can keep track of his changes, and then add them to B.java once C checks it back in, but of course that's really not optimal.

With a concurrent version system, A and C can both check out B.java and make changes. They end up working just on their local copy, and there is no issue until they try to check the code back in. In this scenario, since C is on the shorter deadline, she would be the first to check in. When A gets done with his revisions, he then does an update before checking in (as did C, but the version in the repository hadn't changed since she checked it out). When A does his check-in, CVS reports that there is a conflict, and a diff shows which lines have changed. It is then up to A to resolve the conflict as he sees fit. (Note that he would have had to do this when he checked out C's version of B.java, when, after noting his changes, he tried to reapply them to the file.) In practice, particularly with good communication on the team, it is rare for there to be mutually incompatible changes to a file between developers, and the merge can usually be accomplished simply by accepting both sets of changes. In those rare cases when the merge is more complex, there are often design implications that need to be worked out anyway, and so direct human intervention takes place probably when it's least expensive.

And of course in real development, changes seldom take place just in one file. A change to the API in one object requires changes to all its callers, and as a result can often involve many files. Plus there are often a small number of files that most of the developers have to interact with. In a servlet project, this might be the main servlet file, or developers may need to make modifications to the deployment descriptor when they modify their code. Having these resources locked by one developer creates an unnecessary bottleneck in many cases. As a result of these productivity advantages, CVS is winning a lot of converts. That's not to say there aren't shortcomings. The command-line tools are rather clunky; it is very difficult to rename files, particularly directories; and there are a number of other issues as well. In fact, to paraphrase Winston Churchill's thoughts on democracy, CVS is the worst version-control system there is, except for all the others.

There is an open source project under way to develop a replacement for CVS (called Subversion). Preliminary reports are encouraging, but it's not quite ready for prime time yet. You can learn more about the project at http://subversion.tigris.org/.

For the meantime, let's continue with CVS. Once you have your directory tree set up, it's time to check the project into the repository.

First, log in to the repository. If it's a remote repository, the commands look something like this:

```
[carbon:~/Projects] % cvs -z3 -d :pserver:<username>@<cvs-
hostname>:<path/to/repository/on/remote/host> login
(Logging in to <username>@<cvs-hostname>)
CVS password: <your non-echoed CVS password>
[carbon:~/Projects] % cvs -z3 -d :pserver:<username>@<cvs-
hostname>:<path/to/repository/on/remote/host> import tomcatbook
wiley v1_0
```

whereupon CVS launches your specified editor and asks you to enter a log comment, which you should do. When you save what you've written, CVS uploads the entire project hierarchy up to the CVS repository, in this case to a repository named tomcatbook, with a vendor tag wiley, and a release tag of v1_0. Once the import is complete, you move the original directory aside and check out the files from the repository again:

```
[carbon:~/Projects] % mv tomcatbook tomcatbook-old
[carbon:~/Projects] % cvs -z3 -d :pserver:<username>@<cvs-
hostname>:<path/to/repository/on/remote/host> checkout tomcatbook
```

You won't have to enter all those parameters before the CVS command anymore (the -z3 -d :pserver:<username>@<cvs-hostname>:<path/to/repository/on/remote/host> part) because CVS will keep track of the information it needs to access the right repository. In fact, it keeps a lot of state information locally. This is why we needed to do the checkout once we had imported the project. If you examine the file hierarchy of the new /tomcatbook directory, you will see that each directory now contains a new CVS/ directory, each containing three files: Entries, Repository, and Root. These are the files CVS uses to manage project state locally. In fact, if you examine the Root file, it will contain the big long string we passed in front of the login, import, and checkout commands; and the Repository file will contain the path on the server to the directory containing our project. The Entries file keeps track of each file and directory in the current directory, the revision number, the revision date, and any additional flags to use when sending or retrieving the file—for instance, whether it's a binary file or a text file.

A number of development tools know about CVS and can let you operate on the repository through a GUI. Operations consist of things like adding new files or directories, checking the revision status of a file, showing the differences between the local file and the current version in the repository, committing the local file to the repository, merging the changes, and reverting to the previously saved state. If your favorite tool doesn't do that, you can always use the command-line tools or one of the many standalone tools for CVS repository management. They exist for most platforms.

Once our project is under revision control, changes should be checked in only when the local copy compiles correctly and builds correctly. That way, the version in the repository always remains in a usable state. It is an excellent policy to require a "build clean test" prior to checking anything in, to verify that no new bugs have been introduced and that everything works to spec.

Build Management

This brings up the issue of build management. We like to use Ant for this. Ant is another project of the Apache Software Foundation, and it consists of a portable, Java-based build system, similar in function and purpose to make. Which build system you use is up to you. Ant has some particular advantages, however, when it comes do developing Java applications in general, and servlets in particular.

One of these, as we'll see in a minute when we examine testing and JUnit, is the ease with which you can integrate testing into your build process. Another is the large number of existing Java projects you can turn to for good examples of how to manage an Ant build. Tomcat itself is built using Ant, so you can see how the programmers on the Tomcat project decided to manage quite an elaborate build process. And since it's portable to any platform on which Java will run, it's also convenient if you have a multi-platform build environment. There are also a large number of specialized Ant tasks for doing all sorts of things that relate to the management of Web applications and that support network operations, from email to the sending of a file to a server. (See Chapter 20 for details on installing and using Ant.)

Ant is managed through a build script, in the form of an XML file called build.xml. Like a Makefile, it resides in the directory on which it is intended to operate, so our main build.xml file will live in the root of our project directory. In this file, you specify a number of possible build targets (as well as dependencies between build targets) and what should happen in each of the build targets. What should happen is specified through a series of Ant tasks, which are expressed as XML tags, with parameters appropriate to the given task. Listing 19.2 shows what a build.xml might look like for the examples we've developed in this book.

```
<?xml version="1.0"?>
<project name="tomcatbook" default="build" basedir=".">
<target name="init">
<tstamp/>
<property name="name" value="tomcatbook"/>
<property name="tomcat-root" value="/Library/Tomcat/"/>
<property name="build" value="./build/"/>
<property name="build.classes" value="${build}classes/"/>
<property name="build.lib" value="${build}lib/"/>
<property name="build.warroot" value="${build}war-root/"/>
<property name="deploy" value="${tomcat-root}webapps/${name}/"/>
<property name="debug" value="on"/>
<property name="optimize" value="on"/>
<property name="deprecation" value="on"/>
<property name="src" value="./src"/>
<property name="libs" value="lib/servlet.jar:lib/jdbc2_0-
stdext.jar "/>
</target>

<target name="makedirs" depends="init">
<mkdir dir="${build}"/>
<mkdir dir="${build.classes}"/>
<mkdir dir="${build.lib}"/>
<mkdir dir="${build.warroot}"/>
<mkdir dir="${build.warroot}WEB-INF/"/>
<mkdir dir="${build.warroot}WEB-INF/lib/"/>
</target>

<target name="compile" depends="init,makedirs">
<javac srcdir="${src}"
   destdir="${build.classes}"
   debug="${debug}"
   optimize="${optimize}"
   classpath="${libs}"
   includes="com/wiley/tomcatbook/*.java"
/>
</target>

<target name="copyfiles" depends="init">
<copy todir="${build.warroot}WEB-INF/">
<fileset dir="conf"/>
</copy>
</target>
```

Listing 19.2 The build.xml file for the examples in this book. (continues)

```
<target name="build" depends="compile, copyfiles">
</target>

<target name="jar" depends="build">
<jar jarfile="${build.lib}${name}.jar" basedir="${build.classes}"/>
</target>

<target name="war" depends="jar">
<copy todir="${build.warroot}WEB-INF/lib">
<fileset dir="${build.lib}"/>
</copy>
<jar jarfile="${build}${name}.war" basedir="${build.warroot}"/>
</target>

<target name="deploy" depends="jar">
<copy todir="${deploy}WEB-INF/lib">
<fileset dir="${build.lib}"/>
</copy>
<copy todir="${deploy}WEB-INF/">
<fileset dir="conf/"/>
</copy>
</target>

<target name="clean" depends="init">
<delete dir="${build}" includeEmptyDirs="true"/>
</target>
</project>
```

Listing 19.2 The build.xml file for the examples in this book. (continued)

The build file consists of a number of <target/> nodes, each representing a build target. You can build any of these targets by specifying it on the command line you use to execute Ant. If none is specified, then the default target (specified in the default attribute of <project/> in the second line of the file) will be built. Any dependency specified in a depends attribute will be satisfied by building that target prior to building the specified one.

Let's take a quick look at the build targets, one by one.

The first is the init target, upon which all of the other targets depend. It sets up a number of variables we will use later. By specifying some basic paths as variables (properties, in Ant parlance), we can easily reuse our build file by changing a few lines here. (For example, if your instance of Tomcat is installed in /usr/local/tomcat, then you would change the tomcat-root property, but the rest of your build file could remain the same.) We also place strings in variables when we need to use them several times, as is the case with the libs property. This way, if we add JAR files to our project, we need to change only one line to make sure all of our build targets use the right classpath.

The second target is the makedirs target, upon which the build target depends. This target is responsible for setting up the necessary file hierarchy in our build directory. The build directory is laid out in order to make packaging the app easier. To that end, we include the file hierarchy we will need for building both the JAR file and the WAR file we will be making.

The compile target follows—this is the target that actually compiles our servlets. In it, we specify a pattern that matches the files we want to compile, the directory into which we want the files to be compiled, and a variety of compiler flags.

The copyfiles target is responsible for copying the deployment descriptor from the /conf directory into the /WEB-INF directory for packaging into the WAR file.

The build target simply rolls up the compile and copyfiles targets.

The jar target packages the compiled classes into a JAR file, tomcatbook.jar.

The war target packages the JAR file and the deployment descriptor into a WAR file.

The deploy target copies the deployment descriptor and the JAR file into the local Tomcat webapps directory. You could easily extend this task to deploy to a remote Web server.

The clean target removes all build products and returns the directory to its initial state.

Running the Software You Build

So based on the preceding build.xml, if we wanted to run our newly built application, we could do so by executing

```
ant deploy
```

from the command line. The first time we deploy, we need to restart Tomcat before our new Webapp will appear. This is true also if we change anything in the deployment descriptor. But under most circumstances, you'll be able to make your changes, run *ant deploy*, and see your changes reflected almost immediately in the running server, if you have servlet reloading turned on. This all makes for a very straightforward development cycle.

Testing

Just having revision control and an automated build system goes a long way toward improving your development cycle. Running *ant clean build* before doing a check-in eliminates a lot of broken builds. But in order to make your build system more robust, including automated testing goes far beyond this to ensure that your application not only compiles but actually works according to spec each time you do a check-in. In this section, we consider how to use JUnit to automate unit testing and, to some extent, even integration testing.

Developing Unit Tests with JUnit

JUnit is an open source testing framework for automating unit testing of Java code. You can find the framework, along with documentation, at http://www.junit.org/.

Automated testing has a number of advantages over manual testing. Chief among these are reproducibility and measurability. By codifying requirements into reproducible unit tests, you can add the passing of the tests to check-in requirements, and more important, identify newly introduced bugs before they break anything, while the code changes that produced them are fresh in your mind. This type of testing, where every test is run each time new code is checked in, is called regression testing.

Ideally, your testing framework should have at least one test for each method, as well as adequate tests to verify that each of these functions provides the right results and produces no unintended side effects (based on the range of expected inputs), and further assert that the inputs are in fact within the expected range. In fact, there are a number of development methodologies that advocate developing the tests before writing any code. (These are collectively called Test First methodologies.) They have a number of advantages, but whatever path you decide to take, testing is good for you and for your code!

Let's look at an example of a simple unit test. In this example, we test the output of a simple method on a simple class. Listing 19.3 contains a simplified Client class.

```
package com.wiley.tomcatbook;

public class Client
{
    private String name;
    public void setName(String aName)
    {
        this.name = aName;
}

public String getName()
{
        return aName;
}
}
```

Listing 19.3 com.wiley.tomcatbook.Client.

Our test case extends TestCase from the JUnit framework. Note in Listing 19.4 that we place it in the same package as the class we're testing, so that it will have access to package and protected methods.

```
package com.wiley.tomcatbook;

import junit.framework.*;
```

Listing 19.4 The ClientTest test case. (continues)

```
public class ClientTest extends TestCase
{
    private Client c;

public ClientServletTest(String name)
{
super(name);
}

protected void setUp()
{
        c = new Client();
        c.setName("Test Name");
}

    public void testName()
    {
        assertTrue("Test Name".equals(c.getName()));
    }
}
```

Listing 19.4 The ClientTest test case. (continued)

The JUnit framework requires all TestCases to have a constructor that takes a string as an argument. The setUp() method can be used to do any initialization needed across the contained tests. The rest of the TestCase consists of one or more test methods, all with method names starting with test, with a void return type. JUnit uses reflection to discover methods that match this pattern, and then runs all tests that it discovers in each registered test case.

The AllTests class, shown in Listing 19.5, is responsible for registering each test case, and is used to initiate the testing.

```
package com.wiley.tomcatbook;

import junit.framework.*;

public class AllTests {

    public static void main (String[] args) {
        junit.textui.TestRunner.run (suite());
    }
    public static Test suite ( ) {
```

Listing 19.5 The AllTests class. (continues)

```
        TestSuite suite = new TestSuite("All Tomcat Book Tests");
        suite.addTest(new TestSuite(ClientTest.class));
        return suite;
    }
}
```

Listing 19.5 The AllTests class. (continued)

Each test is registered by creating a TestSuite and passing a new instance for each class to the addTest() method.

Of course, we want to be able to run this test from our build script. The revised build script is shown in Listing 19.6.

```
<?xml version="1.0"?>
<project name="tomcatbook" default="build" basedir=".">
<target name="init">
<tstamp/>
<property name="name" value="tomcatbook"/>
<property name="tomcat-root" value="/Library/Tomcat/"/>
<property name="build" value="./build/"/>
<property name="build.classes" value="${build}classes/"/>
<property name="build.lib" value="${build}lib/"/>
<property name="build.warroot" value="${build}war-root/"/>
<property name="deploy" value="${tomcat-root}webapps/${name}/"/>
<property name="debug" value="on"/>
<property name="optimize" value="on"/>
<property name="deprecation" value="on"/>
<property name="src" value="./src"/>
<property name="libs" value="lib/servlet.jar:lib/jdbc2_0-
stdext.jar:lib/junit.jar:lib/httpunit.jar:lib/xerces.jar"/>
</target>

<target name="makedirs" depends="init">
<mkdir dir="${build}"/>
<mkdir dir="${build.classes}"/>
<mkdir dir="${build.lib}"/>
<mkdir dir="${build.warroot}"/>
<mkdir dir="${build.warroot}WEB-INF/"/>
<mkdir dir="${build.warroot}WEB-INF/lib/"/>
</target>

<target name="compile" depends="init,makedirs">
```

Listing 19.6 The build.xml file with the test targets. (continues)

```
<javac srcdir="${src}" destdir="${build.classes}" debug="${debug}" optimize="${optimize}"
classpath="${libs}"
includes="com/wiley/tomcatbook/*.java"/>
</target>

<target name="copyfiles" depends="init">
<copy todir="${build.warroot}WEB-INF/">
<fileset dir="conf"/>
</copy>
</target>

<target name="build" depends="compile, copyfiles">
</target>

<target name="jar" depends="test,build">
<jar jarfile="${build.lib}${name}.jar" basedir="${build.classes}"/>
</target>

<target name="war" depends="test,jar">
<copy todir="${build.warroot}WEB-INF/lib">
<fileset dir="${build.lib}"/>
</copy>
<jar jarfile="${build}${name}.war" basedir="${build.warroot}"/>
</target>

<target name="test" depends="jar">
 <java
  classname="junit.textui.TestRunner"
  classpath="${build.lib}${name}.jar:${libs}"
  fork="yes">
 <arg value="com.wiley.tomcatbook.AllTests"/>
 </java>
</target>

<target name="testgui" depends="jar">
 <java
  classname="junit.swingui.TestRunner"
  classpath="${build.lib}${name}.jar:${libs}"
  fork="yes">
 <arg value="com.wiley.tomcatbook.AllTests"/>
 </java>
</target>

<target name="deploy" depends="test,jar">
```

Listing 19.6 The build.xml file with the test targets. (continues)

```
<copy todir="${deploy}WEB-INF/lib">
<fileset dir="${build.lib}"/>
</copy>
<copy todir="${deploy}WEB-INF/">
<fileset dir="conf/"/>
</copy>
</target>

<target name="clean" depends="init">
<delete dir="${build}" includeEmptyDirs="true"/>
</target>
</project>
```

Listing 19.6 The build.xml file with the test targets. (continued)

We've added the libraries we need for testing—junit.jar, httpunit.jar, and xerces.jar—and included dependencies on the test task for the jar, war, and deploy targets, so that we'll be assured that the tests are run each time we are ready to make a distributable version of the Webapp. The test build target runs a command-line-oriented test suite. The testgui build target will launch a Swing-based GUI that gives you more control over the tests.

Integration Tests

Unit testing, the testing of individual code modules, is not the whole story. Just because your individual unit tests pass, that doesn't necessarily mean that the code modules will function correctly together. Beyond this, the servlet API presents a few hurdles to simple method-based testing. Simple method calls are easy enough to test with JUnit, but many of the key methods in a servlet—methods like init() and doGet()—depend on a running servlet engine to generate valid inputs to the methods, and they typically don't return anything that we can measure, either.

But have no fear. We can use HttpUnit to automate testing of the output of servlets. The library and documentation can be found at http://www.httpunit.org/. Our next example, shown in Listing 19.7, is a test case based on HttpUnit that tests the ClientServlet we wrote in Chapter 16, "Databases, Connection Pools, and JDBC." We use it to test our completed application and verify that we're getting back the right values in the right places.

```
package com.wiley.tomcatbook;

import java.io.*;
import java.net.*;
```

Listing 19.7 A test case based on HttpUnit. (continues)

```
import junit.framework.*;
import org.xml.sax.*;
import com.meterware.httpunit.*;

public class ClientListServletTest extends TestCase
{
   public ClientListServletTest(String name)
   {
     super(name);
   }

   public void testTableContents()
        throws SAXException, IOException, MalformedURLException
   {
     WebConversation wc = new WebConversation();
        WebRequest req = new GetMethodWebRequest("http://localhost:8080/tomcatbook/client-
list" );
        WebResponse resp = wc.getResponse(req);
        WebTable table = resp.getTables()[0];
     String[][] tableStrings = table.asText();
     assertEquals("First Name", tableStrings[0][0]);
     assertEquals("Last Name", tableStrings[0][1]);
     assertEquals("Phone", tableStrings[0][2]);
     assertEquals("Ian", tableStrings[1][0]);
     assertEquals("McFarland", tableStrings[1][1]);
     assertEquals("+1 415 555 1515", tableStrings[1][2]);
     assertEquals("Peter", tableStrings[2][0]);
     assertEquals("Harrison", tableStrings[2][1]);
     assertEquals("+64 9 555 1551", tableStrings[2][2]);
     assertEquals("Tim", tableStrings[3][0]);
     assertEquals("Ryan", tableStrings[3][1]);
     assertEquals("+1 718 555 5151", tableStrings[3][2]);
   }
}
```

Listing 19.7 A test case based on HttpUnit. (continued)

This test case starts out by creating a new connection to our server. Note that JUnit allows us to throw any exceptions that may occur during a test. Any exception thrown will duly be reported back in your Ant output, or in the GUI if you're using the Swing-based test environment.

Since this test depends on the deployment step in order to provide useful results, we should call it separately from the unit tests, which can be run as soon as the classes are built. To do this, we need to create a new test framework class, which we call PostDeployTests.java (see Listing 19.8.).

```
package com.wiley.tomcatbook;

import junit.framework.*;

public class PostDeployTests {

  public static void main (String[] args) {
    junit.textui.TestRunner.run (suite());
  }
  public static Test suite ( ) {
    TestSuite suite = new TestSuite("Tomcat Book Integration Tests");
    suite.addTest(new TestSuite(ClientListServletTest.class));
    return suite;
  }
}
```

Listing 19.8 PostDeployTests.java.

We also want to add a couple of tasks to our build.xml file, as shown in Listing 19.9.

```
<target name="testdeploy" depends="deploy">
  <java classname="junit.textui.TestRunner" classpath="${build.lib}${name}.jar:${libs}"
fork="yes">
    <arg value="com.wiley.tomcatbook.PostDeployTests"/>
  </java>
</target>

<target name="testdeploygui" depends="deploy">
  <java classname="junit.swingui.TestRunner" classpath="${build.lib}${name}.jar:${libs}"
fork="yes">
    <arg value="com.wiley.tomcatbook.PostDeployTests"/>
  </java>
</target>
```

Listing 19.9 The postdeployment test targets.

We make our testdeploy and testdeploygui tasks depend on the deploy task, so that the modified code will be deployed to our local server before the test is run.

Then we can run our test and verify that the integrated product in fact produces the expected results. Further, when we do introduce a bug, we find out about it in a timely way so that we can fix it before our customer, manager, or client is exposed to it.

For more information on using JUnit, HttpUnit, Ant, and other tools, please see the book *Java Tools for Extreme Programming* by Richard Hightower and Nicholas Lesiecki.

Refactoring

Now that we have a testing framework in place, it is much easier to refactor the code. Refactoring specifically is the process of factoring code out into separate method calls when that code exists in multiple locations in your code base. More generally, it is used to refer to the process of streamlining your code, making it more readable, and breaking complex methods down into simpler methods that are easier to read and maintain.

Refactoring in practice means taking working code and improving the way it is written without changing its functionality. Without testing, this can be a little dangerous. It may not be obvious what the side effects of a given piece of code are, and when you refactor a mysterious block of code, it may appear to work in one case but actually break something else. Typically, this kind of breakage is the result of poor design in the first place; correcting the flaws is part of the purpose of the exercise.

Automated testing, coupled with revision control, allows us to refactor with relative impunity; if we break anything, our tests will let us know, and if we break anything so badly we can't fix it with better code, we can always roll back to the last version that actually worked.

Refactoring has turned into something of a fad at the moment. The downside of this is that people sometimes think that refactoring can cure any shortcoming. The upside is that, to the extent this is true, it is more often being done. A further win for the developer is that a wide range of refactoring tools are now starting to come onto the market and are being included in a wide range of development tools: some free; some not. These refactoring tools do save quite a bit of time in finding and updating references to modified code, and just in generating the basic code blocks for the new methods. Regardless of how good the tools get, however, it is nice to be able to test what was generated and verify that it still works to spec.

Staged Release Environment

Finding out you have a bug right *after* deploying it to your live server is far from ideal. As a result, any even vaguely serious development environment should have a separate development server, and probably one or more separate staging servers for quality assurance purposes. Moving code from the development server to the QA server can be handled from within Ant by writing an additional task, or it can be managed through other means. Whatever works best for your development process is the right thing to do. Of course, testing should take place (both unit testing and integration testing) before you ever release your code to QA.

Setting Up Your Development and Testing Instances

It is important that your development environment, your QA environment, and your live environment all match. Having your application break because of environment differences between these release stages defeats the purposes of having a rigorous testing process. Here are some key things to make sure of when setting up your development, staging, and QA servers:

1. Use the same version of the servlet engine across all environments.
2. Use the same operating system and version across all environments.
3. Use the same versions of any database servers and middleware your application requires across all environments.
4. Try to use matching hardware across environments. There are whole classes of problems that may surface only if you're running on a multiprocessor box, for instance, so if you're running on an 8-processor Sun box at deployment time, try to at least have a 2-processor box in QA. If you can afford another 8-way box for QA, that will help too, and will make it less likely that you will miss race conditions in your software before it goes live.
5. Try to work on similar-sized datasets across environments. If your dataset is very large, this may be prohibitively expensive, but do try to have a database server with a substantial number of records pulled from your live database, so that you can reasonably simulate operational load factors related to dataset size, and so problems that may arise based on peculiarities of your dataset will be more likely to come to light before you launch your application.
6. Load test your applications. We'll talk a bit about how to do that next, but the fact is, a lot of code that seems to work fine when connected to a single client, sending requests one at a time, will fail in a production environment due to thread-safety issues, resource contention, or a variety of other reasons. By load testing, you reduce the likelihood of this class of bug slipping through into production code.
7. Have a rollback procedure. Even with the most rigorous testing, sometimes a bug slips through. Being able to roll back to the last known good build will take a lot of the time pressure off while you're trying to resolve what exactly went wrong.

User Testing

User testing is also an important part of developing solid applications. Do you really know how your users interact with your application? What things do they find intuitive, and what things do they find confusing? Are they always getting stuck in the same place? Are there things you could do to make their experience using your application smoother, more efficient, and more satisfactory? Details of how to approach user testing are beyond the scope of this book, and responsibility for user testing may fall outside your development team, but do consider requirements of user testing when developing your deployment workflow.

Load Testing and Profiling

As we mentioned a couple of paragraphs ago, load testing is an important part of servlet development. Because of the nature of servlets and the networked architecture on which they are based, servlets typically have to handle multiple concurrent requests, and do so without those requests polluting each other. This concurrency affects performance, but it is the data integrity that is in most cases of primary concern. The more sensitive the data involved, the more important the testing of data integrity under load becomes.

There are a number of ways to go about load testing, from simply writing a few scripts to place load on your server (for instance, by calling wget or curl—two command-line utilities that grab content from servers—over and over in a tight loop and measuring performance), to running some of the more lightweight load testers like JMeter (also part of the Apache project), to using commercial load testing products such as LoadRunner (from Mercury Interactive).

Of course, you can only simulate load patterns that your live application will experience. There is a qualitative difference between running thousands of sessions from a machine one hop away on your network and running thousands of sessions, each to a different endpoint, with different network latency, different performance characteristics, and different clients attached. That said, however, load testing, even from a machine one hop away, can provide a wealth of information and expose failure modes that you may not have anticipated.

In all cases, the basic scenario is as follows:

1. Determine the load requirements for your application. How many concurrent users must your application support? Plan for growth. Determine your criteria for success or failure before you start testing. Otherwise, there is a tendency for your criteria to converge on your results, and not vice versa.
2. Set up your load tester on a separate machine. It is important to test how the whole IP stack functions, and testing from another machine also prevents the load generated by the processes initiating the connections from degrading the performance of the servlet you are testing.
3. Run your load test. Monitor memory usage, CPU usage, network traffic, and usage of other key resources on the server, and on any other server or middleware component your application depends on.
4. While the application is operating under load (but not while you are measuring performance), try using the application yourself from a Web browser to see if the application is performing adequately from a qualitative perspective. Just because your application is capable of handling a million simultaneous connections, and 10 billion transactions per minute, that doesn't mean the application is usable under load. If each of those transactions takes 20 minutes to complete, it is unlikely real-life users will stick around to see those results.

Profiling Your Code

A number of profiling tools are available to tell you where your code is eating up most of its CPU time. Concentrate on optimizing these sections first. Don't pre-optimize. Usually, the actual bottlenecks won't be where you think they are. Using a profiling tool can tell you where your real performance issues lie.

You can get started with javap, the profiler that comes as part of the JDK, but it is hard to use and the output is difficult to read. A few excellent commercial products are on the market that let you profile your code. JProbe from Sitraka, and OptimizeIt, recently acquired by Borland, are the two leaders. Sitraka also has a new product designed to help you profile servlets and more complex J2EE applications, called PerformaSure. Consider using these products to improve the performance of your code.

Summary

In this chapter, we provided some common-sense techniques to improve your development process. If you're new to servlet programming, build systems, or automated testing, we hope that this chapter has whetted your appetite to know more about these systems.

CHAPTER

20

Developing Web Applications with Ant and XDoclet

Another Neat Tool (Ant) enables you to automate the build deploy process of your server-side Java Web components, such as custom tags, servlets, and JSPs. In this chapter, we show you how to write Ant build files, and explain how to automate the build and deploy process for your Web component development.

Ant's easy-to-use XML-based syntax overcomes many of the issues with make. Unlike using shell scripts and batch files to create build scripts, Ant works cross-platform and is geared toward Java build files. Ant gets its cross-platform support by relying on Java for file access, compilation, and other tasks.

Ant is extensible through its support for scripting (JPython and NetRexx, among others); Java custom tasks; and the ability to call OS commands, executables, and shell scripts via an Ant exec task (normally a last-resort measure). Ant makes continuous integration possible for server-side components with its automated build script and integration with JUnit, a unit-testing framework for Java.

Developing in the J2EE environment can be tricky, with its multitude of deployment descriptors and configuration files. In addition, these files often need to be configured and reconfigured for each deployment environment, and for each application the components will be deployed in and for each phase in the development process. After all, the advantage of using components is that they can be reused by many applications—and you are not going to deploy your application and components without going through the full development cycle. You may want to deploy to different servers; say you need to deploy to your development server (maybe a local Windows box), then your integration server (Solaris or Linux), then to the QA server—and with some good fortune, one day to your production server. Now, each of these application server instances will likely use different instances of your datastore (MySQL, SQL Server, Oracle, etc.). Then add the fact that you may be trying to deploy your components to different application servers, and your build process can quickly become too complex not to automate.

Ant comes to the rescue, allowing you to automate your build and deploy process. Ant lets you manage the complexities of component development and make continuous integration with J2EE development possible.

NOTE **Ant was developed by the Apache Software Foundation as part of its Jakarta project. Ant 1.5 is distributed with the Apache Software License version 1.1, and you can download it at http://jakarta.apache.org/ant/index.html.**

This chapter starts out with a quick tour of Ant. Then, for those who are already familiar enough with Ant, we cover the XDoclet Ant tasks for generating deployment descriptors and taglib descriptor files. For those of you who want an easier time of it, we present a step-by-step tutorial to using Ant with a limited set of Ant built-in tasks.

Setting Up Your Environment to Run Ant

If you are running Unix, install Ant in ~/tools/ant; if you are running Windows, install Ant in c:\tools\ant. You can set up the environment variables in Windows by using Control Panel. However, for your convenience, we created a Unix shell script (setenv.sh) and a Windows batch file (setenv.bat) that will set up the required environment variables for you.

Your Unix setenv.sh file should look something like this:

```
#
# Setup build environment variables using Bourne shell
#
export USR_ROOT=~
export JAVA_HOME=${USR_ROOT}/jdk1.4
export ANT_HOME=${USR_ROOT}/tools/ant
export PATH=${PATH}:${ANT_HOME}/bin
```

Your Windows setenv.bat file should look something like this:

```
:
: Setup build environment variables using DOS Batch
:
set USR_ROOT=c:
set JAVA_HOME=%USR_ROOT%\jdk1.4set
CLASSPATH=%USR_ROOT%\jdk1.4\lib\tools.jar;%CLASSPATH%
set ANT_HOME=%USR_ROOT%\tools\Ant
PATH=%PATH%;%ANT_HOME%\bin
```

Both of these setup files begin by setting JAVA_HOME to specify the location where you installed the JDK. This setting should reflect your local development environment—make adjustments accordingly. Then, the files set up the environment variable ANT_HOME, the location where you installed Ant.

NOTE **The examples in this chapter assume that you have installed Ant in c:\tools\ant on Windows and in ~/tools/ant on Unix.**

What Does an Ant Build File Look Like?

Ant, which is XML-based, looks a little like HTML. It has special tags called *tasks*, which give instructions to the Ant system. These instructions tell Ant how to manage files, compile files, jar files, create Web application archive files, and much more.

Listing 20.1 shows a simple Ant build file with two targets. Ant build scripts have a root element called project. The project element consists of subelements called *targets*. These elements in turn have *task* elements. Task elements do useful things, such as creating directories and compiling Java source into Java classes. All of the tasks for a given target are executed when the target is scheduled to execute. The project element has a default attribute, which specifies the target that should be executed for the project. In Listing 20.1, the compile target is the default. However, the compile target has a dependency specified by the depends attribute. The depends attribute can specify a comma-delimited list of dependencies for a target.

```
<project name="hello" default="compile">

  <target name="prepare">
      <mkdir dir="/tmp/classes" />
  </target>

  <target name="compile" depends="prepare">
      <javac srcdir="./src" destdir="/tmp/classes" />
  </target>


</project>
```

Listing 20.1 A simple Ant build file.

In Listing 20.1, the compile target depends on the prepare target; thus, the prepare target is executed before the compile target. The prepare target uses the mkdir task to create the directory /tmp/prepare. Then, the compile target executes the javac task to build the Java source files contained in the ./src directory.

Properties, File Sets, and Paths

Ant supports properties, file sets, and paths. Properties are to Ant build scripts as environment variables are to shell scripts and batch files. Properties allow you to define string constants that can be reused. The general rule is that if you use a string literal more than twice, you should probably create a property for it. Later, when you need to modify the string constant, if you've defined it as a property you have to change it only once. In Listing 20.2 we've defined two properties: lib and outputdir.

```
<property name="lib" value="../lib"/>
<property name="outputdir" value="/tmp"/>
...
 <path id="myclasspath">
   <pathelement path=".;${lib}/log4j.jar"/>
   <fileset dir="${lib}">
     <include name="**/*.jar"/>
   </fileset>
 </path>
...
  <javac srcdir="./src" destdir="${outputdir}/classes" >
       <classpath refid="myclasspath"/>
  </javac>
```

Listing 20.2 Defining the properties lib and outputdir.

A property is defined as follows:

```
<property name="lib" value="../lib"/>
```

A property can be used inside another string literal, as shown here:

```
<fileset dir="${lib}">
```

A file set is used to define a set of files. It allows you to group files based on patterns using one or more include subelements, as shown in Listing 20.2. A file set is defined as follows:

```
<fileset dir="${lib}">
   <include name="**/*.jar"/>
 </fileset>
```

A path allows you to define such things as classpaths (for compiling Java source and other tasks that need classpaths). A path consists of pathelements, which is a semicolon-delimited list of subdirectories or JAR files and file sets. Listing 20.2 uses the file set to add all the JAR files in the lib directory to the classpath defined with the ID myclasspath. Later in Listing 20.2, myclasspath is used by the javac task.

A path is defined as follows:

```
<path id="myclasspath">
   <pathelement path=".;${lib}/log4j.jar"/>
   <fileset dir="${lib}">
      <include name="**/*.jar"/>
    </fileset>
</path>
```

A path can be used by a task using the classpath subelement:

```
<javac srcdir="./src" destdir="${outputdir}/classes" >
      <classpath refid="myclasspath"/>
</javac>
```

Using Properties

Look at the number of environment variables being used in Listing 20.3: jdbc.jar, jdbc.driver, jdbc.userid, jdbc.password, jdbc.url, jdbc.jar, and build.sql. Defining properties can quickly become tedious; and often properties vary quite a bit from development environments to integration, QA, and production environments--so it makes sense to define properties in another file.

```
<project name="EJBQL" default="compile" >

  <property environment="env"/>

  <property file="build.properties" />

  <target name="createtables">
        <sql driver="${jdbc.driver}" url="${jdbc.url}"
            userid="${jdbc.userid}" password="${jdbc.password}"
            src="${build.sql}" print="yes">
              <classpath>
                  <pathelement location="${jdbc.jar}"/>
              </classpath>
        </sql>
  </target>
...
```

Listing 20.3 The Zen of property usage.

To import a whole file of properties, you use the property element:

```
<property file="build.properties" />
```

Listing 20.3 defines the target createTables to create database tables using the sql task. Simply by changing the current build.properties file (shown in Listing 20.4) to the one shown in Listing 20.5, we can make the build script build database tables for MySQL instead of PointBase.

```
jdbc.driver=com.pointbase.jdbc.jdbcUniversalDriver
jdbc.userid=petstore
jdbc.password=petstore
jdbc.url=jdbc:pointbase:server://localhost/demo
jdbc.jar=${wlhome}/samples/server/eval/pb/lib/pbclient.jar
build.sql=build.sql
```

Listing 20.4 The PointBase build.properties.

```
jdbc.userid=trivera
jdbc.password=trivera7
jdbc.driver=org.gjt.mm.mysql.Driver
jdbc.url=jdbc:mysql://localhost/trivera
jdbc.jar=c:/mysql/mysql.jar
build.sql=mybuild.sql
```

Listing 20.5 The MySQL build.properties.

In addition, you can import environment variables as properties to make minor tweaks from one environment to another. To import environment variables from your OS as properties prepended with *env.*, you'd use the property element:

```
<property environment="env"/>
```

The environment variables can be used in a property file to define other properties:

```
src=${env.WS}/src
classes=${env.WS}/classes
jardir=${env.WS}/jars
```

This becomes useful if some members of your team use Linux while others use Windows. It appears Linux users are a bit picky about putting directories off the root directory—go figure. Windows users are generally not as picky. Specify the root for the application workspace with an environment variable, and you can keep both developers happy.

Conditional Targets

Targets can be conditionally executed, depending on whether you set a property. For example, to optionally execute a target if the production property is set, you define a target as follows:

```
<target name="setupProduction" if="production">
    <property name="lib" value="/usr/home/production/lib"/>
    <property name="outputdir" value="/usr/home/production/classes"/>
</target>
```

To define a target that executes only if the production target is not set, use this:

```
<target name="setupDevelopment" unless="production">
      <property name="lib" value="c:/hello/lib"/>
      <property name="outputdir" value="c:/hello/classes"/>
  </target>
```

Conditional execution of targets is another way to support multiple deployment environments.

Using Filters

You can use filters to replace tokens in a configuration file with their proper values for the deployment environment (see Listing 20.6). Filters are another way to support multiple deployment environments. Let's look at a case where you have both a production database and a development database. When deploying, you want the production value (jdbc_url in Listing 20.6) to refer to the correct database.

```
<project name="hello" default="run">
  <target name="setupProduction" if="production">
      <filter token="jdbc_url" value="jdbc:rdbms:production"/>
  </target>

 <target name="setupDevelopment" unless="production">
      <filter token="jdbc_url" value="jdbc:rdbms:development"/>
  </target>

  <target name="setup" depends="setupProduction,setupDevelopment"/>

  <target name="run" depends="setup">
      <copy todir="/usr/home/production/properties" filtering="true">
          <fileset dir="/cvs/src/properties"/>
      </copy>
  </target>
</project>
```

Listing 20.6 An example that uses filters.

The setupProduction and setupDevelopment targets are executed conditionally based on the production property, then they set the filter to the proper JDBC driver:

```
<target name="setupProduction" if="production">

      <filter token="jdbc_url" value="jdbc::production"/>

</target>

<target name="setupDevelopment" unless="production">

      <filter token="jdbc_url" value="jdbc::development"/>

</target>
```

In our example, the filter in the setupProduction target sets jdbc_url to jdbc::production, while the filter in the setupDevelopment target sets jdbc_url to jdbc::development.

Later, when the script uses a copy task with filtering on, it applies the filter to all files in the file set specified by the copy. The copy task with filtering on replaces all occurrences of the string @jdbc_url@ with jdbc::production if the production property is set, but to jdbc::development if the production property is not set.

Creating a Master Build File

Applications can include many components that can be reused by other applications. In addition, components can be written to target more than one application server. An application may consist of a large project that depends on many smaller projects, and these smaller projects also build components. Because Ant allows one Ant build file to call another, you may have an Ant file that calls a hierarchy of other Ant build files. Listing 20.7 shows a sample build script that calls other build scripts. The application project can direct the building of all its components by passing subbuild files certain properties to customize the build for the current application.

```
<project name="main" default="build" >
...
 <target name="build" depends="prepare"
        description="build the model and application modules.">

     <ant dir="./model" target="package">
          <property name="outdir" value="/tmp/app" />
          <property name="setProps" value="true" />
     </ant>

     <ant dir="./application" target="package">
          <property name="outdir" value="/tmp/app" />
          <property name="setProps" value="true" />
     </ant>
     ...
  </target>
</project>
```

Listing 20.7 A build script that calls other build scripts.

The ant task runs a specified build file. You have the option of specifying the build file name or just the directory. (The application uses the file build.xml in the directory specified by the dir attribute.) You can also specify a target that you want to execute. If you do not specify a target, the application uses the default target. Any properties that you set in the called project are available to the nested build file.

Here are some examples. First, to call a build file from the current build file and pass a property:

```
<ant antfile="./hello/build.xml">
    <property name="production" value="true"/>
</ant>
```

Next, to call a build file from the current build file (since an Ant file is not specified, it uses ./hello/build.xml):

```
<ant dir="./hello"/>
```

Finally, to call a build file from the current build file and specify the run target that you want to execute (if the run target is not the default target, it will be executed anyway):

```
<ant antfile="./hello/build.xml"  target="run"/>
```

Using the War Task to Create a WAR File

Ant defines a special task for building Web Archive (WAR) files. The *war task* defines two special file sets for classes and library JAR files: classes and lib, respectively. Any other file set would be added to the document root of the WAR file (see Chapter 6 for more information).

Listing 20.8 uses the war task with three file sets. The war task will put the files specified by the fileset into the document root. As you can see in Listing 20.8, one file set includes the helloapplet.jar file, and the other two file sets contain all the files in the HTML and JSP directories. All three file sets will end up in the docroot of the Web application archive.

The war task body also specifies where Tomcat should locate the classes using the file set called classes (<classes dir="${build}" />). Files in the classes directory will be added to the WAR file at the docroot/WEB-INF/classes. Similarly, the lib element specifies a file set that will be added to the WAR file's docroot/WEB-INF/lib directory.

```
<war warfile="${dist}/hello.war" webxml="${meta}/web.xml">
    <!--
        Include the html and jsp files.
        Put the classes from the build into the classes
directory of the war.
    /-->
    <fileset dir="./HTML" />
    <fileset dir="./JSP" />
    <!-- Include the applet. /-->
    <fileset dir="${lib}" includes="helloapplet.jar" />

    <classes dir="${build}" />

    <!-- Include all of the jar files except the ejbeans and
applet. The other build files that create jars have to be run in
        the correct order. This is covered later.
    /-->
    <lib dir="${lib}" >
        <exclude name="greet-ejbs.jar"/>
        <exclude name="helloapplet.jar"/>
    </lib>
</war>
```

Listing 20.8 Using the war task.

The war task is a convenient method of building WAR files, but it does not help you write the deployment descriptors. XDoclet does help you write the deployment descriptors--and so much more, as you'll see in the following section "Using XDoclet's webdoclet Task to Create Deployment Descriptors."

Using XDoclet's webdoclet Task to Create Deployment Descriptors

XDoclet extends the JavaDoc engine to allow the generation of code and other files based on custom JavaDoc tags. XDoclet ships with an Ant task that enables you to create example web.xml files, ejb-jar.xml files, and much more. In this section, we use XDoclet to generate a Web application deployment descriptor with the webdoclet Ant task. Note that XDoclet Ant tasks do not ship with the standard distribution.

NOTE **You can download XDoclet from SourceForge at http://sourceforge.net/projects/xdoclet.**

You will remember from Chapter 6 that the web.xml file is the deployment descriptor for the Web application. XDoclet allows you to generate the web.xml deployment descriptor using JavaDoc tags. We used the code in Listing 20.9 to generate the web.xml file in Listing 20.10.

```
/*
 * BasicServlet.java
 *
 */

package tomcatbook.servlet;

import javax.servlet.*;
import javax.servlet.http.*;
import javax.sql.*;
import java.sql.*;
import javax.naming.*;


/**
 *
 * @author  Rick Hightower
 *
 * @version 1.0
 * @web:servlet name="BasicServlet"
```

Listing 20.9 XDoclet tags in a servlet. (continues)

```
          display-name="Basic Servlet"
          load-on-startup="1"
 * @web:servlet-init-param name="hi" value="Ant is cool!"
 * @web:servlet-init-param name="bye" value="XDoc Rocks!"
 * @web:resource-ref description="JDBC resource"
 *              name="jdbc/mydb"
 *              type="javax.sql.DataSource"
 *              auth="Container"
 * @web:servlet-mapping url-pattern="/Basic/*"
 * @web:servlet-mapping url-pattern="*.Basic"
 * @web:servlet-mapping url-pattern="/BasicServlet"
 */
public class BasicServlet extends HttpServlet {

   /** Initializes the servlet.
    */
   public void init(ServletConfig config) throws ServletException {
      super.init(config);

   }

   /** Destroys the servlet.
    */
   public void destroy() {

   }

   /** Processes requests for both HTTP <code>GET</code> and
<code>POST</code> methods.
    * @param request servlet request
    * @param response servlet response
    */
   protected void processRequest(HttpServletRequest request,
HttpServletResponse response)
   throws ServletException, java.io.IOException {
      ServletConfig config = this.getServletConfig();
      String hi = config.getInitParameter("hi");
      String bye = config.getInitParameter("bye");

      try{
         response.setContentType("text/html");
         java.io.PrintWriter out = response.getWriter();
         out.println("<html>");
         out.println("<head>");
```

Listing 20.9 XDoclet tags in a servlet. (continues)

```
            out.println("<title>Basic Servlet</title>");
            out.println("</head>");
            out.println("<body>");
            out.println("<h1> bye:" + bye + "</h1>");
            out.println("<h1> hi:" + hi + "</h1>");
            getJdbcPool(out);
            out.println("</body>");
            out.println("</html>");
            out.close();
        }catch(Exception e){
            throw new ServletException(e);
        }
    }

    /** Handles the HTTP <code>GET</code> method.
     * @param request servlet request
     * @param response servlet response
     */
    protected void doGet(HttpServletRequest request,
HttpServletResponse response)
    throws ServletException, java.io.IOException {
        processRequest(request, response);
    }

    /** Handles the HTTP <code>POST</code> method.
     * @param request servlet request
     * @param response servlet response
     */
    protected void doPost(HttpServletRequest request,
HttpServletResponse response)
    throws ServletException, java.io.IOException {
        processRequest(request, response);
    }

    /** Returns a short description of the servlet.
     */
    public String getServletInfo() {
        return "XDoc Rules";
    }

    private void getJdbcPool(java.io.PrintWriter out)throws Exception{
        out.println("</ br>");

        Object obj = new InitialContext().
```

Listing 20.9 XDoclet tags in a servlet. (continues)

```
lookup("java:comp/env/jdbc/mydb");
        DataSource pool = (DataSource)obj;
        if (pool == null) return;
        Connection connection = pool.getConnection();

        out.println("<table>");
        try{

            ResultSet rs =
                connection.getMetaData().
getTables(null,null,null,null);
            while(rs.next()){
                out.println("<tr><td>");
                out.println(rs.getString("TABLE_NAME"));
            }
        }finally{
            connection.close();
        }
        out.println("</table>");



        out.println("</ br>");
    }

}
```

Listing 20.9 XDoclet tags in a servlet. (continued)

```
<?xml version="1.0" encoding="UTF-8"?>
<!DOCTYPE web-app PUBLIC "-//Sun Microsystems, Inc.//DTD Web
Application 2.3//EN" "http://java.sun.com/dtd/web-app_2_3.dtd">

<web-app>

...

   <servlet>
      <servlet-name>BasicServlet</servlet-name>
      <display-name>Basic Servlet</display-name>
     <servlet-class>tomcatbook.servlet.BasicServlet</servlet-class>

      <init-param>
```

Listing 20.10 The web.xml deployment descriptor generated with XDoclet. (continues)

```
      <param-name>hi</param-name>
      <param-value>Ant is cool!</param-value>
    </init-param>
    <init-param>
      <param-name>bye</param-name>
      <param-value>XDoc Rocks!</param-value>
    </init-param>

    <load-on-startup>1</load-on-startup>

  </servlet>

  <servlet-mapping>
    <servlet-name>BasicServlet</servlet-name>
    <url-pattern>/Basic/*</url-pattern>
  </servlet-mapping>
  <servlet-mapping>
    <servlet-name>BasicServlet</servlet-name>
    <url-pattern>*.Basic</url-pattern>
  </servlet-mapping>
  <servlet-mapping>
    <servlet-name>BasicServlet</servlet-name>
    <url-pattern>/BasicServlet</url-pattern>
  </servlet-mapping>

...

  <resource-ref>
    <description>JDBC resource</description>
    <res-ref-name>jdbc/mydb</res-ref-name>
    <res-type>javax.sql.DataSource</res-type>
    <res-auth>Container</res-auth>
  </resource-ref>

...

</web-app>
```

Listing 20.10 The web.xml deployment descriptor generated with XDoclet. (continued)

XDoclet may seem intimidating, but the mappings are quite natural. For example, let's look at generating the resource reference in the web.xml for the JDBC connection pool. The Java file includes these JavaDoc style tags:

```
...
 * @web:resource-ref description="JDBC resource"
```

```
 *                    name="jdbc/mydb"
 *                    type="javax.sql.DataSource"
 *                    auth="Container"
...
```

which generate the following elements in the web.xml file:

```
...

   <resource-ref>
      <description>JDBC resource</description>
      <res-ref-name>jdbc/mydb</res-ref-name>
      <res-type>javax.sql.DataSource</res-type>
      <res-auth>Container</res-auth>
   </resource-ref>

...
```

Our code assumes that you have set up the resource in the server.xml file of Tomcat (see Chapter 7, "The server.xml File in Depth," and Appendix A, "Server Configuration (server.xml) Reference," for more detail).

The first step in using webdoclet is defining the servlet element:

```
* @web:servlet name="BasicServlet"
                display-name="Basic Servlet"
                load-on-startup="1"
```

This code generates the following servlet element and subelements in the server.xml file:

```
   <servlet>
      <servlet-name>BasicServlet</servlet-name>
      <display-name>Basic Servlet</display-name>
     <servlet-class>tomcatbook.servlet.BasicServlet</servlet-class>

...

      <load-on-startup>1</load-on-startup>

   </servlet>
```

You may wonder how the servlet class was determined. Since the XDoclet task relies on the JavaDoc API, it can get the full classname of the servlet from the JavaDoc API.

After the servlet is defined using the Servlet element, then you can define mappings and init parameters.

Init parameters are defined in JavaDocs comments like this:

```
 * @web:servlet-init-param name="hi" value="Ant is cool!"
 * @web:servlet-init-param name="bye" value="XDoc Rocks!"
```

These parameters will generate the following init params in the deployment descriptor:

```
   <servlet>
      <servlet-name>BasicServlet</servlet-name>
...
```

```
        <init-param>
           <param-name>hi</param-name>
           <param-value>Ant is cool!</param-value>
        </init-param>
        <init-param>
           <param-name>bye</param-name>
           <param-value>XDoc Rocks!</param-value>
        </init-param>
...

   </servlet>
```

The servlet mappings are also defined with the JavaDoc tags:

```
 * @web:servlet-mapping url-pattern="/Basic/*"
 * @web:servlet-mapping url-pattern="*.Basic"
 * @web:servlet-mapping url-pattern="/BasicServlet"
```

These would generate the following entries in the web.xml file:

```
   <servlet-mapping>
      <servlet-name>BasicServlet</servlet-name>
      <url-pattern>/Basic/*</url-pattern>
   </servlet-mapping>
   <servlet-mapping>
      <servlet-name>BasicServlet</servlet-name>
      <url-pattern>*.Basic</url-pattern>
   </servlet-mapping>
   <servlet-mapping>
      <servlet-name>BasicServlet</servlet-name>
      <url-pattern>/BasicServlet</url-pattern>
   </servlet-mapping>
```

Three short lines of code versus 12 lines of XML elements and subelements. XML was meant to be parsed and human-readable, not written by humans. This is all fine and dandy, but how do you take the Java source files and generate the web.xml file? For this, we need to write an Ant script that uses the webdoclet task from XDoclet, as shown in Listing 20.11. Listing 20.12 shows the build.properties file for our Ant build script.

```
<?xml version="1.0"?>

<project name="tomcatbookWebdoclet"  default="deploy">

   <property file="build.properties"/>

   <path id="cpath">
      <fileset dir="${lib}"/>
   </path>

   <target name="init">
```

Listing 20.11 An Ant script showing XDoclet's webdoclet task. (continues)

```
        <mkdir dir="${output}/war" />
        <mkdir dir="${dest}" />
    </target>

    <target name="clean">
        <delete dir="${output}/war" />

        <delete>
            <fileset dir="${dest}">
                <exclude name="**/*.java" />
            </fileset>
        </delete>

        <delete dir="${webapps}/myapp" />
        <delete dir="${webapps}/myapp.war" />

    </target>

    <target name="compile" depends="init">
        <javac srcdir="${src}" destdir="${dest}" debug="true"
deprecation="true">
            <classpath refid="cpath"/>
        </javac>
    </target>

    <target name="generateDD">
      <taskdef name="webdoclet"
             classname="xdoclet.web.WebDocletTask"
classpath="${xdocpath}"
      />
      <echo message="${xdocpath}" />

      <webdoclet
        sourcepath="${src}"
        destdir="${dest}">

        <fileset dir="${src}">
          <include name="**/*Servlet.java" />
        </fileset>

        <deploymentdescriptor servletspec="2.3"
destdir="${WEBINF}" />


      </webdoclet>
```

Listing 20.11 An Ant script showing XDoclet's webdoclet task. (continues)

```
    </target>

    <target name="package" depends="init,compile,generateDD">

        <war destfile="${output}/war/myapp.war"
webxml="${WEBINF}/web.xml">

            <fileset dir="${docroot}">
                <exclude name="**/build.xml" />
                <exclude name="**/*.bat" />
                <exclude name="**/build.properties" />
                <exclude name="**/web.xml" />
                <exclude name="**/*.nbattrs" />
                <exclude name="**/*.java"/>
                <exclude name="**/*.class"/>
            </fileset>


            <lib dir="${WEBINF}/lib">
                <exclude name="jdbc1.jar"/>
            </lib>

            <classes dir="${WEBINF}/classes">
                <exclude name="**/*.java"/>
                <exclude name="**/*.nbattrs" />
            </classes>
        </war>

    </target>

    <target name="deploy" depends="package">
        <copy file="${output}/war/myapp.war" todir="${webapps}" />
    </target>


</project>
```

Listing 20.11 An Ant script showing XDoclet's webdoclet task. (continued)

```
src=WEB-INF/classes
dest=WEB-INF/classes
lib=/tomcat4/common/lib
antpath=/ant/lib
```

Listing 20.12 The build.properties file for our Ant build script. (continues)

```
xdocpath=${antpath}/xdoclet.jar;${antpath}/log4j.jar;${antpath}/
  ant.jar
WEBINF=WEB-INF
docroot=.
output=/tmp
webapps=/tomcat4/webapps
```

Listing 20.12 The build.properties file for our Ant build script. (continued)

To generate the web.xml file from the Java source, you need to use XDoclet's webdoclet task, as shown in Listing 20.11 under the target generateDD. The input files for the webdoclet task are specified with a sub-file set, and the deploymentdescriptor subtask must specify the location for the generated deployment descriptor, as shown here:

```
        <webdoclet
            sourcepath="${src}"
            destdir="${dest}">

            <fileset dir="${src}">
                <include name="**/*Servlet.java" />
            </fileset>

            <deploymentdescriptor servletspec="2.3"
destdir="${WEBINF}" />


        </webdoclet>
```

As with any custom Ant task, we must declare the task before it can be used:

```
        <taskdef name="webdoclet"
                classname="xdoclet.web.WebDocletTask"
classpath="${xdocpath}"
        />
```

Note that the ${xdocpath} property specifies the JAR files needed to run the XDoclet task. In this case, we copied all of the XDoclet JAR files to our Ant's lib directory. The ${xdocpath} property and many others are defined in the build.properties file for the Ant bulid script. Having a build.properties file for your build script cuts down on the signal-to-noise ratio in your Ant build script, and it makes your build scripts more flexible.

I know what you're thinking: We just hard-coded the servlet init parameters in the source file. This does not seem very sane, I agree. A better way is to set the init parameters to point to a token, as in @bye@ and @hi@, and then later use the technique in filters to pass the right value for the right application. Let's look at an example.

Init parameters are defined in JavaDocs comments as:

```
 * @web:servlet-init-param name="hi" value="@hi@"
 * @web:servlet-init-param name="bye" value="@bye@"
```

This code will generate the following init params in the deployment descriptor:

```
    <servlet>
        <servlet-name>BasicServlet</servlet-name>
```

```
...

      <init-param>
         <param-name>hi</param-name>
         <param-value>@hi@</param-value>
      </init-param>
      <init-param>
         <param-name>bye</param-name>
         <param-value>@bye@</param-value>
      </init-param>
...

   </servlet>
```

Then, you will simply copy the web.xml file with filtering on (after the tokens are set).

Keep in mind that we have not covered everything there is to know about XDoclet and servlets. For more information, please refer to the XDoclet documentation at http://sourceforge.net.

Running Ant for the First Time

To run the sample Ant build file, go to the directory that contains the project files. To run Ant, navigate to the examples/chap20/webdoclet directory and type:

```
ant deploy
```

As we stated earlier, Ant will find build.xml, which is the default name for the build file. (You may have to adjust your build.properties files.) For our example, here is the command-line output you should expect:

```
C:\tomcatbook\chap20\webdoclet>ant deploy
Buildfile: build.xml

init:
    [mkdir] Created dir: C:\tmp\war

compile:
    [javac] Compiling 2 source files to C:\tomcatbook\webdoclet\WEB-
INF\classes

generateDD:
     [echo] /ant/lib/xdoclet.jar;/ant/lib/log4j.jar;/ant/lib/ant.jar
[webdoclet] Generating Javadoc
[webdoclet] Javadoc execution
[webdoclet] Loading source file C:\tomcatbook\webdoclet\WEB-
INF\classes\tomcatbo
ok\customtag\BasicTag.java...
[webdoclet] Loading source file C:\tomcatbook\webdoclet\WEB-
INF\classes\tomcatbo
ok\servlet\BasicServlet.java...
[webdoclet] Constructing Javadoc information...
[webdoclet] Running <deploymentDescriptor/>
```

```
[webdoclet] Running <jspTagLib/>

package:
      [war] Building war: C:\tmp\war\myapp.war

deploy:
     [copy] Copying 1 file to C:\tomcat4\webapps

BUILD SUCCESSFUL
Total time: 14 seconds
```

Notice that the targets and their associated tasks are displayed. That's it!

Using the XDoclet's webdoclet Task to Create Custom Tag TLDs

If you are not already familiar with creating JSP custom tags, then you might want to read Chapter 12 first. Creating custom tags may seem like a daunting task, but after you read this section, you will convert to using custom tags: they are easy, useful, and fun to make. Setting up and syncing the Java source and the tag library descriptor (TLD) file, however, is about as much fun as getting audited by the Internal Revenue Service. If only there was a way to have one file instead of two... XDoclet comes to the rescue. The XDoclet webdoclet task does for custom tags what it does for servlets. You could easily argue that custom tags, with all of its attributes and variables, needs XDoclet support more than servlets do.

The TLD file is the deployment descriptor for a custom tag library. XDoclet allows you to generate TLD files using JavaDoc tags. We used the code in Listing 20.13 to generate the taglib.tld file in Listing 20.14.

```
package tomcatbook.customtag;

import javax.servlet.jsp.tagext.TagSupport;
import javax.servlet.jsp.*;


/**
 * Basic JSP tag.
 *
 *
 * @author    Rick Hightower
 * @created   July 29, 2002
 * @version   1.0
 *
 * @jsp:tag name="BasicTag"
```

Listing 20.13 XDoclet tags in a custom tag source. (continues)

```
 *
 * @jsp:variable name-given="currentIter"
 *             class="java.lang.Integer" scope="NESTED"
 * @jsp:variable name-given="atBegin"
 *             class="java.lang.Integer" scope="AT_BEGIN"
 * @jsp:variable name-given="atEnd"
 *             class="java.lang.Integer" scope="AT_END"
 */
public class BasicTag extends TagSupport {


    /** Holds value of property includePage. */
    private boolean includePage;

    /** Holds value of property includeBody. */
    private boolean includeBody;

    /** Holds value of property iterate. */
    private int iterate;

    public int doStartTag() {
        pageContext.setAttribute("currentIter", new Integer(0));
        pageContext.setAttribute("atBegin", new Integer(0));
        return this.includeBody ? EVAL_BODY_INCLUDE : SKIP_BODY;
    }

    public int doEndTag() {
        pageContext.setAttribute("atEnd", new Integer(iterate));
        return this.includePage ? EVAL_PAGE : SKIP_PAGE;
    }

    public int doAfterBody () {
        this.iterate -= 1;
        pageContext.setAttribute("currentIter", new Integer(iterate));
        if (iterate <= 0) return SKIP_BODY;
        else return EVAL_BODY_AGAIN;
    }

    /** Getter for property includePage.
     * @return Value of property includePage.
     * @jsp:attribute   required="true"
     *                  rtexprvalue="true"
     *                  description="The includePage attribute"
     */
    public boolean isIncludePage() {
        return this.includePage;
```

Listing 20.13 XDoclet tags in a custom tag source. (continues)

```
    }

    /** Setter for property includePage.
     * @param includePage New value of property includePage.
     *
     */
    public void setIncludePage(boolean includePage) {
       this.includePage = includePage;
    }

    /** Getter for property includeBody.
     * @return Value of property includeBody.
     * @jsp:attribute   required="true"
     *                  rtexprvalue="true"
     *                  description="The includeBody attribute"
     */
    public boolean isIncludeBody() {
       return this.includeBody;
    }

    /** Setter for property includeBody.
     * @param includeBody New value of property includeBody.
     */
    public void setIncludeBody(boolean includeBody) {
       this.includeBody = includeBody;
    }

    /** Getter for property iterate.
     * @return Value of property iterate.
     * @jsp:attribute   required="true"
     *                  rtexprvalue="true"
     *                  description="The iterate attribute"
     */
    public int getIterate() {
       return this.iterate;
    }

    /** Setter for property iterate.
     * @param iterate New value of property iterate.
     */
    public void setIterate(int iterate) {
       this.iterate = iterate;
    }

}
```

Listing 20.13 XDoclet tags in a custom tag source. (continued)

```
<?xml version="1.0" encoding="UTF-8"?><!DOCTYPE taglib PUBLIC "-//Sun Microsystems,
Inc.//DTD JSP Tag Library 1.2//EN" "http://java.sun.com/dtd/web-jsptaglibrary_1_2.dtd">
<taglib>
   <tlib-version>1.0</tlib-version>
   <jsp-version>1.2</jsp-version>
   <short-name>basic</short-name>

   <tag>
      <name>BasicTag</name>
      <tag-class>tomcatbook.customtag.BasicTag</tag-class>
      <variable>
            <name-given>currentIter</name-given>
            <variable-class>java.lang.Integer</variable-class>
            <scope>NESTED</scope>
      </variable>
      <variable>
            <name-given>atBegin</name-given>
            <variable-class>java.lang.Integer</variable-class>
            <scope>AT_BEGIN</scope>
      </variable>
      <variable>
            <name-given>atEnd</name-given>
            <variable-class>java.lang.Integer</variable-class>
            <scope>AT_END</scope>
      </variable>
      <attribute>
            <name>iterate</name>
            <required>true</required>
            <rtexprvalue>true</rtexprvalue>
            <description>The iterate attribute</description>
      </attribute>
      <attribute>
            <name>includeBody</name>
            <required>true</required>
            <rtexprvalue>true</rtexprvalue>
            <description>The includeBody attribute</description>
      </attribute>
      <attribute>
            <name>includePage</name>
            <required>true</required>
            <rtexprvalue>true</rtexprvalue>
            <description>The includePage attribute</description>
      </attribute>
   </tag>
</taglib>
```

Listing 20.14 The taglib.tld file generated with XDoclet's webdoclet task.

Listing 20.13 does not appear as intimidating as our previous example. Just like before, the mappings are quite natural. The first step is to define the jsp tag using the @jsp:tag and passing the name of the custom tag as follows:

```
* @jsp:tag name="BasicTag"
```

This code generates the following in the TLD file:

```
    <tag>
        <name>BasicTag</name>
        <tag-class>tomcatbook.customtag.BasicTag</tag-class>
...
    </tag>
```

Remember that XDoclet uses the JavaDoc API to get the full classname of the custom tag. Next, we define any variables that we want available to the JSP. For this example, we defined three variables. One of the variables can be used after the begin tag, one after the end tag only, and one only inside the body, as shown here:

```
* @jsp:variable name-given="currentIter"
 *               class="java.lang.Integer" scope="NESTED"
 * @jsp:variable name-given="atBegin"
 *               class="java.lang.Integer" scope="AT_BEGIN"
 * @jsp:variable name-given="atEnd"
 *               class="java.lang.Integer" scope="AT_END"
```

This code generates the following in the JSP page within the basic tag definition:

```
        <variable>
                <name-given>currentIter</name-given>
                <variable-class>java.lang.Integer</variable-class>
                <scope>NESTED</scope>
        </variable>
        <variable>
                <name-given>atBegin</name-given>
                <variable-class>java.lang.Integer</variable-class>
                <scope>AT_BEGIN</scope>
        </variable>
        <variable>
                <name-given>atEnd</name-given>
                <variable-class>java.lang.Integer</variable-class>
                <scope>AT_END</scope>
        </variable>
```

Now here is a little something different. In the servlet example, all of the special JavaDoc tags were at the *class* level. The custom tag example uses JavaDoc tags at the *method* level to define custom tag attributes for the three attributes in this example: includeBody, includePage, and iterate:

```
    /** Getter for property includePage.
     * @return Value of property includePage.
     * @jsp:attribute   required="true"
     *                  rtexprvalue="true"
     *                  description="The includePage attribute"
     */
    public boolean isIncludePage() {
```

```
        return this.includePage;
    }

...

    /** Getter for property includeBody.
     * @return Value of property includeBody.
     * @jsp:attribute   required="true"
     *                  rtexprvalue="true"
     *                  description="The includeBody attribute"
     */
    public boolean isIncludeBody() {
        return this.includeBody;
    }
...
    /** Getter for property iterate.
     * @return Value of property iterate.
     * @jsp:attribute   required="true"
     *                  rtexprvalue="true"
     *                  description="The iterate attribute"
     */
    public int getIterate() {
        return this.iterate;
    }
```

Note that the JavaDoc tag @jsp:attribute is used to define the property as an attribute. This code generates the following in the TLD file within the BasicTag definition:

```
<attribute>
        <name>iterate</name>
        <required>true</required>
        <rtexprvalue>true</rtexprvalue>
        <description>The iterate attribute</description>
</attribute>
<attribute>
        <name>includeBody</name>
        <required>true</required>
        <rtexprvalue>true</rtexprvalue>
        <description>The includeBody attribute</description>
</attribute>
<attribute>
        <name>includePage</name>
        <required>true</required>
        <rtexprvalue>true</rtexprvalue>
        <description>The includePage attribute</description>
</attribute>
```

Custom tags, with all of their variables and attributes, can be hard to manage and keep in sync. As you can see from the example, XDoclet can make short order of what would otherwise be chaos, and it allows you to define all of this needed metadata in one file instead of two. This makes doing custom tags a lot easier—maybe easy enough for you to start fitting them into your project. This is all well and good, but how do you take the Java source files and generate the TLD file? We need to write an Ant script that uses the webdoclet task from XDoclet. Listing 20.15 modifies the code shown in 20.11 to add support for custom tags under the target generateDD (notice the portions in bold). Just as before, the input files for the webdoclet task are specified with a sub-file set except, this time we added a new include directive to include our task (<include name="**/*Tag.java" />). The jsptaglib subtask generates the TLD file.

```
...
    <target name="generateDD">
      <taskdef name="webdoclet"
            classname="xdoclet.web.WebDocletTask"
classpath="${xdocpath}"
      />
      <echo message="${xdocpath}" />

      <webdoclet
        sourcepath="${src}"
        destdir="${dest}">

        <fileset dir="${src}">
          <include name="**/*Servlet.java" />
          <include name="**/*Tag.java" />
        </fileset>

        <deploymentdescriptor servletspec="2.3"
destdir="${WEBINF}" />

        <jsptaglib jspversion="1.2" destdir="${WEBINF}/tlds"
          shortname="basic" />

      </webdoclet>

    </target>
...
```

Listing 20.15 Changes to the generateDD task.

Granted, this tag is basic and does not do much—but it does work. There is a JSP file called happy.jsp in the docroot of this project. Once you run the Ant deploy target, you can edit the JSP file and try all the alternatives. Essentially, it will iterate the body as many times as you specify with the iterate attribute. The includeBody attribute flags specify whether or not the body should be included, and the includePage attribute specifies whether or not the rest of the JSP file should be evaluated. We tried many permutations and it works as advertised—see Listing 20.16 for more details.

```
<%@page contentType="text/html"%>
<%@taglib uri="/WEB-INF/tlds/taglib.tld" prefix="mytag"%>
<html>
<head><title>I am a happy JSP page</title></head>
<body>

<mytag:BasicTag includePage="true" includeBody="true" iterate="2">
   Current iteration is <%=currentIter%> <br />
</mytag:BasicTag>
<%
int i = 5;
i++;
%>
<h1>I am I and I am <%=i%>
</h1>

</body>
</html>
...
```

Listing 20.16 A JSP file that uses our new tag.

We have only scratched the surface of what you can do with XDoclet and Ant. These are powerful tools in your toolbox. They make Web development easier. Ant is powerful tool, and XDoclet is an example of how Ant can be extended to simplify Web development. We provided a quick tour of Ant. For some, this is enough; for others, a more detailed description is in order. The following sections take Ant at a slower, more deliberate pace.

Standard Targets

Steve Loughran wrote an Ant guide called *Ant in Anger* that is part of the Ant download. This guide explains many pitfalls, and recommends ways to use Ant. Two very useful suggestions are creating a list of names for targets and learning how to divide build files.

The following are some of Steve's recommended names for Ant top-level targets:

test—Runs the junit tests

clean—Cleans the output directories

deploy—Ships the JARs, WARs, and so on to the execution system

publish—Outputs the source and binaries to any distribution site

fetch—Gets the latest source from the Concurrent Versions System (CVS) tree

docs/javadocs—Outputs the documentation

all—Performs clean, fetch, build, test, docs, and deploy

main—Performs the default build process (usually build or build and test)

The following are some recommended names for Ant internal targets:

init—Initializes properties and performs other initialization tasks; read in per-user property files

init-debug—Initializes debug properties

init-release—Initializes release properties

compile—Performs the actual compilation

link/jar—Makes the JARs or equivalent files

ataging—Carries out any pre-deployment process in which the output is dropped off and then tested before being moved to the production site

We'll discuss some of the concepts from *Ant in Anger* in this chapter. We strongly suggest that you read *Ant in Anger* because it contains excellent guidelines for using Ant. The guide is included with the Ant binary distribution under the docs directory.

We'll now begin examining the techniques involved in using Ant to build and deploy Java applications. During the rest of this chapter, we build a "Hello World" example. Because the emphasis is on how to build components with Ant—and not the mechanics of implementing these various components—the example is meant to be as simple as possible. We package the application and the common JAR, construct a build file that creates an applet, and construct a master build file that coordinates the entire build.

The source code for the Hello World example is divided into several directories. Each directory has its own Ant build file, which contains instructions for compiling the components and packaging the binaries. Each directory also includes the requisite configuration files (such as manifest files). The master Ant build file, located in the root directory, calls the other build files and coordinates the entire build.

This divide-and-conquer technique for organizing components into separate directories is quite common with Ant. It may seem like overkill on a simple project like this one, but suppose you were building a system with 50 components. Each component has its own set of deployment descriptors and configuration files, and each component is deployed in different containers. The divide-and-conquer technique becomes necessary to manage the complexity—it also makes it easier to reuse components.

Here is the directory structure for the Hello World project:

```
Model 2 Hello World root
+---Model
+---Application
+---Applet
+---WebApplication
```

The Model directory holds the common code (in this simple project, only the application will access the common code). The Application directory holds the Java application code, including the manifest file that marks the deployment JAR as executable. The Applet directory holds the applet code. The WebApplication directory holds the Web application code.

The Hello World Model Project

This section explains the basic structure for all the build files and directories you use in this example. We introduce the three Java class files: a GreetingBean class, a GreetingFactory class, and a Greeting interface. Then, we discuss how to build these files with Ant and break down the Ant build files' target execution step by step. We also explain how to use the Ant command-line utility to build the files with Ant.

Overview of Model Classes

You use the GreetingFactory class to create a Greeting object. Here is the code for GreetingFactory:

```
package xptoolkit.model;

public class GreetingFactory {
    private GreetingFactory(){}

    public Greeting getGreeting()throws Exception {
     String clazz = System.getProperty("Greeting.class",
                              "xptoolkit.model.GreetingBean");
        return (Greeting)Class.forName(clazz).newInstance();
    }

    public static GreetingFactory getGreetingFactory(){
        return new GreetingFactory();
    }

}
```

Next, we have a Greeting interface that defines the *contract* of a Greeting object—that is, what type of behavior it supports. The Greeting interface looks like this:

```
package xptoolkit.model;

public interface Greeting extends java.io.Serializable{
    public String getGreeting();
}
```

Finally, the GreetingBean class implements the Greeting interface. GreetingBean is defined as follows:

```
package xptoolkit.model;

public class GreetingBean implements Greeting{

    public GreetingBean(){}

    public String getGreeting(){
      return "Hello World!";
    }
}
```

GreetingBean returns the message "Hello World!". To create a Greeting instance, you use GreetingFactory. The default implementation of GreetingFactory gets the implementation class from a property and instantiates an instance of that class with the Class.forName().newInstance() method. It casts the created instance to the Greeting interface.

These two lines of code create the Greeting instance from GreetingFactory's getGreeting() method:

```
String clazz = System.getProperty("Greeting.class",
                        "xptoolkit.model.GreetingBean");
return (Greeting)Class.forName(clazz).newInstance();
```

Thus, any class that implements the Greeting interface can substitute for the Greeting.class system property. Then, when the class is instantiated with the factory's getGreeting() method, the application uses the new implementation of the Greeting interface.

In the book *Java Tools for Extreme Programming* (also published by Wiley), we use this technique to transparently add support for EJBs to the Web application. In that book, we also create an Ant script that can deploy the same Web application to use either enterprise beans or another bean implementation just by setting an Ant property (and some Ant filter magic). We also map the Greeting interface with the use bean action of a JSP when we implement the Model 2 using servlets and JSP.

Creating a Project Directory Structure for Model

This part of the example application uses the smallest build file. Basically, we need to create a JAR file that acts as a common library. We don't need any special manifest file or deployment files. This is the most basic build file and directory structure you will see in this example. Here is the directory structure for the Model directory:

```
Root of Model
|    build.xml
|
+---src
    +---xptoolkit
        \---model
                GreetingFactory.java
                Greeting.java
                GreetingBean.java
```

Notice that there are only four files in the Model directory and subdirectories. Also notice that the name of the Ant file is build.xml. The build.xml file is the default build file; if Ant is run in this directory, it automatically finds build.xml without you having to specify it on the command line. Let's examine the model build file in greater detail.

Creating a Build File for a Shared Library

The model build file has six targets: init, clean, prepare, compile, package, and all. The build files in this example have similar targets:

init—Initializes all the other properties relative to the outputdir.

clean—Cleans up the output directories and the output JAR file.

prepare—Creates the output directories if they do not already exist.

compile—Compiles the Java source files for the model into the build directory defined in the init target.

package—Packages the compiled Java source into a JAR file.

all—Runs all the tags. It is the default target of this build project.

Analysis of the Model Project Build File

Listing 20.17 shows the entire build file for the model project. In this section, we provide a step-by-step analysis of how this build file executes. All the build files in the Hello World example are structured in a similar fashion, so understanding the model project build file is essential to understanding the others. A quick note on naming conventions: As you see from the first line of code in Listing 20.17, the project name for this build file is model. Therefore, we refer to this build file as the *model project build file*. This naming convention becomes essential once we begin dealing with the five other build files in this project.

```
<project name="model" default="all" >


  <property name="outdir" value="/tmp/app/" />

  <target name="init"
                description="initialize the properties.">
     <property name="local_outdir" value="${outdir}/model" />
     <property name="build" value="${local_outdir}/classes" />
     <property name="lib" value="${outdir}/lib" />
     <property name="model_jar" value="${lib}/greetmodel.jar" />
  </target>

  <target name="clean" depends="init"
            description="clean up the output directories
and jar.">
     <delete dir="${local_outdir}" />
     <delete file="${model_jar}" />
  </target>

  <target name="prepare" depends="init"
                description="prepare the output
directory.">
     <mkdir dir="${build}" />
```

Listing 20.17 The Hello World model project build file. (continues)

```
        <mkdir dir="${lib}" />
    </target>

    <target name="compile" depends="prepare"
                description="compile the Java source.">
        <javac srcdir="./src" destdir="${build}" />
    </target>

    <target name="package" depends="compile"
            description="package the Java classes into a
jar.">
        <jar jarfile="${model_jar}"
          basedir="${build}" />
    </target>

    <target name="all" depends="clean,package"
            description="perform all targets."/>

</project>
```

Listing 20.17 The Hello World model project build file. (continued)

Let's go over the model project build file and each of its targets in the order they execute. First, the model project sets the all target as the default target:

```
<project name="model" default="all" >
```

The all target is executed by default, unless we specify another target as a command-line argument of Ant. The all target depends on the clean and package targets. The clean target depends on the init target; thus, the init target is executed first.

Next, the init target is executed. The init target is defined in build.xml as follows:

```
    <target name="init"
                        description="initialize the properties.">

        <property name="local_outdir" value="${outdir}/model" />
        <property name="build" value="${local_outdir}/classes" />
        <property name="lib" value="${outdir}/lib" />
        <property name="model_jar" value="${lib}/greetmodel.jar" />
    </target>
```

The init target defines several properties that refer to directories and files needed to compile and deploy the model project. Let's discuss the meaning of these properties because all the other build files for this example use the same or similar properties. The init target defines the following properties:

local_outdir—Defines the output directory of all the model project's intermediate files (Java class files).

build—Defines the output directory of the Java class files.

lib—Defines the directory that holds the common code libraries (JAR files) used for the whole Model 2 Hello World example application.

model_jar—Defines the output JAR file for this project.

NOTE As a general rule, if you use the same literal twice, you should go ahead and define it in the init target. You don't know how many times we've shot ourselves in the foot by not following this rule. This build file is fairly simple, but the later ones are more complex. Please learn from our mistakes (and missing toes).

Now that all the clean target's dependencies have executed, the clean target can execute. The clean target deletes the intermediate files created by the compile and the output common JAR file, which is the output of this project. Here is the code for the clean target:

```
<target name="clean" depends="init"
         description="clean up the output directories and jar.">

  <delete dir="${local_outdir}" />
  <delete file="${model_jar}" />

</target>
```

Remember that the all target depends on the clean and package targets. The clean branch and all its dependencies have now executed, so it is time to execute the package target branch (a *branch* is a target and all its dependencies). The package target depends on the compile target, the compile target depends on the prepare target, and the prepare target depends on the init target, which has already been executed.

NOTE During development you would probably not use the all target; instead, you would use the compile or package target. However, as a general rule, the default target is preferred as the most complete target with the fewest side effects. You can always override this during development by passing the desired target on the command line when invoking Ant.

Thus, the next target that executes is prepare because all its dependencies have already executed. The prepare target creates the build output directory, which ensures that the lib directory is created. The prepare target is defined as follows:

```
<target name="prepare" depends="init"
                      description="prepare the output directory.">

    <mkdir dir="${build}" />
    <mkdir dir="${lib}" />
</target>
```

The next target in the package target branch that executes is the compile target—another dependency of the package target. The compile target compiles the code in the src directory to the build directory, which was defined by the build property in the init target. The compile target is defined in this way:

```
<target name="compile" depends="prepare"
                    description="compile the Java source.">

   <javac srcdir="./src" destdir="${build}"/>
</target>
```

Now that all the target dependencies of the package target have been executed, we can run the package target. The package target packages the Java classes created in the compile target into a JAR file in the common lib directory. The package target is defined as follows:

```
<target name="package" depends="compile"
              description="package the Java classes into a jar.">

    <jar jarfile="${model_jar}"
       basedir="${build}" />
</target>
```

Running an Ant Build File

In this section, we discuss how to run the Hello World model project build file. There are three steps to running this file:

1. Set up the environment.
2. Go to the directory that contains the build.xml file for the model.
3. Run Ant.

Successfully running the build script gives us the following output:

```
Buildfile: build.xml

init:

clean:

prepare:
    [mkdir] Created dir: C:\tmp\app\model\classes

compile:
    [javac] Compiling 3 source files to C:\tmp\app\model\classes

package:
      [jar] Building jar: C:\tmp\app\lib\greetmodel.jar

all:

BUILD SUCCESSFUL

Total time: 3 seconds
```

If you do not get this output, check that the properties defined in the init target make sense for your environment. If you are on a Unix platform and the build file is not working, make sure that the /tmp directory exists and that you have the rights to access it. Alternatively, you could run the previous script by entering this on the command line:

```
$ ant -Doutdir=/usr/rick/tmp/app
```

Basically, you want to output to a directory that you have access to, just in case you are not the administrator of your own box. If for some reason Ant still does not run, make sure you set up the Ant environment variables.

After you successfully run Ant, the output directory for the model project looks like this:

```
Root of output directory
\---app
    +---lib
    |       greetmodel.jar
    |
    \---model
        \---classes
            \---xptoolkit
                \---model
                        GreetingFactory.class
                        Greeting.class
                        GreetingBean.class
```

Notice that all the intermediate files to build the JAR file are in the model subdirectory. The output from this project is the greetmodel.jar file, which is in ${outdir}/app/lib. The next project, the application project, needs this JAR file in order to compile. In the next section, we discuss how to use Ant to build a stand-alone Java application that uses the JAR file (greetmodel.jar) from the model project.

The Hello World Application Project

The goal of the Hello World application project is to create a stand-alone Java application that uses greetmodel.jar to get the greeting message. The application project build file is nearly identical to the model project build file, so we focus our discussion on the differences between the two. We also explain how to make a JAR file an executable JAR file.

Overview of Application Java Classes

The Java source code for this application is as simple as it gets for the Hello World Model 2 examples. Here is the Java application:

```
package xptoolkit;

import xptoolkit.model.GreetingFactory;
import xptoolkit.model.Greeting;
```

```
public class HelloWorld{

    public static void main(String []args)throws Exception{
       Greeting greet = (Greeting)
         GreetingFactory.getGreetingFactory().getGreeting();

       System.out.println(greet.getGreeting());

    }
}
```

As you can see, this application imports the GreetingFactory class and the Greeting interface from the model project. It uses GreetingFactory to get an instance of the Greeting interface, and then uses the instance of the Greeting interface to print the greeting to the console.

Creating a Project Directory Structure for the Application

The directory structure of the Hello World Java application is as follows:

```
Hello World Application root
|    build.xml
|
+---src
|    |
|    +---xptoolkit
|            HelloWorld.java
|
\---META-INF
        MANIFEST.MF
```

Notice the addition of the META-INF directory, which holds the name of the manifest file we will use to make the application's JAR file executable. The only other file that this project needs is not shown; the file is greetmodel.jar, which is created by the model project (the reason for this will become obvious in the following sections).

Creating a Manifest File for a Stand-alone Application

The goal of this application is for it to work as a stand-alone JAR file. To do this, we need to modify the manifest file that the application JAR file uses to include the main class and the dependency on greetmodel.jar. The manifest entries that this application needs look something like this:

```
Manifest-Version: 1.0
Created-By: Rick Hightower
Main-Class: xptoolkit.HelloWorld
Class-Path: greetmodel.jar
```

The JAR file that holds the Hello World Java application needs to run a certain JAR file (in our case, greetmodel.jar), as specified by the Class-Path manifest entry. The

Main-Class manifest entry specifies the main class of the JAR file—that is, the class with the main() method that is run when the executable JAR file executes.

Creating an Ant Build File for a Stand-Alone Application

Listing 20.18 shows the application project build file; you'll notice that it is very similar to the model project build file. It is divided into the same targets: init, clean, delete, prepare, mkdir, compile, package, and all. The application project build file defines the properties differently, but even the property names are almost identical (compare with the model project build file in Listing 20.17).

```
<project name="application" default="all" >


    <property name="outdir" value="/tmp/app" />

    <target name="init"
                    description="initialize the properties.">
      <property name="local_outdir" value="${outdir}/java_app" />
      <property name="build" value="${local_outdir}/classes" />
      <property name="lib" value="${outdir}/lib" />
      <property name="app_jar" value="${lib}/greetapp.jar" />
    </target>

    <target name="clean" depends="init"
                    description="clean up the output
directories.">
        <delete dir="${build}" />
        <delete file="${app_jar}" />
    </target>

    <target name="prepare" depends="init"
                    description="prepare the output directory.">
        <mkdir dir="${build}" />
        <mkdir dir="${lib}" />
    </target>

    <target name="compile" depends="prepare"
                    description="compile the Java source.">

        <javac srcdir="./src" destdir="${build}">
          <classpath >

              <fileset dir="${lib}">
```

Listing 20.18 The Hello World application project build file. (continues)

```
            <include name="**/*.jar"/>
        </fileset>

      </classpath>

    </javac>

  </target>

  <target name="package" depends="compile"
           description="package the Java classes into a jar.">
    <jar jarfile="${app_jar}"
       manifest="./META-INF/MANIFEST.MF"
     basedir="${build}" />
  </target>

  <target name="all" depends="clean,package"
              description="perform all targets."/>

</project>
```

Listing 20.18 The Hello World application project build file. (continued)

One of the differences in the application project build file is the way that it compiles the Java source:

```
<target name="compile" depends="prepare"
                      description="compile the Java source.">

    <javac srcdir="./src" destdir="${build}">
        <classpath >

            <fileset dir="${lib}">
                <include name="**/*.jar"/>
            </fileset>

        </classpath>

    </javac>

</target>
```

Notice that the compile target specifies all the JAR files in the common lib directory (<include name="**/*.jar"/>). The greetmodel.jar file is in the common lib directory, so it is included when the javac task compiles the source. Another difference is the way the application project build file packages the Ant source:

```
<target name="package" depends="compile"
               description="package the Java classes into a jar.">
    <jar jarfile="${app_jar}"
         manifest="./META-INF/MANIFEST.MF"
       basedir="${build}" />
</target>
```

Notice that the package target uses the jar task as before, but the jar task's manifest is set to the manifest file described earlier. This is unlike the model project build file, which did not specify a manifest file; the model used the default manifest file. The application project build file's manifest file has the entries that allow us to execute the JAR file from the command line.

In order to run the Hello World Java application, after we run the application project build file, we go to the output common lib directory (tmp/app/lib) and run Java from the command line with the -jar command-line argument:

```
$ java -jar greetapp.jar
Hello World!
```

You may wonder how the application loaded the Greeting interface and the GreetingFactory class. This is possible because the manifest entry Class-Path causes the JVM to search for any directory or JAR file that is specified (refer to the JAR file specification included with the Java Platform documentation for more detail). The list of items (directory or JAR files) specified on the Class-Path manifest entry is a relative URI list. Because the greetmodel.jar file is in the same directory (such as /tmp/app/lib) and it is specified on the Class-Path manifest, the JVM finds the classes in greetmodel.jar.

One issue with the application project is its dependence on the model project. The model project must be executed before the application project. How can we manage this? The next section proposes one way to manage the situation with an Ant build file.

The Hello World Main Project

The Hello World Java application depends on the existence of the Hello World model common library file. If we try to compile the application before the model, we get an error. The application requires the model, so we need a way to call the model project build file and the application project build file in the correct order.

Creating a Master Build File

We can control the execution of two build files by using a master build file. The master build file shown in Listing 20.19 is located in the root directory of the Model 2 Hello World Example of the main project. This build file treats the model and application build files as subprojects (the model and application projects are the first of many subprojects that we want to fit into a larger project).

```
<project name="main" default="build" >

  <property name="outdir" value="/tmp/app" />

  <target name="init"
            description="initialize the properties.">
      <property name="lib" value="${outdir}/lib" />
  </target>

  <target name="clean" depends="init"
            description="clean up the output
directories.">
     <ant dir="./Model" target="clean">
        <property name="outdir" value="${outdir}" />
     </ant>

     <ant dir="./Application" target="clean">
        <property name="outdir" value="${outdir}" />
     </ant>

     <delete dir="${outdir}" />

  </target>


  <target name="prepare" depends="init"
            description="prepare the output directory.">
     <mkdir dir="${build}" />
     <mkdir dir="${lib}" />
  </target>


  <target name="build" depends="prepare"
      description="build the model and application modules.">

     <ant dir="./model" target="package">
        <property name="outdir" value="${outdir}" />
     </ant>

     <ant dir="./application" target="package">
        <property name="outdir" value="${outdir}" />
     </ant>
  </target>

</project>
```

Listing 20.19 The Hello World master build file.

Analysis of the Master Build File

Notice that the main project build file simply delegates to the application and model subproject, and ensures that the subprojects' build files are called in the correct order. For example, when the clean target is executed, the main project build file uses the ant task to call the model project's clean target. Then, the main project calls the application project's clean target using the ant task again, as shown here:

```
<target name="clean" depends="init"
                            description="clean up the output
directories.">
        <ant dir="./Model" target="clean">
            <property name="outdir" value="${outdir}" />
        </ant>

        <ant dir="./Application" target="clean">
            <property name="outdir" value="${outdir}" />
        </ant>

        <delete dir="${outdir}" />

</target>
```

A similar strategy is used with the main project's build target. The build target calls the package target on both the model and application subprojects:

```
<target name="build" depends="prepare"
            description="build the model and application modules.">

        <ant dir="./model" target="package">
            <property name="outdir" value="${outdir}" />
        </ant>

        <ant dir="./application" target="package">
            <property name="outdir" value="${outdir}" />
        </ant>

</target>
```

Thus, we can build both the application and model projects by running the main project. This may not seem like a big deal, but imagine a project with hundreds of subprojects that build thousands of components. Without a build file, such a project could become unmanageable. In fact, a project with just 10 to 20 components can benefit greatly from using nested build files. The master build file orchestrates the correct running order for all the subprojects. We could revisit this main project after we finish each additional subproject, and update it. In the next section, we discuss the applet build file.

The Applet Project

The applet project is a simple applet that reads the output of the HelloWorldServlet and shows it in a JLabel. The dependency on the Web application is at runtime; there are no compile-time dependencies to the Web application. Let's take a look at the applet next.

Overview of the Applet Class

The meat of the applet implementation is in the init() method, as shown here:

```
public void init(){
    URL uGreeting;
    String sGreeting="Bye Bye";

    getAppletContext()
         .showStatus("Getting hello message from server.");

    try{
        uGreeting = new URL(
               getDocumentBase(),
               "HelloWorldServlet");

        sGreeting = getGreeting(uGreeting);
    }
    catch(Exception e){
        getAppletContext()
            .showStatus("Unable to communicate with server.");
        e.printStackTrace();
    }
    text.setText(sGreeting);

}
```

The init() method gets the document base URL (the URL from which the applet's page was loaded) from the applet context. Then, the init() method uses the document base and the URI identifying HelloWorldServlet to create a URL that has the output of HelloWorldServlet:

```
uGreeting = new URL( getDocumentBase(), "HelloWorldServlet");
```

The init() method uses a helper method called getGreeting() to parse the output of HelloWorldServlet. It then displays the greeting in the applet's JLabel (text.setText (sGreeting);). The helper method looks like this:

```
private String getGreeting(URL uGreeting)throws Exception{
     String line;
     int endTagIndex;
     BufferedReader reader=null;
    . . .

         reader = new BufferedReader(
                new InputStreamReader (
                        uGreeting.openStream()));

        while((line=reader.readLine())!=null){
            System.out.println(line);

            if (line.startsWith("<h1>")){
                getAppletContext().showStatus("Parsing message.");
                endTagIndex=line.indexOf("</h1>");
```

```
                    line=line.substring(4,endTagIndex);
                    break;
                }
            }
        ...
        return line;
    }
```

Basically, the method gets the output stream from the URL (uGreeting.openStream()) and goes through the stream line by line looking for a line that begins with <h1>. Then, it pulls the text out of the <h1> tag.

The output of HelloServlet looks like this:

```
<html>
<head>
<title>Hello World</title>
</head>
<body>
<h1>Hello World!</h1>
</body>
```

The code that the helper method retrieves appears in bold. Listing 20.20 shows the complete code for HelloWorldApplet.

```
package xptoolkit.applet;
import javax.swing.JApplet;
import javax.swing.JLabel;
import java.awt.Font;
import java.awt.BorderLayout;
import java.applet.AppletContext;
import java.net.URL;
import java.io.InputStreamReader;
import java.io.BufferedReader;

public class HelloWorldApplet extends javax.swing.JApplet {

    JLabel text;


    public HelloWorldApplet() {
        this.getContentPane().setLayout(new BorderLayout());
        text = new JLabel("Bye Bye");
        text.setAlignmentX(JLabel.CENTER_ALIGNMENT);
        text.setAlignmentY(JLabel.CENTER_ALIGNMENT);
        Font f = new Font("Arial", Font.BOLD, 20);
        text.setFont(f);
```

Listing 20.20 The HelloWorldApplet that communicates with HelloWorldServlet. (continues)

```
        getContentPane().add(text,BorderLayout.CENTER);
    }


    public void init(){
        URL uGreeting;
        String sGreeting="Bye Bye";

        this.doLayout();
        getAppletContext()
.showStatus("Getting hello message from server.");

        try{
            uGreeting = new URL(
                this.getDocumentBase(),
                "HelloWorldServlet");

            sGreeting = getGreeting(uGreeting);
        }
        catch(Exception e){
            getAppletContext()
.showStatus("Unable to communicate with server.");
            e.printStackTrace();
        }
        text.setText(sGreeting);

    }

    private String getGreeting(URL uGreeting)throws Exception{
        String line;
        int endTagIndex;
        BufferedReader reader=null;


        try{
            reader = new BufferedReader(
                    new InputStreamReader (
                        uGreeting.openStream()));
            while((line=reader.readLine())!=null){
                System.out.println(line);
                if (line.startsWith("<h1>")){
                    getAppletContext().showStatus("Parsing message.");
```

Listing 20.20 The HelloWorldApplet that communicates with HelloWorldServlet. (continues)

```
                endTagIndex=line.indexOf("</h1>");
                line=line.substring(4,endTagIndex);
                break;
            }
          }
        }
        finally{
          if (reader!=null)reader.close();
        }
        return line;
    }

}
```

Listing 20.20 The HelloWorldApplet that communicates with HelloWorldServlet. (continued)

Creating a Build File for the Applet

The applet project build file is quite simple, as shown in Listing 20.21. It is structured much like the application project build file.

```
<project name="applet" default="all" >


    <property name="outdir" value="/tmp/app" />


    <target name="init"
                    description="initialize the properties.">

        <property name="local_outdir" value="${outdir}/applet" />
        <property name="build" value="${local_outdir}/classes" />
        <property name="lib" value="${outdir}/lib" />
        <property name="jar" value="${lib}/helloapplet.jar" />
    </target>

    <target name="clean" depends="init"
                    description="clean up the output
```

Listing 20.21 The applet project build file. (continues)

```
directories.">
        <delete dir="${build}" />
        <delete dir="${jar}" />
    </target>


    <target name="prepare" depends="init"
                    description="prepare the output directory.">
        <mkdir dir="${build}" />
        <mkdir dir="${lib}" />
    </target>

    <target name="compile" depends="prepare"
                    description="compile the Java source.">
       <javac srcdir="./src" destdir="${build}" />
    </target>

    <target name="package" depends="compile"
          description="package the Java classes into a jar.">
       <jar jarfile="${jar} "
         basedir="${build}" />
    </target>

    <target name="all" depends="clean,package"
                    description="perform all targets."/>

</project>
```

Listing 20.21 The applet project build file. (continued)

Building the Applet with Ant

To build the applet, we need to navigate to the Applet directory, set up the environment, and then run Ant at the command line. First, we build the applet:

```
C:\CVS\...\MVCHelloWorld\Applet>ant
Buildfile: build.xml


init:

clean:
    [delete] Deleting directory C:\tmp\app\lib

prepare:
```

```
    [mkdir] Created dir: C:\tmp\app\applet\classes
    [mkdir] Created dir: C:\tmp\app\lib

compile:
    [javac] Compiling 1 source file to C:\tmp\app\applet\classes

package:
      [jar] Building jar: C:\tmp\app\lib\helloapplet.jar

all:

BUILD SUCCESSFUL

Total time: 4 seconds
```

Now we clean the applet:

```
C:\CVS\...\MVCHelloWorld\Applet>ant clean
Buildfile: build.xml

init:

clean:
   [delete] Deleting directory C:\tmp\app\applet\classes
   [delete] Deleting directory C:\tmp\app\lib

BUILD SUCCESSFUL

Total time: 0 seconds
```

Hello World Recap

It's important to recap what we have done. We created a common Java library called model.jar. This model.jar file is used by a Web application and a stand-alone executable Java application in an executable JAR file. We created an applet that can communicate with the Web application we create in the next section. Once the applet loads in the browser, the applet communicates over HTTP to the Web application's HelloWorld-Servlet.

Hello World Model 2 and J2EE

The following section explains techniques for using Ant to build and deploy J2EE applications. The Hello World example includes an applet, a Web application, an application, support libraries, and other components. This may be the only Hello World example that has an applet, servlet, and JSP; and that attempts to be Model 2.

You're probably thinking, "Why should I implement the most complex Hello World application in the world?" This example—although a bit complex to just say "Hello World"—is as simple as possible while demonstrating how to build and deploy a J2EE application and its components with Ant. By working through this example, you will understand how to use Ant to build these different types of components and applications, and how to combine them by nesting build files.

The Model 2 HelloWorld example for this chapter is the simplest example of Model 2 architecture—also known as Model-View-Controller (MVC)—for JSP servlets. In this example, the applet and JSP are the View; the servlet is the Controller; and the object Model is a Java class.

The Web application build file is set up so that if we add one property, it can talk to the local implementation in the original model library (common code) defined earlier. The WebApplication directory holds HTML files, deployment descriptors, JSP files, and servlet Java source.

Because each component has its own set of deployment descriptors and configuration files, it makes sense to separate components into their own directories; this practice also makes it easier to reuse the components in other projects and applications. Each directory has its own Ant build file, which knows how to compile the components, package the binaries, and include the requisite configuration files (deployment descriptors and manifest files).

In the next section, we cover the Web application build file—the heart of this example.

The Web Application Project

The Web application is another subproject of the Model 2 Hello World application; it consists of a servlet, two JSPs, an HTML file, and a deployment descriptor. This section describes how to build a WAR file with a deployment descriptor. We also explain how to map servlets and JSPs to servlet elements in the deployment descriptor, and how to map the servlet elements to URLs. In addition, this section breaks down the Web application project build file step by step, and shows how to use the build file to build and deploy the Web application.

The Web Application Project Directory Structure

We build these files into a Web application:

```
Web application root directory
|   build.xml
|
+---JSP
|      HelloWorld.jsp
|      HelloApplet.jsp
|
+---src
|   \---xptoolkit
|      \---web
|             HelloWorldServlet.java
|
+---HTML
|       index.html
|
\---meta-data
       web.xml
```

Notice that the Web application project includes only six files. There are four subdirectories: JSP, src, HTML, and meta-data; and the root directory holds the build.xml file. The JSP directory contains two JSPs: HelloWorld.jsp and HelloApplet.jsp. Under the src directory is the Java source for the servlet xptoolkit.web.HelloWorldServlet.java. The web.xml file under the meta-data directory holds the deployment file for this Web application.

HelloWorldServlet.java

The servlet is contained in the class xptoolkit.web.HelloWorldServlet (see Listing 20.22). Like the Java application, it uses the Greeting interface and the GreetingFactory class that are packaged in greetmodel.jar, the output of the model project.

```
package xptoolkit.web;
import javax.servlet.http.HttpServlet;
import javax.servlet.http.HttpServletRequest;
import javax.servlet.http.HttpServletResponse;
import javax.servlet.http.HttpSession;
import javax.servlet.ServletException;
import javax.servlet.ServletConfig;
import javax.servlet.ServletContext;
import javax.servlet.RequestDispatcher;

/* import the classes to create a greeting object or type greeting */
import xptoolkit.model.GreetingFactory;
import xptoolkit.model.Greeting;



public class HelloWorldServlet extends  HttpServlet{

    public void init(ServletConfig config) throws ServletException{
        super.init(config);
          /* Read in the greeting type that the factory should create */
        String clazz = config.getInitParameter("Greeting.class") ;
        if(clazz!=null)System.setProperty("Greeting.class",clazz);

    }


    public void doGet(HttpServletRequest request,
                              HttpServletResponse response)
                                    throws ServletException{
```

Listing 20.22 xptoolkit.web.HelloWorldServlet. (continues)

```
        RequestDispatcher dispatch;
        ServletContext context;
       /*Get the session, create a greeting bean, map the greeting
         bean in the session, and redirect to the Hello World JSP.
       */
        try {


            /* Create the greeting bean and map it to the
session. */
          HttpSession session = request.getSession(true);
          Greeting greet = (Greeting)
              GreetingFactory.getGreetingFactory().getGreeting();
          session.setAttribute("greeting", greet);


            /* Redirect to the HelloWorld.jsp */
           context = getServletContext();
           dispatch = context.getRequestDispatcher("/HelloWorldJSP");
           dispatch.forward(request, response);
        }catch(Exception e){
           throw new ServletException(e);
        }
    }

    /* Just call the doGet method */
    public void doPost(HttpServletRequest request,
                       HttpServletResponse response)
                            throws ServletException{
        doGet(request, response);
    }

}
```

Listing 20.22 xptoolkit.web.HelloWorldServlet. (continued)

Analyzing HelloWorldServlet

HelloWorldServlet is a simple servlet; it reads in the servlet initialization parameters in the init() method, as follows:

```
        String clazz = config.getInitParameter("Greeting.class") ;
```

It uses the value of the initialization parameter "Greeting.class" to set the System property "Greeting.class", as follows:

```
System.setProperty("Greeting.class",clazz);
```

You will recall that GreetingFactory uses the system property "Greeting.class" to decide which implementation of the Greeting interface to load. Now let's get to the real action: the doGet() and doPost() methods.

When the doGet() or doPost() method of HelloWorldServlet is called, the servlet uses GreetingFactory to create a greeting:

```
Greeting greet = (Greeting)
     GreetingFactory.getGreetingFactory().getGreeting();
```

HelloWorldServlet then maps the greeting object into the current session (javax.servlet.http.HttpSession) under the name greeting:

```
session.setAttribute("greeting", greet);
```

Finally, HelloWorldServlet forwards processing of this request to the JSP file HelloWorld.jsp by getting the request dispatcher for HelloWorldServlet from the servlet's context:

```
      /* Redirect to the HelloWorld.jsp */
context = getServletContext();
dispatch = context.getRequestDispatcher("/HelloWorldJSP");
dispatch.forward(request, response);
```

You may notice that the context.getRequestDispatcher call looks a little strange. This is because HelloWorld.jsp is mapped to /HelloWorldJSP in the deployment descriptor for the servlet. Next, let's examine HelloWorld.jsp.

HelloWorld.jsp

HelloWorld.jsp exists to display the message it gets from the Greeting reference that HelloWorldServlet mapped into that session. The HelloWorld.jsp code looks like this:

```
<jsp:useBean id="greeting" type="xptoolkit.model.Greeting"
                                               scope="session"/>
<html>
<head>
<title>Hello World</title>
</head>
<body>
<h1><%=greeting.getGreeting()%></h1>
</body>
```

If you are a Web designer at heart, we understand if you are shocked and horrified by this HTML code. But for a moment, let's focus on the following two lines of code from the JSP:

```
<jsp:useBean id="greeting" type="xptoolkit.model.Greeting"
                                               scope="session"/>

<h1><%=greeting.getGreeting()%></h1>
```

Notice that the jsp:useBean action grabs the Greeting reference that we put into the session with HelloWorldServlet. Then, we print out the greeting with the JSP scriptlet expression <%=greeting.getGreeting()%>.

This sums up what the Model 2 Hello World Web application does. We discuss the other JSP, HelloApplet.jsp, after we examine the applet subproject. For now, the next section explains why the servlet could forward HelloWorldJSP to the JSP HelloWorld.jsp.

The Deployment Descriptor for the Hello World Web Application

In order to configure the JSPs and servlets, we need a deployment descriptor. The following code defines a simple deployment descriptor that assigns names and mappings to the JSPs and servlet. Please note that the deployment descriptor goes in the web.xml file:

```
<?xml version="1.0" encoding="ISO-8859-1"?>

<!DOCTYPE web-app
  PUBLIC "-//Sun Microsystems, Inc.//DTD Web Application 2.2//EN"
  "http://java.sun.com/j2ee/dtds/web-app_2_2.dtd">

<web-app>
    <error-page>
        <error-code>404</error-code>
        <location>/HelloWorldServlet</location>
    </error-page>

    <servlet>
        <servlet-name>HelloWorldServlet</servlet-name>
        <servlet-class>xptoolkit.web.HelloWorldServlet</servlet-class>
        <init-param>
          <param-name>Greeting.class</param-name>
          <param-value>@Greeting.class@</param-value>
        </init-param>
    </servlet>

    <servlet>
        <servlet-name>HelloWorldJSP</servlet-name>
        <jsp-file>HelloWorld.jsp</jsp-file>
    </servlet>

    <servlet-mapping>
        <servlet-name>HelloWorldServlet</servlet-name>
        <url-pattern>/HelloWorldServlet</url-pattern>
    </servlet-mapping>

    <servlet-mapping>
        <servlet-name>HelloWorldJSP</servlet-name>
        <url-pattern>/HelloWorldJSP</url-pattern>
    </servlet-mapping>

</web-app>
```

The deployment descriptor defines two servlet elements: one for HelloWorldServlet and one for HelloWorldJSP. If you are wondering why there is a servlet element for HelloWorldJSP, remember that HelloWorld.jsp is compiled to a servlet before it is used for the first time. The HelloWorldServlet servlet element maps to the servlet (<servlet-class>xptoolkit.web.HelloWorldServlet</servlet-class>). The HelloWorldJSP element maps to the JSP file HelloWorld.jsp (<jsp-file>HelloWorld.jsp</jsp-file>). Then, the servlet mapping elements map the servlet element to specific URL patterns.

Thus, HelloWorldServlet maps to /HelloWorldServlet (<url-pattern>/HelloWorld-Servlet</url-pattern>); this is relative to the Web application location from the root of the server. And the HelloWorldJSP servlet element is mapped to the /HelloWorldJSP URL pattern (<url-pattern>/HelloWorldJSP</url-pattern>).

The build file must deploy the descriptor to a place where the application server can find it. It does this by packaging the HTML files, JSP files, Java servlet, and deployment descriptor in a WAR file. The next section describes the build file for this project.

The Build File for the Hello World Web Application

This project has many more components than the other subprojects. As you would expect, the Web application project build file (see Listing 20.23) is much more complex, but it builds on the foundation set by the model project—that is, the Web application project build file has the same base targets with the same meanings: init, clean, delete, prepare, mkdir, compile, package, and all.

To the base targets, the Web application project build file adds the prepare_metadata and deploy targets. The prepare_metadata target sets up the Ant filtering for the deployment descriptor. The deploy target adds the ability to deploy to both Tomcat and Resin Web application servers. The remaining details of this build file are covered in the applet and the enterprise beans sections later in this chapter.

```
<project name="webapplication" default="all" >

  <property name="outdir" value="/tmp/app" />


  <target name="init"
                description="initialize the properties.">
    <property name="local_outdir" value="${outdir}/webapps" />
    <property name="lib" value="${outdir}/lib" />
    <property name="dist" value="${outdir}/dist" />

    <property name="build" value="${local_outdir}/webclasses" />
    <property name="meta" value="${local_outdir}/meta" />

    <property name="deploy_resin" value="/resin/webapps" />
    <property name="deploy_tomcat" value="/tomcat/webapps" />
```

Listing 20.23 The Hello World Web application project build file. (continues)

```
    <property name="build_lib" value="./../lib" />
    <property name="jsdk_lib" value="/resin/lib" />
  </target>

  <target name="clean_deploy" >

     <delete file="${deploy_resin}/hello.war" />
     <delete dir="${deploy_resin}/hello" />
     <delete file="${deploy_tomcat}/hello.war" />
     <delete dir="${deploy_tomcat}/hello" />
  </target>

  <target name="clean" depends="init,clean_deploy"
               description="clean up the output
directories.">
     <delete dir="${local_outdir}" />
     <delete file="${dist}/hello.war" />
  </target>


  <target name="prepare" depends="init"
               description="prepare the output directory.">
     <mkdir dir="${build}" />
     <mkdir dir="${dist}" />
     <mkdir dir="${build_lib}" />
  </target>



  <target name="compile" depends="prepare"
               description="compile the Java source.">
     <javac srcdir="./src" destdir="${build}">
        <classpath >

           <fileset dir="${lib}">
              <include name="**/*.jar"/>
           </fileset>

           <fileset dir="${jsdk_lib}">
              <include name="**/*.jar"/>
           </fileset>

           <fileset dir="${build_lib}">
```

Listing 20.23 The Hello World Web application project build file. (continues)

```
            <include name="**/*.jar"/>
          </fileset>

        </classpath>
      </javac>

   </target>

   <target name="prepare_meta_ejb" if="ejb">
      <filter token="Greeting.class"
            value="xptoolkit.model.GreetingShadow"/>
   </target>

   <target name="prepare_meta_noejb" unless="ejb">
      <filter token="Greeting.class"
             value="xptoolkit.model.GreetingBean"/>
   </target>

   <target name="prepare_meta"
         depends="prepare_meta_ejb, prepare_meta_noejb">
      <copy todir="${meta}" filtering="true">
         <fileset dir="./meta-data"/>
      </copy>
   </target>

   <target name="package" depends="compile">

      <mkdir dir="${meta}" />

      <antcall target="prepare_meta" />

      <war warfile="${dist}/hello.war" webxml="${meta}/web.xml">
         <!--
            Include the html and jsp files.
            Put the classes from the build into the classes
directory
            of the war.
         /-->
      <fileset dir="./HTML" />
      <fileset dir="./JSP" />
       <classes dir="${build}" />

         <!-- Include the applet. /-->
       <fileset dir="${lib}" includes="helloapplet.jar" />
```

Listing 20.23 The Hello World Web application project build file. (continues)

```
    <!-- Include all of the jar files except the ejbeans and
applet. The other build files that create jars have to be run
in the correct order. This is covered later.
         /-->
      <lib dir="${lib}" >
        <exclude name="greet-ejbs.jar"/>
        <exclude name="helloapplet.jar"/>
      </lib>
    </war>

  </target>

  <target name="deploy" depends="package">
    <copy file="${dist}/hello.war" todir="${deploy_resin}" />

    <copy file="${dist}/hello.war" todir="${deploy_tomcat}" />


  </target>

  <target name="all" depends="clean,package"
              description="perform all targets."/>

</project>
```

Listing 20.23 The Hello World Web application project build file. (continued)

The final output of the Web application project is a single WAR file. The WAR file is built (not surprisingly) by the package target. Here is the code for the package target:

```
<target name="package" depends="compile">

    <mkdir dir="${meta}" />
    <antcall target="prepare_meta" />

    <war warfile="${dist}/hello.war" webxml="${meta}/web.xml">
        <!--
            Include the html and jsp files.
            Put the classes from the build into the classes
            directory
            of the war.
        /-->
       <fileset dir="./HTML" />
       <fileset dir="./JSP" />
       <classes dir="${build}" />
```

```
            <!-- Include the applet. /-->
            <fileset dir="${lib}" includes="helloapplet.jar" />

            <!-- Include all of the jar files except the ejbeans
                    and applet.
              /-->
            <lib dir="${lib}" />
        </war>

    </target>
```

As you can see, this package target is much larger than the other two we've discussed (model and application). For now, we'll offer a detailed discussion of the second and third lines of code:

```
        <mkdir dir="${meta}" />
        <antcall target="prepare_meta" />
```

These lines do some processing on the web.xml deployment descriptor file and put the file in the directory defined by the ${meta} directory (note that the meta property is set in the init target). Next, the package target calls the war task:

```
        <war warfile="${dist}/hello.war" webxml="${meta}/web.xml">
           <fileset dir="./HTML" />
           <fileset dir="./JSP" />
           <classes dir="${build}" />
           <fileset dir="${lib}" includes="helloapplet.jar" />
           <lib dir="${lib}" />
        </war>
```

The WAR file hello.war is put in the distribution directory (dist), which is specified by the war task's warfile attribute (warfile="${dist}/hello.war"). The dist directory is another common directory that is used by the main project build file later to build an enterprise archive (EAR) file; the dist property is defined in the init target. The webxml attribute of the war task defines the deployment descriptor to use; it's the one we processed at the beginning of the package target. The web.xml file is put in the WAR file's WEB-INF/ directory.

In addition, the war task body specifies three file sets. One file set includes the helloapplet.jar file (which we discuss in the section "HelloWorld.jsp Applet Delivery" later in this chapter) and all the files in the HTML and JSP directories. The war task body also specifies where to locate the classes using

```
<classes dir="${build}" />
```

This command puts the classes in the WEB-INF/classes directory.

The Web application project build file defines a slightly more complex compile target:

```
    <target name="compile" depends="prepare"
                           description="compile the Java source.">
        <javac srcdir="./src" destdir="${build}">
            <classpath >

                <fileset dir="${lib}">
                    <include name="**/*.jar"/>
```

```
                </fileset>

                <fileset dir="${build_lib}">
                    <include name="**/*.jar"/>
                </fileset>

            </classpath>
        </javac>

    </target>
```

Notice that this compile target defines two file sets. One file set (<fileset dir="${build_lib}">) is used to include the classes needed for servlets (such as import javax.servlet.*). The other file set (<fileset dir="${lib}">) is used to include the Greeting interfaces and the GreetingFactory class. The only real difference from the application compile target is the inclusion of the JAR file for servlets. The build_lib property is defined in the Web application project's init target, as shown here:

```
<property name="build_lib" value="./../lib" />
```

The good thing about this approach is that if we need additional JAR files, we can put them in build_lib. The second file set (<fileset dir="${build_lib}">) grabs all the JAR files in the ./../lib directory.

The Web application project build file adds a few convenience targets geared toward Web applications. The deploy target copies the WAR file that this build file generates to the /webapps directory of Tomcat and Resin. (Resin is an easy-to-use Java application server that supports JSPs, EJBs, J2EE container specification, XSL, and so on. We show it here to show that the build script would work with more than one app server since it generates J2EE-compliant war files). Without further ado, here is the deploy target:

```
<target name="deploy" depends="package">
        <copy file="${dist}/hello.war" todir="${deploy_resin}" />
        <copy file="${dist}/hello.war" todir="${deploy_tomcat}" />
</target>
```

Both Tomcat and Resin pick up the WAR files automatically, in the interest of doing no harm and cleaning up after ourselves. The Web application project build file adds an extra clean_deploy target that deletes the WAR file it deployed and cleans up the generated directory:

```
    <target name="clean_deploy" >
        <delete file="${deploy_resin}/hello.war" />
        <delete dir="${deploy_resin}/hello" />
        <delete file="${deploy_tomcat}/hello.war" />
        <delete dir="${deploy_tomcat}/hello" />
    </target>
```

"Great," you say. "But what if the application server I am deploying to is on another server that is halfway around the world?" No problem; you could use the following FTP task:

```
<ftp server="ftp.texas.austin.building7.eblox.org"
       remotedir="/deploy/resin/webapps"
       userid="kingJon"
```

```
        password="killMyLandLord"
        depends="yes"
        binary="yes"
>


    <fileset dir="${dist}">
      <include name="**/*.war"/>
    </fileset>

</ftp>
```

The key lesson here is that Ant is powerful and extensible, and if you can think of a whiz-bang task that would be great, there is a good chance it may already exist. Be sure to read the Ant online docs—they are a great reference.

Building and Deploying the Web Application

This section explains how to build and deploy the Web application. The build file assumes that you have Tomcat (or Resin) installed in the root of your drive. You may need to make adjustments to the build file if you installed Tomcat in another directory or if you are using another J2EE-compliant Web application server.

To build the Web application, follow these steps:

1. Navigate to the WebApplication directory, set up the environment, and then enter the following at the command line:

```
C:\CVS\...\MVCHelloWorld\WebApplication>ant
```

2. You will get the following output:

```
Buildfile: build.xml

setProps:

init:

clean_deploy:
   [delete] Could not find file C:\resin\webapps\hello.war to delete.
   [delete] Could not find file C:\tomcat\webapps\hello.war to delete

clean:
   [delete] Could not find file C:\tmp\app\dist\hello.war to delete.

prepare:
    [mkdir] Created dir: C:\tmp\app\webapps\webclasses
    [mkdir] Created dir: C:\tmp\app\dist

compile:
    [javac] Compiling 1 source file to C:\tmp\app\webapps\webclasses

package:
```

```
    [mkdir] Created dir: C:\tmp\app\webapps\meta

prepare_meta_ejb:

prepare_meta_noejb:

prepare_meta:
     [copy] Copying 1 file to C:\tmp\app\webapps\meta
      [war] Building war: C:\tmp\app\dist\hello.war

all:

BUILD SUCCESSFUL
```

3. Deploy the WAR files to the application server. If you install Tomcat off the root directory, then you can run the deploy target. Otherwise, modify the appropriate deploy properties defined in the init target. To deploy the application with Ant, do the following:

```
C:\CVS\?.\MVCHelloWorld\WebApplication>ant deploy
Buildfile: build.xml

...
...

deploy:
     [copy] Copying 1 file to C:\resin\webapps
     [copy] Copying 1 file to C:\tomcat\webapps

BUILD SUCCESSFUL

Total time: 0 seconds
```

4. After we run the application, we start Tomcat, and then hit the site with our browser. We can also clean out the directories when we are ready to deploy a new version:

```
C:\CVS\...\MVCHelloWorld\WebApplication>ant clean
```

5. The output looks like this:

```
Buildfile: build.xml

setProps:

init:

clean_deploy:
   [delete] Deleting: C:\resin\webapps\hello.war
   [delete] Deleting: C:\tomcat\webapps\hello.war

clean:
   [delete] Deleting directory C:\tmp\app\webapps
```

```
    [delete] Deleting: C:\tmp\app\dist\hello.war

BUILD SUCCESSFUL

Total time: 0 seconds
```

6. Notice that we delete the WAR files and the deployment directories. This is just good housecleaning for when we do a build and deploy. In the next section, we run the Web application project.

Running the Web Application

Now that we've built and deployed the Web application project, let's run it. We start our servlet engine and then open the site in our browser—for example, http://localhost/hello/ HelloWorldServlet. (Tomcat's default setup is port 8080, so you may have to adjust the URL.)

You may notice a couple of things. The application URL is defined in a directory called hello (http://localhost/hello/HelloWorldServlet). By default, Tomcat unjars our WAR file in a directory called *<War file File Name>*.

The HelloWorldServlet part of the application's URL is defined by a mapping in the deployment descriptor:

```
<servlet>
    <servlet-name>HelloWorldServlet</servlet-name>
    <servlet-class>xptoolkit.web.HelloWorldServlet</servlet-class>
    <init-param>
      <param-name>Greeting.class</param-name>
      <param-value>@Greeting.class@</param-value>
    </init-param>
</servlet>


<servlet-mapping>
    <servlet-name>HelloWorldServlet</servlet-name>
    <url-pattern>/HelloWorldServlet</url-pattern>
</servlet-mapping>
```

The servlet tag declares the servlet and gives it a name. The servlet mapping assigns HelloWorldServlet the URL pattern /HelloWorldServlet. We could change the URL pattern to /PeanutButter, and the URL http://localhost/hello/PeanutButter would work.

Actually, we mapped the 404 error to HelloWorldServlet as well, so the server sends any URL it does not recognize to HelloWorldServlet to process (for the benefit of people with fumble fingers...not a good idea for a production system).

The next section describes a simple applet project that integrates with the Web application project.

HelloWorld.jsp Applet Delivery

Now, the applets JAR we built earlier becomes part of the Web application. It is put in the Web application where the browser can find it. The Web application has a JSP page,

HelloApplet.jsp, which has a jsp:plugin tag that delivers the applet to the browser. The HelloApplet.jsp with the jsp:plugin action looks like this:

```
<html>
<head><title>Hello World Applet</title></head>
<body>
<jsp:plugin type="applet"
            code="xptoolkit.applet.HelloWorldApplet"
            archive="helloapplet.jar"
            height="200"
            width="200"
            align="center">
    <jsp:fallback>
    <!-- This fallback message will display if the plugin does not work.
/-->
        <p> Java is cool. Get a browser that supports the plugin. </ br>
            Or we will hunt you down and melt your computer!
        </p>
    </jsp:fallback>
</jsp:plugin>

</body>
</html>
```

This shows how the applet is delivered to the browser. How is the applet included in the Web application's WAR file in the first place? We explain in the next section.

Including an Applet in a WAR File

If you look at the Web application project build file, you will note that the war task in the package target does the following:

```
<war warfile="${dist}/hello.war" webxml="${meta}/web.xml">
      <fileset dir="./HTML" />
      <fileset dir="./JSP" />
      <classes dir="${build}" />
      <fileset dir="${lib}" includes="helloapplet.jar" />
      <lib dir="${lib}" />
</war>
```

The fileset directive

```
<fileset dir="${lib}" includes="helloapplet.jar" />
```

tells the war task to include only the helloapplet.jar file from the lib directory. Because this file set is not a classes- or lib-type file set, helloapplet.jar goes to the root of the WAR file. In contrast, the special lib and classes file sets put their files in WEB-INF/lib and WEB-INF/classes, respectively. The end effect is that the browser is able to get the applet.

After we build the applet, we go back and rebuild the Web application and then deploy it. We run Ant in the root of both the projects' home directories (if you get a compile error, be sure you have built the model because the Web application depends on it). After everything compiles and the appropriate JAR and WAR files are built, we deploy the Web application project by using the deploy target of the Web application build file.

Let's review what we've done so far. We've created a common Java library called model.jar. This model.jar file is used by a Web application and a regular Java application that is a stand-alone executable Java application in an executable JAR file. We've also created an applet that is loaded with a JSP page that has the jsp:plugin action. Once the applet loads into the browser, the applet communicates over HTTP to the Web application's HelloWorldServlet. HelloWorldServlet calls the getGreeting() method on the GreetingFactory, which is contained in the model.jar file.

NOTE **In the book *Java Tools for Extreme Programming,* we set up GreetingFactory so that it talks to an enterprise session bean, which in turn talks to an enterprise entity bean. The Web application build file is set up so that after we add one property file, it can talk to either the enterprise beans or to the local implementation in the model library. We achieve this magic by using Ant filters.**

After we define the ejb property, the Web application project has the option of deploying/configuring whether the Web application that is deployed uses enterprise beans. Notice that the prepare_meta target, which is a dependency of the prepare target, has two dependencies: prepare_meta_ejb and prepare_meta_noejb, as shown here:

```
<target name="prepare_meta"
        depends="prepare_meta_ejb, prepare_meta_noejb">
    <copy todir="${meta}" filtering="true">
        <fileset dir="./meta-data"/>
    </copy>
</target>
```

The prepare_meta_ejb target is executed only if the ejb property is set as follows:

```
<target name="prepare_meta_ejb" if="ejb">
    <filter token="Greeting.class"
           value="xptoolkit.model.GreetingShadow"/>
</target>
```

If the ejb property is set, then the target creates a filter token called Greeting.class. Here, we set the value of Greeting.class to GreetingShadow. Conversely, the prepare_meta_ejb target is executed only if the ejb property is not set, as follows:

```
<target name="prepare_meta_noejb" unless="ejb">
    <filter token="Greeting.class"
            value="xptoolkit.model.GreetingBean"/>
</target>
```

Here, we set GreetingBean as Greeting.class. But how is this used by the application? You may recall that HelloWorldServlet uses the servlet parameter Greeting.class to set the system property Greeting.class (which is used by GreetingFactory to create an instance of Greeting). We put an Ant filter key in the Web application project deployment descriptor, as follows:

```
<servlet>
    <servlet-name>HelloWorldServlet</servlet-name>
```

```
        <servlet-class>xptoolkit.web.HelloWorldServlet</servlet-class>
        <init-param>
          <param-name>Greeting.class</param-name>
          <param-value>@Greeting.class@</param-value>
        </init-param>
    </servlet>
```

If we copy this file using the filter command after the filter token Greeting.class has been set, then *@Greeting.class@* is replaced with the value of our token Greeting.class, which is set to xptoolkit.model.GreetingShadow in the prepare_meta_ejb target and to xptoolkit.model.GreetingBean in the prepare_meta_noejb target. Notice that the prepare_meta target copies the deployment descriptor with filtering turned on, as follows:

```
        <copy todir="${meta}" filtering="true">
            <fileset dir="./meta-data"/>
        </copy>
```

Now that is a cool trick. We hope this step-by-step Ant example will help you visualize how you go about using Ant.

Summary

In this chapter, we took a very complex project with a few components and subsystems, albeit a simple implementation, and built it in an orchestrated fashion. We showed how to create a Java application in an executable JAR and a Java applet in a JAR. We also demonstrated how to package a set of classes that is shared by more than one application in a JAR.

This chapter covered the basics of using Ant and the concepts of build files, projects, targets, conditional targets, tasks, file sets, filters, nested build files, and properties. Our discussion included the basic styles and naming conventions for Ant build files.

The chapter also explained the importance of Ant in its relationship to continuous integration.

APPENDIX

A

Server Configuration (server.xml) Reference

We've provided this appendix as a concise reference to the server.xml configuration file, which you can find in the *<$CATALINA_HOME>*/conf directory. See Chapter 7, "The server.xml File in Depth," for a more complete discussion of the information contained here.

The lists in this appendix specify basic usage criteria. First, we list the name of the node. Next, we tell you in which other nodes (*parent* nodes) this node may appear. Then we list the most common *child* nodes, and we indicate how many of each may occur inside that node.

Finally, we list the principal attributes of each node. Required attributes are indicated in bold; attributes that appear only on some implementations (including the default implementation) are listed in italics. We also describe the purpose of the attibute and indicate its default value where appropriate.

Not all classes will support all attributes, and new classes may define additional attributes and allow additional child nodes for further configuration. Because the framework is very flexible, it is impossible to include an exhaustive list of possible attributes. As you know, new implementations with new attributes could be introduced at any time.

NOTE **In the remainder of this chapter, all attributes listed in bold are required; all attributes listed in *italics* are not part of the specification, but are present in the implementation.**

The <Server/> Node

The root node is the <Server/> node. It contains all the other nodes that control the server.

Node: <Server/>

Parent Nodes: None

Child Nodes: <Service/> 1+ required

ATTRIBUTES	DESCRIPTION	DEFAULT
className	Class implementing Serverorg.apache.catalina.core.	org.apache.catalina. StandardServer
port	Port to listen on for shutdown requests	8005
shutdown	Literal string to listen for on shutdown port	SHUTDOWN
debug	Log level for debug information	0

The <Service/> Container

The <Service/> nodes are containers grouping resources that cooperate to handle requests. <Service/> nodes contain one or more <Connector/> nodes (which specify protocol handlers that listen for requests), and they share a single <Engine/> node that dispatches the requests. You should place the <Connector/> nodes before the <Engine/> node in the server.xml file.

Node: <Service/>

Parent Nodes: <Server/>

Child Nodes: <Connector/> 1+ required

<Engine/> 1 required

ATTRIBUTES	DESCRIPTION	DEFAULT
name	The name of this instance; used for logging	N/A
className	Class implementing org.apache.catalina. Service	org.apache.catalina.core. StandardService

The <Engine/> Container

The <Engine/> component is responsible for dispatching all requests. Requests come in through one of the connectors and are processed by the engine, which passes the requests off to the appropriate handlers. The output from the handler is then passed back to the appropriate connector.

Node: <Engine/>

Parent Nodes: <Service/>

Child Nodes: <Host/> 1+ required
<Realm/> 0-1 required
<Logger/> 0-1 required
<Valve/> 0+ required

ATTRIBUTES	DESCRIPTION	DEFAULT
name	The name of the instance, used for logging.	N/A
defaultHost	Must match the name of a child <Host/>. This host will be used if no other host matches the incoming request.	N/A
className	Class implementing org.apache.catalina. Engine	org.apache. catalina.core. StandardEngine
jvmRoute	Identifier used in clustering. Must be unique to the server on which it is specified.	N/A
debug	Log level for debug information	0

The <Realm/> Node

The <Realm/> node configures HTTP authentication for the containing node. See Chapter 8, "Managing Authentitcation with Realms," for more information.

Node: <Realm/>

Parent Nodes: <Engine/>, <Host/>, <Context/>

Child Nodes: None

ATTRIBUTE	DESCRIPTION	DEFAULT
className	Class implementing org.apache.catalina. Realm	N/A

The <Logger/> Node

As you'd expect, you configure loggers in <Logger/> nodes, which, like the <Realm/> node, you may configure as a child of an <Engine/> container, a <Host/> container, or a <Context/> container. Note also that there must be no more than one <Logger/> node per container, although the same scoping rules apply as for the <Realm/> node.

Node: <Logger/>

Parent Nodes: < Engine/>, <Host/>, <Context/>

Child Nodes: None

ATTRIBUTES	DESCRIPTION	DEFAULT
className	Class implementing org.apache. catalina.Logger	N/A
verbosity	Log level. 0 = fatal messages only; 1 = error messages; 2 = warnings; 3 = informational messages; 4 = verbose output	1
directory	Log directory	logs
timestamp	Indicates whether to include a timestamp in the log filename	false
prefix	The beginning of the log filename	catalina
suffix	The ending of the log filename	.log

The <Host/> Container

You use the <Host/> container to configure the default hostname of this server and any virtual hosts.

Node: <Host/>

Parent Nodes: <Engine/>

Child Nodes: <Alias/> 0+ required

<Context/> 1+ required

<Logger/> 0-1 required

<Realm/> 0-1 required

<Valve/> 0+ required

ATTRIBUTES	DESCRIPTION	DEFAULT
name	The principal hostname for this virtual host	N/A
appBase	Directory containing the Webapps for this host	webapps
className	Class implementing org.apache. catalina.Host	org.apache.t catalina.core. StandardHos
autoDeploy	Specifies whether this host should automatically deploy new Webapps	true

ATTRIBUTES	DESCRIPTION	DEFAULT
unpackWARs	Specifies whether WAR files in the appBase of this host should be unpacked on server start	true
liveDeploy	Specifies whether newly unpacked Webapps should be deployed at runtime	true
deployXML	Specifies whether new contexts in context.xml files should be detected and deployed at runtime	true
workDir	Writable directory to be made available to servlets on this host	If not specified, Tomcat will assign an appropriate directory at runtime
errorReport ValveClass	Class implementing org.apache. catalina.Valve	org.apache. catalina.valves. ErrorReportValve
debug	Log level for debug information	0

The <Alias/> Container

Each <Host/> node may contain zero or more <Alias/> nodes, specifying additional hostnames that the host should support. The <Alias/> node doesn't have any attributes but specifies a single hostname as its body.

Node: <Alias/>

Parent Nodes: <Host/>

Child Nodes: None

The <Context/> Container

The <Context/> container relates a URI to a Web application. Every host must have one context with an empty context path, as specified by the path attribute.

Node: <Context/>

Parent Nodes: <Host/>

Child Nodes: <Logger/> 0-1 required

<Realm/> 0-1 required

<Valve/> 0+ required

<Resources/> 0-1 required

<Loader/> 0-1 required

<Manager/> 0-1 required

ATTRIBUTES	DESCRIPTION	DEFAULT
path	Base URI for context	N/A
docBase	Path to directory containing Webapps, or path including WAR file	The appBase directory of the containing host
className	Class implementing org.apache.catalina. Context	org.apache. catalina.core. StandardContext
override	Specifies whether settings on the context should override matching settings on the host	false
reloadable	Specifies whether the servlet engine should modify classes and JAR files under the docBase and reload the context if they change	true
cookies	Specifies whether Tomcat should attempt to use cookies to hold session state tokens	true
crossContext	Specifies whether Tomcat should allow servlets access to the shared context	false
privileged	Specifies whether this context should have access to container servlets	false
wrapperClass	Class implementing org.apache.catalina. Wrapper	org.apache. catalina.core. StandardWrapper
useNaming	Specifies whether this context should create a JNDI initial context	true
workDir	Writable directory to be made available to servlets on this host	If not specified, Tomcat will assign an appropriate directory at runtime
debug	Log level for debug information	0

The <Valve/> Node

You can add Valves to the processing pipeline in order to modify the request and/or response and, as a result, use them to limit access. Valves have widely divergent attributes, so we'll cover only the common ones here.

Node: <Valve/>

Parent Nodes: <Host/>, <Context/>, <Engine/>

Child Nodes: None

ATTRIBUTE	DESCRIPTION	DEFAULT
className	Class implementing org.apache.catalina.Valve	N/A

The <Resources/> Node

The <Resources/> node is used to specify resources available to the context from a JNDI InitialContext. See Chapter 7 for more details.

Node: <Resources/>

Parent Nodes: <Context/>

Child Nodes: None

ATTRIBUTES	DESCRIPTION	DEFAULT
className	Class implementing javax.naming. directory.DirContext	org.apache. naming.resources. FileDirContext
cached	Specifies whether to use caching	true
caseSensitive	Specifies whether case sensitivity should be enforced on non-case-sensitive filesystems like FAT and NTFS	true
docBase	Specifies where to find resources	

The <Loader/> Node

Use the <Loader/> node when you want to configure the class loader for the containing context.

Node: <Loader/>

Parent Nodes: <Context/>

Child Nodes: None

ATTRIBUTES	DESCRIPTION	DEFAULT
className	Class implementing org.apache.catalina. Loader	org.apache. catalina.loader. WebappLoader
delegate	Specifies whether to use the standard delegation model. See Chapter 7.	false
reloadable	Specifies whether to allow class reloading	true

ATTRIBUTES	DESCRIPTION	DEFAULT
checkInterval	Indicates how frequently Tomcat should check whether the app needs reloading	15 (seconds)
loaderClass	Class implementing java.lang. ClassLoader	org.apache. catalina.loader. WebappLoader
workDir	Writable directory to be made available to servlets on this host	If not specified, Tomcat will assign an appropriate directory at runtime
debug	Log level for debug information	0

The <Manager/> Node

Use the <Manager/> node to configure the session manager used in the containing context.

Node: <Manager/>

Parent Nodes: <Context/>

Child Nodes: None

ATTRIBUTES	DESCRIPTION	DEFAULT
className	Class implementing org.apache. catalina.Manager org.apache.catalina.session.	StandardManager
distributable	Specifies whether to enforce conformance with servlet spec distributable session standards	false
maxInactive Interval	Specifies how long sessions can remain inactive before being timed out	60 (minutes)
checkInterval	Specifies how frequently Tomcat should check for expired sessions	60 (seconds)
maxActiveSessions	Specifies how many sessions may be created and maintained active at a time	-1 (no limit)
algorithm	Specifies the digest algorithm to use in generating session tokens	MD5
randomClass	Class implementing java.util.Random	java.security. SecureRandom
entropy	String used to seed random number generator	Tomcat will generate a random seed by default

ATTRIBUTES	DESCRIPTION	DEFAULT
pathname	Name and path of file in which Tomcat should store session state during restarts	SESSIONS.ser
debug	Log level for debug information	0

The <Connector/> Node

<Connector/> nodes connect protocol handlers to IP addresses and ports. They vary substantially in functionality, and so have divergent attributes. We'll follow the standard table with additional tables describing attributes for three of the most common connectors.

Node: <Connector/>

Parent Nodes: <Service/>

Child Nodes: Varies

ATTRIBUTES	DESCRIPTION	DEFAULT
className	Class implementing org.apache. catalina.Connector	N/A
enableLookups	Specifies whether to look up domain names for inbound IP addresses at runtime	true
redirectPort	Contains port Tomcat should redirect to if security is requested but the protocol supported by this connector is not secure. See Chapter 7.	N/A
scheme	URL protocol scheme for protocol supported by this connector	http
secure	Specifies whether this connector uses a secure protocol	false
port	Specifies the port to listen on	N/A
minProcessors	Specifies the minimum number of processor instances to keep in the instance pool	5
maxProcessors	Specifies the maximum number of processor instances to create	20
acceptCount	Specifies the number of requests Tomcat should keep in queue after all processor instances are busy, before refusing additional connections	10
debug	Log level for debug information	0

The Coyote HTTP/1.1 Connector

The Coyote HTTP/1.1 connector is capable of handling HTTP 1.1, HTTP 1.0, and HTTPS connections. To configure this connector to support HTTPS, you will also need to configure a <Factory/> node (we provide the details a little later in this appendix). This node should specify the SSLSocketFactory that Tomcat must build in order to create the secure connection HTTPS relies on. You should set the secure attribute to true and the scheme attribute to https. Use the className org.apache.coyote.tomcat4.CoyoteConnector.

ATTRIBUTES	DESCRIPTION	DEFAULT
address	Local IP address to listen on	Bind to all configured interfaces
connectionTimeout	Specifies how long to wait for the first line of an incoming request before timing the request out	60000 (milliseconds)
bufferSize	Specifies how large a buffer Tomcat needs to create for each connection	2048 (bytes)
tcpNoDelay	Specifies whether Tomcat should set the socket options to use TCP_NO_DELAY	true
proxyName	Specifies the hostname to use when constructing redirects	Primary hostname of the principal IP address the connector is configured on
proxyPort	Specifies the port number to use when constructing redirects	The port set in the port attribute

The JK 2 Connector

The JK 2 connector communicates with the principal Web server using the AJP protocol. This connector supports versions 1.3 and 1.4 of that protocol. Use the className org.apache.coyote.tomcat4.CoyoteConnector.

ATTRIBUTE	DESCRIPTION	DEFAULT
ProtocolHandlerClassName	Must be set to org.apache.jk.server.JkCoyoteHandler	N/A

The Webapp Connector

The Webapp connector communicates with the principal Web server over the WARP protocol.

You should configure the Webapp connector to run in its own service and to use the WarpEngine engine instead of the default engine. The class that defines WarpEngine is org.apache.catalina.connector.warp.WarpEngine, so specify this in the className attribute of the <Engine/> context for this service.

For the Webapp connector, use the className org.apache.catalina.connector.warp. WarpConnector.

ATTRIBUTE	DESCRIPTION	DEFAULT
appBase	Specifies the application base Tomcat should use in hosts created from the Apache virtual hosts configuration	*<$CATALINA_HOME>*/webapps

The <Factory/> Node

The <Factory/> node is used by connectors that need a factory to create their underlying secure socket, particularly those implementing HTTPS.

Node: <Factory/>

Parent Nodes: <Connector/>

Child Nodes: None

ATTRIBUTES	DESCRIPTION	DEFAULT
className	Must contain org.apache.coyote.tomcat4. CoyoteServerSocketFactory	N/A
algorithm	Specifies the algorithm Tomcat should use to authenticate key exchange	SunX509
clientAuth	Specifies whether client-side certificates should be required	false
keystoreFile	File containing the keystore	The .keystore in the home directory of the user Tomcat is running as
keystoreType	Type of keystore	JKS
keystorePass	Keystore password	changeit
protocol	SSL/TLS version Tomcat should use	TLS

APPENDIX

B

The Deployment Descriptor (web.xml) Reference

This appendix is provided as a concise reference to the web.xml configuration file. See Chapter 6, "Configuring Web Applications," for a more complete discussion of the information contained here. The web.xml file is found in the /WEB-INF directory of a Webapp, whether that Webapp is contained in a WAR file or in a directory.

Unlike the server.xml file, which eschews a DTD for purposes of flexibility, deployment descriptors conform to a DTD (found at http://java.sun.com/dtd/web-app_2.3.dtd). This appendix is based on the Servlet 2.3 Specification, Final Release, dated August 13, 2001, and is available at http://jcp.org/aboutJava/communityprocess/final/jsr053/index.html. Note that the order of elements is important. All child nodes must appear in the order listed here for the parent node, or the document will not be valid.

All deployment descriptors must begin with the following preamble:

```
<?xml version="1.0" encoding="ISO-8859-1"?>
<!DOCTYPE web-app
    PUBLIC "-//Sun Microsystems, Inc.//DTD Web Application 2.3//EN"
    "http://java.sun.com/dtds/web-app_2.3.dtd">
```

The lists in this appendix specify basic usage criteria. First, we list the name of the node. Next, we tell you in which other nodes (*parent* nodes) this node may appear. Then we list the most common *child* nodes, and we indicate how many of each may occur inside that node.

Following this information is a list of the principal attributes of the node. Required attributes are indicated in bold type. The attibute name is followed by a description of the purpose of the attribute and then the default value for the attribute, where appropriate.

Nodes and linkages that were added in the Servlet 2.3 specification are in bold, to help you update 2.2-compliant Webapps to take advantage of 2.3 features, and to help if you need to maintain backward compatibility to 2.2.

NOTE **In the remainder of this chapter, all attributes listed in bold are required; all attributes listed in *italics* are not part of the specification but are present in the implementation.**

The <web-app/> Node

The root node is the <web-app/> node. It contains all of the other nodes that constitute the deployment descriptor

Node: <web-app/>

Parent Nodes: None

Child Nodes: <icon/> 0-1 required

<display-name/> 0-1 required

<description/> 0-1 required

<distributable/> 0-1 required

<context-param/> 0+ required

<filter/> 0+ required

<filter-mapping/> 0+ required

<listener/> 0+ required

<servlet/> 0+ required

<servlet-mapping/> 0+ required

<session-config/> 0-1 required

<mime-mapping/> 0+ required

<welcome-file-list/> 0-1 required

<error-page/> 0+ required

<taglib/> 0+ required

<resource-env-ref/> 0+ required

<resource-ref/> 0+ required

<security-constraint/> 0+ required

<login-config/> 0-1 required

<security-role/> 0+ required

<env-entry/> 0+ required

<ejb-ref/> 0+ required

<ejb-local-ref/>

ATTRIBUTE	DESCRIPTION	DEFAULT
id	Node id	Automatically assigned

The <icon/> Node

The <icon/> node specifies a <small-icon/> node and a <large-icon/> node containing icons used to represent this Webapp in certain management contexts.

Node: <icon/>

Parent Nodes: <web-app/>, <servlet/>, <filter/>

Child Nodes: <small-icon/> 0-1 required
<large-icon/> 0-1 required

ATTRIBUTE	DESCRIPTION	DEFAULT
id	Node id	Automatically assigned

The <small-icon/> Node

The <small-icon/> node specifies a file within the Webapp file structure containing a 16x16 icon image.

Node: <small-icon/>

Parent Nodes: <icon/>

Child Nodes: None

ATTRIBUTE	DESCRIPTION	DEFAULT
id	Node id	Automatically assigned

The <large-icon/> Node

The <large-icon/> node specifies a file within the Webapp file structure containing a 32x32 icon image.

Node: <large-icon/>

Parent Nodes: <icon/>

Child Nodes: None

ATTRIBUTE	DESCRIPTION	DEFAULT
id	Node id	Automatically assigned

The <display-name/> Node

The <display-name/> node is used to associate a name (specified in the body of the node) with the parent node, to be used in certain management contexts.

Node: <display-name/>

Parent Nodes: <web-app/>, <servlet/>, <security-constraint/>, <filter/>

Child Nodes: None

ATTRIBUTE	DESCRIPTION	DEFAULT
id	Node id	Automatically assigned

The <description/> Node

The <description/> node is used to associate a textual description (specified in the body of the node) with the parent node, to be used in certain management contexts.

Node: <description/>

Parent Nodes: <web-app/>, <servlet/>, **<filter/>**, <security-role-ref/>, <context-param/>, <init-param/>, <resource-ref/>, **<resource-env-ref/>**, **<run-as/>**, <web-resource-collection/>, <user-data-constraint/>, <auth-constraint/>, <security-role/>, **<security-role-ref/>**, <env-entry/>, <ejb-ref/>, **<ejb-local-ref/>**

Child Nodes: None

ATTRIBUTE	DESCRIPTION	DEFAULT
id	Node id	Automatically assigned

The <distributable/> Node

The <distributable/> node is an empty tag used to indicate that the Web application is implemented in a way that allows it to run correctly in a distributed servlet container—for example, in a Tomcat cluster.

Node: <distributable/>

Parent Nodes: <web-app/>

Child Nodes: None

ATTRIBUTE	DESCRIPTION	DEFAULT
id	Node id	Automatically assigned

The <context-param/> Node

The <context-param/> node is used to pass a parameter, in the form of a name-value pair, into the ServletConfig passed into all servlets associated with this Webapp. (You can pass a parameter to a single servlet by using the <init-param/> node described later.)

Node: <context-param/>

Parent Nodes: <web-app/>

Child Nodes: <param-name/> 1 required

<param-value/> 1 required

<description/> 0-1 required

ATTRIBUTE	DESCRIPTION	DEFAULT
id	Node id	Automatically assigned

The <param-name/> Node

The <param-name/> node specifies the name portion of a name-value context parameter in its body.

Node: <param-name/>

Parent Nodes: <context-param/>, <init-param/>

Child Nodes: None

ATTRIBUTE	DESCRIPTION	DEFAULT
id	Node id	Automatically assigned

The <param-value/> Node

The <param-value/> node specifies the value portion of a name-value context parameter in its body.

Node: <param-value/>

Parent Nodes: <context-param/>, <init-param/>

Child Nodes: None

ATTRIBUTE	DESCRIPTION	DEFAULT
id	Node id	Automatically assigned

The <filter/> Node

The <filter/> node declares a filter that can be mapped either to a URL pattern or to a servlet and is functionally similar to Tomcat Valve classes. (See Chapter 6, "Configuring Web Applications.") Filters can access the parameters specified in child <init-param/> nodes via the FilterConfig interface.

Node: <filter/>

Parent Nodes: <web-app/>

Child Nodes: <icon/> 0-1 required
<filter-name/> 1 required
<display-name/> 0-1 required
<description/> 0-1 required
<filter-class/> 1 required
<init-param/> 0+ required

ATTRIBUTE	DESCRIPTION	DEFAULT
id	Node id	Automatically assigned

The <filter-name/> Node

The <filter-name/> node specifies in its body the logical name by which the filter it is attached to will be associated with zero or more filter mappings. It must be unique to this filter.

Node: <filter-name/>

Parent Nodes: <filter/>

Child Nodes: None

ATTRIBUTE	DESCRIPTION	DEFAULT
id	Node id	Automatically assigned

The <filter-class/> Node

The <filter-class/> node contains the fully qualified Java className of the class implementing javax.servlet.Filter to be used.

Node: <filter-class/>

Parent Nodes: <filter/>

Child Nodes: None

ATTRIBUTE	DESCRIPTION	DEFAULT
id	Node id	Automatically assigned

The <filter-mapping/> Node

The <filter-mapping/> node associates a filter with either a specific servlet or a range of URLs. How you use it will depend on the nature of the filter and what you're trying to do. For example, you might want to write an XSLT filter to translate XML content to WML if it's requested with a .wml at the end, or HTML if it's requested with an .html at the end. You might use a filter to exclude certain hosts from viewing content in a certain subdirectory of your app, or you might want to use the same filter to restrict access to a specific servlet.

Filters are mapped in the order they are found in the deployment descriptor, and more than one filter may be mapped to a single URI, servlet, or request.

Node: <filter-mapping/>

Parent nodes: <web-app/>

Child Nodes: <filter-name/> 1 required. The <filter-mapping/> node must contain *either* a <url-pattern/> node *or* a <servlet-name/> node, but not both; however, multiple mappings can be created if you wish to associate a filter with both a servlet and a URI pattern.

<url-pattern/> 0-1 required

<servlet-name/> 0-1* required

ATTRIBUTE	DESCRIPTION	DEFAULT
id	Node id	Automatically assigned

The <listener/> Node

The <listener/> node associates a class implementing one or more of the four life-cycle event listener interfaces with the context being created for the Webapp. (See Chapter 5, "Anatomy and Life Cycle of a Servlet," for more information.)

Node: <listener/>

Parent Nodes: <web-app/>

Child Nodes: <listener-class/> 1 required

ATTRIBUTE	DESCRIPTION	DEFAULT
id	Node id	Automatically assigned

The <listener-class/> Node

The <listener-class/> node contains the fully qualified Java className of a class implementing one or more of the life-cycle event listener interfaces: javax.servlet.ServletContextListener, javax.servlet.ServletContextAttributeListener, javax.servlet.http.HttpSessionListener, or javax.servlet.http.HttpSessionAttributeListener.

Node: <listener-class/>

Parent Nodes: <listener/>

Child Nodes: None

ATTRIBUTE	DESCRIPTION	DEFAULT
id	Node id	Automatically assigned

The <servlet/> Node

The <servlet/> node identifies key attributes of a servlet. It also assigns a logical name to the servlet, which is used later in the <servlet-mapping/> node to bind the servlet to a URI.

Node: <servlet/>

Parent Nodes: <web-app/>

Child Nodes: <icon/> 0-1 required

<servlet-name/> 1 required

<display-name/> 0-1 required

<description/> 0-1 required

<servlet-class/> 0-1 required. The <servlet/> node must contain *either* a <servlet-class/> node *or* a <jsp-file/> node, but not both.

<jsp-file/> 0-1 required. The <servlet/> node must contain *either* a <servlet-class/> node *or* a <jsp-file/> node, but not both.

<init-param/> 0+ required

<load-on-startup/> 0-1 required

<run-as/> 0-1 required

<security-role-ref/> 0-1 required

ATTRIBUTE	DESCRIPTION	DEFAULT
id	Node id	Automatically assigned

The <servlet-name/> Node

The <servlet-name/> node specifies the logical name to assign to this servlet in its body. This is used elsewhere to reference this servlet--for example, in the <servlet-mapping/> node. The name must be unique within the Web application.

Node: <servlet-name/>

Parent Nodes: <servlet/>
<servlet-mapping/>
<filter-mapping/>

Child Nodes: None

ATTRIBUTE	DESCRIPTION	DEFAULT
id	Node id	Automatically assigned

The <servlet-class/> Node

The <servlet-class/> node specifies in its body the class to use to implement the servlet described in its parent node. The contents of this node must be the fully qualified className of a class extending javax.servlet.GenericServlet or one of its children, and must be on the server classpath at runtime, either by being included in the WEB-INF/classes/ or WEB-INF/lib/ directory, or by being otherwise included on the classpath used by the servlet engine. Note that only in the former case will the Webapp be self-contained and broadly deployable.

Node: <servlet-class/>

Parent Nodes: <servlet/>

Child Nodes: None

ATTRIBUTE	DESCRIPTION	DEFAULT
id	Node id	Automatically assigned

The <jsp-file/> Node

The <jsp-file/> node specifies in its body the relative path to a JSP file contained in the Webapp to use to implement the servlet declared in the containing <servlet/> node.

Node: <jsp-file/>

Parent Nodes: <servlet/>

Child Nodes: None

ATTRIBUTE	DESCRIPTION	DEFAULT
id	Node id	Automatically assigned

The <init-param/> Node

The <init-param/> node is used to pass a parameter, in the form of a name-value pair, into the ServletConfig passed into the servlet configured in the containing node. (You can pass a parameter to all servlets in the context by using the <context-param/> node described earlier.)

Node: <init-param/>

Parent Nodes: <servlet/>, <filter/>

Child Nodes: <param-name/> 1 required
<param-value/> 1 required
<description/> 0-1 required

ATTRIBUTE	DESCRIPTION	DEFAULT
id	Node id	Automatically assigned

The <load-on-startup/> Node

The <load-on-startup/> node specifies whether the containing servlet should be loaded by the servlet container when it starts, rather than waiting for the first request for the URI to trigger its loading. It may optionally contain a positive integer in its body specifying the order of precedence (relative to other servlets specifying this attribute) in which to load. Servlets are to be loaded starting with the lowest-numbered instance. Unnumbered instances, and those specifying non-positive integer values, may be loaded at any time during startup, at the container's discretion.

Node: <load-on-startup/>

Parent Nodes: servlet/>

Child Nodes: None

ATTRIBUTE	DESCRIPTION	DEFAULT
id	Node id	Automatically assigned

The <run-as/> Node

The <run-as/> node specifies which role the servlet should assume when it's run.

Node: <run-as/>

Parent Nodes: <servlet/>

Child Nodes: <description/> 0-1 required
<role-name/> 1 required

ATTRIBUTE	DESCRIPTION	DEFAULT
id	Node id	Automatically assigned

The <security-role-ref/> Node

The <security-role-ref/> node can be used to map a role name used in the servlet to a role name configured for the context in a <security-role/> node. The contained <role-name/> element specifies the name of the alias, and the <role-link/> node specifies the name of the actual role to which to map it. This way, a servlet requiring a specific role need not be rewritten to adapt it to local conditions where the role may exist under a different name, or where privileges from another role are to be extended to grant access to it.

Node: <security-role-ref/>

Parent Nodes: <servlet/>

Child Nodes: <description/> 0-1 required
<role-name/> 1 required
<role-link/> 1 required

ATTRIBUTE	DESCRIPTION	DEFAULT
id	Node id	Automatically assigned

The <role-name/> Node

The <role-name/> node has as its body the name of a role. (See Chapter 8, "Managing Authentication with Realms," for more information.)

Node: <role-name/>

Parent Nodes: <security-role-ref/>
<auth-constraint/>
<security-role/>

Child Nodes: None

ATTRIBUTE	DESCRIPTION	DEFAULT
id	Node id	Automatically assigned

The <role-link/> Node

The body of a <role-link/> node contains the name of a role specified in a <security-role/> node, and is used to reference that role.

Node: <role-link/>

Parent Nodes: <security-role-ref/>

Child Nodes: None

ATTRIBUTE	DESCRIPTION	DEFAULT
id	Node id	Automatically assigned

The <servlet-mapping/> Node

The <servlet-mapping/> node maps a URI pattern to a servlet name defined in a <servlet/> node.

Node: <servlet-mapping/>

Parent Nodes: <web-app/>

Child Nodes: <servlet-name/> 1 required
<url-pattern/> 1 required

ATTRIBUTE	DESCRIPTION	DEFAULT
id	Node id	Automatically assigned

The <url-pattern/> Node

The <url-pattern/> node contains a URI pattern string. When associated with a <servlet-mapping/> node, it is used to tell the servlet container which URIs should be directed to the servlet specified in the matching <servlet-name/> node inside the <servlet-mapping/> element. Similarly, when it is associated with a <web-resource-collection/> node, it is used to define a range of possible request URIs to associate with a security constraint.

The pattern is a regular expression, with * matching any character.

Node: <url-pattern/>

Parent Nodes: <servlet-mapping/>, <web-resource-collection/>,
<filter-mapping/>

Child Nodes: None

ATTRIBUTE	DESCRIPTION	DEFAULT
id	Node id	Automatically assigned

The <session-config/> Node

The <session-config/> node defines the session parameters for the Webapp.

Node: <session-config/>

Parent Nodes: <web-app/>

Child Nodes: <session-timeout/> 0-1 required

ATTRIBUTE	DESCRIPTION	DEFAULT
id	Node id	Automatically assigned

The <session-timeout/> Node

The <session-timeout/> node specifies the default session timeout interval (in minutes) for the Webapp.

Node: <session-timeout/>

Parent Nodes: session-config/>

Child Nodes: None

ATTRIBUTE	DESCRIPTION	DEFAULT
id	Node id	Automatically assigned

The <mime-mapping/> Node

The <mime-mapping/> node maps an extension to a MIME type. It is used to configure the content type: header for files downloaded from the context.

Node: mime-mapping/>

Parent Nodes: <web-app/>

Child Nodes: <extension/> 1 required

<mime-type/> 1 required

ATTRIBUTE	DESCRIPTION	DEFAULT
id	Node id	Automatically assigned

The <extension/> Node

The <extension/> node contains a file extension—for example, txt or jnlp—in its body.

Node: <extension/>

Parent Nodes: <mime-mapping/>

Child Nodes: None

ATTRIBUTE	DESCRIPTION	DEFAULT
id	Node id	Automatically assigned

The <mime-type/> Node

The <mime-type/> node contains the MIME type—for example, text/plain or application/x-java-jnlp-file--in its body. It is associated with the extension specified in the <extension/> node that forms the other half of the tuple contained in the <mime-mapping/> node.

Node: <mime-type/>

Parent Nodes: <mime-mapping/>

Child Nodes: None

ATTRIBUTE	DESCRIPTION	DEFAULT
id	Node id	Automatically assigned

The <welcome-file-list/> Node

The <welcome-file-list/> node is used to specify—in child <welcome-file/> nodes—which file (or files, in order of precedence) should be served from a directory when only a directory path is specified—for example, index.html or index.jsp.

Node: <welcome-file-list/>

Parent Nodes: <web-app/>

Child Nodes: <welcome-file/> 1+ required

ATTRIBUTE	DESCRIPTION	DEFAULT
id	Node id	Automatically assigned

The <welcome-file/> Node

The <welcome-file/> node contains as its body a filename that serves as the default file when a directory URI is requested.

Node: <welcome-file/>

Parent Nodes: <welcome-file-list/>

Child Nodes: None

ATTRIBUTE	DESCRIPTION	DEFAULT
id	Node id	Automatically assigned

The <taglib/> Node

The <taglib/> node maps a URI pattern to a tag library descriptor, or TLD, file.

Node: <taglib/>

Parent Nodes: <web-app/>

Child Nodes: <taglib-uri/> 1 required
<taglib-location/> 1 required

ATTRIBUTE	DESCRIPTION	DEFAULT
id	Node id	Automatically assigned

The <taglib-uri/> Node

The <taglib-uri/> node contains as its body the relative path (from the location of the deployment descriptor itself) to a tag library to be used in this Webapp.

Node: <taglib-uri/>

Parent Nodes: <taglib/>

Child Nodes: None

ATTRIBUTE	DESCRIPTION	DEFAULT
id	Node id	Automatically assigned

The <taglib-location/> Node

The <taglib-location/> node contains the relative path (from the location of the deployment descriptor itself) to the TLD file for this taglib.

Node: <taglib-location/>

Parent Nodes: <taglib/>

Child Nodes: None

ATTRIBUTE	DESCRIPTION	DEFAULT
id	Node id	Automatically assigned

The <error-page/> Node

The <error-page/> node is used to specify an error page that serves in the event of a particular error code being returned or a particular exception being thrown.

Node: <error-page/>

Parent Nodes: <web-app/>

Child Nodes: <error-code/> 0-1 required. You must specify *either* an <error-code/> *or* an <exception-type/>, but not both.

<exception-type/> 0-1 required. You must specify *either* an <error-code/> *or* an <exception-type/>, but not both.

<location/> 1 required

ATTRIBUTE	DESCRIPTION	DEFAULT
id	Node id	Automatically assigned

The <error-code/> Node

The <error-code/> node contains as its body the numerical HTTP return code to match on for this particular error page mapping—for example, 404.

Node: <error-code/>

Parent Nodes: <error-page/>

Child nodes: None

ATTRIBUTE	DESCRIPTION	DEFAULT
id	Node id	Automatically assigned

The <exception-type/> Node

The <exception-type/> node contains as its body the fully qualified className of a Java exception type to match on for this particular error page mapping—for example, java.lang.Exception or java.sql.SQLException.

Node: <exception-type/>

Parent Nodes: <error-page/>

Child Nodes: None

ATTRIBUTE	DESCRIPTION	DEFAULT
id	Node id	Automatically assigned

The <location/> Node

The <location/> node contains as its body the relative path to a resource within the Web application to serve as an error page.

Node: <location/>

Parent Nodes: <error-page/>

Child Nodes: None

ATTRIBUTE	DESCRIPTION	DEFAULT
id	Node id	Automatically assigned

The <resource-env-ref/> Node

The <resource-env-ref/> node contains the declaration of a Web application's reference to an administered object associated with a resource in the Web application's environment.

Node: <resource-env-ref/>

Parent Nodes: <web-app/>

Child Nodes: <description/> 0-1 required
<resource-env-ref-name/> 1 required
<resource-env-ref-type/> 1 required

ATTRIBUTE	DESCRIPTION	DEFAULT
id	Node id	Automatically assigned

The <resource-env-ref-name/> Node

The <res-ref-name/> node contains as its body the environment entry name used in the Web application code to access the environment entry configured in its parent node. It represents a JNDI name, relative to the java:comp/env context, and must be unique within the Web application.

Node: <res-ref-name/>

Parent Nodes: <resource-env-ref/>

Child Nodes: None

ATTRIBUTE	DESCRIPTION	DEFAULT
id	Node id	Automatically assigned

The <resource-env-ref-type/> Node

The <resource-env-ref-type/> node contains as its body the fully qualified className of the type returned by the resource.

Node: <resource-env-ref-type/>

Parent Nodes: <resource-env-ref/>

Child Nodes: None

ATTRIBUTE	DESCRIPTION	DEFAULT
id	Node id	Automatically assigned

The <resource-ref/> Node

The <resource-ref/> node contains the declaration of an external resource.

Node: <resource-ref/>

Parent Nodes: <web-app/>

Child Nodes: <description/> 0-1 required
<res-ref-name/> 1 required
<res-type/> 1 required
<res-auth/> 1 required
<res-sharing-scope/> 0-1 required

ATTRIBUTE	DESCRIPTION	DEFAULT
id	Node id	Automatically assigned

The <res-ref-name/> Node

The <res-ref-name/> node contains as its body the name of the resource factory reference.

Node: <res-ref-name/>

Parent Nodes: <resource-ref/>

Child Nodes: None

ATTRIBUTE	DESCRIPTION	DEFAULT
id	Node id	Automatically assigned

The <res-type/> Node

The <res-type/> node contains as its body the fully qualified className of the type returned by the resource.

Node: <res-type/>

Parent Nodes: <resource-ref/>

Child Nodes: None

ATTRIBUTE	DESCRIPTION	DEFAULT
id	Node id	Automatically assigned

The <res-auth/> Node

The <res-auth/> node specifies whether the container is responsible for signing on to the resource, or whether the Webapp will do this programmatically. Its body contains either CONTAINER or SERVLET.

Node: <res-auth/>

Parent Nodes: <resource-ref/>

Child Nodes: None

ATTRIBUTE	DESCRIPTION	DEFAULT
id	Node id	Automatically assigned

The <res-sharing-scope/> Node

The <res-sharing-scope/> node specifies whether connections obtained through the given resource manager connection factory reference can be shared. Its body either contains Shareable or Unshareable.

Node: <res-sharing-scope/>

Parent Nodes: <resource-ref/>

Child Nodes: None

ATTRIBUTE	DESCRIPTION	DEFAULT
id	Node id	Automatically assigned

The <security-constraint/> Node

The <security-constraint/> node is used to associate security constraints with one or more Web resource collections. It associates URIs and HTTP methods with authorization and security constraints that users must satisfy before they are granted access to those URIs via those methods.

Node: <security-constraint/>

Parent Nodes: <web-app/>

Child Nodes: **<display-name/>** 0-1 required

<web-resource-collection/> 1+ required

<auth-constraint/> 0-1 required

<user-data-constraint/> 0-1 required

ATTRIBUTE	DESCRIPTION	DEFAULT
id	Node id	Automatically assigned

The <web-resource-collection/> Node

The <web-resource-collection/> node contains the relative path (from the location of the deployment descriptor itself) to the TLD file for this taglib.

Node: <web-resource-collection/>

Parent Nodes: <security-constraint/>

Child Nodes: <web-resource-name/>1 required
<description/> 0-1 required
<url-pattern/> 0+ required
<http-method/> 0+ required

ATTRIBUTE	DESCRIPTION	DEFAULT
id	Node id	Automatically assigned

The <web-resource-name/> Node

The <web-resource-name/> node contains a name to associate with the parent <web-resource-collection/> as its body.

Node: <web-resource-name/>

Parent Nodes: <web-resource-collection/>

Child Nodes: None

ATTRIBUTE	DESCRIPTION	DEFAULT
id	Node id	Automatically assigned

The <http-method/> Node

The <http-method/> node contains as its body a string matching an HTTP method—for example, GET or POST.

Node: <http-method/>

Parent Nodes: <web-resource-collection/>

Child Nodes: None

ATTRIBUTE	DESCRIPTION	DEFAULT
id	Node id	Automatically assigned

The <user-data-constraint/> Node

The <user-data-constraint/> node is used to require a particular level of transport security, as specified in the contained <transport-guarantee/> node.

Node: <user-data-constraint/>

Parent Nodes: <security-constraint/>

Child Nodes: <description/> 0-1 required
<transport-guarantee/> 1 required

ATTRIBUTE	DESCRIPTION	DEFAULT
id	Node id	Automatically assigned

The <transport-guarantee/> Node

The <transport-guarantee/> node is used to indicate a particular level of transport security. It can contain as its body one of three keywords: NONE, INTEGRAL, or CONFIDENTIAL. NONE means that the constraint does not require any transport guarantee. INTEGRAL requires that the transport does not allow the data to be modified in transport. CONFIDENTIAL means that the data to be transported should be encrypted to prevent that data from being read by third parties in transit. In most cases, both of these latter requirements have the effect of requiring the server to use SSL/TLS and HTTPS.

Node: <transport-guarantee/>

Parent Nodes: <user-data-constraint/>

Child Nodes: None

ATTRIBUTE	DESCRIPTION	DEFAULT
id	Node id	Automatically assigned

The <auth-constraint/> Node

The <auth-constraint/> node is used to require authentication by a user belonging to a particular role, as specified in the <role-name/> node.

Node: <auth-constraint/>

Parent Nodes: <security-constraint/>

Child Nodes: <description/> 0-1 required
<role-name/> 0+ required

ATTRIBUTE	DESCRIPTION	DEFAULT
id	Node id	Automatically assigned

The <login-config/> Node

The <login-config/> node is used is used to configure the authentication method that should be used; the realm name that should be used for this application; and, if you are using form-based login, the attributes that are needed by the form login mechanism.

Node: <login-config/>

Parent Nodes: <web-app/>

Child Nodes: <auth-method/> 0-1 required
<realm-name/> 0-1 required
<form-login-config/> 0-1 required

ATTRIBUTE	DESCRIPTION	DEFAULT
id	Node id	Automatically assigned

The <auth-method/> Node

The <auth-method/> node specifies the type of authentication to require; it must contain BASIC, DIGEST, FORM, or CLIENT-CERT in the body of the tag.

Node: <auth-method/>

Parent Nodes: <login-config/>

Child Nodes: None

ATTRIBUTE	DESCRIPTION	DEFAULT
id	Node id	Automatically assigned

The <realm-name/> Node

The body content of the <realm-name/> node specifies the name of the authentication realm to use to supply user information (see Chapter 8), which is sent as an HTTP header (typically presented to the user) that allows the browser to retransmit the credential if the same realm is requested.

Node: <realm-name/>

Parent Nodes: <login-config/>

Child Nodes: None

ATTRIBUTE	DESCRIPTION	DEFAULT
id	Node id	Automatically assigned

The <form-login-config/> Node

The <form-login-config/> node associates a login form and an error page with its parent <login-config/> node, and must be present if the <auth-method/> tag contains FORM.

Node: <form-login-config/>

Parent Nodes: <login-config/>

Child Nodes: <form-login-page/> 1 required
<form-error-page/> 1 required

ATTRIBUTE	DESCRIPTION	DEFAULT
id	Node id	Automatically assigned

The <form-login-page/> Node

The <form-login-page/> node specifies the location relative to the Webapp root of a file to be used as a login form.

Node: <form-login-page/>

Parent Nodes: <form-login-config/>

Child Nodes: None

ATTRIBUTE	DESCRIPTION	DEFAULT
id	Node id	Automatically assigned

The <form-error-page/> Node

The <<form-error-page/> node specifies the location relative to the Webapp root of a file to be used as an error page that will be presented to the user if authentication fails.

Node: <form-error-page/>

Parent Nodes: <form-login-config/>

Child Nodes: None

ATTRIBUTE	DESCRIPTION	DEFAULT
id	Node id	Automatically assigned

The <security-role/> Node

The <security-role/> node declares the existence of a security role, which may be referenced by other entries, notably the <security-ref/> node.

Node: <security-role/>

Parent Nodes: <web-app/>

Child Nodes: <description/> 0-1 required

<role-name/> 1 required

ATTRIBUTE	DESCRIPTION	DEFAULT
id	Node id	Automatically assigned

The <env-entry/> Node

The <env-entry/> node declares an entry in the environment, consisting of a key-value pair—with the key defined in the <env-entry-name/> node and the value defined in the (optional) <env-entry-value/> node—of a Java type specified in the <env-entry-type/> node. J2EE-compliant containers are required to accept environment entries and make the specified objects available for JNDI-style lookup. Tomcat does honor this.

Node: <env-entry/>

Parent Nodes: <web-app/>

Child Nodes: <description/> 0-1 required
<env-entry-name/> 1 required
<env-entry-value/> 0-1 required
<env-entry-type/> 1 required

ATTRIBUTE	DESCRIPTION	DEFAULT
id	Node id	Automatically assigned

The <env-entry-name/> Node

The <env-entry-name/> node contains as its body the name of the environment entry. The name is a JNDI name relative to the java:comp/env context, and must be unique within a Web application.

Node: <env-entry-name/>

Parent Nodes: <env-entry/>

Child Nodes: None

ATTRIBUTE	DESCRIPTION	DEFAULT
id	Node id	Automatically assigned

The <env-entry-value/> Node

The <env-entry-value/> node contains as its body the value to be associated with the environment entry. If the associated <env-entry-type/> is java.lang.Character, then the body must contain a single character.

Node: <env-entry-value/>

Parent Nodes: <env-entry/>

Child Nodes: None

ATTRIBUTE	DESCRIPTION	DEFAULT
id	Node id	Automatically assigned

The <env-entry-type/> Node

The <env-entry-type/> node contains as its body the fully qualified className of the type of the environment entry value associated with it. The body must contain one of the following Java types: java.lang.Boolean, java.lang.Character, java.lang.String, java.lang.Byte, java.lang.Integer, java.lang.Short, java.lang.Long, java.lang.Float, or java.lang.Double.

Node: <env-entry-type/>

Parent Nodes: <env-entry/>

Child Nodes: None

ATTRIBUTE	DESCRIPTION	DEFAULT
id	Node id	Automatically assigned

The <ejb-ref/> Node

The <ejb-ref/> node is used to declare a reference to an Enterprise JavaBean. The container must be EJB-aware in order to do anything meaningful with such a reference.

Node: <ejb-ref/>

Parent Nodes: <web-app/>

Child Nodes: <description/> 0-1 required

<ejb-ref-name/> 1 required

<ejb-ref-type/> 1 required

<home/> 1 required

<remote/> 1 required

<ejb-link/> 0-1 required

ATTRIBUTE	DESCRIPTION	DEFAULT
id	Node id	Automatically assigned

The <ejb-ref-name/> Node

The <ejb-ref-name/> node contains as its body the JNDI name of the Enterprise Java Bean, which the servlet code can use to get a reference to the bean, relative to the java:comp/env context. The name must be unique within the Web application. It is recommended that the name start with with ejb/.

Node: <ejb-ref-name/>

Parent Nodes: <ejb-ref />, **<ejb-local-ref/>**

Child Nodes: None

ATTRIBUTE	DESCRIPTION	DEFAULT
id	Node id	Automatically assigned

The <ejb-ref-type/> Node

The <ejb-ref-type/> node specifies whether the referenced EJB is an entity bean or a session bean, and must have either Entity or Session as its body.

Node: <ejb-ref-type/>

Parent Nodes: <ejb-ref/>, **<ejb-local-ref/>**

Child Nodes: None

ATTRIBUTE	DESCRIPTION	DEFAULT
id	Node id	Automatically assigned

The <home/> Node

The <home/> node contains as its body the fully qualified name of the home interface of the EJB.

Node: <home/>

Parent Nodes: <ejb-ref/>

Child Nodes: None

ATTRIBUTE	DESCRIPTION	DEFAULT
id	Node id	Automatically assigned

The <remote/> Node

The <remote/> node contains as its body the fully qualified name of the remote interface of the EJB.

Node: <remote/>

Parent Nodes: <ejb-ref/>

Child Nodes: None

ATTRIBUTE	DESCRIPTION	DEFAULT
id	Node id	Automatically assigned

The <ejb-link/> Node

The <ejb-link/> node is used to specify that an EJB reference is linked to an EJB in an encompassing J2EE application package. It contains as its body the ejb-name of that EJB.

Node: <ejb-link/>

Parent Nodes: <ejb-ref/>

Child Nodes: None

ATTRIBUTE	DESCRIPTION	DEFAULT
id	Node id	Automatically assigned

The <ejb-local-ref/> Node

The <ejb-local-ref/> node is used to declare a reference to the local home of an EJB. As with the <ejb-ref/> node, the container must be EJB-aware in order to do anything meaningful with such a reference.

Node: <ejb-local-ref/>

Parent Nodes: <web-app/>

Child Nodes: <description/> 0-1 required
<ejb-ref-name/> 1 required
<ejb-ref-type/> 1 required
<local-home/> 1 required
<local/> 1 required
<ejb-link/> 0-1 required

ATTRIBUTE	DESCRIPTION	DEFAULT
id	Node id	Automatically assigned

The <local-home/> Node

The <local-home/> node contains as its body the fully qualified name of the local home interface of the EJB.

Node: <local-home/>

Parent Nodes: <ejb-local-ref/>

Child Nodes: None

ATTRIBUTE	DESCRIPTION	DEFAULT
id	Node id	Automatically assigned

The <local/> Node

The <local/> node contains as its body the fully qualified name of the local interface of the EJB.

Node: <local/>

Parent Nodes: <ejb-local-ref/>

Child Nodes: None

ATTRIBUTE	DESCRIPTION	DEFAULT
id	Node id	Automatically assigned

Index

Symbols

A

B

C

D

N

O

P

T

U

X